SCOTTISH ISLANDS

The Western
Isles

D0717188

SCOTTISH ISLANDS SERIES

BOOK 1 — The Western Isles
BOOK 2 — Orkney & Shetland

SCOTTISH ISLANDS

The Western
Isles

James & Deborah Penrith

Illustrations by Mick Siddens

Published by Vacation Work, 9 Park End Street, Oxford
www.vacationwork.co.uk

SCOTTISH ISLANDS BOOK 1 – THE WESTERN ISLES

by James & Deborah Penrith

Editor: Ian Collier

Copyright © Vacation Work 2002

ISBN 1-85458-267-4

Cover Design by
Miller Craig & Cocking Design Partnership

Maps by Andrea Pullen

Typeset by WorldView Publishing Services

Printed by William Clowes Ltd., Beccles, Suffolk, England

Contents

Western Isles: Practical Information

OUTER HEBRIDES

Outer Hebrides: Practical Information

Exploring The Outer Hebrides

LEWIS

HARRIS

NORTH UIST

FIRTH OF CLYDE ISLANDS

MAPS

Acknowledgements

We'd like to thank by name all the people from the Butt of Lewis down to the Firth of Clyde who have helped us in one way or another, but we just don't have the space. The assistance of the following, however, contributed immeasurably in ensuring that what you find between these covers is comprehensively informative, up-to-date, entertaining and, hopefully, at times amusing. More, that we have successfully addressed the prime function of any good guidebook – usability.

Our thanks to Anne-Marie Mooney, of the Scottish Tourist Board; Mike Blair, Marketing Manager, Caledonian MacBrayne; Anna Campbell, Western Isles Tourist Board; Sally Monro of The Highlands of Scotland Tourist Board; Yvonne Preece and Nicola Callaghan of the Argyll, the Isles, Loch Lomond, Stirling & Trossachs Tourist Board; Anique Adamson and Joyce Hall, of the Ayrshire and Arran Tourist Board; Linda Kain, Oban Tourist Information Office; Alasdair Galbraith, Portree Tourist Information Centre; James McMillan, Iain Middleton, and Sharon MacDonald of the Tourist Information Centre, Rothesay, Bute; Bill Lawson, of Northton, Harris; Marleen and John Mitchell, of Ceol na Mara, Harris; Joan MacDonald, of Kilchoan Bay, South Uist; David and Diana Savory, of Northbay House, Barra; Dr Bill Gibbs, Tobermory, Mull; Peter and Janet Hall, Mull; Emily King, Copeland House, Tobermory, Mull; The Hon Mrs Chrissie Anderson, of Ulva Ferry, Mull; Iain Henderson, of Laphroaig Distillery, Isle of Islay; Donald Black, Achnacroish, Lismore; John Taylor, Seil; Peter MacDiarmid, Seil; Charles Soane, The Ardyne-St Ebba, Rothesay, Isle of Bute; Robert AC Liddell, Millport, Great Cumbrae; Professor Keith Branigan of Sheffield University. Special thanks to Pauline Byrom for contributing reference sources we might otherwise have overlooked.

Sources of Information

As Dr Johnson so famously said, to produce even half a book you must ransack a whole library, and in *Further Reading* are sources we have used to check and cross-check the matters of fact we have used to clothe the bones of our personal observations and the information generously provided by all connected with the islands and with the tourism industry in general. For this we cannot praise too highly the combined services of the Scottish Tourist Board and the regional tourist boards responsible for the islands covered in this book, their helpful staffs, and their first-rate publications. Other sources mined were the *Stornoway Gazette* and *West Highland Free Press,* weekly newspapers, *Scottish Islands Explorer* magazine, *West Word,* the community newspaper with regular coverage of The Small Isles, National Trust for Scotland, Royal Society for the Protection of Birds, WWF Scotland, Scottish Wildlife Trust, Scottish Natural Heritage, Historic Scotland, Sustrans, A Taste of Scotland, Bill Lawson Publications, and the Scottish Parliamentary Archives.

Photography

Cover photograph by Garry Peasley. Other photographs of the Western Isles were taken by the authors James and Deborah Penrith.

Preface

At a time when foreign excursions were fast growing in popularity 19th century travel writer George Borrow said there were no places less known by the British than their own islands. He wrote this at a time when the fashionably witty definition of an island was 'a piece of land surrounded by the Royal Navy'. Borrow's words still apply today, but should be counted a blessing by all drawn by the special magic of islands. When it comes to definitions no one seems able to agree on what exactly constitutes an island, or even on how many there are around the coast of Scotland. All do agree that an island is a piece of land surrounded by water but whereas one old measurement says it must also be inhabited or have sufficient vegetation to support one or two sheep, a modern definition excludes islands with bridges to the mainland, which immediately knocks one of the most famous, Skye, off the island-hopper's itinerary. Whoever decided that Scotland's islands number one for each day of the year obviously hadn't done much travelling among them. There are at least twice that number, most of them off the west coast of Scotland and most making up the Outer and Inner Hebrides in the shape of islands, islets, stacks, skerries and plain old rocks. Whatever the definitions and numbers they all have a fascination quite out of proportion to their size; they are all treasure islands.

In this book we have concentrated on those islands which are the chosen destinations of the adventurous, as well as a number which, while off the beaten track, do not require you to mount a full-scale expedition to get there. Coincidentally, there's at least one island for each week of the year. Only a small number of the hundreds of Scottish islands are inhabited but the people of the more remote ones are studies in themselves. Totting up a little old lady's purchases in one tiny island shop the village postmistress asked her, 'Have you got everything you want?' 'No,' replied the little old lady, 'but it's all I can afford.' On another island a nonagenarian shepherd was asked by a television interviewer whether he had lived in the village all his life. 'Not yet,' said the old man. 'Is there anything further west?' we asked a local. 'Aye,' he replied, 'America.'

Yes, there's definitely something engagingly different about islanders.

James and Deborah Penrith
Tobermory, Mull

The Western Isles
Practical Information

Travellers bound for the islands off the west coast have a choice of reaching Scotland by air, sea, rail, or road, depending on which country they are coming from. Trains and long-distance coaches are the prime carriers of passengers. On the main London to Glasgow and Edinburgh routes there are frequent rail and coach departures every day. There are also regular rail services from London to the western seaboard at Mallaig and Oban for ferry links to the Outer and Inner Hebrides. There are also good bus links with the ferry ports around Scotland's coast.

BY AIR

Glasgow is the major hub for onward air travel to the west coast islands. *British Airways* (tel 08457-733377; www.britishairways.com) operated by *Loganair* (tel 0141-848 7594) flies from Glasgow to airports in Lewis, Benbecula, Barra, Islay, and Tiree.

If you are going to Scotland via London check the fares offered by *ScotAirways* (tel 0870-606 0707; fax 01223-292160; www.scotairways.co.uk) against no-frills airlines such as *Ryanair* (tel 0870-333 1231; fax 01279-666201; www.ryanair.com), *EasyJet* (tel 0870- 600 0000; fax 01582-443355; www.easyjet.com), and *Go* (tel 0845-605 4321; www.go-fly.com).

Bikes. If you are planning a cycling holiday and want to take your own bike with you many airlines consider bikes to be part of the normal baggage allowance provided they are carefully packed, but you might be obliged to sign off their liabilities for compensation – Limited Release is the official term. Budget flights usually charge extra to carry a bike and inter-island flights on small aircraft have limited luggage space, so check beforehand.

BY SEA

Numerous regular ferry services link Europe with ports along the southern and east coasts of England. The closest to the Scottish border are Newcastle-upon-Tyne and Hull in northern England. Scandinavian ferries run to Leith, in Edinburgh, as well as Newcastle-upon-Tyne.

For a full list of ferry companies with a breakdown of who sails where browse website www.ferryinformationservice.co.uk, and for a one-stop shop offering the best prices on all ferry lines sailing to and from the UK contact *Ferry Savers* (tel 0870 442 42 43; fax 0870 444 14 84; e-mail customerservices@ferrysavers.com; www.ferrysavers.com).

Alternatively, you can charter or sail your own boat. Contact *Sail Scotland Ltd* (tel 01309-676757; fax 01309-676744; e-mail info@sailscotland.co.uk; www.sailscotland.co.uk), for advice on the options.

CalMac Ferries

In no other part of Britain does the ferry play such an important part in the daily life of communities as along the west coast of Scotland, and as the old poem says:

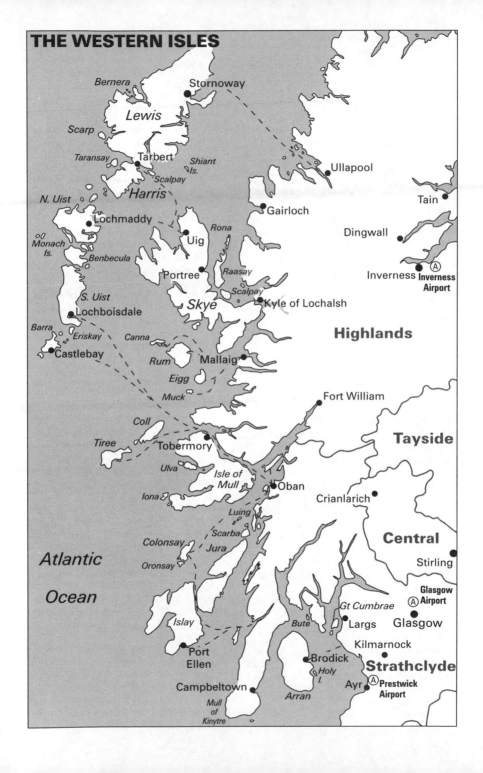

*'The earth unto the Lord belongs
And all that it contains,
Except Western Isles and piers
For they are Caledonian MacBrayne's'*

Caledonian MacBrayne is a name synonymous with ferries to these Scottish islands and for many its operations are truly lifeline services. The arrival and departure of the ferry is still a focal point of the week for most islanders. Mail is always off first and into the red Royal Mail van waiting at the foot of the slipway. The ferry company, better known as CalMac, has its head office in Gourock (The Ferry Terminal, Gourock, PA19 1QP; for reservations tel 08705-650000; fax 01475-635235; e-mail reservations@calmac.co.uk; www.calmac.co.uk. For general enquiries tel 01475-650100; fax 01475-637607).

CalMac runs a fleet of 30 modern roll on/roll off (Ro-Ro) car and passenger ferries serving a wide range of routes, from a quick 'shuttle' across the Clyde to the 7¼-hour voyage from Oban in Argyll to Lochboisdale in South Uist, by way of Barra. Vessels vary from small 'Island Class' ferries which can carry 50 passengers and six cars to vessels capable of carrying up to 1,000 passengers and 120 cars. The largest vessel in the fleet is the 6,573-ton *Isle of Lewis*, operating between Ullapool and Stornoway. The larger vessels have self-service restaurants, fully licensed bars, and shops. A hearty Scottish breakfast (£3.95) is served every day until 11am, and 20 other hot and cold meals, snacks and beverages are available throughout the day on all of the larger ferries. There are also snack and drink vending facilities at most of the major terminals. Many of the larger ferries have comfortable modern lounges and you can even watch a video on board. Ask at reception or cafeteria. All CalMac Ferries are non-smoking, except on deck. There are lifts for mobility impaired passengers, and designated dog areas.

Timetables and Tickets

CalMac's summer timetable runs from Easter to mid-October. There's a reduced services timetable from mid-October to Easter. It is advisable to make reservations well in advance if you are taking a vehicle, especially during the summer months. CalMac's 'Island Hopscotch' and 'Island Rover' tickets offer discounts on the standard single fares. The 'Island Hopscotch' enables you to hop from island to island on a number of different routes for less than the price of the individual journeys. There are more than 20 combinations and these usually offer substantial savings, especially if you are touring by car. The 'Island Rover' ticket gives unlimited travel on most CalMac ferry routes for 8 or 15 consecutive days. A ticket does not automatically ensure a place on any particular sailing, so advance booking for both tickets is advisable, especially in the peak season, as is space for a vehicle. All tickets are valid for one month, from date of first journey, and can be used in either direction.

Regulations which came into force at the beginning of 2000 require details of passengers to be recorded on most routes at the ferry terminal no later than 30 minutes before sailing time. You then have to be on board no later than 10 minutes before sailing time.

Disabled drivers and vehicles carrying disabled passengers. You get 50% off the normal car fare for the single journey on presentation of an orange disability card, supported by the tax exemption certificate or proof of receipt of a Disabled Living Allowance at the higher level; 10% off the normal car fare for the single journey on presentation of the orange card only. For campervans not exceeding 16 ft (5 m) there's a 50% reduction on the normal single fare for the single journey on presentation of an orange card, supported by tax exemption.

Ferry Terminals

Oban, 90 miles (145 km) north of Glasgow, on the west coast of Argyllshire, is often called the 'Charing Cross of the Highlands'. It is the departure port for many of the ferries to the islands, including Mull, Colonsay, Coll, Tiree, Barra, and South Uist. Other CalMac ferry terminals are at Ardrossan, for Arran; Kennacraig, for Islay and Jura; Uig on Skye, for North Uist and Harris; and Ullapool, for Lewis. Passenger ferries also run from Mallaig to the Small Isles of Rum, Muck, Canna, and Eigg, and to Armadale in Skye. Western Ferries (tel 01369-704452) operate services across the Clyde estuary, and to Islay and Jura.

Mainland CalMac Offices:

Colintraive: tel 01700-841235; fax 01700-841342.
Kennacraig: tel 01880-730253; fax 01880-730202.
Mallaig: tel 01687-462403; fax 01687-462281.
Oban: tel 01631-566688; fax 01631-566588.
Ullapool: tel 01854-612358; fax 01854-612433.
Wemyss Bay: tel 01475-520521; fax 01475-522166.

CalMac Cruises

Old CalMac itineraries advertised tempting summer tours along what it called the 'Royal Route' among islands which readers were reminded had seen the likes of Alexander II, King Haakon of Norway, Robert the Bruce, James IV, James V, Bonnie Prince Charlie, Queen Victoria, and King Edward VII sailing the same route. Today's cruises include non-landing evening dinner cruises from Ardrossan, Oban, Uig, Ullapool, and Stornoway. These must be booked no later than two hours prior to sailing on the day of the cruise. Evening cruises are also available on the 3,504-ton *MV Lord of the Isles* from Mallaig on Sundays and Tuesdays to Castlebay, Barra or Lochboisdale, South Uist, sailing past the Small Isles. Passengers return to Mallaig. Buy tickets from the CalMac office in Mallaig. Bookings no later than 4pm on day of departure.

Cruise Options

Puffer Vic 32 (tel 01546-510232) is an appealing old red-funnelled steamship whose hold has been converted into a capacious saloon and comfortable accommodation for a dozen people. If you can't afford an expensive yacht charter or don't fancy an open-boat trip a novel alternative is a week among the isles on the puffer.

The *Hebridean Princess* a 50-passenger small luxury cruise ship, offers a number of cruises from Oban during the summer months. Seven-night trips are available, as well as four-night Hebridean sampler cruises. These take place four times a year, visiting the islands of Colonsay, Iona, Staffa, Mull and Loch Sunart. Contact *Hebridean Island Cruises* (Griffin House, Broughton Hall, Skipton, North Yorkshire, BD23 3AN; tel 01756-704704; fax 01756-704794; e-mail reservations@hebridean.co.uk; www.hebridean.co.uk).

The *Corryvreckan* (Dal an Eas, Kilmore, Oban PA34 4XU; tel 01631-770246; www.corryvreckan.co.uk) is a 64 ft (20 m) sailing boat with room for 10 guests in its twin-birth cabins. It's based in Oban and runs trips of between 6-12 days throughout the year until September.

For yacht charter, bareboat or skippered, contact the *Association of Yacht Charterers* (tel 01369-706727; www.asyc.co.uk).

Note

Scottish Natural Heritage (SNH) has guidelines for visitors to remote islands where there are National Nature Reserves (NNRs), such as St Kilda, North Rona, and The Monach Isles, as well as to islands with the Sites of Special Scientific Interest and Special Protection Areas, such as the Flannan Isles, the Shiant Islands, Mingulay, and Berneray. If you are planning to visit any of these first contact SNH (12 Hope Terrace, Edinburgh, EH9 2AS; tel 0131-447 4784; fax 0131-446 2277; www.snh.org.uk).

BY RAIL

There are eight main stations in London. Euston is the terminus for Western Scotland, and King's Cross for Eastern Scotland. Britain's 25 train companies operate the *National Rail* network and its website (www.nationalrail.co.uk) is a good place to find out what discounts and specials each company is offering or you can telephone for information (08457-484950).You can buy a National Rail timetable at main railway stations and some bookshops. As well as tracking down cheap fares, you can also check the best times to travel at www.thetrainline.com.

The main cross-border rail services are run by *ScotRail* (tel 08457-484950; www.scotrail.co.uk), *Virgin Trains* (tel 08457-222333; www.virgintrains.co.uk), and *GNER* (tel 08457-225225; www.gner.co.uk). All serve Edinburgh and Glasgow, with extensions to Dundee and Aberdeen; GNER also runs trains through to Inverness. Check out the special book-ahead deal on ScotRail's overnight Caledonian Sleepers which run Sunday to Friday from London (Euston), Edinburgh, Glasgow, Aberdeen, Inverness, Dundee, and Fort William. Check out the special book-ahead deal. The journey time from London to Edinburgh is about 4^1/2 hours and to Glasgow about 5 hours. ScotRail's 'Freedom of Scotland Travelpass' allows unlimited train travel, with additional discounts on many connecting bus and ferry services. 'International Student Discount Railcards' can also be used. These are usually cheaper if bought in your country of origin.

The **Jacobite Steam Train** (tel 01463-239026) runs in summer from Fort William to Mallaig, terminus of the West Highland Line, once a day Monday to Friday at 10.20am, and on Sunday at the same time along a route that is scenically stunning. Getting to Kyle of Lochalsh by rail is a classic run-around. While the West Highland Line links Fort William and Mallaig to Glasgow and London, Kyle, only 40 miles (64 km) north of Mallaig on the west coast, can be reached by train only via Inverness on the east coast.

Bikes

Bikes can be taken on most rail services in the UK, although there are no standard regulations. A leaflet on bike rail carriage is available from most railway stations. The Caledonian Sleeper carries up to six bicycles in reservable spaces, except from Inverness, where only three are carried. Both Virgin and GNER trains have space to carry bikes but charge for a one-off journey. Reservations must be made in advance. ScotRail has space for at least two bikes per carriage and carries them free. Bikes which can be dismantled or folded to a maximum dimension of one metre are treated by all rail companies as part of your luggage allowance (two large items and one small).

BY ROAD

In the UK long-distance coaches run cross-border services and serve all major towns and are a relatively inexpensive way to travel. Two of the major companies which operate a nationwide network are *National Express* (tel 08705-808080; www.nationalexpress.co.uk) and *Scottish Citylink* (tel 08705-505050, 8am to 8pm daily; www.citylink.co.uk). Many National Express services – known as 'Rapide' – have toilet facilities, movies and light refreshments. Scottish Citylink coaches have toilet facilities. There are good value discount passes when travelling by bus to most areas of Scotland. The 'Citylink Explorer Pass,' for instance, offers a hefty discount on Caledonian MacBrayne's ferry passenger fares, as well as a small discount off the first night's stay at some of the Independent Backpackers Hostels Scotland establishments. There are a number of other options depending on where you visit and how long you want to travel. The 'Discount Coachcard,' for instance, offers a discount of up to 30% off adult fares on all National Express and Scottish Citylink services. It is available to 16-25 passengers inclusive, and mature students over 26. The 'Advantage 50 Discount' offers the same discount to senior citizens of 50 and over. Children aged 5 to 15 receive this discount automatically. Check discounts and special offers for Eurolines and National Express at www.GoByCoach.com.

Bikes

In general, bus companies will carry dismantled and wrapped bikes, provided there's space and you do not exceed your passenger luggage allowance. Scottish Citylink does not carry conventional bikes, but will carry bagged bikes. The *Bike Bus Company* based in Edinburgh (tel 0131-229 6274) operates a minibus and bike trailer service.

Postbuses

Scottish Royal Mail Postbuses run in many remote areas of Scotland, carrying mail and fare-paying passengers where there is no other form of public transport. If you are using Postbus it pays to study the timetable and route carefully as Postbuses follow postal delivery and collection schedules and do not always travel the same routes on their return journeys. You can flag down a Postbus at any point and it will stop to pick you up. Some Postbuses are adapted for wheelchair users. Space is limited so don't make travel plans that rely totally on the Postbus. Details and timetables are available from Communication Services, Royal Mail (Room 716, 102 West Port, Edinburgh, EH3 9HS; tel 0131-228 7407), or write to Royal Mail Customer Service Centre (Freepost, The Guildhall, 57 Queen Street, Glasgow, G1 3AT. Helpline tel 01246-546329; Customer Services tel 08457-740740; www.royalmail.co.uk).

Driving

By car the **Road to the Isles** is a 46-mile (74 km) journey on the A830 from Fort William to Mallaig, winding through some of Scotland's most magnificent scenery. Ferries sail from Mallaig to the Isle of Skye and the Small Isles – Canna, Eigg, Rum and Muck. Ferries also leave from Arisaig. Although there are no tolls on Scottish roads, some bridges are tolled. The bridge from Kyle of Lochalsh to Skye is an example.

Journey Times. By car from Edinburgh to:

Aberdeen 2½ hours	Oban 3 hours
Glasgow 1¼ hours	Ullapool 4½ hours
Inverness 3 hours	

TOUR OPERATORS

Scotia Travel: 57 Bothwell Street, Glasgow, G2 6RF (tel 0141-305 5050; fax 0141-305 5051; www.scotiatravel.com).

Scotsell for Scottish Island Holidays: 2d Churchill Way, Bishopsbriggs, Glasgow, G64 2RH (tel 0141-772 5928; fax 0141-762 0297; e-mail holidays@scotsell. com; www.scotsell.com). Scottish island specialists with imaginative touring holidays.

MAPS AND GUIDES

Britain's national mapping agency *Ordnance Survey (OS)* publishes a special index of Britain showing the parts of the country covered by all the different OS maps. This mapping index is free from main OS stockists, or you can contact Ordnance Survey (Customer Helpline; tel 08456 05 05 05; e-mail at enquiries@ordsvy.gov.uk, or write to Ordnance Survey, Romsey Road, Southampton, SO16 4GU, which is open Monday to Friday from 8.30am to 5pm). *Map Reading*, by Robert B Matkin (Dalesman, Skipton 2000) is easy-to-understand and inexpensive (£3.50).

Where to Buy. If you are shopping for maps and guidebooks in Britain, among your options are: *Blackwell's* (53 Broad Street, Oxford, OX1 3BQ; tel 01865-792792; www.bookshop.blackwell.co.uk); *Daunt Books* (83 Marylebone High Street, London, W1M 4DE; tel 020-7224 2295); *Newcastle Map Centre* (55 Grey Street, Newcastle upon Tyne, NE1 6EF; tel 0191-261 5622; www.newtraveller.com); *The Map Shop* (30a Belvoir Street, Leicester, LE1 6QH; tel 0116-247 1400); and *The Travel Bookshop* (13 Blenheim Crescent, London, W11 2EE; tel 020-7229 5260; www.thetravelbookshop.co.uk). In London map-seekers usually make a bee-line for the bookshop *Stanford's* (12/14 Long Acre, Covent Garden, London, WC2 9LP; tel 020-7836 1321; www.stanfords.co.uk); there are also branches at 156 Regent Street, London, W1R 5TA (as part of the British Airways Travel Shop); 52 Grosvenor Gardens, London, SW1W 0AG (adjacent to Victoria railway station and part of the Usit Campus store); and 29 C ~n Street, Bristol, BS1 1HT (tel 0117-929 9966). Stanford's also has a mailing servi

The *British Tourist Authority* stocks a comprehensive range o atlases, including Ordnance Survey, motoring, town plans and water and a wide variety of specialist guidebooks. (See list of BTA offices *Information*).

The *Stationery Office* is the official publisher for British Government and other official bodies in Britain. Stationery Office publications can be ordered directly from The Stationery Office Ltd, Publications Centre, PO Box 29, Norwich, NR3 1GN, England; tel 0870-600 5522; fax 0870-600 5533; e-mail book.orders@theso.co.uk.

On-Line

Internet sites providing maps include the following:

Bodleian Library: Map Links: www.rsl.ox.ac.uk/nnj/maplinks.htm.

If you are interested in looking at some early maps of the Scottish islands, the British *Library Map Collections'* website www.bl.uk/collections/maps is a good place to browse. The focal point of the Map Collections is the Map Library which provides access to maps, atlases and globes dating back to the 15th century. Contact The British Library, Map Library, 96 Euston Road, London, NW1 2DB; tel 020-7412 7702; fax 020-7412 7780; e-mail maps@bl.uk.

Multimap (24 Merton Rise, London, NW3 3EN; tel 020-7433 0460 or 020-7681 2094; e-mail info@multimap.com) one of the UK's leading interactive mapping services on the web, provides free access to online street maps and travel directions for the UK and Europe, as well as a range of other options you can access on www.multimap.com. This is one of the UK's top 10 most visited sites and has been providing maps on the Internet since 1997. Its website enables users to search for a particular location by postcode, street name, place name or grid reference, delivering a screen-sized digital map which is accurate to within a few metres.

UK Street Map www.streetmap.co.uk, on-line maps. Geographic map data supplied by Bartholomew and Ordnance Survey.

Harvey (12-22 Main Street, Doune, Perthshire, FK16 6BJ; fax 01786-841098; e-mail winni@harveymaps.co.uk, call credit card hotline 01786-841202, or shop online at www.harveymaps.co.uk) has a reputation for producing high quality specialist maps for adventurous recreation, particularly walking, climbing, cycling, and horse-riding.

Nicolson Maps (1-3 Frazer Street, Largs, Ayrshire, KA30 9HP; tel/fax 01475-689242; e-mail enquiries@nicolsonmaps.com; www.nicolsonmaps.com) supplies all types of maps and books handling street maps for most of Scotland's towns and villages.

Mapsofscotland.com offers a wealth of information on Scotland – maps, charts, atlases, guides, books – and owner Mike Hyatt says if you come across anything you think might be of interest to others he'll consider adding it to his stock list. Check his website www.mapsofscotland.com or e-mail info@mapsofscotland.com.

A comprehensive guidebook looking at all the islands from the yachtsman's point of view is Hamish Haswell-Smith's *The Scottish Islands* (Canongate Books, Edinburgh 1999). While its maps are meant more for route planning than for navigation the book includes information on anchorages and other useful watery things for those who mess about in boats. Haswell-Smith's companion volume is *Island Odyssey – Among the Scottish Isles in the Wake of Martin Martin –* illustrated by the author's own attractive watercolours.

Plastic Cash

Major credit cards are increasingly accepted but it is still advisable to carry cash in UK Sterling or Scottish banknotes in the likely event you come across a place that doesn't have the facility to accept your plastic. Cash dispensers – auto tellers – at the Bank of Scotland, the Royal Bank of Scotland, Clydesdale Bank, and Lloyds TSB Scotland accept most credit cards, among them Eurocard, American Express, Mastercard, Visa Card, Multibanco, and Mistercash.

Banks and Banking

Three of Scotland's traditional banks issue their own banknotes. The Royal Bank of Scotland, the Bank of Scotland and Clydesdale Bank. Banknotes come in £5, £10, £20, £50 and £100 denominations. The £1 coin is in general circulation throughout Scotland, although the Royal Bank of Scotland still produces a £1 banknote. Bank of England and Bank of Northern Ireland notes are welcome in Scotland, although you might have difficulty in changing them the further south of the border you go in England, so convert your Scottish money before leaving. Exchange rates are the same for Scottish and English notes. All Scottish banks use the same basic colours to distinguish the different banknote values – blue for £5, brown for £10, purple for £20, green for £50, and red for £100 (the Bank of England also uses the same colours for Sterling). In the main, the notes differ in their designs.

Good medical services are widely available, but free care under the National Health Service applies only to UK and European Union residents, and nationals or residents of a country with a reciprocal healthcare agreement with the UK. All others are expected to pay. This means that carrying adequate travel insurance is a good policy. If you become ill while in Britain you are eligible for free emergency treatment only at National Health Service accident and emergency departments of hospitals. For details read the *Overseas Visitors' Eligibility to Receive Free Primary Care*, which is available from the Department of Health Distribution Centre (PO Box 777, London, SE1 6XH; tel 020-7210 3000; www.open.gov.uk/doh/coinh.htm).

Hazards

There are no natural hazards to speak of, although dense blizzards of the ferocious Highland midge (*Culicoides impunctatus*) raise irritation levels in summer. Recommended are repellents based on either dimethyl phthalate (DMP, or Dimp) or di-ethyl toluamide (DEET). Shoo! is a popular DMP version. Old fishing manuals recommend pipe smoking; all authorities suggest you should wear light-coloured clothing at dusk, which is the time *Culicoides impunctatus* best likes to dine on humans. It might be smaller than a pinhead but it can make your life a misery. You are likely to meet midges from late May until early September, with the worst months July and August. The female midge is the one with the blood lust. The male can't bite you. Once a female midge has located you, she releases a chemical, a pheromone, that tells all other midges nearby that a meal awaits. There are 37 species of midge in Scotland but only six species bite, and of these *Culicoides impunctatus* does most of the damage. Despite their hordes, midges are a problem only on overcast days, in the evenings, and early mornings. On sunny or windy days you should be safe. In Gaelic the midge is known as *meanbh-chuileag* (pronounced *menuv-hoolag*). *Meanbh* means minute, or tiny, but this doesn't necessarily describe the size of island midges. There's a saying in Rum that if you kill one midge a thousand come to the funeral.

CLOTHING

Pack lightweight clothing, but be flexible enough to allow for the variable weather. May to September is often warm, but an umbrella or light (waterproof) jacket is still advisable to cope with rain or cool evenings. A heavier waterproof jacket and a decent sweater – buy one in Scotland – is a good idea from October and on through the winter months. Pack waterproof trousers and a rainproof hat if you plan to do a lot of walking, and take your stoutest and most comfortable shoes or boots. Even with the most reliable footwear your feet are likely to get wet or, at the very least, damp. Take lots of socks. No one is keen to draw attention to the midges that can sometimes make life a misery in summer, but it is a good idea to get a hat with a veil that covers your face and neck if you intend to spend time outdoors.

While there are lots of guest houses and B&Bs on the islands top-end accommodation is limited. The Scottish Tourist Board produces four accommodation guides, revised annually, which cover Hotels & Guest Houses, Bed & Breakfast, Self-Catering, and Caravan & Camping. Accommodation in these categories is graded on a one to five-star system. The more stars, the better the quality, and this is the determining factor – the quality of the welcome and service, the food, the hospitality, ambience, and the comfort and condition of the establishment – not the size of accommodation or its range of facilities. This easy-to-understand system tells you at a glance the quality standard of all types and sizes of accommodation from the smallest B&B and self-catering cottage to the largest countryside and city centre hotel: Five-star = Exceptional, world-class; Four-star = Excellent; Three-star = Very Good; Two-star = Good; and One-star = Fair and Acceptable.

For caravan holiday accommodation meeting the required high standards STB gives its colourful Thistle Award symbol. Other signs to look out for are the square 'Walkers Welcome' and 'Cyclists Welcome' ones which mean the establishments have met a rigorous string of requirements aimed at making your walking or cycling holiday even more enjoyable. STB also operates a national accessibility scheme, identifying and promoting accommodation that caters for

people with mobility problems. It awards symbols in three different categories: Unassisted wheelchair access; assisted wheelchair access; and access for people with mobility difficulties. For more information contact Quality Assurance Department (Scottish Tourist Board, Thistle House, Beechwood Park North, Inverness, IV2 3ED; tel 01463-716996; fax 01463-717244); or the Scottish Tourist Board (23 Ravelston Terrace, Edinburgh; tel 0131-332-2433; fax 0131-343-1513; www.visitscotland.com).

Accommodation listings can be obtained from Area Tourist Boards. Local tourist information centres can book accommodation for you. Many operate the national 'Book-a-Bed-Ahead' service, reserving your accommodation for a nominal fee.

Nearly 500 hotels and restaurants recognised for their high culinary standards and use of natural ingredients are emblazoned with the distinctive 'Taste of Scotland' stockpot symbol, and the islands have a fair share of these. For more information contact Taste of Scotland Scheme (33 Melville Street, Edinburgh, EH3 7JF; tel 0131-220 1900; fax 0131-220 6102; e-mail tastescotland@sol.co.uk; www.taste-of-scotland.com).

Hostels

The *Scottish Youth Hostels Association* (SYHA, 7 Glebe Crescent, Stirling, FK8 2JA; tel 01786-891400; fax 01786-891333; e-mail syha@syha.org.uk; www.syha.org.uk) runs most of the hostels in the islands, although there are several that are independently owned. SYHA membership offers more than a way to avoid expensive hotel bills. You can also use it to get 5%-25% discount on a wide variety of goods, services and facilities, such as Hertz and Budget car rentals, Stena Line and P&O North Sea Ferries, and National Trust for Scotland entrance fees. SYHA is a member of the Hostelling International network, offering self-catering or meals, common rooms, hot showers, dormitories, and family rooms, as well as central and free fax reservation service. The office is open from Monday to Friday 9am to 5pm.

Independent Backpackers Hostels Scotland (7 Portnalong, Isle of Skye, IV47 8SL; tel/fax 01478-640254; e-mail skyehostel@lineone.net; www.hostel-scotland.co.uk) is a chain of 40 independently run hostels, bunkhouses and bothies. Accommodation varies from historic town houses to converted barns and working crofts. Some rural hostels are fairly remote so you should telephone to confirm a bed is available before you arrive. All hostels are inspected annually to ensure they meet IBH standards. Most are privately owned and the majority are family run. They all provide hostel-style accommodation at a fair price, with a minimum of rules, no curfew, and no membership required. Hostels and their facilities are open all day. All have fully equipped kitchens, common rooms, hot showers, and dormitories. Some hostels have family rooms with a twin room occasionally available and some have a 'Book-a-Bed-Ahead' service. Enquire at individual hostels if you want to take advantage of this. Own sleeping bag is recommended, although many hostels provide full bedding. All offer free blankets or duvets and sheet sleeping bags are always available.

Scottish Farmhouse Holidays (Renton Terrace, Eyemouth, TD14 5DF; tel 01890-751830; fax 01890-751831; e-mail info@scotfarmhols.co.uk; www. scotfarmhols.co.uk) is a central reservation service for working farms and crofts. Contact them for a copy of their free brochure. *Country Cottages in Scotland* (tel 0870-585 1133; www.countrycottagesinscotland.co.uk) and *Scottish Country Cottages* (tel 0141-772-5920; www.scotsell.com or www.scottishcountrycottages. co.uk) are also worth a browse. Fancy staying in a castle? Contact *Scott's Castle Holidays* (tel 0131-229 7111; www.scottcastles.com) for suggestions.

The *National Trust for Scotland* (Wemyss House, 28 Charlotte Square,

Edinburgh, EH2 4ET; tel 0131-243 9331; fax 0131-243 9594; www.nts.org.uk) has croft house accommodation in Skye and a furnished house in Canna. Contact them for details.

Camping. There are not a lot of official camping areas in the islands, but hill and coastal camping is normally easy to find. Get advice and permission from farmers, crofters, or estates where these exist.

SPORT AND RECREATION

WALKING AND CLIMBING

Most Tourist Information Centres have a wide range of local walks guides which include suggested routes, maps, grade of walk, length of walk, estimated duration, local points of interest, and local facilities. Guides come in waterproof plastic covers. Collins publishes a range of practical, easy-to-use Walk Guides. Each guide features a selection of walks with clear colour maps and step-by-step route descriptions. Walks are graded. Information on local amenities, places of interest, natural history and wildlife is also given. Premier among climbing guides is the Scottish Mountaineering Club's district guide *The Island of Scotland, including Skye.*

May, June and September are the **best months** of the year to be walking, scrambling, or rock-climbing among the tops. For walking generally, spring and early autumn are likely to be finer and drier than the height of summer, although the later the month the more you might find routes restricted by deer stalking and grouse shooting. The main **stalking seasons** are 1 August to 31 October and for grouse from 12 August to 10 December. In important hill areas a Hillphones system has been set up, with a recorded message updated at 8am each day indicating where stalking is taking place and which walking routes are likely to be affected, as well as giving a forecast for the next few days. Calls are charged at normal rates. Have the relevant map to hand when phoning. The telephone numbers are on website www.snh.org.uk and details of the Hillphones service can also be obtained from the *Mountaineering Council of Scotland* (MCofS). Some of the finest climbs are in the Cuillin range of Skye, with stretches of the rock that all climbers love, gabbro. Pitches on climbs here range from the simple to the well-nigh impossible. The only Munros, mountains with summits over 3,000 ft (914 m), are on Skye and Mull.

Munros

These mountains get their name from Sir Hugh Munro, first president of the *Scottish Mountaineering Club* (SMC), who listed them in 1891. The list has been updated a few times since then and now recognises 284 Munros. In the 1920s, J Rooke Corbett compiled a list of summits of 2,500-3,000 ft (762-914 m), with the proviso that they had to be separate summits with at least 500 ft (152 m) of re-ascent on all sides. Currently, 221 **Corbetts** meet his criteria. A list of 2,000-2,500 ft (610-762 m) summits was drawn up in 1992 by Fiona Graham and these are now recognised as Grahams. A handy descriptive pocket book is *The Munro Almanac*, by Cameron McNeish.

Mountain Bothies

These are unlocked shelters in the mountains which can be used free of charge by bona-fide walkers and mountaineers. Users should not stay for long periods, although a few days is acceptable. There is no bothy booking system and their location is available from the *Mountain Bothies Association (MBA)* contactable through their website www.mountainbothies.org.uk/.

Club Huts

Huts are available for the use of clubs affiliated to the Mountaineering Council of Scotland (MCofS) and the British Mountaineering Council (BMC) and their members. There are three huts in Skye, one the Glen Brittle Memorial Hut (GBMH), near the Cuillin, and the other two in the Cuillin. These can be used by members of MCofS and its affiliates.

Right of Way

This is a thorny subject. Generally speaking your access to the countryside and to all historic sites is unrestricted, but permission to enter private land should always be obtained. Courtesy and consideration are the keywords. There is free access at all times of the year to areas owned by the National Trust for Scotland, and also to most land owned by Forestry Enterprise. For more information on access, contact the *Mountaineering Council of Scotland* (tel 01738-638227) and the *Scottish Rights of Way and Access Society* (ScotWays, 24 Annandale Street, Edinburgh EH7 4AN; tel/fax 0131-558 1222; e-mail info@scotways.com; www. scotways.com) which works to safeguard your access to the Scottish countryside. Their site contains information about Scottish rights of way in general. The society also publishes rights of way maps covering some hill areas. More clearly defined rights of access to land and inland water are being considered by the Scottish Parliament and you can get more details on the Scottish Executive website; www.scotland.gov.uk.

Walking Holidays

Some companies specialising in these are:

Bespoke Highland Tours: 14 Belmont Crescent, Glasgow G12 8EU (tel/fax 0141-334 9017; e-mail bespoke.tours@virgin.net; www.highland-tours.co.uk). For self-led walking/hiking/trekking in the islands of Skye, Raasay, Harris, Barra, Eriskay, the Uists, Eigg, and Rum.

C-N-Do Scotland: Unit 32, Stirling Enterprise Park, Stirling FK7 7RP (tel/fax 01786-445703; e-mail info@cndoscotland.com). Organises guided walking holidays throughout Scotland all year round, as well as climbing and mountaineering courses.

Lomond Walking Holidays: 34c James Street, Riverside, Stirling FK8 1UG (tel/fax 01786-447752). For guided walking and trekking holidays in Mull and Skye.

Make Tracks Walking Holidays: 26 Forbes Road, Edinburgh EH10 4ED (tel 0131-229 6844; fax 0131-229 6808; e-mail mtracks@dircon.co.uk; www.mtracks. dircon.co.uk). For walks on Eigg and Rum.

Rob Roy Tours: Richard Watt, 630 Lanark Road, Juniper Green, Edinburgh EH14 5EW (tel/fax 01620-850408 or 0131-477 4566; e-mail relwatt@hotmail.com). For guided cultural and walking tours to Skye, Mull, and Iona.

Rua Reidh Lighthouse: Chris Barrett and Fran Cree, Melvaig, Gairloch, Ross-shire IV21 2EA (tel/fax 01445-771263; e-mail ruareidh@netcomuk.co.uk). For guided walks on Harris and Lewis.

Useful Contacts

Boots Across Scotland (BAS): 33 Arnothill Gardens, Falkirk FK1 5BQ (e-mail enquiries@bootacrossscotland.org.uk; www.bootsacrossscotland.org.uk). Organises training sessions, funds courses in mountain safety and provides a free route plan you can download from their website before you set off.

The *British Mountaineering Council:* 177-179 Burton Road, West Didsbury, Manchester M34 2BB (tel 0161-445 4747; fax 0161-445 4500; e-mail info@thebmc.co.uk; www.thebmc.co.uk).

The *John Muir Trust:* tel 0845-458 8356; e-mail membership@jmt.org; www.jmt.org. Named after the Scots-born naturalist (1838-1914) who is regarded as the father of the modern environmental movement. The Trust purchases scenic spots in Scotland to protect them for the use and benefit of all.

The *Mountaineering Council of Scotland:* The Old Granary, West Mill Street, Perth PH1 5QP (tel 01738-638227; fax 01738-442095; e-mail info@mountaineering-scotland.org.uk; www.mountaineering-scotland.org.uk). Represents the interests of mountaineers and climbers in Scotland. This site includes information on the workings and activities of the Council as well as stalking information via Hillphones.

The Ramblers' Association: 2nd Floor, Camelford House, 87-90 Albert Embankment, London SE1 7TW (tel 020-7339 8500; fax 020-7339 8501; e-mail ramblers@london.ramblers.org.uk). **Scottish Office:** Kingfisher House, Auld Mart Business Park, Milnathort, Kinross KY13 9DA (tel 01577-861222; fax 01577-861333; e-mail enquiries@scotland.ramblers.org.uk; www.ramblers.org.uk). A campaigning body protecting the rights of walkers throughout the UK. Local branch groups organise outdoor activities.

The *Scottish Mountaineering Club:* Hon Secretary, 4 Doune Terrace, Edinburgh EH3 6DY (www.smc.org.uk).. One of the oldest and most influential mountaineering clubs in Scotland.

The *Scottish Sports Council Trust Company:* Caledonia House, South Gyle, Edinburgh EH12 9DQ (tel 0131-317 7200; fax 0131-317 7202; www.charitiesdirect.com). Operates several national sports centres, including one on Great Cumbrae. The Sports Council is now known as *Sportscotland.*

The *Scottish Tourist Board's* walking site has advice, links to walking organisers and details of 13 walks; www.holiday.scotland.net/outdoor/walk – frame.htm.

UK Mountain Training Board: Siabod Cottage, Capel Curig, Conwy LL24 0ET (tel 01690-720272; fax 01690-720248; e-mail theukmtb@aol.com; www.ukmtb.org).

CYCLING

The Scottish Tourist Board's *Cycle Scotland* is a mine of information for pedal-pushers.

Cyclists' Touring Club: Cotterell House, 69 Meadrow, Godalming, Surrey GU7 3HS (tel 01483-417217; fax 01483-426994; e-mail cycling@ctc.org.uk; www.ctc.org.uk). Is the largest cycling organisation in the UK and provides a wide range of services. Benefits include touring information, third-party insurance, legal and technical advice, bi-monthly magazine (also available on audio tape), annual handbook, and discounts in many cycle shops. They also provide information sheets on transport, cycle hire and cycle routes.

National Cycle Network: Sustrans Scotland, 3 Coates Place, Edinburgh EH3 7AA (tel 0131-623 7600; fax 0131-623 7761; e-mail sustrans@sustrans-scot.freeserve.co.uk; www.sustrans.org.uk). Good for detailed route maps if you plan to cycle to the ferry point or airport on the mainland.

Scottish Cyclists' Union: The Velodrome, Meadowbank Stadium, London Road, Edinburgh, EH7 6AD (tel 0131652 0187; fax 0131-661 0474; e-mail Scottish.Cycling@btinternet.com. www.btinternet.com/-scottish.cycling).

DIVING

Underwater visibility around the islands is generally good and the underwater scenery can be absolutely stunning. Oban is the diver's gateway to the island dive spots of the Inner and Outer Hebrides. All the marine areas and coastline around Scotland come under the jurisdiction of Scottish National Heritage. As they are protected from the worst of the Atlantic storms, the islands of the Inner Hebrides and the Small Isles of Canna (with Sanday), Rum, Eigg, and Muck are favourite spots with visiting divers.

If you want to learn to scuba-dive or brush up your knowledge and qualifications the best-known diving organisations offering internationally recognised diving are *Professional Association of Diving Instructors* (PADI), *British Sub-Aqua Club (BSAC)*, and the *National Association of Underwater Instructions* (NAUI). Courses involve theory and practical sessions with first stages in a swimming pool or sheltered water. An entire course can be completed in under a week. A PADI Open Water or BSAC Ocean Diver course takes four to five days to complete. The PADI Scuba Diver course can be done in a long weekend. BSAC branches in the UK offer a part-time Club Diver course, which can be done over several weeks. For information about courses at your nearest dive centre in the UK, contact the PADI head office (tel 0117-300 7234; www.padi.com), BSAC (tel 0151-350 6200; www.bsac.com), NAUI (Brian Porter, 2 Queensway, East Didsbury, Manchester M19 1QP; tel 0161-432 6661; fax 0161-443 1700; e-mail naui@prosplash.com; www.prosplash.com).

Regional Centres

Aquatech Diving Centre: 1 Reddish Lane, Debdale, Manchester, M18 7JH (tel/fax 0161-223 5102; e-mail aquatech.diving@freedomnames.co.uk; www.aquatechdivingcentre.co.uk). Offers PADI, BSAC and Scuba Schools International (SSI) courses.

Edinburgh Diving Centre: 1 Watson Crescent, Edinburgh (tel 0131-229 4838). Offers complete PADI and BSAC courses from March to November. Both courses can be completed in two weekends.

Greenock Diving Company: Unit 1-3 Dellingburn Street, Greenock, PA15 4TW (tel 01475-790135; e-mail greenock_diving_co@yahoo.co.uk). A diver training facility offering the full range of Scuba Schools International (SSI) courses from Open Water to Instructor training. Specialist courses on request.

London Underwater Centre/Shoal Divers: The Queen Mother Sports Centre, 223 Vauxhall Bridge Road, London, SW1V 1EL (tel 020-7630 7443). Offers referral courses in theory and poolwork so that you can finish your course elsewhere. Courses are completed in four evenings over several weeks.

Puffin Dive Centre: Port Gallanach, Oban, Argyll, PA34 4QH (tel 01631-566088; fax 01631-564142; e-mail info@puffin.org.uk; www.puffin.org.uk). Offers a PADI Open Water 3-4 day course and you can also do the two-day PADI Wreck Diver course if you are a certified PADI Advanced Open Water diver.

Gear. Dive centres usually provide all the gear you need so don't buy anything unless you are planning to dive regularly, although it's a good idea to have your own mask and fins.

Wreck Diving

War Graves are covered by the Protection of Military Remains Act 1986 and include the wrecks of any Royal Navy ship or merchant vessel lost on active government service and which might hold human remains. You can usually dive on such wrecks but you are not allowed to disturb or remove anything. If you find anything on a wreck you are legally obliged to report your find to the *Receiver of Wrecks and the Maritime and Coastguard Agency.* Failure to do so is a criminal offence and can result in a fine of up to £2,500, forfeiture of salvage rights and liability to pay the owner, or the person entitled to the wreck, double the value of the wreck. All wreck material, no matter how old, could be owned by someone. This could be the individual who originally lost it, an insurance company, or the *Ministry of Defence* (MoD). Chances are good, however, that you will be able to keep finds. Each case is considered on its merits. To find out contact the Receiver of Wrecks (Maritime and Coastguard Agency, Spring Place, 105 Commercial Road, Southampton SO15 1EG; tel 023- 8032 9474; fax 023-8032 9477; e-mail row@mcga.gov.uk. www.mcga.gov.uk/row, 24-hour information; tel 0870 6006505).

Useful contacts

British Sub-Aqua Club branches in Scotland are supported by two regional coaches, each with a team of area coaches, covering northern and southern Scotland. Coaches can be contacted at e-mail Scotland.coach@bsac.com. Branches can be contacted at www.bsac.com. ScotFed is the Scottish Federation of BSAC branches and the current website is www.arcl.ed.ac.uk/scotfed/.

Department of the Environment, Transport and the Regions, War Wrecks: Bay 4/21, Defence Planning Emergencies, Greatminster House, 76 Marsham Street, London SW1P 4DR (tel 020-7890 5139; fax 020-7676 2184).

Royal Commission on Ancient and Historic Monuments of Scotland: John Sinclair House, 16 Bernard Terrace, Edinburgh EH8 9NX (tel 0131-662 1456; fax 0131-662 1477/1499; www.rchams.gov.uk).

Ministry of Defence: Wreck Section, Room 6384, Main Building, Whitehall, London SW1A 2HB (tel 020-7218 7725; fax 020-7218 4702).

UK Hydrographic Office (MOD): Wreck Section, Admiralty Way, Taunton, Somerset TA1 2DN (tel 01823-337900 ext 3308).

FISHING

Accessible water is open to any legitimate method of angling, although even the remotest loch might be the preserve of an hotel, angling association, or individual. In the wilder areas you may find permission is yours for the asking – but ask anyway. Each Area Tourist Board in Scotland can give you information on fishing in its area, the cost of permits, and where to get them. You can also get advice from the Tourist Information Centres, which usually stock fishing guides. Fishing with wet or dry fly is the traditional method of angling for game-fish. Spring and late autumn are the **best times** for salmon. Sea trout start arriving in the rivers and lochs in July. Sea trout waters are not generally free; when not privately owned, they are usually attached to hotels. *Fish Scotland*, one of the Scottish Tourist Board's excellent publications, gives comprehensive information on all aspects of angling, including maps, lists of angling clubs, where permits can be obtained, fishing hotels, and summaries of rivers and lochs where fishing is available.

Open season. For salmon and sea trout this varies from district to district but generally runs from 11 or 25 February to 31 October in the Outer and Inner Hebrides. Check with the local Tourist Information Centre. There is no closed season for coarse fish or rainbow trout.

Sea Angling. Waters off the remote north and west offer excellent sea fishing. Warm Gulf Stream waters and colder currents from the north blend to provide a mixed bag of fish. Twenty-five different species are commonly caught by boats in the Western Isles. Cod, pollack and haddock are the most widely distributed. The monsters of Scottish sea fishing are the porbeagle shark, giant skate, and whopping halibut.

Useful Fishing Books

Directory of Scottish Salmon Waters: Durham Ranger Publishing (tel 0181-747 8707).

The *Fishing Scotland* series: James Coutts, Roy Bridge, Inverness-shire PH31 4AG (tel/fax 01397-712812; e-mail gofishing@fishing-scotland.co.uk; www.fishing-scotland.co.uk).

The *Scottish Federation of Sea Anglers Yearly Handbook:* SFSA, Caledonia House, South Gyle, Edinburgh EH12 9DQ (tel 0131-317 7192).

Scotland for Game, Sea and Coarse Fishing: Pastime Publications, 6 York Place, Edinburgh EH1 3EP (tel 0131-556 1105).

Fishing Associations

Salmon and Trout Association: Fishmongers Hall, London Bridge, London EC4R 9EL (tel 0171-283 5838).

Scottish Anglers National Association: Helen Bull, Administration Office, Caledonia House, Redheughs Ridd, South Gyle, Edinburgh EH12 9DQ (tel 0131-339 8808).

Scottish Federation of Sea Anglers: Brian Burn, Flat 2, 16 Bellevue Road, Ayr, KA7 2SA (tel 01292-264735).

Scottish Sports Association for the Disabled: Fife Sports Institute, Viewfield Road, Glenrothes KY6 2RB (tel 01592-415700).

SAILING

The waters around the islands offer challenging sailing and cruising amid splendid scenery and wildlife. Chartering is a cost-effective way of enjoying sailing where the wind is free and there are plenty of yacht charter companies around. Contact *Associated Scottish Yacht Charters* (Ken Barr, Secretary, 86 Fairhaven, Kirn, Dunoon, PA23 8NS; tel/fax 01369-706727; e-mail mullargy@aol.com; www.asyc.co.uk).

The *Royal Yachting Association* (RYA, RYA House, Ramsey Road, Eastleigh, Hampshire SO15 4YA; tel 01703-627400). is the governing body representing sailing, windsurfing and motor-boating in Britain. The association offers a wide range of benefits and advice, plus full training courses for all types of recreational craft. 'Safety at Sea' booklets for small boat and recreational craft users are available free. The *Royal National Lifeboat Institution* (RNLI) also supplies free booklets, as well as a number of videos on aspects of safety. For more information and prices contact RNLI (West Quay Road, Poole, Dorset BH15 1HZ; tel 01202-663174). RNLI also maintains a sea safety website (www.seasafety.org.uk). There are sailing schools all around the country offering tuition, including lessons in dinghy sailing, cruiser racing, cruising, power-boating, and windsurfing. All levels of RYA qualification can be obtained. Contact the *Sail Training Association* (tel 01705-832055).

The *Coastguard Service* (Clyde MRCC, Navy Buildings, Eldon Street, Greenock, PA16 7QY; tel 01475729988; Oban MRSC, Boswell House, Argyll Square, Oban PA34 4BD; tel 01631-563720; and Stornoway MRSC, Battery Point, Stornoway, Lewis HS1 2RT; tel 01851-702013) maintains regional and district maritime rescue centres around the British Isles. The Coastguard is there is help, and services are free, so talk to them first if you plan to spend any time at sea. In an emergency Dial 999 and ask for the Coastguard.

Scottish Canoe Association (Caledonia House, South Gyle, Edinburgh EH12 9DQ; tel 0131-317 7314; fax 0131-317 7319; e-mail enquiry@scot-canoe.org; www. scot-canoe.org). Contact for guidance if you plan to canoe or kayak around the islands.

GOLF

Mary Queen of Scots is said to have popped out for a quick game after organising the murder of her husband, Lord Darnley. Established as the national game as early as the 14th century, there are golf courses all over the place. There's even a five-hole links course on the deserted Flannan Isles, out in the Atlantic Ocean. Visiting golfers are not likely to experience difficulty in getting a game. For a full list of Golf Tour Operators, contact the *Scottish Tourist Board* (tel 0131-332-2433; e-mail golf@stb.gov.uk).

TOURIST INFORMATION CENTRES

Scotland has a network of Area Tourist Boards which work in conjunction with the Scottish Tourist Board, and each can give detailed information and advice on most things concerning their area. Contact them for information on things to see and do, places to visit, events, transport within their area and full accommodation listings. The central office of the *Scottish Tourist Board* is in Edinburgh (23 Ravelston Terrace, Edinburgh, EH4 3TP; tel 0131-332 2433; fax 0131-343 1513). If you are in London visit the Scottish Tourist Board's London office close to Trafalgar Square for information and a wide selection of maps, guides and books. The in-house travel agency can organise your travel and accommodation bookings. Personal callers only (The Scottish Tourist Board, 19 Cockspur Street, London, SW1 5BL. Open all year, October to April Monday to Friday 9.30am to 5.30pm, Saturday midday to 4pm; www.visitscotland.com). In the *Britain Visitor Centre* (1 Lower Regent Street, London, SW1Y 4NX), a few minutes' walk from STB's London office, STB staff and their commercial partners provide advice, information and a full booking service for Scotland. Open all year, Monday 9.30am to 6.30pm, Tuesday to Friday 9am to 6.30pm, Saturday and Sunday 10am to 4pm, deals only with walk-in enquirers.

Area Tourist Boards

Argyll, the Isles, Loch Lomond, Stirling and Trossachs Tourist Board: Old Town Jail, St John Street, Stirling, FK8 1AE (tel 01786-459208; fax 01786-461994; www.visitscotland.com).

Ayrshire and Arran Tourist Board: Burns House, Burns Statue Square, Ayr, KA7 1UP (tel 01292-262555/288688; fax 01292-269555/288686; www.ayrshire-arran.com).

The Highlands of Scotland Tourist Board: Peffery House, Strathpeffer, Ross-shire, IV14 9HA (tel 01997-421160; fax 01997-421168; e-mail admin@host.co.uk).

Western Isles Tourist Board: 26 Cromwell Street, Stornoway, Lewis, HS1 2DD (tel 01851-703088; fax 01851-705244; e-mail stornowaytic@witb.ossian.net; www.witb.co.uk).

Post Offices

In many rural areas Post Office services are available as part of a shop or general store. Post Offices vary in size and in rural areas may have only one postal collection a day. Local staff are knowledgeable about their area and usually happy to answer questions. Post Offices are generally open Monday to Friday 9am to 5.30pm, Saturdays 9am to 12.30pm or 1pm. Smaller branches (sub-post offices) often close for lunch.

Telephones. Telephone boxes/pay-phones operated by British Telecom can usually be found throughout the islands. These accept coins or BT phonecards. Coin-operated pay-phones do not give change, so start with small value coins and add larger value coins for as long as you want to chat.

Mobile Phones. Check coverage with your service provider before you go as signals in many islands are weak to non-existent, especially in mountainous areas.

Weather

Lots of websites offer weather forecasts, but if you want the most authoritative information, check out the Met Office's home page for detailed three-day regional forecast at www.met-office.gov.uk. Other useful weather websites are www.zetnet.co.uk/sigs/weather and www.euroseek.com/weather. For recorded weather forecasts for the west of Scotland; tel 0891-232791 (calls are charged at 50p a minute).

Traffic. The *Automobile Association (AA)* of the UK provides information and updates on traffic-related issues on its web site at www.theaa.co.uk.

Women Travellers

If you are nervous about travelling alone one solution is offered by *Women Welcome Women World Wide* (88 Easton Street, High Wycombe, Bucks, HP11 1LT; tel/fax 01494-465441; www.womenwelcomewomen.org.uk), a non-profit trust which fosters international friendship by enabling women of different countries to visit one another. Visit, call or write. Their office is open from 9.30am to 1.30pm from Monday to Friday, excluding public holidays.

Disabled Travellers

The Scottish Tourist Board produces *Accessible Scotland*, a useful booklet on accommodation with disabled facilities. *Capability Scotland* is Scotland's largest disability organisation and provides a national advice and information service. For more information on their services contact *Advice Service Capability Scotland* (ASCS, 11 Ellersly Road, Edinburgh, EH12 6HY; tel 0131-313 5510; fax 0131-346 1681; e-mail capability@capability-scotland.org.uk; www.capability-scotland. org.uk). You can also get practical advice and information from *Holiday Care* (2nd Floor, Imperial Buildings, Victoria Road, Horley, Surrey, RH6 7PZ; tel 01293-774535; fax 01293-784647; e-mail holiday.care@virgin.net; www.holidaycare.org.uk). This is a national charity and the UK's central source of holiday and travel information and support for disabled people and their carers. A referral service that can put you in touch with local disability advice centres is *Update* (27 Beaverhall Road, Edinburgh, EH7 4JE; tel 0131-558 5200). Information on the facilities at UK airports for disabled travellers, including those in wheelchairs, can be obtained from *Tripscope* (Alexandra House, Albany Road, Middlesex, TW8 0NE; tel 020-8580 7021; fax 020-8580 7022; e-mail tripscope@cableinet.co.uk; www.justmobility.co.uk/tripscope/maim.htm).

Gay Travellers

Organisations and establishments catering for the needs and interests of gay travellers continue to blossom in the major mainland cities and towns of Scotland. Not so in the islands where a strict Calvinist ethic prevails. One starting point is the *Gay and Lesbian Switchboard* (PO Box 169, Edinburgh, EH1 3UU; tel 0131-556 4049); another is the *Glasgow Gay & Lesbian Centre* (11 Dixon Street, St Enoch, Glasgow, G1 4AL; tel 0141-221 7203, reception tel 0141-400 7203).

USEFUL ADDRESSES AND TELEPHONE NUMBERS

Historic Scotland: Longmore House, Salisbury Place, Edinburgh, EH9 1SH (tel 0131-668 8600; e-mail graeme.munro@scotland.gov.uk; www.historic-scotland.gov.uk. For information about opening times; tel 0131-668 8800) has more than 300 historic sites in its direct care. Proceeds from admissions and purchases at its sites support conservation and presentation work.

National Museums of Scotland: Chambers Street, Edinburgh, EH1 1JF (tel 0131-225 7534; fax 0131-220 4819; e-mail info@nms.ac.uk; www.nms.ac.uk) Includes the Royal Museum, where many of the more striking and important archaeological finds made in the islands are on display. Entry is free.

The *National Trust for Scotland (NTS):* Wemyss House, 28 Charlotte Square, Edinburgh, EH2 4ET (tel 0131-243 9300; fax 0131-243 9301; e-mail information@nts.org.uk; www.nts.org.uk). A conservation charity which aims to protect and promote Scotland's natural and cultural heritage for present and future generations. Membership of the trust literally opens some of the most famous doors in the country.

The *Royal Society for the Protection of Birds (RSPB):* Scotland Headquarters, Dunedin House, 25 Ravelston Terrace, Edinburgh, EH4 3TP (tel 0131-311 6500; www.rspb.org.uk). Associated with bird and habitat conservation organisations worldwide, forming a global partnership called BirdLife International. There are more than 60 RSPB reserves in Scotland, covering more than 118,610 acres (48,000 ha) and ranging from seabird cliffs to moorland, wetlands and farmland. Outside its reserves, RSPB has more than 200 management agreements, mostly to support those who manage their land for corncrakes. The society is a registered charity working throughout the UK and abroad, and has more than 70,000 members in Scotland and more than 1-million in total.

Scottish Natural Heritage (SNH): 12 Hope Terrace, Edinburgh EH9 2AS (tel 0131-447 4784; fax 0131-446 2277; www.snh.org.uk). Works to assure the long-term health of the country's natural high level of biodiversity, and to maintain and improve a rich variety of plants and animals, their habitats, and the natural processes which support them. Much of SNH's work is about caring for special sites and areas which have been designated because of the importance of their plants, animals, habitats, rocks, landforms and scenery. SNH also works with owners and land managers to maintain and, where appropriate, enhance Sites of Special Scientific Interest, National Nature Reserves and the National Scenic Area which have been designated to protect landscapes.

The *Scottish Wildlife Trust (SWT):* Cramond House, off Cramond Glebe Road, Edinburgh, EH4 6NS; tel 0131-312 7765; fax 0131-312 8705; e-mail enquiries@swt.org.uk; www.swt.org.uk). An independent charity which is part of a network of 46 wildlife trusts in the UK working together to protect wildlife. SWT owns or manages 123 wildlife reserves covering more than 61,776 acres (25,000 ha). Membership gives you free entry to all SWT wildlife reserves in Scotland and to its visitor centres.

FURTHER READING

Historic Scotland and *Scottish Natural Heritage* produce a range of illustrated specialist and general interest publications which are available from bookshops and visitor centres, or you can order them from Historic Scotland (Retail Order, Room G1, Longmore House, Salisbury Place, Edinburgh, EH9 1SH; tel 0131-668 8752 for a free publications catalogue; www.historic-scotland.gov.uk) and Scottish Natural Heritage (Publications Department, Battleby, Redgorton, Perth, PH1 3EW; tel 01738-444177; fax 01738-827411; e-mail pubs@redgore.demon.co.uk. You can buy on-line at www.snh.org.uk). Scotland's largest local history publisher is *Birlinn/John Donald* (8 Canongate Venture, 5 New Street, Edinburgh, EH8 8BH; tel 0131-556 6660; fax 0131-557 6250; www.birlinn.co.uk). Contact for free catalogue. *Goblinshead* (130B Inveresk Road, Musselburgh, EH21 7AY; tel 0131-665 2894; fax 0131-653 6566; e-mail goblinshead@sol.co.uk) specialises in Scottish books, most of them written, published and printed in Scotland.

A Book of Scotland, edited by GF Maine (Collins, London and Glasgow 1950).
A Description of the Western Islands of Scotland, Circa 1695, and *A Voyage to St Kilda*, by Martin Martin, with *A Description of the Occidental i.e. Western Islands of Scotland (1549)*, by Dean Donald Monro (Birlinn, Edinburgh 1999).
A Tour in Scotland and Voyage to the Hebrides 1772, by Thomas Pennant (Birlinn, Edinburgh 1998).
A Treasure Lost, by Olive Brown and Jean Whittaker (Brown & Whittaker Publishing, Tobermory 2000).
A Very Civil People, by John Lorne, edited by Hugh Cheape, Campbell (Birlinn, Edinburgh 2000).
The Alban Quest, by Farley Mowat (Weidenfeld & Nicolson, London 1999).

The Ancient Celts, by Barry Cunliffe (Oxford University Press, Oxford 1997).

Arran Shipwrecks, 1890-1899, by Donald Johnston (Johnston's Marine Stores, Lamlash 1997).

Barra: Archaeological Research on Ben Tangaval, by Keith Branigan and Patrick Foster (Sheffield Academic Press, Sheffield 2000), focuses on the Tangaval peninsula where nearly 250 sites and monuments have been found.

From Barra to Berneray, by Keith Branigan and Patrick Foster (Sheffield Academic Press, Sheffield 2000), presents the results of 13 years of archaeological research on 12 islands.

Birds of Britain & Europe, by J Nicolai, D Singer and K Wothe, translated and adapted by Ian Dawson (HarperCollins, London 1994).

Bonnie Prince Charlie, by Susan Maclean Kybett (Unwin Hyman, London 1988).

Cille Bharra, by Alan Macquarie (Grant Books, Worcestershire 1989).

The Complete Scotland (Ward, Lock and Co Limited, London and Melbourne).

Discovering Lewis and Harris, by James Shaw Grant (John Donald Publishers, Edinburgh 1998).

Dive Islay Wrecks, by Steve Blackburn (Bucknall Publications, 1986).

Diving and Snorkelling Guide to Scotland, by Lawson Wood (Pisces Books, Houston 1996).

Gaelic-English/English-Gaelic Dictionary (Lomond Books, Scotland 1998).

Gaelic-Scots Wordbook, by James S Adam (Arbroath Herald Ltd, 1998).

Hebridean Journey, by Halliday Sutherland (Geoffrey Bles, London 1939).

The Highlands and Islands of Scotland, by Allan Campbell McLean (Collins, Glasgow 1979).

The Inner Hebrides and their Legends, by Otta F Swire (Collins, London 1964).

Invaders of Scotland, by Anna Ritchie and David J Breeze (Historic Scotland, Edinburgh 1991).

Island Quest, the Inner Hebrides, by Prunella Stack (Collins and Harvill Press, London 1979).

The Islands of Scotland, including Skye, by DJ Fabian, GE Little, DN Williams (Scottish Mountaineering Trust, Glasgow 1989).

The Isles, by Norman Davies (Macmillan, London 2000).

The Isle of Taransay, by Bill Lawson (Bill Lawson Publications, Northton, Harris 1997; www.billlawson.com).

The Lewis Chessmen, by Michael Taylor (British Museum Press, 1978), a division of British Museum Publications Ltd, 46 Bloomsbury Street, London WC1B 3QQ.

Lewis, The Story of an Island, by Christine Macdonald (Acair, 1998).

The Lighthouse Stevensons, by Bella Bathurst (Flamingo, London 2000).

The Little Book of Scottish Folklore, by Joules and Ken Taylor (Parragon, Bath 1999).

Midges in Scotland, by Dr George Hendry (Mercat Press, Edinburgh 1996).

Mingulay, An Island and Its People, by Ben Buxton (Birlinn, Edinburgh 1995).

The Munro Almanac, by Cameron McNeish (Neil Wilson Publishing, Glasgow 1991) names them all for climbers and scramblers.

The Outer Hebrides Handbook and Guide (Kittiwake Press, Wales 1995).

Picts, by Anna Ritchie (Historic Scotland 1999).

Polly, by Roger Hutchinson (Mainstream Publishing, Edinburgh 1990) recounts the true story behind *Whisky Galore*, the shipwreck that rocked Eriskay during World War II.

Prehistoric Scotland, by Ann MacSween and Mick Sharp (BT Batsford, London 1989).

Recipes from Scotland, by F Marian McNeill (Albyn Press, Edinburgh 1946).

Reflections on Scotland, by Ian Wallace (Jarrold Colour Publications, Norwich,

UK 1988).

Road to the Isles, Travellers in the Hebrides 1770-1914, compiled by Derek Cooper (Routledge & Kegan Paul, London 1979).

Rum: Nature's Island, by Magnus Magnusson (Luath Press, Edinburgh 1997).

Scotland, an Oxford archaeological guide to more than 200 sites from earliest times to AD 1200, by Anna and Graham Ritchie (Oxford University Press, Oxford and New York 1998).

Scotland – History of a Nation, by David Ross (Lomond Books, 1999).

The Scottish Islands, by Hamish Haswell-Smith (Canongate Books Ltd, Edinburgh 1999).

The Scottish Nation 1700-2000, by TM Devine (Allen Lane, The Penguin Press, London 1999).

Shell Guide to Scotland, by Moray McLaren (Ebury Press, London 1965).

Shipwrecks of the West of Scotland, by Bob Baird (Nekton Books, Glasgow 1995).

St Kilda, by David Quine (Colin Baxter Photography, Grantown-on-Spey 1995).

St Kilda, Island on the Edge of the World, by Charles Maclean (Canongate Classics, Edinburgh 1972).

Times Subject to Tides, by Roy Calderwood (Kea Publishing, Erskine, Renfrewshire); tells the story of Barra's airport, whose runway disappears under the waves twice a day.

Travels in the Western Hebrides (1782-1790), by Rev John Lane Buchanan, originally published in 1793 (MacLean Press, 1997).

The Western Islands Handbook, by David Perrott (Kittiwake Press, Wales 1998).

Wild Flowers of Britain & Europe, by W Lippert and D Podlech, translated and adapted by Martin Walters (HarperCollins, London 1994).

Books from British publishers can be ordered directly from British booksellers, among them:

Blackwell's: Hythe Bridge Street, Oxford, OX1 2ET (tel 01865-261381; fax 01865-261355; e-mail bob.online@blackwell.co.uk; www.blackwcll.co.uk).

Hatchards Ltd: 187 Piccadilly, London W1V 0LE (tel 020-7439 9921; fax 020-7494 1313; e-mail books@hatchards.com; www.hatchards.co.uk).

Heffers Booksellers: 20 Trinity Street, Cambridge, CB2 1TY (tel 01223-568568; fax 01223-568591; e-mail heffers@heffers.co.uk; www.heffers.co.uk).

British exporting booksellers are listed on the Internet website www.britishcouncil.org/infoexch/publishing/sellers.htm.

Outer Hebrides

Whalebone Arch

'*Away beyond Skye, and seen from it in misty outline on the edge of the ocean, stretches a series of islands from the Butt of Lewis to Barra Head...As seen on the map the group looks like a stranded icthyosaurus of geological times, the Lews forming its skull, the Uists its chest, and the Barra Isles the detached vertebrae of its lower spine. At the very point of the saurian tail rises the rocky islet of Bernera, terminated by the grand cliff, where gleams the lighthouse of Barra Head.*'

The vivid impression made on a visiting schools inspector to the Outer Hebrides is still as descriptive as it was when he wrote it in 1883, and while the islands may seem bleak at first sight, they have a captivating elemental beauty. Once you have caught a whiff of their unforgettable essence on the wind – a strange mingling of riotous wild flowers, salt spray, and the throat-catching haze of smoking peat fires – you'll begin to appreciate something of their magic. You'll also understand why islanders see nothing odd about the notice once posted in a church porch after the minister was called to the mainland. It said: 'No service on the Sabbath, the minister has gone abroad.'

GEOGRAPHY

The islands of the Outer Hebrides lie in the Atlantic Ocean between 30 and 60 miles (48-97 km) off the north-west coast of Scotland, an archipelago of around 200 islands, islets and skerries forming an arc some 130 miles (209 km) from north to south. Only 14 of the islands are inhabited and barely 20 of them have an area of more than three square miles (7,7 sq km). The rest reduce in size down to mere pinpricks on the map. The entire archipelago was known to the Vikings who first ravaged and then settled the islands as *Havbrødøy*, or the 'Islands on the Edge of the Sea' and the earliest maps show them lying between what was then known as the *Deucaledonius Oceanus*, the Caledonian Ocean, in the north and the *Mare Hibernicum*, the Irish Sea, in the south.

The island chain begins in the north with **Lewis** which, attached to **Harris**, is the largest and most densely populated island. Then come **North Uist, Benbecula, South Uist, Eriskay, Barra,** and **Vatersay.** Once separate islands they are now all joined by road, bridge or causeway, with the exception of the Uists and Barra. The island chain is often referred to as the 'Long Island', a name that will be even more appropriate when the *Comhairle nan Eilean Siar* (Western Isles Council) finally establishes an integrated spinal route through the islands from top to bottom.

Bounded all the way along its western seaboard by the Atlantic Ocean the eastern shores of the islands are washed in the south by the Sea of the Hebrides, in the centre between North Uist and Isle of Skye by The Little Minch, and in the north between Lewis and the mainland by The Minch. The narrowest stretch of The Little Minch is 14 miles (22 km) and the greatest width of The Minch is between the Butt of Lewis and Scotland's north-western tip, Cape Wrath, a distance of about 62 miles (100 km). The total area of the Outer Hebrides is nearly 1,158 sq miles (3,000 sq km), although almost a quarter of this is water held in the lochs and lochans that account for 16% of Britain's fresh water areas. With 536,677 acres (217,186 ha) Lewis and Harris make up the largest of the populated islands, and at 289 acres (117 ha) Grimsay, between Benbecula and North Uist, is the smallest inhabited isle. The many isles scattered around the central chain include the Monachs, the Flannans, the Shiants, North Rona, the islands south of Barra and Vatersay known as **The Bishop's Isles**, Taransay, of television's *Castaway 2000* fame, and Scalpay. Forty-one miles (66 km) out to the west from Benbecula and truly on the edge of the sea are the islands of **St Kilda – Hirta, Soay,** and **Boreray.** With such a multitude of islands it is not surprising that a number of them share the same name, given the Norse and Gaelic penchant for naming places after prominent features or profiles, and this can cause confusion when tracking a route on the map.

Geology

Nearly all the islands of the Outer Hebrides are founded on the extremely ancient rock known as Lewisian gneiss, which takes its name from the largest island in the archipelago and is estimated by geologists to have been deposited around 3,000-million years ago, when the planet was young. This archaic gneiss is largely grey in colour, with coarse bands of white and dark minerals. Most of Lewis and Harris are made of this rock, as well as the Uists and Barra. Along almost the whole length of the east coast of the island chain outcroppings of this barren grey gneiss

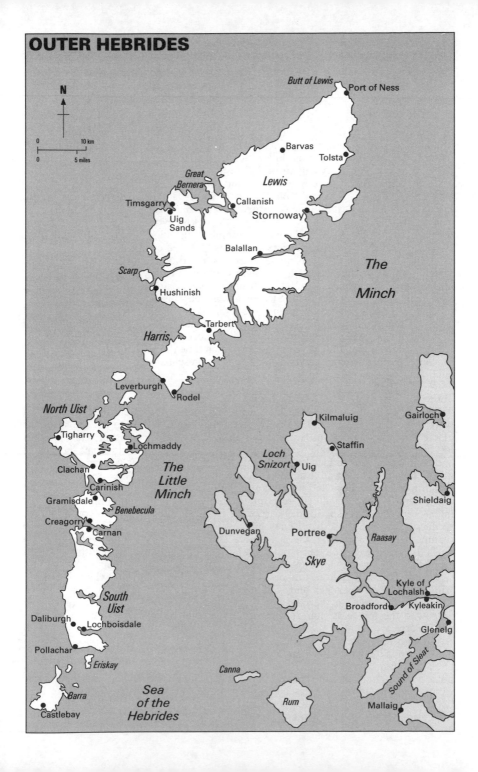

give the landscape a stark appearance, as the impermeable rock weathers to a thin, acidic soil in which very little will grow.

The hilly regions of Uig and North Uist are the result of later intrusions of younger granite, which can have a startling pink and white complexion shot through with silvery mica flakes and dark red garnet crystals. The pink rock is a coarsely crystallised granite known as pegmatite, which is largely made up of feldspar and quartz. Outstanding examples of this pinkish banded rock can be seen in southern Harris on the hilly Chaipaval promontory, north-west of Northton. It forms a distinct line across the hill which is visible from a considerable distance. As well as very large crystals of pink feldspar the granite here also has chunks of whitish quartz, flaky muscovite (clear) and biotite (glossy black) micas. Feldspar was quarried during World War II, when South Harris produced most of the feldspar needed in Britain to make porcelain electrical insulators. In the area of the east coast of Harris known as 'The Bays' the rock-strewn landscape is dotted with whalebacks, ice-moulded rocks which resemble surfacing whales, and the blocks of rock dumped by melting glaciers known as 'perched erratics.'

Near the pier at Rodel in South Harris is a bed of metamorphosed limestone which is unique in the Western Isles. There's not much rock younger than the granites laid down in the islands about 18,000 million years ago, with the exception of a significant sandstone areas in the Stornoway district. This is around 200 million years old and by a quirk of location escaped the aeons of pulverising erosion which scoured away all the other geologically young rocks which once covered the fundamental Lewisian gneiss. After some 2-million years of successive waves of glaciation the last Ice Age ended about 10,000 years ago, by which time the geological vertebrae of the Western Isles had been rasped and polished to its present shape.

Topography

Today's landscape was effectively born at the end of the Pleistocene Ice Age, which for roughly 2-million years had locked up seawater to the extent that ocean levels were more than 450 ft (137 m) below what they are today. With the retreat of the glaciers and the melting of the ice sheets all over Scotland the vast dips and hollows left gouged out in their wake were flooded by sea and melt-water to create the islands and their wild, loch-studded scenery. From the hill tops of Harris you get a clear view of the drowned landscape resulting from the startling post-Ice Age rise in sea levels, which filled the valleys and left many of the hills as small isolated islands. Upland corries and U-shaped valleys are prime examples of a topography moulded by the intense activity of ancient ice that carved the islands in such a way that you'll find the shortest distance by road between two points is often a lengthy and convoluted drive or hike. Broadly speaking, the islands are characterised by long stretches of steep cliffs fretted by long sea lochs and deep bays along the east coast, and by the vivid green belt of pasture land, known as *machair*, on the low coastal plain of the western seaboard. This is a rich mix of peaty soil and alkaline shell-sand which invariably fringes wonderful beaches and is ablaze with wildflowers in spring and summer. From north to south as the inhospitable grey gneiss spine of the east becomes ever narrower, the fertile stretch of *machair* grows ever broader in the west, and it is particularly abundant in the Uists and Benbecula where nearly 14,826 acres (6,000 ha) of *machair* make up about 8% of the land area. This had led to a concentration of agriculture in the west and a predominance of fishing in the east.

The central areas of the island chain are covered by an immense blanket of peat, a stark environment relieved only by dark lochs and lochans, and too acidic to support any plant-life less hardy than moorland heather. Crofters have long used the peat moorland as rough grazing for their livestock and there is an increasing trend towards sanding, fertilising and seeding it to improve its quality and create more pasturage for animals. As well as using it for grazing crofters also cut their supplies of peat for fuel from the moorland. Peat is cut with a *tairsgeir*, a wooden-handled iron cutting tool and spade which is used to dig out chunks like hefty slabs of dark chocolate. This is stacked and left on the moor to dry before being taken home where you'll see it in a neat *cruach*, or stack, outside most island houses. Peat with an average depth of 5 ft (1.5 m) covers nearly 230 sq miles (596 sq km) in Lewis alone, which is why the island's Gaelic name is Lèodhas, a derivation of the word for marshy terrain.

The islands are fairly flat and largely treeless and nearly all the mountains of any significance to walkers and climbers are in Lewis and North Harris where the largest continuous upland range stretches from Lochs in the east to Uig in the west. This is where you'll find vast areas of exposed rock and steep scree-covered slopes. Clisham, the highest peak in the Western Isles, lies in this range. Its distinctive conical shape rises to 2,621 ft (799 m). Spectacular cliffs include Sron Ulladale in North Harris, which claims the biggest overhanging rock face in Britain.

CLIMATE

Islanders will tell you that it rains only twice a year in the Hebrides – from June to September and October to May. This led novelist Sir Compton Mackenzie, long-time Barra resident, to say that the 'prudent topographer' should refrain from suggesting which months to visit, adding: 'If it should happen to have been wet in the month you chose, the water-lilies in the lochans will make you glad that you did take your holiday then.' Considering the regular dousing the islands get it is surprising that stone crosses known as Water Crosses were once erected by islanders to bring rain. When they thought it had rained enough they laid the crosses flat on the ground. Some also relied on an old man who began to sneeze a day or two before rain. The more he sneezed the bigger the drenching they could expect. He was known as the 'Rain Almanach'.

The weather around the Western Isles is strongly influenced by the fast-moving oceanic current known as the Gulf Stream, which brings warm water up from the Caribbean. This current is deflected by the North Atlantic Drift as it approaches the west coast of Europe to send tendrils of warm water around the shores of Britain. The climate of the Western Isles is generally much milder than that of the nearby Scottish mainland, and despite all the horror tales of never-ending downpours, rainfall is at least lower than in the Scottish Highlands. The sunniest and driest months are usually May and June; July and August are warmer, but wetter. The average summer temperature is around 55°F (13°C) and the winter average is about 41°F (5°C). The highest recorded temperature was 77°F (25°C) in July 1948, and the lowest 10°F (-12°C) in January 1960. The sun shines for an average of 210 hours in May, nearly twice as long as in September. Although temperatures in summer are generally lower than those in the south of Scotland and England the islands enjoy many more hours of summer daylight. On the eve of the longest day the sun sets after 11pm and islanders take advantage of the long daylight hours in summer to cut peat for winter. The islands are in the path of the prevailing south-westerly, rain-bearing winds from the Atlantic, so the west coast tends to be wetter than the east. Rainfall averages 47 inches (120 cm) a year, with about 40% of the total coming down between April and September. Gale-force winds blow for about 50 days a year, lesser strength winds during the rest of the year for two days out of every three. The relative warmth of the surrounding sea means that many of the islands can go all winter without frost at sea-level and this also usually keeps air temperatures above freezing in winter. Snow occasionally falls in winter, but rarely lies for more than a few days.

For a weather forecast before or while you are travelling call *Weather Check* (tel 09001-333111), *Weathercall* (tel 09068-500481) for a seven-day report (60p a minute), or visit the *Met Office* website (www.metoffice.com), which will give you a Western Isles as well as a three-day North Scotland forecast.

HISTORY

The Stone Age

Historians believe that the earliest inhabitants of the Outer Hebrides were probably hunter-gatherers who arrived from the south in the wake of the last Ice Age, probably when the English Channel was still dry land. No definite evidence has yet been found to substantiate this, but archaeologists think that this is because any dwellings they might have had would have been in coastal areas long submerged by rising sea levels. Permanent communities are thought to have been established by Neolithic, or New Stone Age, farmers who settled in the islands around 6,000 years ago, grew crops and raised domesticated goats and cattle. What forests there were at the time disappeared as these early settlers cleared the trees to extend their animals' pasture land. Archaeological digs have revealed traces of such Neolithic settlements at Udal and Loch Olabhat in North Uist, and at Northton in Harris. These early farmers are most renowned, however, for the remarkable chambered cairns, massive communal stone tombs, they built for their dead. One outstanding example is Barpa Langass, the great chambered cairn in North Uist.

The Bronze Age

Around 1800 BC people using Bronze Age technology arrived in the Western Isles. These new settlers are known as Beaker People, after the distinctive style of the pottery found during excavations. As well as a new metal-working technology the Bronze Age settlers introduced a new form of burial. Their dead were interred in individual stone cists, or coffins, often with fine beaker ware. Arrowheads and wrist-guards also sometimes found with their pottery identify them as archers, whose warrior elite were often buried with bronze and even gold artefacts. The groups of standing stones which are such a striking feature in some areas of the islands date back to the late Neolithic and early Bronze Age. The most impressive are the Standing Stones of Callanish, on the western side of Lewis.

CALLANISH STONES, LEWIS.

The Iron Age

The Celts began to settle in the Western Isles more than 2,500 years ago during an historical migration that carried them from central and Western Europe at the beginning of the Iron Age to Britain, Ireland and the Scottish islands. As well as introducing the technology to make iron weapons, tools, and other artefacts they dotted the landscape with constructions that indicate they lived in dangerous, unsettled times – defensive hill and promontory forts, the dwellings on artificial islands built in lochs and known as *crannogs,* and the impregnable drystone *brochs,* or towers, with their double walls hiding stairs, galleries, and chambers. One impressive example is Dun Carloway Broch in Lewis, whose ruined walls still reach 30 ft (9 m), another is the broch of Dun Bragar, on an island in Loch an Duna, in north-west Lewis. By the time Christianity was spreading in the islands times were more peaceful and the people more interested in sheltering themselves from the elements than in defending themselves from enemies and were building snug sunken stone wheelhouses, so-called from their layout of a central chamber with rooms radiating from it like the spokes of a wheel.

The Vikings

The old fortified and defensive structures, however, came in handy when the wild Norsemen started arriving in their dragon-prowed longboats on pillaging and slaving raids until, around AD 850-875, the Vikings swapped their swords and battle-axes for the plough and colonised the Western Isles. Once settled and farming the Vikings liked their islands so much that, according to local folklore, they tried to tow them closer to Norway. They passed a rope through a hole in the rocks at the Eye of the Butt on Lewis, tied it to a fleet of galleys and hoisted sail. The rope broke to leave the fragmented islands scattered in the fleet's wake – where they still lie. You can still see the huge natural hawse-hole in the rocks.

Towards the end of the 11th century the islands were home to Norse families who had run their own affairs for more than 250 years with little contact with their old homeland. These joined with the Viking colonists of the Isle of Man to set up the independent Kingdom of Man and the Isles and refused to pay further allegiance to Norway. King Magnus Barelegs reasserted Norway's claim to the Western Isles in AD 1098, sweeping through the isles of the west from Lewis down to the Isle of Man to bring the Viking colonies to heel with a good old Norse-style drubbing of sword and fire. On the mainland King Edgar of Alba (Scotland) grudgingly acknowledged Magnus ruler of the Outer and Inner Hebrides. It was during this time of Norse overlordship that the islands became known to the Celts of the mainland as *Innse Gall,* or 'Isles of the Foreigners,' a named that has persisted in Gaelic to the present day. The Norsemen held on to their Scottish possesions until King Haakon IV lost them in 1263 at the Battle of Largs. The most enduring legacy of the Vikings in the islands is the predominance of place-names which derive from Norn, the Old Norse language. Their ingenious watermills are another. The design of the traditional island 'blackhouse' is also thought to echo the longhouse of Viking times.

The Clans

After Scotland took control of the Western Isles some of the Norse families left to settle in Iceland, but the majority stayed on to become Norse-Gaelic clans under the Lord of the Isles, the chief of Clan Donald better known to them as *Buchaille nan Eilean* ('Herdsman of the Isles'). The ruling clan took its name from Donald of Islay. In Lewis emerged the clans of Macleod, the Morisons of Ness, the Macivers, Macauleys, and Macraes of Uig, and the Macleods of Harris, who ancestral seat is Dunvegan Castle, in the Isle of Skye. In 1493, King James IV of Scotland asserted his wavering authority over the Hebrides by making the title Lord of the Isles forfeit to the Crown. By ending the islands' unifying hereditary rule he unwittingly strengthened the clans, whose first loyalty was to their chiefs, rather than to the Crown. The people responded with the lament *Ni h-eibhneas gun chlainn Dòmhnaill* ('There is no joy without Clan Donald'), and then embarked on a century of destructive inter-clan warfare.

James V of Scotland made a personal visit to Lewis in 1540 with a fleet of 12 warships which a contemporary account says 'bred great fear in those islanders and savages'. The king was there to put an end to the clans' destructive feuding, which he temporarily halted by making Lewis clan chief Roderick Macleod a prisoner for a year.

After James VI of Scotland succeeded to the English crown in 1603 he resorted to trickery to bring the rebellious islands to heel. All the Hebridean clan chiefs were invited to a council meeting on Mull in 1608 and taken prisoner. They were freed a year later after pledging that they would respect the king's law. Edinburgh was a long way from the Western Isles, London even further, and when Scotland joined England in the Act of Union in 1707 to form the United Kingdom of Great Britain the legislative marriage meant little to most islanders, even though it gave Scotland vital entry to English and colonial markets, and British privileges and protection for Scottish merchant ships. For the Catholic minority hoping one day to see a Catholic Stewart restored to the kingdom the article in the Act ensuring a Protestant succession was a bitter blow.

The Jacobites

After Bonnie Prince Charlie and his Jacobite followers were vanquished at the Battle of Culloden in April 1746 the Young Pretender, pursued by the British, sought refuge in the Western Isles for nearly two months, where he astounded the clansmen by drinking a bottle of brandy a day while waiting for the French to come to his rescue. Even though the Prince's island sympathisers were in the minority no one sought to claim the immense reward of £30,000 offered by the British for his capture. Disguised in women's clothing, he was eventually spirited over the sea to Skye from Benbecula as 'Betty Burke', the Irish maidservant of young Flora MacDonald. After several close calls with the searching British the hunted prince left Scotland forever on 20 September 1746. Thereafter the government announced its decision to 'smoak out' Jacobitism. Among other things the wearing of the tartan plaid and kilt was forbidden (until 1782), the use of Gaelic was discouraged, the clansmen were disarmed, and even the bagpipes were banned, being considered 'wild and tempestuous' and an implement of war. The clan chiefs were shorn of their hereditary legal powers and this more than any other measure radically changed the traditional relationship between chief and clansman and helped to pave the way for the cruel Clearances of the late 18th and early 19th centuries.

The Clearances

To this day the story of how many islanders, like the clansmen of the Highlands, were cleared from the land their families had occupied for generations is an emotional issue. Once it was discovered that hardy Cheviot sheep flourished in the islands and Highlands with next to no attention landowners – clan chiefs and Lowland lairds alike – began to clear their lands of tenants. Where there was good pasture for sheep in Lewis areas were cleared and the evicted families moved to congest remaining areas; people in Harris were moved by a new landlord to the rocky east coast, where there was hardly enough soil to bury the dead and plots for growing crops consisted of 'lazybeds', peat and seaweed laboriously built up in rocky hollows. It took four carts of fresh seaweed to make one cart decayed sufficiently for the beds, and 13 carts of rotting seaweed to produce a single barrel of potatoes. The potato blights of the 1840s piled more misery on people living largely on fish and potatoes. Compulsory immigration, assisted and otherwise, denuded large areas of the Western Isles of their people and helped to swell the populations of Canada and Australia.

The Land Struggle

The islanders periodically rioted and agitated for help through petitions, land raids, and squatting but it was not until 1884 when voting rights were extended to farm labourers that they were able to elect to Westminster men who were sympathetic to their cause. Within two years Gladstone's government had passed the Crofters' Holding Act giving security of tenure to tenants and the right to pass on tenancies to their heirs. At the end of World War I servicemen returned to the islands expecting the government to honour its promise to provide land 'fit for heroes'. When this was not forthcoming some took by force what they felt was their due and land ownership remained a focal point for grievances which the Land Settlement Act of 1919 moved to address by buying land throughout the isles to establish new crofts. Land tenure remained a contentious issue and crofting rights were bolstered by legislation in 1955 which through loans accelerated the building of new houses to replace the picturesque but insanitary old blackhouses known in Lewis and Harris as *taighean dubh*, and the thatched cottages (*taighean tugha*) of the southern isles. In 1976 the Crofters' Reform Act gave tenants the option of buying their crofts. The various crofting statutes were consolidated in 1993 in the Crofters' (Scotland) Act, giving crofters unprecedented protection. So far has the pendulum now swung that, although privately owned, most of the estates in the Western Isles have tenant crofters whose tenure gives them housing, agricultural and grazing rights, leaving the legal landowners with hardly any control of their properties, apart from rights to shooting, fishing, and minerals. In recent years monuments have been raised to commemorate some of the bloodier and more memorable of the riots and land struggles that punctuated this period in history, among them Aignish, Coll and Gress, Bernera, and Pairc.

Blackhouses

All over the islands blackhouses in various stages of dilapidation dot the landscape. Some have become cow byres and others with only their walls standing are used as sheep *fanks* (enclosures). They were all once literally black houses, coloured by the smoke from a smouldering peat fire that was never allowed to go out. The roof was thatch held in place against the winds by ropes anchored with heavy rocks. The walls were often more than three feet (a metre) thick, but little above the height of a man. Beds were usually in *neuks*, or cavities in the walls.

Local Government

In the past, the people of the Outer Hebrides had good reason to feel neglected and far from the powers that be. The restructuring of Scotland's local government from the 1970s radically changed forms that in some instances had been around since the 13th century and saw Lewis divorced from Ross-shire, and Harris and the other islands from Inverness-shire, to fall in 1975 under the newly established Western Isles Council (*Comhairle nan Eilean Siar*). For the first time in their long history the islands were grouped under a single local authority independent of the mainland and with effective control of their own destiny. Since 1991, Western Isles Enterprise (*Iomairt nan Eilean Siar*) has been a partner with the Council in a European Community initiative tailored especially to meet the needs of remote areas and its thumb-print is to be seen in such areas as infrastructural development, land improvement, fish farming, and tourism. Now that devolution has given Scotland its own parliament again for the first time since the Act of Union of 1707 islanders are keeping an expectant eye on proceedings in Edinburgh. They are hoping that the 1999 return of constitutional power will ensure a better deal for them than they have had in the past.

ECONOMY

The Western Isles are balancing on an economic tightrope. Out of an estimated population of 27,180 (mid-2000) fewer than 10,000 have paid, full-time jobs and 37% of these work for the Western Isles Council, the largest single employer in

Enduring Harris Tweed

Harris Tweed, the durable cloth long associated with sensible skirts, floppy fishing hats and hacking jackets, is the best known of the islands' products. It doesn't come only from Harris, but from weavers throughout the Western Isles. Originally the tweed, known as the *clò mór*, great or big cloth, was woven by islanders exclusively for their own use, but in the early 1840s Lady Dunmore, the wife of a prominent Harris landowner, introduced the tweed to her aristocratic friends and its popularity was established. By 1909 it was famous and the Harris Tweed Association had been formed to protect the industry from imitators.

Over the years since then the industry has contributed greatly to the local economy and is a substantial fulltime and part-time employer of weavers making cloth for the mills. The mills buy the raw virgin wool and wash, dye and spin it ready for delivery to the weavers with instructions for the specific pattern required. All genuine Harris Tweed is hand-woven on treadle looms by weavers in their own homes. The Lewis-based *Harris Tweed Authority* requires all weavers to sign a statement before starting work, promising that they will weave only by hand. Older weavers use traditional Hattersley looms, which produce single-width 30-inch (75 cm) wide fabric, the younger weave with modern Griffith looms, which were introduced to the island in 1995 to weave double-width fabric. The woven tweed in lengths of about 85 yards (78 m) is collected from the crofts and returned to the mills.

After finishing, the tweed is checked by Harris Tweed Authority inspectors, and if all the necessary regulations have been met, the length is stamped with the Certification Mark, the world-famous trademark Orb and Maltese Cross, which is the recognised mark of authenticity. This confirms that the Harris Tweed is made from 100% pure virgin wool, dyed, spun and finished in the Outer Hebrides and certified by the Harris Tweed Authority as hand-woven by islanders at their homes 'in the islands of Lewis, Harris, Uist, Barra and their several purtenances'. Each finished product also carries a number which can be traced back to the weaver who produced the cloth. The tweed comes in three weights – standard, light and bantam/feather – which gives it tremendous versatility. The lighter weights combined with a new range of colours have made it a favourite with top designers in Rome, Paris, London and New York.

Harris Tweed, has come a long way since its was first woven by island women as a prickly, heavy but hard-wearing *clò mór* from wool dyed in various infusions of bark, flowers, heather, scrub and lichen to produce the muted natural colours of the landscape they saw around them. Cloth weight has been halved, the material is softer, and Harris Tweed is now seen on the world's catwalks in such vibrant colours as dusty pink, pomegranate red, and lemon yellow. Mill workers and weavers are being recruited for the first time in years on Lewis after a flood of orders from fashion houses in France, Germany, Italy, Japan, and America. There are 150 mill workers and 250 weavers in four mills on the islands; at its height, the industry's seven mills employed 500 workers and 1,200 weavers.

Don't leave Lewis and Harris without a visit to a Harris Tweed weaver. For details contact the Harris Tweed Authority (6 Garden Road, Stornoway, Lewis HS1 2QJ; tel 01851-702269; fax 01851-702600; e-mail enquiries@ harristweed.org; www.harristweed.org).

the region. The average household income in 2001 was the lowest in Scotland and declining, as is the population, where the proportion of elderly to young people is higher than anywhere else in Scotland. Compounding this is a steady, high exodus from the islands of men and women between the ages of 18 and 21, lured to the mainland by the prospect of better jobs and a different lifestyle. With unemployment at a high of 6.4% and a Gross Domestic Product (GDP) per head of population only 65% of the UK average the islands – at least on paper – are economically in crisis. One saving grace is that crisis is a way of life in the islands, which for centuries have seen and survived a succession of economic highs and lows; another is that underlying the trappings of the modern economy is an age-old strain of self-reliance and independence bred by working the land and the sea. The main economic activities of the area are crofting agriculture, fishing, fish-farming, fish processing, construction, quarrying, tourism, and services, with small-scale industry and the manufacture of Harris Tweed and various craft products also contributing to the regional economy.

Agriculture

The islands are largely given over to subsistence crofting agriculture which is environmentally friendly in its approach to land management and is commonly regarded as the glue which holds rural communities together. It is the foundation of the island way of life, its culture and its language, and as a form of land use crofting has been extremely successful in maintaining rural populations in areas from which they would otherwise have undoubtedly disappeared. Many Hebrideans still live on rural crofts, although the vast majority are now worked as part-time or spare-time agricultural units which usually oblige crofting families to have other jobs as well. There are 6,000 individual crofts distributed among 250 settlements and nearly 80% of the land is held under complex crofting legislation which has given rise to the wry island definition of a croft as a piece of land surrounded by regulations. A parcel of crofting land typically averages 7 acres (3 ha) in size, which explains why 94% of all crofts call for fewer than two days of work a week. Some full-time farms are worked in a few areas but they tend to be small and agriculturally marginal. The quality of land and the size of crofts and grazing areas varies considerably throughout the islands, but generally, the smallest crofts are to be found on the poorest land and most of the large full-time crofts are in Uist. There are around 145,000 sheep on the islands and raising store lambs is the most important crofting activity. The rearing of calves as store or as hardy breeding stock is also carried out, mainly in the Uists and Barra, although the number of cattle, at around 3,000, is only a fraction of what it was a century ago.

Fishing

This is another traditional industry which is having to re-invent itself, having declined dramatically over the past century or so. The most significant change has been the composition of the fleet, which over the last decade has seen a decline in the number of boats, especially larger craft. Fishing boats now tend to be small, are often family-owned, and work out of local harbours and the emphasis has shifted from pure fishing to the more lucrative harvesting of shellfish – prawns, scallops, lobsters and crabs – which find a ready market in mainland Scotland, England and continental Europe. Such shellfish account for about 90% of total fishery landings.

Fish farming. This is a growing sector of the fishing industry and both freshwater and sea lochs are dotted with floating rafts of cages holding farmed fish, generally salmon, which are first cultivated in freshwater cages before being transferred to saltwater pens to complete their growth in a replication of their natural environment.

Fish processing is concentrated in Stornoway and Barra, and together with ancillary activities, merchants, ice-making, administration and advisory services, provides several hundred jobs. Local producers have joined forces to form retail co-operatives for salmon and shellfish, and there are ongoing plans for the improvement of the processing, packaging, and marketing sectors to capitalise on the reputation for high quality enjoyed by marine products from the Western Isles.

Tourism

Many islanders have become accustomed to taking in summer visitors on a bed and breakfast basis, but most of them have not placed undue emphasis or reliance on the extra income this generates. This haphazard approach is changing as the Western Isles Council and the Western Isles Tourist Board take the lead in establishing tourism or a sound and well defined basis. A survey undertaken for the Council, Western Isles Enterprise and the Western Isles Health Board in 2000 found that visitors were pumping at least £33-million a year into the local economy and this leaves no doubt that the unspoilt environment of the islands is a major economic asset. There is a campaign to improve accommodation and facilities, the variety and quality of local information, and the local interpretation available to visitors. The idea is not to emulate other holiday destinations, but rather to continue to develop the traditional skills and attributes which set the Western Isles apart. To boost tourism the islands are placing greater emphasis on aspects which focus on the islands' natural and cultural resources. Plans recognise that local people must share in the economic benefits of tourism, take account of their contribution to the total tourism experience, and be guided by their wishes. In tune with growing public interest in the environment and conservation issues development initiatives are turning increasingly to wildlife and eco-tourism ventures. Experts are looking at ways to develop these areas without any adverse impact on such species as whales, dolphins, seabirds, seals and otters.

Education

The islands offer a highly educated workforce. More than 40% of all school-leavers on the islands go on to higher education compared with 31% in the rest of Scotland. The main school in Stornoway, the *Nicolson Institute*, sends 52% of its pupils on to higher education establishments and Lews Castle College, part of the *University of the Highlands and Islands*, has 3,000 students and offers degrees in six subjects. At the end of 2000 it opened a new campus which is a major centre for education and training in information and communications technologies.

LANGUAGE

Gaelic is an ancient Celtic language which shares common roots with the Gaelic of Ireland and the old Manx language of the Isle of Man. It is also closely related to Welsh, Cornish and Breton, but only Irish and Scottish Gaelic are reasonably mutually intelligible. Gaelic's Scottish heartland is in the Outer Hebrides where it is the everyday lyrical mother tongue of the majority (75%) of the people, from the Butt of Lewis in the north to Barra in the south. Western Isles Council promotes a bilingual language policy and the first evidence of this to strike the visitor is the number of green and white road signs full of apparently unpronounceable words seemingly dotted with more accents than French. Luckily for non-Gaelic speakers the signs usually have black and white English equivalents – but not always. Make sure your map is bilingual or you'll never know that to catch the ferry at Leverburgh you have to look for *An t-Ob* in *Ceann a Deas Na Hearadh* (South Harris) and that to get to the Butt of Lewis (*Rubha Robhanais*) from Stornoway (*Steornabhagh*) you have to pass through South Dell (*Dail Bho Dheas*). One of the first signs you'll see on arrival is the warm Gaelic greeting *Ceud Mìle Fàilte* ('A Hundred Thousand Welcomes'), pronounced *kate meele falltche*. The traditional greeting between strangers is *Co leis thu?* which means 'Whose son (or daughter) are you?' and is how Gaels establish family and clan ties. *Mac* in a surname means 'son of' and *Nic* is Gaelic for 'daughter of'.

The Gaelic spoken in the islands is as musical as it is poetic and in common with the old Norn language of the Vikings that it eventually supplanted it is unusually descriptive. A place-name invariably describes the locality's distinctive physical features. Gaelic-speaking islanders display their innate courtesy by switching to English if they know you are English-speaking. Sadly, it is estimated that for every child born into a Gaelic-speaking Scottish family four elderly speakers die. Despite this sobering statistic the islanders are not giving up the struggle to preserve and invigorate a language that was the dominant tongue north of the border for more than a thousand years.

Acair, originally established to produce Gaelic texts for schools, publishes a wide range of Gaelic, English and bilingual books for the general reader. One of Acair's popular publications is *Gaelic is Fun!*, a pocket-size book of cartoons which teach beginners the language in an amusing way. For a free book catalogue contact Acair (7 James Street, Stornoway, PA87 2QA; tel 01851-703020; fax 01851-703294). A handy bilingual pocket dictionary is published by *Lomond Books* and is available in bookshops and at tourist offices. The first Gaelic translation of the Bible was published in 1609 by the Rev Robert Kirke, who wrote *The Secret Commonwealth of Elves, Faunes and Fairies* the following year.

Most islanders speak English and Scots as well as Gaelic. Scots is a language in its own right and not, as is generally supposed, a corrupt form of English. It has grown from a Northumbrian dialect of Anglo-Saxon, absorbing French, Germanic and Norse influences and was the standard speech at court until James VI of Scotland inherited the English crown in 1603 and moved to London. Recording and preserving the Scots language is the concern of the *Scottish National Dictionary Association* (27 George Square, Edinburgh; tel 0131-650 4149), and also of the *Scots Language Society* (Secretary Mr I Murray, 60 Victoria Road, Falkirk FK2 7AX; tel 01324-621567, evenings). A useful little book showing some linguistic links between Gaelic, Scots and English is the *Gaelic-Scots Wordbook*, by James S Adam (Arbroath Herald Ltd, Arbroath 1998).

RELIGION

The austere tenets of John Calvin still shape religious belief in most of the Hebridean islands, although there is concern among the older adherents of the Presbyterian kirks that today's youngsters are more familiar with the designer label of Calvin Klein than they are with the doctrines of the 16th century theologian and reformer. Broadly speaking, the northern islands are Protestant, the southern islands of Barra and South Uist are Catholic, and in-between Benbecula is a mixture of the two. Despite this sectarian split there is none of the friction that characterises similar situations in other countries and the islands are a model of religious tolerance. What does strike the visitor is the deathly silence of the northern half of the archipelago on a Sunday, compared to the more relaxed atmosphere of the south. Sunday Observance means just that in the north: no shops, restaurants or bars are open, you can't buy petrol for your car, and there's no public transport available. The only people you are likely to see are those either going to church or leaving it after attending a service. It's as well to remember this so that you can plan your itinerary accordingly and also show due respect for local sensibilities.

Christianity came to the islands by a circuitous route. It was already widespread in the southern parts of Britain by the last century of the Roman occupation and the first Christian church was established in Scotland at Whithorn in AD 397 by St Ninian. The faith spread to Ireland in AD 432, carried there from Britain by the Welshman who became the patron saint of Ireland, St Patrick. From Ireland the Christian faith of the Celtic Church was carried to the isles of the west by Columcille, or St Columba, who founded a monastery on the island of Iona in 563. There is no evidence that St Columba ever set foot in the Outer Hebrides, and it is believed that the islands were evangelised by missionary monks from his Celtic order during the half-century after he died in AD 597. In AD 620 St Barr established a monastic community at Cille Bharra on the island of Barra and there were religious settlements and colleges at Carinish and Howmore in the Uists, which attracted scholars from Britain, Ireland and continental Europe. These centres of learning were abandoned at the time of the Reformation, but the lessons learned of the value of a good education were not wasted on the islanders. While visiting English-speaking travellers were making derogatory remarks about the locals, their hosts were often fluent in Gaelic, English, Latin, French, and frequently several other European languages. The Celtic Church maintained its independence of Rome until AD 664 when, at the Synod of Whitby, it agreed to accept the authority of the Pope and the islands effectively became Roman Catholic. By the time the Vikings had begun to settle in the islands to make them a Norse colony Christianity was sufficiently rooted for the islands to have their own bishop. Within the next century or so many of the pagans who had arrived worshipping the Norse gods Thor and Odin were building churches as newly converted Christians. A gravestone dating to AD 900 and engraved with both a Celtic cross and a Norse inscription was found on Barra in 1865 and is evidence that there were Christianised Vikings at an early stage of their occupation of the islands.

The great religious ferment of the 16th century led by Martin Luther, John Calvin and John Knox and known as the Reformation started by agitation for a reform of the doctrines and corrupt practices of the Roman Catholic Church; it ended with the Church's fragmentation and the establishment of the Reformed or Protestant churches. John Knox put his own strict stamp on the Protestantism that emerged in Scotland. The Scottish reformers opted to ditch episcopacy – government of the church by bishops – and replace it with Presbyterianism, or rule by ministers and church elders. In the troubled period following the Reformation the islands gradually moved away from the Roman Catholic Church to become Protestant in the mould laid down by Knox and influenced by Calvin.

Lewis has some of Scotland's largest Free Church congregations. They are distinguished from other Presbyterians by their popular name, the 'Wee Frees', and by their devotion to what they regard as the purest and most traditional form of Presbyterianism. The devout of all Presbyterian denominations usually attend church services twice on Sundays, as well as prayer meetings and other services throughout the week.

OUTER HEBRIDES
Practical Information

Getting There

Transport links have undergone a revolution since the days when Dr Samuel Johnson and James Boswell made their celebrated tour of the Hebridean isles in the late 18th century. Glasgow is the hub for air travel to the islands and links are comfortable and frequent. Modern car ferries ply back and forth every day from Oban, Ullapool, and from Uig on the Isle of Skye. These sailings serve five island ferry ports – Castlebay, Lochboisdale, Lochmaddy, Tarbert and Stornoway – making it easy to reach any destination along the length of the island chain.

BY AIR

Nearly a million passengers a year use the airports operated and maintained by *Highlands and Islands Airports* (HIAL) and providing, with the ferry links, lifeline services to some of the remotest areas in Britain. There are HIAL airports on Stornoway (tel 01851-702256), Benbecula (tel 01870-602310), and Barra (tel 01871-890283), which make the islands easily accessible. Barra has one of the world's most novel airports. Planes land here between tides on the wide sandy beach of the Cockle Strand.

British Airways (tel 0845 77 333 77; www.britishairways.com), in conjunction with its operators *British Regional Airways* (same telephone number as British Airways) and *Loganair* (St Andrew's Drive, Glasgow Airport, Paisley, Renfrewshire, PA3 2TG; tel 0141-848 7594; fax 0141- 887 6020), flies direct to Stornoway. A 'Highland Rover' ticket gives you five separate flights on Scottish domestic routes operated by British Airways and Loganair. Tickets can be bought only outside Scotland.

BY SEA

This is the traditional way to get to the isles of the west and, naturally, the most scenic. Book well ahead, especially if you are taking a vehicle. About 80% of ferry passengers travel to the islands between April and October. *Caledonian MacBrayne* (The Ferry Terminal, Gourock, PA19 1QP; tel 01475-650100; fax 01475-637607; or reservations tel 08705-650000; fax 01475-635235; e-mail reservations@calmac.co.uk; www.calmac.co.uk) runs a fleet of well-equipped car and passengers ferries to five ports in the Outer Hebrides, and also operates some of the inter-island ferry services within the Outer Hebrides. The company – better known as CalMac – is literally a lifeline service for the islands and its history under one name or another has been inextricably intertwined with the story of the islands for more than a century and a half. On mainland Scotland you can board one of their ferries at Ullapool and Oban, or sail from Uig (Skye) to the Outer Hebrides. All sailings are subject to weather and tidal conditions, but you can rest assured that if a CalMac ferry departure is cancelled the weather really must be ferocious.

Caledonian MacBrayne's 'Island Rover' – a runabout ticket valid for 8 or 15 consecutive days from the date of the first journey with unlimited travel – and 'Island Hopscotch' – valid for one month from the date of the first journey with 12 combinations – tickets are available on the Outer Hebridean routes. Discounted 'Five-Day Return' and 'Six-Journey' tickets are also available. Contact CalMac for information on the best option.

BY ROAD

There are regular coach services to the ferry ports at Ullapool, Oban, and Uig (Skye) which tie in with ferry arrival and departure times. The main coach operator is *Scottish Citylink Coaches* (Buchanan Bus Station, Killermont Street, Glasgow, G2 3NP; tel 08750-505050; fax 0141-332 4488; e-mail info@ citylink.co.uk; www.citylink.co.uk). *Rapsons Coaches* (1 Seafield Road, Inverness, IV1 1TN; tel 01463-710555; fax 01463-711488; e-mail info@rapsons.co.uk; www.rapsons.co.uk) also operate between Inverness and Ullapool, Monday to Saturday.

You can also get to Ullapool on the 'hop-on, hop-off' bus service run by *Haggis* (tel 0131-557 9393). This starts four times a week on a circular route from Edinburgh, through Stirling and Glencoe to Ullapool and then Loch Ness. You can take from three days to three months to cover the route and this makes it a favourite choice of backpackers. *MacBackpackers* (tel 0131-558 9900; www.macbackpackers.com) runs a similar route, though in the opposite direction. The company says anyone using this service is guaranteed cheap accommodation in hostels along the route. *Wild in Scotland* (tel 0131-478 6500; www.wild-in-scotland.com) runs tours designed for age group 18-30.

BY RAIL

ScotRail (Caledonian Chambers, 87 Union Street, Glasgow, G1 3TA; tel 08457-484950; www.scotrail.co.uk) has a 'Freedom of Scotland Travelpass' which offers unlimited travel on most scheduled rail services in Scotland, and discounts on Caledonian MacBrayne ferries and selected Citylink coach routes. The ticket is available for four out of eight consecutive days, or 12 out of 15 days. You can travel as far as Oban, Mallaig and Kyle of Lochalsh by train on some of the most scenic lines in Britain. There are coach connections across Skye from Armadale and Kyle of Lochalsh to Uig. To get to Ullapool, you can take the train as far as Inverness, and then go by coach to Ullapool. Contact ScotRail or the National Rail Enquiry Service (tel 08457-484950) for timetables and fares.

Note. If you'd prefer to let others make your arrangements *Scotia Travel* (tel 0141-305 5050) can usually offer some tempting deals out of Glasgow. ScotRail and CalMac are also worth checking for offers on island holidays.

TOUR OPERATORS

Classique Coaches: 8 Underwood Road, Paisley, Renfrewshire, PA3 1TD (tel 0141-889 4050; fax 0141-848 7616; www.classiquecoaches.co.uk). Coach tours to the islands using modern and vintage coaches.

Going Forth Tours; 9 South St Andrews Street, Edinburgh, EH2 2AU (tel 0131-478 6500; fax 0131-478 6501; e-mail info@goingforth.com; www. goingforth.com). Tours of the islands for backpackers and independent travellers.

Natureguide (Travel): 12 Albany Business Centre, Gardeners Street, Dunfermline, Fife, KY12 0RN (tel/fax 01383-625874). Small group holidays by mini-coach, specialising in birds, flowers and other wildlife of the islands.

Scotia Travel: tel 0141-305 5050; fax 0141-305 5051; e-mail failte@ scotiatravel.com; www.scotiatravel.com. Has four fly-drive, four-day breaks. These are the 'Harris Heritage' (bays of Harris), 'Island Fling' (Lochboisdale and Eriskay), 'Hebridean Flora and Fauna' (Uig and Bernera), and 'Now You're

Talking Gaelic' (Lewis). All four packages include flights from Glasgow or Edinburgh, hire car at airport, and B&B accommodation on a half-board basis.

You can also have a day out in Lewis and Harris with *Harris Coaches* (tel 01859-502441) where you sail on a Saturday from Uig, Skye, at 9.40am on the *Hebridean Isles* and arrive at Tarbert at 11.25am. The coach then takes you on a tour of Callanish, West Lewis and Stornoway before the 8.30pm ferry departure. Alternatively you can sail from Uig on Tuesday, Thursday or Saturday, from April to October, for a tour of Grand Harris, Sound of Harris and North Uist.

Getting Around

Not too long ago it cost a packet to ferry your car from island to island, an expense which tended to dampen enthusiasm for Hebridean motoring holidays. Now, once you have reached the islands from the Scottish mainland by air or sea it is possible, apart from two unavoidable ferry trips, to drive from one end of the Outer Hebrides to the other, roughly the equivalent of the 110-mile (177 km) journey from Oxford Circus in London to the Bull Ring in Birmingham. Island communities such as Vatersay, Berneray, Scalpay, and latterly Eriskay, have benefited from European Community funding to have their first causeways and bridges built so that they are no longer dependent on ferry services. The inter-island car and passenger ferries are still operating and a reliable public transport system should enable you to explore all corners of the islands.

Maps and Guides

The 1:125,000 Western Isles Tourist Map produced for the *Western Isles Tourist Board* by Estate Publications (£4.50) gives both Gaelic and English place-names, shows beaches, and details points of interest, as well as airports, ferry routes, youth hostels, and even tea rooms. It's available from Tourist Information Centres and is a good overall quick-scan map for planning routes and estimating distances. For more detail there's the 1:50,000 − 1$^{1}/4$ inches to the mile (2 cm to 1 km) − Ordnance Survey Landranger Series in OS sheets 8 (Stornoway and North Lewis), 13 (West Lewis and North Harris), 14 (Tarbert and Loch Seaforth), 18 (Sound of Harris and St Kilda), 22 (Benbecula), and 31 (Barra and surrounding islands). This series has replaced the old one inch to one mile maps and is the one popular with walkers and climbers. At the end of 2000 *Ordnance Survey* (OS) announced a unified approach to Gaelic names on its maps. The OS will seek consensus on the accepted form and spelling of Gaelic names used on its maps and will collect names in English and Gaelic for towns, roads, streets, buildings and man-made forestry. Tourist Information Centres are also good places to pick up free maps, information leaflets, as well as guides and specialist books.

BY AIR

Loganair (Barra: tel 01871-890282/388; Benbecula: tel 01870-602290; Stornoway: tel 01851-703067) operates inter-island flights between Barra-Benbecula (twice a day Monday to Friday), and Benbecula-Stornoway (twice a day Monday to Friday). Flights to Barra land on the famous Cockle Strand beach, known in Gaelic as *Traigh Mor*, or the Big Beach (airport tel 01871-890283). You can get a bird's-eye view over the islands by booking a special 'Sightseer' ticket on the Loganair flights from Barra and Stornoway to Benbecula. You can buy a ticket at the airport virtually right up to the time the prop begins to spin.

BY SEA

Ferries

A Caledonian MacBrayne (Harris: tel 01859-502011; North Uist: tel 01876-

500337; South Uist: tel 01878-700288: Barra tel 01871-810306) vehicle ferry connects Harris with North Uist with up to four sailings a day Monday to Saturday. The adult single fare is £4.75, and a car £21.90. CalMac also connects South Uist with Barra once a day on Tuesday, Thursday, Friday and Sunday. The single adult fare on this route is £5.30, and a car £30.50. The Western Isles Council (tel 01851-701702) runs a passenger-only ferry between Eriskay and Barra. There are two sailings a day, Monday to Saturday, to the pier at Eoligarry, and daily sailings, Monday to Friday, to Northbay (Ardveenish) pier. The adult single fare is £5, and concession/children £2.50, bicycles £2.50.

Boat Trips

Boat operators offer trips from one-hour-long to two-week charters with full crew. More than 30 operators regularly run trips out into The Minch, half of them on a daily basis between April and October, depending on weather conditions. The others operate on a charter basis and undertake general cruises only on demand. Short outings cost £5-£10, although this increases with duration. Most of the trips last 1-3 hours, although some operators also offer full day outings.

Longer Cruises

Twenty-five operators offer cruises in The Minch, most of them using yachts based outside the area. They operate only between April and October. Cruises range from one to 14 days, with three-quarters of them lasting for one week

Engebret Hebridean Holidays: Charles and Margaret Engebretsen, Sandwick Road, Stornoway, HS1 2SL (tel 01851-702304; fax 01851-702305; e-mail charles. engebretsen@virgin.net). Wildlife, sightseeing and fishing in the Loch Roag area. Twin-engined rigid inflatable from Miavaig or Valton Pier, West Loch Roag.

Eriskay Seascapes: William Rusk, Portpatrick, Eriskay (tel/fax 01878-700215). Trips around South Uist, Eriskay and Barra. Leisurely cruises round Eriskay, visiting the wreck of the *SS Politician*, Weaver's Castle, and Prince's Bay.

Island Cruising: Murdo Macdonald, 1 Erista, Uig, Lewis, HS2 9JG (tel 01851-672381; fax 01851-672212; e-mail cuma@sol.co.uk; www.island-cruising. com). Offers diving, bird-watching, and wildlife cruises aboard the *MV Cuma* as far north as North Rona and Sula Sgeir, as far west as the Flannan Isles and the St Kilda archipelago, and to the southern uninhabited islands of Mingulay, The Monachs, Scarp and Taransay.

Malcolm Macleod: Cnoc Cottages, 5a Knock, Point, Lewis (tel 01851-870537; fax 01851-706384). Boat trips on *Elena C*. Wildlife trips from Stornoway. Charter trips to Shiant Isles.

Scenic Cruises: Hamish Taylor, Tigh an Tobair, Flodabay, Harris (tel 01859-530310; fax 01859-530289; e-mail Hamish@scenic-cruises.co.uk). Coastal mini-cruises and coastal exploration along the east coast of Harris on *MV Lady Catherine*, visiting depopulated homesteads, wildlife observation and fishing.

Sea Trek: Murray Macleod, 16 Uigen, Miavaig, Uig, Lewis, HS2 9HX (tel/fax 01851-672464; e-mail murray@seatrek.co.uk; www.seatrek.co.uk). Offers seal, dolphin, and whale, and seabird-watching around the scenic areas of Uig, Bernera, and Callanish. Excursions last about 2¹/₂ hours and cost about £20 a person. Specialists in visits to the remotest islands. Fishing trips also available.

Strond Wildlife Charters: Andrew and Alison Joubert, 1 Strond, Harris, HS5 3UD (tel/fax 01859-520204; e-mail aj@erica.demon.co.uk). Has a 19 ft (5.8 m) launch *Petrel* based in Leverburgh. Cruises for a maximum of five passengers. Wildlife watching a speciality. Longer trip or 'water taxi' by arrangement. Booking essential.

Sulaire Trust: Kenneth Morrison, 18 Napier Hill, Stornoway, Lewis (tel 01851-703814). Traditional dipping lugsail fishing boat which sails regularly around the Western Isles.

Western Edge Limited: Iain Murray, 51 York Street, Aberdeen, AB11 5DP (tel 01224-210564; fax 01224-210563; e-mail murrayiain@compuserve.com). Yacht *Annag* based at Berneray Harbour in North Uist in the summer months and sails weekly to St Kilda. Places available for 6 to 8 guests on board this sailing sloop for 3-6 day cruises.

BY ROAD

Old travel diaries and guidebooks always evaluated road conditions as well as mileages. During the Scottish tour she made in 1803 Dorothy Wordsworth, the sister of Lakeland poet William Wordsworth, rated roads she travelled on from 'tolerable' to 'wretchedly bad'. She'd be pleasantly surprised if she were travelling now. Millions of pounds have been spent on the inter-island route from Ness to Barra, via Stornoway, and the road network is being improved all the time. Where other parts of Britain has built motorways and bypasses to supplement existing roads, in most cases the islands have had to build roads, bridges and causeways where none existed before and this has created an extensive road network within the island chain. This has had the effect of preventing islands such as Great Bernera, Vatersay, Scalpay, Berneray and Eriskay from becoming victims of the depopulation which over the past century has left other once vibrant little islands forlorn and uninhabited. As you travel you can look out to a number of depopulated islands, such as Mingulay, Pabbay, and the Monach Isles. Toll-free road bridges connect the islands of Scalpay to Harris and Great Bernera to Lewis. Causeways join the islands of Berneray with North Uist, Eriskay with South Uist, Barra with Vatersay, while Benbecula is linked to the Uists north and south by causeways which replaced the old hazardous fords.

Road Signs. In line with its bilingual policy, the Western Isles Council has erected Gaelic road signs throughout the islands. Get a leaflet giving the English equivalents from a local Tourist Information Centre on arrival.

Driving

While the islands tend to attract such outdoor enthusiasts as hikers and cyclists, four wheels are always a sensible option on the bigger islands. Lewis and Harris, for instance, are deceptively large. Bus services do operate but having to arrange your days around their timetables can put a crimp in your travel plans. If you are not taking your own vehicle, you can usually hire a car, although this should be organised well in advance of your arrival. Although many of the smaller roads are single-track there's no such thing as rush-hour traffic. Remember to use the passing places to allow other vehicles to pass or overtake and watch out for sheep or other animals on the roads. Should you see a pair of ghostly horns appear in your headlights at night you've spotted a ram belonging to a crofter in Uig, Lewis. He has painted the horns of his flock's black sheep a bright reflective orange to stop them being run over on unlit roads. To give you an idea of scale the distance between Stornoway (Lewis) and Tarbert (Harris) is 38 miles (61 km) and it's 45 miles (72 km) between Lochmaddy (North Uist) and Lochboisdale (South Uist).

Fuel. Petrol pumps are dotted all over the islands, with garages, filling and service stations mainly in Stornoway, Tarbert, Northton, Lochmaddy, Balivanich, Howmore, Lochboisdale, and Castlebay. Petrol is widely available on the island, but at a premium which usually adds 10p a litre or more to the mainland price.

Cycling

You have to pay to take a bike on the ferry, but meandering roads through spectacular scenery make cycling a worthwhile option. The downside to pedal-power isn't so much the uphill sections of road or the unpredictable soakings you get, but rather the windy conditions that can take all the fun out of cycling. Bumpy island roads also mean that male riders could suffer from what's jokingly known among the fraternity as 'scrotal trauma'. Bikes are available for rent.

Buses

Services run throughout the islands, usually running hourly from Stornoway to many of the surrounding villages. There's a north-south network, via ferry links, which allows travel from Ness in the north of Lewis to Castlebay in Barra, linking the main communities and ferry ports. Services operate on most routes until about 6.15pm. There are also evening services on certain routes radiating from Stornoway, and within the town itself. The main routes operate Monday to Saturday. Buses do not operate on Sundays. Fares are reasonable, especially for long journeys. Day returns are available. The main routes are (summer schedule):

Overland Route. Services connecting with the Sound of Harris and Sound of Barra ferries. Linking Lewis, Harris, the Uists and Barra. Up to three services a day.
Postbus. On Lewis, the Uists, and Barra you can travel with the postman on his Postbus (tel 01246-546329) routes for a small fee.

Hitching. If you are not pressed for time thumbing your way around is also a possibility, although you are unlikely to get lifts at the weekend, especially in the northern islands on Sunday.

Guided Walks

Most of these are led by guides from a public or voluntary body and are available in summer (April-October). At the height of the season regular walks take place twice a week and can last from one to six hours, with most taking 2-6 hours. A third of the walks are partly coastal. The price depends on the mileage covered.

Mail

The main Post Office is in Lewis (Francis Street, Stornoway; tel 01851-702166). This is open Monday to Friday between 9am and 5.00pm. On Saturdays the hours are 9am until midday. You will find sub-post offices throughout the islands (see Help and Information in each section), usually as part of a local shop or store. Their hours of business can be variable in the extreme.

Telephones

You can usually find a phone box, no matter where you are, although be warned that some accept only prepaid phonecards. To get local or national directory help dial 192 and 153 for overseas directory assistance. 100 will get the local operator and 155 should raise the international operator. The only mobile phones which seem to work in the Western Isles are Vodafone and BT Cellnet.

MEDIA

Radio

The *British Broadcasting Corporation* (BBC) operates from Stornoway, Lewis, and a number of small studios are situated at key locations throughout the area. This service, and in particular *BBC Radio nan Gaidheal*, the Gaelic radio station on 103.4FM, reaches virtually every home and provides an important social service. *Isles fm* (tel 01851-703333; fax 01851-703322; e-mail ann@ islesfm.uk.org; www.islesfm.uk.org), on 103 MHz, is a Stornoway-based community radio station. Contact the station for information on programmes or check the *Isles fm* schedule published every week in the *Stornoway Gazette*. Tune in for the latest breaking news, music, chat, information about *ceilidhs* and whatever else is happening in the islands. *Reidio.com* caters for the Gaelic-speaking communities with regular updates, information, and entertainment.

Television

The islands receive all the usual mainland channels, with the exception of Channel 5. Recent years have seen an increase in economic and creative activities relating to the expansion of Gaelic television (*telebhisein*) broadcasting. In 1991, the *Gaelic Television Committee* was established to focus on improving the TV service provided for the Gaelic-speaking community. This committee has its headquarters in Stornoway. A small number of Scottish independent production companies have been established to produce local and international programmes for national television and the number of films and documentaries shot on location in the islands is growing. Grampian Television has a branch studio in Stornoway and BBC Gaelic TV screens regular programmes.

Newspapers

The *Stornoway Gazette* (10 Francis Street, Stornoway, HS1 2XE; tel 01851-702687; fax 01851-706424) is a weekly newspaper, on sale every Wednesday afternoon, which serves all the islands. *Fios* – 'news' or 'information' – is a North Lewis newspaper published weekly by *Cuan Ard Press Ltd* (6 Lionel, Port of Ness, Lewis; tel/fax 01851-810110; e-mail fios@cuanard.freeserve.co.uk). You can read selected extracts from *Fios* on www.reidio.com/fios, as well as listen to Gaelic songs and music clips. *De Tha Dol?* (Room 2, Old Hostel, Tarbert; tel 01859-502171) is a community newspaper published once a fortnight by the *Harris Council of Voluntary Services*. Its name means 'What's On?' Mainland publications available locally include Scottish and English newspapers flown in every morning, and regionals such as the *West Highland Free Press* (tel 01471-822464; e-mail admin@whfp.co.uk; www.whfp.com), published every Thursday. WHFP's priorities are summarised in its Gaelic masthead slogan: *An Tir, an Canan 'sna Daoine* ('The Land, the Language, the People'), a slogan borrowed from the Highland Land League which, in the late 19th century, fought to win security of tenure for crofters. The land issue is at the heart of the newspaper's politics down to the present day, and it also champions the Gaelic language by giving it political support and by publishing more Gaelic text than any other newspaper.

Eating and Drinking

EATING

The Scots were not amused when Dr Samuel Johnson described oats in his famous 1755 *Dictionary of the English Language* as a 'grain, which is generally given to horses, but in Scotland supports the people'. It wasn't until he travelled north to the Hebrides with his biographer James Boswell nearly 20 years later that he discovered just what Scottish food was all about. In his account of their travels, *A Journey to the Western Isles of Scotland*, Dr Johnson wrote: 'Not long after the dram, may be expected the breakfast, a meal in which the Scots...excel us'. He added, 'If an epicure could remove by a wish in quest of sensual gratification, wherever he had supped, he would breakfast in Scotland'.

Dr Johnson's remarks are still as valid today throughout the isles as they were when he wrote them more than 200 years ago. Other breakfasts pale in comparison with the gargantuan platters that face you in the morning in even the most modest hotel or B&B, and an island breakfast will keep you fuelled and going all day long no matter how you travel or how far you go. Not for nothing did HV Morton write that Scotland is 'the best place in the world to take an appetite'. A Barra B&B served us up a typical breakfast of fruit, porridge, smoked haddock, eggs, bacon, tomatoes, mushrooms, potato cakes, sausages, black pudding, beans, toast, marmalade, honey, jam, the whole washed down with a choice of tea or coffee. We were then asked if we'd like more of anything 'to fill the corners'.

The island tables didn't groan to this extent in the old days, at least not in the blackhouses of the crofting communities. For them, their staples of barley, oatmeal, and potatoes were – with luck – served as accompaniments to fish or a fat seabird. *Brochan Air Sgarbh* (cormorant porridge) called for a cormorant or puffin to be cooked with barley meal or oatmeal and served with mashed potatoes; *Ceann Cropaig* (stuffed fish-heads) required a seasoned mix of chopped fish liver, preferably cod, stuffed into fish-heads and boiled; *Maragan Dubha* is a black pudding made from finely chopped suet, oatmeal, and onions, seasoned and mixed with the blood before being stuffed into a casing and boiled in water. Once cool, the black pudding is sliced and fried in hot fat. *Maragan Geala* (white pudding) is the same, but without the blood. *Sgeit Gort* was even more of an acquired taste. Skate wings were hung up for a few days so that their gooey oil could drain away. In some areas of Lewis they left the skate on a dung heap for a few days until it developed a strong smell of ammonia, treatment that echoes the way the old Norse dealt with the shark they ate. If you are visiting Lewis in the autumn you might be invited to sample one of the 2,000 *gugas* (plump young gannets) that are collected every year from the uninhabited islet of Sula Sgeir, 40 miles (64 km) north of the Butt of Lewis. These are usually served with boiled potatoes and a glass of milk and are usually described as 'better meat than any fish and better fish than any meat'.

As Dr Johnson observed, oats do have a prominent place in island meals, with various types of oatmeal being used for different dishes. Pinhead goes into haggis and oatmeal loaves, rough is used for porridge or brose, medium-rough is favoured by butchers for meal puddings, medium-fine is used in porridge, brose, skirlie, and for everyday baking; superfine quality oats are reserved for special baking and for fine oatcakes. With its remarkable filling properties porridge was once a dish eaten by crofters every day of their lives. Crofters' wives would make a large pot of porridge at the beginning of the week and, once cold, it was cut into slices for the men in the family to take every day for their midday meal. One common story is that crofters would fill a wooden drawer with cooked porridge at the beginning of winter and cut a slice from it whenever they felt peckish.

Most seaweeds are edible and dulse (*Rhodymenia palmata*), which grows on rocky shores, was once eaten widely in the islands. Carragean (*cruaigean*) was chewed fresh or dried and boiled in milk with sugar then left to set to make a type of jelly. Cakes of laver seaweed (*Porphyra umbilicalis*) are still eaten today in coastal communities. The laver is rolled in oatmeal and fried as a tasty breakfast accompaniment. This is the sloke of Ireland and the laverbread of Wales.

Gullible foreign tourists are often told stories about the wild haggis, supposedly a beast looking like bagpipes, with one set of legs shorter than the other so that it can easily run round hillsides to escape hunters. Haggis is undoubtedly Scotland's best known traditional food, although it's very much a love it or hate it dish. Poet Robert Burns extolled it as the 'Great chieftain o' the pudden race'. In an unkind moment travel writer HV Morton described it as 'looking remarkably like a piece of boiled grey granite'. Haggis is made from the windpipe, lungs, heart and liver of the sheep, which are first boiled and then minced. Mixed with beef suet and lightly toasted oatmeal, it is stuffed into a sheep's stomach and sewn up. The haggis is prepared by further lengthy boiling. Haggis is traditionally served with bashed neeps and tatties – mashed turnips and creamed potatoes – which are flavoured with a little grated nutmeg. Haggis, neeps and tatties are traditionally eaten with a dram of malt whisky, which is poured down the throat, not over the haggis. These days there is even a vegetarian haggis, which is quite tasty, even though the only ingredient it has in common with the original is oatmeal. One we tried in Harris contained mixed veg, oil, nuts, seasoning and honey, as well as oatmeal. If traditionalists find this an affront to Robert Burns, how about the version being promoted in startling Indian guise – Haggis Pakora. For this delight, the haggis is gutted and its innards mixed with chilli before being rolled into balls and dipped in a batter of garam flour, turmeric, coriander, more chilli, and water. Deep fried, the reconstituted haggis has been hailed by one leading food writer as 'the most futuristic' of Scotland's culinary delights. 'Great chieftain o' the curry race...'?

At one time many crofts made their own cheese but the most you'll find these days is *crowdie*, a simple semi-cooked soft white cheese made without rennet from the whey of slightly soured milk, seasoned with salt and a touch of pepper. This is then squeezed in a muslin bag to remove excess water, left to rest for a couple of days and finally rolled in oats before serving.

DRINKING

Waiting to board an inter-island ferry one day we were concerned to see an elderly woman wheeling a young man off the vessel in a barrow. Thinking he had been involved in an accident we asked the ferryman what had happened. He grinned and replied: 'He's been to a wedding and that's his mother taking him home'. In his *A Description of the Western Isles of Scotland, Circa 1695* Martin Martin noted:

> *'The chief men of the isles...continued drinking sometimes 24, sometimes 48 hours. It was reckoned a piece of manhood to drink until they became drunk, and there were two men with a barrow attending punctually on such occasions. They stood at the door until some became drunk, and they carried them upon the barrow to bed, and so carried off the whole company one by one as they became drunk.'*

In a changing world it's nice to know that some things never change.'

In the old days everyone started off the day with an eye-opener, a dram of whisky, or *uisge beatha* – the 'water of life' in Gaelic. This was usually a fiery, illicitly distilled potion. Today, pubs and bars can usually oblige with any drink you fancy, so long as you are not in Lewis, Harris, or North Uist on Sunday. The Presbyterian Free Church is the guardian of Protestant morality on these isles and very little opens, or moves, on the sabbath. The Catholic islands of South Uist and Barra are more relaxed and do not frown on Sunday drinking. When the film *Whisky Galore!* was being made on Barra the producer took a bottle to the local priest and in the approved manner turned it upside down before he cracked the cap and poured the Father a dram. Seeing the priest looking askance at the ritual the producer asked whether this was the wrong thing to do. 'It's a good idea right enough' replied the father gravely, 'if you have the time'. Where they are open for business most pubs are open all day and they are generally cheaper than hotel lounges or restaurants if you feel like a bracer. Unlike the Inner Hebrides, none of the islands of the Outer Hebrides has an established distillery or a brewery, although the blended stuff of *The Whalers Whisky Company* (21 Gress, Lewis, HS2 0NB; tel 01851-701265; fax 01851-701272) is worth sampling. You'll find this sold under the label 'The Whalers Dram', a name inspired by islander John Murray, who produced a potent firewater from a crude still on the ice-bound island of South Georgia during the time many Hebridean men went south to the Antarctic with the whaling fleet.

If someone raises a glass to you and says *Slàinte mhath!* (slanju va) – 'Here's to your health!' – you should, if you can, reply with the old Jacobite toast: *Slainte mhor a h-uile la a chi's nach fhaic* (slanju vore a hoola la a chee is nach highchk), which means 'Great health to you every day that I see you and every day that I don't'.

With the emphasis placed nowadays more on the economic and political similarity of nations rather than their differences more and more people are beginning to appreciate distinctive regional and minority cultures and the Gaelic and Norse heritage of the islands has produced a legacy of music, song and dance going back close on a thousand years. Gaelic arts and music can be found in both formal and homely settings throughout the islands. Festivals, Highland Gatherings, informal house *ceilidhs*, exhibitions, dances, and the annual *Mods*, or competitions, all ensure that traditional entertainment is readily accessible to visitors throughout the year. Events attract top international performers and artists and the various gatherings and agricultural shows held throughout the islands highlight such attractions such as piping competitions, Hebridean and Highland dancing, Gaelic singing, and music played on such instruments as the fiddle, accordion, clarsach (Celtic harp), chanter and recorder. As well as some fine music you'll also hear the unaccompanied Gaelic singing for which the Western Isles are famous. These range from the *puirt-a-beul*, or 'mouth music', to the songs about people, places, and local events which are common at *ceilidhs*. Other distinctive island songs are those known as waulking songs (*orain luaidh*) which were sung by women while making Harris Tweed. Waulking refers to the fulling or beating of the cloth to shrink and thicken it. Viscount Leverhulme's niece Emily Macdonald explains the process in her *Twenty Years of Hebridean Memories*:

> *Then comes the shrinking and finishing process of waulking, as it is called, and this is a great social occasion...The tweed having been made thoroughly wet, is spread out yard by yard over a long table. The women sit on each side of the table and pull and push and thump the tweed till it has shrunk as much as it will ever do. The work is carried on at differing speeds, first slow, then quicker, then quick and very quick, and it is accompanied by songs in the appropriate time. Very often each woman sings an impromptu verse and all join in a chorus.*

You can hear waulking songs sung at the *Lewis Loom Centre*, at Bayhead, Stornoway, which features the history of Harris Tweed. A compilation of such songs has been published by *An Comunn Gaidhealach* in the collection *Eilean Fraoich*. The standard work on island waulking songs is Dr JL Campbell's three-volume *Hebridean Songs*, published by the Oxford University Press.

Mods

These are competitive assemblies and local *mods* usually offer three days of competitions for piping, solo and choral singing, instrumental music, drama and poetry, followed by prize-winners' concerts and various fringe events. The Royal National Mod is the premier festival of Gaelic music, language and culture and is held in a different place each year during October. For more information contact *An Comunn Gaidhealach* (The Highland Society; tel 01851-703487).

Piping

The annual **Pipe Major Donald Macleod Memorial Piping Competition** is held in April and is recognised as one of the most prestigious in the piping world. Pipe Major Macleod was a prolific composer of tunes for the instrument and regarded as one of Scotland's finest players of the great highland bagpipe. The Lewis Pipe Band, formed in 1904, is a major attraction and plays a key role in events and festivals throughout the year. The band performs regularly throughout the summer in Stornoway Town Centre. The *Lewis and Harris Accordion and Fiddle Club* meets regularly and performances by visiting bands and musicians as well as local artists are held at the Royal British Legion in Stornoway. Visitors are always welcome. For further details contact Stornoway Tourist Information Centre (tel 01851-703088).

Festivals

Fèis (pronounced *faysh*, plural *fèisan*) is the Gaelic word for a festival or feast and has become associated with music, song and dance tuition festivals. These tuition festivals are mainly for the young, and take place throughout the summer. *Fèis Bharraigh* – the Barra Festival – is one of the principal *fèisean* in Scotland and attracts visitors and tutors from around the world during its two-week run. If you are lucky, you might see a display of the unique story-telling Hebridean dancing rescued from the brink of extinction by Barra enthusiasts. There are similar festivals in the islands of Uist, Harris and Lewis during the summer months which offer an opportunity for you to experience some great music and attend various *ceilidhs* held locally throughout the festival. For more information contact *Fèisean nan Gàidheal* (Meall House, Portree, Skye, IV51 9BZ; tel 01478-613355; fax 01478-613399; www.feisean.org).

Fèis nan Coisir (tel 01851-702482) is a festival of Gaelic choirs attracting visiting singers from across Scotland for a week of choral concerts and evening entertainment featuring world-renowned Gaelic singers. Most island festivals take place in July-August. Some contact numbers: North Uist (tel 01876-500247); Harris (tel 01859-502050); Lewis (tel 01851-702520); Barra (tel 01871-810779); and Benbecula (tel 01870-620322).

The **Hebridean Celtic Festival**, the largest festival of its kind in the north of Scotland, is staged in the grounds of Lews Castle, Stornoway, during July and draws large international audiences. The festival mixes indigenous Gaelic music from home-grown professional musicians with a wide range of top performers from the Celtic nations. Past performers have included master fiddler Alasdair Fraser, 'new roots' folk-rock group Wolfstone, La Bottine Souriante, Natalie MacMaster, Sharon Shannon, Davy Spillane, singer-songwriter Dougie MacLean, and the pioneering Gaelic rock group Runrig, which climbed over the years from the relative obscurity of North Uist to become UK chart-busters and world-class musicians. In addition to the main concerts there are lots of fringe events, music sessions and workshops. From the intimacy of the early evening events to the late-night party atmosphere in the festival tent there's something for everyone. Contact the Festival Office (PO Box 9909, Stornoway, HS2 9DW; tel 07001-878787; e-mail celftfest@sol.co.uk; www.hebceltfest.com and www.hebrides.com/celtfest).

Ceilidhs

The *ceilidh* (pronounced *kaylee*) is an ancient form of home entertainment and takes its name from the Gaelic for 'visit', and goes back to the times when villagers would gather in someone's cottage to gossip, sing, dance, and recite poetry. Today, *ceilidhs* are usually riotous affairs held in a village community hall or hotel. Many hotels, especially in Barra and the Uists, have free live entertainment at weekends. Try to attend at least one *ceilidh* before leaving the isles. Information is posted in shop windows and on noticeboards. In Harris, dates and times of *ceilidhs* appear in the local newspaper *De Tha Dol* ('What's On?'). Check times and dates of all events or find out what else is on locally by contacting the Tourist Information Centre (tel 01851-703088; e-mail stornoway@ witb.ossian.net) the website www.witb.co.uk updates the diary of events.

FLORA AND FAUNA
Wildlife is caught in a lucky time warp in the islands. As they are not suited to highly mechanised farming techniques traditional crofting methods have left large areas of untouched habitat where many species which have long since vanished or are trembling on the edge elsewhere in Britain continue to survive, if not flourish.

Two-thirds of all Britain's **corncrakes** are concentrated in the Hebrides; a significant proportion of Britain's **corn buntings** breed here; a third of the **dunlin** population of the UK and a quarter of its population of **ringed plover** and 20,000 pairs of **lapwings** breed on the coastal machair. **Golden eagles** are not uncommon in the mountainous areas of the islands and even the rare **white-tailed sea eagle**, reintroduced to Scotland from Norway in 1975 by Scottish Natural Heritage (SNH) and the Royal Society for the Protection of Birds (RSPB), is a periodic visitor. The islands form one of the last strongholds of the engaging **otter** and some of the more remote islets support internationally important breeding colonies of grey seals. Nearly 300 types of seaweed have been recorded, 600 species of beetle, and eight different kinds of bee. The famous moorland bumblebee *bombus jonellus var.hebridensis* is found nowhere else.

FLORA
More than 800 plant species have been recorded. For sheer volume and variety nothing can beat the rich coastal strip known as the machair, which supports a wide range of vegetation and in summer a surprising range of wild flowers, with dense growths of **red and white clover, eyebright, self-heal, birdsfoot-trefoil, daisies, kidney** and **tufted vetch, yellow pepperwort, heartsease** and **corn marigold**. Common plants along the coast include the pink **sea thrift** and white or lilac **scurvy grass**, and **silverweed**, whose fleshy roots were once eaten boiled or roasted and ground into flour by the islanders in times of famine, as well as such rarities as the spiral **tasselweed** of North Uist. Orchids, some of them endemic to the Western Isles, further enliven this display. **Frog orchids, northern marsh orchids, early purple orchids** and **early marsh orchids** are plentiful. In autumn, **Devil's-bit scabious** and the lilac **field gentian** are also plentiful. The international importance of the machair for flora and fauna, and the fine balance of environmentally friendly land use which protects it, has resulted in much of it being declared Environmentally Sensitive Areas and Sites of Special Scientific Interest.

As well as the lime-rich machair, habitats ranging from acidic peaty moorland and windy summits of rocky gneiss to spray-splashed coastal grassland add to the wide diversity of flora. Rare **rock sea spurrey** can be found on low cliffs along the eastern side of the Uists. **Sea campion** and **sea pearlwort** decorate the cliffs, and **sea plantain** carpets the sandy coastal saltmarshes which are under water at high tide. On the beaches are **sea sandwort** and pink **sea rocket**, and on the fringing dunes tough **marram grass** helps to stabilise the sand. The moorland which covers most of the central and eastern parts of the islands supports **heath spotted orchid** in profusion and white expanses of **hare's-tail** and **common cottongrass, heath milkwort**, and insect-eating **sundews** whose sticky spoon-shaped leaves trap unwary prey. Botany buffs are drawn by oceanic peatland flowers such as **marsh St John's-wort, bog myrtle, pale butterwort, lesser skullcap** and **white beak-sedge**. In seasonal sequence come purple **bell heather**, pink **cross-leaved** and **purple heather**. The blue-flower **milkwort** and yellow **tormentil** add colour to the browns and purples of the peatlands. Bright yellow **marsh marigolds** grow in roadside ditches, with the **yellow iris** attractive to corncrake favouring the damper areas. White and sometimes yellow **water-lilies** brighten the edges of dark inland lochs. The range of aquatic plantlife varies from loch to loch. The shallow, sandy machair lochs are rich in nutrients, while the peat lochans of the moorland are dark and acidic. Brackish water lochs with a mix of salt and fresh water are characteristic of the islands and the plants which flourish in these salty conditions add yet another dimension to local botanical interest. Flowers of the upland include **Alpine lady's-mantle**, **Alpine meadow-rue**, and **mountain sorrel**. **Purple** and **starry saxifrage** and such ferns as **parsley** and **beech fern** share exposed heights with **dwarf willow**.

Useful Plants

Bog myrtle's aromatic leaves were traditionally used to flavour beer, and the **bitter centaury** of the gentian family was macerated in whisky to make a tonic drink. The roots of the pretty, yellow-flowered **lady's bedstraw** were used to make a red dye; **tormentil** roots were used for tanning and chewed to heal sore lips; the root of sneezewort was used as tobacco. A preparation of the aquatic **bogbean** was used to treat constipation. On South Uist, the flowers of the **red poppy** were once used as an ingredient in a mixture for teething babies, and **meadowsweet, fleabane** and **bog myrtle** were used to cover the floor to produce a pleasant insect-repelling fragrance when trodden underfoot. On North Uist the ashes of **bladder-wrack** seaweed were used to preserve seal meat and cheeses, and it was also used as a fertiliser which improved the flavour of potatoes as well as promoting their growth. Other plants provided the islanders of old with food, shelter, medicine, dyes, fibres and many other benefits. The knowledge of how island plants can be used has been passed from generation to generation and plants have taken deep root in the language, local place-names and mythology. *Flora Celtica* (Royal Botanic Garden, Edinburgh, EH3 5LR; e-mail Celtica@ rbge.org.uk) is a project documenting and promoting the knowledge and use of wild plants with the aim of increasing awareness of their past and present diverse roles and promoting their sustainable use for local benefit. The project would like to hear from you if you know of, or have come across, any uses for wild plants or can contribute associated folklore.

Woodlands

Grazing deer and sheep have prevented the renewed growth of wild trees and the remnants of past natural woodlands survive mostly as stunted clumps on islets in the middle of lochs or in steep-sided gullies where fire and grazing animals have been unable to destroy them. Modern plantations consist largely of stands of profitable commercial timber, or as exotic and coniferous species such as those ornamenting Lews Castle in Stornoway. In a largely treeless environment the woodlands in the grounds of Lews Castle are a delight. They were planted on imported soil in the mid-19th century by Sir James and Lady Matheson. Some 70 species of conifers and broad-leaved trees flourish here in what is now known as Lady Lever Park, providing cover which supports plant, bird and insect populations that could not otherwise thrive locally. The only **walnut tree** in the islands grows here.

FAUNA

The **otter** is the only indigenous land mammal in the islands, although the introduced **red deer** is a regional native. Otters can be seen all around the islands; deer herds are confined to certain areas of the islands, such as North and South Uist, Uig, North Harris, the Pairc district of Lewis, and the island of Pabbay in the Sound of Harris. The **rabbit, blue hare, brown rat, feral cat** and **polecat** have all been introduced by man. **Mink** which escaped from local mink farms, now closed down, have become well established in the islands and are now so widespread that they are posing a serious threat to many ground-nesting birds. Black or 'ship' **rats** have colonised the Shiant Islands, off the east coast of Lewis, since surviving a shipwreck there in 1876. As they are among the last plague rats of mediaeval Europe they are a protected species on the islands. No one is sure where rodents such as **mice** and **voles** come from. Introduced **hedgehogs** are common in southern South Uist and in the Stornoway area and are reportedly spreading, also with dire results predicted for ground-nesting birds. The only reptile you might see is the harmless **slow-worm**, a legless lizard. No native amphibians are known and any **frogs, newts** or **toads** you come across have been introduced. **Pipistrelle bats** occur in and around Stornoway. The short-legged **Eriskay pony** is one of Scotland's last remaining native breeds of pony and has a lineage popularly believed to go back at least to the hardy little grey ridden by Robert the Bruce when he vanquished the army of England's King Edward II at the Battle of Bannockburn in 1314. The Eriskay pony bears a striking resemblance to carvings on Pictish stones of more than a 1,000 years ago, so it could even have been around in those days. The *Eriskay Pony Society* was established in 1972 to preserve this unique breed from extinction. The Uist Community Riding School in Balivanich trains ponies to prepare them for riding. They are also easily trained to pull small carts or traps.

Atlantic grey seals and **common seals** are abundant in the waters around the islands. Greys prefer the more isolated islets of the west coast; the common seal is more prevalent in the east. Other marine mammals include various species of whale, dolphin and porpoise. Around 20 different species have been recorded in the waters of the west coast and unusual marine visitors have included **harp** and **hooded seals**, a stray **beluga**, or toothed white whale, and even the occasional **walrus**. The most common sightings are of **white beaked dolphin** and **porpoise**. **Minke whales** are also fairly common and often approach close to boats. **Killer whales**, orcas, are easily identified by their tall dorsal fins. All these, as well as huge **basking sharks**, are most frequently spotted between April and October. A worrying development for whale-watchers is the news that the Ministry of Defence (MoD) is investigating reports that naval submarine-hunting sonar equipment could be killing whales. The investigation began late in 2000 after a number of dead whales were found off the islands. Scientists say naval equipment could be interfering with the mammals' own sonar communications, confusing them and driving them away from their breeding and feeding grounds to strand on beaches. It could also kill them at short distance. **Turtles**, mainly loggerhead and leathery, are occasionally seen in coastal waters. **Brown** and **rainbow trout** as well as **wild salmon** are common in the lochs and rivers, **eels** are widespread, and **Arctic char** are found in a number of lochs.

BIRD-WATCHING

Some 327 species of birds have been recorded, of which more than 100 breed in the islands. The islands lie on the natural flight path for migrating landbirds to and from their Arctic grounds and also provide a refuge for windblown vagrants from America and northern Europe. Unusual vagrants have included a **pied-billed grebe**, a **bufflehead, American wigeon, green-winged** and **blue-winged teal**, and **pintail**. Sea cliffs and islets provide sites for millions of seabirds, among them **gannet, fulmar petrel, puffin, storm** and **Leach's petrel, kittiwake, common** and **black guillemot**. Hills and moors are home to such breeding birds as **red grouse, golden plover, greenshank,** and **skylark. Oystercatcher, turnstone, dunlin, redshank**, numerous varieties of **sandpiper** and other waders can be seen on sandy and rocky shores, along with various **gulls, skuas**, and **terns**. The rare **corncrake** and **corn bunting** share the landscape with the more common **wheatear, mallard**, and **lapwing**. Regular visitors include wintering **redwing, Greenland white-fronted geese**, and **barnacle geese**. Other rarities include the **golden eagle, peregrine, merlin, red-necked phalarope** and **little tern**, as well as the occasional **white-tailed sea eagle**. Golden eagles quarter the uplands of Lewis, Harris and North and South Uist, a few pairs of peregrine falcons survive on coastal cliffs, and merlin and **buzzard** are quite common on hills and moorland. The absence of voles and adequate numbers of other suitable prey animals in Lewis and Harris confines **hen harriers, long** and **short-eared owls**, and **kestrels** to the southern isles. Twitchers come particularly to see birds such as the skua and red-necked phalarope breeding at the southern limit of their range and other birds peculiar to the area, such as the Hebridean sub-species of song-thrush, wren, twite, and dunnock. The Stornoway woodlands of Lews Castle are the haunt and breeding ground for many species of birds. **Treecreeper, blue** and **great tits**, and **mealy redpolls** are found nowhere else in the islands, except as vagrants. **Warblers** such as willow, chiffchaff, garden, wood and grasshopper turn up regularly, along with the more exotic **great spotted woodpecker**. The woods at Lews Castle hold the only **rookery** and one of the few tree colonies of **herons** in the Western Isles. Some 6,000 sea and freshwater lochs and lochans have been counted throughout the Western Isles, providing ideal habitats for a wide variety of birds. **Red-throated divers** nest on countless small lochans and a few **black-throated divers** on bigger lochs, mainly in Lewis. **Arctic skuas** are spreading south from Lewis as far as South Uist but the **great skua** breeds only in Lewis, St Kilda, North Rona, the Shiant Isles and Barra Head. Winter bird-watching offers a great diversity of wildfowl. **Eider** and **long-tailed duck** are common in the shallow waters around Lewis, while the Uists and Benbecula are noted for their breeding **mute swan** and **greylag geese**, as well as **whooper swan** and **white-fronted geese**. The only RSPB Reserve in the Outer Hebrides is at Balranald, North Uist, which is a draw in summer for twitchers hoping to see, or at least hear, the elusive corncrake.

CONSERVATION

The international environmental importance of the Outer Hebrides has been recognised by the number and extent of conservation initiatives undertaken by the local authority in conjunction with a variety of other organisations. Several different types of environmental designations have been awarded to protect both landscape and important natural resources. These include four **National Nature Reserves** with a total areas of 7,999 acres (3,237 ha), or 1.12% of the Western Isles; 53 **Sites of Special Scientific Interest (SSSI)** covering 92,295.2 acres (37,350.6 ha) or 12.9%; 15 **Special Protection Areas (SPA)** covering 77,933.2 acres (31,538.5 ha), or 10.88%; 11 **Candidate Special Areas of Conservation (CSAC)** covering 81,443 acres (32,958.9 ha); and three **National Scenic Areas (NSA)** covering 288,124 acres (116,600 ha).

SSSI is one of the most widespread designations of the 53 in the Outer Hebrides, with 31.5 in Lewis and Harris, and 21.5 in the Southern Isles. The Lewis and Harris sites cover 45,101.8 acres (18,252.1 ha) or 8.54% of Lewis and Harris; the Southern Isles sites cover 47,193.3 acres (19,098.5 ha) or 25.12% of the Southern Isles. Individual sites vary in size from North Harris SSSI covering 31,927.4 acres (12,920.6 ha) to Cnoc a' Chapuill, which covers just half an acre (0.2 ha).

There are **Marine Special Areas of Conservation (mSAC)** at Loch Roag, Western Lewis; Loch Maddy and Loch Euphort, North Uist; the Monach Islands, 5 miles (8 km) west of North Uist; North Rona, 44 miles (71 km) off the north-east Lewis; and the archipelago of St Kilda, some 40 miles (64 km) west of North Uist.

SPORT AND RECREATION

WALKING

More than a dozen recognised and waymarked trails cover many parts of the islands, with routes over mountain, moor and machair, where you can see and enjoy birdlife, animals and flowers, and explore ancient places and unspoilt landscapes, as well as interact with the people who live in the isles. Each trail is clearly marked and has a self-guide leaflet giving route details and safety information, and insights into places of interest and history along the way. The 13 designated routes are Tolsta-Ness; Calanais; Great Bernera; Rhenigidale; Scalpay; Stockinish/Luskentyre; Berneray; Lochmaddy; Langass; Druidibeg; Eriskay; Eoligarry; and Vatersay. Leaflets on all these walks are written by local experts and are illustrated. They are available from Tourist Information Centres and local outlets throughout the islands for 50p each.

Walks vary from easy 2-mile (3.2 km) strolls around Calanais or Langass to demanding treks of 10 miles (16 km) or more, such as the Tosta-Ness route, or the Rhenigidale circuit in Harris. You can walk through a nature reserve at Druidibeg, cross from The Minch to the Atlantic on the Stockinish walk, or just enjoy a relaxing stroll at Eoligarry. Some of the walks are on the smaller islands, but all are easily accessible. New trails are being developed by local communities throughout the islands and it is hoped that these will link up to become the 'Western Isles Way'.

Crofting Code

This is something all walkers should respect. Leave dogs behind or make sure they are kept on a leash; use parking areas provided and don't drive vehicles on the machair; fasten gates and use stiles to cross fences; do not litter; avoid damaging archaeological sites; try not to disturb breeding birds; protect wildlife and plants. The weather can be unpredictable and the ground boggy after wet weather, so wear sensible clothing and footwear. Take an OS map of the area and a compass. Tell someone where you are going and by what route, or leave a note visible on the dashboard of your car saying where you are going and when you expect to be back.

For guided walks contact the following:

Balranald Nature Reserve: North Uist. Guided walks from visitor centre May to August, 2pm Tuesdays and Fridays.

Crann Tara Tours: 207 Stoneybridge, South Uist HS8 55D (tel 01870-620323).

Mike Briggs Sports: Bun-na-Gille, Bunabhainneadar, Harris, HS3 3AL (tel 01859-502376). Guided walks in Harris for groups or individuals.

Northton Machair Guided Walks: Co Leis Thu (tel 01859-520258). From the Macgillivray Machair Centre, mid-May to mid-September.

North-West Frontiers: 18a Braes, Ullapool, Ross-shire, IV26 2SZ (tel/fax 01854-612628). Guided walking holidays.

Stornoway Trust Ranger Services: Leverhulme House, Perceval Square, Stornoway, HS1 2DD (tel 01851-702001). For guided walks around Stornoway past and present, during April to October.

Southern Isles Amenity Trust: Langais, Lochmaddy (tel 01870-602039). Various summer guided walks.

Western Isles Tour Guide Association: tel 01859-520330; fax 01859-520244. Whose island-based guides offer a wealth of local experience.

You can also contact the *Hebridean Walking and Climbing Club* (tel 01851-643297 or 01851-860562), which caters for a wide range of abilities and interests. For a seven-day regional forecast contact Weathercheck (tel 09001 333 111 code 101).

FISHING

The Outer Hebrides accounts for only 1.3% of Britain's land area, but the islands encompass 16% of its fresh water. Fishing guides are on hand in some areas to give visiting anglers the opportunity to improve their fishing skills or to guide them to the best lochs. Loch Roisnavat Trout Fishery, outside Stornoway, offers fishing for rainbow and blue trout, and also teaches fly fishing. Sea angling centres include Stornoway, Tarbert, Harris, and Castlebay, in Barra. Stornoway has hosted several major sea angling festivals in recent years. Visitors can apply for temporary membership of the *Stornoway Sea Angling Club* (South Beach Street; tel 01851-702021).

Brown Trout

Apart from those available on some estates, there are not many boats for hire and bank fishing is usual. The wild brown trout is territorial so if you are bank fishing keep on the move and fan out your casts. You can use bait or spin on some lochs, but most anglers rely on a fly rod and fly fishing is the rule on estate waters, as well as those controlled by angling associations. The brown trout season is from 15 March to 5 October. The **best months** for wild trout, however, are May, June, early July and September.

Sea Trout and Salmon

Salmon in the isles are summer fish averaging 6-7 lb (2.7-3.2 kg), though much larger fish are regularly taken. Sea trout can be found almost anywhere in a loch, but salmon prefer to lie in shallow water close to the shore of a loch or island where turbulence oxygenates the water. The season for salmon and sea trout runs from 11 February to 15 or 30 October, although there might be slight variations in some districts. Salmon begin to run in late June. From then until late September are the **best months** locally.

Flies

You should find the following suitable for all island gamefish: Butchers, Black Zulu, Soldier Palmer, Black Pennell, Peter Ross, Blae and Black, Cinnamon and Gold, Bibio, Grouse/Mallard and Claret, Invicta, Kate McLaren, Camasunary Killer, Teal Blue and Silver, Alexandra, Claret and Golden Olive Bumbles, Irish Dabblers, Goat's Toe, Connemara Black. The Western Isles Clan Chief and Green French Partridge are recommended. Salmon flies around sizes 10 and 8 work well, including Stoat's Tail (and Silver), Hairy Mary, Blue Charm, Thunder, Sweep, Garry Dog, Kenny's Killer and others.

No rod licence is required but you do need permission to fish for salmon and sea trout from the controlling estates. A fee is sometimes charged. For brown trout fishing you can usually get a day ticket for a modest fee, or take out temporary membership of a local angling association.

Sunday Fishing

It is illegal to fish for salmon and sea trout on Sundays. Although Sunday fishing for brown trout is legal, anglers are asked not to fish on Sunday as this offends religious beliefs in most areas. An exception to this is Barra, where brown trout fishing on Sunday is acceptable.

Sea Angling

There's unsurpassed sport for the sea angler, and local sea angling clubs fish regularly for nearly 30 different species, from deepwater bluemouth to the blue shark. There are excellent pollack and saithe in the tidal races around the rocky headlands, haddock and whiting over a variety of sea-bed conditions, cod and ling around the underwater reefs, and thornbacks and flatfish in the mud and sand, often in inshore shallows. There are also conger eel and mackerel, along with skate. Noteworthy is the common skate record of 195 lb (88 kg). Contact the Stornoway Sea Angling Club for information on tagging as common skate must be returned alive to the sea. The club has a 36 ft (11 m) boat, and sea angling trips take place most weekends in summer. The club also organises the Western Isles Open Boat Championship every July and the Western Isles Cod Championship in

August, both well established events. There are also competitive sea angling events in Harris, Benbecula, and Uist. Check with the Western Isles Tourist Board or a local Tourist Information Centre. Local suppliers have an extensive range of rods, reels and tackle for hire.

SAILING AND CRUISING

If you don't know you luff from your leech but you'd still like to go sailing or cruising we recommend that you go out with an operator experienced in local waters, as there are unexpectedly tricky reaches even in the calmest of conditions. You can sail to the Outer Hebrides, St Kilda, or other islands on the Bermuda ketch rig *Corryvreckan* (Dal an Eas, Kilmore, Oban, PA34 4XU; tel/fax 01631-770246; e-mail yacht.corryvreckan@virgin.net; www.corryvreckan.co.uk). No experience is necessary. All cruises start and finish in Oban, which is easy to reach by road or rail. The yacht is equipped for distance sailing in safety and comfort and complies with the Department of Transport Code of Practice for charter yachts. Accommodation is in five two-berth cabins. Prices start at £495 for a berth for six days.

Island Cruising (Murdo Macdonald, 1 Erista, Uig, Lewis, HS2 9JG; tel 01851-672381; fax 01851-672212) cruises in the Outer Hebrides with its 67 ft (20 m) *MV Cuma*, formerly a fishing research boat, now converted into a comfortable vessel for up to 12 passengers. The boat has six cabins, each with hot and cold water and central heating. There are also three toilets and two showers.

If you want to get closer to sea level for some whale and bird-watching *Hebridean Exploration* (Stephanie Sergeant, 19 Westview Terrace, Stornoway, HS1 2HP; tel 01851-705655/701851; www.hebex.co.uk) provides guided sea kayak tours for novices to experts. All equipment is supplied.

DIVING

For well qualified, experienced scuba-divers the islands of St Kilda and the Flannan Isles off the west coast of Lewis offer the ultimate in Atlantic diving in Britain, but excellent diving spots also abound from Lewis south to Mingulay. Dive operators, though few and far between, should be contacted through the Scottish or Western Isles Tourist Board as local knowledge of dive sites is a must, as is the use of a boat or inflatable. Once organised, the rewards are great – from untouched ancient wrecks and prolific marine life forms to breathtaking visibility and the opportunity to harvest in unpolluted water the ingredients for a bumper seafood supper.

GOLF

There are five well distributed golf courses in the islands on Lewis, Harris, Benbecula, South Uist, and Barra. While the Stornoway course is parkland-moorland in nature, the other four are natural machair turf, with seaside links' characteristics. Long daylight hours and relatively uncrowded fairways add to golfing pleasure and visitors are welcome on all the courses. Those in Stornoway and Harris courses are closed on Sunday.

HEBRIDEAN CHALLENGE

If you want to stretch yourself to the limit, are in good shape, and can spare the necessary four days, you can take part in this taxing event, an adventure race through the islands from south to north, calling for a mixed team whose five members will share some arduous hill running, mountain biking, road biking, sea kayaking, and sea swimming. The race is staged annually and the 2002 race is scheduled for 6-10 May. You can get more information from events director Martin Stone (Sleagill Head Farm, Sleagill, Penrith, CA10 3HD; tel 01931-714106; fax 01931-714107) or local event co-ordinator Stephanie Sargent (e-mail stephanie@hebrideanchallenge.com).

Help and Information

TOURIST INFORMATION CENTRES
(Ionadan Failte)
Western Isles Tourist Board: 26 Cromwell Street, Stornoway, Lewis, HS1 2DD (tel 01851-703088; fax 01851-705244; e-mail stornowaytic@witb.ossian.net; www.witb.co.uk). The tourist office in **Tarbet**, Harris (tel 01859-502011), is open all year but with restricted hours during winter. There are also seasonal area tourist offices in **Lochmaddy**, North Uist (tel 01876-500321), **Lochboisdale**, South Uist (tel 01878-700286), and **Castlebay**, Barra (tel 01871-810336). There are 24-hour Public Access Information systems available at all centres all year round. An accommodation booking service is also offered and tickets are available for some local tours and attractions. All the tourist offices are situated close to the ferry terminals and offer a wide range of information, maps, guidebooks and other publications and useful accessories and gifts.

USEFUL ADDRESSES AND TELEPHONE NUMBERS
British Airways: Stornoway Airport; tel 01851-703240.

Loganair: Stornoway (tel 01851-703673); Barra (tel 01871-890283/388); and Benbecula (tel 01870-602290).

Caledonian MacBrayne: Ferry Terminal, Stornoway (tel 01851-702361); Harris (tel 01859-502444); North Uist (tel 01876-500337); South Uist (tel 01878-700288); and Barra (tel 01871-810306).

The main **Police Sation** is in Church Street, Stornoway; tel 01851-702222. There are also police stations in Harris (tel 01859-502002); Lochmaddy, North Uist (tel 01876-500328); Lochboisdale, South Uist (tel 01878-700261); and Benbecula (tel 01870-602374).

Western Isles Tour Guides Association: 9 Cluer, Harris, HS3 3EP (tel 01859-530294; e-mail dbroadbent@linoone.net). Professional guides with local knowledge.

Harbour Master: Western Isles Council, Balivanich, Benbecula; tel 01870-602425 (office), 01870-604294 (home); e-mail calum-macleod@cne-siar.gov.uk.

Western Isles Council (Comhairle nan Eilean Siar), Sandwick Road, Stornoway, Lewis HS1 2BW; tel 01851-703773; fax 01851-705349; e-mail nscott@cne-siar.gov.uk; www.cne-siar.gov.uk.

Western Isles Enterprise: James Square, 9 James Street, Stornoway HS1 2QN; tel 01851-703703; fax 01851-704130; e-mail wie@hient.co.uk.

Royal Society for the Protection of Birds (RSPB): Druidibeg Cottage, Grogarry, South Uist; tel 01870-620369; www.rspb.org.uk.

Scottish Natural Heritage (SNH): 32 Francis Street, Stornoway, Lewis HS1 2ND; tel 01851-705258; fax 01851-704900; www.snh.org.uk.

Scottish Marine Wildlife Association: 34 Valtos, Uig, Lewis HS2 9HR; tel/fax 01851-672373.

Museum nan Eilean: Francis Street, Stornoway HS1 2NF; tel 01851-703773; fax 01851-706318.

Banks are open Monday to Friday, closed Saturday and Sunday. Opening times vary.

Bank of Scotland: Stornoway; tel 01851-704000; Tarbert; tel 01859-502453; Lochmaddy; tel 01876-500266/323; and Benbecula; tel 01870-602044.

Royal Bank of Scotland: Stornoway; tel 01851-705252; Lochboisdale; tel 01878-700399; and Barra; tel 01871-810336.

Clydesdale Bank: Stornoway; tel 01851-703555.

Lloyd's TSB: Stornoway; tel 01851-702368.

CALENDAR OF EVENTS

Apart from the recognised national public and religious holidays the islands also have a number of local holidays throughout the year when offices and businesses are closed. You can check the dates with the Western Isles Tourist Board or visit www.cne-siar.gov.uk/holidays.

March   *Feis nan Coisir*, Stornoway, Lewis.

April   *Pipe Major Donald Macleod Memorial Piping Competition*, Stornoway, Lewis.

May   *Western Isles Challenge*, endurance team race, Barra-Lewis.
               Lochmaddy Boat Festival, North Uist.
               Lewis Half Marathon, Stornoway.

June   *Harris Mod*, Tarbert.
               Lewis Mod, Stornoway.
               Benbecula Half-Marathon.
               Uist Mod, Iochdair, South Uist.
               Sea Angling Championships, Stornoway, Lewis.
               Uist to Barra Yacht Race.

July   *Harris Half Marathon*.
               Berneray Week, North Uist.
               Celoas Music Festival, South Uist.
               Barra Festival.
               Hebridean Celtic Festival, Stornoway, Lewis.
               Feis Tir un Eorna, Paible, North Uist.
               Barra Highland Games.
               Harris Gala.
               Feis na Hearadh, Harris.
               North Uist Highland Games, Hosta.
               South Uist Highland Games, Askernish.
               Lewis Highland Games, Tong.
               Barra Live music festival.
               Lewis Golf Week, Stornoway.
               Hebridean RIB Challenge, around Western Isles coast.
               West Side Agricultural Show, Barvas, Lewis.
               South Uist Agricultural Show, Iochdar.
               South Harris Agricultural Show, Leverburgh.
               Feis Eilean an Fhraoich, Stornoway.
               North Uist Agricultural Show, Hosta.

August   *Highlands Festival*.
               Carloway Agricultural Show, Carloway, Lewis.
               Feis Tir a Mhurain, Lionacleit, Benbecula.
               Harris Arts Festival, Tarbert.
               Sail Hebrides Maritime Festival, various locations.
               Brevig Regatta, Back, Lewis.
               Lewis Carnival, Stornoway.
               Fish Festival, Stornoway.
               Uist and Benbecula Heritage Events.
               Twin Peaks Hill Race, North Uist.
               Sea/Surf Kayak Symposium, North Uist.

October   Royal National Mod, various venues.

Exploring Outer Hebrides

Lewis

In Gaelic, Lewis is known as *Leodhais*, and gets its name from the word *leogach*, meaning marshy ground, but it's better known locally as 'the Lews' and is the most populous of the islands, with 21,737 people. It is the most northerly of the islands in the Outer Hebrides and at 850 sq miles (2,201 sq km) is the largest, stretching more than 50 miles (81 km) from the tip to the North Harris border and 8-28 miles (29-45 km) across. Although Lewis and Harris are regarded as two distinct islands, they are not in fact separate and a distinct geographical boundary exists where the Lewis moorland reaches the natural barrier of rugged mountains to the north of the Forest of Harris. For centuries the two areas were cut off from one another by this physical hurdle comprising 2,622 ft (799 m) Clisham and its surrounding hills, and this isolation of old is today reflected by the fact that even the Gaelic spoken by each community is different. Lewis is well-known for its large inland blanket of peat, a broken moorland pocked with hundreds of shallow lochs. The coastline is a succession of sea-lochs, cliffs, sandy and pebble beaches, all of which make for ideal walking, bird-watching, and fishing. The island rises to 1,885 ft (575 m) at the summit of Mealisval in the south-west, and to 1,874 ft (571 m) on Beinn Mhor's summit in the south. The island is broken up into half a dozen districts: **Point**, to the east of Stornoway; **Back**, going north along the east coast; **Ness** at the northern tip; **Westside** and **Uig** heading down to North Harris; and **Lochs**, between Loch Seaforth and Loch Erisort in the south-east.

STORNOWAY *(Steornabagh)*

This is the bustling administrative capital and only town in the Outer Hebrides, a lively seaport halfway up the east coast sheltered in all weather and accessible from the sea no matter what the tide, a factor that has for centuries made it the centre of the local fishing industry and a popular port of call for cruise ships and yachts. It has a population of about 8,000.

After ousting the Macleods in the 17th century the Mackenzie Earls of Seaforth held sway over Lewis until 1844 when the last of the family sold the island to returned Scottish merchant trader James Matheson, a founding partner in the famous Jardine Matheson Company of Hong Kong, which had made him enormously wealthy. Matheson, later to receive a baronetcy, paid £190,000 for title to Lewis and took control at a time when potato blight had brought many islanders to the verge of famine and too weak to offer much resistance to the Clearances which saw lairds and landlords clear their lands through mass evictions to make way for sheep or deer parks. Matheson took part in these Clearances, providing subsidised passages to Canada in the 1850s for his uprooted, poverty-stricken tenants. Matheson's monument is **Lews Castle**, which can be seen to the west of the town high above the harbour.

The castle stands on the site of Seaforth Lodge, the old seat of the Mackenzies, which at the end of the 17th century was in turn built on the site of the even older Macleod stronghold of Stornoway Castle. Cromwell's troops demolished this and the broken masonry was used as rubble to provide foundations for Stornoway's

Number One Pier. Cromwell was remembered by Stornoway's Presbyterian town fathers centuries later when they named the main street after the Puritan leader of the anti-royalist Roundheads. The conqueror was obviously a man after their own hearts. Matheson planted 1,000 acres (405 ha) of the grounds around Lews Castle with extensive woodlands comprising a huge variety of trees, including rare imported species, shrubs and bushes which surround the castle in a riot of colour during the summer and autumn months.

In 1918, the island changed hands again when the Matheson family sold it to the energetic Liverpool soap magnate William Lever, Viscount Leverhulme. Lord Leverhulme was seduced by Lewis and decided he would turn it into a modern fishery and fish-canning centre and drag the islanders into the 20th century. Lord Leverhulme gave Stornoway a gas supply, a laundry, and a dairy and also intended to use electricity to light the streets. The post-war collapse of the European herring market, plus the intransigent conservatism usual in island communities, put an end to his grandiose schemes. The final nail in the coffin was the return of World War I servicemen who staged a series of land raids to claim crofts they felt rightly belonged to them as returning war heroes. A disgruntled Lord Leverhulme closed down all his operations in Lewis, gifting Lews Castle and its grounds, now the public Lady Lever Park, to the community and even offering them the island. He then moved to try to modernise Harris instead, but died during the attempt and both places sank back into a welcome torpor.

Lews Castle is not open to the public, although you can enjoy the woodlands for which Matheson imported soil by the shipload. In the grounds of Lews Castle are **three walks** designed to highlight the main features of shoreline, woodland, river, and open moorland. A number of vantage points give excellent views of the town, the harbour and surrounding area. The three walks are: Willoglen Walk 2 miles (3.5 km), Gallows Hill Walk 3 miles (5 km), and Creed River Walk 3.7 miles (6 km). A brochure detailing them is available from *The Stornoway Trust* (Estate Office, Leverhulme House, Stornoway, HS1 2DD; tel 01851-702002; fax 01851-706915) or the Tourist Information Centre. The *Millennium Forest* project funding along with funding from *European Objective 1*, *Forest Authority*, Scottish Natural Heritage and The Stornoway Trust, has made possible extensive improvements to the paths and trails within the castle grounds. For the past half century **Lews Castle College** has been educating and training students in a variety of subjects useful in the industry and commerce. The college, surrounded by parkland, a golf course, woodland and with its own croft, now has 3,000 students with 500 of these in full-time education and is part of the *University of the Highlands and Islands*, a university linked by modern technology to other campuses in the most sparsely populated parts of Britain and to universities around the world. Overlooking the town to the north of the golf course is the **Lewis War Memorial** whose opening by Lord Leverhulme in 1920 was his last public act in Lewis. More than 1,000 names of servicemen who fell in World War I are commemorated. World War II losses were added later.

The central area of the town offers an interesting hour's walkabout and you can get a leaflet detailing the highlights. It's called *Stornoway* and it's by Mary Bone. The **Public Library** (19 Cromwell Street, Stornoway; tel 01851-708632; fax 01851-708676) in the town centre offers an extensive local reference section, café and Internet facilities. The Library Coffee Shop is open Monday to Saturday from 10am to 4.30pm. On nearby North Beach Quay stands what is probably the oldest building in the town, an 18th century net-loft. The nearby **Fish Market**, built in 1980, is owned by the Stornoway Pier and Harbour Commission. The site of Luskentyre House, the house in which the great Canadian explorer Sir Alexander Mackenzie (1764-1820) was born is marked by a plaque on the corner of **Martin's Memorial Church** in Francis Street. Mackenzie was the first

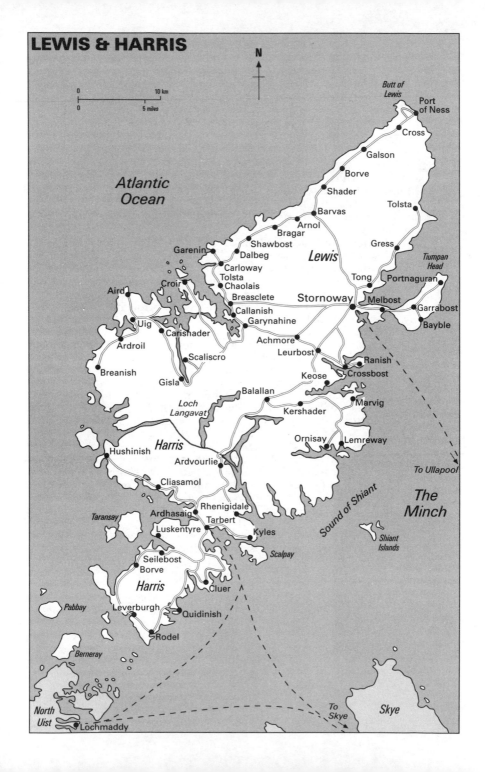

European to make the overland crossing of Canada from the east coast to the Pacific Ocean. He was knighted for this achievement. He used vermilion and grease to record his feat by painting on a rock, 'Alex MacKenzie from Canada by land 22nd July 1793'. There are no memorial plaques to another of Stornoway's sons, James Morrison, who was bo'sun's mate on the *Bounty* during the famous mutiny in 1789, but he is remembered in local folk tales. Stornoway can also boast of another son known for his association with two great explorers, 'Scott of the Antarctic' and Sir Henry Shackleton. This was stoker Thomas MacLeod, who sailed with both men on their last polar voyages. The Bible used by David Livingstone on his African travels can be seen in **St Peter's Episcopal Church** at the upper end of Francis Street. In the heart of the town *An Lanntair* ('The Lantern') centre (Town Hall, South Beach, Stornoway HS1 2BX; tel/fax 01851-703307; e-mail lanntair@sol.co.uk; www.lanntair.com) stages exhibitions of the best available in the visual arts and promotes a variety of Gaelic and other cultural events.

A major development is due to begin late in 2002 which will give the centre a gallery, a 250-seat theatre/cinema, community workshops, offices, foyer bar and café restaurant, shops, visitor centre, and gift shop. All areas will have disabled access. The coffee shop serves light meals, lunches, home-baking, snacks and hot and cold drinks are available and the centre is also licensed. Open all year Monday to Saturday from 10am to 5pm. **Museum nan Eilean** (Francis Street, Sornoway, Lewis, HS1 2NF; tel 01851-703773 ext 266; fax 01851-706318; e-mail: rlanghorne@w-isles.gov.uk; www.cne-siar.gov.uk), close to the town centre, hosts exhibitions showcasing the archaeology, history, fishing, crofting and other aspects of island life. It's open April to September, Monday to Saturday from 10am to 5.30pm; October to March, Tuesday to Friday from 10am to 5pm, and Saturday 10am to 1pm. Admission is free.

On the eastern headland of Stornoway Harbour at Holm Point (*Rubha Thuilm*) is a simple monument looking out to the scene of the worst tragedy in recent island history, the group of rocks known as 'The Beasts of Holm' (*Blastan Thuilm*), which tore the bottom out of *HM Yacht Iolaire* in the early hours of New Year's Day 1919. The yacht was carrying a crew of 23 and 260 servicemen returning after World War I. Only 78 men survived, even though the yacht struck the rocks barely 20 yards (18 m) from the shore. Almost every village on Lewis lost family members in the disaster; one man who had previously survived for 36 hours in the sea after his ship had been torpedoed drowned within sight of his home. The monument erected in 1969 stands some distance from the side road leading to Holm Farm. On the opposite headland at Arnish Point (*Rubha Airinish*) is a memorial cairn to Bonnie Prince Charlie, who spent some hectic weeks in the islands while dodging soldiers and ships of the pursuing British in 1746.

POINT

Stretching out further east from the town is Point (*An Rubha*), on the Eye (*Ui*) Peninsula, which gets its name from the Norse word *eidh*, meaning neck of land. The Point is almost an island, separated by a narrow isthmus of sand at Branahuie, which carried the road to **Tiumpan Head** and the lovely little village of Port nan Giuran The access road across the isthmus is protected by sea walls from the huge waves which roll in from The Minch. The 14th century church of **St Columba** at Aiginish was once the parish church of Stornoway. In mediaeval times it was the burial place of the Macleods of Lewis and the tombstones are of considerable historical importance. Nineteen Macleod chiefs are reputedly buried here, as well as one Mackenzie. On the south side of the ruined church is an impressive effigy of Ruairidh (Roderick) MacLeod, the

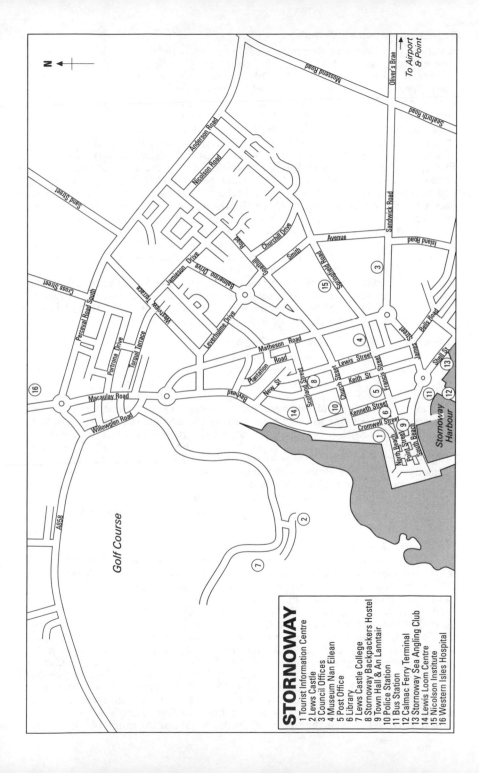

STORNOWAY

1 Tourist Information Centre
2 Lews Castle
3 Council Offices
4 Museum Nan Eilean
5 Post Office
6 Library
7 Lews Castle College
8 Stornoway Backpackers Hostel
9 Town Hall & An Lanntair
10 Police Station
11 Bus Station
12 Calmac Ferry Terminal
13 Stornoway Sea Angling Club
14 Lewis Loom Centre
15 Nicolson Institute
16 Western Isles Hospital

Golf Course

Stornoway Harbour

To Airport
& Point

seventh chief and a contemporary of James the 4th of Scotland. The female figure is said to be of Margaret, his daughter, who died in 1503 and was the mother of the last Abbot of Iona. The church is signposted from the main A866 road. Access is by track from the parking area. Close to St Columba's church is the **Aignish Riot Memorial** cairn, an award-winning project which commemorates the local land raiders who in January 1888 drove the cattle from Aignish Farm in the hope that it would be divided into crofts. On the opposite, southern shore of the Peninsula at **Swordale** (*Suardail*) is a spectacular fringe of sheer cliffs which are the rendezvous for an interesting variety of seabirds. Further along the coast is **Bayble** (*Pabail*), where the bay shelters a small harbour with a sandy beach in the lee of the pier. Good for watersports, fishing, and bird-watching. Bayble Hill is the highest point in the peninsula, with good views from the top. **Tiumpan Head lighthouse** at the extremity of Point also has excellent views across The Minch to the Scottish mainland hills. Basking sharks and whales can sometimes be seen cruising below. In 1955, during a Royal Visit to Lewis, six-year-old Prince Charles – now Prince of Wales and Lord of the Isles – inaugurated a new foghorn at the lighthouse, marking his first official function with a resounding blast.

To tour Lewis from Stornoway you can take the B895 road north for an out-and-back trip along the coast as far as the Garry River beyond the village of Tolsta; the A857 or A858 across to the west coast and north to the Butt of Lewis; or the A859 south across the moors in the direction of Harris.

Back/North Tolsta *(Am Bac/Tolastadh)*

The B895 road runs through an area of lovely beaches, green croft land unusual for the usually rocky east coast, and villages straggling along the sea. At **Gress** (*Griais*) is the ruined church of St Olaf believed to be the only one in the Western Isles dedicated to a Norse saint, and an 18th century farm mill once used to grind barley and grain for local crofters. One of Lord Leverhulme's ambitious schemes was to build a road along the east coast from Stornoway to Ness. He left before it was completed and the road now peters out into the moorland across the Garry Bridge, just beyond the village of Tolsta. This bridge is still known as 'The Bridge to Nowhere'. **Tolsta** lies above the rocky promontory of Tolsta Head, which has beaches of silvery sand on both sides. The long beaches of *Tràigh Mhòr* and the adjoining stretch at *Port Geiraha* are regarded as among the finest in the isles. On a fine day you can look from Tolsta across 40 miles (64 km) of sea to mainland Scotland. The **Bay of Geiraha** is one of the most picturesque in Lewis.

NESS *(Nis)*

The A857 road from Stornoway swings north-west across the island through moorland speckled with lochans to where it forks near Barvas (*Barabhas*) to follow the west coast to Port of Ness and the Butt of Lewis at the northern extremity of Lewis. About 4 miles (6 km) along this road a signposted left turn leads to the 19 ft (5.7 m) tall monolith near Shader (*Siadar*) known as the **Thrushel Stone** (*Clach an Truiseil*), overlooking the sea at **Ballantrushal** (*Baile an Truiseil*). This is the tallest standing stone in the Outer Hebrides. It tapers skywards from a base about 15 ft (4.7 m) around and is popularly supposed to mark the site of a great prehistoric battle. To the east of the road at Shader is *Loch an Duin* where **Steinacleit**, a 52 ft (16 m) diameter impressive but enigmatic chambered cairn dated at 3000-1500 BC, is encircled by stones in an oval enclosure. It stands on the skyline near the end of a rough track. Down the slope from the cairn a narrow causeway connects a fine example of an Iron Age galleried island dun to the shore of the loch. About 30 miles (48 km) from

Stornoway is the island's most northerly point, the Butt of Lewis (*Rubha Robhanais*), which has commanding views from sea cliffs towering 656-984 ft (200-300 m). The rugged headland above the cliffs is crowned by a 126 ft-high (38 m) red brick automated lighthouse. A mile (1.6 km) south of the Butt lies the village of **Europie** (*Europaidh*), where there is a restored 12th century church dedicated to St Moluag (*Teampall Mholuaidh*) and probably built on an earlier religious site. About 1.2 miles (2 km) to the south-west is the mysterious tiny tidal stack of **Luchruban**, known as **Pygmies Isle** because of a quantity of small bones discovered there. They were not, however, the skeletal remains of pygmies, but leftovers from meals eaten by the early Christian anchorite who once lived here. At the summit of the stack is a chambered cairn. A deep cleft separates it from the Lewis mainland, except at low water. The Ness district is one of the most densely populated rural areas in the Western Isles and this is obvious from the closeness of the houses and the narrowness of the crofts, particularly on the road to the Butt of Lewis. **Loch Stiapavat** is one of the island's most fertile lochs and its varied plant and animal life provide a rich larder for birds. This is one of the best wildfowl sites in Lewis, holding whooper swan, wigeon, teal, mallard, pochard and tufted duck. About 200 pairs of black-headed gulls breed here, the largest colony in Lewis. To the south of the small harbour at nearby **Port of Ness** (*Port Nis*) is a large sandy beach which is ideal for a spot of relaxation.

The Ness area is noted for the skill and bravery of its seamen and their Norse origins are reflected in the name of this, the most northerly parish of Lewis. The people of Ness are also known for their traditional annual *guga* (young gannet, or solan goose) expeditions to the islet of **Sula Sgeir**. Each autumn they sail out 40 miles (64 km) beyond the Butt of Lewis to this 52-acre (21 ha) windswept rock which, although with Rona part of a National Nature Reserve, is the only place in Britain where these fat young seabirds can legally be taken for food. According to an old Ness saying: 'When the barley is ripe, so is the guga.' Some 12 miles (20 km) east of Sula Sgeir and about 44 miles (71 km) north-north-east of the Butt of Lewis, is the much larger (269 acres/109 ha) uninhabited island of **Rona** (*Ronaidh*) rising in its south-east corner to 354 ft (108 m) above the Atlantic and still revealing the 'lazybed' pattern of cultivation indicating past settlement. A Celtic Christian hermit, St Ronan, is thought to have been the first inhabitant in the 8th century and the ruins of his cell and tiny chapel lie in the southern part of the island. A polished ball of green marble the size and shape of a sheep's heart, thought to be a piece of marble from the Celtic Mother Church, was found under the altar in St Ronan's cell. In the 17th century visiting writer Martin Martin noted that the five families who lived there 'take their surname from the colours of the sky, the rainbow and the clouds.' He described how one man in want of a wife sent a shilling with a missionary to Lewis and a wife was duly despatched to him by the next annual supply boat. No one has lived on the island since 1884. In that year Rona had two inhabitants, men who had quarrelled with their minister at Ness and settled on the island. The following summer a boatman found them dead. They had kept track of the days by notching a stick. The last notch had been made in February, months earlier. The island has been a National Nature Reserve since 1956 and is particularly important as a breeding place for Atlantic grey seals. More than 7,000 gather on the island from September to December each year when about 2,500 pups are born. By the peak of the breeding season the seal nursery on the peninsula of Fianais is churned up by their constant comings and goings. When the pups are born they weigh an average of 33 lb (15 kg), but they can grow to 165 lb (75 kg) in the space of three weeks on a diet of milk that is 60% fat. Every day they consume the equivalent of six half-pound (250 g) packs of butter. There are also important colonies of Leach's and storm petrel on the island, and large numbers of guillemot, razorbill, kittiwake, puffin and fulmar nest on the cliffs. For permission to visit contact Barvas Estate (tel 01851-840267) and Scottish Natural Heritage (tel 01851-705258).

Ness Heritage Centre (Habost, Ness HS2 0TG; tel 01851-810377) in the village of Habost provides a fascinating insight into local history and the folklore of the area. Thousands of photographs and artefacts cover a century of changing times and there's genealogical information spanning 250 years. The museum is open during summer. Browse and enjoy tea with fresh homebakes. Just before the centre is *Taigh Dhonnchaidh*, the restored cottage of Major Duncan Morrison, who was an internationally known pianist. It's now used as an **Arts and Music Centre** (tel 01851-810377).

WEST SIDE *(An Taobh Siar)*

By taking the alternative left fork near Barvas on the A857 from Stornoway you can enjoy a walk on the wild side and visit some of Lewis's major west coast monuments, including the **Standing Stones at Callanish**, the broch at Dun Carloway; and the blackhouse at Arnol. From Barvas the road passes the expanse of *Loch Mòr Bharabhais*, a refuge for wildfowl, before reaching Arnol, off the A858, 11 miles (18 km) north-west of Stornoway. At the far end of the township of Arnol is the **Black House Museum** (tel 01851-710395). This *tigh dubh*, last occupied in 1964, has walls 6 ft (1.8 m) thick, with a roof of thatch over turf, weighted with ropes and stones. A peat fire burns in the open hearth in the centre of the floor. There is no chimney. It was occupied as a functioning croft house until well into the 1960s and up until the end of World War II nearly half of all croft houses in Lewis were similar to this. Families often lived in one end of the house in the living room known as *aig an teine*, literally 'at the fire', while their animals occupied the other. The museum is fully furnished and complete with the barn, byre, and stockyard. It is open every day except Sunday all year round and is in the care of *Historic Scotland* (Longmore House, Salisbury Place, Edinburgh, EH9 1SH; tel 0131-668 8800; fax 0131-668 8888; e-mail stuart.mclean@scotland.gov.uk; www.historic-scotland.net). Admission for adults is £2.80, reduced £2, children £1. There's also a normal island 'white house' *(tigh geal)* and a Visitor Centre with a shop at the site.

In the village of **Bragar** there's a curious attraction that is one of the west coast's best-known landmarks. It recalls an autumn evening in 1921 when local boys spotted what they thought was the hull of an upturned ship out at sea. By morning the 'ship' had washed ashore – an 85-ft (26 m) blue whale with a harpoon still sticking out of its back. After the whale's blubber was melted down the local postmaster erected the enormous jaw-bone and harpoon over the gate to his garden, where you can still see the **Whalebone Arch.** At the western end of Bragar on an island in *Loch an Dùna*, a stone causeway leads to *Dun Bragar*, a broch whose ruins indicate that it must once have been an impressive defensive structure.

In the next village along the road, Shawbost (*Siabost*), is a folk museum which was established by local schoolchildren. **Shawbost Crofting Museum** (Shawbost, HS2 9BQ; tel 01851-710212; fax 01851-710582) is housed in an old church next to the school. Its display of implements reflects a crofting era that lasted until the 1950s. Open beginning-April to end-September, but all year access is available. If closed, the key is available from the school caretaker. The two small thatched buildings housing **Shawbost Norse Mill and Kiln** (*Shawbost Norse Mill Society*: tel 01851-710208) illustrate how barley grain was processed into meal at a time when this was a crucial part of crofting life. The grain was dried in a kiln and then milled in a water-driven horizontal mill of the type originally introduced by the Vikings. Mills and kilns of this type were used in Lewis up until the mid-20th century. All-year access.

Once derelict blackhouses and crofts have been meticulously restored at **Gearrannan Blackhouse Village** (5A Gearrannan, Carloway, HS2 9AL; tel 01851-643416; fax 01851-643488; e-mail info@gearrannan.com; www. gearrannan.com), about 25 miles (40 km) from Stornoway, to recreate an authentic settlement above a sheltered shingle bay at the end of the track from Carloway (*Carlabhagh*). Developments at the village include quality accommodation and improved facilities for visitors who want to experience blackhouse living. Guided tours and on-site interpretation are available. All-year access. The local community trust *Urras nan Gearrannan* (The Garenin Trust) has been restoring the old blackhouses since 1989 and traditional methods have been used to recreate the drystone masonry and thatched roofing of the original croft houses with the discreet integration of mod cons. Ten blackhouses are once more in everyday use. The central building offers an interpretative view of the overall project providing insight into the restoration process and local historical background through information panels and an interactive presentation. There's also a tearoom and a retail outlet for local crafts. Open April to September, 10am to 4pm Monday to Saturday. Accommodation is available in self-catering blackhouses or in a residential blackhouse for groups of up to 16 people (see *Accommodation*).

DUN CARLOWAY BROCH

About a mile (1.6 km) beyond Carloway heading south is the **Dun Carloway Broch**, still standing 30 ft (9 m) high, and one of the best-preserved Iron Age brochs in the Outer Hebrides. The 2,000-year-old stone tower looks out over *Loch Chàrlabhaigh*. Although half of the broch is now broken down, what remains is striking evidence of how secure such a refuge must have been for the Picts or Celts who built its massive 11 ft-thick (3 m) galleried walls. Such brochs have been likened to modern air-raid shelters as they were intended to protect civilians from marauders. Long after Dun Carloway had ceased to defend its builders, a group of Morrisons returning from a raid in Macaulay territory in Uig hid inside from their pursuing enemies. The irate Macaulays used their dirks to make a ladder up the outside wall and killed the hiding clansmen by smothering them with burning heather. All-year access; car park.

There's an unobtrusively sited Interpretation and Visitor Centre near the broch. The megaliths forming the **Standing Stones of Callanish** (*Calanais*) are tall, slender pillars of Lewisian gneiss set in a circle on a whaleback ridge overlooking East Loch Roag. They rank in grandeur second only to Stonehenge on Salisbury Plain, Wiltshire, but built around 5,000 years ago are considerably older. The main formation has a central monolith 15 ft 6 inches (4.7 m) high surrounded by a 37 ft (11.25 m) diameter circle of stones. In the mid-19th century 5 ft (1.5 m) of peat was dug away to reveal the stones as they were when first erected, and a small chambered tomb which contained cremated human remains in pottery vessels. Giant stones extend in the rough shape of a Celtic cross from the central circle. One legend says the huge stones are petrified giants, turned to stone for making merry instead of converting to Christianity. The stones have given rise to many theories, one that they are part of an ancient astronomical observatory, another that it is a site of considerable pre-Christian religious significance, possibly sun worship. Whatever the reasons they were erected the old grey stones continue to attract, and perplex, thousands of people every year. The site is cared for by Historic Scotland. The **Calanish Visitor Centre** (Calanais, Lewis, HS2 0QW; tel 01851-621422; fax 01851-621446) is discreetly situated away from the Standing Stones. It is open all year, Monday to Saturday from 10am to 7pm April-September, and 10am to 4pm October-March. Entry is free. Graphic panels, models and audio-visual explore how the Standing Stones were built and used. There's a restaurant and gift shop and public toilets with disabled facilities. Three companies offer day coach trips to the Calanish site: *Galson Motors* (from Stornoway Bus Station; tel 01851-840269), *W MacDonald & Co* (from Stornoway Pier; tel 01851-706267) and *Harris Coaches* (from Tarbert Pier; tel 01859-502441).

UIG

Heading south-west by way of Garynahine along the B8011 road you pass through a landscape full of sparkling lochs and lochans. The **River Grimersta** draining a long chain of small lochs here into the headwaters of East Loch Roag, has since Victorian times been regarded as the finest salmon water in Scotland, if not in Europe. There's a turn-off to the right (B8059) to the island of Great Bernera before it traverses some of the remotest areas in the west around **Little Loch Roag** and goes through the impressive narrow gorge of **Glen Valtos** to reach Timsgarry and the famed **Uig Sands** (*Traigh Chapadail*). This is a magnificent 1.2 mile (2 km) long tidal stretch where *Loch Suainaval* exits into the great Bay of Uig (*Camas Uig*). The loch has depths of more than 200 ft (61 m) and is the deepest in Lewis. The famous 12th century Lewis Chessmen were found in the dunes here by chance in 1831 (see *Shopping*). At the eastern end of the bay is *Baile-na-cille* ('village of the church'), which is associated with *Coinneach Odhar Fiosaiche* ('Sombre Kenneth of the Prophecies'), the famous Brahan Seer whose 'second sight' predictions were often startling – and true. The Seer, who was born in Uig, correctly foretold in graphic detail the decline and demise of the island's Seaforth family line:

> *I see into the far future and I read the doom of the race of my oppressor. The long descended line of Seaforth will, ere many generations have passed, end in extinction and sorrow. I see a Chief, the last of his House, both deaf and dumb. He will be father of four fair sons, all of whom he will follow to the tomb. He will live careworn and die mourning, knowing that the honours of his House are to be extinguished for ever and that no future Chief of the Mackenzies shall bear rule in Kintail. After lamenting over the last and most promising of his sons, he himself shall sink into the grave*

and the remnant of his possessions shall be inherited by a white-coifed lassie from the east; and she is to kill her sister.

All this did indeed happen and the Seaforth title became extinct in 1923.

At Crowlista, on the northern headland of the bay, is the **Uig Community and Heritage Centre** (tel 01851-672481/456), where soup, toasted sandwiches, baked potatoes, homebakes, tea, coffee, and soft drinks are available. It's open mid-June to mid-September, Monday to Saturday from midday to 5pm. Access to the beach is more convenient from the Ardroil shore road than from Crowlista. Carnish beach cannot be reached by car, but the views from there will repay the short walk from the end of the road. **Berie Sands** (*Traigh na Berie*) is another favourite among the many excellent beaches in the West Uig area, reached from the B8011 by a scenic circular route through Clioff (*Cliobh*), Valtos (*Bhaltos*), Kneep (*Cnip*), and Uigen (*Uigean*). Vehicles have caused serious erosion to the machair around the beach, so don't drive or park anywhere except in designated areas, which have protective covering. The western coastal road ends at Mealista, where you'll find the ruins of a chapel and a nunnery known as 'the house of black-veiled women' (*tigh nan cailleachan dubhe*). There are large stretches of fine cliff scenery around **Gallan Head**, looking north over island-studded Loch Roag and far out on the horizon to the lonely **Flannan Islands**, which are also known also as the 'Seven Hunters.' This group lying 21 miles (33 km) north-west of Gallan Head are among the remotest of the western islands. They were at one time regarded by islanders as a place of special sanctity and the 8th century ruins of St Flannan's chapel can be seen on Eilean Mór ('Big Island'). This island was the scene of one of the most mysterious events in island history. Just before Christmas in 1900 the beam of the lighthouse built there in 1899 failed to shine. After investigation it was found that all three of the keepers on duty had disappeared and no trace of them has ever been found. There is an air of *Marie Celeste* mystery about reports of the time. The men who went out to see what was wrong with the light found the lighthouse kitchen table set with an untouched meal of meat, potatoes and pickles. The lighthouse was built on the summit of the island 288 ft (88 m) above high water and it would have needed a freak wave of titanic proportions to wash them away. The mystery inspired composer Sir Peter Maxwell Davies to write his modern opera *The Lighthouse* (1979). Since the lighthouse became automatic what must have been one of the most exclusive golf links in the world has been abandoned. This is the rough five-hole course made by the last of the keepers to while away their days. There's good grazing on the islands and Flannan mutton was once considered a delicacy. Bernera crofters still make the most of it by fattening sheep there.

LOCHS *(Lochan)*

South-west from Stornoway, the A859 road to Harris passes numerous small lochs, as well as the larger lochs of Erisort and Seaforth, to reach the boundary of North Harris at Vigadale Bay, opposite Seaforth Island, which is half in Lewis and half in Harris. Some of the most beautiful villages in Lewis are in the parish of Lochs, which falls into three parts, Kinloch, North and South Lochs. The only inland village is Achmore (*Acha Mor*). The area is ideal for cycling, fishing and walking, but many also visit for photography, to paint, to watch for the wildlife, or simply to relax. South Lochs, more commonly known as *Pairc*, was the scene of the great Park Deer Raid in 1887, where impoverished and displaced crofters drew the attention of the British Press to the injustices and hardships they suffered by moving into the area and slaughtering some of the laird's red deer, which they barbecued and fed to the visiting journalists. A broch-like cairn at the Eishken junction commemorates this event. Only the northern area is now inhabited. Sir

James Matheson cleared settlements from the south in the 19th century. Red deer still roam the treeless forest which lies in a privately owned 57,000-acre (23,067 ha) estate, much of it is still reserved for stalking and fishing. You can still make out the outline of the wall, the *Garadh an Tighearna*, or Laird's Dyke, Lord Seaforth built across the narrow neck of land between Loch Seaforth and Loch Erisort in the early 17th century. The highest point here is *Beinn Mhór* at 1,874 ft (571 m), with neighbouring Crionaig reaching 1,581 ft (482 m). Offshore from the mountainous headland lying between the lochs of Shell and Seaforth are the **Shiant Islands** (*Na h-Eileanan Mora*), some 10 miles (16 km) out. Centred on the Lewis-Harris border is **Loch Langavat**, the largest inland loch on the island, about half a mile (1 km) wide and 7 miles (12 km) long. There's another loch of the same name in Harris.

At Kershader (*Cearsiadar*) on the southern shore of Loch Erisort, 22 miles (35 km) from Stornoway on the A859, is **Ravenspoint Visitor Centre** (tel 01851-880236) a refurbished hostel that makes an ideal base from which to explore the surrounding area. Open by arrangement January-December, 14 beds, showers, central heating, café, shop, parking. Home-made soup, light lunches and afternoon teas are available, as well as suppers from 4.45pm to 7pm on Friday evenings. Public toilets nearby. The lochside road east will take you to *Eilean Chaluim Chille*, where a ruined church dedicated to St Columba can be seen, and to Cromore. The main road ends at Lemreway (*Leumrabhagh*), at the back of a small bay sheltered by *Eilean Iubhard*.

It's difficult to imagine anything in this wild and remote corner of Lewis being connected with Space Age technology, but when US astronauts went to the moon in 1969 their notebooks were fire-proofed with an alginic compound made from seaweed processed in the tiny village of Keose (*Ceos*) on the north shore of Loch Erisort.

FLORA AND FAUNA

Loch Branahuie

On the narrow neck of land connecting Point to the rest of Lewis this little loch offers shelter to gulls and ducks in bad weather, among them **tufted** and **long-tailed ducks**, **wigeon**, **scaup** and **red-breasted mergansers**, most of which may also be seen in the adjacent bays. **Shags** are frequent offshore and in late summer and winter they are joined by **black-throated** and **great northern divers**.

Tiumpan Head

The car park at the automatic lighthouse on the point of the Eye Peninsula is a good place to watch dolphins and whales. There are resident **Risso's dolphins**, and large numbers of **white-beaked dolphins** appear in summer. You might also see an occasional **minke whale** inshore in the deep water around this point. The cliffs to the north have a **kittiwake** colony of about 100 pairs which can be viewed in comparative safety. **Tufted ducks** and **goldeneye** are often found on nearby *Loch an Siùmpan*, a bird sanctuary owned by Stornoway Trust, while *Loch an Dùin* usually has a small **tern** colony.

Tong and Steinish

This large inlet north of Stornoway combines sand dunes, saltmarsh and sand flats. Large numbers of terns nest on and around this area in summer. Other breeding species include **skylark, shelduck, oystercatcher** and **ringed plover**. In winter, the flats are often thronged with migrating or wintering waders, ducks, geese and gulls, and the occasional **common seal** may also be seen. Note that below high water mark the flats have areas of dangerous sinking sand.

Coll

Inland are pools with large numbers of mallard and teal in winter, along with small numbers of **whooper swans**. About 300 **eiders** winter offshore here.

Gress

The river estuary and machair here attract similar birds to those at Coll, but there's a greater range of plantlife. Small numbers of **arctic terns** breed here and **great** and **arctic skuas** breed on the moor to the north of Gress. **Grey** and **common seals** may be seen from the shore.

Garry

Sea stacks are a well-known feature of Garry Beach, particularly the one which looks like Queen Victoria in profile. Another stack, *Caisteal a' Mhorair*, is topped by the remains of a small defensive settlement. Grass on the cliff-top to the south of the beach can be treacherously slippery. *Loch na Cartach* is covered with **water lilies** in summer and its spectacular setting makes it a popular site.

Barvas Moor and Muirneag

Northern Lewis has one of the largest expanses of blanket bog remaining in Britain. The landscape is best seen from above, making a trek to the summit ridge of Muirneag worthwhile. From here you can see the great expanse of peatland spread out below and get views of both east and west coasts, with the Harris range of hills to the south. About 80% of Lewis north of the Leurbost to Garynahine road is covered by peat, deposited over 7,000 years to an average depth of 5 ft (1.5 m). It is a vital source of fuel for islanders and it usually takes about a fortnight for a family to cut a year's supply. Peatland pools are the breeding grounds of waders such as **dunlin, golden plover** and **greenshank**.

Barvas

Loch Mòr Barvas is very shallow, and is the northernmost of a series of lochs on the north-west coast of Lewis separated from the sea by narrow shingle and boulder beaches. Huge areas of an extensive machair have been laid bare by erosion, but despite this there is a good variety of machair plants and numbers of waders can be seen. **Oystercatcher, ringed plover, dunlin**, and **curlew** are often present, and **otters** can sometimes be spotted.

    Achmore. *Loch Acha Mòr* has **teal, tufted duck, goldeneye** and **pochard**, while the surrounding moors are home to **golden plover** and **dunlin**. There's an excellent panoramic view over the moorlands of southern Lewis and the hills of Uig and Harris from the A858 road, though you'll get even better views from the high ground of Eitshal to the north.

Mangersta Sands

A large area of bare sand stretches inland from this beach, demonstrating machair erosion in its final stages. The cliffs here are the highest vertical cliffs on mainland Lewis and Harris, with **lovage, roseroot** and other cliff plants growing in profusion. From higher parts of the road, the outline of St Kilda can sometimes be seen in fine weather, as well as the famous lighthouse of the Flannan Isles.

Loch Orasay

The islands in this loch support remnants of the woodland which was once much more widespread. Most of the trees are **willows** and **rowans**, with some **aspen** and **birch**. One of the islands in the south-east of the loch is a *crannog*, a prehistoric man-made islet. **Greylag geese** breed here and large numbers of gulls roost on the far side of the loch. This is one of the few lochs in the Western Isles where that rare Ice Age fish, the **Arctic char**, is found.

Loch Cromore. Good for wildfowl, including wintering **whooper swans**. **Common seals** frequent the inlets.

GETTING THERE

Late in November 2000 an opinion poll carried out for the BBC Gaelic television programme *Cunntas* showed that the majority (72%) of people in Lewis and Harris were in favour of a referendum on the vexed issue of Sunday travel to and from the islands. Members of *Comhairle nan Eilean Siar* islands authority, however, decided by 17 votes to 8 against spending £14,000-£20,000 on such a referendum, so it seems that the elders of the community will at least keep the northern isles incommunicado on the sabbath for the foreseeable future.

By Air

British Airways (tel 08457-733377; www.britishairways.com), through its operators British Regional Airways and Loganair (tel 0141-848 7594), flies to Stornoway, Lewis, from:

Aberdeen: two a day from Monday to Friday.

Belfast: Monday to Friday.

Benbecula: two a day from Monday to Friday.

Edinburgh: one a day Monday to Friday, with an additional flight on Saturday from March to October.

Glasgow: up to three times daily from Monday to Friday, with an additional flight on Saturday during May to September.

Inverness: twice a day from Monday to Friday, and one flight on Saturday.

Connecting flights to Glasgow, Edinburgh, and Inverness are available from from **London**, **Birmingham**, and **Manchester**, Monday to Friday, with an additional flight on Saturday during May to September.

On the islands contact *British Airways* (tel 01851-703673) directly to check the fares and times of flights.

Charters: Bristows Helicopters; tel 01851-705577.

Airport: Stornoway airport provides a key access point to the islands from Inverness and Glasgow, as well as inter-island services to Benbecula and Barra. It also serves as a base for the search and rescue helicopter operated by HM Coastguard. Located on the east coast of Lewis, about three miles (5 km) from Stornoway, the airport is clearly signposted from the A866 road. It is open Monday to Friday 8.15am to 5.30pm. Saturday 8.15am to 3.45pm (summer) and 8.15am to 3pm (winter), and by arrangement. Closed on Sunday. Disabled facilities exist within the terminal and staff are always available to assist. The Melbost bus to the airport gate runs hourly. For timetable information tel 01851-704327. Taxis are available at the airport.

By Sea

The Caledonian MacBrayne (The Ferry Terminal, Gourock, PA19 1QP; tel 08705-650000; fax 01475-635235 for reservations; e-mail reservations@calmac.co.uk; www.calmac.co.uk) car ferry sails to Stornoway from Ullapool on the Scottish mainland on Monday at 4.15am, 10.45am and 5.15pm on Monday; 9.30am and 5.15 on Tuesday; 9.30am, 4pm and 10.30pm on Wednesday and Friday; and 11am and 5.30pm on Thursday and Saturday during summer. In winter it sails at 9.30 am and 5.15pm every day Monday to Saturday. The journey takes 2 hours 40 minutes. A single adult return costs £13, car and motorhome £62, and an additional £62 for a caravan and boat/baggage trailer, motorcycle £31, and bicycle £2. Discounted 'Five-Day Return' and 'Six-Journey' tickets are available on this route.

The mainland CalMac office is at Ullapool pier (tel 01854-612358) and the ferry terminal in Stornoway (tel 01851-702361) on South Beach, close to the bus station.

Tours
Albanach Tours: 1 Tomair, Balallan, HS2 9PT (tel/fax 01851-830433; e-mail l.mcinulty@talk21.com). With fully qualified Scottish Tourist Guide.
Archaeological Tours. Margaret Curtis (Callanish; tel 01851-621277) offers comprehensive guided tours of Callanish Standing Stones and other interesting sites.

GETTING AROUND
By Air
British Airways (tel 08457-733377; www.britishairways.com), through its operator Loganair (tel 01851-703067), flies from Stornoway to Benbecula twice a day, Monday to Friday. The adult return fare is £80.

By Sea
You can take an all-inclusive, non-landing 'Evening Dinner Cruise' from Stornoway. The cruise leaves Stornoway at 7.15pm on Wednesday and Friday from end-June to end-August and arrives back at 1.10am the following morning. Contact the local Caledonian MacBrayne (Ferry Terminal, South Beach, Stornoway; tel 01851-702361) office not later than two hours prior to sailing on the day of the cruise.

By Road
Altogether, there are around 200 miles (322 miles) of good motoring roads in Lewis and Harris, with those in the northern island being more easily negotiated than those in an around Harris, particularly South Harris, where they tend to be more narrow and winding.

Buses
Regular bus services are operated by:
Galson Motors: 1 Lower Barvas, Lewis, HS2 0QZ (tel 01851-840269; fax 01851-840445; e-mail galson@sol.co.uk).
MacLennan Coaches: 24 Inaclete Road, Stornoway, HS1 2RN (tel/fax 01851-702114). Discount Rover tickets round Westside of Lewis visiting Callanish Stones, Carloway Broch and Arnol Blackhouse.
Royal Mail: tel 01246-546329; www.royalmail.co.uk. Operates a 14-seater Postbus service from Stornoway Bus Station to Timsgarry Post Office, Monday to Friday during school term; to Brenish on Monday, Wednesday and Friday; and to Carnish on Tuesday and Thursday. It stops at about 10 points along the way. Check routes and times at Stornoway Bus Station, as they change during school holidays.

Taxis: *Central Cabs:* 20 Macmillan Brae, Stornoway, HS1 2YU (tel 01851-706900).

Vehicle Rental
Arnol Car Rentals: Arnol, Lewis (tel 01851-710548; fax 01851-710248; e-mail arnolmotors@aol.com). Has cars available direct from Stornoway airport and ferry terminal, £20 a day for a small car for one to six days, seven days and over £18; medium cars cost £22 per day for one to three days, £20 for 4-6 days, and £19 for seven days and over.
Autohire: Unit 7, Mossend Industrial Estate, Stornoway, HS1 2SG (tel 01851-706939; fax 01851-705541; mobile 0374 180845; e-mail autohire@ btinternet.com). Delivers and collects free from Stornoway airport, ferry terminal, local guest houses, B&Bs and hotels. No mileage charge.

Hebridean Campervan Holidays: 18 Plantation Road, Stornoway, HS1 2JS (tel/fax 01851-704578).

Jackies Car Hire: Barvas, Lewis, HS2 0RA (tel/fax 01851-840343). Hires out cars and vans.

Lewis Car Rentals: 52 Bayhead Street, Stornoway (tel 01851-703760; fax 01851-705860; e-mail lewis@carrentkiwi.freeserve.co.uk). Delivers and collects from the airport, ferry terminal, local guest houses, hotels and B&Bs. Daily rates from £16. Open Monday to Saturday from 9am to 6pm.

Lochs Motors Car Hire: 33 South Beach, Stornoway, HS1 2BN (tel/fax 01851-705857).

Mackinnon Self-Drive: 18 Inaclete Road, Stornoway, HS1 2RB (tel 01851-702984; fax 01851-705596; e-mail mackinnonhire@hotmail.com). Car, van and minibus hire.

Cycle Hire

Alex Dan's Cycle Centre: 67 Kenneth Street, Stornoway, Lewis (tel 01851-704025; fax 01851-701712). Open six days a week, from 9am to 6pm, for cycle hire.

Stornoway Motorcycle Club: 7 Kenneth Street, Stornoway (tel 01851-705456). Welcomes all motorcyclists visiting the island. The club is open Monday to Friday from 7.30pm to 11pm and on Saturday from 10am to 11pm.

ACCOMMODATION

You've got a choice of the usual types of accommodation on Lewis but if you want to try something really different you should consider a spell in a traditional island blackhouse – complete with peat fire but minus the discomforts the original inhabitants had to endure. The cluster of thatched, drystone buildings at *Gearrannan Blackhouse Village* (Carloway, HS2 9AL; tel 01851-643416; fax 01851-643488; e-mail info@gearrannan.com; www.gearrannan.com), overlooking the Atlantic Ocean on the west side of Lewis have been restored and upgraded to provide all mod cons. There's self-catering accommodation in three blackhouses, with fully fitted kitchens, showers, bedrooms, and living space. Rates vary from £200 a week January to March, to £450 June to August. There's also a self-catering facility for larger groups or families, with four bedrooms and two shower rooms in a blackhouse at rates from £90 a night in low season to £110 in high season. There's also the option of staying in a four-star blackhouse with a sumptuous seven-course dinner served at nearby *Taigh 'an Chòcair*, all for £50 per person a night. From your blackhouse door you can walk along rugged Atlantic cliffs, past an old illicit still, until you reach the white sands of Dalbeg beach and the rich flora and fauna of Loch Dalbeg, or you can walk south to the Iron Age Dun Charlabhaigh Broch, the burial cairn at Breascleit and the Callanish Standing Stones.

Hotels

Caberfeidh Hotel: Manor Park, Stornoway, HS1 2EU (tel 01851-702604; fax 01851-705572; e-mail cabarfeidh@calahotels.com; www.calahotels.com). Three-star, all rooms en suite. Open January to December, double from £46.

Caledonian Hotel: 6 South Beach, Stornoway (tel 01851-702411; fax 01851-701932). Has a wide range of dishes to suit all tastes. Lounge open all year, Monday to Saturday midday to 2pm and 5pm to 9pm. Dining room open Friday and Saturday from 5pm to 9pm, and Thursday and Friday midday to 2pm.

Crown Hotel: Castle Street, Stornoway (tel 01851-703181/703734; fax 01851-701912). Bar meals, high teas, a la carte menu. Lunches served midday to 2pm, high tea and dinner from 5pm to 9pm, bar meals 5pm to 9.30pm.

Doune Braes Hotel: Doune, Carloway (tel 01851-643252; fax 01851-643435; e-mail hebrides@doune_braes.co.uk). Three-star, comprehensive bar meal menu, moderately prices, also a la carte using local produce. Open all year, from £28 B&B.

Royal Hotel: Cromwell Street, Stornoway, HS1 2DG (tel 01851-702109; fax 01851-702142; e-mail royal@calahotels.com; www.calahotels.com). Two-star, centrally situated with views of Lews Castle and harbour. Open January to December, double from £50.

Scaliscro Lodge Hotel: Scaliscro, Uig, Lewis (tel 01851-672325; fax 01851-672393). One-star. Open April to December, from £28. Specialises in seafood, also serves home-produced lamb and beef and wild venison. Restaurant open Tuesday to Saturday from 11am to 2.30pm and 5pm to 11pm.

Seaforth Hotel: 9 James Street, Stornoway, HS1 2QN (tel 01851-702740; fax 01851-703900). Two-star, en suite rooms. Open March to October, double from £40.

Guest Houses

Baile na Cille Guest House: Timsgarry, HS2 9JD (tel 01851-672242; fax 01851-672241; e-mail RandJGollin@compuserve.com). Two-star. Open Easter to October, from £24 B&B.

Eshcol Guest House: 21 Breascleit, Callanish, HS2 9ED (tel/fax 01851-621357; e-mail donlewis@madasafish.com). Four-star, within walking distance of the Callanish Standing Stones, good views. Open all year, from £29 B&B.

Galson Farm Guest House: South Galson, Ness, Lewis, HS2 0SH (tel/fax 01851-850492; e-mail galsonfarm@yahoo.com). Four-star, fully-restored 18th century farmhouse on an 18-acre (7 ha) croft, double and twin rooms, traditional home cooking, dinner and packed lunches on request. No smoking. Open all year, from £30.

Greenacres Guest House: 8 Smith Avenue, Stornoway, HS1 2PY (tel 01851-706383; fax 01851-703191). Three-star, family-run, eight minutes' walk from town. Open January to December, from £16 B&B.

Hal O The Wynd Guest House: Graham Lowder, 2 Newton Street, Stornoway, HS1 2RE (tel/fax 01851-706073). Three-star, opposite ferry terminal, five minutes' walk to town. Open January to December, from £20 B&B.

Hebridean Guest House: 61 Bayhead Street, Stornoway, HS1 2DZ (tel 01851-702268; fax 01851-701791; e-mail hebgh@sol.co.uk). Two-star, close to town centre, overlooking golf course. Open January to December, from £20 B&B.

Loch Roag Guest House: 22a Breasclete, Callanish (tel/fax 01851-621357; e-mail lochroag@madasafish.com; www.lochroag.com). Three-star. Open January to December, from £23 B&B.

The Old House: 4 Lewis Street, Stornoway, HS1 2QH (tel 01851-704495; fax 01851-700356; e-mail ricollins@genic.co.uk). Two-star, family-run detached house in town centre. Open January to December, from £23 B&B.

Park Guest House: 30 James Street, Stornoway, HS1 2QN (tel 01851-702485; fax 01851-703482). Three-star, family-run stone Victorian guest house in the centre of town, not far from the ferry terminal. Open all year except 24 December-5 January. B&B from £24, facilities for non-residential disabled visitors. Restaurant serves Hebridean produce. Vegetarians welcome. The restaurant closed Sunday and Monday. Taste of Scotland member.

Seaside Villa: Mrs M Fraser, Back, Lewis, HS2 0LQ (tel/fax 01851-820208). Four-star, good home cooking, overlooks the beach.

B&B

Alexandra's: Kildun, 14 Goathill Road, Stornoway, HS1 2NL (tel 01851-703247). Three-star, family home, five minutes walk from town centre. Open January to December, from £16.

Crois Ailien Lodge: Mrs J Barker, Gravir, South Lochs, Lewis, HS2 9QX (tel/fax 01851-880409). Two-star. Open January to December, from £18.

Dolly's B&B: 33 Aignish, Point, HS2 0PB (tel 01851-870755). Three-star, 10 minutes from Stornoway, five minutes from airport. Disabled facilities.

Fernlea: Mrs M Macmillan, 9 Matheson Road, Stornoway, HS1 2NQ (tel 01851-702125). Three-star, Victorian listed building, close to ferry. Open January to December, from £18.

Handa: Murdo and Christine Morrison, 18 Keose Glebe, Lochs, HS2 9JX (tel 01851-830334; e-mail handakeose@supanet.com). Four-star, 1½ miles off A859, 12 miles south of Stornoway, 25 miles north of Tarbert, from £18, overlooking a private loch. Open 4 May to 5 October, no smoking throughout. Taste of Scotland member. Unlicensed.

Pairc House: Anne Morrison, Habost, Lochs, HS2 9QB (tel 01851-880480; fax 01851-880386; e-mail donnic@sol.co.uk). Three-star. Open April to November, from £24.

Ravenswood: 12 Matheson Road, Stornoway (tel 01851-702673). Four-star, one double, two twins.

Mrs C Slater: 31 Jamieson Drive, Stornoway, HS1 2LE (tel 01851-704122). Two-star. Open January to December, from £16.

Westwinds: Mrs Marie Maclennan, 34 Newton Street, Stornoway, HS1 2RW (tel 01851-703408). Two-star, on the sea front. Open January to December, from £18.

Self-Catering

Mrs Margaret Engebretsen: 21 Braighe Road, Stornoway, HS2 0BQ (tel 01851-702304; fax 01851-702305). Three-star, five minutes' from Stornoway, three bedrooms, sleeps 6. Open January to December, from £280 to £300 a week.

Mrs Helen Graham: Aird Cottage, South Dell, Ness, HS2 0SP (tel 01851-810207). Two-star, country cottage near Butt of Lewis, two bedrooms, sleeps four. Open January to December, from £150 to £200 a week.

Mrs Frances Macleod: 51 Matheson Road, Stornoway, HS1 2LA (tel 01851-705230). Two-star, modern chalet, two bedrooms, sleeps four. Open January to December, from £100 to £190 a week,

Neil and Rhoda MacLeod: 25 South Shawbost, Lewis, HS2 9BJ (tel/fax 01851-710461; e-mail kabuis@madasafish.com). Three-star, stonebuilt house with 6 acres (2.5 ha) of croft land.

Mrs A Nicolson: 25 Borve, Lewis, HS2 0RX (tel 01851-850225). One-star, five bedrooms, sleeps 2-9. Open April to October, from £110 to £260 a week.

Hostels

Galson Farm Bunkhouse: Galson Farm, South Galson, HS2 0SH (tel/fax 01851-850492; e-mail galsonfarm@yahoo.com). Eight beds, open all year, from £8 a night.

Garenin Hostel: Carloway, Lewis, HS2 9AL. One-star, restored blackhouse. This is one of the blackhouses restored by the *Garenin Trust*. Run by the *Gatliff Hebridean Hostels Trust* (30 Francis Street, Stornoway, HS1 2ND), a charitable organisation which helps local people to run traditional crofts as simple hostels. No advance bookings accepted. Bedlinen is not provided. Open all year. 14 beds, two rooms with 5-8 beds, wheelchair access, shop a mile away, bus 1½ miles, ferry 25 miles at Stornoway. Walkers and cyclists welcome.

Kershader Youth Hostel: Ravenspoint, Kershader, South Lochs, HS2 9QA (tel 01851-880236). A community-run hostel halfway between Tarbert and Stornoway. Open all year. 14 beds, two rooms with 4 beds, one room with 5-8 beds, laundry, hostel store, shop next door, bus nearby, ferry 23 miles (37 km) away. Walkers and cyclists welcome.

Stornoway Backpackers Hostel: 47 Keith Street, Stornoway, HS1 2JG (tel 01851-703628; e-mail stornoway@bigfoot.com; www.stornoway-hostel.co.uk). One-star, near local amenities, ferry and buses, 24-hour access. Open January to December, from £9, including breakfast.

Camping

Eilean Fraoich Camp Site: North Shawbost, Lewis, HS2 9BQ (tel 01851-710504). Three-star, 10 sites on an acre (0.4 ha) of grassy, level terrain. Disabled facilities. Open May to October, from £3 to £7.50.

Laxdale Holiday Park: 6 Laxdale Lane, Laxdale, Lewis, HS2 0DR (tel 01851-706966/703234; fax 01851-706966; e-mail Gordon@laxdaleholidaypark. force9.co.uk). 42 sites on 2¹/₂ acres (1 ha), 2 miles (3 km) from Stornoway ferry terminal. Open April to October, from £8 a night. Three holiday caravans to let from £130 a week.

EATING AND DRINKING

Eating

Baile na Cille: Timsgarry, Uig (tel 01851-672242; fax 01851-672241; e-mail RandJGollin@compuserve.com). Local produce dinners, lunches by arrangement. Open 15 March to 15 October.

Barnacles Harbour Bistro: The Royal Hotel, Cromwell Street, Stornoway (tel 01851- 702109; fax 01851-702142). Offers snacks, chargrills, seafood, pizzas, vegetarian selections, and home baking. Open 7 days from March to October, closed Sundays. Dinners served 11.30am to 2.30pm and 4.30pm to 9.30pm. Also *The Boatshed Restaurant*, which specialises in local seafood, prime Scottish meats, game and vegetarian dishes. Table d'hote and a la carte menus are offered seven days a week. Dinner served from 6pm to 9.30pm, High Tea from 4pm to 6pm, and Lunch 12.30pm to 2pm.

Bonaventure: Aird Uig, Timsgarry, HS2 9JA (tel/fax 01851-672474). Licensed Scottish/French restaurant offering local produce, views over West Loch Roag. Open all year, summer from Tuesday to Saturday 10.30am till late, winter 10.30am until late Friday and Saturday only. It's a bit of a trek to get there, but the Franco-Scottish cooking has a good reputation.

Chumleys Restaurant & Bar: Seaforth Hotel, James Street, Stornoway (tel 01851-702740; fax 01851703900). A five-minute walk from the town centre. High teas served from 5.30pm to 7pm and table d'hote and a la carte from 7pm to 9.30pm.

Copper Kettle: 5 Dalbeg, Lewis, HS2 9AE (tel 01851-710592). Small tearoom overlooking Loch Dalbeg, high teas and evening meals, home-baking. Bookings required for evening meals. Open 10.30am to 5pm.

Crom-lus: 9 Bayhead, HS1 2DU (tel 01851-703337). Gaelic for poppy and pronounced 'crowm loose', has a variety of crafts for sale including Coll Pottery and Gisla Woodcraft. A few minutes' walk from the town centre. Tea, coffee and snacks available. Open all year, Monday to Saturday 10am to 5pm. In winter closes early on Wednesday.

Islander Shellfish: Site 2, Rigs Road, Stornoway, HS1 2RL (tel 01851-706772; fax 01851-703486; e-mail ronnie.isf@excite.co.uk). Fresh fish and shellfish daily. Smoked fish available.

The Manor Restaurant: Cabarfeidh Hotel, Manor Park, Stornoway, Lewis, HS1 2EU (tel 01851-702604; fax 01851-705572). On the outskirts of Stornoway, using only the finest local produce. Open all year, seven days a week from midday to 2.30pm and 7pm to 9.30pm.

Park Guest House and Restaurant: 30 James Street, Stornoway (tel 01851-702485; fax 01851-703482). Specialises in local seafood, shellfish and game.

Open all year, Tuesday to Saturday, chargrill and salad bar from 5.30pm to 7pm, and a la carte from 7pm to 9pm. Taste of Scotland member.

Smugglers: Aird, Uig (tel 01851-672351/474). Situated within a remote Gaelic community above cliffs on the rugged Uig coast and offers a range of seafood, vegetarian, game and meat dishes. Lunch served from 12.30pm to 2.30pm and evening meals from 7.30pm to 9.30pm. Coffees, teas and snacks are available from 11am to 4pm.

Tigh Mealros: Garynahine, Callanish (tel/fax 01851-621333). Local seafood, fish, scallops, and meat. Unlicensed (BYO). Open January to March, Friday and Saturday at 7pm, April to December, Monday to Saturday at 7pm.

Drinking

A drink with a story somehow always seems to taste better. How about this one? Generations of men from the islands once earned their living from whaling in the stormy oceans of the Antarctic. These men were as resourceful as they were hardy and even in the icy wastes of the south they produced their own dram from illicit stills. This fiery spirit helped to make a tough life tolerable for the men who shared it. One of these was young John 'Jock' Murray, who spent many hours at his still in South Georgia. The result was far removed from the famous products of Scotland but he vowed that one day he would create his own blend of whisky. He did and *The Whalers Dram* is the result, a blend of Islay and peated malt whiskies. Bottled by *The Whalers Whisky Co* (21 Gress, Lewis, HS2 0NB; tel 01851-701265; fax 01851-701272) in two sizes, 1.5 litre and 70cl, it's available from most shops, or appropriately from the lounge and public bar of *Whaler's Rest* (19 Francis Street, Stornoway, HS1 2ND; tel 01851-701265; fax 01851-701272; e-mail jockmurray@talk21.com), in the centre of town, five minutes' walk from ferry terminal.

Licensing hours in Stornoway are from 11am to 11pm. No Sunday opening.

ENTERTAINMENT

You can access information on the latest screening, venues, and membership details of the *Lewis Film Society* on its website (www.lewis-filmsociety. fsnet.co.uk). Membership for the season is £5, which means you can watch a movie for £1.50 where guests and non-members pay £2.50.

The award-winning *Lanntair Arts Centre* (An Lanntair, Town Hall, South Beach, Stornoway; tel/fax 01851-703307), is the main public arts facility in the Western Isles. It provides a forum for local, national and international arts and stages monthly exhibitions and events from traditional to rock music, as well as promoting all aspects of Gaelic culture. As well as local artists, performers from all over the world appear here to dance, sing and play all kinds of music. Contact the centre for an update on its programme.

SPORT AND RECREATION

Walking

Look out for the 'Walkers Welcome' symbol on accommodation as this ensures such useful services as a drying facility for wet clothes, hot drinks on arrival, packed lunch and flask filling, and late evening meal/early breakfast, as well as information on local walks, public transport, and daily weather forecast.

For a pleasant amble, *The Stornoway Trust* (Leverhulme House, Perceval Square, Stornoway, HS1 2DD; tel 01851-702002; fax 01851-706915; e-mail colin@stornowaytrust.org.uk) has guided walks around Lews Castle Grounds. Contact the Trust or the Tourist Office for dates and times.

There's an exacting, but fascinating, walk of 10 miles (16 km) from Tolsta (*Tolstadh*) on the east coast, to Ness (*Nis*) in the north. Allow 4-6 hours for the trek, which is waymarked by green and yellow posts and takes you across Lord Leverhulme's 'Bridge to Nowhere' spanning the Garry River, and on to the spectacular waterfall at *Abhainn na Cloich*. Open moorland and stunning coastal scenery make for a memorable walk. Along the way you can see across The Minch on a clear day to Cape Wrath in the north-west corner of mainland Scotland.

The **Westside Walk** is a moderate to demanding four-mile (6 km) coastal route from Garenin (*Gearrannan*) to Dalbeg (*Dail Beag*). Allow three hours for the walk. To the south-west as you climb from Gearrannan, you'll see the islands at the mouth of Loch Roag – the dome-shaped one is called *An t-Seana Bheinn* (The Old Hill). Local folklore says a giant horse leapt from this island to the headland at the northern tip of Loch nan Geàrrannan and left its imprint on the rock known as *Bròg an Eich* ('The Horse Shoe'). The shape is visible from the sea. On a clear day, the Flannan Isles can be seen on the horizon. The Norwegian sailing vessel *Ruth* ran aground in *a' Gheodha Ruadh* ('The Red Cove') in 1905, which was also the scene of the recent wreck of Carloway fishing boat *Three Greeks*.

The boundary fence between Gearrannan and Dail Mòr runs alongside a much older turf dyke. Inland, it runs along the stream *Allt na Muilne* ('Mill Burn'), which has the remains of two mills – one about 900 yards (823 m) inland between *Sgairbheiseal Mòr* and *Cnoc a' Choin*, and the other where the stream runs into the sea at *Geodha na Muilne*, near *Dail Mòr Beach*. Many such mills similar to the restored Norse Mill at Shawbost were used throughout the islands. *Dail Beag* was cleared of its families as early as 1850 to free more grazing land for the local innkeeper's animals. Records show that the inn there, although one of very few on the island, sold a mere 218 gallons (991 litres) of whisky in the three years to 1850. It was also one of the first places in Lewis to see tea. A ship ran aground in the bay and among the goods salvaged was a chest of tea. Not knowing what it was, the residents spread it on their fields as fertiliser.

Climbing

For rock-climbing of any significance in Lewis head for the Uig district, either on its inland crags, or on the challenging sea-cliffs at *Ard More Mangersta*. The inland crags are of striated but generally firm, dark grey gneiss. The finest inland rock-face, and one of the least climbed, is *Creag Dhubh Dibadale* on the northeast face of Tamanaisval at the head of Loch Dibadale. *Sgò Climbing and Abseiling* (20a Coll, Back, HS2 0JR; tel 01851-820726; e-mail sgor.climbing@virgin.net; www.sgor.co.uk) offers climbing in Lewis and Harris.

Cycling

There are many out and back rides from Stornoway along quiet dead-end roads such as the A866 east to Tiumpan Head, on the Eye Peninsula, on the B895 north-east to Tolsta Head, and the B897 south to Crosbost. Circular routes tend to be much longer, for example the 48 miles (77 km) circuit north from Stornoway along the A857 to Barabhas then west and south to Callanish (Calanais) Standing Stones.

Golf

Stornoway Golf Club at Willowglen (Huw Lloyd, Secretary, Willowglen Road, Stornoway, HS2 0XP; tel 01851-702240; e-mail stornowaygolfclub@lineone.net) has a well-designed and professionally maintained 18-hole parkland par 68 course in the grounds of Lews Castle, with panoramic views of Stornoway Harbour and The Minch. At only 5,250 yards (5,741 m) the course may appear short by modern standards, but there are plenty of hazards. There's a clubhouse with a golf shop for club hire, a bar, locker and changing rooms. You can often enjoy *ceilidhs* in the evenings. Playing and non-playing visitors welcome. Green fees £20 a day.

Fishing

You don't have to go far from Stornoway to cast a line. About 5 miles (8 km) from town there's good fishing for **trout** and **salmon** in the lochs *Clachan* and *An Ois*, joined by *Abhainn Ghrioda*, the River Creed. Permits with boat cost £22. Contact the **Stornoway Trust Estate Office** (20 Cromwell Street, Stornoway; tel 01851-702002). The **Soval Angling Association** has brown trout fishing on several lochs close to Stornoway. Check with N Mackenzie (tel 01851-830242). In the Lochs area is 90-acre (36 ha) Loch Keose, which is good for brown trout. You can get permits and information from Murdo Morrison (tel 01851-830334).

Game Fishing Contacts:

Aline Estate: James McGarrity, Aline Lodge (tel 01859-502276). Has a salmon fishery and a dozen brown trout lochs where specimens of up to 10 lb (4^{1}/2 kg) have been landed.

Barvas Estate: D Macdonald (tel 01851-840267).

Eishken Estate: C Macrae (tel 01851-830486).

Garynahine Estate: Malcolm Macphail (home tel 01851-621383).

Island Flies: Mike Reed, 23 Gravir, South Lochs (tel/fax 01851-880233).

Loch Roisnavat Trout Fishery: Barvas Road, Barvas (tel 01851-701404). Offers angling association fishing for rainbow and blue trout. Fly fishing tuition is available.

Scaliscro and North Eishken Estates: James Mackenzie (tel 01851-672325). Salmon, brown trout and sea trout fishing available, as well as sea angling in West Loch Roag.

Soval Angling Association: Stile Park, Willowglen Road, Stornoway (tel 01851-703248).

Soval Estate: Soval Lodge, John Macleod (tel 01851-830223).

Sportsworld: Donnie MacIver, 1/3 Francis Street, Stornoway (tel 01851-705464). Fishing permits for Stornoway area and for Loch Langavat, where there's Arctic char. Guided fishing trips arranged.

Stornoway Angling Association: Hamish Fraser, 5 Laxdale (tel 01851-703990).

Uig and Hamanavay Estate: Graeme Sinclair, 10 Ardroil (tel 01851-672421). Fly only, salmon and sea trout fishing.

Uig Lodge Estates: Kenny Angus Mackay (tel 01851-672250).

Sea Angling

Stornoway is the major centre for sea angling in the islands and *Stornoway Sea Angling Club* (South Beach Street, Stornoway, HS1 2BT; tel 01851-7020210) is the place to touch base. Sea angling trips are available daily. Take advantage of local experience and a modern clubhouse where there's live music every Saturday night. Temporary membership is available.

The *Elena C* (5a Knock, Point; tel 01851-703000) takes out fishing parties and is ideal for families or beginners. Equipment is supplied if required. For the serious sea angler there are day trips for rough ground or wreck fishing, mainly for ling, cod, pollack and coalies from Bevig or Stornoway harbour, or half-day and day trips to fish the west coast waters from Kirkibost Harbour. The boat is usually on station at the island of Great Bernera, strategically situated for exploiting the prolific west coast grounds which every summer and autumn produce some magnificent catches. Bird-watching trips are also offered. All sailings are subject to numbers and weather conditions. Take your waterproofs, warm clothing and non-slip footwear.

Sailing

The **Hebridean Maritime Festival** is held at Stornoway every year, usually in August. The event is organised by Sail Hebrides and includes windsurfing and canoeing, as well as a regatta. For more information contact *Sail Hebrides* (9 Goathill Road, Stornoway, HS1 2NJ; tel 01851-703562; fax 01851-709205; e-mail kkennedy@madasafish.com; www.sailhebrides.co.uk).

Diving. For diving from Lewis contact *Murdo MacDonald* (tel 01851-672381).

Sea Kayaking

To get seal's-eye views of Lewis and Harris try sea kayaking with *Hebridean Exploration* (19 Westview Terrace, Stornoway, HS1 2HP; tel 01851-705655 or 870716; e-mail steffisar@aol.com). You might see whales, dolphins, otters and a variety of birds. They take 1-10 people for a day to one-two week camping expeditions. All kayaking and camping basics are supplied.

Surfing

Lewis has some of the finest empty beaches and clearest waters in the Outer Hebrides and 'Hang Ten' enthusiasts can also take advantage of a North Atlantic coastline where pounding rollers and swells build waves for consistent quality surfing all year round. The months from September to April in particular attract surfers looking for hardcore conditions. In midsummer the long daylight hours mean you can actually surf all night long. The Gulf Stream ensures that water temperatures reach 60°F (16°C) in summer and never drop below 48°F (9°C) in late winter. Check out *Hebridean Surf Holidays* (28 Francis Street, Stornoway, HS1 2ND; tel/fax 01851-705862) for more information about local conditions, board and equipment hire, and even tuition. The company can also provide comfortable and informal accommodation at hostel prices for surfers and other outdoor enthusiasts. Breakfast and evening meals, car hire or bus tour and transport to the surf are also options. If you visit Stornoway they'll be happy to discuss local hot spots.

Other Activities

If the weather lets you down you can limber up at the *Sports Centre* (Sandwick Road; tel 01851-702603), which has a swimming pool, fitness gymnasium and sports hall. There's also a *bowling club* (Bayhead Street; tel 01851-701007) which caters for indoor and outdoor enthusiasts and holds regular competitions and friendly matches.

SHOPPING

Wherever you go you are likely to come across squat yet strangely attractive little chess pieces which, even singly, are unusual mementoes of the Outer Hebrides. Behind them is an intriguing story. The year was 1831. Near Ardroil in Uig, a crofter was pursuing one of his cows across the beach when he stumbled across a sand dune that the day's exceptionally high tide had eroded to reveal a small, stone-built chamber. Inside he was horrified to see a host of small figures he was convinced were angry trolls and goblins. What he had discovered were the 78 stunning walrus teeth ivory chess pieces now known as the **Lewis Chessmen**. These are believed to be of Norse origin, dating from the 12th century, and come from at least eight incomplete sets. They have been described as the most outstanding ancient chessmen in the world. Their depiction of characters such as church dignitaries and Norse warriors shows highly skilled craftsmanship. The crofter sold his haul for £84; today they are considered priceless. Of the original find, 67 are in the British Museum, London, and 11 are in the National Museum in

Edinburgh. *Hebridean Replicas* (15A Arnol, Lewis, HS2 9DB; tel 01851-710562; e-mail coleen@hebreplicas.demon.co.uk) produces striking hand-made copies of the chessmen using stone from local beaches.

Arts & Crafts

The Barn Gallery: 2 Eagleton, Lower Bayble Point, Lewis, HS2 0QD (tel 01851-870704). A small gallery with a selection of pictures by local painters on sale at reasonable prices. Call any time. If no reply, call at house opposite. Closed Sunday.

Borgh Pottery: Sue and Alex Blair, Fivepenny House, Borgh, Lewis, HS2 0RX (tel 01851-850345; e-mail borghpottery@yahoo.co.uk; www.borgh-pottery.com). On the main road to the Butt of Lewis. All pots are hand-thrown or hand-built using traditional techniques. There's domestic and decorative ware, one-off pieces, and highly individual frost-resistant terracotta garden pots. Open all year Monday to Saturday 9.30am to 6pm. 17 miles (27 km) north-west of Stornoway.

Breanish Tweed: 1a Melbost, near Stornoway, HS2 0BD (tel/fax 01851-701524). Hand-woven tweed, cashmere and lambswool. Made-to-measure jackets, suits, and skirts.

Celtic Art Gallery: Arnol, Lewis (tel 01851-710531).

Coll Pottery and *Scotia Ceramics:* Back, Lewis, HS2 0JP (tel 01851-820219; fax 01851-820565; e-mail collpot@sol.co.uk). 6 miles (10km) from the centre of Stornoway produces Hebridean pottery, including the Coll Range – hand-modelled earthernware figures, such as the now famous Hebridean Peat Lady – which reflect aspects of island life now dying out. Pottery, viewing gallery, craft shop, coffee and light snacks available. Toilets with facilities for the disabled. Open all year, October to March Monday to Saturday from 9am to 5pm; April to September 9am to 6pm.

Crom-Lus: 9 Bayhead Street, Stornoway, HS1 2DU (tel/fax 01851-703337, carol.edwards@currantbun.com). Gisla woodcraft and Coll pottery.

Eilean Oir: Beech Cottage, Keose, Lochs, HS2 9JT (tel 01851-830479; e-mail EileanOir2@aol.com). Leslie Lankester designs and produces hand-crafted gold and silver jewellery with Celtic, Viking, wildlife and Art Nouveau themes in a village workshop overlooking Loch Erisort.

Gisla Woodcraft: Gisla Lodge, Gisla, HS2 9EW (tel/fax 01851-672371; e-mail carol.macdonald0@talk21.com). Hand-turned wooden gifts and other crafts. Open end-April to end-September from 9am to 6pm. Phone to arrange a visit at other times.

Harbour View Gallery: Anthony and Kate Barber, Port of Ness, Lewis, HS2 0XA (tel/fax 01851-810735; e-mail AJB@harbourview.freeserve.co.uk www.harbourview.freeserve.co.uk). A working studio/gallery near the Butt of Lewis. Displays original watercolours, fine art prints and greeting cards of island scenes by Anthony J Barber. Visitors welcome Easter to October. Open daily except Sunday. November to March by appointment.

Jenor Jewellery: 4 Bayhead Street, Stornoway, HS1 2DU (tel/fax 01851-703338).

Loch Erisort: 63 Cromwell Street, Stornoway. Has a range of silverware, wall hangings, and glass in Celtic designs, and a collection of books of island interest.

James R Mackenzie's *Lewis Loom Centre:* Old Grain Store, 3 Bayhead, Stornoway, HS1 2DU (tel 01851-704500; e-mail lewisloomcentre@ madasafish.com; www.lewisloomcenter.co.uk). Exhibition and shop are housed in a building going back to 1799. Harris Tweed was produced here from 1860 to 1910. Stone peat-burning fireplaces, ship's mast wooden beams, wooden window lintels of greenheart harbour fenders, and old granite blocks from harbour piers all give this building character and atmosphere. Spinning wheels, dyes, wools and loom are on view at the exhibition, as well as charts detailing everything you've ever wanted to know about such important discoveries as Arkwright's water wheels, Hargreaves' spinning jenny, Compton's mule and the power loom. Exhibition entrance for adults is £1, 50p for children. Guided tours £2.50. The shop is well-stocked with locally made products, including Harris Tweed clothing, knitwear, crafts, and gifts.

Kenneth Macleod Harris Tweed Mill: 9 North Shawbost, Lewis, HS2 9BS (tel 01851-710251; fax 01851-710567; e-mail KM.Harris.Tweed@aukgateway.net). Guided tours, Harris Tweed for sale.

Morven Gallery: Janis Scott, Upper Barvas, Lewis, HS2 0QX (tel/fax 01851-840216; e-mail morvengal@email.msn.com). Sells original paintings, prints of Christine Dodd watercolours, ceramics, tapestry and textiles. Coffee shop.

Mosaic: 97 Cromwell Street, Stornoway, HS1 2DG (tel/fax 01851-700155). Scottish and international ethnic crafts and jewellery.

Oiseval Gallery: Brue, Lewis, HS2 0QW (tel/fax 01851-840240; e-mail jamessmith@oiseval.co.uk; www.oiseval@demon.co.uk). In the crofting village of Brue on the Atlantic west coast, is where the work of Lewis-based photographer James Smith, a member of the Royal Photographic Society, is displayed for sale. The gallery is open all year 10.30am to 5.30pm Monday to Saturday, or by arrangement.

PQA: 27 Achmore, Lochs, HS2 9DU (tel 01851-860551). Harris Tweed crafts. Open Monday to Thursday 10am to 5pm.

Scottish Island Crafts: tel 01851-706527; e-mail sicrafts@madasafish.com). Handcrafts ornamental replicas of island blackhouses in Lewis stone.

The Studio Gallery: Simon Rivett, North Shawbost, Lewis, HS2 9BQ (tel 01851-710672; e-mail simon@tullochard.demon.co.uk; www.tullochard. demon.co.uk). An open studio on the west coast. Drawings and paintings interpret the landscape of Lewis and Harris. Tuition offered. Opening times vary, so phone to make an appointment.

Books

Bookshops in Stornoway include:

Acair Ltd: Unit 7, 7 James Street, Stornoway, HS1 2QN (tel 01851-703020; fax 01851-703294; e-mail acair@sol.co.uk). Full range of books in Gaelic and English.

R Smith's (Baltic Bookstore). Opposite the Library, in Cromwell Street, Stornoway.

Stornoway Gazette Card and Book Shop: 10 Francis Street, Stornoway.

Miscellaneous

Music Room: 27 Bayhead Street, Stornoway (tel/fax 01851-701027). Has an extensive range of local, Scottish, and Gaelic music. Mail order service. Check out tapes or CDs *A Song of Lewis,* by Jean G (Murray) Clarke, performed by Jennifer Clarke, Skromeda and Wild Mountain Thyme, *An Iomall* ('The Edge'), by Lewis-born Gaelic songstress Alyth McCormack, and *Tri Nithean* ('Three Things'), by actress, singer and BBC presenter Anna Murray, of Back, Lewis.

You can also buy on-line from the *Celtic Music Room* (8 North Street, Sandwick, HS2 0AD; tel 07754 614498; e-mail karen@celticmusicroom.com; www.celticmusicroom.com).

The Hebridean Cottage (7 Bennadrove Road, Stornoway, Lewis, HS2 0DL (tel/fax 01851-701633; e-mail info@hebrideancottage.co.uk) is a one-stop Internet shop for all things Hebridean and showcases local producers. It is in daily contact with suppliers of smoked salmon, and also stocks books on history, culture and folklore, and music from Gaelic folksongs to modern Celtic rock. Available through their website www.hebrideancottage.co.uk.

The *Whalers Dram Scotch Whisky:* 21 Gress, Lewis, HS2 0NB (tel 01851-701265; fax 01851-701272). Bottled in two sizes, 1.5 litre and 70cl, it has a special label offering you the opportunity to personalise your purchase with an appropriate message or greeting. A novel gift.

HELP AND INFORMATION

Western Isles Tourist Board: 26 Cromwell Street, Stornoway, HS1 2DD (tel 01851-703088; fax 01851-705244; e-mail stornowaytic@witb.ossian.net; www.witb.co.uk). Open all year, Monday to Friday from 9am to 5pm. *Bureau de Change* available.

Police Station: Church Street, Stornoway (tel 01851-702222). Other police stations are at: Back (tel 01851-820222); Balallan (tel 01851-830222); Barvas (tel 01851-840222); Carloway (tel 01851-643222); Garrabost (tel 01851-870222) and Ness (tel 01851-810298).

Archway Medical Practice: Francis Street, Stornoway (tel 01851-703588).

Bayhead Dental Practice: 56 Bayhead Street, Stornoway (tel 01851-702548); 42 Church Street, Stornoway (tel 01851-702334).

Health Centre: Springfield Road, Stornoway (two practices; tel 01851-703145/704888); Bank Street (tel 01851-703588).

Western Isles Hospital: Macaulay Road, Stornoway (tel 01851-704704).

Western Isles Council (Comhairle nan Eilean Siar): Sandwick Road, Stornoway, HS1 2BW (tel 01851-703773; fax 01851-705349; e-mail nscott@cne-siar.gov.uk; www.cne-siar.gov.uk).

Western Isles Enterprise: James Square, 9 James Street, Stornoway, HS1 2QN (tel 01851-703703; fax 01851-704130; e-mail wie@hient.co.uk).

British Airways: Stornoway Airport (tel 01851-703240).

Bus Station: South Beach Street, Stornoway (tel 01851-704327).

Caledonian MacBrayne: Ferry Terminal, Stornoway (tel 01851-702361).

Loganair Ltd: The Airport, Stornoway (tel 01851-703067).

Stornoway Pier and Harbour Commission: Amity House, Esplanade Quay, Stornoway, HS1 2XS (tel 01851-702688; fax 01851-705714; e-mail sphc@sol.co.uk).

Post Office: Francis Street, Stornoway (tel 01851-702166).

Bank of Scotland; Cromwell Street (tel 01851-704000).

Clydesdale Bank: South Beach Street (tel 01851-703555).

Lloyd's TSB: Francis Street (tel 01851-702368)

Royal Bank of Scotland: 17 North Beach Street, Stornoway, HS1 2XH (tel 01851-705252; fax 01851-702509).

Sea Angling Club: South Beach Quay, Stornoway (tel 01851-702021).

Sports Centre: Sandwick Road, Stornoway (tel 01851-702603).

Stornoway Golf Club: Lady Lever Park, Stornoway (tel 01851-702240).

Lewis Dolphin Project: Joe Platt (tel 01851-621349; e-mail jd.platt@hotmail.com).

Library: Keith Street, Stornoway (tel 01851-703773).

There are *public toilets* in Perceval Square Car Park, Stornoway, and automatic public toilets at North Beach, Point Street, and South Beach. **Free car parking** at Perceval Square, Kenneth Street, South Beach Quay, and (on street) Bayhead and Scotland streets.

Great Bernera

(Bearnaraigh)

Great Bernera (known simply as Bernera) is a small island lying in Loch Roag off the west coast of Lewis, linked to the main island by a road bridge which in effect is a bridge across the Atlantic Ocean. The bridge was built in 1953 after fed-up locals threatened to blow up the cliffs to create a causeway across the narrow channel. The construction was a major breakthrough for British civil engineering, being the first example in the country of a bridge made of pre-stressed concrete girders. Once over the bridge you'll see four standing stones to the left of the road and a further mile (1.6 km) or so a walk of about a mile (1.5 km) across the moor to the left of the road will bring you to the east shore of **Loch Baravat** (*Bharabhat*) where a causeway runs out to an island dun, or broch, possibly dating back to the Iron Age. Bernera and its outlying islands are owned by resident Count Robin de la Lanne Mirrlees, Prince of Coronata, who lives on the main island, which has a population of about 275. Although the island stretches only 5½ miles (9 km) at its greatest length and is only 2¾ miles (4 km) at its widest it is the largest of the more than 40 islets in the loch. It is a gem. Nowhere did we see more pristine white sands or more sparkling blue waters than at the road's end near the deserted (1878) village of Bosta, at the tip of the island. You can look out from the beach here to Little Bernera and the islets of Floday, Old Hill, Campay – pierced by a natural tunnel about 395 ft (120 m) long – and Bearasay, small in size but big in local history. On this small rocky island west of Little Bernera Neil MacLeod of Lewis held out for three years against his enemy, Mackenzie of Kintail. He gave himself up after the authorities stranded his wife and children on one of the skerries at low tide. In 1613, Neil Macleod was executed in Edinburgh where he died, it is recorded, 'verie Christianlie,' leaving the Mackenzies in possession of Lewis.

A more recent area of interest on the lovely beach at Bosta is the site of an excavated **Iron Age village** and reconstructed Iron Age house. The reconstruction is open during the summer months from Tuesday to Saturday from midday to 4pm. Replicas of artefacts and demonstrations of craft skills are on site during opening hours (*Bernera Historical Society*, Bernera Museum, Lewis, HS2 9LZ; tel 01851-612285; fax 01851-612331; e-mail cesb@zoom.co.uk). It had long been known that there was a prehistoric site somewhere on the beach but it was not until the spring of 1993 that gales and high tides revealed its precise location. In the dunes archaeologists found Norse material, including soapstone bowls, carved antler pins, and bone combs. Beneath the Norse layers were three subterranean buildings. Each was shaped like a figure of eight, which has given them their nickname of 'jelly baby' houses. Like the wheelhouses of earlier times, they were designed to be largely underground dwellings and only the roofs would have been visible above the surface. The three houses are thought to date from Pictish times and recall features of the prehistoric village of Skara Brae, Orkney, constructed some 3,000 years earlier. Intriguing small cells found at the entrances of two of the houses were possibly once used as peat stores or dog kennels. You'll find the replica house close to the main archaeological site where the excavation work was done by the *Centre for Field Archaeology*, funded by Historic Scotland. The site has been laid out with easy access and information boards. Nearby toilets, refreshments are available at the Community Centre. The **Community Centre and museum** are the focal point for local activity. Throughout the summer season, the community runs a café where teas and coffees, fresh homebakes, snacks, lunches and takeaway meals are available. The museum houses all the records, photographs, and archives of the local history group and mounts various exhibitions. During the summer the main museum display is on the lobster fishing which has sustained Bernera for many generations. The museum is open from April to mid-September, Monday to Saturday from 11am to 5pm. All other times by appointment only. Admission is £1.50.

As well as its other archaeological attractions – a restored Norse mill, standing stones and duns – Bernera also has numerous freshwater lochs with **good trout fishing**, and wildlife includes **seals, otters, dolphins, eagles, gannets**, and a host of land and seabirds. *Ceilidhs* and dances are organised throughout the year and 'Bernera Nights' are renowned throughout the isles for their liveliness. Scottish Evenings with traditional food and entertainment by local artists and Bernera's own acclaimed Highland Dancers are especially popular. A shop, post office, primary school, the doctor's surgery, and two churches are located in Breacleit, about 1½ miles (2.4 km) from the bridge.

Walks

A moderate waymarked circular route of 7½ miles (12 km) will take you from Bernera Community Centre at Breacleit in the centre of the island round the north through Bosta and back by way of the banks of Loch na Muilne, where you can take a track from the shore to the village of Tobson, the oldest continuously inhabited settlement in Bernera. The cairn at Tobson crossroads commemorates the Bernera Rioters, island raiders who in 1874 won a famous legal battle over land rights.

ACCOMMODATION
B&B

Garymillis: Catherine Macaulay, 6 Kirkibost (tel 01851-612341; fax 01851-612271; e-mail ailtenis@globalnet.co.uk). Three-star, four double en-suite rooms, from £18. Open February to November.

Mrs Macdonald: 17 Tobson (tel 01851-612347). Three-star, from £16.

Self-Catering

Elsa Hutchison: 5 Hacklete (tel 01851-612269). One-star, three bedrooms, sleeps five, from £120-£150 a week. Open all year.

Anne Ryan: 25 Valasay, HS2 9NA (tel/fax 01851-612288; e-mail aryan25v@aol.com). Semi-detached croft house overlooking the Kyles of Valasay, two bedrooms, sleeps four. Oil-fired central heating and coal included, bed linen supplied. No pets permitted due to livestock. Open all year.

SCARP

On 23 July 1934, German inventor Gerhardt Zucher tried to convince the British government that irrespective of wind and weather mail and medicines could be delivered by rocket to remote islands. He had chosen Scarp as the island for his innovative demonstration as a woman there had given birth to the first of her twins in her cottage earlier that year because a wild storm had prevented the doctor from crossing to attend to her. Two days later the weather calmed and she gave birth to the second child, but this time in a Stornoway hospital. On the day of the experiment, celebrated by the issue of a special postage stamp and watched by an expectant crowd, the experimental rocket exploded and thousands of burnt and singed letters fluttered down to the beach. A similar attempt made a few days later in the grounds of Amhuinnsuidhe Castle was also a spectacular failure. Although those experiments were disasters Zucher later played a part in the Third Reich's development of the destructive V2 rockets the Germans launched on London during World War II. Zucher vanished mysteriously during the war and is thought to have been liquidated on Hitler's orders. As a result of all this Scarp can claim to be a tenuous link in the technological development that led to men landing on the moon. *The Rocket Post*, a movie about this idealistic and decidedly eccentric German, was filmed on the island of Taransay in 2001. It tells the true story of how Zucher came to the Outer Hebrides to develop his mail-transporting rocket and how, when he arrived in this then extremely remote corner of Scotland, he had to deal with local hostility not only to new technology, but also to Germans. During World War I the Highlands and Islands lost more servicemen in ratio to their populations than any other part of the British Isles, something the islanders had not forgotten when Herr Zucher and his rocket arrived.

Scarp's 2,580 acres (1,044 ha) are largely hilly and rocky. There are a number of small lochs scattered around the island, with the largest, Loch Uidemul, lying between high point Sròn Romul (1,010 ft/308 m) and the hill above the deserted village, Beinn fo Thuath (587 ft/179 m). Although the island has been uninhabited since the last two crofting families left at the end of 1971 the occasional shepherd visits and cottages in the old village in the south-east are used as holiday homes. In 1884, after some of the islanders evicted elsewhere during the Clearances had settled here the population peaked at about 200. By 1900, it was down to 120 and thereafter the drift away from the island was steady. Apart from the difficulty of scratching a living, one major complaint was the lack of a landing place to cross the Sound of Scarp. By the time the authorities heeded their request and built a pier near Hushinish the last of the islanders had left for good.

SHIANT ISLANDS

The Shiants are known in Gaelic as the 'Big Islands'(*Na h-Eileanan Mora*), something of a misnomer for this 353-acre (143 ha) group of rock and grass islands and islets 10 miles (16 km) into The Minch and halfway between Lewis and the Isle of Skye. These islands (they're pronounced 'Shant') comprise *Garbh Eilean* ('Rough Island'), which is connected to *Eilean Tighe* ('House Island') by a shingle ridge, and fertile *Eilean Mhuire* ('Mary's Island'), a short distance to the east. The ruins of a chapel dedicated to the Virgin Mary give the smallest island its name. The islands rival Staffa for spectacle, with cliffs of columnar volcanic basalt rock towering up to 492 ft (150 m). They are also famed in local folklore as 'The Enchanted Isles' and the Sound of Shiant, a place of furious currents and wild water, is one of the reasons. The Sound is known in Gaelic as the 'Stream of the Blue Men,' weird, dripping semi-human creatures who come aboard your boat and sit beside you singing a Gaelic song or reciting a poem. If you can't continue the song or the poem, say fishermen, the creatures sink the boat and drown you.

The islands are also famous as one of the last remaining hideouts in Britain of the ship or black rat, a rodent whose fleas carried the plague known in mediaeval times as the Black Death.

The Shiants were once owned by the novelist Sir Compton Mackenzie and later by British author and publisher Nigel Nicolson, who bought them as a Balliol undergraduate in 1937 for £1,300 from a Colonel Macdonald of Skye. For some reason Macdonald never visited the islands after buying them. Nicolson gave the islands to his son Adam, who periodically lives in the restored two-roomed croft house built by Compton Mackenzie in the 1920s on the site of an older building on the shore of *Eilean Tighe*. The novelist used this as his summer writing refuge. Half a million burrowing **puffins** arrive in the Shiants every year late in April and early May – always on a Sunday, according to the Scalpay fishermen – along with hordes of **razorbills** and **guillemots**. There is a huge puffin colony on a scree of large boulders next to a fine natural arch on *Garbh Eilean*. **Seals** haul out on the tidal rocks offshore, **otters** hunt along the beaches, and the waving forests of kelp are full of exquisite soft corals, all good reasons why the Shiants are a designated Site of Special Scientific Interest (SSSI) and an Area of Outstanding Natural Beauty.

About 10 years ago, a fisherman from Scalpay recovered a 2 ft (0.6 m) length of twisted 'wire' from the sea off one of the Shiant skerries. He threw it in his boat and forgot about it. One evening a crew member happened to see a bracelet of similar design on a TV show about antiques. The result was that the old piece of wire was sent to the National Museum in Edinburgh for examination. It turned out to be the only late Bronze Age gold torc ever to have been found in Scotland and was probably made in Ireland around 1200 BC. The torc, which would once have decorated the neck or arm of a warrior chieftain, is now on display in the National Museum. Ask about boat hire at the Tourist Information Office in Tarbert, or talk to local fishermen if you'd like to visit the Shiants.

Harris *(Na Hearadh)*

Apart from playing a role in the wanderings of Bonnie Prince Charlie in 1746, Harris has not placed much of a stamp on Scottish history, but neither has its history been marred by the battles and bloodshed that marked the early days of neighbouring Lewis. The Macleods held sway over Harris for nearly 500 years until the Earl of Dunmore bought their fief in 1834. The Earl hived off North Harris in 1868 and it was sold to Sir Edward Scott, along with the islands of Scalpay and Scarp, and the village of Tarbert. South Harris was in turn bought by Lord Leverhulme in 1919, after his debacle in Lewis. The Earl of Dunmore's family had a more beneficial impact on the island's economy than frustrated Lord Leverhulme. Thanks to the promotional activities of the Dowager Countess of Dunmore, Harris Tweed became *the* material for Britain's landed gentry and today's thriving industry was born.

NORTH HARRIS *(Ceann a Tuath na Hearadh)*

North Harris is separated from Lewis by the deep inland thrusts of Loch Resort on the west coast and Loch Seaforth on the east, as well as a belt of six miles (10 km) of mountainous terrain moulded by glaciation, and an oddly treeless deer forest. The scenery here changes noticeably from the lochan-strewn flatland of Lewis to hilly country with the lofty, bare peaks of North Harris in the west, dominated by the 2,622 ft (799 m) peak of Clisham. North Harris is separated from South Harris by the narrow isthmus of land at Tarbert, situated on the pinched waist where another two great sea lochs almost meet. Harris is generally considered to be scenically more spectacular than partner Lewis. Along the western Atlantic coast are some remarkable beaches while in contrast the east side has large areas of exposed rocky terrain where picturesque little hamlets and scattered settlements lie around the sea lochs. Peat is cut by local families in summer and enormous black stacks drying ready for use as fuel are integral features of the landscape at this time of the year.

TARBERT *(An Tairbeart)*

Tarbert is the village capital of Harris and the ferry port for Uig in Skye and Lochmaddy in North Uist. It's perched on the steep sides of a narrow valley between East Loch Tarbert, opening into The Minch, and West Loch Tarbert, debouching into the Atlantic. Its name indicates that this was where the Norse rovers of old used the isthmus as a place over which they manhandled their longships from The Minch to the Atlantic Ocean. The village itself is not all that old. It was established in 1779 as a fishing settlement. It now holds about a quarter of Harris's total population of 2,000. Tarbert is the main point of entry to Harris and the island's focal point, with a Tourist Information Office, Community Centre, a Post Office, Mountain Rescue Post, shops, two churches, restaurant, and a pleasant hotel where three of Britain's leading literary figures signed the visitor's book in 1912: the playwright JM Barrie, Sir Anthony Hope Hawkins, author of *The Prisoner of Zenda*, and Edward Verrall (EV) Lucas, essayist and novelist who also wrote for *Punch* magazine. Hawkins and Lucas were guests of Barrie, who had rented nearby Amhuinnsuidhe Castle.

About eight miles (13 km) out of Tarbert along the A859 road north a minor road leads down to Maraig (*Maaruig*) on the shores of Loch Seaforth, regarded as one of the great beauty spots on the island. From here a winding track passes the Laxadale Lochs and traverses wild rocky terrain before reaching Urgha, on East Loch Tarbert. Alternatively, you can follow the minor road along Loch Seaforth to the tiny village of Rhenigidale (*Reinigeadal*), where there's an isolated hostel (see *Accommodation*). Loch Seaforth has some wonderful fjord-like scenery and gave its name to the famous Scottish regiment originally raised as 'Seaforth's Highlanders' by Mackenzie, Earl of Seaforth. A recruitment poster of 1793 promised 'High bounties and soldier-like Entertainment,' as well as the opportunity for 'a Stroke at the Monfieurs' to all who enlisted. There are many views of this 18-mile-long (29 km) sea loch from the A859 road as it crosses the boundary from Lewis to Harris.

On the main road along West Loch Tarbert towards Ardhasaig is the little village of **Bunavoneadar** (*Bun Abhainn Eaddara*), with its ruins of an old Norwegian whaling station established in 1904. Lord Leverhulme bought this in 1922, along with three Norwegian vessels which he planned to use to catch whales as part of his plan to develop a modern fishery based at Leverburgh, a spot he chose because of its access to the waters of both The Minch and the Atlantic Ocean. Both schemes had foundered by 1924, when he left the Western Isles for the last time. Lord Leverhulme died in May 1925 following a visit to the Belgian Congo and his far-sighted, if grandiose, schemes were abandoned by his associates.

Some 10 miles (16 km) west of Tarbert along the narrow lochside road is **Amhuinnsuidhe Castle**, where dramatist JM Barrie conceived his play *Mary Rose*, inspired by one of the small islets in Loch Voshimid, 4½ miles (7 km) to the north-east (the 'island that likes to be visited,' according to the play). The castle overlooks a river cascading into the sea over a rock slide, where in season you might see salmon leaping the falls. It was built by the Earl of Dunmore in 1868 and stands by the pretty inlet of Loch Leosavay. The castle is now owned by the Bulmer cider family and is available for weekly lets if you can afford it (see *Eating and Drinking*). The road runs past the castle's front door and beyond to end at Hushinish Point. Looking out north-west from here you'll see the island of Scarp, which lies about half a mile (0.8 km) from the jetty to the north of Hushinish. This small pier was built too late to serve the island community of Scarp, whose last members left in December 1971. The island is now uninhabited, although former tenants living on mainland Harris still graze their sheep here. A walk along the mountain path from Hushinish to Cravadale on the shores of Loch na Cleavag presents some fine views of the island of Scarp, but don't be tempted to wade across to the island at low tide. Though the water can become very shallow, the currents are dangerously strong. In the other direction from Tarbert along East Loch Tarbert the road leads to Kyles Scalpay (*Caolas Scalpaigh*) and the bridge across to the island of Scalpay.

SOUTH HARRIS *(Cean Deas na Hearadh)*

The A859 road south from Tarbert enters South Harris and loops to the west to follow the coast all the way down to the ferry port of **Leverburgh** *(An t-Ob)*, the largest village in South Harris and the terminal for the ferry to Otternish, gateway to the Uists and Barra. On the way down the road goes through Glen Laxdale and passes a succession of lochs, many of them linked by the River Laxdale, which winds down from the South Harris Forest above the wide sandy beach of Luskentyre Bay. When the tide is out the gleaming Luskentyre sands *(Tràigh Losgaintir)* are 2 miles (3 km) long and more than ¹/₂ mile (1 km) wide. The heights of *Beinn Dubh* (1,660 ft/506 m) above Luskentyre look out across the Sound of Taransay to the uninhabited island of Taransay. This became a household word during the screening of the BBC Television documentary *Castaway 2000*, which was made there over a period of 12 months (see *Taransay*). South Harris is almost an island, measuring roughly 7 miles (12 km) from west to east, and 11 miles (18 km) north to south. Its west coast with its widespread fertile machair and its magnificent long beaches is a complete contrast to the eastern shores, where the terrain is so rock-bound that people once had to take their dead to the west coast for burial. The village of Leverburgh has many associations with soap magnate Lord Leverhulme, who gave it his name. After he had given up his attempts to revolutionise Lewis he moved here to concentrate his efforts on Harris. He intended to establish Leverburgh as the hub of a modern fishing industry and built houses for what he planned to be a flourishing community.

The End of a Dream

The village of Leverburgh was originally named Obbe. It was renamed Leverburgh in 1919 when Lord Leverhulme, Bolton-born soap tycoon and one of the founders of the giant conglomerate Unilever, bought the South Harris estate from the Earl of Dunmore for £36,000. He planned to turn Obbe into a major fishing centre and with this intention he bought what was to be the first in a chain of 400 fish shops throughout Britain, known as MacFisheries. Fish would be landed at Obbe and then distributed to these shops. Lord Leverhulme set up a fish processing site at Leverburgh Pier consisting of curing sheds, a smoke-house, refrigeration facilities, accommodation blocks, store sheds, houses for his managers, as well as a harbour that was capable of providing berths for 50 herring drifters. The second phase of the development would have been the conversion of Obbe into an inner harbour. Unfortunately, the project was doomed to failure. It was 1924 before the first herrings were landed at Leverburgh from 12 drifters from Great Yarmouth. He developed pneumonia after returning from a trip through Africa the following year and on 7 May 1925 William Hesketh Lever, Viscount Leverhulme of the Western Isles, died in Hampstead. When the news reached Harris the sirens were hooted on Leverburgh pier and all work was halted. The workforce was subsequently laid off and the 33,000-acre (13,355 ha) South Harris Estate put up for sale. In October 1925 the pier site at Leverburgh was sold for £5,000 and the vast lands of the estate in South Harris went for £900. All that remains of Lord Leverhulme's works are the houses built in Leverburgh and a local school, Leverhulme Memorial. The village that was named after him reverted to the original Gaelic *An t-Obb*.

Heading west along the coastal road from Leverburgh, the A859 road passes through Glen Coishletter (*Gleann Choisleitir*), to fork at Northton (*Taobh Tuath*) where a track runs to Chaipaval, rising to 1,198 ft (365 m), on the peninsula of Toe Head (*Gob an Tobha*). A short walk along the south coast of the peninsula brings you to a ruined chapel on a small headland at *Rubh' an Teampuill*. On the north coast of the peninsula the natural arches offer more challenging scrambles. The walk to the top of Chaipaval gives some splendid views. On a clear day you can make out St Kilda some 45 miles (72 km) to the west and the Cuillin of Skye 50 miles (80 km) to the south-east. Just over a mile (1.6 km) to the west is the tiny island of Coppay, haul-out ground for a seal colony. At different times in history this area of Harris has been occupied over thousands of years by different cultures. Excavation has revealed Neolithic, Beaker, and Iron Age settlements spanning from about 2500 BC to 500 BC-AD 500. Scarasta's long dune-fringed beach lies to the north of the peninsula and often attracts couples looking for memorable surroundings in which to exchange their marriage vows. Nearby are the Scarista golf links and the **Scarista Standing Stone**.

The **McGillivray Centre** at Northton (tel 01859-502367; fax 01859-502283) is dedicated to the work of the noted naturalist and ornithologist and gives an insight into the natural attractions of the area. Unmanned centre, picnic area, toilets with facilities for the disabled, and car parking. The centre is open all year. Also at Northton is the **Seallam! Visitor Centre** (tel/fax 01859-520258; e-mail seallam@cs.com; www.Seallam.com), a place offering a genealogical research service called *Co leis thu?* (which means 'Whose son, or daughter, are you?'). If you want to know about your Scottish ancestry writer-broadcaster Bill Lawson (tel 01859-520488) is the man to talk to here. He also arranges guided walks. You can see a variety of exhibitions at the centre and there's a café and shop on site, with facilities for the disabled. The retail area stocks books, videos, CDs and tapes. The centre, whose Gaelic name means 'Let me see,' is open all year, Monday to Saturday from 10am to 6pm, and by appointment.

EAST COAST

Along the way from Tarbert to Rodel (*Roghadal*) in the south-east the road passes the conspicuous bulk of 1,509 ft/460m Roneval (*Roineàbhal*), the mountain that almost wasn't. Plans to turn it into a super-quarry for its deposits of pink anorthosite were shelved in 2000 only after a protracted battle led by outraged conservationists. Had the development of the quarry been given the green light it would, over a period of 50-60 years, have turned the mountain into a sea loch. At Rodel is the well-known cruciform **Church of St Clement** built on the site of a much older religious structure in the 16th century by Alasdair Crotach, the 8th chief of the Macleods of Harris and Dunvegan, a family known as *Siol Tormoid* ('The seed of Norman, son of Leod'). The tombs in this otherwise empty church are among the most spectacular in Scotland, and the finest of them all is the tomb Alasdair Crotach had built for himself in 1528, even though he didn't occupy it until his death 19 years later. His tomb lies in an arched recess in the wall on the south side of the choir. The arch above the stone coffin is intricately carved. Below the arch and above the crumbling effigy of the Macleod chief in armour are Latin inscriptions, a religious panel showing St Michael and Satan weighing souls, a castle and a galley, and a Celtic stag-hunting scene. The Twelve Apostles also appear, dressed in quilted coats typical of the 16th century western Highlands. Tradition says one of Scotland's greatest female bards – Màiri nighean Alasdair Ruaidh – is also buried in the church. She is said to lie face downwards, the fate of all female bards so that their songs couldn't escape to prick the consciences of the living. Bard Mary Macleod was reputedly 105 when she died and in life enjoyed both snuff and whisky. Among the other tombs in the churchyard is that of a Macleod of Berneray who once fought for Bonnie Prince

Charlie. The 66 ft (20 m) square church tower looks out over the village of Rodel to the small harbour built in the late 16th century and sheltered by the little island of Vallay. The church lost its roof after the Reformation but was restored and reinforced by the Countess of Dunmore in 1873. It is no longer used for public worship. Today St Clement's is owned and maintained by Historic Scotland. It is unmanned but open all year round.

Four miles (6 km) north-east of Rodel is the small port of Finsbay, on the loch of the same name. From here north the eastern seaboard region is known as the 'Bays' (*Na Baigh*). Innumerable little inlets along this coast provide harbours for fishing boats and sheltered areas for tiny scattered villages, many of them with names ending in 'bay.' The 'Golden Road,' a narrow, twisting road full of blind corners and wicked bends skirts the east coast, winding around the heavily indented coastline where, in some places, bays and fresh-water lochans are separated by no more than the width of the road. The road gets its name because of its exorbitant building cost in the 1930s. There's a viewpoint on this rocky east coast road at **Manish** (*Manais*) with lovely views of The Minch and the dramatic heather-clad landscape of this part of Harris. The road eventually passes the head of Loch Stockinish to rejoin the main A859 road leading back to Tarbert. West of the southern half of the Bays district is Loch Langavat, not as big as the loch of the same name in Lewis, but still 2¹/₂ miles (4 km) long from north to south and nearly ¹/₂ mile (1 km) across at its widest.

FLORA AND FAUNA

Flora

From June to August is the **best time** to see the floral splendour of the *machair*, the white shell-sand blended with peaty soil by wind and rain to form a rich fertile coastal meadowland which each year bursts with more wild flowers than grass. Some of the finest machair is found in South Harris at Northton and Chaipaval and closely resembles the superb machair of the Uists. The machair around Hushinish is famous for its **creeping willow** and its **harebells**. Marshy ground is the place for the **marsh marigold** and the **march** and **northern orchid**. In summer, the lochans are covered with **waterlilies** and **sea pinks** carpet the coastline. The southern part of the Seilebost peninsula in South Harris encloses a large area of saltmarsh vegetation which is noted for its high percentage of 'turf fucoids' – seaweeds so small that they resemble mosses.

Fauna

Harris has a wide and varied wildlife population and several species that are rare elsewhere are quite common here. **Otters** are found almost everywhere on Harris and if you are keen to see them it's unlikely you'd leave without coming across a family. On the slopes of Clisham you'll see **red deer** and even **wild goats**. There are large colonies of the **blue hares** introduced over the last century and **rabbits**, **polecats**, **fieldmice** and **hedgehogs** are equally common.

The **grey** or **Atlantic seal**, rarer elsewhere, is frequently seen and the **common seal** is a resident. As well as several types of **dolphin** and **porpoise**, you may see whales. Of the baleen or toothless whales, visitors include **minke**, **fin** and **sei whales**, as well as toothed **pilot** and **killer whales**. The great **humpback whale** is also believed to frequent the waters around Harris.

Bird-Watching

Golden eagles nest at a higher density here than almost anywhere else in Europe and the hills of North Harris are particularly good areas in which to spot this majestic raptor gliding on the thermals. **Buzzards** are more common. Twitchers can also tick off **peregrine falcons**, **black-throated divers**, **oyster catchers**, curlews, **redshanks, puffins,** and **kittiwakes.** Seabirds are prolific on the windy and spray-swept peninsula to the south-west of Hushinish where the hills and low cliffs of pinkish gneiss offer nesting sites to **guillemots, fulmars, shags, rock doves** and many other common coastal birds. Large populations of **gannet** are common and the *bonxie,* or **great skua,** is also a visitor. The machair is the home of the **corncrake** and **wheatear, larks, cuckoos,** and the **pewit,** or **lapwing,** also abound. The Sound of Taransay is one of the **best places** in Harris to see ducks such as **eider, long-tailed duck, red-breasted merganser** and **scoters.** The machair around Northton and Chaipaval attracts huge numbers of birds, among them **skylark, dunlin** and **redshank.** On occasion there may also be significant numbers of **greylags** and **barnacle geese. Goldeneye** and **whooper swan** may be seen in the lochs around Rodel, in South Harris, as well as the more familiar **mallard.**

GETTING THERE

From Skye

Caledonian MacBrayne (The Ferry Terminal, Gourock PA19 1QP; tel 08705-650000; fax 01475-635235 for reservations; e-mail reservations@calmac.co.uk; www.calmac.co.uk) operates a car ferry service across The Little Minch from Uig, Skye, to Tarbert, Harris, on Monday, Wednesday and Friday at 2pm; Tuesday, Thursday and Saturday at 9.40am and 6pm. From end-May to 3 September there are additional sailings on a Monday at 5.30am and Saturday at 8pm. The journey takes about 1 hour 40 minutes. The single adult fare costs £8.50, car or motorhome £40, and caravan, boat/baggage trailer an additional £40, motorcycle £20, and bicycle £2. The ferry office is at Uig pier; tel 01470-542219.

From North Uist

If you are travelling to Harris from North Uist the car ferry leaves Otternish pier from end-April to 1 September on Monday, Wednesday and Friday at 7.10am, 10.40pm, 1.25pm, and 4.00pm; on Tuesday, Thursday and Saturday at 7.10am, 12.05pm, and 4pm. The trip takes about 1½ hours. A single adult fare is £4.75, car and motorhome £21.90, and caravan or boat/baggage trailer £21.90, motorcycle £10.95, and bicycle £1. Times change from mid-April to end-April, 3 September to 22 September, and 24 September until 20 October, so it's best to contact CalMac for sailing times. The ferry offices are at Tarbert pier, Harris (tel 01859-502444), and Lochmaddy, North Uist (tel 01876-500337).

GETTING AROUND

From Leverburgh in South Harris the inter-island ferry operated by CalMac links Lewis and Harris to North Uist.

Harris and Lewis are connected by road across a narrow neck of land between Loch Seaforth and Loch Erisort. From Stornoway to South Harris takes about1 hour and 20 minutes by car. By road from Tarbert to Leverburgh (*An t-Ob*) it's 20 miles (32 km). To Stornoway and Port of Ness, Lewis, it's 37 and 65 miles (60/105 km) respectively.

Bus

There is a good daily bus service run by *Harris Coaches* (Scott Road, Tarbert, HS3 3BG; tel 01859-502441; fax 01859-550278) linking Leverburgh with the rest of Harris and Lewis. It connects with the ferry services to the mainland and the other islands.

Vehicle Rental

Gaeltech Car Hire: Grimisdale Guest House, Leverburgh, HS5 3TS (tel 01859-

520460; fax 01859-520461; e-mail farky@grimisdale.co.uk). Self-drive vehicles, pick up and return from Leverburgh or Tarbert ferry terminals.
Harris Car Service: Tarbert (tel/fax 01859-502221).

Cycle Hire. Bicycles are available for hire near the pier (tel 01859-502271), and from *Blazing Saddles* (tel 01859-502417).

ACCOMMODATION

Hotels

Harris Hotel: Tarbert (tel 01859-502154; fax 01859-502281; e-mail Cameronharris@btinternet.com). Family-owned, two-star, 24 rooms, built around 1865. JM Barrie (1860-1937) of *Peter Pan* fame visited Harris in 1912, where he got the idea for his play *Mary Rose*. You can still see where he scratched his initials on a dining-room window in the hotel. A la carte and table d'hote dinner menus feature fresh local produce, seafood, lamb and game. Open all year, seven days a week from 7pm to 9pm. The *Crofter's Table Restaurant* has a bistro type menu, open April to October, Monday to Saturday 6pm to 9.15pm. From £34 a night B&B. Dinner £19. The hotel has the largest selection of single malt whiskies on the island, 64 to taste, and others for display only. The friendly public bar is at the side of the hotel, across the road, and has pool, darts, and a juke box.

Macleod Motel: Pier Road, Tarbert (tel 01859-502364; fax 01859-502578). Two-star, beside ferry terminal. Open May to September, from £28. Lively lounge bar and a restaurant serving traditional Scottish cuisine, Monday to Saturday, midday to 2.30pm and 6pm to 8.30pm. Bookings only on Sunday.

Guest Houses

Allan Cottage Guest House: Tarbert, HS3 3DJ (tel/fax 01859-502146; www.witb.co.uk/links/allancottage.htm). Four-star, lochside Victorian guest house, a mile (1.6 km) from Tarbert on A859 to Stornoway. Open 1 April to 30 October, B&B from £30, no smoking in dining-room and bedrooms. Imaginative cooking of fish, seafood, Harris lamb, and a sensational 18th century nutmeg cheesecake with brown bread ice cream. Taste of Scotland member. Vegetarians welcome by prior arrangement.

Ardvourlie Castle Guest House: Ardvourlie, HS3 3AB (tel 01859-502307; fax 01859-502348). Five-star, restored Victorian hunting lodge in North Harris. Open 1 April to 31 October, B&B from £65, no smoking in dining-room, which offers views over the wooded grounds to the mountains. Kitchen uses as much local produce as possible. Taste of Scotland member. Vegetarians welcome, but prior notice essential.

Carminish House: Alex and Mary Borthwick, 1A Strond, Leverburgh (tel 01859-520400; fax 01859-520307). Four-star, double and two twin en-suite rooms. Open April to September, from £20 B&B. 10-minute walk to Leverburgh ferry, private car park. Dinner and packed lunches available.

Leachin House: Tarbert, HS3 3AH (tel/fax 01859-502157; e-mail leachin.house@virgin.net; www.leachin-house.com). Four-star guest house, overlooking the sea, a mile (1.6 km) from Tarbert on road to Stornoway. Open all year except Christmas and New Year, B&B from £45, no smoking in dining-room or bedrooms. Modern Scottish cuisine, such as flaky smoked salmon with an avocado salsa, collops of Scotch beef with Drambuie cream sauce. Taste of Scotland member. Unlicensed.

Scarista House: Tim and Patricia Martin, Scarista, HS3 3HX (tel 01859-550238; fax 01859-550277; e-mail tnpmartin@ukgateway.net; www.scaristahouse.com). Four-star Georgian guest house, 15 miles (24 km) south-west of Tarbert. Open all year, but closed occasionally in winter, B&B from £63. No smoking in dining-room, bedrooms and drawing room, although permitted in library. Creative cooking using organic produce wherever possible. Fish and shellfish dishes such as ravioli of Sound of Harris langoustines with squat lobster butter sauce. Taste of Scotland member. Vegetarians welcome.

St Kilda Guest House: Leverburgh, HS5 3UB (tel 01859-520419).

Tetherstone Guest House: Northton, HS3 3UB (tel 01859-520357).

B&B

Ceol na Mara: Mr and Mrs J Mitchell, 7 Direcleit, Harris, HS3 3DP (tel 01859-502464; e-mail midgie@madasafish.com; www.colenamara.com). Delightful three-star, beautifully appointed and refurbished old Hebridean house in 55 acres (22 ha) of crofting land. Views over Loch Kindebig and beyond to The Minch. A few minutes from Tarbert ferry terminal. Private lounge with local books and videos. Open January to December, from £20 a night. Dinner on request at £12.50 a person.

Caberfeidh House: Mrs C Mackenzie, Leverburgh, HS5 3TL (tel 01859-520276). Four-star, overlooking sea loch, minutes from ferry terminal. Open all year, from £17.

Dunard: Christina Morrison, Tarbert, HS3 3DJ (tel 01859-502340). Four-star, original 19th century house, two minutes' from ferry terminal. Open all year, from £29.

Grimisdale: Farquhar MacLeod, Leverburgh, HS5 3TS (tel 01859-520460; fax 01859-520461; e-mail farky@grimisdale.co.uk; www.grimisdale.co.uk). Four-star, open all year, from £20.

Langracleit: Catherine MacLeod, Kendibig, HS3 3HQ (tel 01859-502413). Three-star. Open all year, from £18.

Minchview House: Corinne Miller, Tarbert, HS3 3DB (tel 01859-502140). Two-star, close to ferry terminal. Open April to October, from £18.

Moravia: Morag Macleod, Luskentyre, HS3 3HL (tel 01859-550262). Three-star, close to beach, open March to October, from £17.

Seaview: Margaret Morrison, North Bowglass, Harris, HS3 3AD (tel 01859-502383).

Skyeview: Annie Mackinnon, 1 Scott Road, Tarbert, HS3 3DL (tel 01859-502095). Two-star. Open April to October, from £16.

Sorrel Cottage: Paula Williams, Leverburgh, HS5 3TY (tel 01859-520319; fax 01859-520416; e-mail sorrelcottage@talk21.com). Two-star, open all year, from £17.

Self-Catering

Beul na Mara: Catherine Morrison, Seilebost, HS3 3HP (tel 01859-550205; e-mail morrisonc1@talk21.com). Two well-equipped four-star cottages overlooking sandy beaches, views to Taransay. Open all year, from £245 a week.

Dolina MacLeod: 1 Carragreich, Kyles, HS3 3BP (tel 01859-502225), two-star, views across Minch, 1 bedroom, sleeps 3. Open all year, from £100-£160 a week.

Fernhaven: John MacAuley, Flodabay, HS3 3HA (tel 01859-530340), two-star, 150-year-old croft house, two bedrooms, sleeps 4. Open all year, £250 to £280 a week.

Hugh MacLean: 12 Ferry Road, Leverburgh, HS5 3UA (tel/fax 01631-562663; e-mail kilchrenanhouse@netlineuk.net). Two-star, 3 bedrooms, sleeps 5/6. Open all year, from £210 to £260 a week.

Kirklee Terrace Cottages: Angus Macleod, Tarbert, HS3 3DG (tel 01859-502364; fax 01859-502578). Four-star, four cottages overlooking loch. Open all year, from £250 to £320 a week.

Mrs Effie Morrison: 3 Amhuinnsuidhe, Harris, HS3 3AS (tel 01859-560230). One-star, 3 rooms, sleeps 6. Open all year, from £180 to £200 a week.

Seaside Cottage: Katie MacLeod, 5 Old Pier Road, West Tarbert, HS3 3BG (tel 01859-502033). Three-star, three rooms, sleeps 6. Open all year, from £180-£280 a week.

Seaview Chalet: Mrs J Ross, Bunavoneadar (tel 01859-502482; e-mail gordon_ross20@hotmail.com). Three-star in quiet village. Open all year, from £120-£220 a week.

Tigh na Seileach: Mr and Mrs Tittmar, Bowglass, Harris, HS3 3AD (tel 01859-502411; e-mail tittmars@bigfoot.com). Two-star, 100-year-old restored thatched blackhouse close to Ardvourlie Castle, sleeps two-four. Open all year, from £100-£250 a week.

Hostels

Am Bothan Bunkhouse: Ruari Beaton, Leverburgh (tel 01859-520251; e-mail ruari@ambothan.com; www.ambothan.com). Three-star, a bunkhouse with a difference, tastefully decorated in a nautical theme, views of the Sound of Harris, close to ferry. Accommodation includes cabins of four berths, one cabin of six bunks, a loft with futons, and a communal room with an open peat fire and TV. Excellent kitchen facilities, toilets and showers, disabled bathroom. Open all year. £12 a night. Shop, café and restaurant nearby.

Drinishader Bunkhouse: 5 Drinishader, near Tarbert, HS3 3DX (tel/fax 01859-511255; e-mail roddy@drinishader.freeserve.co.uk). 12 beds, open all year, from £7 a night.

Rhenigidale Youth Hostel Rhenigidale, Harris, HS3 3BD. Owned by the *Gatliff Hebridean Hostels Trust* (GHHT). No advance bookings accepted. Bed linen provided. This traditional croft house is situated in a remote hamlet looking out to the Sound of Shiant. East from Tarbert along the road towards Kyles Scalpay you'll find the four-mile (6 km) footpath signposted for Rhenigidale. A three-hour walk in total. Open all year. 11 beds, three rooms with 4 beds. No telephone. Shop 6 miles (10 km) away, bus (Maaruig) 5 miles (8 km), ferry from Tarbert 6 miles (10 km). Good local fishing and hillwalking. Walkers and cyclists welcome. For more information write to GHHT (30 Francis Street, Stornoway, Lewis, HS1 2ND).

Rockview Bunkhouse: Main Street, Tarbert, HS3 3DJ (tel 01859-502626; fax 01859-502211). Near ferry terminal, two-storey building in the main village, well-equipped kitchen, lounge, showers, dorms, sleep 32, £8.50 a night. Bike hire arranged.

The *Scaladale Centre*, a residential centre in Ardvourlie, is run by the *Lewis and Harris Youth Clubs Association* (Ardvourlie, HS3 3AB; tel/fax 01859-502502; e-mail scaladale@ukonline.co.uk; www.scaladale.co.uk) and accommodates 28 people on a self-catering basis. It can also be used as a conference or training base for up to 60 people.

Camping

Catherine MacKinnon: 5 Grosebay, Grosebay, HS3 3EF (tel 01859-511246). Has two holiday **caravans** which sleep six. Open all year, from £100-130 a week. You will find them beside the main road, about 6½ miles (10 km) from Tarbert.

EATING AND DRINKING

Non-residents can eat in most hotel dining-rooms or you can get a plate of decent, inexpensive food in a bar. For something really special, try the slap-up dinner at *Amhuinnsuidhe Castle* (pronounced *Avin-suey*), about 12 miles (19 km) up the B887 road from Tarbert. This Victorian baronial pile is owned by cider heir Jonathan Bulmer whose decision to let resident chef Rosemary Shrager appear in the TV Channel 5 series *Rosemary: Castle Cook* has placed it firmly on the itinerary of all visiting serious foodies. Rosemary Shrager also runs five-day cookery courses at the castle every year in April, May, and June, and in September and October, when she shows what can be done with such local ingredients as turbot, halibut, langoustines, lobsters, crabs, and scallops, venison and lamb, all fresh from the sea or from the 50,000-acre (20,234 ha) estate, as well as lessons in patisserie, island baking, sauces and soufflés. For more information contact The Estate Office (tel 01876-500329; fax 01876-500428; e-mail northuistestate@ btinternet.com; www.castlecook.com).

If your funds don't run to gourmet meals there's a fish and chip shop next to the bunkhouse in Tarbert's main street, which is open every day, except Sunday, April to October.

An-Clachan T-Room: An Clachan, Leverburgh (tel 01859-520370; fax 01859-520449). For home-made soup, filled rolls, home-baking. Craft shop sells island knitwear and Harris Tweed. Open Monday to Saturday, March to May at 10am to 4pm; May to September 10am to 5pm; and September to October 10am to 4pm.

First Fruits Tearoom: Pier Road Cottage, Tarbert (tel 01859-502439). Serves breakfast, lunches, snacks, afternoon tea. Vegetarian choice. Take-away service available. Open April to September, Monday to Saturday 10.30am to 4.30pm.

ENTERTAINMENT

Every Wednesday evening from May to September you can experience and learn about local culture at the Harris Hotel, Tarbert, organised by the Harris Arts & Heritage. Entertainment includes music, songs, stories and slides of Harris and St Kilda. For more information contact local historian Bill Lawson (tel 01859-520488).

SPORT AND RECREATION

Walking and Climbing

At 2,621 ft (799 m) Clisham in North Harris is the highest mountain in the Outer Hebrides, and running along East and West Loch Tarbert on either side of this peak is a range holding no less than nine summits over 1,969 ft (600 m). This sweep includes the mountains of Tirga Mor, Beinn Dubh, Teinnasval, Roineabhal, Bleabhal, and Scarp at 984-2,297 ft (300-700 m) and the whole area is wild walking and scrambling country.

Walking. From the car park at Urgha, about a mile (1.6 km) to the east of Tarbert, you can follow a waymarked nature trail to Rhenigdale (*Reinigeadal*) on one of the most spectacular walks in Harris. Allow 2-4 hours to cover the 3¹/₂ miles (5¹/₂ km), depending on your level of fitness and how long you want to dawdle. Highest point on the trail is around 919 ft (280 m). Strong walkers can add two more legs to the circuit, from Rhenigdale to Maraig (4 miles/6 km), and Maraig back to the Urgha track (3³/₄ miles/6 km). Allow 8-10 hours for the entire circuit. For amblers rather than scramblers other waymarked walks are being developed on Harris, such as the one at Ardvourlie, where you can ramble through a new forest and enjoy impressive views of Loch Seaforth. Check with the Tourist Information Centre for *Western Isles Walks* leaflets.

Climbing. The most challenging rock climbing is on the dramatic west and north-east faces of Sron Ulladale, which is at the end of the northern summit ridge of Ullaval, above Loch Ulladale. A huge overhanging cliff towers 886 ft (270 m) above the head of the loch and its West Wall is 820 ft (250 m) high for over a kilometre from the Nose above the loch to the South Buttress in Glen Ulladale. To get the most out of this area serious walkers and climbers should consider using a local guide.

Mike Briggs: Bunabhainneadar, Harris (tel/fax 01859-502376; e-mail mikebriggs@isleofharris.swinternet.co.uk). Offers a professional hill walking guide service. You can climb the highest peak to catch a glimpse of St Kilda on the western horizon, go in search of puffins, otters, eagles or deer, and follow ancient pathways.

North-West Frontiers: 18A Braes, Ullapool, Ross-shire IV26 SSZ (tel/fax 01854-612628; e-mail NWF@compuserve.com). Offer walking holidays in Harris, taking in the Clisham range and several other mountains.

Fishing
There are plenty of opportunities to fish for **brown trout, sea trout** and **salmon** and permission is readily given in most cases. Angling charges are low and licences are reasonably priced. Most of the brown trout, salmon and sea trout fishing in North Harris lies around Amhuinnsuidhe Castle and belongs to the North Harris Estate (tel 01876-500329; fax 01876-500428). If you are renting the castle for the week you get the fishing thrown in. Mere anglers should contact the head keeper at Amhuinnsuidhe, Roddy Macleod (tel 01859-560232).

The Lacasdale Lochs, owned by the Harris Hotel, are well known for their salmon and sea trout. There's fly and bank fishing around Tarbert. Contact *The Anchorage* at Ardhasaig (tel 01859-520225). At Scarista, *Borve Lodge Estate Fisheries* has fishing on sea trout lochs and day tickets are sometimes available. *Finsbay Fishing* (4 Ardslave, HS3 3EY; tel 01859-530318) has access to more than 100 lochs for brown trout, sea trout and salmon fly fishing.

Sea fishing from the shore or from boats can be very rewarding, and no licence is needed. *Harris Sea Angling Club* arranges trips and competitions from June to August. Contact Ian Macleod (tel 01859-502364). Boats with crew are readily available and reasonably priced. Hamish Taylor (Tigh an Tobair, Flodabay, Harris, HS3 3HA; tel 01859-530310; fax 01859-530289) arranges coastal exploration, scenic and sea angling trips from Flodabay.

Game Fishing Contacts:
Borve Lodge Estates: Tony Scherr, factor (tel 01859-550202).
Finsbay, Flodabay and Stockinish Estates: A Mackinnon (tel 01859-530318).
Lacasdale Lochs: James MaGarrity (tel 01859-502276).
Rodel Estates: Roddy Coles, 5 Lever Terrace, Leverburgh (tel 01859-520426).
    Has salmon and sea trout fishing.

Cruising
Strond Wildlife Charters: Andrew and Alison Johnson, 1 Strond, Harris, HS5 3UD (tel 01859-520204, mobile 07833 967778; e-mail aj@erica.demon.co.uk). Run wildlife boat trips in the Sound of Harris. You'll see grey and common seals, fishing gannets, red-throated divers, Arctic tern colonies, and maybe whales, dolphins, and basking shark. Trips leave from the fishery pier at Leverburgh, Monday to Saturday weather permitting.

Diving
Ruari Beaton (tel 01859-520251), who runs the Am Bothan Bunkhouse in Leverburgh, takes divers out on trips in his own boat, and also supplies air from his own compressor. Dive on five wrecks in the area and pick up crabs and queen scallops. One of the wrecks is that of the 1,685-ton Panamanian steamship *Stassa*, which drove on to the rocks in July 1966. She was lifted off by high tide and towed by the Stornoway lifeboat into Rodel Bay, where she took four days to sink in 66 ft (20 m) of water.

Golf
At the *Harris Golf Club* in Scarista Mhor (Andrew Haddow, Secretary; tel 01859-520236; e-mail harrisgolf@ic24.net; www.harrisgolf.com) massive sand dunes, small greens and the ever-present wind more than compensate for the modest yardage of the 9-hole, par 68, links course, which has breathtaking views of the

Atlantic. Top professional Nick Faldo once played here and the green fee which he signed and deposited in the honesty box is known as the 'Faldo Fiver' and it is now competed for annually at the club. Green fees are £7.50 a day.

Tennis

At Bunavoneadar, overlooking West Loch Tarbert, is what must be one of the most scenic tennis courts in Britain (tel 01859-502376), an all-weather facility where professional coaching is available.

SHOPPING

Think Harris, think Harris Tweed. Although this world-famous cloth is woven on other islands in the Outer Hebrides there's nothing quite like buying your hat, jacket, or skirt on the island where it all began.

For extra cachet check out the tweeds woven by *Mrs Alex MacDonald* at Drinishader, three miles (5 km) south of Tarbert on the shore of East Loch Tarbert. She produced the tweed presented by the islands as a gift to Queen Elizabeth II.

Harris Tweed Shop: Tarbert, HS3 3DJ (tel 01859-502493). Not far from the ferry terminal in Tarbert, stocks a wide range of tweed apparel, as well as knitwear, souvenirs and gifts.
Luskentyre Harris Tweed Co: 6 Luskentyre, Harris, HS3 3HL (tel 01859-550261; fax 01859-550308). Hand-woven Harris Tweeds and tartans, hats, caps, scarves, Harris wool sweaters. Open all year, except October, Monday to Friday.
Joan MacLennan Tweeds: 1a Drinishader, Harris, HS3 3DX (tel 01859-511266). Has hand-woven Harris Tweed and knitwear. Open May to October 9am to 6pm, Monday to Saturday. Closed Sunday.
Soay Studio: West Tarbert, HS3 3BG (tel 01859-502361; e-mail soaystudio@talk21.com). Uses traditional natural dyeing methods based on plants and lichens. Hand-knitted accessories, knitting wool, and gifts for sale.
Tweeds and Knitwear: 4 Plockropool, Drinishader, Harris, HS3 3EB (tel 01859-511247; fax 01859-511249). Weaving demonstrations, knitwear and wool. Open Monday to Saturday.
For something different:
Rose Cottage Industries: Leverhulme Road, Tarbert, HS3 3DD (tel/fax 01859-502226; e-mail chessmen@rosechess.co.uk; www.rosechess.co.uk). This is a workshop dedicated to producing small quantities of high-quality, hand-crafted collectors' chess sets and Celtic tile boards. The pieces are made of ground stone and resin mix, and the Celtic board is made from single tiles of ground stone. As well as replica sets of the most famous chess pieces in the world, the Lewis Chessmen, there are also the popular Harris Crofters and Scottish v English chess sets.

HELP AND INFORMATION

Harris Tourist Office: Pier Road, Tarbert (tel 01859-502011). Open all year but with restricted hours during the winter. Normally open to coincide with ferry arrivals and departures. There's a 24-hour Public Access Information system available all year round.
Tarbert Police Station: Harris (tel 01859-502002).
Surgeries: Leverburgh (tel 01859-520278); Tarbert (tel 01859-502421).
Caledonian MacBrayne: Tarbert (tel 01859-502444).
Tarbert Pier: tel 01859-502444.
Uig Pier: tel 01470-542219.
Bank of Scotland: Tarbert (tel 01859-502453).
Harris Development Ltd: The Old Hostel, Tarbert, Harris, HS3 3BG (tel 01859-502367; fax 01859-502283) is the community-led local development group.

Scalpay *(Scalpaigh)*

The island of Scalpay in the mouth of East Loch Tarbert has been part of Lewis and Harris since it was permanently joined to North Harris by a £7-million 330-yard-long (300 m) bridge completed in the autumn of 1997. Relative to its size – about three by two miles (5 km x 3 km) – the island is fairly heavily populated, with a tight-knit community of some 350 people sharing the prosperity brought largely by offshore trawling in the fishing grounds of The Minch and inshore prawn and scallop fisheries. Another factor could be the strict Free Church presence which keeps the island 'dry.' This is definitely a BYO island – bring your own. That's what Bonnie Prince Charlie did when he stopped here on his way to Stornoway in 1746 after his defeat on the battlefield at Culloden. Local legend says that a young man giving his name as 'Sinclair' landed on Scalpay from a small boat with some crewmen. Local tacksman Donald Campbell put them up for some days and 'Sinclair' helped around the household. He went fishing with Campbell's son and even helped to pull a cow from a bog. Campbell's suspicions about the identity of his lodger were confirmed when men arrived to arrest him. Campbell refused to hand him over and directed him to a cave where he hid until the coast was literally clear. For many years the Gaelic inscription *'n uair a bha e air alaban na fhogarach na Rioghachd dhleighich fhein* ('When he was wandering as an exile in his own legitimate Kingdom') adorned the lintel of a house built on the site of Scalpay House, where the Young Pretender had sought refuge, but was covered over by harling when it became a Free Church manse.

Scalpay has the advantage of good anchorages with a fine natural harbour in the north-west and another further along the heavily indented west coast. In the far south-east is the *Eilean Glas* lighthouse built of Aberdeen granite in 1788 by the grandfather of Robert Louis Stevenson's, at least officially. An Act of Parliament of 1786 charged the Northern Lighthouse Board (NLB) with the task of establishing four lighthouses on the Scottish coast. *Eilean Glas* (Grey Island) was the first of them. After moves to construct the lighthouse ground to a halt the local tacksman obtained the NLB blueprints and hired local labour to build it. The following summer a passing ship reported the building activity to Edinburgh and agitated NLB officials arrived to find the lighthouse nearly completed. Work had been done to such a high standard that the locals were paid the going rate for their efforts, but the lighthouse was finished by skilled workmen and finally lit in October 1789, 73 years before the Butt of Lewis light. *Eilean Glas* was the first relatively modern lighthouse to be built in islands, but was superseded by a 19th century light, now automatic. The old keepers' houses are used as holiday homes.

ACCOMMODATION

B&B

Hirta House: Mr and Mrs Morrison, Scalpay, HS4 3XZ (tel 01859-540394; e-mail mmackenzie@lineone.net). Three-star, 10 minutes' from ferry. Open all year, from £18.

New Haven: Mairi MacLennan, 15 Scalpay, HS4 3XZ (tel 01859-540325; e-mail Newhaven@madasafish.com). Three-star, five miles (8 km) from ferry terminal. Open April to October, from £16.

Seafield: Rachel Cunningham, Scalpay, HS4 3XZ (tel 01859-540250; e-mail seafieldscalpay@hotmail.com). Two-star. Open February to November, from £16.

Self-Catering
Bridge Side: Mrs A Morrison, Scalpay, HS4 3XY (tel 01859-540282). Two-star, two bedrooms, sleeps 4-5. Open all year, from £200 to £230 a week.
Enfield House: A Cunningham, Scalpay, HS4 3XZ (tel 01859-540344). 3 bedrooms, sleeps 6. Open all year, from £150 to £200 a week.

Walks
The interior is awash with lochs, lochans, and peat bogs and walks tend to be rather marshy. There's a waymarked circular walk round the island of about 8 miles (13 km) which takes about four hours to complete. It starts at the Community Centre and takes in Ceann a' Bhàigh, where at the road's end you can look out to the wreck of the 2,750-ton Antiguan-registered cargo ship *Golf Star*, which has been wedged between two reefs since striking in October 1995. Unfortunately, unlike *SS Politician* of *Whisky Galore* fame (see Eriskay) she was carrying only an uninteresting cargo of gravel. **Bonnie Prince Charlie's Cave** is at Lagna Làire, marked by a yellow pole; you can't miss *Eilean Glas lighthouse*, and the summit of **Ben Scorabhaig** (341 ft/104 m), will reward you with panoramic views of Lewis, North and South Harris, the Uists, the Shiant Islands and across The Minch to Skye.

Diving
Scalpay Divers (Phil and Anne Jones, 34 Outend, Scalpay; tel/fax 01859-540328; e-mail scalpaydivers@madasafish.com; www.scalpaydivers.co.uk) offer tailor-made diving holidays for small groups, buddied pairs, or single divers (buddy provided). The area has dive sites to suit all tastes, from shallow, sandy bays, kelp forests, wall dives, offshore reefs and pinnacles, as well as high energy sites and drift dives. Macro-photography dives are a speciality in August and September. **Minke whale** are frequent summer visitors along with the occasional **orca** and **basking shark**. There are also **otters** fishing around the islands and you might spot such rarities as **sunfish** and **turtle**. The Gulf Stream runs close to the islands, making the water temperature ideal for profuse growths of marine life and for comfortable dry-suit diving all year round. Temperatures never drop much below 50°F (10°C) and go up to 57°F (14°C) in less than 33 ft (10m), and 53°F (12°C) in 66 ft (20 m). The water is clear with visibility around 49 ft (15 m), but less with plankton bloom. The fully equipped RIB 20 ft (6 m) dory with twin 40hp engines and diver/cox will take you to 30-plus recognised sites or you can explore virgin territory. Philip Jones, a Scottish Sub-Aqua Club Regional District PADI divemaster, dives six to seven months of the year. He takes only qualified divers – at least PADI Open Water level. Keeps spare tanks, weights, DVs and fins, but no suits. Recommends dry suits or full 7mm wetsuits.

SHOPPING
There is a general store in the village centre, about a mile (1.6 km) from the bridge, where you can buy the unusual knitwear for which the island women have gained a reputation. *Scalpay Linen* (Rover Cottage, Outend, opposite Eilean Glas lighthouse branch road, Scalpay, HS4 3XX; tel 01859-540298) stocks woven and hand-finished linen products. The loomshed is open April to October, Monday to Saturday from 2pm to 5pm.

Local group *Bothan* record their music at Scalpay Digital Audio (10 Parkview Terrace, Scalpay, HS4 3XX; tel 01859-540246). You can buy their first album/CD *The Bridge* from the studio or you can write to them (Dachaidh, Scalpay, HS4 3XU; e-mail bothan@scalpay.com; www.scalpay.com/bothan). *Bothan* is Gaelic for a shebeen, or illicit drinking place, and the group chose this name so they could say they were the only *Bothan* on this officially 'dry' island.

TARANSAY *(Tarasaigh)*

The island lies off the west coast of Harris, about 10 miles (16 km) north of Leverburgh. Although the distance between Taransay and the Harris mainland across the Sound of Taransay is less than two miles (3 km), locals say it is not advisable to make the crossing in a small boat unless there's an, unlikely, calm sea. The Sound is usually full of turbulent swells. The best plan for would-be visitors is to charter a fishing boat from Leverburgh. Check with the local Tourist Information Centre. There are three good viewpoints of Taransay from the coastal road in West Harris: between Seilebost and Horgabost, the headland of Aird Niosaboist with its *Clach Mhic Leòid* Standing Stone, and from the parking place between Horgabost and Na Buirgh, from where you can see the southern coast of the island. Until the mid-19th century there were three small settlements on the island, Raa, Uidh and Paible, scratching a living from fishing and crofting. They were merged into one holding at Paible in 1901 when a new farmhouse was built there. For years this was the only household on Taransay, but these inhabitants were also eventually obliged to move to the Harris mainland, leaving the island populated only by a flock of sheep and a small herd of red deer.

In 2000, Taransay was home to a disparate group of 36 people, strangers to each other, who were marooned on the island for a year in a televised experiment to see how they would adapt to a simple lifestyle. Their progress, or otherwise, was featured in the regular BBC TV *Castaway 2000* series of programmes, which documented their experience and brought Taransay into living rooms all over Britain. All but seven of the modern 'castaways' stayed the full year. Until they arrived Taransay had been uninhabited since the early 1970s, although there are signs of settlement going back to the Bronze Age, and indications of Norse occupation more than a thousand years ago.

Taransay's 3,645 acres (1,475 ha) are almost cut into two unequal parts by Loch na h-Uidhe. The south-western chunk, Aird Vanish (*Aird Mhanais*), is joined to the main part by a sandy isthmus called the Uidhe. Aird Vanish is a bleak place with sea caves and a wild storm beach around the twin nubs of Bullaval (272 ft/83 m) and Herraval (289 ft/88 m). At its south-west point is Rubha Sgeirigin, with the shining white sands of Traigh Shanndaig close by. The larger part of the island is dominated by 876 ft-high (267 m) Beinn Raa, the highest point on the island, with Loch an Duin in the valley below harbouring a prehistoric dun on an island approached by causeway. As well as two Iron Age duns, the island is dotted with unexplored and unexcavated prehistoric and later sites. On the south-east coast are the sites of two ancient Celtic chapels, one dedicated to St Keith and the other to St Tarran, who gave his name to the island. When the peripatetic writer Martin Martin visited around 1700 he was fascinated by the local tradition stipulating that no woman could be buried in St Keith's and no man in St Tarran's, otherwise their corpses would be found the next day lying on the ground outside the grave. Martin thought this 'a most ridiculous fancy' and was subsequently proved right when a man was interred at St Tarran's, and stayed underground. A satisfied Martin wrote 'his Corps is still in the Grave, from whence it is not like to rise until the general Resurrection'.

The owners of Taransay, Norman and Angus MacKay of Horgabost, Harris, have plans to create self-catering accommodation for visitors who want to sample the castaway life for themselves. The MacKay family bought Taransay for a few hundred pounds in 1967; since the TV programme brought it unsolicited fame the island could now fetch around £1-million, according to estate agents. The movie *The Rocket Post* was made in 2001 on Taransay, which doubled for Scarp, the island to the north where the events portrayed in the movie actually took place. Scarp's owner would not allow filming there, so film construction teams spent four weeks on Taransay building a replica of a 1930s island village, complete with jetty and church hall. Everything from building materials to fresh water had to be transported from Harris by barge and helicopter.

North Uist

(Uibhist a Tuath)

Following earlier Norse and clan rule the history of North Uist over the past 500 years has not been a happy one for the islanders. The Macdonalds of Sleat, in Skye, were granted title in 1495 by King James IV. They are chiefly remembered for their savage eviction of tenants during the Clearances of 1850, only five years before they sold North Uist. The fertile district of Sollas alone was cleared of 603 inhabitants. Some of these were forced to spend a winter at Langass in atrocious conditions, before being shifted to the newly created western crofting township of Locheport. At that time three families attempted to scratch a living from the barren soil; by 1883 they had been joined there by a further 37 families. Many islanders emigrated. Until the 19th century Clearances nearly 5,000 people lived on the island. The population has steadily declined and now stands at around 1,800. In 1855, North Uist was bought from the Macdonalds by Sir John Powlett Ord. North Uist is now largely owned by the Granville family, through the *North Uist Estate Trust*. In contrast to Catholic South Uist, North Uist has been Protestant since the late 18th century.

North and South Uist are separated by Benbecula, which sits between the two. The main A865 road runs down their length, joining all three from top to bottom by means of bridges and causeways. The road system is simplicity itself. A circular road begins and ends at Lochmaddy, forking in the middle of the island to head south through Benbecula to South Uist. The entire North Uist road system covers 45 miles (72 km). The road keeps mainly to the machair coastal plain of the west where the beaches run for miles and the land is broken into cultivated crofts. The eastern coast is scenically more interesting, deeply bitten into by the two deep sea lochs of Maddy and Eport. South of Loch Eport, North Uist's highest hill, 1,138 ft (347 m) Eaval, is almost completely surrounded by water. Near Lochmaddy are North Lee (823 ft/251 m) and South Lee (919 ft/280 m), both hills offering fine prospects of the watery west. North Uist has an area of about 75,000 acres (30,351 ha), but the eastern half of the island is almost all water – an angler's paradise of sea lochs, freshwater lochs, and lochans bursting with brown trout and the result of a post-glacial rise in sea level nearly 6,000 years ago which partially submerged the Uists. Loch Maddy alone, although only a mile (1.6 km) wide at its entrance and half a dozen miles (10 km) long, has a wandering coastline of no less than 300 miles (483 km). The nooks and crannies of freshwater Loch Scadavay mean the shores of this serrated loch of only 1½ sq miles (4 sq km) are 47 miles (75 km) long.

LOCHMADDY *(Loch nam Madadh)*

Lochmaddy is the port and natural centre of North Uist with a population of about 300. It gets its name either from the offshore rocks covered in 'maddies,' or black mussels, or from the rocks guarding the entrance for the sea and known in Gaelic as *madadh* ('dogs'). Another more convoluted story says that the original name of the whole Lochmaddy area was Chearsabhagh. Apparently a Viking who waded ashore here after his longboat ran aground shouted the Norse equivalent of 'We've got the wrong bay', which sounded like 'Chearsabhagh'. At one time the area was the haunt of pirates who found ideal hideaways along its fretted coastline. The Sheriff Court sits at Lochmaddy, presiding over all minor legal cases in the islands south of Harris, and it was here that sentence was passed on those unfortunates caught by HM Customs & Excise 'rescuing' whisky from the famous 'Whisky Galore' ship *SS Politician*, which foundered off Eriskay in February 1941.

Taigh Chearsabhagh Museum and Arts Centre (Lochmaddy, HS6 5AA; tel 01876-500293; e-mail taigh-chearsabhagh@zetnet.co.uk; www.taigh-chearsabhagh.co.uk), once an inn, is situated by the old harbour slipway. The harbour was an important centre for the herring fishing industry as early as the 17th century when the site was used for salt making. There's an annual museum exhibition on local history, a changing monthly exhibition in the art gallery, a large photographic archive, and a wide variety of arts and crafts workshops for adults and children. There's also a café and a shop selling pottery, postcards, prints by local artists, photographs, including reproductions from the museum collection, tapes of local music, and books. Public toilets. Open all year from 10am to 5pm, disabled access. An unusual attraction at Sponish is the award-winning **Sea/Sky Chamber**, which acts as a camera obscura to create ever-changing images of sky, sea, wind and waves.

North Uist is dotted with the remains of great Neolithic burial cairns and other prehistoric ruins, evidence of early settlers attracted by the island's fertility. Buildings of later generations were often erected on these ancient mounds. The circular A865 route north from Lochmaddy takes in some of the more remarkable. Along this road is the 358 ft (109 m) hill of Blashaval (*Blathaisbhal*) above the loch of the same name. On its western slopes are **The False Men** (*Na Fir Bhreige*) standing stones which mark the spot where three men suspected of spying were buried alive, although another tale says they were unfaithful husbands turned to stone. Opposite the hill a minor road branches off to the east to Loch Portain and Cheese Bay (*Bàgh a'Chàise*), a 7-mile (11 km) road winding through the low-lying ground that makes an excellent outing by bike. The area is sprinkled with lochans and has a number of duns and other prehistoric remains. In tidal Loch an Dùin, a causeway runs out to an island where a pile of stones is all that remains of the broch **Dun Torcuill**. There's another broch in Loch an Sticir just off the B893 road on the way to Berneray. This is **Dun Sticir**, which is also built on a causeway island and is reputedly the last dun to be inhabited in North Uist. It was occupied until 1602 and is still well preserved. The last man to use it as a refuge was Hugh MacDonald, who met a harrowing end locked in the dungeon of Duntulm Castle, on Skye. MacDonald was imprisoned with only a piece of salt beef and an empty water jug by a jailer with a grim sense of humour.

The site of a **Neolithic pottery workshop**, the earliest known in Europe, has been discovered on Eilean an Tighe, close to where the A865 road skirts the shore of Loch nan Geireann. Further out is the island of Oronsay (*Orasaigh*). At Grenitote (*Greinetobht*) you can walk across the wide beach (*Tràigh Ear*) to the Aird á Mhòrain peninsula, where there are Norse and Iron Age sites and the **mausoleum** of the MacLeans of Boreray (*Boraraigh*), the deserted island which lies off the headland. Boreray's highest point is Mullach Mòr, rising over 184 ft (56 m) above a large central loch. As you pass through **Sollas** heading west you'll see a memorial commemorating the crofting resettlement here of communities evicted during the mid-19th century in one of the cruellest of the local Clearances. On the peninsula north of Sollas excavations by Edinburgh University have found evidence of a Norse settlement and indications of continuous human habitation for nearly 4,000 years. From Malacleit you get a lovely view across a large sandy expanse of *Tràigh Bhàlaigh* to the island of **Vallay** (*Bhalaigh*), which is cut off at high tide. There are lots of prehistoric sites on the island as well as the large house

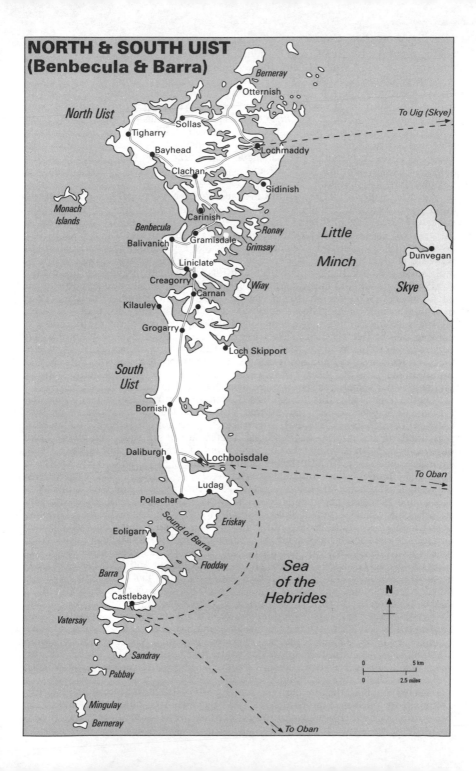

NORTH & SOUTH UIST
(Benbecula & Barra)

North Uist

Berneray

Otternish

Sollas

Tigharry

Bayhead

Lochmaddy

To Uig (Skye)

Clachan

Sidinish

Monach Islands

Carinish

Benbecula

Ronay

Little

Balivanich

Gramisdale

Grimsay

Minch

Liniclate

Dunvegan

Creagorry

Wiay

Skye

Kilauley

Carnan

Grogarry

Loch Skipport

South Uist

Bornish

Daliburgh

Lochboisdale

To Oban

Ludag

Pollachar

Eriskay

Eoligarry

Sound of Barra

Flodday

Sea of the Hebrides

Barra

Castlebay

N

Vatersay

Sandray

Pabbay

0   5 km

0   2.5 miles

Mingulay

Berneray

To Oban

belonging to the family of Lord Granville, which owns large areas of North Uist, and the ruins of Vallay House, the once imposing home of mill owner and antiquary Erskine Beveridge.

At a curve in the road opposite Vallay a minor road turns off to the left to rejoin the A865 on the west coast between Bayhead (*Ceann a Bhàigh*) and Cladach Kirkibost (*Cladach Chireboist*). This road, built as famine relief work during the 19th century, passes several cairns and standing stones and is a good short-cut to the **Unival** chambered cairn, where rich deposits of pottery and the bones of a young Neolithic woman have been found. The burial cairn is on the slopes of *Uineabhal* (459 ft/140 m) and is a slog across marshy ground. Nearby is a souterrain, or underground structure.

To the north-west of the island archaeologists have found a 5,000-year-old submerged Neolithic village on a crannog, or man-made island, in the shallow waters of Loch Oileabhat, near Griminish village. The timbers and foundations of the crannog are remarkably well preserved. At **Griminish Point** is a natural rock arch 30 ft (9 m) high and a water-spouting cave. Eight miles (13 km) out to the west are Haskeir Island and the smaller Haskeir Eagach, a small group with rock arches, skerries, and stacks popular with puffins and Atlantic grey seals. Just off the A865 where it starts to curve south is **Scolpaig Tower**, a folly situated on a small island in Loch Scolpaig. The tower was built in the 19th century from the remains of a dun as part of local famine relief work. It is the only folly in the Outer Hebrides. About half a mile (800 m) south of Scolpaig Tower, at Cille Pheadair, is conspicuous **St Peter's Cross**. This was discovered and re-erected in 1830 by Dr Alex MacLeod, the man who built the folly. The coastal road passes Hosta, where there's a rock arch and another spouting cave, appropriately known as the **Kettle Spout**, in the cliffs of Tigharry. When waves break in here during Atlantic storms a plume of water sometimes shoots more than 197 ft (60 m) in the air.

On the next headland is the RSPB's **Balranald Nature Reserve** (see *Flora and Fauna*). At Bayhead is the **Uist Animal Visitor Centre** and **MacAskill's Leisure Café** (tel/fax 01876-510223/706). This is a great place for children with a play area, pony trekking and rare Scottish animals. There's also a gift shop, and horse-drawn gypsy caravans can be hired (see *Getting Around*). Open Wednesday 11am to 10pm, Thursday and Friday 10am to 10pm, Saturday midday to 11pm, Sunday midday to 7pm. The **Claddach Kirkibost Centre** (tel/fax 01876-580390) offers views west to the white shell beaches of Kirkibost, as well as a conservatory café with homebakes, snacks and refreshments. It sells local craftwork and is open throughout the year from 10am to 5pm. Closed on Sundays. Public toilets with disabled access. Offshore from Claddach Kirkibost is the uninhabited machair island of **Kirkibost**. At Clachan na Luib the road south forks, with the A867 swinging back to Lochmaddy. About 2 miles (3 km) along this, look out for the sign to **Barpa Langass**, which is on Ben Langass (*Beinn Langais*), the only hill between Clachan and Lochmaddy. On its north-west shoulder is a 5,000-year-old chambered cairn that is thought to be the burial place of a Neolithic chieftain. The great bare stone cairn is 70 ft (21 m) in diameter, and exceeds 16 ft (5 m) in height. This is the most impressive of North Uist's Stone Age sites. It is largely intact and in a good state of preservation. Don't be tempted to crawl through the cairn's short entrance tunnel. It's not safe. A track from nearby Langass Lodge hotel and restaurant leads to a Neolithic stone circle on the south side of the hill that is regarded as the finest of its kind in North Uist. This is known as **Pobull Fhinn** ('Finn's People'). The name refers to the warrior followers of Gaelic folk hero Finn MacCool.

Almost touching the southern point of Kirkibost Island is **Baleshare**, a fertile, sandy island joined to mainland North Uist by causeway. Its Gaelic name (*Baile Sear*) means East Township, indicating that there must once have been a corresponding West Township. No one knows where this was, although it's thought likely that it must have been one of the casualties of the ferocious tidal waves and storms which washed away various other villages, channels and sand bars late in the 16th century. Ringed plover, oystercatcher, lapwing, dunlin, redshank, and snipe breed on Baleshare, while the machair lochs attract breeding mute swan, mallard and moorhen. Breeding arctic terns prefer the shingle areas.

Standing on a small eminence near Carinish in the south-west are the ruins of the **Church of the Holy Trinity** (*Teampull na Trionaid*), once an important monastery with a college that was a centre of learning in mediaeval times. It was founded around 1203 by Beathag, daughter of Somerled, and built on an earlier Celtic site. The complex was enlarged in 1350 by the wife of John MacDonald of Islay, first Lord of the Isles. Associated with this ecclesiastical centre in the Middle Ages was the famous Franciscan philosopher and theologian Duns Scotus (1265-1308), whose name is now a label for an unscholarly 'dunce.' Alongside is *Teampull Clan A'Phiocair*, chapel of the MacVicars, who were teachers at the college. Close by is the site of the last horrendous battle between the Macdonalds of Uist and the MacLeods of Harris. A reminder of the slaughter in 1601 is a ditch known as the **'Ditch of Blood'** (*Feithe Na Fala*), which got its macabre name for obvious reasons.

A few miles further south the A865 road runs across the western tip of the low-lying island of **Grimsay** (*Griomasaigh*). In September 1960, the Queen Mother opened the North Ford causeway between Carinish, in North Uist, and Gramasdail, in Benbecula, joining the two via Grimsay and making possible an unbroken journey of about 75 miles (121 km) from North Uist to Ludag, in South Uist. Grimsay is the centre of the fishing industry in North Uist and is a good place to buy fresh fish and lobsters. Surrounded by some 40% of Britain's unpolluted waters it's not surprising that the fish and seafood caught or farmed here bring premium prices in continental Europe. An information panel at Kallin (*Na Ceallan*) Harbour describes the role the fishing industry plays in the economy of the islands. A narrow road follows the coast right round the island. East of Grimsay are several islands, the largest of which is hilly **Ronay** (*Ronaigh*), which has been uninhabited since the 1920s.

FLORA AND FAUNA

Lochmaddy (*Loch nam Madadh*) is a Marine Special Area of Conservation (mSAC), one of only three in Scotland. **Balranald Reserve** on the other side of the island, 3 miles (5 km) north of Bayhead, is famous for its **corncrakes** and is one of only three Royal Society for the Protection of Birds (RSPB) reserves providing sanctuary for this, one of Europe's most endangered birds. This elusive migrant usually arrives in April and early May and begins its exodus to its warmer winter haunts in Africa in August. As well as a possible glimpse of this prized visitor twitchers can also expect a more likely sighting of another rarity, the **red-necked phalarope**, whose breeding grounds the reserve to the west of the A862 road was originally established to safeguard. Terrain in the 1,623 acre (658 ha) reserve changes from saltmarsh in the south around Loch Paible through a variety of marshland habitats to the north. Sandy beaches and a rocky foreshore are separated from the machair and marshes by sand dunes and there are also a number of shallow lochs. The wetlands around Loch nam Feithean, the core of the reserve, provide breeding and feeding grounds for a variety of birds. The reserve has one of the highest concentrations of breeding wading birds in Europe. Waders include **lapwing, redshank, oystercatcher, snipe, ringed plover**, and **dunlin**. The area also attracts raptors – birds of prey – such as **merlin, hen harrier**, and **peregrine falcon**, and songbirds such as **corn buntings, reed buntings** and **sedge warblers. Arctic tern** and **little tern** breed on the silver-grey sandy beaches and dunes, **shag** and **black guillemot** on the rocky headlands. More than 180 species have been recorded in the reserve and around 50 of these nest annually here.

The **best times** to visit Balranald are late in May for the waders and corncrakes and the end of June and July for wild flowers. Eight species of butterflies have also been recorded in the reserve, along with 56 kinds of moth. Balranald Reserve includes the tiny rocky island of **Causamul**, where **Atlantic grey seal** breed and **porpoises, dolphins** and **whales** are possibly sightings.

The reserve is managed by the RSPB in association with surrounding crofters and it maintains a small Visitor Centre (wheelchair access) which explains the importance of traditional crofting land use for the corncrake and other wildlife in the reserve. The summer warden regularly leads 1-1¹/₂ hour guided walks from the centre in July and August on Tuesday and Thursday at 10am. A 3¹/₂ mile (5¹/₂ km) nature trail takes you from the Centre out to the coast, where you'll find breathtaking beaches and at Ard an Rùnair a fine viewpoint for sea mammals and birds of passage, such as the numerous **long-tailed pomarine** and **skuas** which pass here in mid-May. The trail is not suitable for wheelchairs. Both the reserve and the Visitor Centre are open all year round. Facilities include a car park and toilets with disabled access.

The nearest ferry terminal is at Lochmaddy. If you don't have your own transport there is a postbus service. For more information contact the reserve (9 Grenitote, North Uist, HS6 5BP; tel 01876-560287) or the RSPB North Scotland Office (Etive House, Beechwood Park, Inverness IV2 3BW; tel 01463-715000).

The whole of North Uist east of high point Marrival (755 ft/230 m) presents a drowned landscape of inland and sea lochs, inlets, bays, and channels. This makes it an **otters'** heaven and you'll find their holts everywhere. You are more likely to spot otters on a rising tide, 2-4 hours before high water being the **best time**. **Common seals** feed in the coastal waters and use the islands and skerries for basking and breeding. Waders, wildfowl and raptors, some of national importance, also nest or overwinter in this area.

GETTING THERE

Lochmaddy developed in the 19th century because of its fine natural harbour, and is still a ferry port with regular sailings to and from Uig on Skye.

From Skye

Caledonian MacBrayne (The Ferry Terminal, Gourock PA19 1QP; tel 08705-650000; fax 01475-635235 for reservations; e-mail reservations@calmac.co.uk; www.calmac.co.uk) car ferry sails from Uig, Skye, to Lochmaddy, North Uist, at 9.45am and 6pm on Monday, Wednesday and Friday; 2pm on Tuesday, Thursday and Saturday; and at 2pm on Sunday. There is an additional sailing at 9.45am from late May until beginning September. The journey takes 1 hour 40 minutes. The single adult fare is £8.50, car or motorhome £40, caravan or boat/luggage trailer an additional £40, motorcycle £20, and bicycle £2. Discounted 'Five-Day Return' and 'Six-Journey' tickets are available on this route. There is also a day return 'Sunday Saver' for £69 for a car with up to four occupants.

From Harris

If you are travelling to North Uist from Harris the ferry leaves Leverburgh pier for Otternish four times a day on Monday, Wednesday and Friday; and three times a day on Tuesday, Thursday and Saturday (See *Harris: Getting There* for times and fares). You can contact the local Calmac offices in Uig (tel 01470-542219) and in Lochmaddy (tel 01876-500337). There's a ticket office and waiting room at the Otternish jetty, which is at the end of a branch road joining the B893 to Lochmaddy, six miles (10 km) away.

GETTING AROUND

Causeways join North and South Uist by way of the islands of Grimsay and

Benbecula. The small island of Berneray in the Sound of Harris is also linked to the Uists by causeway. The airport is on Benbecula at Balivanich (*Baille a' Mhanaich*).

Buses

The *Royal Mail* (tel 01246-546329; www.royalmail.co.uk) operates a 14-seater **Postbus** service from Lochmaddy to Balivanich Monday to Saturday. A 10-seater serves Bayhead-Lochmaddy-Sidinish-Baleshare-Clachan, and Lochmaddy-Cheesebay-Sidinish-Baleshare-Grimsay-Tigharry routes, Monday to Saturday. Check with the local post office for times and fares.

Taxis

Alda's Taxi-minibus can be contacted in Lochmaddy at No 1 Kersavagh (tel 01876-500215), and *Ferguson's* taxi and minibus also operates from the village.

If you fancy getting around at sedate 'Old Dobbin' pace contact *Hebridean Horse-Drawn Holidays* (Sue and Tim, Kyles Road, Paible, HS6 5DS; tel 01876-510706; fax 01876-510223; e-mail castawaywad1fr@supanet.com) who can fix you up with a gypsy caravan.

Distances. From Otternish to Lochmaddy is six miles (10 km) and to Balivanich, in Benbecula, is 26 miles (42 km). To Lochboisdale and Ludag in South Uist it's 50 and 54 miles (80/87 km) respectively.

ACCOMMODATION

Hotels

Carinish Inn: Carinish, HS6 5EJ (tel 01876-580673; fax 01876-580665). Three-star. Open all year, from £35 a night. Serves bar and a la carte meals, including fresh local fish and shellfish. Open all year for lunch from 12.30pm to 2.30pm and dinner 6.30pm to 9.30pm.

Langass Lodge: Locheport, HS6 5HA (tel 01876-580285; fax 01876-580385; e-mail langass@aol.com). Three-star small hotel, offers the old-world comfort of a traditional shooting lodge. Open all year except Christmas Day, B&B from £36. Facilities for disabled visitors. Menu features mainly fish dishes and selection of seafood. Try Uist prawns wrapped in cod fillet and grilled with a herb crust, malt whisky cheesecake. Food available all day. Vegetarians welcome. Taste of Scotland member.

Lochmaddy Hotel (1864): Lochmaddy, HS6 5AA (tel 01876-500331/2; fax 01876-500210). Two-star, five minutes' from the ferry terminal, 15 en-suite bedroom. Meals using local produce and seafood served in the bar – fish and chips £5 – and dining-room. Open all year, from £33 a night B&B. Can organise fishing, stalking and wildfowling trips (see *Sport and Recreation*).

Stag Lodge: John and Jacqueline Handyside, Lochmaddy, HS6 5AE (tel/fax 01876-500364; e-mail jacquie@staglodge.freeserve.co.uk). A three-star guest house with accommodation for eight people, two double, two twins. The lodge dates back to 1763 and was the first post office in North Uist. Open all year, from £25 B&B. Café by day, a la carte restaurant for 35 people by night serves light snacks, hot and cold food at affordable prices. Sample scallops sautéed with spring onions in cream for £5.50, fresh salmon at £10.25. Open all year Monday to Saturday from 11am to 3pm and 6pm to 9.30pm.

Temple View Hotel: Carinish, HS6 5EJ (tel 01876-580676; fax 01876-580682). Four-star family hotel, room with disabled facilities. Open all year, from £33 a night B&B. Restaurant open all year from 1pm to 11pm has table d'hote menu using seasonal local produce.

B&B

Bonnieview: Mrs H Morrison, 19 Carinish, HS6 5HN (tel 01876-580211; e-mail h.morrison@amserve.net), four-star croft house in Baleshare. Open all year, from £20.

The Old Courthouse: Margaret Johnson, Lochmaddy, HS6 5AE (tel/fax 01876-500358; e-mail mjohnson@oldcourthouse.fsnet.co.uk), two-star. Open all year, from £21.

Old Shop House: Morag Nicholson, Bayhead, HS6 5DS (tel 01876-510395). Three-star, near beaches. Open all year, from £18 a night.

Sealladh Traigh: Mr and Mrs WJ Quarm, Cladach Kirkibost, HS6 5EP (tel 01876-580248; fax 01876-510360). One-star, food views, home-cooking. Open all year, from £18 a night.

Sheillaidh: Mr and Mrs K MacCuish, Solas, HS6 5BS (tel 01876-560332), three-star. Open April to October, from £16 a night.

Self-Catering

Mrs Grace Beaton: 16 Knockintorran, Bayhead, HS6 5ED (tel/fax 01876-510353). Two-star cottage, three bedrooms, sleeps four. Open all year, from £180 to £300 a week.

William MacDonald: 18 Illeray, Clachan, HS6 5HF (tel 01876-580672; e-mail clachan@golbalnet.co.uk). Two-star, first floor three-bedroomed flat, sleeps five. Open May to September, from £150 to £190 a week.

Mrs AJ Nicolson has a **caravan** available at Knockqueen (Coel na Mara, 4 Knockqueen, Lochmaddy, HS6 5HW; tel 01876-580608; e-mail mark@knockquien.freeserve.co.uk), close to moor and beach, centrally located for ferries, sleeps 4-6. Open all year, from £100 a week.

Smithy Croft: Angus Dingwall, Lochmaddy, HS6 5AA (tel 01876-500391). Four-star, modernised cottage, 2 bedrooms, sleeps 4-6. Open all year, from £190 to £270 a week.

Struan House: Norma Shepherd, 11 Solas, HS6 5BY (tel 01876-560282). Three-star, croft house overlooking beach, three bedrooms, sleeps seven. Open all year, from £170 to £260 a week.

Tigh na Boireach: Neil Nicholson, Clachan Sands, HS6 5AY (tel/fax 01876-580237). Four-star, thatched cottage, one bedroom, sleeps 2-4. Open all year, from £250 to £380 a week.

Hostels

Taigh Mo Sheanair: Carnach, Claddach, Baleshare (tel 01876-580246). Three-star, family-run hostel in a renovated croft house, inexpensive self-catering accommodation, 10 beds and camping sites available, two rooms sleep four. No smoking. Open all year, from £9 a person a night.

Uist Outdoor Centre: Niall Johnson, Lochmaddy, HS6 5AE (tel/fax 01876-500480; e-mail info@uistoutdoorcentre.co.uk). Has an independent one-star hostel, five bedrooms, each with four bunk beds. Open all year.

Camping

Mrs A MacDonald (8 Knockqueen, Carinish, HS6 5BW; tel 01876-580635) has a **caravan** which sleeps 4-6. Open March to October, from £90-100, minimum let two days.

EATING AND DRINKING

Most of what's good to eat in North Uist can be sampled in the hotels, but you can also try the *Taigh Chearsabhaigh Café* in Lochmaddy (tel/fax 01876-500293), which serves soups, homebakes, filled rolls, sandwiches, tea, coffee and cold drinks. Open all year except January, Monday to Saturday, from 10am to 5pm. For take-away smoked salmon for an outdoor picnic visit *Mermaid Fish Supplies* (Anne and Fergus Granville, Clachan, Lochmaddy, North Uist; tel 01876-580209;

fax 01876-580323; e-mail sales@mermaidfish.com) whose Lochmaddy salmon is smoked over local peat, giving it an addictive Hebridean savour. Peat smoke is more assertive than wood smoke and imparts a taste quite different from the commercial smoked salmon found in supermarkets. There's also a mail order service.

SPORT AND RECREATION

Walking

Self-guided walks have been created around Lochmaddy and from the prehistoric burial cairn at Langass near the main road, 5 miles (8 km) to the west of the village. For *Western Isles Walks* leaflets detailing these check with the local Tourist Information Centre. A 4-mile (6¹/2 km) walk starts and finishes at Taigh Chearsabhagh Museum, Lochmaddy, which takes about 2-3 hours. Mostly on reasonable paths and roads, though boots are recommended. Turn right at the Post Office in Lochmaddy and take the next fork to the right, down to the old 'Wee Pier'. Turn right as the crossroads in front of the New Court House (1875), and follow the road past the Uist Outdoor Centre. It becomes a track through a plantation, past a small harbour and over a footbridge. To the left is the burnt-out ruin of Sponish House, built in 1804 for Lord Macdonald's factor. You are quite likely to see otters which come from the sea up the lagoon to the freshwater lochs inland. Follow the path around the coast. It's marked by green posts. There's usually plenty of birdlife around, including herons and, in summer, colonies of terns. Turn right at a track and then left on to the road. Walk along the road for about 1.4 miles (2.3 km) to a T-junction, and turn left towards Lochmaddy. You soon reach *Cnoc na Fèille*, or Market Stance, where livestock fairs were once held in July and September. From here carry on along the road to Lochmaddy. Round off the walk with a tour of *Taigh Chearsabhagh*. It was built as an inn in 1741 but became an excellent museum and art centre in 1995.

Fishing

The fishing on North Uist is controlled by two bodies, *North Uist Estate*, which with 16 **brown trout** lochs and 11 **salmon** and **sea trout** lochs controls the larger part of available fishing, and the *North Uist Angling Club* (NUAC), which controls Newton and Balranald Estates.

Seasons. Brown trout: 15 March to 30 September; salmon: 25 February to 15 October; and sea trout: 15 February to 31 October.

Fishing on all inland lochs is exclusively by fly but you can use fly, bait or spinning in the sea pools controlled by North Uist Estate. There is no fishing on a Sunday. Any brown trout under a half pound (250 g) should be returned to the water. NUAC boats are blue, North Uist Estates are grey. NUAC provides flotation jackets (recommended for all boat anglers), rowlocks and a bilge pump.

Newton Estate comprises the large area of **Lochportain** and beyond, providing you with a choice of innumerable lochs. The lochs vary in nature; many of them rarely see an artificial fly. Many are within easy access of the road; others offer the opportunity to combine hill-walking with fishing. Most lochs contain free-rising brown trout, with the occasional loch presenting more of a challenge with larger, but more elusive trout. While you may encounter sea trout on the Newton Estate, NUAC retains only the rights to brown trout. Any sea trout caught must therefore be returned to the water. **Loch Fada** is an expansive water which contains large numbers of average-sized trout and some weightier specimens. Small numbers of sea trout and salmon are also present, along with char. Most productive fishing is located on the shelving shoreline and there are reefs and islands in the channel between the north and south basins which often hold good-sized fish. Be aware that rowing between the two basins can take up to two hours.

Brackish **Loch an Duin** promotes good fish growth and you'll occasionally get into such species as pollack, coalfish, and even sea trout. **Loch Armuinn** and **Deadman's Loch** at the top are well worth fishing. **Geireann Mill Loch**, 7.4 miles (12 km) from Lochmaddy, is an expanse where you can try the various arms of the loch as well as the main body of the loch itself. NUAC retains the rights only to brown trout here.

Fishing guide. Jock Handyside of Stag Lodge (tel/fax 01876-500364) charges £40 a day and holds all NUAC waters. He can organise permits, boats and loch fishing, as well as **sea fishing** for all common saltwater species. He specialises in conger and skate.

Game Fishing Contacts:

Clachan Stores: J Matheson (tel 01876-580257). Has NUAC brown trout permits for Newton Estate waters.

Lochmaddy Hotel: John Coles (tel 01876-500331/2).

North Uist Angling Club: Secretary, Philip Harding, Claddach (tel 01876-580341).

North Uist Estate and Amhuinnsuidhe Estate: George Macdonald, Lochmaddy (tel 01876-500329; fax 01876-500428).

Uist Outdoor Centre: Niall Johnson (tel 01876-500480). Arranges sea-angling trips from Lochmaddy.

Diving

Uist Outdoor Centre (Cearn Dusgaidh, Lochmaddy, North Uist, HS6 5AE; tel 01876-500480; e-mail alyson@keiller.u-net.com) can take you diving in the sheltered sea lochs around The Minch, or in the Atlantic Ocean off the west coast. You can charter a 19 ft (5.8 m) Sea Fury RIB with 90 hp engine. There's also canoeing and kayaking, water-skiing, rowing, boat-handling, navigation and seamanship, coasteering, orienteering, rubber tubing, and power boating available, as well as hill, coastal, and ridge walks, rock climbing, abseiling, island exploration, overnight expeditions, and survival skills. Hill-walking routes have varying degrees of difficulty, but there are also many low-level rambles. You can also go wildlife watching, and take part in field studies. Open to groups, clubs, families, individuals, and colleges. The centre has accommodation for 20 people in four-person bunk rooms. You can choose self-catering or opt for full board. Open daily all year from 9am to 5.30pm. Five minutes from Lochmaddy Pier (signposted). Toilets and disabled facilities.

Stalking

Contact staff of Lord Leversohn-Gower (tel 01876-500329) for deer stalking on the North Uist Estate, as well as for wildfowling. Lochmaddy Hotel (tel 01876-500331/2; fax 01876-500210) can point you in the right direction if you are after trophy red deer. The best stag has been a 17-pointer and the North Uist deer forest is home to an unusually high number of big old stags.

SHOPPING

Island Crafts (Main Street, Lochmaddy, under the Royal Mail sign; tel 01870-602418) stocks the Hebridean Woolhouse range of products, scarves, rugs, hats and sweaters made from 100% undyed natural Hebridean sheep wool. They also stock books, local pottery, and traditional tweeds. Open Monday-Friday from 10.30am to 5.15pm and on Saturday June-October from 1pm to 5pm. You'll need to make an appointment to visit the *Hebridean Woolhouse* (Sandbank, Grimsay, HS6 5HU; tel/fax 01870-603180; e-mail sales@hebrideanwoolhouse.com; www.hebrideanwoolhouse.com) or order by post or e-mail. Classic range of 100% natural undyed Hebridean wool products, with made-to-measure range made by hand in Uist. Check the range out at their website (www. hebrideanwoolhouse.com). Mail order or visit by appointment. For more general requirements you'll find the *Weehaveit* shop, on the main road in Lochmaddy.

HELP AND INFORMATION

North Uist Tourist Office: Pier Road, Lochmaddy (tel 01876-500321). Seasonal opening from early April to mid-October.

Uist On Line: Unit 3 Lochboisdale Pier, Lochboisdale, HS8 5TH (tel/fax 01878-700007; www.uistonline.com). Has information on local news and weather, what's on, shopping, island history, places to visit and accommodation.

Police: Lochmaddy (tel 01876-500328).

Lochmaddy Hospital: tel 01876-500325.

Surgery: Lochmaddy (tel 01876-500333).

Southern Isles Amenity Trust: (Ranger Service), James MacLetchie (www. siat.org.uk).

Caledonian MacBrayne: Lochmaddy (tel 01876-500337).

Bank of Scotland: Lochmaddy (tel 01876-500266/323).

BERNERAY *(Beàrnaraigh)*

Berneray, 3 miles (5 km) long by 1¹/₂ miles (2 km) wide, is connected by causeway to the mainland of North Uist and is now the only inhabited island in the Sound of Harris and well worth a visit. Berneray and Pabbay are the largest of the islands in the Sound and should not be confused with islands of the same names and similar size which lie to the south of Barra. Berneray is a favourite holiday hideaway of HRH Prince Charles. There's not a great deal to do or see on the island, which is probably why the Lord of the Isles and future King likes to get away from it all here. He can also rely on the close-mouthed islanders not to publicise his presence. The first time he stayed on Berneray in May 1987 to live the life of a crofter for three days no one outside the community – apart from Buckingham Palace – knew he was there. He stayed in one of the oldest croft houses on Berneray, Burnside Croft, hosted by Donald 'Splash' MacKillop and his wife. He also enjoyed a bracing walk on the three miles (5 km) of unbroken sands on Beneray's famed west beach, a stretch he first saw as a child when he visited the Outer Hebrides on the *Royal Yacht Britannia* during the 1956 Royal Tour.

A popular traditional island song pities people who were not born on Beneray, but the sentiment hasn't halted the steady depopulation that's been going on since the mid-19th century, when there were more than 700 people living there. The population is now 141 and the local primary school has just 10 pupils. Children must go to Harris for secondary schooling. The island is fertile, but has no peat, and the islanders are mainly occupied raising sheep and fishing for prawns, velvet crabs and lobsters. Waters in the area have given up one monster lobster which measured 35 inches, nearly a metre, from head to tail. Half of the island is machair, but there are no rabbits – at least there were none before the £6.6-million causeway was officially opened by Prince Charles in April 1999. At the opening ceremony the Prince approved of the efforts being made to keep rabbits off Berneray so that they could not destroy its unique ecology. He also praised the way the causeway blended into its setting and the provision of thoughtful facilities such as otter culverts.

Settlements are concentrated around Bays Loch and Loch Borve, whose splendid sands dry out completely at low tide. The drainage course of Loch Bhruist, which once flowed to the shore over the machair, was changed in the past and directed south, into shallow Loch Borve. The village of Siabaidh was covered by sand in the storm of 1697, which also buried Baile Meadhanach on nearby

Pabbay. There's a circular 7¹/₂ mile (12 km) walk around the island which is particularly pleasant in summer when the machair is full of wild flowers. Nearly 200 species have been recorded. Huge dunes run along the full 3 miles (5 km) of Berneray's sandy west shore, and for a mile (2 km) along its north shore. The dunes are 49 ft (15 m) high in places. On the circular route both **Borve Hill** 279 ft (85 m) and **Beinn Shléibhe** 305 ft (93 m) are easy climbs and give fine views of the Sound and North Harris. There are several prehistoric sites scattered around the island, including the remains of a stone circle, a souterrain and a dun. A Bronze Age 8 ft (2 m) standing stone, *Clach Mhòr,* overlooks Loch Borve. About 130 yards (120 m) south of this is an unobtrusive rock ledge known as *Leac an Righ* ('Flat Stone of the King'). Carved into it is the imprint of a small foot and it's thought this was once used to initiate Pictish kings. At Baile is the oldest surviving building on Berneray, **MacLeod's Gunnery,** dating back to the 16th century.

The island used to be the seat of the Macleods of Berneray and was long recognised as a vibrant centre of Gaelic culture. Though small, it has produced some extraordinary characters. Among them was an enormous strongman known as Giant MacAskill, born in 1825. Magnificently proportioned, Angus MacAskill stood 7 ft 9 in (2.38 m) tall and weighed 425 lb (193 kg). At the age of 24 he toured with the circus of Barnum and Bailey. Another notable was Donald Macleod, known as the 'Old Trojan,' who fought for Bonnie Prince Charlie and hid out in a cave in southern Harris while Cumberland was cutting a swathe through the Scottish Highlands after the Battle of Culloden in 1746. Donald Macleod married his third wife when he was 75 and fathered nine children. Old tales have it that in spite of his age, the 'Old Trojan' celebrated his third marriage by performing the amazing Highland 'salmon leap' on his wedding night – springing into bed beside his bride from a crouching position on all fours on the floor. He is fondly remembered in these parts.

There's a regular car ferry to Berneray from Leverburgh, Harris (tel 01859-502444). Locals run a mini-bus service on the island, and there's a shop, tearoom, post office, and a lively community centre with a café. The community hall is the focal point for *Seachdain Bheàrnaraigh* (Berneray Week) during the third week of every July and hosts a succession of *ceilidhs*, concerts, dances and other excitements.

PABBAY *(Pabbaigh)*

Records show that until about the 16th century, Berneray was almost connected to Pabbay by a long spit of sand, but over time strong winds and tides slowly scoured this away until the two islands became separated by what is now the 1.8-mile (3 km) wide Sound of Pabbay. Though not so striking as those on Berneray, Pabbay's south-east coast has some fine dunes. In the north, the island's one hill, *Beinn a' Charnain* lifts a sharp profile (643 ft/196 m). Pabbay is remembered locally for the storm of 1697 which created havoc both here and on Berneray. The storm changed the features of Pabbay and was regarded by the abstemious as divine punishment for its long history of illegal whisky distilling. This probably took place in the centre of Pabbay, around Loch Heddal More, away from Excisemen and close to the island's only peatlands. Scattered around are Iron Age duns and in the south near the landing place the ruins of **Mary's Chapel** (*Teampull Mhóire*) close to those of an earlier church, probably dedicated to St Moluag. There's an old burial ground on the south shore. Another notable ruined site is that of the ancient castle (*Seana-Chaisteal*) built and occupied by the Macleods until they decided that their other fortress at Dunvegan, on Skye, suited them better.

The small islands of **Shillay** (*Siolaigh*), about a mile (1.6 km) to the north, are breeding grounds for **Atlantic grey seals,** and for migrant **Leach's** and **storm petrel**.

Accommodation

Berneray Youth Hostel is right on the beach, overlooking the Sound of Harris. It is run by the *Gatliff Hebridean Hostels Trust* (30 Francis Street, Stornoway, HS1 2ND) and has 16 beds, three rooms with 5-8 beds. No advance bookings are accepted and no bed linen is provided. It's open all year.

Burnside Croft: Donald MacKillop, Berneray, HS6 5BJ (tel/fax 01876-540235). Three-star, croft house. This has been given the Royal seal of approval by Prince Charles, who has stayed here during unofficial getaways.

Mrs C MacAskill: Morven, Berneray, HS6 5BJ (tel/fax 01876-540230). Three-star, self-catering, traditional croft house, 4 bedrooms, sleeps nine. Open all year, from £180 to £280 a week.

MONACH ISLANDS

The Monach Islands lie some five miles (8 km) west of North Uist, a group of five small islets with a total area of about 1,426 acres (577 ha). They are still known locally by their old Norse name, Heisker ('Bright Skerry'), even though this has been changed to Monach on the charts and maps to avoid confusion with the nearby Haskeir group of islands. The machair of the main islands of *Ceann Iar* and *Ceann Ear* has the appearance of a well-tended golf course – flat, green and pocked with sand bunkers. The highest point on these low-lying islands is in the north-east of Ceann Ear, where there's a hillock rising 59 ft (18 m). The main islands bracket tiny Shivinish – connected to both at low water – and in turn lie between dots on the map eastern Stockay, a grey seal nursery, and Shillay. As Shillay is the furthest west this is where the nuns and later monks who settled on the Monach ('Monk') Islands in the Middle Ages tended a beacon fire at night to warn passing ships of the reefs and rocks which menace from the surrounding waters. A lighthouse was built on Shillay in 1864, but as the area did not attract much shipping – and after two of its keepers had been drowned – the lighthouse was decommissioned in 1942. On one of its stones was the poignant inscription carved by a past keeper: 'Eternity oh Eternity.' A small solar-powered light was installed on Shillay in 1997.

The Monachs are thought to have been connected to North Uist until about 6,000 years ago, although there is a strong support for a local tradition which states that it was possible to walk over a 5-mile (8 km) stretch of sand to the islands from North Uist within relatively recent times. It's said the connecting sands were obliterated in the 16th century by the same giant tidal wave that swept away the sand bar that once virtually linked the islands of Berneray and Pabbay. The Monachs have a long history of fertility and had a reputation for keeping their inhabitants in good health. The islands were finally abandoned in the 1940s and subsequently became a sheep farm, though fishermen still often stay here in summer. The old village, now in ruins, can be seen in the south-east of Ceann Ear. In the north, beyond Dead Man's Point, is *Cladh na Bleide*, thought to be the site of the old monastery/convent and its churchyard. In the mid-18th century Ceann Ear was the island chosen by MacDonald of Sleat to hide Lady Grange for two years before she was eventually shipped off to St Kilda. Her offence was that she had prattled about her husband's Jacobite sympathies and a plot she heard him discussing with conspirators at their home in Edinburgh. Her husband, an eminent judge and pillar of the Church, concealed her abduction by holding a 'funeral' for her at Greyfriars cemetery in Edinburgh. There's a memorial cairn on Ceann Iar which serves to confirm the superstitious belief of old Hebridean fishermen that if they should drown at sea their body would eventually wash up on their home island. The cairn marks the grave of Lieutenant RNR MacNeill, who drowned off Northern Ireland in 1917 when the ship in which he was serving, *HMA Laurentic*, sank after striking a German mine. The sea carried his body to this island, which is part of traditional Clan MacNeill territory.

The extensive and undisturbed machair has a rich variety of plants and is an important feeding area for several hundred wintering **barnacle** and **white-fronted geese.** It is also home to large numbers of seabirds, including an immense population of **black guillemots,** along with **eider, shags, arctic terns** and **fulmars.** The islands support the largest breeding colony of **Atlantic grey seals** in Europe. The Monachs are a National Nature Reserve, managed by Scottish Natural Heritage (SNH). They are difficult to get to but well worth the effort, especially for bird-watchers and scuba-divers. Check with the Tourist Information Centre for suggestions, or Murray MacLeod at the remote island specialists *Sea Trek* (tel 01851-672464; fax 01851-672464; e-mail webmaster@seatrek.co.uk; www.seatrek.freeserve.co.uk) for details about boat trips.

Benbecula

(Beinn na Faoghla)

A government report of 1895 says of Benbecula, 'Though little better than a patch of wilderness, half swamped in ocean, Benbecula was an ancient property of the chiefs of Clanranald...and much land since about the year 1830 has been reclaimed from a state of moss'. As you travel through the stepping stone island of Benbecula between North and South Uist you quickly understand these remarks. Your overriding impression will be one of a water maze of lochs and lochans, relieved only by 407 ft (124 m) Rueval (*Ruabhal*), the solitary hill that gives the island its name 'The Mountain at the Ford'. This refers to a time before causeways and bridges, when crossing to the Uists meant fording dangerous stretches of tidal sands. From the main road there's a track and a path from **Market Stance** (*Stansa na Fèille*) that leads you to the summit of Rueval. The walk to the top is an easy one and offers excellent views. The path passes close to a cave in the south-east where Bonnie Prince Charlie hid for two days in June 1746 while waiting for Flora MacDonald to arrange his escape from the island. The Prince was in hiding for weeks before he sailed over the sea to Skye from Rossinish, in the east, disguised as Flora MacDonald's maid. The main artery is the A865 road, which runs the length of the island, with narrow roads branching off mainly to the west. In the east is a seemingly endless area of wet, peaty moorland; in the western half of the island, which holds most of Benbecula's 1,300 population, the road passes through low-lying machair land and tidy crofts. The inhabitants are a mixture of Protestants and Catholics, a harmonious blend of the religions of the north and south.

BALIVANICH *(Baile a Mhanaich)*

Balivanich is the biggest town on the island and the administrative and shopping centre for the Uists. A monastery was built here soon after the Outer Hebrides became Christian, and to the south is a reminder of those times, the ruins of **Columba's Church** (*Teampull Chaluim Chille*). Benbecula has had a long, if ambivalent, association with the military going back to World War II. RAF Benbecula operated there from June 1942 as part of Coastal Command. The original RAF airfield has expanded into the modern airport on the outskirts of Balivanich, where an army base was established in 1958 and is now one of the main sources of employment and a lucrative component of the island's economy. Benbecula is the headquarters of the forces and civilian technicians who service the South Uist missile testing range. North of the army base is the site of an Iron Age fort, *Dun Gainmhich* (Dunganachy) where you can still find traces of the original walls. About a mile to the south of Balivanich is the bay of **Culla**, where there's a beautiful sandy beach. Tons of tangle, the seaweed *Laminaria*, are cast up at Culla and at nearby Poll nan Crann ('Pool of the Masts') by winter gales. This is collected to fertilise the croftlands as well as for processing into alginates. Poll nan Crann reputedly gets its name from a Spanish Armada galleon wrecked here by autumn gales in 1588. Behind the dunes of Culla beach, near Aird on the B892, are the ruined walls of early 14th century Nunton **chapel and nunnery**. Lady Clanranald of **Nunton House** provided the clothes that Bonnie Prince Charlie used to disguise himself as a maidservant before escaping to Skye. **Nunton Steadings** (tel 01870-602039; www.siat.org.uk) is an art and exhibition centre housed in buildings which have been restored from the derelict steadings originally built in the 19th century for the Clanranald family. Contact the centre for information on events and activities, including the *Uist Countryside Ranger Service*, which is based here. One of its tasks is to look after footpaths and walking trails and assist in interpretation at archaeological sites.

The coastal road continues to Borve, where the ruined walls of 14th century Borve Castle (*Casteal Buirgh*) stand in a field. The castle was once the principal stronghold of the ruling Clanranald chiefs of Benbecula. Opposite are the remains of a ruined chapel, *Teampall Bhuirgh*. At Lionacleit is the **Museum nan Eilean** (Sgoil Lionacleit, HS7 5PJ; tel 01870-602864; fax 01870-602053; e-mail danamacleod@cne-siar. gov.uk) which has a varied programme of art, heritage and natural history exhibitions throughout the year, run by the local authority Museums Service in the new Community School. Access to an excellent public swimming pool and other sports facilities, library, theatre, café and public toilets. Open throughout the year. Disabled access in all areas. Lively *ceilidhs* and other entertainments are held in summer.

The B891 road branches off from the main road near Lionacleit and divides into two routes to the east coast. Off Benbecula's rocky south-east corner there's a well-made pier at **Peter's Port** where the B891 road ends, facing **Wiay** (*Fuidhaigh*). The pier was built in 1896, long before there was an access road, and consequently it's never been much used. Wiay is a flat island of 927 acres (375 ha), where the highest hill, Beinn a'Tuath, rises no more than 335 ft (102 m). The island is a bird sanctuary.

GETTING THERE

British Airways (tel 08457-733377; www.britishairways.com), in conjunction with its operators *British Regional Airways* and *Loganair* (tel 0141-848 7594), flies direct to **Benbecula** from:

Barra: twice a day Monday to Friday.
Glasgow: once flight a day, Monday to Saturday.
Stornoway (Lewis): twice a day Monday to Friday.
There are also connecting flights (stop in Glasgow) from:
Belfast: twice a day on Saturday.
Birmingham: once a day Monday to Friday.
Inverness: once a day Monday to Friday.
London: twice a day Monday to Friday.
Manchester: once a day Monday to Friday.

Airport

Benbecula's Balivanich Airport (Highlands and Islands Airports, Balivanich, HS7 5LW; tel 01870-602051), is on the west coast of the island, clearly signposted from the B892 road. The airport provided important services to the government's *Defence Evaluation and Research Agency* (DERA) Hebrides Ranges, split since mid-2001 into two separate bodies, *Defence Science and Technology Laboratory* (DSTL) and *QinetiQ*. There are ramp facilities at the entrance to the airport terminal and staff are available to assist disabled passengers. The airport is open Monday to Friday 9am to 4pm, and on Saturday 11am to 12.30pm (and by arrangement). It is closed on Sunday.

Buses run regularly between the airport and points within Benbecula, North and South Uist. Contact *Hebridean Coaches* (tel 01870-620345). You can also use the *a2b Travel TravelCall* hotline (tel 0906 915 0106) for timetable and fare information. Lines are open 7am to 10pm seven days a week. There is also a **Postbus** service which runs from Lochboisdale and Ludag piers, as part of the North Uist route, which will stop at the airport on request.

Helicopter Charter: Available from *Bristows Helicopters* (tel 01950-460 6010), which also does Coastguard duties.

Taxis from the airport are operated by:
   Benbecula Taxi Service: tel 01870-602464.
   Buchanans: tel 01870-602277.
   Buster: tel 01870-610374.
   Donald John: tel 01870-603007.
   MacVicars: tel 01870-602307.

GETTING AROUND

A **Postbus** service operates from North Uist to Balivanich Post Office, Monday to Saturday. Check times and fares at the Post Office.

Ask Car Hire: Liniclate, HS7 5PY (tel 01870-602818; fax 01870-602933).

Maclennan Bros Ltd: Balivanich, HS7 5LL (tel 01870-602191; fax 01870-603191).

ACCOMMODATION

Hotels

Creagorry Hotel: Creagorry, HS7 5PG (tel 01870-602024; fax 01870-603108; e-mail darkislandhotel@msn.com). One-star, from £30, open all year. Extensive bar snack menu available lunchtime and evenings. Dining-room table d'hote menus. Local seafood a speciality. Open all year for lunch at midday to 2.30pm, dinner 6pm to 9.30pm.

   Dark Island Hotel: Liniclate, HS7 5PJ (tel 01870-603030; fax 01870-602347; e-mail darkislandhotel@msn.com). 6 miles (4 km) from the airport, two-star, from £88 for a double room, open all year. Meals served throughout the day until 10pm.

Guest House

Borve Guest House: Greta Campbell, 5 Torlum, HS7 5PP (tel 01870-602685; fax 01870-603235; e-mail campbell.m3@talk21.com).

B&B

Creag Liath: Mr and Mrs MacDonald, 15 Griminish, HS7 5QA (tel 01870-602992; e-mail creagliath@aol.com). Three-star, two en-suite rooms, from £25. Open all year.

   Mary Robertson: 9 Liniclate, HS7 5PY (tel 01870-602532), two-star, two rooms, from £18. Open January to November.

Self-Catering

Mr and Mrs A MacDonald: 3 Gramsdale Road, Balivanich, HS7 5LZ (tel 01870-

602432). Two-star, three bedrooms, sleeps 7. Open all year, from £170 to £250 a week.

Mrs Esther MacDonald: 2 Kyles Flodda, Gramsdale, HS7 5QR (tel 01870-602536). Four-star, thatched stone-built croft cottage, one bedroom, sleeps 2-4. Open all year, from £200 to £300 a week.

Mrs Margaret Shepherd: Heisker, Liniclate, HS7 5PJ (tel 01870-602235). Three-star, three bedrooms, sleeps 6-7. Open all year, from £150 to £260 a week.

Camping
Shellbay Caravan and Camping Park: Liniclate, HS7 5PJ (tel 01870-602447). Two-star, two holiday caravans, and 25 pitches. Open April to October, caravans £100 to £150 a week, pitches £5 per person a night.

EATING AND DRINKING
Stepping Stone Restaurant: Balivanich, HS7 5DA (tel 01870-602659; fax 01870-603121). Food available all day from 10am to 9pm, including a mixture of sandwiches, rolls and homebakes to more substantial meals. Table d'hôte menu in the evenings offering three, four or five-course meals, including Scottish cheeses. Try pan-fried local cockles in oatmeal, roast Uist venison with rowanberry jelly. Take-away food available. Open all year, seven days a week. Vegetarians welcome, facilities for disabled, no smoking throughout. Taste of Scotland member.

Locals also recommend the *Dark Island Hotel* for its excellent spread, and the table at *Creagorry Hotel*, on the A865 just before the causeway to South Uist.

SPORT AND RECREATION
Golf. *Benbecula Golf Club* (Bank House, 12 Aird, Benbecula, HS7 5LT; tel 01870-602467. Or Iain Macrury, Secretary; tel 01870-602126) is one mile (1.6 km) north of Balivanich on the B892 road, next to the airport. A naturally flat par 62 nine-hole machair course features some tricky holes and natural hazards include rabbit scrapes. Originally founded by the RAF in 1945. Visitors welcome. Green fees £5 a day.

Horse-Riding. *Uist Community Riding School* (The Stables, Balivanich, HS7 5LA; tel 01870-604283), is a centrally located riding school. Daily rates, and lessons with the option for indoor or outdoor tuition. All ages and levels welcome.

SHOPPING
MacGillivrays, Hebridean gift house (Balivanich, HS7 5LA; tel 01870-602525; fax 01870-602981) is an Aladdin's Cave of souvenirs, clothing – real McCoy Harris Tweed – books, crafts, and fishing tackle. There's a *Spar* supermarket in Balivanich which is open every day. This used to be the NAAFI store for military personnel but was used by every shopper in the Uists.

HELP AND INFORMATION
For information on Benbecula contact the *Tourist Information Offices* in Lochboisdale, South Uist (tel 01878-700286), open April-mid October and Lochmaddy, North Uist (tel 01876-500321), open April-mid October.
Balivanich Police Station: tel 01870-602374.
Surgery: Griminish (tel 01870-602215).
Balivanich Airport: tel 01870-602051.
British Airways: Benbecula (tel 01870-602310).
Loganair: tel 01870-602290.
Western Isles Enterprise: tel 01870-602646.
Bank of Scotland: Balivanich (tel 01870-602044).

South Uist

(Uibhist a Deas)

At 22 miles (35 km) from north to south and seven miles (11 km) across South Uist is the second largest of the islands and is regarded as a centre of Gaelic culture and tradition. South Uist has produced many famous pipers and it has a strong military tradition. The family of Marshal Macdonald, who fought for Napoleon Bonaparte, came from here. The population numbers about 2,200. The A865 main road runs from Carnan in the north to Daliburgh and then, as the B888, to Pollachar in the south. Small roadside shrines along the way are evidence of the fact that 95% of the people on South Uist are Catholic. To the east of the road lies hilly, peat moorland dotted with 190 freshwater lochs providing good bags of **brown trout**. The high ridge of mountains in the east below Loch Skipport is dominated by the twin peaks of 2,034 ft (620 m) Beinn Mhor and Hecla (*Thacla*) rising to 1,988 ft (606 m). To the west the land is largely fertile machair and this is where most of the crofting townships are situated. The network of minor roads off the A865 link most of these little settlements and give easy access to many of the island's remarkable prehistoric and mediaeval sites. The western coastline is crammed with archaeological sites. In some places there are about 15 sites for every square mile (2.5 sq km). There are more than 230 sites on the western machair alone, mostly settlements dating from the Early Bronze Age, more than 4,000 years ago, to the 19th century. Some have also been identified as Viking settlements and this is one of the few places in Britain where so many Viking sites can be matched to the names of present townships. More recent history concerns events which were in some respects the roots of the damaging Clearances suffered by South Uist. From the mid-18th century the price brought by Hebridean kelp soared over 50 years to unbelievable levels. As 24 tons of the seaweed were needed to produce a single ton of the alkaline ash used in the production of glass and soap it was especially labour intensive. As a consequence, the population of South Uist had increased to more than 11,000 by the early 1800s. With a production cost of about £5 a ton and a sale price of more than £20 a ton the kelp industry generated enormous profits for the landowner, Macdonald of Clanranald, but little for the islanders who had to gather and burn the kelp under the terms of their tenancy. While they struggled, MacDonald was living the life of Riley. At the height of the kelp boom his wine bill alone was the equivalent of £20,000 over a 16-month period. By the late 1820s new methods of producing alkali caused profits from kelp to slump and mounting debts forced many landowners to sell off most of their lands, paving the way from 1838 for the widespread evictions carried out to make room for the sheep of South Uist's new owner, Colonel John Gordon of Cluny. By the early 1840s it's estimated that he had evicted and shipped to Canada nearly 2,000 people, and at one stage he offered both South Uist and Benbecula to the government as a possible penal colony.

LOCHBOISDALE *(Loch Baghasdail)*

Lochboisdale is the ferry port for the island, connecting with Oban on the Scottish mainland and Castlebay in Barra. In its heyday it was a major herring port, bustling with fishermen, herring gutters, and buyers. Today, the settlement of 300 shows most signs of life when the car ferry berths. It has a Tourist Information Office, a few shops, a bank, and public toilets. At the entrance to Loch Boisdale is the island of **Calvay** where Bonnie Prince Charlie once again took refuge during his wanderings in 1746. There's a ruined 13th century castle on the island and an automatic light which replaced the one erected in 1857. Most of South Uist's scenic attractions and interesting sites lie to the north of Lochboisdale and you should leave the main north-south road whenever possible to get the real flavour of this island.

Starting at the north-west tip is **Ardivachar Point**, composed of rock which is more than 3-billion years old, the oldest known in Britain. From this headland 20 miles (32 km) of beach stretch to the southern tip of South Uist, broken only by another headland, Rubha Ardvule (*Rubha Aird a' Mhuile*). Close to Ardivachar is the military range at Eochar (*Iochdar*), west of Loch Bee, from which the Royal Artillery has been firing guided missiles into the Atlantic since 1961. Some of them are tracked from the radar station on St Kilda, 41 miles (66 km) to the north-west. Warning flags fly when the rocket range is active. A glance at the Ordnance Survey map will show you a number of danger spots associated with the rocket range in areas along an otherwise lovely coast, so watch out for suspicious chunks of metal. **Loch Bee** is a huge brackish stretch of salt and fresh water, connected to both the Atlantic and – by a floodgate – to The Little Minch in the east through Loch Skipport. South of the loch is the 'Hill of Miracles,' 285 ft-high (87 m) **Rueval**. A 30 ft (9 m) granite statue of **Our Lady of the Isles** towers above the heathery slopes. It was erected in 1957 by the local community to commemorate Marian Year. On the summit above the Madonna and Child sculpted by Hew Lorimer are the masts and aerials of the control installation for the Royal Artillery rocket range. This conglomeration is known to locals as 'Space City.' Down the road is the fascinating expanse of the **Loch Druidibeg Nature Reserve**, stretching inland for about four miles (6 km) (see *Flora and Fauna*).

At **Howmore** (*Tobha Mor*) are some interesting examples of restored thatched cottages and the ruins of five mediaeval churches and chapels. This was an important ecclesiastical site in the 12th or 13th century and was the burial ground of the ruling Clanranald chiefs. The village also has a modern Church of Scotland, one of only two in Scotland still retaining a central communion pew. **Rubha Ardvule** is one of the few rocky headlands of any size on the west coast of South Uist. This is a good spot for watching the many seabirds in the area, including a small tern colony. There is a small loch in the middle of the headland and there are distinct signs that the Vikings dug a canal from it into the sea so that they could shelter their longships inland. Purple loosestrife, uncommon in the Outer Hebrides, grows on the headland. **Ormacleit Castle** took seven years to build and was completed for the Clanranald chief in 1708. Seven years later it was accidentally burnt down during a drunken party on the eve of the Battle of Sheriffmuir, in which the chief was killed fighting for the Old Pretender, James Stewart, in the (first) Jacobite Rebellion of 1715. In the ruins you can see an armorial plaque in the north wall. One of the largest ever Norse settlements has been uncovered at **Bornish** (*Bornais*) and finds of bone combs and bronze pins indicate close contact with the Irish trading centres of Dublin and Waterford. Other finds at Bornish include soapstone weights, vessels, and coins, which also indicate links with the Northern Isles and with Scandinavia.

The road into **Loch Eynort** (*Loch Aineort*) branches north and south of the loch, making it possible to see lots of this lovely area. South Uist's highest hills lie to the north of the loch and offer excellent hill-walking. A day out here along the ridge between the peaks of **Beinn Mhor** and **Hecla** will give you a good idea of the strenuous dance Bonnie Prince Charlie led the searching redcoats in 1746. You'll also get excellent views across to Skye and the Cuillins. There's a **Prince's Cove** on the south-east side of Hecla, where the Prince spent a night while fruitlessly searching for a boat. Tradition has it that French gold today worth £2-million is buried in a cave in this area, cash that was to have been used to pay the clansmen of the '45 Rebellion. Also on the coast here is **Nicolson's Leap**, named after an islander legend says leapt a 50 ft (15 m) gap to the top of a sea stack, clutching in his arms the baby son of the Clanranald chief. The chief had surprised him in bed with the Lady Clanranald. From this eyrie the man tried to bargain with the enraged chief. When he realised it was hopeless he jumped off the stack with the child to perish in the boiling sea below.

Uist Craft Producers safeguard and promote both traditional and contemporary crafts in the Uists, creating a wide variety of crafts from knitwear, painting, and woodwork, to flowercraft. Examples can be seen at the **Kildonan Museum** (tel 01878-710258), along with local history exhibitions. There's also a tearoom/restaurant. Open 20 April to end-September, Monday to Saturday from 10am to 5pm, Sunday 2pm to 5pm. Toilets with disabled facilities. The museum sells an informative booklet which makes it easy to follow the South Uist archaeological and wildlife trail. Near Milton, to the west of the A865 road, a rough stone cairn and plaque inside low tumbled walls mark the **birthplace of Flora MacDonald**, the young woman famous for helping Bonnie Prince Charlie to escape after his defeat on the battlefield of Culloden.

Flora and the Bonny Prince

The ruins of a farmhouse just north of Milton might seem unlikely as a place where an imperishable romantic legend was born, but this is the birthplace of Scottish heroine Flora MacDonald and from here on 20 June 1746, while staying with her brother Angus, she went out to meet Prince Charles Edward Louis Philippe Casimir Stuart – Bonnie Prince Charlie. He had been hiding with two clansmen in Glen Corodale, north-east of Milton, and was now desperate to escape from the British troops closing in on him. A plan was devised which called for the Prince to disguise himself as Flora's maidservant and go with her to Skye. There the Prince expected to be sheltered by Lady Margaret MacDonald of Sleat at Kingsburgh House, Trotternish, even though her husband, Sir Alexander MacDonald of Sleat, was serving at Fort Augustus in the headquarters of the redcoats who had put a bounty of £30,000 on the Prince's head. Details of the plan were settled at Lord Clanranald's residence at Nunton, in Benbecula. The Prince and his attendants were advised to make their way to Rossinish, in north-east Benbecula, where Flora and the Clanranalds would meet them with a boat for the voyage across The Little Minch to Skye. On 27 June, Flora arrived at Rossinish with her brother Angus, Lady Clanranald, and her daughter Margaret. Lady Clanranald brought with her the clothes for the lanky Prince to wear in his disguise as Irish maid 'Betty Burke.' The Prince set sail with Flora and one attendant and after a rough crossing landed at the little bay of Kilbride, on the west side of Skye's Trotternish peninsula, below Monkstadt.

When the Prince subsequently said farewell to Flora in Portree their parting, far from being the stuff of legend, was rather prosaic. The Prince said, 'I believe, Madam, I owe you a crown of borrowed money.' She replied that it was only half a crown, which he then gave her. He did at least salute her, saying, 'For all that has happened I hope, Madam, we shall meet in St James' yet.' History has shown that this was not to be but the adventure did prompt an Englishman, Sir Harold Edwin Boulton, to write the well-known song that goes:

Speed bonnie boat like a bird on the wing,
'Onward,' the sailors cry:
Carry the lad that's born to be King.
Over the sea to Skye.'

South of Daliburgh between the B888 and the sea is **Kilpheder** (*Cille Pheadair*), where the remains of a wheelhouse dated at around AD 200 have been excavated. The nearby village of **Garrynamonie** (*Gèarraidh ma Mònadh*) is notable among locals for its school, where the headmaster from 1890-1913 ignored the common language of his pupils and taught them only in English. During earlier attempts to stamp out Gaelic in schools any children heard using their mother tongue had to hang a baton around their neck – the *Maide Gàidhlig*, or 'Gaelic Stick' – to remind them it was forbidden. There are excellent views of Eriskay and Barra from the south coast. Near the inn at **Pollachar** is one of the few large shingle beaches in the Outer Hebrides, above which is a prehistoric standing stone. **Bottle-nosed dolphins** are often seen here in the Sound of Barra, even in winter. At **Ludag** ferry port is a *Clach Shanais* information panel recounting the story of Bonnie Prince Charlie, as well as the tale of the whisky ship *SS Politician*, whose shattered remains lie in the Sound not far to the east (see *Eriskay*).

FLORA AND FAUNA

In November 2000, a dozen ardent twitchers chartered a fishing boat to take them from the mainland to South Uist, where a **long-tailed shrike** from Central Asia had been sighted. Britain's last **Steller's eider**, which breeds in the Siberian tundra, was seen in the Western Isles in 1984. You probably won't see either of these rare vagrants, but the celebrated **Loch Druidibeg National Nature Reserve** is one of the best places in the Western Isles to see the full range of island wildlife and habitats. It's particularly rich in birdlife. The 4,144-acre (1,677 ha) reserve stretches across the northern part of South Uist on either side of the main A865 road from the Atlantic coast almost to The Minch and is an important site for breeding **greylag geese**, as well as being a sanctuary for many other birds, including the rare **corncrake**. The greylags here form one of the few populations of these birds in Britain that do not fly north in spring to breed. At 1,988 ft (606 m) Hecla is one of the highest hills in South Uist and forms an impressive backdrop to the reserve. **Golden eagles** often quarter its slopes, and **red grouse, golden plover**, and **red deer**, a recent introduction to South Uist, may also be seen. The reserve is always open but depending on the season you might need a permit to enter from the SNH warden at Grogarry Lodge, where the B890 road branches east to Loch Skipport (*Loch Sgiopoirt*). This little road runs through rugged countryside to the ruined pier at the mouth of the sea loch, where you can park. There is a sign and information panel at the start of the circular nature trail route about 1¹/2 miles (2.4 km) down this road, or you can start at the other end on the main A865 at Stilligarry (*Stadhlaigearraidh*). Leaflets and information about the reserve and self-guided walks are available from Scottish Natural Heritage (135 Stilligarry, South Uist, HS8 5RS; tel 01870-620238; fax 01870-620350).

You are expected to keep to existing tracks and footpaths in the reserve and the south-west corner of the loch should be avoided during the nesting season (April-August). There are a number of islands in shallow Loch Druidibeg where such native woodland species as **birch, rowan, juniper, bluebell** and **royal fern** survive away from grazing animals. The only other tree cover on the reserve is in a small plantation beside the Loch Skipport road which attracts a variety of insects and woodland birds. One of the islands in the loch has been colonised by herons. Raptors you might spot in the reserve include **kestrel, peregrine, short-eared owl, merlin**, and **hen harrier**. Other breeding birds found in the eastern part of the reserve include **buzzard, red-breasted merganser, mute swan, common gull** and **wren**. Within the western section lie two crofting townships, a series of shallow lochs, lagoons and marshes, and a stretch of dunes with their associated machair. The patchwork of cultivated, fallow and uncultivated wet and dry areas on the western coastal machair is a riot of colour during the summer months, when **corn marigold**, **wild pansy**, **thyme** and a host of **orchids** come into bloom. The rare **American pondweed** is found in its natural state only in the Uists. The coastal areas and croftland are important breeding areas for waders such as **dunlin**, **redshank**, **lapwing** and **ringed plover**, and **long-tailed duck** may often be seen offshore in winter. In the north-west, Loch Bee (*Loch Bì*) is also excellent for bird-watching. Its resident population of 300 **mute swans** is joined in winter by migrant **whooper swans**.

Conservationists are struggling to contain the **hedgehogs** which are devouring the eggs of ground-nesting birds. The hedgehog population has grown from the five brought from the mainland in 1974 by a school teacher who wanted pets to control garden slugs. Away from their mainland predators, hedgehogs have since multiplied and have snuffled along roads and causeways into Benbecula and North Uist. They are now roaming internationally renowned bird reserves and it's estimated that over the past 15 years they have reduced the numbers of waders on the Uists by up to 63%. Researchers say that the hedgehogs eat half the eggs laid in nests along the coastal dunes each year which, with natural predation, means that only one in 10 pairs of birds successfully raises young. Most seriously affected is the chestnut-coloured dunlin, a small, unagressive bird protected by international law.

GETTING THERE

Caledonian MacBrayne (The Ferry Terminal, Gourock PA19 1QP; tel 08705-650000; fax 01475-635235 for reservations; e-mail reservations@calmac.co.uk; www.calmac.co.uk) car ferry sails to Lochboisdale, South Uist, via Barra **from Oban** on Monday, Wednesday, Thursday, and Saturday at 2.50pm; and direct Oban to Lochboisdale at 2.50pm on Friday. The journey takes 6 hours 40 minutes via Barra and 4 hours 50 minutes on the direct route. The peak single adult fare is £18.75, car and motorhome £89, and caravan and boat/luggage trailer an additional £89, motorcycle £44.50, and bicycle £2. Discounted 'Five-Day Return' and 'Six-Journey' tickets are available on this route.

You can also take a ferry **from Mallaig** to Lochboisdale on Tuesday at 6.10pm. The journey takes 3¹/₂ hours and the single adult fare is £13.85, car and motorhome £49.50, caravan and boat/luggage trailer an additional £49.50, motorcycles £24.75, and bicycles £2. The 'Six-Journey' ticket is also available on this route.

For more information contact the CalMac offices in Oban (tel 01631-566688), Mallaig (tel 01687-462403), or Lochboisdale (tel 01878-700288).

GETTING AROUND

Causeways and bridges are the vital links that connect the two Uists by way of Benbecula. The A865 road traverses the entire length of this large island from Carnan, in the north, where the original South Ford crossing point from South Uist to Benbecula was bridged in 1943. It then crosses a narrow, raised causeway over Loch Bee. This road is more than 20 miles (32 km) in length and forks at Daliburgh to Lochboisdale and south to Pollachar, near Kilbride, on the Sound of Eriskay. From points along this road St Kilda, 60 miles (97 km) out in the Atlantic, can at times be seen. Across the sound you look south-eastwards to the island of Eriskay, where Bonnie Prince Charlie first set foot on Scottish soil in 1745.

Bus: *Royal Mail* (tel 01246-546329; www.royalmail.co.uk) operates an 8-seater **Postbus service** from Ludag and Lochboisdale piers to Balivanich and the airport, Monday to Saturday, stopping at about 13 points on the way.

Vehicle Rental: *Laing Motors* (Lochboisdale, HS8 5TH; tel/fax 01878-700267), self-drive car hire, 5 minutes' walk from Lochboisdale ferry terminal.

Cycle Hire: *Rothan Cycles* (9 Howmore, HS8 5SH; tel/fax 01870-620283, mobile 07720 558064; e-mail rothan@btnternet.com).

Tours

Crann Tara Tours: 207 Stoneybridge, HS8 5SD (tel 01870-620323; e-mail cranntaratours1@tinyonline.co.uk). Offers guided tours, either in your own vehicle, by coach, bike or on foot.

ACCOMMODATION

Hotels

Borrodale Hotel: Daliburgh, HS8 5SS (tel 01878-700444; fax 01878-700446; e-mail darkislandhotel@msn.com). Two-star, from £30. Good food, such as roast of the day, seafood, home-made meat and vegetarian dishes, bar meals and a la carte. Open all year, seven days a week from 8am to 9.30pm. Free golf and fishing can be arranged.

Lochboisdale Hotel: Lochboisdale, HS8 5TH (tel 01878-700332; fax 01878-700367; e-mail hotel@lochboisdale.com; www.lochboisdale.com). Three-star, at ferry terminal. Open all year, from £38 a night. A la carte and daily specials menu feature seafood and game. Open all year for lunch from 12.30pm to 2pm and dinner 6pm to 9pm. Light snacks available.

Orasay Inn: Lochcarnan, HS8 5PD (tel 01870-610298; fax 01870-610390; e-mail: orasayinn@btinternet.com). Two-star inn, two miles (3 km) from Lochboisdale, B&B from £29. Nine en suite rooms. Open all year except Christmas Day, facilities for disabled visitors. Dining-room has great views across The Minch and serves smoked salmon duo: a mix of Hebridean hot-smoked and cold-smoked salmon, served with green salad; medallions of venison with redcurrant and port sauce, garnished with chestnuts. No smoking in dining-room, vegetarians welcome. Taste of Scotland member.

Pollachar Inn: Pollachar, HS8 5TT (tel 01878-700215; fax 01878-700768). Three-star, family-run hotel with licensed restaurant with views across Sound of Barra. Open all year, from £30 a night. Bar serves traditional bar food, a la carte menu, available on request, uses fresh local seafood and venison. Open all year, seven days a week, Monday to Saturday, from 12.30pm to 2.30pm and 6.30pm to 9.30pm; and Sunday 12.30pm to 9.30pm.

Guest House

Brae Lea House: Patricia Murray, Lasgair, Lochboisdale, HS8 5TH (tel/fax 01878-700497; e-mail braelea@supanet.com). Three-star, a mile (0.8 km) from ferry terminal, overlooking Lochboisdale Bay, reduced rates for three or more days. Open all year, from £25 B&B.

B&B

Anglers Retreat: 1 Ardmore, Iochdar, HS8 5QY (tel/fax 01870-610325; e-mail billy@wfelton.freeserve.co.uk). Two-star, set in lochside croftland, cycle shed. Open March to December, from £15.

Karingeidha: Morag Walker, Daliburgh, HS8 5SS (tel 01878-700495; fax 01878-700795). Two-star, three rooms. Open all year, from £20.

Joan MacDonald: Kilchoan Bay, 455 Lochboisdale, HS8 5TN (tel 01878-700517). Three-star, on main bus route and a mile (0.8 km) from ferry terminal, will collect. Open April to September. Excellent value B&B from £18.

Isabel Mackenzie: 5 Gearraidh Bhailteas, Bronish, HS8 5RY (tel 01878-710371). Three-star, modern croft house, six miles (10 km) from Lochboisdale ferry. Access for the disabled.

Christina MacPhee: 363 South Boisdale, HS8 5TE (tel 01878-700586). Three-star, near beach, two rooms. Open all year, from £16.

Mr and Mrs M MacRury: Cross Roads, Stoneybridge, HS8 5SD (tel 01870-620321). Two-star, disabled access.

Monach View: Mary Mackay-Hood, Kilaulay, Iochdar, HS8 5RE (tel/fax 01870-610347; e-mail glennhood@hotmail.com). Three-star, on sandy beach. Open all year, from £17.

Self-Catering

Roderick and Fiona MacInnes: 364 South Boisdale, HS8 5TE (tel 01878-70037/347; fax 01878-700371). Four-star, five minutes' walk to beach. Open all year, from £160 to £350 a week.

Mrs Kate Ward: 209 Stoneybridge, HS8 5SD (tel 01870-620322). Three-star, one bedroom, sleeps four. Open all year, from £90 to £160 a week.

Marion Morrison: Loch Bee View, West Gerinish, HS8 5RW (tel 01870-620202; e-mail flojoe@lochbee.freeserve.co.uk). Two-star, beside fishing loch, sandy beaches, three bedrooms, sleeps five. Open all year, from £150 to £200 a week.

Self-catering caravans are available from:

Mrs Marion Felton: Ardmore (tel/fax 01870-610325; e-mail billy@ wfelton.freeserve.co.uk). Sleeps 4-7. Open all year, from £100 to £110 a week.

Neil John MacDonald: Lochside Cottage, Lochboisdale, HS8 5TH (tel 01878-700472). Beside fishing loch, near ferry port, will collect. Open all year, from £100 a week.

Mrs Shona MacIntyre: 6 North Locheynort, Bornish, HS8 5SN (tel 01878-710363/700707). Beside the sea, sleeps 4-6. Open all year, from £95 to £110 a week.

Hostel

Howmore Youth Hostel: Howmore, South Uist, HS8 5SH. Run by the Gatliff Hebridean Hostels Trust. The accommodation is simpler than the usual youth hostel. Basic equipment is provided but you are advised to bring a sleeping bag. No advance bookings are accepted. 17 beds, two rooms with four beds, two rooms with 5-8 beds, shop and bus ³/4 mile (1.2 km) away, ferry 13 miles (21 km) away in Lochboisdale. Cycling, entertainment, fishing, 18-hole golf course, hill-walking, swimming. Walkers and cyclists welcome. Signposted from the main Lochboisdale to Lochmaddy A865 road. From £7 over 18, £5 under 18, and £4 camping. Open all year.

ENTERTAINMENT

The annual **Ceolas Music Summer School** is a highlight of the summer in South Uist. This is a lively tuition festival with daytime classes and evening performances which are usually packed to capacity. The festival sets out to explore the links between dance, song, Gaelic language, fiddle and piping. Staged in July, it draws participants and tutors from around the world. For more information contact Ronald MacKinnon (tel 01878-700543; e-mail raoinaidh@aol.com), or Mary MacInnes (tel 01878-710376; e-mail cmacinnes@aol.com).

The **South Uist Games**, an annual exhibition of such Highland pastimes as tossing the caber, dancing, and piping, take place every July. This is followed by the **South Uist Agricultural Show**, and later on a Gaelic festival.

SPORT AND RECREATION

Walking and Climbing

The west coast is a good place for walkers who enjoy rambling, especially the areas around Howmore, Kildonan, and Askernish. Adding a frisson of excitement to beach walks all down the west coast are signs reminding you not to touch anything suspicious in case it explodes. These refer to the bits of rocket which sometimes wash up from the missile firing range on the island. There's more demanding hill-walking on Hecla (1,988 ft/606 m), Beinn Corradail (1,729 ft/527 m), and Beinn Mhor (2,034 ft/620 m), and these three summits make an excellent day's outing if you are fit and experienced. Allow 6-8 hours.

The north-facing Hellisdale Buttresses on Bheinn Mhor offer some testing **rock climbing**. These are divided by six gullies into seven distinct buttresses and can be reached in two hours from Loch Dòbhrain, alongside the main A865 road, over the Bealach Hellisdale. There are good climbs here of 328-492 ft (100-150 m) on pitches which vary from moderate to very severe. Only top-notch cragsmen should attempt these.

Golf

On the west coast *Askernish Golf Club* (Neil Elliot, Secretary, Askernish, Lochboisdale, HS8 5ST; tel 01878-700298) has an 18-tee/9-hole, par 68 course originally laid out in 1891. The tees are spread enough to give variety in the two sets of nine holes. Green fees are £10 a day. Turn off the A865 for Askernish village. From the club you can also get access to the beautiful sandy beach which runs along all South Uist's western seaboard.

Fishing

The north-east corner and west coast in particular offer good opportunities for angling. The Lochboisdale Hotel (tel 01878-700332) sells a booklet detailing the area's 70 trout-fishing lochs and is a good source of information. It issues permits for brown trout fly-fishing and has boats on some of the lochs.

Game Fishing Contacts:
Creagorry Hotel (Stephen Peteranna; tel 01870-602024).
Hector MacLean (tel 01870-602575) arranges sea-angling trips from Loch Carnan.
Lochboisdale Hotel and South Uist Estates (Captain John Kennedy; tel 01878-700332, hotel, or 01878-710366, home).
South Uist Angling Club (Secretary, WP Felton; tel 01870-610325) has trout fishing in lochs in both South Uist and Benbecula. Boats available. Permits available in South Uist from Mrs Kennedy at Bornish Stores, Bornish.

SHOPPING

Hebridean Jewellery: Cochdar, HS8 5QX (tel 01870-610288; fax 01870-610370). Craft shop and jewellery workshop producing Celtic silver and gold jewellery, and stocking a large range of gifts.

Salar Fish Farm Shop and Smokehouse: The Pier, Loch Carnan, HS8 5PD (tel 01870-610324; fax 01870-610369; e-mail sales@salar.co.uk; www.salar.co.uk). Sells delicious, award-winning Salar flaky salmon. Fresh salmon are harvested regularly then prepared and smoked by a special process, using a variety of wood shavings to bring out the best possible flavour and texture. You can sample freshly smoked salmon on the spot, take some home with you, or use the mail order despatch service. Open Monday to Friday from 9am to 5pm.

Studio Gallery (Bill Neill, Askernish; tel 01878-700237) has a permanent exhibition, including work by other local artists. Landscape, wildlife, watercolours, limited editions and cards. Open April to September, Monday to Saturday from 10am to 5pm. The studio is close to the main road.

HELP AND INFORMATION

Tourist Information Office: Pier Road, Lochboisdale (tel 01878-7002860. Seasonal opening from early April to mid-October.
Police: Lochboisdale (tel 01878-700261).

Surgery: Lochboisdale (tel 01878-700302).
Caledonian MacBrayne: Lochboisdale (tel 01878-700288).
Ludag-Eoligarry ferry: passenger ferry only (tel 01878-720233).
Royal Bank of Scotland: Lochboisdale (tel 01878-700399).
Scottish Natural Heritage (SNH): 135 Stillgarry, South Uist, HS8 5RS (tel 01870-620238).

Eriskay *(Eiriosgaigh)*

The island of Eriskay lies two miles (3 km) off the southern tip of South Uist across a tricky strait. Until 2000 this channel had to be crossed by boat. It is now permanently linked to the islands to the north by causeway. The island belonged to the MacNeils of Barra until 1758, when it passed to the MacDonalds of Clanranald. Eriskay, Barra, Benbecula and South Uist were sold in 1838 to Lieutenant-Colonel John Gordon of Cluny Castle, Aberdeenshire. He cleared the island for sheep but allowed a few evicted crofters to settle on Eriskay as he thought the land too poor even for his sheep. As well as a pub, the main village has a church, primary school, post office, a health clinic, and shop. Islanders supplement their crofting with fishing for lobsters, prawns, and crabs. The women are well known for the sweaters they knit in distinctive patterns peculiar to Eriskay. The patterns depict Eriskay's fishing way of life. Eriskay is a small place, only 2¹/₂ miles long by 1¹/₂ miles wide (4 km by 2¹/₂ km), with a population that has fallen by 70% in the last 70 years to its present 126 people, but it is an island firmly anchored in history. It is famous as the spot where Bonnie Prince Charlie first set foot on Scottish soil in 1745 at the start of his ill-starred Jacobite uprising. In Gaelic circles it is also renowned as the source of the lovely melody known as the *Eriskay Love Lilt*, as well as many other songs popular in the Gaelic musical repertoire and preserved for posterity in the collection of Father Allan MacDonald (1859-1905), who was the scholarly parish priest of Eriskay. Non-Gaels might be equally interested in the island's rare breed of pony, the sturdy Eriskay of 12-13 hands which has been saved from extinction by dedicated enthusiasts, and is registered as endangered with the *Rare Breeds Survival Trust*. It's said that these are the mounts the Picts rode into battle. All are fascinated by the event which turned Eriskay upside down during World War II and made it the subject of a smash-hit novel and a hilarious movie. This was the wreck of the *SS Politician*.

Eriskay is said to take its name from the Gaelic for Eric's Isle. Its west coast has several lovely shell-sand beaches and the most southerly of these is the half-mile long **Prince's Beach** (*Coilleag a'Phrionnsa*), where the Young Pretender landed from the French ship *Du Teillay*. The white-striped pink sea bindweed (*Calystegia soldanella*), or convolvulus, which grows at the back of the beach is known locally as the 'Prince's Flower.' It usually blossoms in July-August and it is said to have grown and spread from French seeds which fell from the Prince's pocket when he landed here in 1745. Local schoolchildren have erected a cairn on the dune above *Sgeir na h-Airidh Samhraidh*, the rocky spot where he stepped ashore. Unfortunately, the blackhouse in Bala where the Prince slept his first night on Scottish soil was demolished around the turn of the 19th century with the consent of landowner Lady Gordon Cathcart.

Apart from his famed collection of Gaelic songs and folklore, Father Allan MacDonald's memorial is **St Michael's Church**, which he built in 1903 in an elevated position at Rubha Bàn. It is dedicated to the patron saint of the islands. The church bell is the one that used to ring the watches on the German battle-cruiser *SMS*

Whisky Galore

The 8,000 ton *SS Politician* took a wrong turn on her way to Jamaica on the morning of 5 February 1941 and went aground just off Eriskay's Rosinish Point. In Hold Number Five of the 450 ft (137 m) merchantman were 264,000 bottles of bonded whisky, 90 crates of stout and 60 cases of sherry. Three days later the *SS Thala* also ran aground within a mile of the ship soon to be famous as the 'Polly,' but her cargo of iron ore couldn't compete with the whisky as a magnet for the islanders, who had liberated more than 2,000 cases of the stuff, an estimated 24,000 bottles, before the first of them was hauled up before the beak in Lochmaddy to face charges of theft. Novelist Compton Mackenzie, living in nearby Barra, wove the events into his 1946 world best-seller *Whisky Galore*, made into the movie of the same name by British film makers Ealing Studios, famed for their post-war comedies. The film was released in 1949. Compton Mackenzie appeared briefly in the film as Captain Buncher of the *SS Cabinet Minister*, but the bottles of whisky at the centre of the plot were not real. Post-war rationing meant whisky was in short supply and Ealing Studios had to use dummy bottles made of wax for the filming. Before all this happened the 'Polly' had been refloated in September 1941 then allowed to settle closer to the South Uist shore, still with 3,000–4,000 cases of whisky on board as well as thousands of bottles rolling around loose. Despite further attempts at salvage throughout the war, which included cutting her in two and towing the bow section to Rothesay, the weather had the last word and sank her where she now lies embedded in sand in the Sound of Eriskay, to the east of the new causeway, her stern section cut down to spring low water level.

In August 1942, sticks of gelignite were dropped into the remains of the ship and it was blown up by HM Customs and Excise officers with the intention of finally destroying any dutiable alcohol left in the hold. One officer reported that if any bottles survived the explosion 'I am satisfied that it could not be removed except by a diver in diving gear' – which is precisely what happened. In the 1960s scuba-divers from sub-aqua clubs all around Britain were making a bee-line for the Sound of Eriskay and starting to scratch around the remains of the old wreck. Soon it was a prime diving spot, with the added attraction of a souvenir bottle or two of duty-free whisky. For non-divers the best place to see one of the fabled bottles is in the bar of the island's only pub, *The Politician* (see *Eating and Drinking*). When the pub opened in the main village in 1988, nearly half a century after the sinking, a bottle of 'Polly' whisky was opened for the occasion. It was pronounced delectable by 86-year-old Donald MacInnes, the only survivor of the islanders who had helped to lighten the wrecked ship's stimulating cargo in 1941.

Derfflinger, scuttled in 1919 at Scapa Flow, Orkney, and salvaged in 1939. The church's altar base is made from the bow of a lifeboat from the British aircraft carrier *HMS Hermes*. Father MacDonald is buried in the old cemetery near Prince's Beach.

There is a 5¼-mile (8½ km) self-guided waymarked walk around the island, which takes about three hours to complete. In the south this gives a panoramic view of Skye, Soay, Canna, Rum, Eigg, and Muck. If the weather is clear you might also see as far as Mull, Tiree, and Coll. Look out for the rare Eriskay ponies running wild around Loch Crakavaig (*Cracabhaig*). The loch supplies Eriskay with fresh water.

Off the southern tip of Eriskay is the scattered group of the Stack Islands. On the largest, *Eilean Leathan*, are the ruins of **Weaver's Castle** which was once the stronghold of a pirate and wrecker. Near the end of the walk is a secluded little bay where you might see otters.

GETTING THERE

On 20 November 2000, for the first time since the Ice Age, people walked across the Sound of Eriskay with the closing of the final gap in the new 1.2-mile (2 km) causeway link between the island and South Uist. The causeway is part of a planned £9.4-million integrated transport route from the Butt of Lewis in the north to Vatersay in the south aimed at linking all the islands on a spinal route through the Western Isles. The causeway liberated Eriskay's residents from the rule of the ebb tide, which at its lowest, prevented the small car ferry from operating for up to six hours at a time. A 66 ft (20 m) steel bridge in the centre of the causeway provides an opening at low tide for whales, porpoises, and small boats to pass through the Sound of Eriskay from The Little Minch to the Atlantic.

There's a *Western Isles Council* (Balivanich, Benbecula, HS7 5LA; tel 01870-602425; fax 01870-602988) passenger-only ferry to Ceann a Gharaidh, Eriskay, from Eoligarry and Ardveenish, Barra. There are two sailings Monday to Saturday from Eoligarry and daily sailings from Ardveenish Monday to Friday, with occasional Saturday sailings. No services on Sunday. The service from Eoligarry is limited to 29 passengers and from Ardveenish to 12 passengers. The crossing from Eoligarry takes 40 minutes and from Ardveenish one hour. The single fare for adults is £5, children/concession £2.50, bicycles/parcels £2.50. Special hires from 7am to 7pm cost £44.65 plus fare, and from 7pm to 7am £66 plus fare. The ferry operates throughout the year and the timetable is published on a monthly basis. For enquiries and bookings contact *Faire*, tel 01851-701702 which is open Monday to Saturday from 9am to 5pm.

ACCOMMODATION

Mrs Marion Campbell: 2 Village, Eriskay, HS8 5JL (tel 01878-720274/236), three-star self-catering chalet, beside the beach, 2 bedrooms, sleeps 4. Open all year, from £180 a week, with a minimum let of one week.

For B&B try *Sue Macdonald* (tel 01878-720220).

EATING AND DRINKING

In the *Am Politician* pub, displayed with other recovered memorabilia, are two original bottles of whisky from the *SS Politician*, which sank en route to Jamaica in 1941 along with its cargo of bicycle parts, the equivalent of £3 million in Jamaican currency, and a hold full of whisky. Once you've seen the whisky and Jamaican money in the lounge bar have a dram before tasting the local seafood in the beer garden beside Ruba Bàn beach.

Am Politician: 3 Baile, Eriskay, PA81 5JJ (tel 01878-720246; e-mail Poli@btconnect.com). Serves meals at any time when the bar is open. Open all year every day:

	Lunchtime	Evening
January to May:	midday to 2pm	5pm to 8pm.
Sunday:	12.30pm to 2.30pm	7pm to 11pm.
June to September:	11am to 11pm.	
Sunday:	12.30pm to 11pm.	
October to December:	midday to 2pm	5pm to 8pm.
Sunday:	12.30pm to 2.30pm.	

We give these opening hours in full as many who make the long trek to the scene of this famous shipwreck have been disappointed to find the renowned bar closed.

Barra *(Barraigh)*

For Barra, small is beautiful. Some eight miles (13 km) long and four miles (6 km) wide, the island is a microcosm of all that's best in many of the other islands. Not too long ago Barra came first in a 'Beautiful Island' competition. The award was well deserved. Its central high landmass surrounded by wild moorland and the coastal areas are a beckoning blend of hills, springy machair and spacious white beaches. There are seven lochs, most of them good for fair-sized **brown trout** and **sea trout**. Barra is said to get its name from the island's mysterious patron saint, St Finbarr, also known as St Barr or Barrfinn, who built a church here in the 7th century. When the first Catholic priest to visit Barra since the Reformation arrived in 1625 he found that although there was no resident priest, the memory of St Finnbarr was still strong. Barra has been predominantly Catholic ever since, with two churches to the Church of Scotland's one. The name Barra once belonged to a whole group of islands, of which Barra is the largest. The islands to the north are Fiaray, Fuday, Orosay, Gighay, Hellisay, Flodday, and Fuiay; to the south lie Vatersay, Sandray, Flodday, Pabbay, Mingulay, and Berneray, which are also numbered among The Bishop's Isles. Barra has a population of around 1,400 within its 27 sq miles (70 sq km). Their mainstay is crofting and fishing.

CASTLEBAY

Castlebay is the port and main town of Barra. Although it has little architectural appeal, it has a humming life of its own. Though Gaelic is their mother tongue all inhabitants are happy to speak English. The Barraman is known as a great raconteur and some of the most ancient Hebridean legends have been preserved over the centuries by this island's story-tellers. Overlooking the centre of the town is the Catholic church of **Our Lady, Star of the Sea**, which was built in 1889. Nearby is the Castlebay Hotel, where trade was brisk in 1948 when film stars Joan Greenwood, Basil Radford, Gordon Jackson, James Robertson-Justice and a film crew of 80 spent three months in Barra during the making of the Ealing Studios classic comedy *Whisky Galore!*.

   The cadet branch of the MacNeil family that originally emigrated to Canada established its hereditary claim in 1915 when American architect Robert Lister MacNeil matriculated arms as the MacNeil of Barra in the Court of the Lord Lyon in Edinburgh. In 1937 he regained the ancestral estate and took over ruined Kisimul Castle and restoration work started in 1938. Members of the MacNeil clan throughout the world contributed to the restoration and except for some work requiring specialists it was carried out by descendants of the men who originally built the castle. The castle is now owned by the clan's 46th chief, Iain MacNeil, who teaches law in Chicago. He flies his standard from the tower when he's at home. **Kisimul *(Chiosmuil)* Castle** (tel 01871-810313) sits on a tiny rocky island in the bay. By far the oldest date attributed to the castle is AD 1030 but it's most likely that it was built around 1427, when the MacNeils were entrenched in Barra by title as well as right (and might). As you near the castle you'll see a large circle of rocks to the east of the landing place, which was once a basin built to trap fish left by the receding tide. Carved in stone above the entrance is the MacNeil coat of arms. On the far side is a stone bollard, worn smooth by the ropes used to moor the galleys of old. A folk tale says that a MacNeil chief declined to join Noah on his ark, saying that he had a galley of his own. There are parts of the castle you cannot enter but you can see the well conveniently fed by a natural underground pipe of fresh water, the 60 ft (18 m) Great Tower, the watch tower and dungeon, the barracks room, parapet walk, and the Great Hall. Steps inside the tower wall are of different heights to trip up invaders. It's said that a herald used to announce from the Great Tower: 'The MacNeil has dined. All the other princes of the earth may now eat' – although this is a legend also attributed to chiefs of other Scottish isles. Like the MacNeil's private apartment and the dungeon, the Great Tower has a toilet that's ingeniously flushed clean twice a day by the tide. Kisimul Castle is now in the care of the Historic Scotland, which pays £1 a year for the lease, plus a bottle of whisky. The boat trip from the jetty in Castlebay takes five minutes, weather permitting. The castle is open in summer from 9.30am to 6.30pm; October, Monday to Wednesday from 9.30am to 4.30pm, Thursday 9.30am to 12.30pm, Friday closed; Saturday 9.30am to 4.30pm, Sunday 2pm to 4.30pm. Admission for adults £3, reduced £2.30, children £1.

Barra Heritage and Cultural Centre (tel/fax 01871-810413) is the place for local history exhibitions and cultural activities. Open April to September, Monday to Friday from 11am to 5pm. Disabled access and toilets. Craft shop and café serving snacks, homebakes, coffee, and other refreshments. The centre is next to **Castlebay Community School** (tel 01871-810471), where you are welcome to use the swimming pool, library, sports hall, and other facilities. Outside the Tourist Information Centre in Castlebay a *Clach Shanais* information panel gives details in Gaelic, English, French and German of other sites and attractions around the island.

Further Afield

The highest of Barra's hills, Heaval (1,257 ft/383m), lies to the north of Castlebay. An easy walk to the top will give you views of the southern islands of Vatersay, Sandray, Pabbay, Mingulay, and Berneray. On the south-east flank of the hill is a white marble statue of Our Lady, Star of the Sea. A well-maintained 12-mile (19 km) road circles the island and going anti-clockwise from Castlebay passes through the settlements of Brevig, Skallary, Earsary, Boinabodach, Bruernish, Borve, and Tangusdale, most of which are Norse place-names.

Along the way is an islet where a statue of St Barr, holding aloft a shepherd's crook, was fixed in 1975 by local artist Margaret Somerville. Close to the dam near Northbay is **Queen Victoria's Rock**. This stands beside the A888 road and, when viewed from the Northbay side, looks remarkably like the old monarch in profile. The first aircraft to land on Barra arrived in 1933. The rocky terrain of the island meant that the planes had to land at the north end of the island on a vast expanse of tidal sand known as the **Cockle Strand**. They still do. The airport is at the edge of the beach that serves as a runway and it's pleasant to sit watching the plane from Glasgow or Benbecula apparently landing in the sea. The cockles here are big and particularly prized by locals who harvest them by hand. Until recently a company based in Sir Compton Mackenzie's old house at nearby *Suidheachan* used cockle shells to produce the rough harl facing favoured by many islanders for their houses. Nearby is **Cille Bharra**, the site of the 7th century Church of St Barr and the ruins of a 12th century monastic community with its mediaeval burial ground. A gravestone with a Celtic cross on one side and an inscription carved in Norse runes on the reverse was discovered here in 1865 and is regarded as evidence of Norse conversion to Christianity. One of Cille Bharra's two ruined chapels has been restored and contains a replica of this grave slab. The original is in the National Museum, in Edinburgh. Sir Compton Mackenzie, who lived and wrote in Barra from 1933 to 1945, is buried here. Overlooking Cille Bharra is Ben Eoligarry, rising to 335 ft (102 m). Beyond, past ruined **Eoligarry House** where the MacNeil chief lived after Kisimul Castle was destroyed by fire in 1795, the peninsula narrows to **Scurrival Point**, and high point Ben Scurrival (259 ft/79 m).

On the west coast is a wing of the Castlebay Heritage Centre, the thatched cottage of **An Dubharaigh**, which has been restored as a small museum and houses a collection of local artefacts and culture. It's open in summer only, Monday to Friday from 11am to 5pm. Its isolated location means a one mile (1.6 km) walk uphill from

Craigston village, near Borve Point. On the slopes above to the north is the chambered cairn of **Dùn Bharpa**, and there's another chambered cairn to the east of the cottage. On the coast near Borve Point are the ruins of an ancient chapel dedicated to Saint Brendan and thought to be a Christian relic from the time before the first Vikings stepped ashore. In a field between the road and the sea are the **Borve Standing Stones**. Stretches of white sandy beach punctuate the west coast. The one at **Halaman Bay** near Tangusdale, is one of the more beautiful. The hotel here was where the children of the Shah of Iran went to ground with their Barra nurse at the start of the revolution that stripped him of his title and brought Ayatollah Khomeini to power. Between Halaman Bay and Castlebay a path goes down to freshwater Loch Tangusdale where a mediaeval tower house, Dùn MhicLeòid, sits on top of an earlier Iron Age roundhouse on an island. This fortified tower of the Macleods, also known as Castle Sinclair, once had three storeys. Near the loch is a well dedicated to St Columba and there's a perfumery in the area where visitors are welcome.

Barra has a wealth of wildlife. Its varied habitats are rich in birdlife and plants and **seals, otters, dolphins, porpoises, whales** and **basking sharks** may be seen in the surrounding waters. More than 150 species of birds and 400 types of plants have been recorded.

GETTING THERE

British Airways (tel 08457-733377; www.britishairways.com), operated by Loganair (tel 0141-848 7594), flies to Barra from Glasgow on Monday to Friday at 9am and 1.35pm, and on Saturday at 11.35am, with an additional flight at 2.35pm from June to September. There is also a flight from Benbecula on Monday to Friday at 11am and 3.35pm. For its Glasgow flights Loganair operates two 18-seater Twin Otter aircraft which fly Barra-Benbecula-Barra and back to Glasgow.

You can experience the unique Barra beach take-off and landing and enjoy the breathtaking scenery on a quick excursion flight to and from Benbecula. The sightseer trip is bookable only on the day of departure at Barra airport. Once booked, the fare is non-refundable. Time for the out-and-back flight is one hour and 10 minutes. For sightseeing the plane flies at about 2,000 ft (610 m), compared to Glasgow flights at 5,000-8,000 ft (1,524-2,438 m). For more information contact the Highlands and Islands Airport manager or Loganair at Barra airport (tel 01871-890283).

Airport

Famed throughout the world as the airport with a runway that is washed twice a day by the tide, the Cockle Strand has been operating since 1935. The modern terminal building was opened on the north-east coast of the island in 1978. The airport is open Monday to Friday 9.45am to 12.15pm or 2pm to 4.30pm, depending on tide; Saturday 12.45pm to 2pm (and by arrangement). Disabled facilities exist within the terminal and staff are always available to assist. Keep off the beach when the windsock is flying.

Bus. The postbus which collects the mail from the aircraft will also take passengers to Castlebay.
Taxis from airport:
J Campbell: tel 01871-810216.
M Hatcher: tel 01871-810486.
D Sinclair: tel 01871-890253.

BY SEA

From Oban

Caledonian MacBrayne (The Ferry Terminal, Gourock PA19 1QP; tel 08705-650000; fax 01475-635235, reservations, and 01475-650100; fax 01475-637607, general enquiries; e-mail reservations@calmac.co.uk; www.calmac.co.uk) runs a car-passenger ferry service from Oban to Castlebay at 2.50pm on Monday, and Wednesday to Saturday. The journey takes about five hours. The single adult fare is £18.75, car and motorhome £67, and an additional £67 if you are towing a caravan or boat/baggage trailer, motorcycle £33.50, and bicycle £2. Discounted 'Five-Day Return' and 'Six Journey' tickets available.

From Mallaig

Alternatively, you can take the car-passenger ferry from Mallaig on Sunday at 6.10pm, arriving 9.55pm. The single adult fare is £18.85, car and motorhome £49.50, an additional £49.50 for a caravan or boat/baggage trailer, motorcycle £24.75, and bicycle £2. There is no 'Five-Day Return' ticket on this route but the 'Six-Journey' ticket is available. The local CalMac office is at the ferry terminal (tel 01871-810306).

From South Uist

The ferry leaves Lochboisdale at 7.30am on Tuesday and Thursday, 7.50pm on Friday, and 8.30am on Sunday. This costs £5.30 for a single adult ticket, car and motorhome £30.50, and an additional £30.50 for a caravan or boat/baggage trailer, motorcycle £15.25, and bicycle £2 single. 'Five-Day Return' and 'Six-Journey' tickets are available.

From Eriskay

The *Western Isles Council* (Balivanich, Benbecula, HS7 5LA; tel 01870-602425; fax 01870-602988) operates a passenger-only ferry from Ceann a Gharaidh, Eriskay, to Eoligarry and Ardveenish, Barra. There are two sailings Monday to Saturday to Eoligarry and daily sailings to Ardveenish Monday to Friday, with occasional Saturday sailings. No services on Sunday. The service to Eoligarry is limited to 29 passengers and to Ardveenish is limited to 12 passengers. The crossing between Barra and Eriskay takes 40 minutes and from Ardveenish one hour. Single fare for adults is £5, children/concession £2.50, bicycles/parcels £2.50. Special hires from 7am to 7pm cost £44.65 plus fare, and from 7pm to 7am £66 plus fare. The ferry operates throughout the year and the timetable is published on a monthly basis. For enquiries and bookings contact *Faire* (tel 01851-701702), which is open Monday to Saturday from 9am to 5pm.

GETTING AROUND

By Sea

Yachting around Barra is a favourite pastime and about 200 yachts a year visit Castlebay. It can become crowded in July and August. There are a dozen mooring buoys in Castlebay. There are no marina facilities, although there are pleasant anchorages in Vatersay Bay and at Northbay (Ardveenish). There are strong currents between the islands and a good pilot book should always be studied before venturing out. Current Admiralty or Imray charts should also be carried. Note that you can't buy these locally. Weather conditions can change dramatically within 2-3 hours, even in summer. Weather forecasts are broadcast by Stornoway MRSC on channels 10 and 73. Channel 16 announces the correct channel for the forecast, which is broadcast six times a day, starting at about 1am. The local harbour master can be contacted at the Caledonian MacBrayne office on the pier (tel 01878-720233).

By Road

A good if winding and narrow road starts in Castlebay and circles the island, with a smaller branch to the airport and the northern tip of the island, and another to

Vatersay via a causeway in the south. There's not much private traffic. One oddity is that Barra is a MOT-free island.

Bus

Royal Mail (tel 01246-546329; www.royalmail.co.uk) operates a 14-seater **Postbus** from Castlebay to Eoligarry, via Borve, on a circular route stopping at Cleat, Cockle Strand airport, Northbay, Bruernish, and Earsary. The Postbus also goes to Vatersay via Caolis and Uidh. The service operates from Monday to Saturday.

Taxis

Hatcher's Taxis Barra: 172 Earsary, Barra, HS9 5UR (tel 01871-810486, mobile 0771 404 8456; e-mail hatcher@isleofbarra.com). Taxi services and island tours.

Vehicle Rental

Barra Car Hire: Taigh a' Dot, Castlebay, HS9 5XD (tel 01871-810243). Cars for hire from £20 per day. Small, medium and large cars available all year. Free delivery to airport and ferry terminals, and throughout Barra and Vatersay. Reduced rates for weekly hire. All cars come with a map and guidebook.

MacMillan Self Drive: 30 Eoligarry, Barra, HS9 5YD (tel/fax 01871-890366). Self-drive and van car hire. Free delivery and collection on Barra. Cars from £20 per day. Discount for weekly hire.

Hector MacNeil: 68 Seann, Tangasdale, HS9 5XD (tel 01871-810262; e-mail ronnie.m@virgin.net). Has buses and minibuses for hire.

Cycle Hire

Cycling is popular so booking ahead is recommended.

Barra Cycle Hire: 29 St Brendan's Road, Barra, HS9 5XJ (tel 01871-810284). 220 yards (200 m) east of Castlebay, hires out bikes from £10 a day, weekly rates on request. Open Sundays.

Tours

Barra Boat Trips: George MacLeod (tel 01871-810223). Offers day trips by boat to Mingulay and other remote islands in The Bishop's Isles group.

ACCOMMODATION

Hotels

Castlebay Hotel: Castlebay, HS9 5XD (tel 01871-810223; fax 01871-810445). Three-star, family hotel overlooking the bay, en suite rooms. Open all year, from £35 B&B. Bar meals and snacks, teas and coffee. Open all year all day to 9pm. In the bar next door there's music on Saturday nights in winter and Friday and Saturday and the rest in summer.

   Craigard Hotel: Castlebay, HS9 5XD (tel 01871-810200; fax 01871-810726; e-mail craigard@isleofbarra.com). Three-star, family-run hotel, above the main village, overlooking the castle, en suite rooms. Open all year, from £31 a night. Good food using local beef, lamb, venison, prawns, scallops and lobsters. Open all year every day from 11am to 11pm.

   Isle of Barra Hotel: Tangasdale Beach, HS9 5XW (tel 01871-810383; fax 01871-810385; e-mail barrahotel@aol.com). Three-star, family run hotel, overlooking Atlantic beach, en suite rooms. Open end March to beginning-October and at New Year (Hogmanay), from £32 B&B. Four-course table d'hote menu specialising in local seafood, also an extensive bar menu. Open all week April to September, restaurant from 7pm to 8.30pm, cocktail bar from 12.30pm to 2.30pm and 6pm to 9pm.

Guest Houses

Tigh-na-Mara: Linda MacLean, Castlebay, HS9 5XD (tel 01871-810304; fax 01871-810858; e-mail tighnamara@isleofbarra.com). Three-star, traditional stone house, views of Castlebay harbour, two minutes' walk from ferry. Open April to October, from £22 a night.

B&B

Aros Cottage: Mrs C MacPherson, Bolnabodach, HS9 5UT (tel/fax 01871-890355; e-mail arosbarra@aol.com). Three-star, courtesy car will collect guests from airport and ferry terminals. Open April to October, from £20.

Barradale: Donald Campbell, 41 Kentangaval, Castlebay, HS9 5XL (tel 01871-810601). Two-star, overlooking Castlebay. Open May to September, from £18.

Faire Mhaoldonaich: Castlebay, HS9 5XN (tel 01871-810441; e-mail fm@isleofbarra.com). Three-star, overlooking Castlebay, 1 1/2 miles (2.4 km) from ferry terminal. Open April to October, from £20.

Grianamul: Mrs Anne MacNeil, Castlebay, HS9 5XD (tel 01871-810416; fax 01871-810319; e-mail macneilronnie@aol.com). Four-star, overlooking bay, 500m from ferry terminal, en suite rooms. Open April to October, from £22.

Northbay House: David and Diana Savory, Balnabodach, HS9 5UT (tel 01871-890255; e-mail northbayhouse@isleofbarra.com). Four-star, formerly Northbay School and Schoolhouse, built in 1882, in a sheltered hollow at the head of Loch na Obe. It is on the island bus route, 15 minutes from the ferry port at Castlebay, and from the airport. Self-catering and B&B accommodation. *Sgoil a' Mhorghain* is a self-contained self-catering unit sleeping four, suitable for disabled. B&B in twin-bedded room en-suite with shower and bath on ground floor, wheelchair access, and a 1st floor double en-suite bedroom with shower. B&B costs £22-26, self-catering costs £225-300 a week. Coin-operated washing machine and tumble dryer. Guest lounges. Private parking. No smoking and no pets allowed. Open all year. Book direct by telephone or e-mail, or through CalMac and Tourist Board.

Ocean View: Chrissie Beaton, 78 Borve, HS9 5XR (tel 01871-810590). Two-star, croft house near sandy beach, 2 1/2 miles (4 km) from ferry terminal. Open April to October, from £14.

Self-Catering

Arnamul: Mrs CP MacLeod, 3 Green, Castlebay, HS9 5XU (tel 01871-810376). Detached self-catering cottage on the west side, two twin bedded rooms, from £130 to £200 a week.

Margaret M Campbell: 77 Borve, HS9 5XR (tel 01871-810408). Two-star, two bedrooms, sleeps four. Open all year, from £80 to £180 a week.

Ceum a Bhealaich: 36 Kentangaval, Castlebay, HS9 5XL (tel 01871-810644; e-mail Mmac202477@aol.com). Three-star, self-contained flat just outside Castlebay, one mile (1.6 km) from ferry terminal, shops, post office and bank. Sleeps two, from £150 to £200 a week or £30 a night (electricity included).

Sheila MacIntosh: 137 Brevig, HS9 5UN (tel 01871-810580). Two-star, two miles (3.2 km) from Castlebay, one bedroom, sleeps two. Open May to September, from £195 a week.

Morag MacNeil: 1 Bogach, Northbay, HS9 5UX (tel/fax 01871-890286). Three-star, two bedrooms, sleeps four. Open all year, from £120 to £200 a week.

Caravans are available from:

Mrs Nan MacLean: 7 Leanish, Castlebay (tel 01871-810363; e-mail barramail@another.com). Fully-equipped, sleeps four people in two bedrooms, 2 miles (3.2 km) from Castlebay. Open April to September, from £80 to £100 a week.

Mrs Doreen MacNeil: Hillside, 25 Glen, Castlebay, HS9 5UQ (tel 01871-

810293; fax 01871-810493; e-mail macneil@lineone.net). Sleep 2-7. Open all year, from £80 to £135 a week.

Hostel

Dunard: Castlebay, HS9 5XD (tel/fax 01871-810443; e-mail dunard@ isleofbarrahostel.com). Family run, three minutes' walk from ferry terminal, 16 beds with four beds a room, twin, double and family rooms, non-smoking. From £10 a night, family room £32, double/twin £20 to £32 a night.

Camping

There are no official camping grounds on Barra but the Tourist Information Office will direct you to two or three spots near Castlebay, otherwise just ask a householder for permission to camp on their land.

EATING AND DRINKING

Best food is the pub grub found in the local hotels. For filling breakfasts and snacks try the café at the *Kisimul Gallery* in The Street, Castlebay, or the *Traigh Tearoom* in the airport terminal in Eoligarry. It's open all day throughout the summer and at arrival and departure times during the winter, serving a range of hot and cold snacks. You can look out to the beach through the windows and watch incoming planes landing on the beach.

ENTERTAINMENT

The *Feis Bharraigh* (Barra Festival) is the highlight of summer. It's one of the principal festivals in Scotland and attracts visitors and tutors from around the world during its two-week run. Otherwise, look out for advertised *ceilidhs*, film shows, and music and sing-songs in hotel bars.

SPORT AND RECREATION

Golf

Barra Golf Club (Cleat, Castlebay; tel 01871-810667; fax 01871-810658; e-mail golf@isleofbarra.com, or Donald Mackinnon, Secretary, Greian Head; tel 01871-810591; fax 01871-810418) claims to be the most westerly golf club in the UK, with possibly the world's largest natural bunker at the 4th hole. The fairways in this north-west corner of the island are a triumph of local ingenuity over an undulating landscape with rocky outcrops. Wire and post fencing to protect the greens from livestock are part of the golfing challenge on this nine-hole, par 68, golf course. Day tickets available from Castlebay Hotel, Craigard Hotel, Isle of Barra Hotel, Heathbank Hotel, Co-Chomunn Bharraidh shop, and the Tourist Information Centre. Visitor green fees £5 a day.

Fishing

Permits for all **trout fishing** are available from the Community Co-operative shop in Castlebay (tel 01871-810354). All lochs are suitable for float tubes, but it is advisable to wear a life-jacket. Of Barra's seven lochs **Loch Tangusdale** is the most attractive and productive. Wild brown trout of 1 lb-2 lb (500 g-1 kg) are taken fairly regularly. The **Barra Challenge** involves fishing all of the named lochs on Barra in one day and catching at least one fish in each. For more angling information contact:
Barra Angling Club: 40 St Brendans Road, Castlebay (tel 01871-810562). For fishing permits and boat hire.
Bill Donnelly: tel 0141-649 0170; e-mail bill496@aol.com.
Boat Hire: William Rusk, Eriskay Seascapes, 10 Port Patrick, Eriskay (tel 01878-720233). Has a 38 ft (12 m) charter boat *Brendan* for wildlife and dolphin tours in Sound of Eriskay and Barra, also inter-island ferry trips.

SHOPPING

The *Co-Chomunn Bharraidh* shop (Castlebay; tel 01871-810354), next to the tourist office has a wide range of goods, books and postcards. Open Monday to Saturday. Fishing permits are available from the shop.

The *Craft Shop Gallery*, on the main road at Skallary, three miles (5 km) from Castlebay, displays paintings of Barra and Vatersay, and retails handknits, pebble and shellwork. Open Monday to Friday 10am-5pm. Saturday 10am to midday.

Kisimul Gallery: The Street, Castlebay (tel 01871-810645). Situated between the Post Office and the bank, three minutes from the pier. It has a wide selection of Gaelic, Scottish and 'Sound of Barra' CDs and cassettes, and cards are a speciality. This gift shop, café and home bakery has take-away meals, snacks, tea and coffee, as well as craft items. It's open seven days a week in summer.

Hebridean Toffee: tel 01871-810898; fax 01871-810899; e-mail hebrideantoffee@ukonline.co.uk. Manufactures traditional handmade Scottish tablet in its Castlebay factory, overlooking Kisimul Castle. The toffee comes in a 350g and 200g gift boxes and can be sent anywhere in the world by the company's 'Sweet Thoughts' postal service. *Artyfacts* is a craft shop area within the factory selling unusual jewellery, hand-crafted gifts and ornaments.

HELP AND INFORMATION

Barra Tourist Office: Main Street, Castlebay (tel 01871-810336). Seasonal opening from early April to mid-October.

Castlebay Police Station (tel 01871-810276).

Doctor: Castlebay (tel 01871-810282).

Caledonian MacBrayne: Castlebay (tel 01871-810306). Ludag/Eoligarry/Ludag, passenger ferry only (tel 01878-720233).

Airport: Loganair (tel 01871-890283/388).

Northbay Post Office: tel 01871-890200. Is in St Barr's Church Hall and provides postal services to the north end of the island saving many the journey to Castlebay. It's open each morning from 10.30am to 12.30pm, Monday to Friday.

The *Royal Bank of Scotland* in Castlebay (tel 01871-810281) does not have an ATM cash machine, but the Co-op and Spar stores offer Switch and Delta cash-back facilities.

Co-Chomunn Bharraigh: Barra Community Co-operative (tel 01871-810354).

Voluntary Action Bureau: tel 01871-810401.

Comhairle nan Eilean Siar: tel 01871-810431.

There is a public library at Castlebay Community School (tel 01871-810471) where Internet access is available for a small charge.

Guth Bharraidh: Castlebay (tel 01871-810401). Is Barra's weekly newspaper. It's produced by *Voluntary Action Barra and Vatersay* and is a way of distributing information and news around the island. It is known locally as the *Guth*.

The Bishop's Isles

Vatersay and the uninhabited islands of Sandray, Pabbay, Mingulay, and Berneray, also known as Barra Head, make up the southern chain of The Bishop's Isles.

VATERSAY *(Bhatarsaigh)*

Vatersay has been the most southerly inhabited island of the Outer Hebrides since Mingulay, further south, was abandoned in 1912. The H-shaped island lies about

1½ miles (2.4 km) across the water from Castlebay, Barra. The two have been linked since 1990 by causeway. The strip of machair land representing the crossbar has beaches on both sides and connects the two main areas of the island. The islands on the western side are dangerously exposed, but the beach on the east side is one of the safest in Barra for swimming. It was on the west side that the *Annie Jane*, an emigrant sailing ship bound for Canada, was wrecked in 1853 with more than 400 people on board. A monument stands on the dunes at *Traigh Siar* (West Beach) marking the burial site of the 350 emigrants who died when the 1,294-ton three-master struck and foundered. The inscription on the granite column reads: 'On 28th September 1853 the ship *Annie Jane* with emigrants from Liverpool to Quebec was totally wrecked in this bay and three-fourths of the crew and passengers numbering about 350 men, women and children were drowned and their bodies interred here.' Bob Charnley recounts the full story of this tragedy in his book *Shipwrecked on Vatersay!* (Maclean Press, Isle of Skye, 1992). Wreckage from another era lies above the bayside road, the remains of a World War II Catalina flying boat that crashed in May 1944, killing three of its nine-man crew.

The remains of a 2,000-year-old circular fortified dwelling house, *Dun Bhatarsaigh*, occupy a prominent hilltop to the south of West Beach. From the dun you can see the village in the southern part of the island and in the foreground the ruins of **Vatersay House**, which was built in the early 19th century during the time Colonel Gordon of Cluny owned the island. Survivors of the *Annie Jane* shipwreck were given grudging shelter here after the sinking. On the rocky ground to the south of Vatersay House there's evidence of a Bronze Age settlement, including a burial cairn and a solitary standing stone. From here there are spectacular views of the uninhabited islands to the south and to the east lies the beautiful beach at South Bay (*Bagh a Deas*).

The main hills on Vatersay are Theisabhal Mòr (623 ft/190 m) and Theisabhal Beag (554 ft/169 m) – Big and Little Heishival – facing Barra, and Beinn Ruilibreac (272 ft/83 m) in the south, looking out to Sandray. They are joined by the narrow neck of sand and machair which holds the north and south halves of Vatersay together. In the south is the island's main settlement, which is also called Vatersay. Most of the island's residents – just over 70 – live here. It has a school and a post office. Off the north-eastern tip beyond the road-end at Uidhe is the small tidal island of Uinessan, where there are the remains of an old chapel dedicated to St Brendan. Tradition says that Marion of the Heads is buried on Uinessan. She lived in the early 15th century and got her name from her habit of ordering the beheading of anyone she disliked, including her stepsons. Beyond is the Sea of the Hebrides where a 1.8-mile (3 km) chain of islets, skerries, and stacks runs out to the dark 499 ft (152 m) hump of *Maol Dòmhnaich*. This 193-acre (78 ha) island once had a chapel thought to have been named for St Duncan and was at one time used as a deer park by the MacNeil of Kisimul Castle.

In the late 19th century Lady Gordon Cathcart inherited Vatersay. She only once visited the island during the 54 years she owned it and the entire island was farmed as a single holding at a time islanders everywhere in the Western Isles were desperate for land. In 1906, a group of men, incensed by the lack of crofting land, took over the island and began farming after one man had invoked ancient island rights to land title by erecting a thatched makeshift dwelling on Vatersay and lighting a fire – all within the space of a day. Ten men, six from Barra and four from Mingulay – known to history as the Vatersay Raiders – were arrested, tried and sentenced to imprisonment but because of the subsequent public outcry were soon released. In 1909, the government's Congested Districts Board – later the Department of Agriculture – bought the island and created 58 crofting holdings and divided them between four small settlements, after which Vatersay flourished. Following the land distribution the village of Eòrasdail was established by Mingulay crofter-fishermen in the south-east. This was inhabited as recently as the 1970s. Today it is a ghost village. The island is rich in wildlife and the Vatersay *Clach Shanais* ('Interpretation Stone') information panel conveniently located above the Barra end of the Vatersay causeway near the War Memorial details some of the island's distinctive plants, birds and other wildlife, as well as interesting historical facts. The coastal machair grassland – naturally enriched with calcium from the shell-sand blown from the shore – cliffs, and sandy beaches provide a variety of habitats, each with its distinctive plants, birds and other wildlife. In summer the plantlife of the machair grows rapidly, and grazing cattle help to keep down tall grass, allowing smaller plants to flourish in the sunlight and create the splendid display of wild flowers associated with this unique habitat. The **golden eagle** sailing on a 7 ft (2 m) wingspan is not uncommon, and usually frequenting the same territory is the **buzzard**. Twitchers should also spot **ravens**, **hooded crows**, **lapwings**, **oystercatchers**, **golden plovers**, **snipe**, **redshank** and even **corncrakes** around the machair. Over the sea look for **cormorants**, **gannets**, **eiders**, and **shags**.

Vatersay Walk. This is a moderate to demanding Heritage Trail of 4 miles (6 km) and should take about 3 hours to complete. A leaflet giving details of the walk is available from the Tourist Information Centre, in Castlebay.

GETTING AROUND

Until the Vatersay causeway was built in 1990 it was customary for crofters on Vatersay to swim their cattle across the Sound of Vatersay to Barra on their way to market. Agitation for a permanent link with Barra reached a peak in the late 1980s after a prize bull called Bernie was swept away and drowned. The causeway also helped to rejuvenate the island where the population had dropped to about 60 people and the school was down to six pupils. Barra people say a policeman used to take the ferry across to Vatersay once a year, just to let the residents know they still lived in Britain. They lived in a world of their own, a world where children drove cars and no one paid for a TV licence. The causeway has changed all that. Now the Barra doctor – and a policeman – can get across to Vatersay in less than 10 minutes. There are only five miles (8 km) of surfaced single-track road on Vatersay, so walking and cycling are the best ways of seeing what the island has to offer.

ACCOMMODATION

Self-Catering

School House: Patricia Barron, Vatersay, HS9 5YW (tel/fax 01871-810283; e-mail vatersayschool@aol.com). Converted school, overlooking Vatersay bay and beach, no smoking, three bedrooms, sleeps 6-8. Castlebay five miles (8 km) away. Open April to December, from £350 to £550 a week.

Mrs E Sinclair: 113 Nightingale Lane, London, N8 7LG (tel 020-8348 6770), two-star, three-bedroomed cottage, sleeps 7. Open all year, from £125 to £200 a week.

SANDRAY *(Sanndraigh)*

Sandray is the most northerly of the four isolated islands which, with Vatersay, make up The Bishop's Isles. Virtually all the other islands scattered in the waters to the west and south of the Outer Hebrides are shaped like bits of a fiendish jigsaw puzzle. Sandray is the exception: it's roughly circular – a bit like an amoeba getting ready to split – with a diameter of about 2 miles (3 km) and an area of 950 acres (384 ha). Vatersay lies to the north about half a mile (0.8 km) away and Pabbay is 2¹/₂ miles (4 km) to the south-west. More or less in between are the hilly and rocky islets of Flodaigh, Lingeigh, and Greanamul. Flodaigh is unique, not for its central natural rocky arch or its **Atlantic grey seal** nursery, but for the fact that it is the only known home of a sub-species of the **Scottish dark green fritillary butterfly**. Sandray gets its name from the Gaelic, which is thought to derive in turn from the Old Norse for 'Sand Isle.' Along its eastern shore is a high, broad stretch of white sand dunes that makes Sandray a distinctive landmark from the sea. The island's high point, Cairn Galtar, is a grassy summit rising 679 ft (207 m) in the middle of the island. Between this and the eastern dunes is Carnat at 587 ft (179 m).

There are several beaches where boats can land on Sandray, there are no high cliffs to worry about, pleasant grassy areas near the coast, two streams and freshwater Reed Loch (*Loch na Cuilce*), all of which combined to attract settlers in prehistoric times. Archaeologists have turned up evidence of sites going back as far as Neolithic times. As well as Neolithic chambered tombs, Bronze Age cairns and Standing Stones, there's an Iron Age dun, prominent on a ridge on Cairn Galtar's western slopes. Its walls survive in places to a height of nearly 6¹/₂ ft (2 m). In an old sand-covered graveyard above White Bay (*Bàgh Bàn*) in the northeast are traces of the mediaeval chapel dedicated to St Bride or Bridget (*Cille Bhride*). The chapel was used by the island's crofting families as late as the early 18th century. Round about 1835, Sandray was turned over to grazing for sheep and the tenant population was evicted. The last people to live there were land raiders from the nearby island of Mingulay, five families who settled in the northwest at Sheader in 1908. Their ruined houses, built end-to-end, can still be seen. Early in 1911 the last of these left Sandray to settle on Vatersay, where croft land had been bought by the government for distribution to the landless. The island has not been permanently inhabited since then. Sandray is now used by a group of Barra crofters as grazing grounds for their sheep, which share the island's grassland with a constantly multiplying population of rabbits.

An odd story about Sandray concerns the disappearance in the early 18th century of a girl from the village of Sheader. The girl vanished on her way home from a village where her mother had sent her for milk. Her broken pail was discovered but no trace of the girl was ever found on the island. Many years later some Scottish seamen were sitting in a bar in the West Indies when a woman asked them where they came from. It was the missing Sandray girl. She said she had been abducted by the crew of a passing boat and sold into slavery. It was not uncommon in the 1700s for people from the more remote islands to be tricked into boarding Irish vessels and then carried off to be sold as slaves in the sugar plantations of the West Indies.

PABBAY *(Pabbaigh)*

Pabbay's Gaelic name comes from the old Norse *Papa-ey*, Hermit's Isle or Priest's Island, a reference to the occupants of the island at the time the Norse arrived to settle. Pabbay was a name given by the Vikings to a number of islets in the Hebrides, which indicates that they were all occupied in early Christian times. Like its many namesakes off the west of Scotland the island was chosen for its isolation by Celtic hermits seeking a remote religious retreat. The island, lying roughly half-way between Sandray and Mingulay, is smaller than either of its neighbours and measures about 1¹/₄ miles (2 km) in length by a mile (1.6 km) wide. Pabbay's highest point and one hill is The Hoe (*An Todha*) whose summit rises 561 ft (171 m) above a conspicuous headland in the south-west with massive arched overhanging cliffs. From its heather-clad hill the land slopes grassily to a steep sand dune in the east sheltering White Bay (*Bàgh Bàn*) and its dazzling beach, above which there is the site of an old chapel and burial ground. In the north-east corner of the island, where it joins the tidal island of Rosinish is an Iron

Age dun, or galleried broch, known as the Red Fort (*Dunan Ruadh*). The finger-like Rosinish peninsula takes its name from the old Norse for 'Horse Headland.'

Apart from a rogueish history of illicit whisky distilling, Pabbay is especially of interest to archaeologists because it is the site of one of only two Pictish symbol stones or incised slabs found in the Outer Hebrides. The symbol stone slab is 3 ft 6 inches (1.1 m) long. It is incised with characteristic Pictish symbols, a crescent and V-rod, and a lily, which date the slab to sometime during the two centuries before the Picts were converted to Christianity around the 8th century. The slab also bears a cross carved on it at a later date. The symbol stone was found in 1889 on the mound between the bay and the ruins of an old settlement. Three other slabs bearing incised crosses have also been found. Two of them stand near the top of the mound, and probably mark ancient graves. Pabbay was undoubtedly occupied in Neolithic or Bronze Age times, as is indicated by hut circles, round houses, and a standing stone. Neolithic chambered tombs have been found around the old settlement and other possible burial cairns have been discovered on the island and on the Rosinish peninsula. There are short stretches of cliff up to 400 ft (120 m) high in the west but for some reason they do not seem to be attractive to the breeding seabirds which flock to surrounding islands, although there are plenty of ground nesters around and lots of rabbits. There is a steep-sided depression in the middle of the island full of marshy peat bog.

In 1844 a Mingulay girl had a second-sight vision in which she saw an island fishing boat capsize, drowning all the men in it. After she recounted this to villagers they pin-pointed the area as the 'Sea of the Ghosts' and it was in this precise area that disaster struck the community in 1897. Its only boat sank in a storm and all five crew members were drowned, four of them the main breadwinners on Pabbay. Some saw the tragedy as an act of God and divine retribution for the whisky distilling secretly taking place. The island never recovered from this blow and its people started to drift away. By 1912 Pabbay was deserted and has since been used only for grazing. Just over a mile (1.6 km) out in the Atlantic to the south-west is the islet of Outer Heisker (*Theisgeir a-muigh*), which is also traditionally Pabbay grazing ground.

MINGULAY *(Miughlaigh)*

It was described in 1897 as 'an island so remote that it is easier to reach America than to get there' and 19th century school inspector William Jolly likened it to a 'rude figure eight written with a shaky pen.' Both reports were referring to the island of Mingulay, 'Big Isle' in the Old Norse tongue, and the last but one in the chain of small southern islands. Mingulay is 2½ miles (4 km) from north to south, and 1¾ miles (3 km) across. In area it covers 1,581 acres (640 ha). It has the highest uplands of all the surrounding islands, rising at the rounded grassy summit of Cànan to 891 ft (273 m). The sea cliffs in the west are awesome, with **Biulacraig** rising sheer for a height of some 751 ft (229 m). The island was once owned by the MacNeil of Barra and this stupendous cliff was the crest of the clan and its name the clan's battle cry. On a clear day its top can be seen from Barra. The cliffs of Mingulay are recognised as one of the most important breeding sites for seabirds off the west of Scotland and along with nearby Berneray they were created a Site of Special Scientific Interest in 1983 and a Special Protection Area in 1994. Breeding birds include nearly 17,000 pairs of **razorbill**, some 12% of the British population; 31,000 individual **guillemot** (3%); 10,500 pairs of **fulmar** (2%); 8,600 pairs of **kittiwake** (2%); and more than 700 pairs of **shag** (2%). In addition to these, twitchers can expect to see **storm petrel**, **common** and **arctic terns**, **great skua**, **black guillemot**, and **puffin**, as well as four varieties of **gull**, which also breed on the island. To see them, however, you've first got to get to

Mingulay and this is not always easy. To get there from Barra, 12 miles (19 km) distant, boats have to contend with the fierce tidal races, as well as with unpredictable and rapidly changing sea and weather conditions. There are no sheltered landing places on the island. The normal landing place is Mingulay Bay (*Bàgh Mhiùghlaig*), also known as Village Bay, which gets lashed by wind and swell from virtually every direction except the west. To get ashore you have to jump on to the rocks. Boats with reliable engines mean it's now easier getting there than it was in the days of oars and sail, but landing still depends on the size of the swell. Parish priest Father Allan McDonald once sailed to Mingulay to hold a service, meaning to return the same evening in order to marry a young couple the next day in Barra. Wind and waves kept him an unwilling guest and it was more than seven weeks before he could get home. One of the MacNeill's rent collectors had a longer enforced stay, but for a different reason. He landed on Mingulay to find most of the islanders dead or dying from the plague. When they heard this news his boatmen took fright and rowed away, leaving him alone on the island. He had to stay on Mingulay for a year before it was thought safe to pick him up. The 735 ft (224 m) hilltop in the north where he used to sit looking out in hope of relief bears his name, **Macphee's Hill**.

The towering sea stack of 368 ft (112 m) **Lianamul** off the western coast was once connected to Mingulay by a rope bridge. Men used to heave their sheep across this flimsy contraption to take advantage of the grazing. The islanders also used to climb the cliffs and crags to gather sea birds' eggs. Puffins today nest here on ledges among the stacks and caves. Over the years they have ousted the Manx shearwaters the islanders used to harvest in the late 18th century for food and to pay the rent. As on the remote island of St Kilda, Mingulay's cragsmen 'never wore a shoe, nor a bonnet' and girls always looked for a husband who was 'stout-footed and thick ankled' to keep the cottage stocked with food. The cliffs are riddled with chasms, arches and caves which boom and bellow when the sea rushes into them. The resulting snort and spray used to be described by the islanders as 'the old woman taking snuff.' Supposedly hidden in one of the sea caves on the west coast is a chest of French gold intended to pay the clansmen who joined Bonnie Prince Charlie in the 1745 Jacobite Rising, but then legend also says the gold was stashed in a cave on Benbecula, or in another on Barra.

A stone cist, or burial chamber, dating back to the Bronze Age has been discovered on the island and there are at least two Iron Age sites, a midden north of the deserted village, and **Dun Mingulay** in the south-west, where a stretch of 6 ft (2 m) thick wall reinforces a rock face across the neck of a narrow peninsula. There are several Christian era sites with religious associations, including a chapel, but little is known about them and whatever structures there were have mouldered away or vanished under the sand. The Gaelic-speaking people of Mingulay used to call their home *Eilean Mo Chridhe*, the 'Isle of My Heart.' They did not believe there was any better place to be, but gradually the people whose forebears had lived on the island for centuries were forced to leave. In the 1880s, Mingulay had a population of about 150 people; by 1912 the island was deserted and areas of the settlement above the head of Village Bay were soon covered by wind-blown shell sand. Today, the lower parts of the village have disappeared under sand up to 5 ft (1½ m) deep. Weeds associated with cultivation have thinned out or vanished completely, while bracken and formerly rare heather are now common. **Sea holly** grows well on Mingulay, and **sea milkwort**, normally found only at sea level, grows on the cliff-tops encouraged by the spray and seagull guano. Mingulay belongs to The *National Trust for Scotland* (NTS), which bought the island in mid-2000. Scottish Natural Heritage (SNH) should be contacted by anyone planning a visit so that they can advise on any particular sensitivities (Stornoway; tel 01851-705258, or South Uist; tel 01870-620238).

BERNERAY *(Bearnaraigh)*

Berneray, or Barra Head, is as far south as you can go in the Outer Hebrides and only the most determined island-hopper ever gets here, although either the pier in a northern sheltered inlet or the heli-pad at the lighthouse can facilitate your visit. It's the smallest of The Bishop's Isles. The island is two miles (3 km) long by less than a mile (1.6 km) wide and gets its name from the old Norse *Bjarnaray*, meaning Bjorn's Isle. From the sea it looks like a tilted wedge of cheese. From the eastern end the land rises to an awesome beetling cliff of 622 ft (190 m) in the west, surmounted by the 60 ft-high (18 m) Barra Head lighthouse, first lit on 15 October 1833, from which a light beams out at an elevation of 682 ft (207 m) above the sea. It was designed and built by famous Scottish lighthouse engineer Robert Stevenson for the Commissioners of Northern Lighthouses, later the Northern Lighthouse Board, who wanted to improve marine navigational aids and make the area safer for shipping. Barra Head was chosen as the site for the lighthouse because it would be visible from almost every direction. In clear weather, the light could be seen for a distance of 33 miles (53 km). There were resident keepers until the lighthouse was automated in 1980. These days the light is powered by batteries charged by two generators, which are remotely controlled from Edinburgh, nearly 200 miles (322 km) away as the gull flies.

The island is surrounded by deep water and the tall cliffs at Skate Point and the nearby lighthouse promontory take the full pounding of the Atlantic Ocean in frequent storms. During the construction of the lighthouse Robert Stevenson wrote: 'On the face of the precipitous cliffs the winds and seas acquire a force...never experienced elsewhere. It is not indeed uncommon to be actually struck down by the more violent and sudden gusts of wind, while the seas remove incredible masses or rock.' Small fish have been found on top of the cliffs after wild storms and in 1836 there were reports that a rock weighing 42 tons had been shifted nearly 5 ft (1½ m) by the violence of one storm. After spending time in the lighthouse in 1868, visiting naturalist Captain Elwes wrote:

> It was the grandest sight I ever experienced, to look out of the window of the lighthouse on a very stormy day, and see oneself hanging, as it were, over the ocean, surrounded on three sides by a fearful chasm in which the air was so thickly crowded with birds as to produce the appearance of a heavy snowstorm, whilst the cries of these myriads, mingled with the roar of the ocean and the howling of the tremendous gusts of wind coming up from below as it forced through a blast pipe, made it almost impossible to hear a person speak.

A plane crashed into the cliffs near the lighthouse during such a storm in World War II but no one heard it. The wreckage was discovered by accident years later. Cliffs aside, Berneray is less interesting than the surrounding islands. It has no glen, bay or beach, and its streams are small and few. The only flattish area is to the north-east, which was once the preferred area of settlement. A surfaced track wanders across the middle of the island from the pier on the north shore to the lighthouse on the cliffs in the west. For such a small island a large number of prehistoric sites have been identified – more than 80 so far – with the earliest being Neolithic chambered tombs and Bronze Age burial cairns. Signs of possible Iron Age hut circles have also been found. On the promontory near the lighthouse are the remains of two ancient forts. The most prominent of these sites is the Iron Age dun, Dùn Sròn an Dùin. North of the lighthouse the promontory was once cut off by a massive defensive stone wall known as Dùn Briste and also probably dating from the Iron Age. Around the settlement area are later boat-shaped sites resembling the Viking boat graves known elsewhere and are regarded as evidence of past Norse occupation.

Berneray was declared a Site of Special Scientific Interest (SSSI) in 1983, along with Mingulay, and in 1994 was also made a Special Protection Area (SPA). This designation is given to the breeding grounds of internationally important seabird populations. Colonies of **kittiwake, guillemot, auks, razorbills**, and **puffins** used to be caught for food by the islanders. They also provided a handy supply of eggs to eat and feathers to sell. One man was recorded in the late 1880s as catching about 600 birds with a pole and noose in a single day. In 1863 the *Shamrock*, commanded by a Captain Otter, visited Berneray while mapping islands for the Admiralty. On board the *Shamrock* was indefatigable world traveller and writer Isabella Bird, who noted for posterity that the crinoline had made it to Berneray and was worn by some island women, although their fashion statement was made out of the hoops from barrels they had salvaged from a shipwreck. The common currency of Berneray was dried skate, and this is what the locals offered during the three hours they spent on board the *Shamrock* bargaining for items that took their fancy. One of the crew members of the *Shamrock* in particular had the islanders rubber-necking. 'It seemed they were never weary of the sight of the black cook, whom at first they had taken for the devil,' wrote Ms Bird. After many years of dwindling occupation Berneray was effectively deserted in about 1910. It is now used for grazing, and breeding ewes are kept there by Barra crofters.

St Kilda

If any name is guaranteed to stir excitement among island lovers that name is St Kilda, so remote that it has long been known as 'The Island on the Edge of the Sea,' although it is not a single island at all, but an archipelago of eight small islands and sea stacks, lying 41 miles (66 km) out in the Atlantic Ocean to the west of the Outer Hebrides. On a good day you can see St Kilda from there as a dark smudge on the horizon. As no saint of this name has been traced St Kilda is thought to derive from the Old Norse *skildir*, meaning 'shields,' while main island Hirta is believed to get its name from the Old Norse for deer, because its peaks and jagged sea stack pinnacles resemble stags' antlers when seen from the sea.

If you can get to St Kilda its spectacular scenery and vast seabird populations make for a truly memorable trip. First impressions on approaching St Kilda by sea are of the scale and ruggedness of the islands and of the great throngs of seabirds – a snowstorm of gannets, circling and plunging off Boreray, puffins whirring up and down the steep grassy slopes of Dun, and guillemots bobbing over the surface of the sea as far as you can see. A naturalist who visited wrote in 1947: *Whatever he studies, the future observer of St Kilda will be haunted the rest of his life by the place, and tantalised by the impossibility of describing it to those who have not seen it.* The National Nature Reserve is managed by Scottish Natural Heritage and the entire St Kilda group is owned by the National Trust for Scotland, which takes work parties out to the islands throughout the summer. Once you have visited you can join the *St Kilda Club*, once exclusively for people who had spent at least 24 hours on the islands but which now also offers 'Friend of St Kilda' membership to anyone genuinely interested in the St Kilda group. Sailing membership is open to anyone who has sailed to and landed on St Kilda. For more information contact Colin Govier, secretary/treasurer (7 Montpelier Terrace, Edinburgh, EH10 4NE; tel 0131-229 0876, evenings).

GEOGRAPHY
Hirta, Dun, Soay, and Boreray are the main islands of the St Kilda archipelago lying 41 miles (66 km) off North Uist in the Outer Hebrides, and 110 miles (177 km) from the Scottish mainland. The principal island in the group is Hirta (*Hiort*), 1.9 miles miles (3 km) east to west and barely 1.2 miles (2 km) from north to south. It is the remotest inhabited island in Britain and has the highest sea cliff in the British Isles, a precipice of nearly 1,411 ft (430 m) on the north face of Hirta's highest point, Conachair. The other sizeable peaks on the island are Mullach Mór (1,184 ft/361 m), Mullach Bi (1,181 ft/360 m), Oiseval (961 ft/293 m), and Ruabhal (728 ft/222 m). Hirta's 1,575 acres (637 ha) are kept green and fertile by constant manuring, courtesy of its vast population of seabirds, and this is the only island in the group ever to have been permanently settled. **Dun** is the mile-long (1.6 km) outer arm of Village Bay, and acts as a huge natural rocky breakwater to protect both anchorage and bayside village from west and south-west gales and the relentless pounding of the Atlantic. Dun is separated from Hirta by a narrow channel little more than 50 yards wide which it's said can be boulder-hopped across if the tide is exceptionally low. Dun's jagged steep spinal ridge varies from 100 ft (30 m) to 200 ft (60 m) wide and is honeycombed with numerous caves and tunnels, including two that bore through to the Atlantic. The largest is the Dun Arch. Nearly two miles (3 km) out from Dun is the southern outlier of Levenish, a blunt precipitous rock pyramid which stands like a sentinel at the approach to Village Bay. **Soay** lies only 550 yards (500 m) off the north-west point of Hirta, cut off by a narrow sound that's only 26 ft (8 m) deep at low water. It lies opposite The Cambir in Hirta's north-west corner, sheltering Glen Bay from the fury of the westerlies. Surrounding Soay are satellites **Stac Soay**, **Stac Dona**, and **Stac na Biorach**. **Boreray** lies about four miles (6 km) to the north-east of Hirta. Off its rock-bound shores are **Stac Lee** and **Stac an Armin**, at 643 ft (196 m) the highest sea stack in the British Isles. Britain's last great auk was beaten to death on Stac an Armin in 1840 by visiting St Kildan bird hunters who, incredibly, thought it was a witch responsible for calling up a violent storm.

Geology
St Kilda is all that remains above sea level of a large volcano that was probably active around 55-60-million years ago. The ancient volcano's rim is defined by Soay, the west and south coastline of Hirta, Dun, Levenish and an undersea ridge that swings north towards Boreray. The underlying rocks – granite, gabbro and dolerite – have been eroded into rugged coastlines on all four main islands and into staggering pinnacles on their offshore stacks. Some of the rock is highly magnetic and enough so to make compass readings unreliable. The cliffs of the western edge of Hirta are splintered dark gabbro; the eastern side, where the rounded hills of Conachair and Oiseval have weathered into tenements of slabs and ledges, are largely buff-coloured granite. Unlike the Western Isles, St Kilda was probably never covered by the grinding glaciers that deeply scored and polished most of Britain and sent it into deep freeze during the last Ice Age, more than 10,000 years ago, and so its skyline rocks remain virtually as sharp and jagged as they were when they first rose from the sea.

CLIMATE
St Kilda has a micro-climate all its own; it even makes its own clouds, thanks to its lofty heights. The first sign of St Kilda from the sea is usually the sight of these clouds shrouding the summits of high points Conachair and Oiseval. Weather on and around the islands can be extreme, so be prepared for all conditions. Wind can sometimes gust up to 130 mph (209 km/h) and the now long-gone islanders used to fill their boat with stones in winter to stop it being blown away. If you are

sailing your own boat note that the anchorage in Village Bay is especially exposed to east winds and boats sometimes have to race back to North Uist for shelter when the easterlies are blowing. It can also rain for two or three weeks without let-up. On average, annual rainfall is about the same as in the Outer Hebrides, around 50 inches (1,270 mm), falling mostly in December and January. Days are short in winter and it can get frosty and sometimes snows, but this never lies long and the climate is generally mild. Summer brings long hours of daylight and it can even get really hot and sunny. Nights last only an hour in midsummer. One of the first visitors to record his impressions of St Kilda was clergyman Donald Munro, High Dean of the Isles, who was there in 1549. He approached through seas that were, he wrote, 'stark and verie evill.' Like the Dean you can experience serious bad weather which, even in summer, can delay your arrival or departure for days. Be prepared for this, and remember that you can't buy supplies on St Kilda.

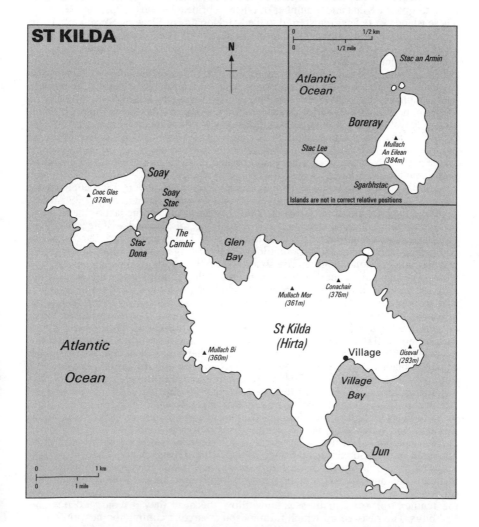

HISTORY

The earliest settlers probably arrived on Hirta around 5,000 years ago and from that time the island was inhabited virtually continuously until the last 36 St Kildans left the island in August 1930. Archaeological investigations have turned up Neolithic flaked stone tools and indications of structures dating back to the Bronze Age, and others suggesting an Iron Age presence. Intriguingly, palaeobotanists have done pollen research which shows the existence 5,000 years ago of plants usually associated with the arrival of humans. The Vikings either established a settlement on Hirta or at least used it regularly as a stop-over to replenish their longships as not only do Norse names like Oiseval ('East Hill'), Soay ('Sheep Isle') and Boreray ('North Isle') refer to landmarks easily seen from the sea, but they left pottery shards, a sword, and the odd brooch lying around.

Scottish King Robert II ratified a charter in 1373 which allowed John, Lord of the Isles, to give St Kilda and a number of other Hebridean islands to his son, Reginald. These islands were later transferred to the MacDonalds of Sleat, on Skye. From them it passed in the mid-15th century to the Macleods of Harris, who had their seat at Dunvegan, on Skye. It remained Macleod property until the Fifth Marquis of Bute, a keen 'twitcher,' bought it as a bird sanctuary in 1934. He bequeathed it to the National Trust for Scotland in 1957 and NTS in turn leased the entire archipelago to Scottish Natural Heritage's predecessor, the Nature Conservancy Council, to manage as a National Nature Reserve. Some land on Hirta was sub-leased to the Ministry of Defence in 1957 as the site for a radar-tracking station for the rocket range on South Uist. A Royal Artillery unit ran this until 1998, when the base on Hirta was taken over by a civilian contract management company. The base itself is something of an eyesore on the foreshore, but on the plus side it provides a lot of the infrastructure and services that make operations easier for the conservation bodies working on St Kilda, and for the 2,000 or so people who visit every year.

Hirta's population reached its peak in 1697, when there were 180 people living there. The number dwindled until by 1930 only 36 were left. On Friday 29 August 1930 the fisheries protection cruiser *HMS Harebell* took off the last of these. They left their doors open and in each house a small pile of oats and a Bible. Hirta then remained deserted until the arrival of the military. The evacuation of the last of the St Kildans from Hirta was a traumatic event which over the years has haunted the popular imagination and given rise to a flood of articles, books, poems, songs, and films. The general theme has been of people living a utopian life away from the evils of the world, and their departure a modern Paradise Lost. Life in St Kilda was, in fact, anything but utopian, with eight out of 10 babies dying of tetanus within eight days of birth because the old midwives insisted on smearing the navel of the newborn with a poultice of fulmar oil and dung. Daily fare was a monotonous diet of seabirds, seabirds' eggs, and young seabirds, with the occasional bit of mutton or fish. Birds were either smoked or wind-dried in the drystone beehive structures known as *cleits*, which are still to be seen in their hundreds all over the island. Eggs were also preserved in the *cleits*, buried in peat ash for up to eight months to heighten the flavour. In one year in the late 17th century, 16,000 eggs and more than 22,000 gannets were consumed in the village. In the mid-19th century Sir William Jardine declared, 'We have eaten them boiled like ham and found them neither strong, fishy, nor unpalatable.' The eggs, said to be best eaten hard-boiled with salt and celery, were sold in London and even appeared on the Buckingham Palace dining table during Queen Victoria's reign. As well as providing food the bones of gannets made useful implements and turned inside out their skins made passable lightweight shoes. Fulmar feathers and oil were exported to the mainland and used to pay rent. The government bought the feathers for army mattresses and pillows because they discouraged lice and bed bugs. The rust-red oil which fulmars spit at anyone coming too near their nest was extracted for heating and lamp fuel, as a balm and medicine, and used as a sure-fire rust-proofing for iron. St Kildans usually drank water or milk, although when Martin Martin visited in 1697 he noted that they occasionally made beer by fermenting barley with nettle juice. This resulted in 'good ale, so that when they drink plentifully of it, it disposes them to dance merrily.'

Nowhere in the world were men such nimble climbers, going barefoot or in stockinged feet down the highest cliffs in Britain, dangling a dizzy thousand feet above the waves, held only by a slender hand-made rope while they snared seabirds or collected eggs. They were filmed doing this in 1908 and 1910 by Oliver Pike who recounted:

'The natives were the finest climbers I have ever known; they were absolutely fearless on the steepest cliffs. I have seen them perform feats which would make our hair stand on end in fright. They worked in pairs, one man attached to a rope, and the other in charge at the top of the cliff. I watched one man take a run at a cliff, eight hundred feet high, with a sheer drop to the sea, fall face downwards when he reached the edge and, while his brother at the top allowed the rope to run through his hands, the climber actually ran down the cliff side, then, when the rope had almost run its full length, the one above put on the brake and the one below gave a twist, turned on his back so that he could see us above, and waved.'

Before a young man was allowed to marry, he had to show he could support a wife and family. To do this he had to demonstrate that he had the nerve to climb the terrifying cliffs in the hunt for birds and eggs by standing on one foot on the edge of a steep, tilted rock known as the **Lover's Stone**, 850 ft (259 m) above the sea. As if this wasn't enough he also had to bend and hold the other foot in his hand. It was said that men rarely died in bed in St Kilda, they either drowned or broke their necks climbing the cliffs. Politics and government for St Kildans were simple, but democratic, matters which had nothing to do with the mainland. Decisions concerning the community were the responsibility of the men. They met every morning except Sunday in the only street in the village in an assembly that became known as the Mòd, or the 'St Kilda Parliament.' This decided what work had to be done and who should do it. Some days the village parliamentarians spent the entire working day debating this weighty problem. Even in those days the islanders were noted for their laid-back lifestyle and one writer observed that if an Olympic 'Go Slow for Britain' team were ever needed the St Kildans would slowly saunter away with all the gold medals.

Occasionally over the centuries their isolation was shattered. In 1734 Lady Grange was moved from her exile in the Monach Islands to Hirta, where she was effectively a prisoner for eight years. This prompted Dr Johnson to say that 'if M'Leod would let it be known that he had such a place for naughty ladies, he might make it a very profitable island.' During the hunt for fugitive Bonnie Prince Charlie in 1746 British warships went to see if he was on St Kilda. The islanders had neither heard of the Prince, nor of the Jacobite Rebellion. In July 1838 the steam yacht *Vulcan*, left the Clyde on an excursion to St Kilda, taking curious Victorians to peer at Britain's most backward people. This historic excursion was the precursor of the regular summer cruises which started in 1877, marking the end of St Kilda's isolation. It was not long before the islanders had contracted 'stranger's cough,' a chest infection also known as the 'boat cough,' from the hordes of excursionists. The first apple ever seen on the island was bought by one of these tourists and was regarded with amazement. World War I brought a real shake-up. A naval detachment was stationed on Hirta and in 1918 a German U-boat fired 72 shells at its radio transmitting aerial. Most went wide, destroying the village store, damaging the church and its Manse, as well as two cottages and two boats, but no one was killed.

EXPLORING

HIRTA

To walk around the village and its surrounding hilly acres is to step back in time. A maze of cottages, buildings, drystone walls and enclosures testify to a departed way of life. Prominently dotted all over the island are *cleits*, the beehive-shaped, turf-topped drystone enclosures with walls that allow the wind through to dry the masses of seabirds that used to fill them. The heart of the village is its main, and only, street, lined by the cottages built mainly in 1860 to replace most of the ancient 'but and ben' blackhouses the St Kildans once shared with their livestock. This is where NTS work parties have concentrated most of their restoration efforts.

After the islanders left in 1930 the **Kirk** gradually decayed but it was restored and re-dedicated in 1980 as part of the commemoration of the 50th anniversary of the evacuation. At the end of the 17th century the village population of 180 people had a choice of three churches, St Columba's, St Brendan's, and Christ Church. No trace of these survives. **The Store** was built by the Macleods of Skye sometime before 1815 and destroyed by the U-boat gunfire of 1918. It was restored in 1986. Above the kirk is the **Coffin Cleit** where the St Kildans kept wood ready for their coffins. The **Factor's House** was probably built in the late 1860s for the use of the Macleod steward during his visits to collect the rent paid by St Kildans in feathers, fulmar oil, wool and tweed. It is now the summer home of the Warden. **Cottage No 3** was once the home of the MacDonald family. It is now an extremely well laid-out little museum, with exhibits reflecting life on St Kilda, as well as information on the islands' flora and fauna. Not far from Cottage No 11 is a large *cleit* which is said to stand on the site of the dwelling where the unfortunate Lady Grange spent her eight years of enforced exile in the mid-18th century.

RUINED SETTLEMENT. ST KILDA.   M.S.

Also known to St Kildans as *Taigh an t-Sithiche*, or the 'House of Fairies,' the **Earth House** behind the main street is one of St Kilda's earliest buildings and thought to date to between 500 BC and AD 300. It could once have been an ice-

Blackhouse (tigh dubh) restored as a museum, Lewis

The main road passes the front door of Amhuinnsuidhe Castle, South Harris

Stornaway's snug haven for Lewis fishing boats

Butt of Lewis Lighthouse

Port Nis harbour, Lewis

Fishing Boats on Loch Skipport, South Uist

Novel decoration for a South Uist blackhouse

Barra Airport's Cockle Strand runway

house for storing perishable food. This souterrain, discovered in 1876, is the only one preserved on St Kilda. One of the most unusual buildings on Hirta is the **Mediaeval House** and its beehive annexe. It was originally a dwelling connected to the beehive chamber by a low tunnel. St Kildans used it to store hay. Inland from the village, the remains of field walls, enclosures, old tracks and *cleits* of varying shapes and sizes are all that's left of an older settlement.

A walk taking in the tops of the hills forming an amphitheatre around Village Bay is a pleasant outing. Circle **Oiseval** and visit **The Gap** between Oiseval and **Conachair** where the cliff falls vertically to the sea for nearly 656 ft (200 m). Killer whales can sometimes be seen below, hunting the Atlantic grey seals which frequent the caves undercutting the cliff. These northern sea cliffs were first scaled from their foot in 1987 by an ITN-sponsored team of climbers which pioneered 19 first ascent routes on Conachair's cliff face. The climbers had to start their ascents from bobbing inflatable dinghies. The cliffs at The Gap and round Conachair were regarded by St Kildans as the best place to harvest fulmars (when roasted they were said to taste like pork). The extraordinary wall ascending Oiseval was built to keep animals from falling over the cliffs. At the foot of the Conachair cliffs, separated by a deep channel, is the high rock of **Mina Stac**. In the 16th century it was connected to the cliffs by a narrow archway until a fleeing Spanish Armada galleon, forced through the channel by storm, struck it and brought it crashing down, destroying both arch and galleon. There's a track most of the way to the top of St Kilda's highest peak, Conachair. From the summit beacon you get panoramic views of Hirta out to Boreray and the stacks and, some 40 miles (64 km) north-east, the Flannan Isles and the Outer Hebrides. On the far horizon, 100 miles (160 km) to the east, are Skye's Cuillin mountains. Near the top of Conachair are the remains of a Beaufighter aircraft which crashed on the south side of the hill in June 1943.

There's an unusual perspective of the jagged ridge of nearby Dun from the summit of **Ruaival** (*Ruabhal*). Below the summit is the 'Old Woman's Cave' where a village woman hid after two Lewis men frightened the islanders into the Kirk by pretending that pirates were coming. They then set fire to it. Huge boulders are visible at low water in the narrow sound between Dun and Hirta. St Kildans used these to get to the foot of the cliff on Dun, which they free-climbed until they reached a fixed chain. Part of this rusty chain is still in place. North-west of Ruaival's summit is the **Mistress Stone**, a triangular block of gabbro precariously bridging a gully, which can just be seen from the west end of the village. The story about the Lover's Stone also applies to this rock. At the head of the **Great Glen** (*Gleann Mór*) in the north-west corner of the island, is the **Earth Dyke**, a continuous turf wall built to keep the cattle of an ancient settlement grazing in the glen during the summer, away from the crops of barley and oats. The area was also known as the 'Female Warrior's Glen' and holds the remains of a beehive structure called the **Amazon's House**. This was probably built in Neolithic or Iron Age times. Many of the *cleits* around the glen now shelter nesting storm petrels. They were once used to dry Great Glen peat, regarded as the best on the island. Scattered over the glen are the remains of a Sunderland flying-boat which crashed in June 1944. A plaque in the Kirk commemorates the crew members who lost their lives here. At 1,181 ft (360 m) **Mullach Bì** is the highest point on the western cliffs, offering fine views in all directions and looking down on the remains of the earlier settlement above Glen Bay. Close to Glen Bay is the **Well of Virtues** (*Tobar nam Buadh*), a low stone building with a stone roof covering a pool fed by a refreshing spring. Its water was believed to have healing properties; they are certainly diuretic. Atlantic grey seals abound in the waters and caves of Glen Bay. There's no beach, but a path on the headland leads down to an eroded rock arch which is a wonderful natural peephole to Boreray and its stacks.

SOAY *(Soaigh)*

Soay is separated from Hirta by a narrow channel. The Vikings who arrived in St Kilda in the 9th or 10th century called this island 'Sheep Island,' either because of the long-legged, yellow-eyed sheep they found running around here, or which they themselves brought from Scandinavia and left there as mutton on the hoof. Although it's close to Hirta the turbulent narrows between them and the difficulty in landing make Soay one of Britain's least visited islands. The south-east corner is the usual landing place, but landings are possible barely three days out of the month in summer. The three rock stacks in the sound between Hirta and Soay are also rarely visited. **Stac Soay** (236 ft/72 m) is a fantastic shape pierced by a hole, **Stac Dona** (87 ft/27 m) was called 'Bad Stack' by St Kildans because it attracted so few nesting birds, and steeple-like **Stac Biorach** (236 ft/72 m) calls for such climbing skills that even the peerless St Kildans gave it special status. They regarded Stac Biorach as the most rigorous test of their climbing ability as it was the most difficult and dangerous of all to scale. Stac Biorach was first climbed by an incomer in 1883, Charles Barrington, the man who conquered the Eiger. Barrington also climbed Boreray's Stac Lee. Perpendicular cliffs overlook Soay's shingle beach and its jumble of enormous boulders where Atlantic grey seals haul out to breed in October and November. To the east of the grassy summit plateau of Cnoc Glas (1,240 ft/378 m) are the remains of an ancient stone altar. Below the cliffs are more recent remains, the wreckage of a World War II Wellington bomber. Soay's cliffs attract large numbers of puffin, shag, fulmar, guillemot, razorbill, kittiwake, gannet, great skua, storm and Leach's petrel.

BORERAY *(Boraraigh)*

Boreray and its sea stacks rise almost vertically out of the sea, and its splendid cliffs towering in the west more than 1,000 ft (305 m) above the Atlantic are an impressive introduction to this small (190 acres/77 ha), but very special, nature reserve. Landing on this uninhabited volcanic island is a rare privilege and permission to do so must be obtained from the warden on Hirta. If you get this, allow yourself at least two hours to explore the island. Attendant sea stacks are towering **Stac an Armin** to the north, and **Stac Lee** to the south-west. Stac an Armin is like a giant wedge, its southern sloping side made up of a series of giant rock steps separated by boulder scree. The stack is a mass of awesome vertical faces above water and a knife-edge ridge below the surface. The most impressive view of Stac Lee is from the south-east, although it is spectacular from every angle. It rises vertically 720 ft (220 m) from the sea bed and then soars another 564 ft (172 m) above sea level. Sir Julian Huxley called it 'the most majestic sea rock in existence.' Boreray and its stacks hold the world's largest gannetry, a colony of more than 60,000 breeding pairs. Two or three pairs of St Kilda wrens and rock pipits also often nest here among thousands of fulmars, guillemots, razorbills, puffins, and kittiwakes. St Kildans used to visit the island regularly at night in March and April to harvest adult gannets, in May to gather eggs, and in summer to tend their sheep. In September and October the highlight of the year was when they collected *gugas*, young gannets or 'fat fellows.' As bad weather sometimes prevented them getting back to Hirta they evolved a novel means of signalling, which involved removing turf near a prominent spot. A bare patch to the left of the spot meant that food and water was needed; to the right, that someone was ill or injured. A large patch signalled the death of someone in the group. Scottish Blackface sheep were introduced late in the 19th century and there are now several hundred of their extremely wild descendants, which have survived untended since the St Kildan evacuation in 1930.

FLORA AND FAUNA

St Kilda is world-famous for its seabirds and was designated Scotland's only World Heritage Site in 1986. The world's largest colony of **gannets** – more than 60,000 pairs – breeds on Boreray and its adjacent sea stacks and an estimated 300,000 pairs of **puffins** and 64,842 pairs of **fulmars** are the biggest colonies of these birds in Britain. The fulmars were painstakingly individually counted by ornithologists during a survey in 1999. More than a million seabirds make St Kilda Europe's most important breeding site and one of the main breeding grounds in the North Atlantic. Among them are **guillemots, razorbills, kittiwakes, Manx shearwaters, storm petrels, Leach's fork-tailed petrels** and several species of gull. Gannets migrate from St Kilda in November and start returning in early spring. One species of seabird, though small in numbers is an aggressive presence on Hirta. This is the **great skua**, which has colonised the grassy moorland areas.

St Kilda's extreme isolation means only a few plant and animal species have found a home on the windswept islands. For instance, of the 367 butterflies and moths recorded 50 miles (80 km) away in the Western Isles, only 58 have made it to St Kilda, and there are only seven species of land birds, although some migratory species touch down on the islands. Animals that do live here, however, either exist in large numbers or have taken on a character all their own. There have been no trees on St Kilda for the past 1,500-2,000 years, but pollen analysis has shown that before this alder, hazel, birch, pine, elm, and oak were common. Since they disappeared wrens have learnt to perch and breed on sea stacks, rocks and cliffs instead of branches and this has made them bigger and stronger than mainland wrens to the point where they are now a different sub-species. There are about 113-117 pairs of these unique **St Kilda wrens**. The island house mouse – recognised in 1885 as St Kilda's only indigenous wild animal – became extinct shortly after the islanders were evacuated in 1930, but the **field mouse**, less dependent on humans, continues to flourish. Primitive sheep survive on Soay and 107 of them transferred from there to Hirta in 1932 after the evacuation run wild in the hills and now number 600-1,200, their total in any one year dependent on the grazing. It's likely they are either descended from the sheep brought to St Kilda by the Vikings, or they have been around since Neolithic times. The Soay's long legs give it the look and agility of a mountain goat, but the resemblance doesn't end there. Scientists studying them have noted that the more dominant rams can mate up to 13 times a day. Feral Blackface sheep also remain cut off on Boreray, where they've been since they were brought from Lewis in the 19th century. **Grey seals** are more recent arrivals and breed in considerable numbers around Hirta and Dun. Plantlife is impressive considering the inhospitable habitat and the depredations of the Soay sheep.

A total of 174 species of flowering plants has been recorded, including **purple saxifrage, honeysuckle, roseroot, moss campion, primrose, sorrel, buttercup** and **iris**. Marine life abounds around St Kilda. As well as **seals**, larger denizens such as **basking sharks** and **minke whales** patrol the rich inshore waters. It's expected that St Kilda's World Heritage Site status will be extended to include its marine environment. Scottish Natural Heritage supports a survey and programme of wildlife research on the islands, which includes a long-term study of the Soay sheep, monitoring of the seabird populations, and detailed vegetation mapping.

GETTING THERE

Unless you join a cruise, own your own boat, or can afford to charter one, the most practical ways of getting to St Kilda is as a member of one of the National Trust for Scotland's working parties between mid-May and August every year. Access by air is discouraged. Depending on the type of boat, the route and the weather the boat trip from Oban can take 14 hours minimum to 48 hours, or even longer; from the Outer Hebrides it takes a minimum of eight hours. Anyone prone to motion sickness should see a doctor or pharmacist beforehand for a reliable preventive. The quickest route from Oban goes through the Sound of Mull, west of Rum and through the Sound of Canna, where some vessels stay the night. From there the boat heads for Neist Point, in Skye, and then north-west across The Little Minch at its narrowest stretch, with perhaps a night at Lochmaddy, North Uist, or Leverburgh, Harris. Then, passing through the Sound of Harris, the northern route heads due west for St Kilda. Boats taking the southern route stay overnight at Lochboisdale, South Uist, before heading for St Kilda. Village Bay is a safe haven provided there's no east wind blowing. Getting out of a small boat or tender on landing calls for caution and what's called the 'St Kilda two-step.'

Scottish Natural Heritage has guidelines for cruise ships, yachts, and other visitors. Unauthorised landings are not permitted on any of the St Kilda stacks and islands, other than Hirta itself. If in doubt, check with the SNH/NTS Seasonal Warden who is present on Hirta from April to September. When planning a visit to St Kilda contact, well in advance, the National Trust for Scotland office in Oban (Lochvoil House, Dunuaran Road; tel 01631-570000; fax 01631-570011) to arrange suitable dates. Try to avoid arriving on Sundays, and also on Tuesdays and Fridays, which are busy supply days.

Byelaws have been drawn up for St Kilda and are on display at the Factor's House, where the Seasonal Warden is based. You should, however, familiarise yourself with them before you go. Some of the main ones are:

* Contact the Seasonal Warden before landing on Hirta, so that he can meet you and brief you. Guided walks of the Village Area are available and the Warden may be able to accompany you around Boreray and the stacks to point out features of interest, provided you take him/her back to Hirta afterwards.

* There is a small pier/breakwater in Village Bay, Hirta, but it is not safe for even small vessels to berth alongside, nor is it encouraged because of the risk of rats getting ashore.

* The National Nature Reserve of St Kilda has a threshold sign near where visitors normally come ashore. This includes a map and information about the island. There are also a few icons explaining activities that can be damaging to the reserve and its wildlife. An SNH leaflet is available from the Seasonal Warden or the SNH Office in South Uist (tel 01870-620238). NTS and Historic Scotland also have an informative leaflet on the islands' archaeology and antiquities. Respect the historic buildings, ruins, graves and archaeological sites; many have been scheduled Ancient Monuments.

* There are no public toilet facilities on any island, even Hirta, so you should take advantage of the facilities on your boat before landing. Don't expect to find any privacy or cover on the islands. Dogs and cats are not allowed ashore.

* There are no landing facilities on any of the other islands and the rocks can be dangerously slippery. Be careful stepping ashore. Wear stout footwear with good, non-slip soles, and be prepared to get your feet wet.

* Visitors are asked not to wander around the islands alone and unaccompanied, in case of accidents. Do not to venture too close to the cliff edge. Not only can this be unstable in places but strong winds or sudden gusts can make it even more dangerous. There are no cliff rescue facilities and it is a long way to the nearest hospital.

* Do not pick flowers, hammer the rocks or take any plants, rocks or other specimens away or otherwise disturb the landscape, vegetation or animals. Animals may appear tame and approachable but you should resist the temptation to get that little bit closer.

* Take care not to introduce any alien plants or animals. Mud on your boots, for example, can carry seeds. Nesting birds, breeding seals and sheep with young lambs are especially vulnerable to disturbance so avoid them at all times. If you come across a nest or chicks leave the area immediately to allow the parent birds to return. Gulls and skuas are always ready to carry off unguarded eggs and young.
* Ground-nesting birds have eggs and young that are well camouflaged and difficult to spot, so be careful where you place your feet. Terns and some waders lay their eggs on bare sand or shingle along the shore and are especially vulnerable. Gulls and terns – and especially skuas – are protective of their nests and often dive-bomb anyone coming too close. It is best to avoid their colonies altogether. Try not to linger or to congregate at one spot too long as studies show that visitor pressure, especially near landing sites, can significantly reduce the breeding success and survival of young birds and seal pups.
* No anchorage is secure in bad weather. Village Bay is especially exposed to easterly winds and downdraughts from the hills. Changes in the weather can be swift and unpredictable making departure from the island dangerous. Adhere rigidly to all arrangements made with your boat crew and do not venture so far away that you cannot be summoned if the weather suddenly deteriorates.

Charters and Cruises

Bute Sailing School: Cannon House, Battery Place, Rothesay, Bute (tel 01700-502819; www.butesail.clara.net). Organises adventure cruises around St Kilda.

    Corryvreckan: Dal-An-Eas, Kilmore, Oban, PA34 4XU (tel/fax 01631-770246; e-mail yacht.corryvreckan@virgin.net; www.corryvreckan.co.uk). A 60 ft (18 ft) yacht for active sailing holidays to St Kilda.

    Gaelic Rose: Bob Jones, Kirk Brae, Lochaline, Morvern, Oban (tel 01967-421654).

    Island Cruising: 1 Erista, Uig, Harris, HS2 9JG (tel 01851-672381; fax 01851-672212; www.island-cruising.com). Based on the west coast of Lewis, says it has managed to land people on St Kilda every year since it began running its four-and six-day trips round the island in 1997. Costs on the *MV Cuma* from £76 per person per day inclusive.

    JDL Marine: Fiona Brown, Shore Manager, 14 Woodbine Terrace, Edinburgh, EH9 8DA (tel 0131-554 6551). Offers 7-10 day voyages around the islands in working square-rigger *Jean de la Lune*.

    Kylebhan Charters: Jim Kilcullen, 3 Dal-an-Alseig, North Connel, Oban (tel 01389-877028) or 3 Barclay Court, Old Kilpatrick, Glasgow, G60 5HX. Has fishing boat *MV Kylebhana*, sleeping 12. Cruises to St Kilda and other islands. Departures from Oban.

    Maiden International: Woodpeckers, Rokley, SO24 0DU (tel 01962-772252; fax 01962-772099). Skipper charter on *Maiden* or sister ship *Ice Maiden* to St Kilda.

    Northern Light Cruising Co: Cameron Farm, Lochbuie, Mull, PA62 6AA (tel 01680-814260; fax 01680-814270; e-mail mv-chalice@northernlight-uk.com; www.northernlight-uk.com). Has Oban-based purpose built *MV Chalice* taking up to 12 people for cruises to St Kilda, and *MV Poplar Diver* (c/o Harbour Master, North Pier, Oban; tel 01740-620562), a 71 ft (22 ft) converted all-weather lifeboat which can accommodate 12.

    Western Edge: 51 York Street, Aberdeen, AB2 1DP (tel 01224-210564; fax 01224-210563. Also 5D Plantation Road, Stornoway, HS1 2JS; tel 01851-705965; e-mail murrayiain@compurserve.com; www.hebrides.com/busi/annag). Operates

4-6 day cruises to St Kilda and other islands on *MV Annag*, a 40 ft (12 m) modern cruising vessel, sleeping six.

Western Isles Sailing and Exploration Co: Prospect House, Hollands Road, Haverhill, Suffolk, CB9 8PJ (tel 01440-702454). Has a fishing boat converted to sail, the *Marguerite Explorer*.

If you plan to arrive at St Kilda by private charter boat you must first inform the NTS Regional Secretary (Lochvoil House, Dunuaran Road, Oban, PA34 4NE; tel 01631-570000) who will then advise the Seasonal Warden of your intended visit.

ACCOMMODATION

There is no accommodation in the usual sense, and what there is on Hirta is limited, consisting of six renovated cottages and campsites for up to six tents. All visits are co-ordinated by The National Trust for Scotland, so if you want to stay on Hirta you should book through them (Wemyss House, 28 Charlotte Square, Edinburgh EH2 4ET; tel 0131-243 9331; fax 0131-243 9594; www.nts.org.uk). Yachties usually stay on board their boats during their visit.

Each year between mid-May and August the NTS takes six work parties of 12 people to St Kilda for a two-week stay. Although these are organised to undertake building, conservation and maintenance work, or archaeological digs, the emphasis is on experiencing life on this unique island, living communally in the restored 19th century cottages of the old village. As well as the cottages, one of the buildings restored is the old village store, which was damaged by German submarine gunfire during World War I. Work party numbers are strictly limited, and you must be fit and in good health. They are open to all between 18 and 70. No special skills are required, although a sense of humour is a help. It costs £450 to join an archaeological work party and £500 for a restoration and maintenance expedition. Applications must be in by 31 January each year for summer travel. For more details check out www.kilda.org.uk or send a self-addressed and stamped envelope to St Kilda Work Parties, The National Trust for Scotland, Lochvoil House, Dunuaran Road, Oban, Argyll PA34 4NE (tel 01631-570000).

SPORT AND RECREATION

Diving

Scuba-divers say that the Flannan Islands aside, waters around St Kilda offer the most spectacular diving in the Outer Hebrides. Off the north-western edge of Soay the Atlantic has drilled a tunnel all the way through the jagged tooth of *Am Plastair*, and the finest underwater arch in the islands is said to be at *Sgarbhstac* ('Cormorant Rock'), off south-west Boreray. The arch, which starts at a depth of 100 ft (30 m), is about 65 ft (20 m) wide and more than 98 ft (30 m) long and divers swimming through it are often accompanied by seals and puffins. Hirta's sheltered Village Bay offers some interesting night dives and '**The Sawcut'** which slices into the long finger of Dun on the south side of the bay is a particularly interesting boat dive. The entrance to this 10 ft (3 m) wide vertical fracture is at 92 ft (28 m), but it shallows to 60-10 ft (18-3 m). It opens into a 60 ft (18 m) cave with walls full of jewel, sagartia, and plumose anemones, sea squirts, yellow sponge, and bunches of the startling orange soft corals known as 'dead man's fingers'. For some odd reason the visibility here is always exceptional. Strong currents and surge noticeable at even 100 ft (30 m) down make diving around St Kilda only for the well-qualified and experienced. If you can handle this it's a great dive destination, where visibility is regularly a crystal 100-130 ft (30-40 m) and the marine life is kaleidoscopic.

HELP AND INFORMATION

You can't buy much on Hirta, so take all the food and supplies you need for your stay with you. Report to the warden on arrival, who will tell you where everything is to be found. Any queries or complaints should be routed through the warden.

A sub-post office was opened in St Kilda in September 1899, but islanders preferred to send their letters the way they had for years, by 'mailboat.' This was a piece of wood shaped like a crude toy boat and hollowed out to hold a bottle or cocoa tin to keep the letters dry. On the outside it said 'Open Me,' and inside were instructions for the finder to post the contents, along with money for the stamps. Once a float made of an inflated sheep's bladder and a small red flag had been fixed to the 'mailboat' it was launched when the wind was in the north-west. Amazingly, two-thirds of the letters posted like this reached their destination. Most washed ashore in the Western Isles and on the west coast of Scotland, but on occasion they reached Norway. 'Mailboats' were used in emergencies right up until all the islanders were evacuated in 1930. On 1 July 1999 a work party on St Kilda sent greetings by St Kilda 'mailboat' to the new Scottish Parliament in Edinburgh. This arrived within a few weeks and brought a more speedy reply. Records of 'mailboats' and where they wash up are compiled and published in the *St Kilda Mail*, the annual magazine of the St Kilda Club.

Mail. These days outgoing mail goes in the post box near the shop and leaves the island whenever and on whatever transport is available.

Telephone. There is a British Telecom call box, but it can be used only with a phonecard.

Puff Inn. This, the remotest pub in Europe, is primarily for the use of the contract staff at the island base, but visitors are welcome and bar opening times are displayed at the entrance. It was originally opened by soldiers of the Royal Artillery unit who used to man the missile tracking station.

Shop. The shop, run by the St Kilda Club and staffed by NTS volunteers, is open only for short periods during the summer. Check times on arrival. Stocks are limited.

Medical Cover. Base medical staff on Hirta can be contacted at any time for serious problems, but there's little hope of immediate evacuation in an emergency.

Washing Facilities. The ablutions block is opposite the Factor's House. It is for the use of NTS work parties, who have priority, those staying in NTS accommodation, and campers.

Maps and Charts. Take OS 1:50,000 (Landranger Sheet 18) and 1:25,000 (Sheet 1373). For boats, Admiralty Charts numbers 2653 and 2721.

For more information contact either Scottish Natural Heritage (John Love or Anne Shepherd, 135 Stilligarry, South Uist, HS8 5RS; tel 01870-620238; fax 01870-620350) or the National Trust for Scotland (Lochvoil House, Dunuaran Road, Oban, PA34 4NE; Anne May, administrator, Alasdair Oatts; tel 01631-570000; Robin Turner, archaeologist based in Perth; tel 01738-636711).

If you are interested in doing research of any kind on St Kilda send full details of your proposed project to SNH in Stilligarry, South Uist.

Skye and the Small Isles

Dunvegan Castle

Bonnie Prince Charlie is a tragic if romantic figure, but he did at least focus attention on the Inner Hebrides during the aftermath of the failed Jacobite rebellion. Spin Dr Samuel Johnson and his companion James Boswell also did their bit to lift the tartan curtain on the area, and Sir Walter Scott followed to set the seal of popularity on all things Scottish with some florid historical novels popular with the Victorians. Unsung is the redcoat General George Wade (1673-1748), whose achievement in the construction of roads and bridges throughout the Highlands – with benefits for tourists the last thing on his mind – helped to open the ports to the Inner Hebrides. A century later David MacBrayne's steamboats made the islands accessible to all who could afford the fare.

Skye

Thanks to its stunning scenery, romantic associations and its easy access, Skye is the most visited of all the western islands and has been for more than a century since the railroads and steamships of the Victorians brought the islands of the Inner Hebrides that much closer to the bursting cities of the mainland. There are some purists who insist that Skye is no longer an island, and that somehow it's not the same singing the *Skye Boat Song* while speeding over the bridge that has linked it firmly to the mainland at Kyle of Lochalsh since 1995. You either love the idea of the bridge or you hate it, but it does at least cut down the time you might otherwise spend waiting for your turn on the ferry in the height of the tourist season. The **best time** to go depends, as with all the other islands from Shetland and Orkney to the Outer and Inner Hebrides, on what you want to do. Months that are good for climbers and walkers are not necessarily the best for fly fishermen, scuba-divers, birdwatchers, and other visitors. If you can, try to avoid the crowds of midsummer. Skye is increasingly being promoted as the 'Mild Winter Isle.' That's a thought.

GEOGRAPHY

The Isle of Skye (*An t'Eilean Sgitheanach*) is the most northerly and largest island of the Inner Hebrides. It is arrestingly beautiful and arguably the best known of all Scotland's islands, with the exception of Iona. It is also the most accessible from the mainland and for all these reasons Skye attracts an estimated 400,000 visitors every year. The island is about 50 miles (80 km) long, 30 miles (48 km) across at its widest point and four miles (6 km) at its narrowest. Skye is often called the 'Winged Isle' and if you look at Waternish in the north-west and Trotternish in the north-east on the map you'll see them unfolding from the island like a pair of clumsy wings. The numerous sea lochs that crenellate its coast give the island a coastline running for more than 350 miles (563 km). Skye's most celebrated mountain ranges are the Black and Red Cuillin in the south-west centre, and the island's longest continuous high ridge is at Trotternish in the north, stretching 19 miles (30 km) and taking in The Quiraing, The Storr – the highest point on the peninsula at 2,359 ft (719 m) – and the startling pinnacle of the Old Man of Storr. A road starting in Portree encircles the Trotternish peninsula. The island capital and only town on Skye is Portree, *port-righ*, or 'Port of the King,' named to commemorate the visit to Skye in 1540 of King James V. Lying close to Skye's eastern shore across the Sound of Raasay is the island of Raasay, which shelters the approaches to Portree. North of Raasay is the uninhabited island of Rona, also known as South Rona, and off Raasay's southern tip is Scalpay. A mere 1% of Skye's 535 sq miles (1,385 sq km) area is standing water. Most lochs are small, and rivers and streams are short and weather-dependent, often being either raging torrents or reduced to a trickle. The moist climate has resulted in widespread and extensive peatland and bog.

Geology

Skye and its attendant islands appeared on the map about 50-60 million years ago, a surviving part of the wreck of a vast volcanic chain which had stretched from Britain to Greenland and also included the islands of Mull, Arran and Rum. This dramatic upheaval thrust up one of the most stunning mountain ranges in Britain, the Black Cuillin. Most of the Black Cuillin comprises coarse-grained gabbro, a rock popular with climbers for its rough, adhesive qualities. Occasionally, grey basalt intrudes to give climbing pitches a dangerously smooth surface. The pinkish granitic rock of the Red Cuillin was the result of a later volcanic explosion and unlike the jagged peaks of the Black Cuillin, the Red Cuillin have weathered into rounded hills with extensive scree slopes. The huge lava flows poured out by the ancient craters can be seen to this day in basalt sheets and terraces of enormously tough rock, in some places still 4,265 ft (1,300 m) thick, covering the area northwards from the Cuillin. This has weathered to leave flat-topped hills such as Macleod's Tables in north-west Skye, and Dun Caan on Raasay. On the west side of the island the basalt has formed high sea cliffs running northwards from Glen Brittle to rise to nearly 984 ft (300 m) in places such as Dunvegan Head; on the east side of the Trotternish peninsula collapsed sedimentary rock has caused massive landslipping in the basalt, creating the ridge of cliffs running north from Portree to Staffin and the contorted rock of The Storr and The Quiraing. In the south the Sleat Peninsula is an area of low rounded hills of old Lewisian gneiss – 1,500-million years old – and later Torridonian sandstone. Vast limestone pavements and bands of marble cross Skye between Strath Suardal and Torrin make this one of the most extensive areas of limestone in Britain.

CLIMATE

Skye's climate is regulated by its mountains, the sea and the oceanic currents of the Gulf Stream that warm it. Even though the island lies at the same latitude as Hudson Bay and Labrador this combination of natural factors means that it never gets extremely cold and never becomes uncomfortably hot. As in all areas with mountainous districts there's plenty of rain and mist, which is why Skye's name comes from the Old Norse word *skuy* for 'cloud' and why it's called *Eilean à Cheo* ('The Misty Isle') in Gaelic. Annual rainfall averages about 47 inches (1,200 mm) at the coast and around 118 inches (3,000 mm) in the hills. Though westerly Atlantic winds are less severe than in the Outer Hebrides, they still blow sufficiently to make summer daytime temperatures lower than on the mainland. The average summer temperature is about 60°F (16°C) and the island gets about 1,200 hours of sunshine a year. Most fine days are in June and September. Winter snow does not normally last long, and the island escapes the severe winters of mainland Scotland, which has led to an increase in the number of visitors between November and March.

HISTORY

There is ample evidence of prehistoric settlement on Skye – standing stones, chambered cairns, brochs, and duns or forts – and stones carved with enigmatic symbols have been found indicating that this innermost isle of the Hebrides was also once occupied by Pictish people. Saint Columba, who was active in Scotland from AD 563 to 597, is said to have met a non-Gaelic speaking native of Skye, called Artbranan, a name that was probably Pictish. Celts from his native Ireland spread the Celtic version of Christianity and the Gaelic language and built monasteries and chapels whose names beginning with *cille* or the Anglicised *kil* today show where they established churches or religious settlements.

Towards the end of the 8th century the Vikings arrived, first as raiders, and then as settlers. They left their mark in the large number of Norse place-names and today such name endings as *-aig* ('bay'), *-bost* ('farm') and *-shader* ('homestead') all point to Norse origins. Skye did not officially become part of Scotland until 1266, when it was ceded by its Norse rulers to Alexander III, three years after the Scots defeated King Haakon's Vikings at the Battle of Largs.

At first Skye was part of the Earldom of Ross, but later came under the jurisdiction of the Lord of the Isles. The main Skye clans were the MacDonalds of Sleat, descendants of Somerled, first Celtic Lord of the Isles, whose clan centre is still in the south at Armadale, and the MacLeods, who claim descent from the Norse King of Man, and whose seat is in the north at Dunvegan. These two great clans came to Skye at roughly the same time during the 13th century. For the next 400 years they warred incessantly. The climax of the feuding came with the 'War of the One-Eyed Woman,' which began because the MacDonald of the day, Donald Gorm Mor, had ill-treated Margaret MacLeod, sister of Rory Mor MacLeod of Dunvegan. It was the custom for a couple to spend a trial year together before marriage. Instead of marrying Margaret after such a trial, Donald Gorm returned her to her brother. One of her eyes was badly injured, and Donald added insult to injury by sending her back on a one-eyed horse, escorted by a one-eyed groom, and followed by a one-eyed dog. Two years of warfare followed until in 1601 the two clans came face to face in their final conflict. The MacDonalds routed the MacLeods in *Coire na Creiche* ('Corry of the Spoil') in the last clash of the clans to take place in Skye. A picnic spot now overlooks the site.

Skye stayed in the wings of Scottish history until the Jacobite Rebellion of 1745. Although the island's clan chiefs didn't 'come out' for the Young Pretender, Prince Charles Edward Stewart (Stuart in French), there was widespread sympathy for his cause. Skye entered Scottish legend when Flora Macdonald smuggled Bonnie Prince Charlie into the island in 1746, disguised as her maid, while the British were ransacking the islands of the western seaboard for him.

In the latter part of the 18th century and early in the 19th century Skye suffered the misery of the Clearances which saw evicted tenants and their families forced out to the cities of Lowland Scotland and virtually transported to Canada and Australia. It's estimated that nearly 30,000 people left the island between 1840 and 1888, a staggering displacement. As a result of several violent revolts by crofters and increasing public consternation Gladstone's government established the commission of enquiry which resulted in the Crofters' Holding Act of 1886 and the beginning of a new dispensation for tenant crofters. Their protected position remains to this day, reinforced by subsidies and by subsequent legislation. Today Skye is one of the most heavily crofted islands in the Hebrides.

ECONOMY

Skye's main industries are agriculture and tourism. Crofting is a major activity, along with hill and upland farming; though good land for cultivation is scarce, the climate is well suited to pasture and stock rearing and Skye's main source of income comes from the sale of produce from crofts, such as sheep, cattle and wool. A croft is not a building or house, but a smallholding of usually between one and 10 acres (4 ha) although there are crofts of up to 50 acres (20 ha) and more. Most crofters generally have another job as well. Tourism is Skye's biggest developing industry and without it the population would quickly decline, as it did in the mid-19th century when the prosperity brought by the kelp industry vanished almost overnight with cheaper imports. After the collapse of the kelp industry men left Skye in their hundreds to look for jobs on what they referred to as 'the Continent,' meaning mainland Scotland. The population is now around 10,000.

LANGUAGE

Arriving in the area in 1818 John Keats was able to report quite truthfully to his brother in London that he was 'for the first time in a country where a foreign language is spoken.' He was referring to Gaelic, which is now enjoying an unprecedented revival. Skye and Lochalsh are pivotal in the remarkable resurgence of Gaelic culture and there are regular festivals celebrating Gaelic music, literature and drama. Ceilidhs are also a regular feature in local pubs and hotels. You'll find at least one of the Sunday services in Portree's five churches is conducted in Gaelic. English as well as Gaelic is spoken throughout Skye, with children being taught in Gaelic, especially in primary school. *Sabhal Mòr Ostaig* (An Teanga, An t-Eilean Sgitheanach, Alba, IV44 8RQ; tel 01471-888000; fax 01471-888001; e-mail oifis@smo.uhi.ac.uk), is a Gaelic teaching college in Sleat which runs courses for anyone wishing to learn the language.

| **Practical** | *i* | **GETTING THERE** |
| **Information** | | **By Road** |

The Kyle of Lochalsh ferry service was discontinued when the Skye toll bridge opened in 1995 and since then the 'Road to the Isles' has meant exactly that. Driving from Glasgow and the south the usual approach is by way of the A82 and the A87 to Kyle of Lochalsh and the Skye Bridge. From Edinburgh take the M90 across the Forth Road Bridge to Perth. At Perth follow the A9 and turn off to go through Dalwhinnie, on the A899. Follow the A899 to join the A86 to Spean Bridge, take the A87 north to Invergarry and join the A87 to Kyle of Lochalsh. From Inverness, head west on the A82 to Invermoriston, then the A887 to Bunloyne Junction where you join the A87 to get to the bridge. The distance by road from Glasgow and Edinburgh is 200 miles (322 km) and from Inverness it's 82 miles (132 km).

The Skye Bridge (Crossing Centre, Kyle IV40 8BG; tel/fax 01599-534880) spans the 437-yard (400 m) wide channel from Kyle of Lochalsh to Kyleakin in Skye. The bridge carries two traffic lanes with a pedestrian and cycle path on both sides of the carriageway. Skye Bridge toll for a car during high season is £5.70 and £4.70 in low season. A car and caravan costs £11.40 and £9.40, and a motorbike £2.90 and £2.40. These toll fees are payable both entering and leaving Skye. High season is 1 May to 30 September, and low season 1 October to 30 April. Books of discount tickets are available from the main administration building. Customers using books of tickets are required to present the full book at the toll booth. Single or unattached tickets are not accepted.

Buses

Scottish Citylink (tel 08705-505050; www.citylink.co.uk) has a complex network of services from Edinburgh, Glasgow, Fort William, and many other centres on the mainland to the Kyle of Lochalsh and across to Kyleakin, Broadford, Sconser, Sligachan, Portree and Uig. Check the timetable and routes with Citylink. There are cheaper fares for off-peak and mid-week travel, and a Citylink Smart Card saves 16 to 25-year-olds, students and over-50s around 30% on adult fares. Scottish Citylink provide connections to and from the National Express nationwide coach network.

Skye-Ways Express Coaches: 4 Station Road, Kyle of Lochalsh IV40 8AE (tel 01599-534328; fax 01599-534862; e-mail info@skyeways.co.uk; www. skyeways.co.uk). Operate services from Glasgow and Inverness to Portree, extending as far north as Uig, seven days a week. Check the latest fares and routes with Skye-Ways.

By Sea

If you want to ignore the concrete bridge and sail over the sea to Skye from the mainland you can still do so from Mallaig to Armadale and Glenelg to Kylerhea. You could, of course, also take the original route followed by Bonnie Prince Charlie and Flora Macdonald from the Outer Hebrides to Uig. The ferry crossing from Mallaig to Armadale is run by Caledonian MacBrayne and the ferry to Kylerhea is a private operation run in summer from Glenelg, 30 miles (48 km) south of Kyle of Lochalsh. To get to Mallaig by road, take the A830 off the A87 just north of Fort William. If you have lots of time to spare and don't mind driving on single-track roads to get there the crossing from the wooded banks of Glenelg to the pier at Kylerhea is a pleasant option.

Caledonian MacBrayne (The Ferry Terminal, Gourock PA19 1QP; tel 08705-650000; fax 01475-635235, reservations; tel 01475-650100; fax 01475-637607, general enquiries; e-mail reservations@calmac.co.uk; www.calamc.co.uk) operate a car and passenger ferry from Mallaig to Armadale seven times a day Monday to Saturday; Sunday from June to August only. The crossing takes about 30 minutes and the single fare is £15.65 for a car, £2.80 each for driver and passengers, £15.65 for caravan, and boat or baggage trailer, and £7.85 for motor cycles. Bicycles free. 'Five-Day Return' and 'Six-Journey' tickets are available. From mid-April to mid-October, Monday to Friday, an 'Early Bird Saver' ticket is available which costs £28.50 for a car and up to four occupants. This is valid on the first sailing of the day, normally at 8.40am, returning to Mallaig on the last sailing of the same day. You can also stay overnight at Mallaig each night (except Tuesday and Sunday) from 4 July to 4 September in a two-berth cabin (with toilet and shower) followed by a hearty full Scottish breakfast before disembarking on Skye the next morning. Single berth cabins are also available. The additional charge for this is £18 a person and £5 for a single supplement. Contact the CalMac offices in Mallaig; tel 01687-462403, or Armadale; tel 01471-844248. There are also day trips on the *MV Lord of the Isles* from Mallaig to Armadale on Monday to Saturday, also Sunday during summer. There are six sailings a day from 8.40am to 4.45pm. The day return fare is £4.75 a passenger and £27 for a car. The ferry has a self-service restaurant for full meals and snacks and a fully licensed bar.

Skye Ferry (tel 01599-511302; fax 01599-511477; e-mail roddy@ skyeferry. co.uk; www.skyeferry.co.uk) operates from Glenelg to Kylerhea. To get to Glenelg travelling north, follow the A87 to Shiel Bridge then take the road to Glenelg and follow the signs to the ferry. The *Glenachulish* takes up to six cars with standing-room only for foot passengers. It takes five minutes to cross to or from Skye. During the following times the ferry crosses every 15 minutes when busy and every 30 minutes when quiet. 17 April to 20 May, Monday to Saturday from 9am to 6pm, no Sunday service; 22 May to 3 September, Monday to Saturday 9am to 8pm, Sunday from 10am to 6pm; 4 September to 28 October, Monday to Saturday from 9am to 6pm, Sunday 10am to 6pm. Car with up to four passengers costs £6, day return £10, additional passengers 50p. A 'Six-Journey' ticket costs £18. Caravans and trailers cost £6, motorcycles £3, cycles £1, and foot passengers 70p. The ferry does not operate in winter. The Kylerhea ferry was Skye's first regular ferry service. This was also the route drovers once used to swim their cattle across the narrows on their way to market in central Scotland.

Cruise

Voyages Jules Verne (21 Dorset Square, London NW1 6QC; tel 020-7616 1000; www.vjv.com) has a Scottish lochs and islands cruise which includes visits to Skye, Mull, and Iona. The cruise leaves from Oban and disembarks in Inverness. The *MV Lord of the Glens* has 27 luxury state cabins for 54 passengers. There's a restaurant, a bar lounge, and a small library. The cruise includes seven nights full board accommodation, shore excursions and sightseeing.

By Rail

Mainland rail services extend to the railheads at ferry ports Mallaig and Kyle of Lochalsh. Victorian engineers spent four years blasting and hewing their way through iron-hard rock which often demanded cuttings as deep as 80 ft (24 m) to finally link Fort William with Kyle of Lochalsh in 1897. The result is one of the most exhilarating rail journeys in Britain. *ScotRail* (Caledonian Chambers, 87 Union Street, Glasgow G1 3TA; tel 08457-484950; www.scotrail.co.uk) operates the Kyle Line from Inverness to the Kyle of Lochalsh. The West Highland Line runs from Glasgow Queen Street to Fort William and takes 3³/4 hours. From Fort William to Mallaig takes a further 1 hour 20 minutes.

The *Jacobite Steam Train*, operated by The West Coast Railway Company (Warton Road, Carnforth, Lancashire LA5 9HX; tel 01524-732100; fax 01524-

735518; www.westcoastrailway.co.uk), follows the famous 'Road to the Isles' railway between Fort William and Mallaig. The 84-mile (135 km) round trip starts near Ben Nevis, visits Britain's most westerly mainland railway station at Arisaig, passes Loch Morar, and finally arrives next to the deepest seawater loch in Europe, Loch Nevis. The train leaves Fort William at 10.20am and returns to Fort William at 4pm, with an 1¹/2 hour stop in Mallaig. It operates Monday to Sunday from June to September. To reserve tickets telephone 01463-239026.

TOUR OPERATORS

A1 Cabs and Tours: 1 Quay Street, Portree (tel 01478-611112; fax 01478-612851; e-mail a1cabs@dial.pipex.com). Air-conditioned car tours for up to four people.

Dunvegan Private Hire: tel 01470-521560. Private hire/taxi for all areas of north Skye. Open all year.

Glenedin Coaches: tel 01470-582306; fax 01470-582396. Local tours of Skye with courier driver, all areas covered. Private coach and contract hire. Open all year.

Kyleakin Private Hire and Taxi: tel/fax 01599-534452. Guided tours of Skye and the north-west Highlands. Taxi service available to/from air, rail, and ferry connections.

The Picture House: Ard Dorch, Broadford (tel/fax 01471-822531; e-mail holidays@picture-house.demon.co.uk; www.picture-house.demon.co.uk). Offers photographic holidays on Skye. Holidays include full-board accommodation and a series of full and half-day excursions. Transport in a mini-bus is included in the cost of the holiday. Photographic tuition or guidance is also available. As well as the usual mod cons there's a well-equipped darkroom for the use of guests. Collection from the coach stop in Broadford or from the railway station in Kyle of Lochalsh.

Red Deer Travel: An Nead, 10 Shullishadder, Portree (tel 01478-612142). Historical and cultural tours of Skye and western Scotland. Open all year.

Skye & Lochalsh Tourist Guides: 1 Balmeanach, Glenhinnisdale (tel/fax 01470-542484; e-mail SLTGA@word.demon.co.uk). Accredited tour guides for groups and individuals. Coaches, driver guiding, special interest, guided walks. Various languages.

Skye Tours: Duncan Hostel, The Pier, Kyleakin (tel 01599-534087; fax 01599-534795; e-mail nickstours@aol.com). Fully guided day tour of Skye. Open all year.

MEDIA

The local newspaper is the *West Highland Free Press* (Ian McCormack, Editor, West Highland Publishing Co Ltd, Broadford, Skye, IV49 9AP; tel 01471-822464; e-mail admin@whfp.co.uk; www.whfp.com), which is published every Thursday. It's regarded as a radical newspaper. Its Gaelic masthead slogan is *An Tìr, an Canan 'sna Daoine* ('The Land, the Language, the People'), a slogan borrowed from the Highland Land League which, in the late 19th century, fought to win security of tenure for crofters. The land issue is at the heart of the newspaper's politics down to the present day, and it also champions the Gaelic language by giving it political support and by publishing more Gaelic text than any other newspaper. The company also publishes a free tabloid holiday guide called *The Visitor*.

GETTING AROUND

Maps and Guides

The official 1:130,000 tourist map to Skye and Lochalsh is produced by *Estate Publications* for the *Highlands of Scotland Tourist Board*. Both this and the 1:250,000 (about 1 inch = 4 miles/2.5 cm = 6 km) Western Highlands Ordnance

Survey map (Sheet 4) are equally good for motorists and for orienting yourself. More useful for walkers, cyclists and climbers are Ordnance Survey Landranger maps: North Skye, Dunvegan and Portree (Sheet 23), South Skye and Cuillin Hills (Sheet 32), and Raasay & Applecross (Sheet 24), all 1:50,000 (1¼ inches = 1 mile/2 cm = 1 km). The 1:25,000 Cuillin and Torridon Hills Outdoor Leisure map (Sheet 8) gives you double the detail. Climbers should look for the Scottish Mountaineering Club's guide to Skye, and if possible, get its large-scale map of the Black Cuillin. You should find everything you need to know in the guidebook you are reading, unless you also plan to visit Orkney and Shetland, in which case you'll find our companion guidebook *The Scottish Islands – Orkney & Shetland* equally useful.

The best way to see Skye is by Shanks' pony, but if you haven't the time to walk everywhere you can hire a car, a bike, join a coach tour or even go horse riding and pony trekking. Island roads are single-track with scooped-out passing places. Keep a sharp look-out for sheep and cattle if you are driving as many of the cattle are black and difficult to see at night on unlit roads. If you hit an animal, try to move it to the side of the road. If it is still alive, try to find help. In any event report the accident to the police.

Buses

The Highland Council: tel 01463-702695. Operates a bus service with stops along the way to:

Armadale-Kyleakin-Broadford-Portree	Fiscavaig-Portree
Portree-Dunvegan	Vatten-Portree
Portree-Glendale	Waternish-Dunvegan
Portree-Flodigarry	

Timetables are complex, so it's a good idea to buy *The Highlands, Orkney, Shetland and Western Isles* public transport map from the Tourist Information Office for 10p.

Highland Country: Rapson Group (tel 01478-612622 or 01463-222244; e-mail info@rapsons.co.uk; www.rapsons.co.uk). Operates a bus service on the following routes, Monday to Friday:

Kyleakin-Broadford-Portree	Armadale-Broadford-Portree
Torrin-Broadford-Portree	Isle Oronsay-Broadford-Kyleakin (during school term)
Kyle of Lochalsh-Skye Bridge-Kyleakin	Portree-Flodigarry

Check fares and timetables with the bus company. Ask if day return tickets are available.

Royal Mail: tel 01246-546329 (for the helpline) or 08457-740740; www.royalmail.co.uk. Operates a four-seater **Postbus** service on three routes. From Glendale Post Office to Dunvegan Post Office return, Monday to Saturday, with stops at Fasach, Borreraig, Colbost, Skinidin, Milovaig, and Neist Point. There is also a service from Glendale Post Office to Ramscraig return on Monday and Wednesday. From Somerled Square, Portree, to Waternish and Dunvegan return, Monday to Saturday. This includes stops at Borve, Skeabost, Bernisdale, Kildonan, Edinbain, Fairy Bridge, Hallin, and Gillen. From Broadford to Glasnakille return, Monday to Friday, with stops at Suardal, Kilbride, Kilmarie, Drynan, and Elgol.

Taxis

A1 Cabs: tel 01478-611112. Accept credit cards.
A2B Taxi's: Matheson Place, Portree, IV51 9JA (tel 01478-613456). Day and night service. Tours arranged. Open all year.
Dunvegan: tel 01470-521560. Private hire and 24-hour taxi service.
Gus's Taxis: tel 01478-613000; fax 01478-613614. Tours and mini-bus hire.

Vehicle Rental
Ewan Macrae: West End Garage, Dunvegan Road, Portree, IV51 9HD (tel 01478-612554; fax 01478-613269). Car hire, open all year.

PC Portree Coachworks: Industrial Estate, Portree (tel 01478-612688, fax 01478-613281). Self-drive car hire.

Skye Car Rental: Broadford, IV49 9AB (tel 01470-822225; fax 01471-822759; e-mail sutherlandsb@lineone.net). Has cars and bicycles for hire. Collection and delivery can be arranged. Free collection from Skye Bridge. Open all year.

Sutherland Garage: Broadford (tel 01471-822225). Free collection from Kyleakin.

Cycle Hire
In the summer of 1800 a Cambridge undergraduate became the first man to pedal a tricycle through Skye, the climax of a 2,467-mile journey round Scotland on his Coventry-built Cheylesmove. His arrival was a minor sensation locally. Today, you'll see helmeted cyclists spinning along the roads all over the island, though not on trikes.

Fairwinds Bicycle Hire: Elgol Road, Broadford, IV49 9AB (tel/fax 01471-822270; e-mail stan.donaldson@talk21.com). Hourly, daily and weekly rates, open all year 9am to 7pm.

Glendale Post Office & Stores: Glendale, IV55 8WJ (tel 01470-511266; e-mail s.e.blackmore@talk21.com). Open all year 9.30am to 6.30pm.

Island Cycles: The Green, Portree, IV51 9BT (tel 01478-613121; fax 01478-511750; www.islandcycles-skye.co.uk). Open Monday to Saturday 9.30am to 5pm. Restricted opening during winter.

Skye Bicycle Hire: Orasay, Uig, IV51 9XU (tel 01470-542316; e-mail barbara@orasay.freeserve.co.uk). Daily and half-daily rates, open all hours.

Horse and Pony
Heavy Horse Tours: Annie Rose, 1 Holoman Park, Raasay, IV40 8PE (tel 01478-660233; fax 01478-660200; e-mail raasay.house@virgin.net). Based at Armadale Castle, Gardens and Museum. There is a 'castle trip' which takes about 10 minutes up the long drive to Armadale Castle. It costs £1.50 an adult and £1 a child. There's also a coastal excursion with views across the Sound of Sleat where you can spot seals basking on the rocks, oystercatchers along the shore and great black-backed gulls. This takes ¹/2 hour and costs £5 an adult, £2.50 a child. The tours run seven days a week from mid-May to mid-September from 10am to about 4.30pm.

Skye Riding Centre: Suladale, between Borve and Dunvegan on the A850 (tel 01470-582419). Horses and ponies, no riding experience necessary.

CRUISES
There's a wide choice of cruises to choose from, including scenic cruises, wildlife tours, fishing trips, boat hire and chartered sailings. Members of the *Skye and Lochalsh Marine Tourism Association* (Donald and Bella MacKinnon, c/o Bella Jane Boat Trips, Elgol, IV49 9BJ; tel/fax 01471-866244; e-mail info@ slmta.co.uk; www.slmta.co.uk) include:

Bella Jane Boat Trips: Elgol, by Broadford, IV49 9BJ (freephone 0800 731 3089; fax 01471-866244; e-mail bella@bellajane.co.uk; www.bellajane. demon.co.uk). Sightseeing trips to Loch Coruisk and the seals in the heart of the Cuillin. Trips leave from Elgol jetty every day from April to October (weather permitting) and take about three hours. Adult fare £13 and children 4-12 years £6.50. Also excursions to Rum, departing Elgol at 8am (crossing time about one hour), disembark at Kinloch and stay ashore for the day before being collected at 6.30pm. A day return costs £22, non-landing return £12, one way trip £12. Booking essential, phone between 7.30am to 10am and 7.30pm to 10pm. All Rum trips must be booked at least a day before departure and a minimum of six passengers applies. No dogs allowed.

Brigadoon Boat Trips: tel 01478-612641. Specialises in fishing trips and scenic tours.

Family's Pride II: Bruaich Mhor, 5 Scullamus, Breakish, IV51 8QB (tl/fax 01471-822037). Scenic glass-bottom boat trips in Broadford Bay.

Kaylee Jayne Boat Trips: Soay, Elgol, IV49 9BJ (tel 01687-462447). Takes a maximum of 12 people to Coruisk visiting seal colonies, with 1¹/₂ hours ashore. Operates June to September.

Sea.fari Adventures: Armadale Pier, Sleat (tel 01471-833316, mobile 07973 509387; e-mail safari_skye@yahoo.co.uk; www.seafari.co.uk/skye). Sea-life adventure boating specialists using custom-made 28 ft (8.5 m) rigid inflatables. Tour the south of Skye and Loch Nevis, 2 hours, 25 miles departing from either Armadale or Isleornsay.

Seaprobe Atlantis: Kyle of Lochalsh (tel/fax 01471-822716; e-mail seaprobe@ msn.com). Offers cruises above and below the waves, with underwater viewing gallery for all-round vision. You can see the wreck of the *Port Napier*, kelp forests, and seals and otters in their natural environment. Open April to October, seven days a week.

Skye Sail Yacht Charters: Kiltaraglen House, Staffin Road, Portree, IV51 9HR (tel 01478-613426; e-mail skipper@skye-sail.co.uk; www.skye-sail.co.uk). Has a 40ft (12 m) yacht for all-inclusive day sails, mini-cruises (2 nights), standard cruises (6 nights), or extended cruises (12 nights) for up to five people. All cruises are fully inclusive of meals and light refreshment, skippered by ex-RNLI coxswain. Waterproof gear essential.

South Skye Boats: tel 01471-844321, mobile 07803-766922; e-mail southskyeboats@skye.co.uk. Skippered boat charter, offers cruising around the Sound of Sleat, Small Isles, Loch Hourn and Nevis.

Staffin Bay Cruises: tel 01470-562217; e-mail angus@ultramail.co.uk. Offers a 1¹/₂ hour cruise to Staffin Bay aboard *MV Sea Eagle*, a 30ft (9 m) motor cruiser. Private charter and fishing trips by arrangement.

DRINKING

Isle of Skye Brewery (Uig; tel 01470-542477; fax 01470-542488; e-mail info@skyebrewery.co.uk; www.skyebrewery.co.uk) was established in 1995 with the aim of producing high quality cask-conditioned ales. Tours and tastings are available but there are no regular times so phone first. There is a charge of £2 per adult. The brewery produces five main ales:

Red Cuillin, a 4.2% abv smooth, malty, nutty, reddish-hue ale; **Black Cuillin**, a dark ale brewed with stout ingredients with the addition of rolled roast oats and Scottish heather honey; **Young Pretender** was originally brewed to commemorate the 250th anniversary of the ending of the Jacobite Rising in 1746. At 4% abv this is the driest and hoppiest of the Skye ales; **Blaven**, Norse-Gaelic for 'Blue Mountain,' at 5% abv is the strongest ale; **Hebridean Gold Porridge Oat & Malt Ale**, is a unique ale, brewed with porridge oats which produce an exceptionally smooth and flavoursome drink at 4.3% abv.

Historic ales add interest to the usual beers on sale in Skye. Try *Fraoch* – Heather Ale (5%); *Grozet* – gooseberry and wheat ale (5%); *Alba* – pine and spruce shoots (7.5%); and *Ebulum* – elderberry black ale (6.5%). All come in 330ml bottles at around £1.90.

Heather ale is probably the oldest type of ale still made. It's produced from an ancient Celtic recipe and like all things Celtic it has taken off. The Picts were known to be accomplished brewers. One legend tells of a Scottish king who, after killing all the Picts in battle except for the chief and his son, wanted the recipe for their famous heather ale. The two survivors were tortured to gain the secret. The Chief agreed to give it if they would kill his son quickly. After the boy was thrown to his death from the cliff the chief faced the king and said: 'Now in vain is the torture, fire shall never avail, here dies in my bosom the secret of the heather ale.' He then grabbed the King and jumped with him from the cliff.

Talisker Distillery and Visitor Centre (Carbost; tel 01478-614308; fax 01478-614302; www.scotch.com). Adult admission charge of £3.50 for a tour of the distillery includes a discount voucher, redeemable in the well-stocked shop when you buy a 700 ml bottle of malt whisky from a range of six classic malts. Open April to June and October Monday to Friday 9am to 4.30pm; July to September Monday to Saturday 9am to 4.30pm; November to March Monday to Friday 2pm to 4.30pm. Last tour 4pm. Complimentary dram after all tours.

You can also enjoy a sample and view a display of historic items related to *uisge beatha* at *Pràban na Linne* (tel 01471-833266; fax 01471-833260) in Sleat. The name means 'The little whisky centre by the Sound of Sleat'. This is located on the private fishing harbour at Eilean Iarmain, and was founded by Sir Iain Noble in 1976 to supply whisky to the Gaelic-speaking islands. All the brand names are Gaelic (said to 'greatly improve the flavour'). On offer are *Té Bheag* ('The Little Lady'), *Poit Dubh* ('Black Pot'), and *MacNaMara* ('Son of the Sea'). These are distilled in the traditional way, without the chill-filtering introduced 50 years ago to remove the proteins which could make the whisky hazy. Since it returned to the old Gaelic method the company has won gold in several international shows.

Stein Inn (Waternish; tel 01470-592362) is Skye's oldest pub. The bar is the heart of the inn, stocking more than 60 single malt whiskies as well as Skye Brewery ales and its own special 'Reeling Deck' ale. Good pub grub, too.

ENTERTAINMENT

Skye is famous for its pipers and the MacCrimmons, hereditary pipers to the MacLeods of Dunvegan, were acknowledged by all to be supreme. The MacCrimmons set up a college in Skye in the 16th century, and pipers from all over the Highlands and Islands came to learn from them. Near to the original site of the college is the **Piping Heritage Centre** at Borreraig, where you can learn all about the musical instrument once outlawed by the English as 'an instrument of war'. Throughout the summer you can also hear the skirl of the pipes at festivals from Dunvegan down to Armadale.

Music and theatre are organised throughout the year in various venues in south Skye by *Seall Community Arts* (Ostaig House, Sleat; tel 01471-844207). There are also week-long courses in Gaelic, fiddle, dance, bagpipes, clarsach, and singing at *Sabhal Mòr Ostaig* (tel 01471-844373), the Gaelic college in Sleat. *Talla Shomhairle* (Sorley Maclean Hall, Aros Centre, Viewfield Road, Portree, IV51 9EU; tel 01478-613649; fax 01478-613775; e-mail aros@demon.co.uk) is named after the internationally acclaimed poet and provides a setting for the promotion of Gaelic arts and culture. Events staged here include evenings of traditional music, drama, poetry and talks. There are also film shows featuring the latest releases and shows of archive material. Check with the Tourist Information Centre or the newspaper to find out what's on and when. *Skye Aros Centre* (tel 01478-613750; www.gaelicmusic.com) in Portree promotes traditional music concerts. There are *ceilidhs* and music sessions all over the place in season. The *Edinbane Hotel*, at Edinbane, near Dunvegan, has traditional music most weekends. Call Bill (tel 01470-582263) for more information. On a more modern note you'll find traditional music fused with folk and rock by a number of groups and singers, such as *Runrig*, *The Peatbog Faeries*, *Anne Martin*, *Blair Douglas*, and *Lorna Cormack*. Check out titles at *Skye Camanachd* (Paire nan Laoch, Portree, IV51 9EG) and *Whitewave Music* (tel 01470-542414; e-mail music@whiteact.demon.co.uk).

FLORA AND FAUNA

Flora

Nowhere on Skye is further than five miles (8 km) from the sea, so coastal plant communities extend well inland, giving rise to maritime heath and grassland and accounting for the presence of sea plantain on moorland. Conversely some mountain flowers grow near sea level, including **roseroot, hoary whitlowgrass** and **moss campion**. Arctic and alpine plants grow at unusually low altitudes in the Cuillin and along the Trotternish Ridge, among them **alpine lady's-mantle, alpine meadow-rue, arctic mouse-ear, purple, yellow** and **mossy saxifrages**, and the rare **alpine rock-cress** and **Iceland purslane**. The only known site of this rock-cress is in the Cuillin and Icelandic purslane grows only on the Trotternish Ridge and on Mull. A study of the island's flora has revealed an astonishing 589 species of flowering plants and ferns, as well as an abundance of lichens and mosses. In summer you'll see the tiny deep blue flower of the **milkwort, yellow tormentil**, and **pink lousewort**. Insect-eating plants such as **butterwort, sundew** and **bladderwort** thrive in damp hollows. The white flowers of **bogbean** and red and green **sphagnum bog moss** brighten dark peaty pools. Other distinctive plants are **lesser skullcap** and **white beak-sedge**. Many lochs carry fine clumps of white **water-lily, bogbean** and **bottle sedge**, and near Sligachan you might find the rare **pipewort. Royal fern** grows on islands in some lochs. Meadows contain more than 100 plant species, including **birdsfoot-trefoil, devil's-bit scabious, tufted vetch, ox-eye daisy**, and several types of orchid. Hay meadows, particularly in north Skye between Staffin and Earlish, are good places to see orchids, from the commoner **marsh** and **spotted orchids** to the rarer, more delicate, **butterfly orchids**. On the seashore in July you'll find purple **sea thrift, sea aster, stonecrop** and **scurvygrass**.

Broadleaved woodland is more extensive in the south than in the exposed north of Skye, although native trees such as **oak, ash, birch, rowan, willow, alder, aspen** and **bird cherry** grow in sheltered gorges throughout the island. The sheltered southern end of Skye, especially the Sleat peninsula, has large areas of natural woodland. The **ash** and **hazel** woods at Kinloch are owned and managed by *Forest Enterprise*. Spring and summer are the best seasons to see the many woodland birds and flowers. The beautiful Coille Dalavil woodland on the shores of Loch a'Ghlinne is owned and managed by the *Clan Donald Lands Trust* and has been deer-fenced to encourage forest regeneration. The *Clan Donald Ranger Service* organises seasonal guided walks from its base at the Clan Donald Visitor Centre, in Armadale.

Fauna

Otters thrive all around the coast and can often be seen near the Skye Bridge, which has special otter tunnels to let them through. You may also spot them hunting near Suisnish pier, on Raasay. Dunvegan, Kyleakin, and Raasay are good **seal-watching** areas, although seals can be seen in most inshore waters. Woodland areas are the haunt of **hedgehogs, mice, rabbits, foxes** and **deer**, but as woodland areas decrease some species are adapting to more open terrain and deer and foxes can also be seen on the moors and hills. Two types of deer occur on the islands, red deer, which range freely over the hills, and the smaller roe deer. Roe deer are not common and are found mainly in the woodlands of Sleat. The **brown hare** is also found on Skye. Two species of bat are the common **pipistrelle** and the less common **long-eared bat**. Also present but rarely seen are stoats. **Harbour porpoise** are common around the coast and several types of **dolphin**, as well as **killer, pilot** and **minke whales** can be seen further out, especially off the north and west of Skye. On calm days in spring and summer you might even see huge

(40 ft/12 m) **basking shark**. The Inner Sound is home to the *British Underwater Test and Evaluation Centre* where the Royal Navy tries out equipment. Conservationists worry about the danger this activity poses to whales and other cetaceans around Skye, especially since a dead minke whale was found floating in the Sound during Nato exercises. Whales in the vicinity during these exercises deserted the area and unusually large numbers have been stranded near military test areas.

Bird-Watching

More than 200 species of birds have been recorded on Skye. Many of them, however, are infrequently seen, while others are found only in small populations. Despite its sea cliffs seabird colonies on Skye are small. **Black guillemot, shag, cormorant, kittiwake,** and **fulmar** are the main species, while a few **puffin, razorbill,** and **tern** nest at isolated sites on outlying islands. North-west Skye is the best place to see large gatherings of seabirds and in June and July hundreds of **auks** can be seen off this coast. A few wildfowl and waders winter along the coasts, with large numbers of eider in the Inner Sound of Raasay, and small groups of **wigeon** round the coast at Broadford, Portree and Dunvegan. **Mallard, red-breasted merganser, eider, shelduck, oystercatcher** and **ringed plover** are among the summer nesting birds. **Greenland white-fronted geese** settle on the islands in the winter months, **greylag geese** migrating to and from Iceland can be seen over the islands in autumn and spring, **barnacle geese** are winter visitors from October to April, **Brent geese** stop over on Skye and Raasay in September and October, and **pink-footed geese** can often be seen over Skye and Raasay in the autumn and spring.

Freshwater lochs attract limited numbers of wintering birds, such as **whooper swan** and **golden-eye**, and more rarely **tufted duck** and **pochard**. In summer, **common sandpiper** nest by lochs and streams, while here and there you'll see **pied** and **grey wagtail, dipper,** and a few pairs of **little grebe**. Birds in the mixed woodlands include **woodcock, tawny owl, great, blue** and **coal tit, redstart, woodpecker, willow** and **wood warbler, spotted flycatcher, treecreeper,** and **tree pipit**. Moorland provides nesting habitats for such small birds as **meadow pipit, skylark** and **wheatear**, and for waders including **dunlin, curlew,** the rare **greenshank,** and **golden plover**. The moorland lochs may be occupied by breeding **red-throated** and occasionally **black-throated diver**. Moorland and mountain provide territories for birds of prey, especially the **buzzard** and **hen harrier**, which also frequents woodland. **Golden eagle** and **peregrine falcon** may be seen, as well as **kestrel, sparrowhawk** and **merlin**. **Short-eared owl** and **white-tailed sea eagle** can also occasionally be spotted. Other common birds include **martin, swallow, crow, rook, raven, dove, pigeon, wren, thrush, lark, finches** and **buntings**. There are **heronries** on Skye and in the forest on Raasay. All birds and their nests are protected by law.

SPORT AND RECREATION

Walking and Climbing

The spectacular **Black Cuillin** of south-west Skye are renowned among walkers and climbers so outrage greeted the announcement in 2000 by John MacLeod, 29th chief of Clan MacLeod, that he was putting the Cuillin up for sale for £10-million. Since the announcement the National Trust for Scotland has been negotiating with him to buy the mountains for the nation. MacLeod says 12th century Dunvegan Castle, his family seat, needs repairs costing millions of pounds. Conservation groups have valued the 23,000 acres (9,308 ha) of wilderness surrounding the Cuillin range at a maximum of £2.5 million.

These are peaks that should be attempted only by fit and experienced walkers and climbers. Take the paths into the foothills of the Black Cuillin through Glen Brittle and into the **Red Cuillin** from Sligachan. Well-maintained footpaths also run from the Sligachan Hotel to Coire Riabhach ('Grey Corry') on the slopes of Sgurr nan Gillean and for eight miles (13 km) along Glen Sligachan to Camasunary. The popular Glen Sligachan path leads as far as Loch Scavaig near Elgol, so the round trip is a long trek. A trip that should not be missed is the short cruise across Loch Scavaig from Elgol, to walk along the path by the River Scavaig to Loch Coruisk ('Cauldron of Water'), in the heart of the Cuillin.

In the north of the island in a scenically outstanding area is the **Trotternish Ridge**, taking in The Storr, the 164 ft (50 m) rock pinnacle known as The Old Man of Storr, and the bizarre rock formations of The Quiraing, where another pinnacle appropriately named The Needle jabs the skyline. The ridge stretches north from Portree and is a tough but rewarding 20-mile (32 km) route to Rubha Hunish on the northern tip of Skye. This can be covered in two days. You don't have to walk the entire length of the Trotternish Ridge to enjoy some spectacular views. One high point, Beinn Edra, can be climbed from Uig in north-west Skye, where the twin peaks of **MacLeod's Tables** rise above Glendale. There are lots of excellent walks along the coast, including the ramble to Neist Point lighthouse, the most westerly point on Skye, and the walk to the **otter sanctuary** at Kylerhea, which is notable not just for the opportunity to watch otters, but also for the spectacular views across the Sound of Sleat. *Isle of Skye & Lochalsh – A Guide to Forest Walks & Trails*, a free leaflet published by Forest Enterprise, details some of these walks.

Munros

Skye offers 30 significant summits, and more than a dozen peaks of 3,000 ft (914 m) and above beckon from the Cuillin area. Skye has more of these high peaks, known as **Munros**, than any other Scottish island. Forming a horseshoe about eight miles (13 km) long around the head of Loch Coruisk in the Black Cuillin are 11 Munros – *Sgurr Dubh Mor*, 3,097 ft (944 m); *Sgurr nan Eag*, 3,037 ft (924 m); *Sgurr Alasdair*, 3,254 ft (992 m); *Sgurr Mhic Choinnich*, 3,110 ft (948 m); *Sgurr Dearg* (Inaccessible Pinnacle), 3,235 ft (986 m); *Sgurr na Banachdich*, 3,166 ft (965 m); *Sgurr a' Ghreadaidh*, 3,192 ft (973 m); *Sgurr a' Mhadaidh*, 3,012 ft (918 m); *Sgurr nan Gillean*, 3,166 ft (965 m); *Am Basreir*, 3,086 ft (935 m); and *Bruach na Frithe*, 3,143 ft (958 m). All these are on Sheet 32 of the Ordnance Survey's Landranger map series. The traverse of the **Cuillin main ridge** with its 11 Munros and various lesser tops is regarded as the finest in Britain. Nowhere along the 8-mile (13 km) traverse from first to last peak does the ridge height fall below 2,461 ft (750 m). The traverse calls for sustained scrambling, and several pitches require rock climbing skill up to 'Very Difficult' standard. A high level of fitness and skill is needed to complete the traverse in a day (12-14 hours), starting and finishing at sea level, and two days with an overnight bivouac is more usual. The ridge was first traversed in 1911. Between Loch Scavaig and Loch Slapin is 3,045 ft (928 m) high *Bla Bheinn* (Blaven), first climbed in 1857. A clergyman, the Rev Smith, made the first recorded ascent in the Cuillin in September 1835 and in July 1836 Sgurr nan Gillean was climbed by Professor David James Forbes, a geologist who compiled the first accurate map of the Cuillin. For many years Inaccessible Pinnacle, projecting from the south-east side of Sgurr Dearg's summit, was considered unclimbable. It was finally scaled in 1880 by the Pilkington brothers. Every peak was climbed between 1895 and 1907 by Ashley P Abraham.

To the east of Glen Sligachan is the stretch of round scree-covered granite hills known as the Red Cuillin. Two of the four tops are easily climbed; the other two call for some scrambling on steep slopes. A notable annual event at Sligachan every July is the **Glamaig Hill Race**. The imposing scree-covered cone of 2,543 ft (775

m) Glamaig is the closest summit to the hotel. In 1899, a Gurkha by the name of Harkabir Thapa ran barefoot from the Sligachan Hotel to the top of Glamaig and back again in 75 minutes. On hearing this the MacLeod of MacLeod refused to believe it, so poor Thapa was asked to do it again. The second time he completed the run in 55 minutes and this remained the official record for nearly a century. The record now stands at 44 minutes, 41 seconds, and was set by Mark Rigby in 1997.

The **best time** to tackle the Cuillin is in late spring or early autumn and, as there's brochure weather and there's real weather, always check the forecast before setting out. All hillwalkers and climbers know how cold it can get among the tops, even when it's sunny down below. The rate of cooling is called the lapse rate and works out at an average drop of 35°F (2°C) for every 1,000 ft (305 m) of ascent, meaning that while the valley is experiencing a cool spring day at 39°F (4°C), it is freezing at 2,000 ft (610 m), the height of a large hill.

Mountain Huts

The Mountaineering Council of Scotland's **Glen Brittle Memorial Hut** is at the edge of the Cuillin, near Glenbrittle House. It has 18 bunks, sleeping bags required, £2.50 a night. Keys are available from the resident warden in summer, otherwise contact the secretary (Mrs Sandra Winter; tel 01882-632240; e-mail bhasteirtooth@aol.com). Open April to October, other times possible by arrangement. The *Junior Mountaineering Club of Scotland's* **Coruisk Memorial Hut** is on the shore of Loch Scavaig, near the landing stage. There are nine bunks, some blankets, cookers, and heaters. Access by boat from Elgol or on foot from Sligachan via Glen Sligachan and Druin Hain, or from Strathaird via the 'Bad Step'. Hut accommodation is £5 a night, camping day charge of £1. Book through Mr AW Dunn (474 Dumbarton Road, Glasgow, G11 6SQ; tel 0141-577 9415). Boat from Elgol should be booked with Donald MacKinnon (11 Elgol, Broadford; tel 01471-866244). Both huts are available for the use of MCofS and British Mountaineering Council members and their affiliated clubs.

Guides

Local guides conduct walks into the mountains, moorlands, woodlands, and along coastal trails. For guided walks in the Sleat area, contact the *Countryside Rangers* (Clan Donald Visitor Centre, Armadale; tel 01471-844305/227).

George Yeomans: Portree (tel 01478-650380). Mountain guiding on Skye, Munros and classic scrambles. Hill and coastal walks. Daily guiding or weekly courses.

Hebridean Pathways: PO Box 6340, Broadford (tel 0771-257 7121; fax 01733-33 1254; e-mail info@hebrideanpathways.co.uk). Walking and climbing guiding service based on Skye. Open April to November.

Pinnacle Ridge: Colin Threlfall, 12 Portnalong, Carbost (tel 01478-640330). Offers guided scrambling and climbing outings. Introductory summer scrambles include four days in the Cuillin for £120, tackling 12 Munros costs £160, classic scrambles £180, rock climbing £200, and the Cuillin ridge traverse costs £300.

Scottish Youth Hostels Association: 7 Glebe Crescent, Stirling, FK8 2JA (tel 01786-891400; fax 01786-891333; e-mail info@syha.org.uk). Also arranges hillwalking holidays in Skye. There are two grades of walks based at the Glenbrittle Hostel. An 'Introduction to the Cuillin' with lots of ascents over rough terrain is suitable for fit and experienced hillwalkers. The 'Munros Holiday' covers very rugged and demanding terrain, with steep ascents. Scrambling experience, a high level of fitness and a good head for height is required.

Skye Guides Mountaineering: Mike Lates, 3 Luid, Broadford (tel 01471-822116). Places emphasis on teaching basic skills with an experienced professional guide. Itineraries to suit individual abilities.

Skye Highs Mountain Guiding: Broadford (tel 01471-822116). Rock climbing, abseiling and mountain guiding. Beginners welcome. Open all year.

Skyetrak Safari: Skeabost Farmhouse, Portree (tel/fax 01470-532436; e-mail rosie@skytrak.demon.co.uk). Interpretive guiding for walkers. Open all year.

Wildlife Guiding: 3 Waterstein, Glendale (tel 01470-511265). Guided walks to Neist Point lighthouse, each walk about 45 minutes. Open all year.

Diving

You can dive all year round in Skye. There is always somewhere safe and the visibility is usually around 49-98 ft (15-30 m). Take your pick of shallow, scenic, deep, cliff, drift or wreck diving, from novice to advanced divers, at depths of 49-115 ft (15-35 m). No wrecks lie deeper than 98 ft (30 m) and include the 1,463 ton British collier *SS Chadwick*, the 9,600 ton mine-layer *HMS Port Napier*, the 1,381 ton Norwegian cargo ship *SS Doris*, and the 6,850 ton cargo vessel *SS Urlana*.

Dive and Sea the Hebrides: Gordon MacKay and Aileen Robertson, Shorepark, Lochbay, Waternish, IV55 8GD (tel 01470-592219; fax 01470-592399, mobile 0798 010 6263; www.dive-and-sea-the-hebrides.co.uk). Offers shore-based comfort in a modern dive centre with accommodation and all facilities. Bedrooms sleep 10 people in two rooms for two, one room for six in ship's cabin-style bedrooms. All you need to bring is your food and your diving gear. On-site is compressor and airbank, changing and drying rooms. Another self-catering unit provides accommodation for eight people in total, ideal for mixed group expeditions.

Portree Diving Services: 5 Achachork, Portree (tel 01478-612274).

Skye Diving Centre: Harlosh, Dunvegan (tel 01470-521366).

Both these latter companies will do air fills if you are in their areas.

Fishing: *Isle of Skye Sea Angling Club:* Secretary J McInnes, Golf View, Kilmuir, Dunvegan (tel 01470-521724).

Golf

Isle of Skye Golf Club (Sconser; tel 01478-650414/351; fax 01478-650351; e-mail iselofskye.golfclub@btinternet.com), halfway between Broadford and Portree. Nine-hole course laid out with 18 tees for golfers of all standards. Spectacular views of the Red Cuillin and the Isle of Raasay. Golf clubs and trolleys for hire. Small shop and tea-room open to all visitors. Green fees (day ticket) £15 adult; £7.50 junior. Country membership available from £55.

Horse-Riding

Portree Riding and Trekking Stables: Graham Long, Garalapin (tel 01478-612945; e-mail long@garalapin.idps.co.uk; www.lochalsh.com). BHS-approved. Out-rides, qualified instruction, large sand school, cross-country course. All standards catered for.

Skye Riding Centre: Trudi Robertson, 2 Suledale, Portree (tel 01470-582419; fax 01470-532282; www.skye-riding.co.uk). See Skye from the saddle. No experience necessary. Caters for all ages and standards. Hard hats provided. TRSS approved. Local authority licensed. Open all year.

Trotternish Trekking: Borve (tel 01470-532233). Off-road riding into the hills for all ages and standards of riders. Open July and August.

Uig Pony Trekking Centre: The Uig Hotel (tel 01470-542205; fax 01470-542308). Rides to suit all abilities. Open all year, seven days a week.

Other Activities
Isle of Skye Swimming Pool: Camanachd Square, Portree (tel 01478-612655; fax 01478-613259). Local authority swimming pool. Open all year, Monday to Saturday.

Whitewave: 19 Linicro, Kilmuir (tel 01470-542414; fax 01470-542443; e-mail activities@whiteact.demon.co.uk). Outdoor centre offers kayaking, windsurfing, archery and guided walks. Open all year.

HELP AND INFORMATION
Skye Tourist Information Centres:
Portree: Bayfield House, Bayfield Road (tel 01478-612137; fax 01478-612141). Open all year, Monday to Friday 9am to 5pm, Saturday 10am to 4pm. Closed Sunday.

Broadford: Car Park (tel 01471-822361; fax 01471-822141). Seasonal opening.

Dunvegan: 2 Lochside (tel 01470-52181; fax 01470-521582). Limited opening hours in winter.

Uig: Caledonian MacBrayne Ferry Offices (tel/fax 01470-542404). Seasonal opening.

Mainland:
Kyle of Lochalsh: Car Park (tel 01599-534276; fax 01599-534808).

Mallaig: tel 01687-462170; fax 01687-462064.

Ullapool: Argyle Street (tel 01854-612135; fax 01854-613031).

Emergency Services:
For police, fire or ambulance services in an emergency telephone **999**.

Police: Portree (tel 01478-612888), Broadford (tel 01471-822222), Dunvegan (tel 01470-521333), Uig (tel 01470-542222), Ardvasar, Sleat (tel 01471-844222).

Mountain Rescue: tel 01478-612888.

Portree Hospital: tel 01478-613200.

Portree Medical Centre: tel 01478-612013.

Hospital: Broadford (tel 01471-822491).

Doctor: Sleat (tel 01471-844283).

Caledonian MacBrayne: Armadale (tel 01471-844248); Mallaig (tel 01687-462403).

Glenelg-Kylerhea Ferry: Skye Ferry (tel 01599-511302; fax 01599-511477; e-mail roddy@skyeferry.co.uk).

Post Offices: Gladstone Building, Quay Brae, Portree (tel 01478-612533); Broadford (tel 01471-822201); and Glendale (tel 01470-511266).

Library Service: tel 01478-613830. There are libraries at Portree and Broadford. Portree library has lots of local reference material, as well as the Dualchas local history collection.

Museums and Heritage Service: tel 01478-613857. Information on the history and culture of the area. A large collection of historic photographs, archaeological records and other material is available for inspection by appointment.

Clan Donald Ranger Service: tel 01471-844305.

Scottish Natural Heritage: Bridge Road, Portree (tel 01478-613329).

Royal Society for the Protection of Birds: tel 01471-822882.

CALENDAR OF EVENTS

Check the 'What's On' display at the local Tourist Information Centres and the local Press. For up-to-date details access www.host.co.uk.

April   *Southern Cairn Terrier Club Championship Show.* Contact honorary secretary, J Berrecloth, Cairn Terrier Club (tel 01382-457601).

May   *Isle of Skye Classic Vehicle Rally:* Portree and North Skye
Isle of Skye Story Telling Festival: Portree and Isle of Rona.
Highland Festival (information line: tel 01463-711112; www.highlandfestival.org.uk). A massive celebration of the uniquely rich and vibrant cultural traditions of the Highlands, featuring the area's finest indigenous artistes complemented by world-class performers from further afield. Various venues.
Garden and Craft Fair: Armadale.
Skye Scene (Braigh-Uige, Uig, IV51 9YB; tel/fax 01470-542228; e-mail braighuige@aol.com). May to September. Ceilidh with piping, Highland dancing, fiddlers, accordionists, singers, *clarsach* (harp) playing and audio-visual tour of Skye.

June   *Isle of Skye Half-Marathon.*
Donald MacDonald Quaich Piping Recital Competition: Armadale.
Celtic Festival: Dunvegan.

July   *Archery Competition:* Armadale.
Glamaig Hill Race: tel 01478-650204.
Feis an Eilean: tel 01471-844207.

August   *Skye Agricultural Show:* Portree.
Skye Highland Games: Portree.
Silver Chanter Piping Competition: Dunvegan.
Talisker Sheepdog Trials: Portree.

September   *Skye Terrier Convention:* Portree.
Skye and Lochalsh Food and Drink Festival: various venues throughout the area.

November   *Fireworks Spectacular:* Dunvegan Castle.

SLEAT AND THE SOUTH

The Skye Bridge has one of its feet planted on Eilean Bàn ('White Island'), which in the 1960s was the home of Gavin Maxwell, famous as the author of the otter book *Ring of Bright Water.* To the south of the bridge is Kyleakin, once the busy Skye terminal for the ferry from Kyle of Lochalsh. At the entrance to the harbour is ruined 12th century Castle Moil (*Caisteal Maol*). Legend says that a Viking princess known as 'Saucy Mary' used to levy tolls on passing vessels by raising a chain to prevent their passage. About a mile (1.6 km) left of the Skye Bridge is the **Bright Water Visitor Centre** (The Pier, Kyleakin IV41 8PL; tel/fax 01599-530040), displaying the cultural and natural history of Eilean Bàn. Open May to November, Monday to Saturday 9am to 5.30pm. At **Kylerhea** you are virtually certain to catch a glimpse of the elusive otter from the **Otter Haven** hide. A remote viewing system has been installed at the hide using TV cameras with high-powered lenses. These can be controlled by visitors, giving close-up views of life on the seashore. The Otter Haven is open from 9am until one hour before dusk each day.

From Kylerhea, a narrow road climbs steeply through Glen Arroch before joining the coast road from Kyleakin to Broadford. You have got to go to **Broadford** to pick up the A851 road to the green and wooded Sleat (pronounced *Slate*) peninsula in the south, known as 'The Garden of Skye.' **Kinloch Lodge** (see *Accommodation*) is near the narrow neck of land where the peninsula effectively begins. A woodland walk near Kinloch takes you through oaklands where, at the end of the waymarked Forest Enterprise track, is the deserted village of Leitirfura. With a good map and stout shoes the fit could continue the walk to Kylerhea.

Most of Sleat is divided between two private estates and both welcome enquiries about access and facilities. The 20,000-acre (8,094 ha) southern half, as far as the road to Ord on Loch Eishort, is owned by the *Clan Donald Lands Trust*, and the northern half is owned by Sir Iain Noble, an Edinburgh merchant banker. His office can be contacted at the *Hotel Eilean Iarmain*, in **Isleornsay**, a village notable for once being a thriving west coast herring port as well as the site of Skye's first public toilet in 1820. It also has a pretty harbour, shop, and an art gallery, Talla Dearg. Offshore is the small island of **Ornsay**. You can walk to it at low water to inspect a ruined nunnery chapel and a lighthouse (1857). On the road to **Armadale** is one of the many ruined MacDonald strongholds which dot the area, 14th century **Knock Castle**, though there's not much to see apart from the creeper-covered stones of the keep. At nearby Kilmore are the ruins of 17th century *A' Chill-Mhor* ('Big Church'). Old gravestones include those of various MacDonalds. The Parish Church of Scotland was built in 1876. Down the road is castellated **Kilmore Manse** (1811). The rapidly expanding Gaelic College of *Sabhal Morr Ostaig* ('Big Barn of East Bay') was once a MacDonald farm. The college runs short courses in Gaelic, music, culture and the environment during the holidays. Full-time students are taught such subjects as business, computing, Gaelic television work and drama.

The ferry from Mallaig to Armadale brings you to the heart of MacDonald country. Here is the renowned **Clan Donald Visitor Centre** which includes the ruins of **Armadale Castle** and the fascinating **Museum of the Isles** (Armadale, Sleat, IV45 8RS; tel 01471-844305/227; fax 01471-844275; e-mail office@cland.demon.co.uk; www.cland.demon.co.uk). There are guided walks around the estate or you can stroll at will among the remarkable Victorian gardens. The planted woodlands around the castle include an extensive and long-established arboretum with some fine tree specimens. Leading from the formal gardens are nature trails which run throughout the surrounding 20,000 acres (8,094 ha). The Centre is a place of pilgrimage for MacDonalds from all over the world who want to trace their ancestors at the family history research centre. There is a small fee for this research. The **Clan Donald Library** has one of the most significant archives on the history of the Highlands and the Hebrides, more than 7,000 reference books in all. The library and Centre are open seven days a week from April to the end of October, from 9.30am to 5.30pm. The admission charge of £10 for family tickets covers the castle gardens, museum, and nature trails. Most facilities are suitable for people with disabilities.

Nearby is **Ardvasar**, a pretty village and one of the social centres of the area with a grocery store, hotel, B&Bs and a post office. The coastal road ends at the **Aird of Sleat**, a crofting township with beautiful views of the mainland and the Small Isles. From here the two-mile (3 km) track to the **Point of Sleat** is a popular and beautiful walk. You are asked to respect the privacy of the tiny community around the harbour and not to cross croft fields to reach the white lighthouse at the Point. To get to the other side of the peninsula you have to retrace your steps to **Ostaig**, where a narrow road crosses to Loch Eishort. A track to the left half-way along the road is the beginning of a satisfying walk to **Dalavil Glen** and Skye's only canal, connecting large freshwater Loch a' Ghlinne to the sea. This walk calls

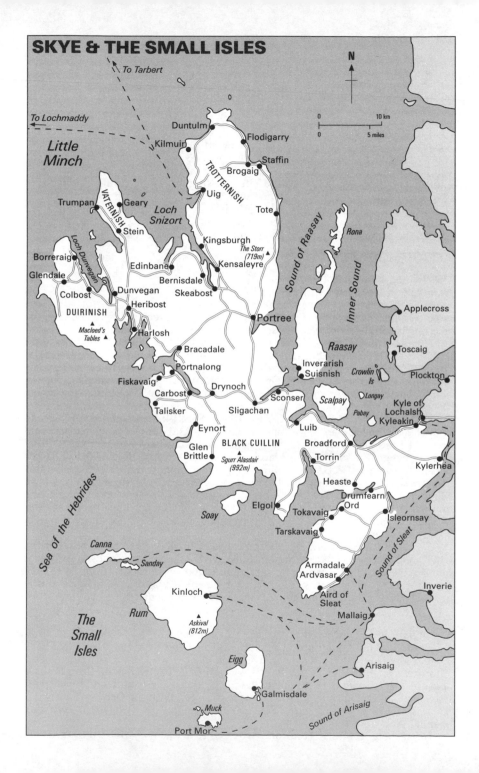

for a good map and waterproof boots. Loch Dùghaill ('Dougal's Loch') lies alongside the cross-peninsula road in the shadow of Sgurr na h-Iolaire ('Eagle Hill'). **Tarskavaig** and **Tokavaig** are pretty villages along the shores of Loch Eishort. The ruins of **Dunsgaith Castle** can be seen on the cliffs just north of Tokavaig. This was the original seat of the MacDonalds before they moved north in the early 1600s to Duntulm. Legend says the castle was built on its isolated rock in a single night with the help of a local witch. It was also where the legendary Irish hero Cúchulainn learned the art of war at the 'School for Heroes' run by Sgàthach, the Celtic warrior queen of Skye. His name lives on in the Cuillin mountain range. **Ord** is the place to watch splendid sunsets over the Cuillin and Blaven. It is also the site of 8th century **St Comgan's Chapel** (*Teampuill Chaon*). A private garden with its entrance gate on the shore, has a remarkable selection of plants. The little islands in the mouth of the loch have coral-like beaches favoured by common seals. From Ord a hilly little by-way crosses the peninsula to join the main Broadford-Armadale road.

ACCOMMODATION
Hotels
Ardvasar Hotel: Sleat IV45 8RS (tel 01471-844223; fax 01471-844495; e-mail christine@ardvasar-hotel.demon.co.uk). Three-star hotel, near Armadale ferry. Nine en suite rooms, from £40 B&B. Open all year. Accomplished cooking. No smoking in dining-room. Vegetarians welcome. Taste of Scotland.

Hotel Eilean Iarmain: Sleat, Isleornsay IV43 8QR (tel 01471-833332; fax 01471-833275; e-mail bookings@eilean-iarmain.co.uk; www.eileaniarmain. co.uk). Three-star hotel on the small rocky bay of Isle Ornsay, 16 en suite rooms and four suites, from £60 B&B. Open all year. Award-winning restaurant. Sip the hotel's own *Té Bheag* whisky. No smoking in restaurant. Vegetarians welcome. Taste of Scotland. AA one rosette.

Kinloch Lodge: Sleat IV43 8QY (tel 01471-833214; fax 01471-833277; e-mail kinloch@dial.pipex.com; www.kinloch-lodge.co.uk). Four-star hotel and ancestral home of Lord and Lady Macdonald, dating from 1540, 14 en suite rooms, from £55. Between November and March, winter rates range from £75 to £85 per person for dinner, B&B, with a third night's accommodation free provided that dinner is taken (£35 a head). Open all year except Christmas. Lady Claire Macdonald is one of Scotland's best known cooks and cookery writers. She presents a five-course take it or leave it table d'hôte menu. Most people take it. Member of the Scotch Beef Club. Vegetarians welcome, but prior notice required. Taste of Scotland.

Skeabost House Hotel: Skeabost Bridge IV51 9NP (tel 01470-532202; fax 01470-532454; e-mail skeabost@sol.co.uk; www.sol.co.uk/s/skeabost). Three-star hotel in the grand old manner, former hunting lodge, 26 rooms, from £40 B&B. Open March to November, facilities for disabled visitors. A buffet menu is available during the day and table d'hôte menu changing daily.

B&B
Mrs P Barton: Hazelwood, Post Office, Ardvasar (tel 01471-844200).

Fernlea: Mrs A Harrison, Upper Breakish, IV42 8PY (tel 01471-822107). Three-star, open March to October, from £19.

Fiordhem: Mrs B la Trobe, Ord, IV44 8RN (tel 01471-855226). Private house accommodation with three double/twin room with private facilities and sea views. Non-smoking establishment. DB&B from £37. Open Easter to October.

Mrs M Fraser: 10 Calgarry, Sleat, IV45 8RU (tel 01471-844312). One-star, open all year, from £20.

Home Leigh: Mrs R Houlton, Ardvasar, Sleat, IV45 8RU (tel/fax 0471-

844361). Three-star, open February to December, from £16 a night.

Nethallan: Mrs W Hyndman, 12 Lower Breakish, Breakish, IV42 8QA (tel 01471-822771; e-mail nethallan@currantbun.com). Four-star, open all year, from £30.

Mrs P Nicolson: Marsco, Ord (tel 01471-855249).

Mrs P Phillips: 4 Camuscross, Isleornsay (tel 01471-833237).

The Old Schoolhouse: Mrs P Newman, Aird of Sleat, IV45 8RN (tel 01471-844218). Two-star, open March to October, from £20 a night.

Strathgorm: Mrs A Graham, 15 Upper Breakish, Breakish, IV42 8PY (tel/fax 01471-822508). Four-star, open February to December, from £18.

Self-Catering

Armadale Castle Cottages: Armadale, Sleat, IV45 8RS (tel 01471-844305/227; fax 01471-844275; e-mail office@cland.demon.co.uk). Four-star, luxury self-catering cottages in the grounds of the castle. Open all year, from £325-£575 a week.

Calligary Cottage: Mrs Janet MacLure, 10 Aird, Ardvasar, IV45 8RN (tel/fax 01471-844205). Three-star, two bedrooms, sleeps 5. Open all year, from £150-£325 a week.

Cedar Cottage: 10 Waterloo, Breakish, IV42 8QE (tel 01471-822506; fax 01471-822465). Two-star, two bedrooms, sleeps 6. Open all year, from £150-£305 a week.

Mrs C MacKinnon: Armadale (tel 01471-833285).

Sandaig Cottage: Duisdale (tel 01471-833212).

Shore Cottage, in Ord, Sleat (Mrs E White, 66 Woodend Drive, Glasgow G13 1TG; tel/fax 0141-954 9013). One-star, four bedrooms, sleeps 9. Open all year, from £190-£550 a week.

Hostels

Armadale Youth Hostel: Ardvasar, Sleat, IV45 8RS (tel 01471-844260). One-star. Open March to October. Hostel reception opens at 5pm. Access until 11.45pm. Total of 42 beds with three rooms with 9+ beds. Shop about a mile away, closes at lunchtime on a Saturday. Bus 1/4 mile (0.4 km) away, ferry 1/2 mile (0.8 km). Cycle hire locally.

Dun Caan: Castle View, Kyleakin, IV41 8SL (tel 01599-534087; fax 01599-534795).

Fossil Bothy Independent Hostel: 13 Lower Breakish (tel 01471-822644, weekdays; tel 01471-822297, evenings and weekends; e-mail fiona. mandeville@talk21.com). On the seashore, five miles (8 km) from the Skye Bridge. Six bunks in the open-plan main room and two in a separate bedroom, fully equipped kitchen. Open all year, from £7.50 a night.

Hairy Coo Backpacker Hotel: Toravaig House, Knock Bay, Sleat, IV44 8RE (tel 01471-833231; fax 01471-833393; e-mail stotty@hairycooskye. freeserve.co.uk). Independent hostel with 26 beds, open all year, from £9 a night.

Kyleakin Youth Hostel: Kyleakin, IV41 8PL (tel 01599-534585) two-star. Continental breakfast included in overnight price. Premier rooms available. International Booking Service. Hostel reception opens at 2pm. Late access until 2am. Open all year. 125 beds, 35 rooms with 4 beds, three rooms with 5-8 beds, family rooms (aged 5+), wheelchair access, train (Kyle) two miles (3 km) away, bus nearby, laundry, hostel store.

Skye Backpackers: Benmhor, Kyleakin, IV41 8PH (tel/fax 01599-534510), 35 beds, open all year, from £10 a night.

Sleat Independent Hostel: The Glebe, Kilmore, Sleat IV44 8RG (tel 01471-844440; fax 01471-844272). Independent hostel with 24 beds, open all year, from £8.

EATING

Serious foodies will doubtless recognise the name Lady Claire MacDonald. She and her husband own and run *Kinloch Lodge* (Sleat; tel 01471-833214; fax 01471-833277), which is home to her cookery school as well as a mecca for meals which are country fare with flair. Open to non-residents.

The Seagull Restaurant: The Old School, Upper Breakish, Breakish IV 42 8PY (tel 01471-822001). Modern and traditional dishes with fish and seafood from local fish merchant. Offers a range of meat and fish dishes and a selection of vegetarian meals. Open all day from Easter to early October.

Stables Restaurant: Armadale Castle Gardens (tel 01471-844305/227; fax 01471-844275). Designed in 1822, it was built to accommodate Lord MacDonald's attendants as well as his horses and coaches. Now a licensed restaurant serving freshly prepared meals in surroundings reminiscent of a baronial hall.

SHOPPING

Crafts route maps are available from the *Skye and Lochalsh Arts and Crafts Association* (chairman Stuart Whatley; tel 01470-582234) and the *Dunvegan and North-West Skye Crafts Group* (chairman Terry Wilding; tel 01470-511240).

Gallery an Talla Dearg: Eilean Iarmain, Isleornsay, Sleat IV43 8QR (tel/fax 01767-650444) stone and bronze sculptures. Open August to September, weekdays 9.30am to 6.30pm, Saturday 9.30am to 1pm.

Octave: The Old Post Office, Ardvasar (tel 01471-844426). Has contemporary works in wood, glass, ceramics, textiles and paper by local people. Normally open Monday to Saturday from 10.30am to 5pm, or by arrangement.

Skye Batiks: Armadale (tel 01471-844396; fax 01471-844496) and Portree (The Green; tel 01478-613331; fax 01478-613338; e-mail info@skyebatiks. demon.co.uk; www.skyebaticks.demon.co.uk). Voted best craft shop in Scotland for two years running. Celtic designs transformed by batik and colourful handloomed cotton and soft wearable tweed garments, and other gift ideas. Open seven days a week.

BROADFORD AND THE CUILLIN

This part of Skye was Mackinnon country, a clan whose men were renowned for their great personal strength. One chief choked a wolf to death with his bare hands, holding it at arm's length to avoid its claws. **Broadford** is the second largest village on Skye. It's about eight miles (13 km) west of Kyleakin and this is the first township you reach by road from the Skye Bridge. The road here goes north to Portree, west to Elgol, and south to Sleat. There's a cluster of shops, hotels and restaurants and the Broadford Hotel, which is where Bonnie Prince Charlie is said to have left the secret recipe of Drambuie liqueur. The village is home to the **International Otter Survival Fund** at the **Skye Environmental Centre** (Broadford, IV49 9AQ; tel/fax 01471-822487, emergency line tel 0788 431 7911; e-mail sec@otter.org), which has talks, walks, and ongoing research projects. Open all year. The **Skye Serpentarium** (The Old Mill, Harrapool, Broadford IV49 9AQ; tel/fax 01471-822209/533; e-mail nik@snakebite.com) is a refuge and breeding centre for some rare reptiles, and snakes, lizards, frogs and tortoises from all over the globe can be seen here in their natural surroundings. Frequent snake handling sessions. Open Easter to October. The **World of Wood** (Old Corry Industrial Estate, Broadford; tel 01471-822831) highlights the ecological importance of trees. There's a tree museum and a display of common trees and woodcraft, with many items for sale. Free entry. Open April to October.

To the west of Broadford are Beinn Dearg Mhor (2,326 ft/709 m), and Beinn na Caillich (2,403 ft/732 m), which is Gaelic for 'The Hill of the Old Woman' and supposedly refers to 'Saucy Mary' of Kyleakin. The large cairn on the summit is said to mark the grave of a Norwegian princess, maybe Mary's. Evidence of Neolithic occupation has been discovered on the Crowlin islands, across the Sound from Broadford. The closest island in the bay is Pabay, which is known for its fossils. A pleasant excursion from Broadford takes you to the lochs of Scavaig and Coruisk along a hilly and narrow road by way of Loch Slapin, dominated by the 3,042 ft (927 m) peak of Blaven, an outlier of the Black Cuillin. At the head of Loch Slapin on the north side of the river is **Clach Oscar**, a remarkable bell rock that rings when struck. A large fragment is even more resonant than the main rock. If you want to hear what they sound like, they are on the CD *The Kilmartin Sessions* (Kilmartin House Trust, Kilmartin, Argyll PA31 8RQ; tel 01546-510278; fax 01546-510330; e-mail museum@kilmartin.org; www.kilmartin.org.uk). The road crosses the low Strathaird peninsula to **Elgol**, where you can take a motorboat across Loch Scavaig to within easy walking distance of Loch Coruisk, one of the most impressive sheets of water in Scotland.

The A850 road from Broadford leads to **Sligachan**. On the way is the **Crofters House Museum**, at Luib on the shore of Loch Ainort, where you can see a restored traditional blackhouse, complete with the smoky peat fire that gave such dwellings their name. During restoration work two guns from the Jacobite rebellion of 1745 were found hidden in the thatch. About 16 miles (26 km) from Broadford is the **Sligachan Hotel**, famous among walkers and climbers. The nearest Munro to the hotel is 3,167 ft (965 m) *Sgurr nan Gillean* ('The Peak of the Young Men'). This is the most popular of the Black Cuillin, even so it should not be attempted by the inexperienced. Several people have lost their lives on its slopes. If you have the necessary experience, the ascent from Sligachan should take 3-4 hours and the descent 2-3. Much more easily climbed is 3,143 ft (958 m) *Bruach na Frithe* ('The Ridge of the Forest'). This takes about four hours up and three hours down. A memorial to the north of Loch Sligachan commemorates the 'Battle of the Braes' where in 1882 policemen who came to evict the tenants and were beaten back by angry crofters.

Glen Brittle, the mountaineering centre, is about 14 miles (23 km) from Sligachan along the hilly turn-off from Drynoch, or along a delightful and easy waymarked walk of three hours or so from Sligachan through Bealach a' Mhàim. Skye's mysterious 'ghost car' is said to appear at night where the road runs through Glen Drynoch, an apparition that has been seen by many reliable witnesses. Most people see headlights coming towards them but the car never arrives. The ghostly car has also been seen in broad daylight. Above Glen Brittle is 150 ft (46 m) high **Eas Mor waterfall** and there's a lovely sandy beach and safe bathing close to the hamlet. There are motorboat trips to Canna, Eigg, Rum, the Isle of Soay, and Loch Coruisk. A more strenuous way to get to Loch Coruisk is to walk from Elgol on the eastern shore of Loch Scavaig. A path follows the loch shore to Camasunary and on to Loch na Creitheach, below the peak of Blaven. The path then turns west to reach Loch Coruisk, which is separated by a narrow ridge from Loch Scavaig. Across the Strathaird peninsula from Elgol is **Spar Cave**, with its curious stalagmites, best visited by boat. South of the cave is **Dun Grugaig**, ('The Wretched Woman's Dun') which occupies a small promontory.

From Glen Brittle to Rubh' an Dùnain ('Headland of the Dun') is a three-mile (5 km) walk, but it's well worth the effort. Almost at the end of the promontory is a lochan where there are two Neolithic burial cairns, one of which has yielded the remains of five adults, along with Neolithic and Beaker pottery. A cave in the hillside nearby has revealed evidence of early human activity, possibly dating to 7,000 BC. Overshadowed by the ruined walls of an Iron Age fort a stone-lined channel runs from the lochan to the sea. This is known locally as 'The Viking Canal,' although it's too small for boats. Just over a mile offshore is the small flat island of **Soay**, three miles long by one mile across (5 km x 1.6 km), which was used as a base for a shark-fishing operation after World War II by Gavin Maxwell, who wrote about his adventures hunting basking sharks in *Harpoon at a Venture*. In June 1953 the local community was officially cleared and all boats and services were withdrawn from the island. Maxwell's old harpooner bought the 2,560-acre (1,036 ha) island in 1993.

On the shore of Loch Harport at **Carbost** is the distillery of **Talisker** (see *Eating and Drinking*), which is also the name of a bay and a hamlet. At the bay is a beautiful sandy beach, about a mile (1.6 km) beyond the end of the road from Carbost. The road along Loch Harport ends at the pier past the crofting township of Portnalong. On the cliffs near the lighthouse is the D-shaped galleried broch of **Dun Ardtreck**. Across the loch, near **Bracadale**, is another well-preserved Iron Age broch, **Dun Beag** ('Little Fort'), which is regarded as the finest on Skye. Although now only about 14 ft (4.3 m) high, there are still signs of rooms and steps within its thick circular walls. The remains of a round house and a souterrain, or earth house, can also be seen in the vicinity. The road divides near Bracadale, the main road continuing round Loch Beag to Sligachan through the Cuillin and a narrower road known as the 'hill road' going off to the left to Portree. Halfway along you are 4^1/2 miles (7 km) from the sea, the greatest distance on Skye you can get from the briny.

ACCOMMODATION
Hotels
Broadford Hotel: Elgol Road, Broadford, IV49 9AB (tel 01471-822253). Two-star, open February to December, rooms from £24 a night, bar meals, public bar and entertainment.

Dunollie Hotel: Broadford, IV49 9AE (tel 01471-822253; fax 01471-822060). Three-star, open March to October, from £30.

The Old Inn: Carbost, IV47 8SR (tel/fax 01478-640205). One-star, open all year, from £22.

Rowan Cottage: 9 Glasnakille, Elgol, IV49 9BQ (tel 01471-866287; fax 01471-866287; e-mail rowan@rowancott.demon.co.uk; www.rowancott. demon.co.uk). Four-star B&B, views over Loch Slapin, three rooms, from £20 B&B. Open 23 March to 30 November, no smoking throughout. Good home cooking. Vegetarians welcome. Taste of Scotland.

The *Sligachan Hotel:* Sligachan, IV47 8SW (tel 01478-650204; fax 01478-650207; www.sligachan.demon.co.uk). Two-star, stands where the roads to Portree and Dunvegan fork at a bridge over the River Sligachan. Close to the Cuillin hills, the hotel was a popular base for early climbers and walkers. It still is, although today's mountaineers seem to prefer the well-equipped campsite across the road from the hotel. Climbing guides can be contacted through the hotel; the nine-hole golf course at Sconser is only three miles (5 km) from the hotel and discounted rates are available for residents. Fishing for sea trout, salmon and brown trout is also available in the River Sligachan with permits from the hotel. The hotel has 22 en-suite bedrooms, a large public bar, cosy lounge bar, and the *Cairidah Restaurant* serving fresh local produce and excellent wines. The lounge bar has its own exclusive range of whiskies together with the usual wide range of spirits and beers, including Mackenzie's Ale, brewed specially for the Sligachan Hotel by the Isle of Skye Brewery. Real ales are a speciality in Seumas' Bar, with up to eight different beers available at any one time. The bar also hosts a Real Ale & Music Festival each year, usually in September or October. The hotel also has self-catering accommodation. A large bunkhouse sleeps up to 20 people, two cottages sleep eight people each, and a house sleeps 10. Open all year, rates vary, depending on the time of year. During July and August the rate is £40 per person,

Tobermory whisky distillery, Mull

Caledonian MacBrayne ferry

Skye's Black Cuillin range seen from the beach at Ord, Sleat

Pretty Port Askaig, one of Islay's two ferry points

Lochranza Castle, Arran

All roads on Bute lead to Rothesay

The Cowal ferry leaves Colintraive for Rhubodach, Bute

The 13th Century Augustinian Nunnery of St Mary, Iona

per night for B&B and £35 per person for the rest of the year. Discounted rates are offered during the winter months. The Sligachan Cuillin-Cam allows visitors and residents to sit inside and scan views of the Cuillin all day, every day, no matter what the weather. If it's dark, or rain obscures the view you can enjoy a panoramic scenic view instead.

Taigh Ailean Hotel: Portnalong, IV47 8SL (tel 01478-640271). Three rooms and a croft annexe with two en suite rooms overlooking Loch Harport. Evening meals available in the dining room or bar.

Guest Houses

The Skye Picture House: Ard Dorch, Broadford, IV49 9AJ (tel/fax 01471-822531; e-mail holidays@picture-house.demon.co.uk). Three-star, open all year, from £22 B&B.

Talisker House: Talisker, Skye, IV47 8SF (tel 01478-640245; fax 01478-640214; e-mail jon_and_ros.wathen@virgin.net; www.talisker.co.uk). Four-star, open March to October, from £50 B&B, no smoking throughout, limited facilities for disabled guests. Visited by Johnson and Boswell in 1773. Interesting menus. Vegetarians welcome. Taste of Scotland.

B&B

Bay View House: Talisker Bay, Talisker, IV47 8SF (tel/fax 01478-640244). Two-star, open all year, from £20.

The Blue Lobster: Mr RJ van der Vliet, Glen Eynort, near Carbost, IV47 8SG (tel 01478-640320). One-star, open April to January, from £23.

Earsary: Mrs M Robertson, 7-8 Harrapool, Broadford, IV49 9AQ (tel 01471-822697; fax 01471-822781). Four-star, open all year, from £20.

Fairwinds: Mrs J Donaldson, Elgol Road, Broadford, IV49 9AB (tel/fax 01471-822270). Four-star, open March to October, from £25.

Hillcrest: Mrs C MacRae, Blackpark, Broadford, IV49 9AE (tel 01471-822375). Two-star, open March to October, from £17.

Lime Stone Cottage: 4 Lime Park, Broadford, IV49 9AG (tel 01471-822142). Three-star, open all year, from £30.

Strathaird House: tel 01471-866269. 10 miles from Broadford, has doubles for £25 per person.

Swordale House: Swordale, Broadford, IV49 9AS (tel 01471-822272). Three-star, open February to November, from £18.

Tigh-Na-Mara: Mrs JM Scott, Lower Harrapoll, Broadford, IV49 9AQ; tel/fax 01471-822475). Two-star, open April to October, from £20.

Self-Catering

Cuillin Side Cottage: Donann, Fernilea, Carbost, IV47 8SJ (tel 01478-640375). Two-star, two bedrooms. Open all year, from £180-£250 a week.

Kilbride House: Kilbride, by Broadford, IV49 9A (tel/fax 01471-822245). Three-star, one chalet, one flat, 1-2 bedrooms, sleeps 2-4. Open April to October, from £120-£200 a week.

The Old Schoolhouse: Glendrynoch Lodge, Carbost, IV47 8SX (tel 01478-640218; e-mail peppe@drynoch.demon.co.uk). One-star, former school, well-equipped, three bedrooms, sleeps 8. Open all year, from £100 a week.

Ptarmigan: Broadford, IV49 9AQ (tel 01471-822744; fax 01471-822745; e-mail Ptarmigan7@aol.com). Five-star, one bedroom, sleeps two. Open all year, from £350-£700 a week.

Hostels

Broadford Youth Hostel: Broadford, IV49 9AA (tel 01471-822442). Three-star, standard grade. Open March to October. Hostel reception opens at 5pm. Access until 11.45pm. 66 beds, eight rooms with four beds, six rooms with 5-8 beds, family rooms (aged 5+), laundry, hostel store, shop and bus $^1/_2$ mile (0.8 km) away.

Croft Bunkhouse & Bothies: 7 Portnalong, IV47 8SL (tel/fax 01478-640254; e-mail skyehostel@lineone.net). Independent hostel with four separate fully equipped hostels each with kitchens. The Bunkhouse sleeps 14 on alpine sleeping shelves; the Bothy sleeps six in 1st floor dormitory; Bothy Beag sleeps 4, built-in bunks in kitchen/living room; and the Cabin is an en suite bijou room for two. Open all year, from £7.

Glenbrittle Youth Hostel: Glenbrittle, Carbost, IV47 8TA (tel 01478-640278). Two-star open March to October. Access until 11.45pm. 39 beds, two rooms with 5-8 beds, one room with 9+ beds, hostel store, shop $1^1/_2$ miles away, bus nearby (May to September). Usually bursting with climbers and serious walkers.

Skyewalker Independent Hostel: The Old School, Fiscavaig Road, Portnalong, IV47 8SL (tel 01478-640250; fax 01478-640420; e-mail skyewalker.hostel@ virgin.net). Tastefully converted from the old village school, 36 beds, open all year, from £7 a night. Village Post Office housed within the hostel and there is a well-stocked shop. There is also a small campsite. Full facilities for disabled.

EATING

Claymore Restaurant: Broadford (tel 01471-822333; fax 01471-820017). Family restaurant specialising in local seafood. Open April to October from 11am to 11pm, October to March from 5pm to 11pm.

Coruisk House: Elgol (tel 01471-866 3301). Speciality is squat lobster tails. A feast costs £15.50 for two. 'Our record for getting a lobster from sea to plate is under an hour,' says proprietor Robin Banks. Open daily for lunch and dinner until mid-October.

Pipers Moon Coffee Shop: 4 Luid, Broadford (tel/fax 01471-822594). Serves Skye salmon sandwiches, cream teas, and homebakes. Open March to November, seven days a week from 9am to 6pm.

SHOPPING

Broadford Gallery and Sandbank Studio: Old Pier Road, Broadford (tel 01471-822064/011). Specialises in mixed media and watercolours. Open Monday to Saturday from10.30am to 5.30pm.

Craft Encounters: Broadford Post Office (tel 01471-822201/754). Has a range of Scottish crafts produced locally. Also features an interesting display of finds from various archaeological excavations on Skye. Open in the low season from 9am to 1pm and2pm to 5.30pm; high season 9am to 6pm (Sunday from 11am).

The Little Gallery: 7 Portnalong (tel/fax 01478-640254). Has a wide range of etchings, prints and watercolours by local artist Jean Thomas, depicting local scenes and flora and fauna. Open daily 10am to 6pm.

Skye Jewellery: Shore Road, Broadford (tel/fax 01471-822100; www.skyejewellery.co.uk). Has become famous for its intricate silver and gold designs. Their Celtic rings are becoming a firm favourite and they also produce a range of hand-crafted marble products, with the grey-green stone taken from the marble quarry at Torrin nearby.

Three Herons Studio: High Road, Broadford (tel 01471-822152). Produces photographs, paintings, woven tapestries, handloom weaving, spinning, batik, natural dyeing and pottery. Tuition in these arts and crafts can be arranged. Open April to September 9.30am to 5.30pm, closed Sunday.

DUNVEGAN AND THE WEST

Dunvegan nestles in the crook between the peninsulas of Duirinish and Waternish, on Loch Dunvegan, where the most historic attraction is **Dunvegan Castle** (MacLeod Estate, Dunvegan; tel 01470-521206; fax 01470-521205; e-mail info@dunvegancastle.com; www.dunvegan.com) the oldest continuously inhabited castle in Scotland and ancestral home of Clan MacLeod for nearly 800 years. The name is said to be Old Norse. The castle wall was built in 1270 by Leod, son of Olaf the Black, the Norse King of Man, who also built the dungeon and the sea-gate which was the castle's only entrance until the middle of the 18th century. There are many fascinating relics on display in the castle, including the massive two-handed sword of the 7th Chief, William, killed off Mull at the 1480 Battle of Bloody Bay, Flora MacDonald's embroidered pincushion, and a lock of Bonnie Prince Charlie's hair. There's also an enormous horn from a mad bull killed by a 14th century chief armed only with a dagger. This is filled with claret and drained at one draught by each chief at his inauguration. The horn used to hold about five pints (2.5 litres), but a false bottom has reduced the volume to make the customary tipple easier.

More intriguing is the **Fairy Flag**, a wispy piece of faded yellow silk said to possess miraculous powers. This clan banner is preserved under glass in the drawing-room, with the inscription: 'Given by the fairies to Ian, 4th Chief, about 1380. It brought victory to the Clan at the battle of Glendale in 1490, and at the battle of the Wall, Trumpan (Waternish) in 1580.' Experts at the Victoria and Albert Museum in London believe the material was probably woven in Syria or Rhodes, suggesting that the flag might have been captured from the Saracens by Olaf the Black's father, King Harold Hardrada. The castle and its 18th century gardens are open all year round. There are two craft and souvenir shops, one at the castle car park and the other in the castle itself. The castle is open daily from 10am to 5.30pm (adults £6.50, children £3, family ticket £15). You can take one of the regular loch cruises from the castle slip on the *MacLeod of MacLeod* (tel 01470-521500), which goes out into the sea loch around Lampay island, with its colony of seals and Arctic terns, and sometimes beyond to the islands of Isay and Mingay. Depending on time and weather the islet of Clett, host to a multitude of seabirds, may also be visited.

Giant Angus MacAskill Museum (Tigh na Bruaich, Dunvegan; tel 01470-521296) displays a model of Scotland's tallest man, Angus MacAskill, with exhibits and stories relating to his feats of strength. He stood 7ft 9in (2.38 m) and weighed 425 lb (193 kg). He died in Nova Scotia, Canada, in 1863 at the age of 38. Open Easter to October, daily from 9.30am to 6.30pm. South of Dunvegan, on a long promontory poking into Loch Bracadale are some chambered cairns near Vatten, which legend says are mounds built on the site of a great battle between the rival Macdonald and the MacLeod clans. The carnage was so complete that only women and old men were left to bury the dead. They made two piles of bodies, one for each clan, and covered them with rocks – the chambered cairns of Vatten.

Duirinish Peninsula. At **Borreraig**, about eight miles (13 km) north-west of Dunvegan, is a memorial beehive cairn to the MacCrimmons, the hereditary pipers to the Macleods and founders of the greatest college of piping Scotland has ever known. Nearby is the **Piping Heritage Centre**, open every day except Monday, 11am to 5.30pm, April to October. **Borreraig Park Museum** (Borreraig Park; tel 01470-511311) has a private collection of bagpipes, silver, knitwear, wool and an eclectic display of agricultural implements and machinery. Open all year, 9am to 7pm.

South of the black cliffs of Dunvegan Head, a short walk from Waterstein, is

Neist Point, the most westerly in Skye, where a lighthouse overlooks The Little Minch and a waterfall cascades into the sea. You can tour the lighthouse between 2pm and an hour before sunset. To the south-west of Dunvegan are the two flat-topped hills known as **Macleod's Tables**, Helabhal Mhor and Helabhal Bheag, both around 1,600 ft (488 m) high and overlooking Loch Bracadale. Below these truncated hills the Duirinish peninsula ends at Idrigill Point. Offshore are the three isolated basalt sea stacks known as **Macleod's Maidens**, named after a chief's wife and daughters who drowned here. Backed by cliffs up to 700 ft (213 m) high, the tallest of these stacks is 200 ft (61 m) high, while the others are only about half as lofty. A stiff walk from **Orbost** will take you to the Point. Four miles (6 km) from Dunvegan on the Glendale road is the **Colbost Croft Museum** (Colbost, by Dunvegan, IV55 8WA; tel 01470-521296). The blackhouse museum depicts how islanders lived in the 19th century and contains implements and furniture of the period. There's a replica of an illicit whisky still at the rear of the museum. Open Easter to October, daily from 10am to 6.30pm. In **Glendale** village is the **Toy Museum** (Holmisdale House; tel 01470-511240; e-mail skye.toy.museum@ukf.net), an award-winning hands-on experience on the Glendale visitor route that should delight children. Open all year, Monday to Saturday from 10am to 6pm.

Waternish Peninsula. Head east from Dunvegan on the A850 and you come to the **Fairy Bridge**, where three rivers and three roads converge. According to legend this is the spot where the fairy wife of a MacLeod chief said farewell to him before returning to her own people, the wee folk. It was also the scene of fiery open-air meetings, both religious and political, in the 19th century. The B886 bearing left for **Trumpan** off the main road at the Fairy Bridge seems dotted with more craft than croft workers. Halfway up the peninsula the road passes **Anait an Waternish**, an early – probably 6th century – Christian site whose name *anait* indicates that it was the first or mother church of the district. The photogenic settlement of **Stein** sits on the shore of Loch Bay. It was designed by Thomas Telford, but it's probably better known as the village with Skye's oldest pub, the Stein Inn, whose oldest bits date to around 1648. Near the end of the Waternish peninsula is **Trumpan Church**, the scene in 1580 of two particularly gruesome massacres on the same day. A raiding party of MacDonalds from Uist beached their galleys in Ardmore Bay and set fire to the church at Trumpan, burning to death all but one of the MacLeods who were at Mass. The woman who escaped raised the alarm and a party of MacLeods from Dunvegan arrived and slaughtered the MacDonalds, who were unable to escape as the tide had gone out and stranded their galleys. A turf and drystone wall was knocked down to cover the bodies of the massacred invaders, which gave the conflict its name, the 'Battle of the Spoiled Dyke.' The little ruined church of Trumpan is now a protected Ancient Monument. In the ruins is a small holy water stoup which is said never to dry out even in the hottest weather and among the gravestones is an ancient four-foot (1.2 m) monolith with a hole in it. One legend says this is the **Heaven Stone**, which tells you whether or not you are bound for heaven by your success in poking your finger through the hole with your eyes shut. Another version says it's a **Trial Stone** which, by the same means, once determined the guilt or otherwise of criminals. In the churchyard a grey slab marks the grave of a noblewoman who had three funerals, two of them while she was still alive. She was Lady Grange, the wife of a high official. After she threatened to reveal his Jacobite sympathies he connived at her abduction. She was then exiled to several remote islands, including St Kilda, for 14 years. Her husband first held a mock funeral in Edinburgh to account for her disappearance. When she died in 1742, three years after being released in Skye, another fake funeral was held in Duirinish, before her third and final funeral at Trumpan.

ACCOMMODATION

Hotels

Atholl House Hotel: Dunvegan, IV55 8WA (tel 01470-521219; fax 01470-521481; e-mail reservations@athollhotel.demon.co.uk; www.athollhotel.demon.co.uk). Three-star hotel, in the centre of the village at the head of Loch Dunvegan. Nine rooms, from £40 B&B. Open March to December, facilities for disabled. Blend of traditional and contemporary Scottish cooking. No smoking in restaurant. Vegetarians welcome. Taste of Scotland.

Dunorin House Hotel: Herebost, Dunvegan, IV55 8GZ (tel/fax 01470-521488; e-mail stay@dunorin.freeserve.co; www.dunorin.com). Four-star small hotel with views across Loch Roag to the Cuillin Hills, 10 en suite rooms, from £36 B&B. Open 1 April to 15 November except for two weeks in October, facilities for disabled visitors. All bedrooms on the ground floor and en-suite. Vegetarians welcome. Taste of Scotland.

Harlosh House: Harlosh, Dunvegan, IV55 8ZG (tel/fax 01470-521367/512; e-mail harlosh.house@virgin.net). Four-star, open Easter to mid-October, from £53 B&B. Built in 1755 as a Factor's house and offers modern restaurant cooking in a traditional setting overlooking Loch Bracadale and the Black Cuillin. Open from 7pm to 8.30pm.

Stein Inn: Waternish, IV55 8GA (tel 01470-592362, angus.teresa@ steininn.co.uk; www.steininn.co.uk). This two-star inn dates from 1790, although parts are known to be even older than this, making it the oldest inn on Skye. Four double rooms and one single room. No two are the same and all offer stunning and uninterrupted views across Loch Bay. Prices from £23.50 to £28.50 B&B. Well-behaved dogs are also welcome. There's also a three-star self-contained apartment with its own entrance and one bedroom. Costs £200 to £250 a week (including electricity). The inn benefits from four council moorings in Loch Bay and also has its own personal mooring. There's a special yachties' shower facility.

Tables Hotel: Dunvegan, IV55 8WA (tel/fax 01470-521404; e-mail bookings@thetableshotel.idps.co.uk). Two-star, central to the village, view across Loch Dunvegan, imaginative home-cooking. Open all year, from £25 B&B.

Ullinish Lodge Hotel: Struan, by Dunvegan, IV56 8FD (tel 01470-572214; fax 01470-572341), two-star, open Easter to October, from £35 B&B.

Guest Houses

Roskhill House: tel 01470-521317; fax 01470-521761; e-mail stay@ roskhill.demon.co.uk; www.roskhill.demon.co.uk. Four-star, two miles (3 km) from Dunvegan, traditional croft house built in 1890, four rooms. Open all year (Christmas and New Year half-board only), from £32 B&B, no smoking throughout. Vegetarian and special diets catered for. Taste of Scotland.

B&B

Clar-Inis: Mrs DJ Hosking, 2 Ardmore, Harlosh, Dunvegan, IV55 8ZJ (tel 01470-521511). Three-star, open all year, from £25.

Easandubh: Mrs I Stewart, Dunvegan, IV55 8WA (tel 01470-521424). One-star, open January to November, from £20.

Mrs GA Milne: Kilmuir Park, 2 Kilmuir, Dunvegan, IV55 8GU (tel/fax 01470-521586; e-mail gmmilne@aol.com). Four-star, open all year, from £25.

Moorfield: Mrs E MacDonald, Dunvegan, IV55 8GU (tel 01470-521315; fax 01470-521416; e-mail sales@skyetronics.co.uk). Three-star, open April to October, from £30.

Shorefield House: Mrs Hilary Prall, Edinbane, IV51 9PW (tel 01470-582444; e-mail shorefield.house@virign.net). Three-star, open all year, from £24.

Self-Catering
Dunvegan Castle Holiday Cottages: MacLeod Estates, Estate Office, Dunvegan, IV55 8WF (tel 01470-521206; fax 01470-521205; e-mail info@dunvegancastle. com). Two-star, four cottages in the grounds of the castle, three bedrooms, sleeps 4-7. Open all year, from £170-£480 a week.

Greshornish Cottages: Mary Eadie, Ceol na Mara, Edinbane, IV51 9PR (tel/fax 01470-582318). Three-star, 2-3 bedrooms, sleeps 4-5, on large hill farm. Open all year, from £200 a week.

Neist Point Lighthouse: Glendale, IV55 8WU (tel/fax 01470-511200). Three cottages, 2-3 bedrooms, sleeps 6-12. Open all year, from £325-£425 a week.

Ose Farm: Struan, IV56 6FJ (tel/fax 01470-572296). Four-star, 80 acres (32 ha) in lochside setting, one cottage, two bedrooms, sleeps 4. Open all year, from £250-£395 a week.

Silverdale Cottage: Skinidin, Dunvegan, IV5 8ZS (tel/fax 01470-521251; e-mail anne@silverdalebb.idps.co.uk). Four-star, one bedroom, sleeps two. Open all year, from £230-£330 a week.

EATING
Lochbay Seafood Restaurant: 1/2 McLeod Terrace, Stein, Waternish (tel 01470-592235). Two fishermen's cottages on the shores of Lochbay. Specialises in local fish and shellfish dishes, non-smoking. Open from Easter to October from 11am to 4pm and 6pm to 11pm. Accommodation in two en-suite rooms and a self-catering cottage available.

MacLeod's Table Restaurant: Dunvegan Castle, MacLeod Estate Office (tel 01470-521206/310). Serves Scottish fare, hot drinks and snacks. Vegetarian menu available. Open from March to October from 10am to 5.30pm; 17 May to 12 September from 10am to 8pm.

Munro's Tables: Struan (tel 01470-572293/312). Family-run restaurant on village green specialising mainly in traditional Scottish fare, using local produce. Local seafood available during the high season. Vegetarian options. Open from Easter to end-October from 11am to 9pm.

The Old School Restaurant: Main Street, Dunvegan (tel 01470-521421). In the original village school. Serves Skye meat, fish and shellfish, homemade soups, and homebakes. Vegetarians and vegans catered for. Open all year from 10.30am to 10pm. In winter months (January to March) opening is dependent on bookings.

An Strupag Restaurant: Lephin, Glendale (tel 01470-511204). Offers local lamb, mussels, lobster, prawns, crab, pollack, mackerel and salmon, Scottish beef, pork and venison. Value for money prices and crofter-size portions. Take-away service, craft shop and licensed grocer attached. Open all year, in summer Monday to Saturday from 11am to 9pm, Sunday 11am to 5pm; in winter Monday to Saturday from 11am to 6.30pm, Sunday 2pm to 4pm.

The Three Chimneys Restaurant and *The House Over-By* (1 Colbost, near Dunvegan; tel 01470-511258; fax 01470-511358; e-mail: eatandstay@ threechimneys.co.uk www.threechimneys.co.uk) are about 50 miles (80 km) from the Skye toll bridge and five miles (8 km) from Dunvegan. Five-star restaurant with rooms. Open every day for lunch from 12.30pm to 2pm (except Sunday and during winter), dinner from 6.30pm (reservations essential). Disabled access. Member of the Scotch Beef Club. Vegetarians welcome. Taste of Scotland member. Shirley Spear's cooking draws gourmets unfazed by the restaurant's remoteness and the food here is a byword. Across the courtyard *The House Over-by* has half a dozen five-star suites which cost £130-£155 for a double bedroom with breakfast. A la carte dinner £45.

SHOPPING

Aurora Crafts: Norma Barnes, 2 Ose, near Struan (tel 01470-572208). A craft shop where you can watch lace-making. Knitwear, hand-spinning, wood turning, candles, embroidery are some of the craft items handmade on the premises. Open April to October, daily from 9am to 7pm. Wheelchair access.

Croft Studio: Portree Road, Dunvegan (tel 01470-521383; e-mail croftstudio@hotmail.com). Original artwork produced at the studio, paintings, prints, Celtic myths, and jewellery. Open all year, every day.

Dandelion Designs: The Captain's House, Stein, Waternish (tel 01470-592218/223). Original craftwork and a variety of other gifts. Open every day Easter to October from 11am to 5pm; winter months by arrangement.

Dunhallin Crafts: 8 Dunhallin, Waternish (tel 01470-592271/213). Wide range of knitwear made on the premises, and a small selection of other crafts. Open all year.

Edinbane Pottery: Edinbane (tel 01470-582234; e-mail stuart@edinbane-pottery.co.uk; www.edinbane-pottery.co.uk). Specialists in wood-fired and salt-glazed pottery. Visit the workshop and showroom, open daily 9am to 6pm, seven days a week from Easter to October.

Orbost Gallery: near Dunvegan (tel 01470-521207). Displays works by professional painters and printmakers who either live on the island or are frequent visitors.

Shilasdair, the Skye Yarn Company: Waternish (tel/fax 01470-592297; www.shilasdair-yarns.co.uk). Natural dyed and coloured yarn knitwear and knitkits. Open seven days a week, April to end September, 10am to 6pm, or by appointment.

Skye Silver: The Old School, Colbost, Dunvegan (tel 01470-511263; fax 01470-511775; www.skyesilver.com). Original sterling and gold jewellery. Open seven days a week from 10am to 6pm. Mail order service available.

Skyeskyns: 17 Loch Bay, Waternish (tel 01470-592237; www.skyeskyns. demon.co.uk). Tannery and showroom with a range of fleeces and leather goods. Free guided workshop tour. Open daily April to October from 10am to 6pm, or by arrangement.

PORTREE AND THE NORTH

Portree is the administrative centre of the island, a village of about 2,500 whose population doubles every summer with the influx of visitors. The picturesque little harbour is sheltered by black cliffs and the pyramid shape of Ben Tianavaig (1,355 ft/413 m) and looks out to the long, narrow island of Raasay. The village sits at the foot of Fingal's Seat, which is easily climbed and gives good views across the island. The headland jutting out into the bay on Loch Portree is known as the 'The Lump' and was the scene of the last public hanging in Skye. Its natural amphitheatre is now the setting for the annual Skye Games, held on the first Wednesday in August. The Royal Hotel on Bank Street stands on the site of MacNab's Inn, where in 1746 Bonnie Prince Charlie said goodbye to his courageous helper, Flora MacDonald, and gave her the half-crown he owed her.

Portree's oldest buildings surround the port. Along the waterfront quay you'll find the old jail and courthouse, the old temperance hotel and ice-house. In the centre of Portree is Somerled Square, the busy commercial hub. Overlooking the river mouth on the south side of Portree is the superb heritage centre known as **The Aros Experience** (Viewfield Road, Portree; tel 01478-613649; fax 01478-613775; e-mail aros@demon.co.uk). This is a multi-functional centre incorporating exhibition, audio-visual show, theatre-cinema, shops, and restaurant. The award-winning exhibition is a celebration of the people who shaped and influenced Skye's cultural heritage. A

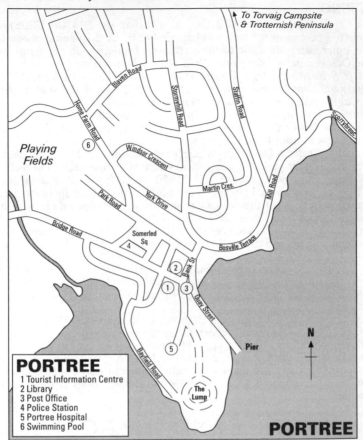

To Torvaig Campsite
& Trotternish Peninsula

Playing
Fields

PORTREE

1 Tourist Information Centre
2 Library
3 Post Office
4 Police Station
5 Portree Hospital
6 Swimming Pool

N

Pier

The
Lump

PORTREE

headset commentary in a choice of six languages guides you through the fascinating displays and tableaux. There is full access for the disabled in the centre, which is open all year, daily from 9am to 11pm, and during the off-season from 9am to 6pm. You can also wander along one of the nearby forest walks to enjoy the wildlife, notably the herons which nest nearby. Up the road from the Co-op Supermarket is **An Tuireann Art Centre** (Struan Road, Portree; tel 01478-613306; fax 01478-613156; e-mail noran@antuireann.demon.co.uk), a lively gallery for contemporary visual arts and crafts, with a licensed café. Open all year, Monday to Saturday 10am to 5pm. Café late opening Wednesday to Saturday until 9.30pm (summer only). Wheelchair access.

Trotternish Peninsula

Portree lies at the base of this matchless peninsula, which on the map has the shape of a traditional 'thumbs-up' sign. Along its length the spinal ridge of The Storr and The Quiraing dominate an area of wild and contorted peaks and pinnacles. Trotternish is said to derive its name from the Old Norse for 'Thrond's Headland' and the whole area carries echoes of the Viking tongue with the names like Uig, Quiraing, Staffin and Flodigarry. From Portree a road circles the entire peninsula, and a minor road cuts across the top through The Quiraing and golden eagle country to link the west coast ferry port of Uig with Staffin on the east coast. Heading north from Portree on the A855, the east coast road passes **Dun Gerashader**, a large prehistoric fort built on the summit of a high rocky eminence, which is an introduction to a chain of these and other ancient structures scattered all over the peninsula. The road narrows and winds along the **Storr Lochs**. When Bonnie Prince Charlie came to leave Skye, two Raasay MacLeods carried a boat from one of these lochs down the cliffs, and got him away safely. The single black finger of rock which can be seen for miles around is the Old Man of Storr, a 160 ft (49 m) detached pinnacle of rock below The Storr which was not climbed until 1955. The crags of The Storr are part of the long, central ridge, averaging some 2,000 ft (610 m) in height. Halfway up the coastal road are the **Lealt Falls**, one of the island's most spectacular waterfalls and gorges. Further on is another stunning cascade, the 300 ft (91 m) **Mealt Falls**. From the cliff-top picnic area at Loch Mealt is a viewpoint from which you can see **Kilt Rock**, a curious formation of vertical basalt rock columns which look like the patterned folds of a gigantic kilt dipping into the sea. At **Ellishader**, near the viewpoint, is the **Staffin Museum**, which has a collection of fossils which include the first dinosaur bones found in Scotland. These Jurassic remains were discovered in 1994. You can also see a dinosaur footprint, the largest ammonite ever found in Skye, and Bronze Age arrowheads. Open Monday to Saturday from 9am to 6.30pm. Admission for adults £1.25, children 50p.

    Staffin lies at the foot of the confused mass of cliffs, rocky spikes and pillars known as The Quiraing. The village has a delightful bay with a sandy beach. The wreck of a Spanish Armada galleon is said to lie out in the bay near Staffin Island. Overlooking Staffin Island on the eastern point of the bay is **An Corran**, where a prehistoric rock shelter is said to provide the first clear evidence of Mesolithic occupation of Skye around 8,000 years ago. The skeletal remains of at least four prehistoric people have been uncovered here. A fascinating find was a 500-600 BC piece of bronze brooch, one of the first examples from Scotland of a so-called swan's neck pin, used to hold a cloak together.

    You have a choice of routes at **Brogaig** either west over the hills to Uig or north to Flodigarry and the most northerly point on Skye. The cross-peninsula road passes **The Quiraing**, whose weird rock formations are easily reached on foot from the path opposite the car park at the top of the hill. To reach the flat area known as **The Table** and its nearby **Prison** keep to the south-eastern slope of the mountain just below the scree and walk between the main mountain and the projecting 120 ft (37 m) rock spine known as **The Needle**. The Table is an area of smooth green turf hemmed on almost every side by enormous cliffs. It was used in the 15th and 16th centuries as a hiding place for stolen cattle. Clefts on the eastward side give you an eagle's-eye view of the little township of **Digg** far below. Looking down on the whole area from a height of 1,781 ft (543 m) is Meal na Suiramach. The walk to Uig is an easy ramble across heath moorland or you can walk on the metalled road all the way.

    Stay on the coastal road north and you come to **Flodigarry**, famous for its association with Flora Macdonald. Her old cottage is in the grounds of the Flodigarry Country House Hotel. Flora and her husband, 'Allan MacDonald of Kingsburgh', settled in the cottage in 1751 and she had five of her seven children here. You can look around the cottage with permission from the hotel. Offshore is little **Eilean Flodigarry**, where 150 fairies are said to have once harvested an entire corn crop in two nights, then asked for more work. The road swings across the top of the peninsula through the township of **Kilmaluag**, named after a Celtic missionary who had a cell here, to the ruined ancient fortress of **Duntulm Castle**. Originally a Pictish fort, it was taken over by the Vikings before becoming a castle and the seat of the MacDonalds. The last MacDonald to occupy the castle was *Domhnull a' Chogiadh* ('Donald of the Wars'). According to legend, the MacDonalds abandoned Duntulm after a nurse accidentally dropped the chief's baby son from the castle window on to the rocks below. For this she was set adrift in a leaky boat.

Heading south along Score Bay is **Kilmuir**, famous as the burial place of Flora Macdonald. When she died in 1790 she was wrapped in a sheet in which Bonnie Prince Charlie had slept while a fugitive. The present memorial replaced the original mausoleum, which over the years was chipped away by souvenir hunters. In the cemetery is a stone slab known as the 'Crusader's Grave' because of the dress of the engraved figure. The costume, however, is typical of the Middle Ages battledress of a Scottish island chieftain. The graveyard lies a little to the north-east of the road. Also in the area, known as the 'Granary of Skye,' is the **Skye Museum of Island Life** (Kilmuir; tel 01470-552206). This cluster of thatched blackhouses near Flora MacDonald's monument displays relics of crofting life 100 years ago. Open Easter to October, Monday to Saturday from 9.30am to 5.30pm.

At **Kilvaxter** an Iron Age underground structure, known as a souterrain, is being excavated, one of more than 20 that have been discovered on Skye. With the help of an archaeologist the local community is undertaking the excavation with the intention of making the souterrain a tourist attraction. At **Balgown**, two miles (3 km) south of Kilmuir, is **Loch Chaluim Chille** (St Columba's Loch), which was drained in 1824. On what were once islands you can see the remains outlining a Celtic monastic settlement. The settlement also gave its name to another famous house associated with Flora MacDonald, **Monkstadt House**, which is now a ruin on the south side of the dry loch. This is where Flora MacDonald first came to seek food and shelter for Bonnie Prince Charlie, who was hidden nearby, disguised as her Irish maid. British officers were dining at Monkstadt when they arrived so the Prince spent the night further south at Kingsburgh, where hostess Mrs MacDonald recalled that after a hearty supper a bottle of brandy was brought. The Prince said he would pour his own drink 'for I have learned in my skulking to take a hearty dram'. It was Mrs MacDonald who asked the Prince for the lock of his hair that is now displayed at Dunvegan Castle. Once Flora's part in the Prince's escape became known to the authorities she was arrested and sent to the Tower of London. Released under the Act of Indemnity, she returned to Skye and married Alexander MacDonald of Kingsburgh. They lived at Flodigarry before moving to Kingsburgh, where in 1773 she was visited by Dr Johnson and James Boswell. Dr Johnson noted that on 13 September he slept in 'the very bed in which the grandson of the unfortunate King James the Second lay on one of the nights after the failure of his rash attempt in 1745-46, while he was eluding the pursuit of emissaries of government.'. Flora and her family emigrated to America, but returned to Kingsburgh in 1779-80 and lived there until she died at the age of 68.

Uig is a crofting township and ferry terminal whose pier was officially opened in 1902 by King Edward VII, even though it had been in use for eight years. The round tower opposite the pier is a folly built by a Captain Fraser. Uig's name comes from a Norse word meaning 'bay.' It is spectacularly sited no matter from which direction you view it. This was once a centre for the herring fishing industry but there are now fewer fishing boats and the main catch is shellfish destined for foreign tables. From picturesque Uig Bay you look out to the Ascrib Islands and the Waternish peninsula. On the coast to the north-west is rugged **Stack Skudiburgh**. Above Uig, where the cross-peninsula road comes down through Glen Rha, the Rha River cascades through the woods in a spectacular two-stage waterfall and in nearby Glen Conon the river also cascades in a series of waterfalls through a wooded glen. To the south of Uig are prehistoric standing stones at South Cuil and the ruined castle near Cuidrach, **Caisteal Uisdein** ('Hugh's Castle'), built in 1580 as the stronghold of Hugh MacDonald, who plotted to murder his chief at a castle-warming party, but sealed his own fate when he messed up the party invitations and sent the murder instructions to the chief instead of to the assassin. About six miles (10 km) off the road leading south from

Uig towards Loch Snizort Beag stands the successor to the former Kingsburgh House. A nearby well where the Prince quenched his thirst is still known as **Prince Charles's Well**. There are standing stones at Kensaleyre, and there's a big well-preserved Neolithic burial cairn near the head of Loch Snizort Beag.

The valley between Waternish and Trotternish carries the shortest route between Portree and Dunvegan. It is also the location of Skye's most important religious site, **St Columba's Isle** at Skeabost. Columba's Isle was the Cathedral of the Hebrides for 400 years until this honour passed to Iona around 1495, and 28 chiefs of Skye's prominent Nicolson clan are buried on the island. If you feel like a break from ancient monuments and sites **KC MacKinnon** (Dalson, Bernisdale; tel/fax 01470-532331, mobile 07780 771095), Scottish and International Sheep Dog Brace Champion, invites you to join him on his croft in Bernisdale to watch him and his dogs doing what they do best. Hour-long demonstrations and ample parking with full facilities for the disabled. Demonstrations Monday to Friday: May-June 11.30am and 4pm, July-August 11.30am, 2pm, and 4pm; September-October 11.30am and 4pm. Advance booking is essential. There are also three self-catering cottages for rent throughout the year in a secluded site overlooking Loch Snizort.

ACCOMMODATION

Hotels

Bosville Hotel and Chandlery Seafood Restaurant: Bosville Terrace, Portree, IV51 9DG (tel 01478-612846; fax 01478-613434; e-mail bosville@macleodhotels. co.uk; www.macleodhotels.co.uk/bosville/). Four-star hotel, in the town centre, on a terrace above Portree harbour, 15 en suite rooms, from £38 B&B. Open all year, facilities for disabled visitors, no smoking throughout. *Chandlery Restaurant* produces meals relying on local produce. Vegetarians welcome. Taste of Scotland.

Cuillin Hills Hotel: Portree, IV51 9QU (tel 01478-612003; fax 01478-613092; e-mail office@cuillinhills.demon.co.uk; www.cuillinhills.demon.co.uk). Four-star hotel in 15 acres (6 ha) of private grounds, overlooking Portree Bay, 30 en suite rooms, from £40 B&B. Open all year, facilities for disabled visitors. Daily changing menu. No smoking in restaurant. Vegetarians welcome. Taste of Scotland.

Duntulm Castle Hotel: Duntulm, IV51 9UF (tel 01470-552213; fax 01470-552292). One-star, unrivalled coastal setting at the northernmost tip of the island, sea views across The Minch to the Outer Isles, adjacent to the ruins of Duntulm Castle. Open March to November, from £26.

Flodigarry Country House Hotel and *The Water Horse Restaurant:* Staffin, IV51 9HZ (tel 01470-552203; fax 01470-552301; e-mail info@flodigarry.co.uk; www.flodigarry.co.uk). Four-star hotel, B&B from £50. Open all year, facilities for disabled visitors. No smoking in restaurant, conservatory or bedrooms. Bar meals served in the conservatory and on the terrace. Vegetarians welcome. Taste of Scotland.

Glenview Inn and Restaurant: Culnacnock, Staffin, Isle of Skye, IV51 9JH (tel 01470- 562248; fax 01470-562211; e-mail valtos@lineone.net www. smoothhound.co.uk/). Two-star, traditional island house, 12 miles (19 km) from Portree on Staffin road, B&B from £25. Open mid-March to early November. Smoking restricted. Vegetarians welcome. Taste of Scotland.

Greshornish House Hotel: Greshornish, by Portree, IV51 9PN (tel 01470-582266; fax 01470-582345; e-mail campbell@greshornishhotel.demon.co.uk). Three-star, open all year, from £45.

The Isles Inn: Somerled Square, Portree, IV51 9EH (tel 01478-612129; fax 01478-612528; e-mail islesinn@hotmail.com). Two-star inn, open all year, from £22. Lively bar, open Monday to Thursday, 11am to 11pm, Friday and Saturday

1am to midnight, Sunday from 12.30pm to 11pm. Food available.

Portree Hotel: Somerled Square, Portree, IV51 9EH (tel 01478-612511; fax 01478-613093; e-mail portree@hendersonhotels.com; www.hendersonhotels. com). Two-star, open all year, from £30, in the centre of town, 24 en-suite room *Clansman Restaurant* themed to depict the clans of Skye, specialises in modern highland cooking. There is also the lively famous *Camanachd Bar* which has regular live entertainment, and meals and snacks are available in the *Square Meal Bistro*.

Rosedale Hotel: Beaumont Crescent, Portree, IV51 9DB (tel 01478-613131; fax 01478-612531; www.rosedalehotelskye.co.uk). Four-star hotel close to village square. Family-run on the waterfront, at the harbour with views over the bay to Raasay and Ben Tianavaig, 23 en suite rooms, from £38 B&B. Open May to September, no smoking in restaurant and all bedrooms. First floor restaurant. Vegetarians welcome. Taste of Scotland member.

The Royal Hotel: Bank Street, Portree, IV51 9BU (tel 01478-612525; fax 01478-613198). Three-star, overlooks working harbour, 25 rooms. Open all year, from £36 B&B. Health and leisure club has full gym, steam room, spa bath, and solarium.

The Uig Hotel: Uig, IV51 8YE (tel 01470-542205; fax 01470-542308). Two-star, old coaching inn overlooking Uig Bay, a mile (1.6 km) from ferry to Outer Hebrides, open all year, from £35.

Viewfield House: Portree, IV51 9EU (tel 01478-612217; fax 01478-613517; www.skye.co.uk/viewfield). Three-star, 12 rooms, from £40 B&B. Open mid-April to mid-October, facilities for disabled visitors. In 20 acres (8 ha) of woodland gardens, 10 minutes' walk from the town centre. Traditional Scottish cooking. No smoking in dining-room. Vegetarians welcome. Taste of Scotland.

Guest Houses

An-Airidh: Mrs C MacLeod, 6 Fisherfield, Portree, IV51 9EU (tel 01478-612250). One-star, open all year, from £18 B&B.

Ard-na-Mara: 11 Idrigill, Uig, IV51 9XU (tel 01470-542281; fax 01470-542289). Shoreside location, close to ferry and bus terminals. Open all year.

The Kings Haven: Portree IB51 9DG (tel/fax 01478-612290). Two-star, restored Georgian house overlooking the harbour, all bedrooms en-suite, close to all village amenities and bus terminal. Open all year, from £22 a night.

Quiraing Guest House: Viewfield Road, Portree, IV51 9ES (tel/fax 01478-612870). Four-star, open all year, from £22.

The Pink Guest House: 1 Quay Street, Portree, IV51 9BT (tel 01478-612263; fax 01478-612181). Three-star, open all year, from £18.

The Shielings Guest House: 7 Torvaig, Portree, IV51 9HU (tel 01478-613024). Two-star, open all year, from £17.

B&B

Almondbank: Viewfield Road, Portree, IV51 9EU (tel 01478-612696; fax 01478-613114; e-mail jansvans@aol.com). Four-star, open all year, from £34.

Balloch: Mrs E Macphie, Viewfield Road, Portree, IV51 9ES (tel 01478-612093). Four-star, open Easter to October, from £20.

Burnside: Mrs S Boyd, 5 Budhmor, Portree, IV51 9DJ (tel 01478-612669). Three-star, open all year, from £20.

Ceol na Mara: Mrs M Matheson, Stenscholl, Staffin, IV51 9JS (tel 01470-562242). Three-star, open all year, from £30.

Drumorell: Mrs C Matheson, 15 Fraser Crescent, Portree (tel 01478-613058). Out of town.

Gairloch View: Mairi MacDonald, 3 Digg, Staffin (tel 01470-562718). Bungalow with sea and mountain views, two family rooms, from £18 a night.

Kilmuir House: Mrs SC Phelps, Kilmuir, near Uig, IV51 9YN (tel 01470-542262; fax 01470-542461; e-mail phelpskilmuirhouseskye@btinternet.com). Three-star, old manse in walled garden, fresh home cooking. Open all year, from £19.

Mrs M MacKenzie: 2 Heatherfield, Penifiler, Portree, IV51 9NE (tel 01478-612820). Three-star, open March to October, from £17.

Mrs N MacLeod: 6 Kitson Crescent, Portree, IV51 9DP (tel 01478-612596). Two-star, open all year, from £16.

Richard and Clare's Place: 5 Penifiler, Portree, IV51 9NF (tel 01478-612476; e-mail rsmith.skye@currantbun.com). Three-star, open all year, from £15.

Woodbine House: Mrs L Hudson, Uig, IV51 9XP (tel 01470-542243). Two-star, open all year, from £17.

Self-Catering

Beaton's Croft House: National Trust for Scotland (tel 0131-243 9331; fax 0131-243 9594; www.nts.org.uk). A late 18th century traditional thatched house in the crofting township of Bornesketaig, about 21 miles (34 km) north-west of Portree. Superb views across The Minch to Harris, Lewis and North Uist. Simple accommodation but with modern amenities. One twin bedroom, sitting-room with original fire opening for burning peat or coal, a small kitchen and shower room, sleeps two.

Mr C Buchanan: 17 York Drive, Portree, IV51 9EB (tel 01478-612995). One-star, three bedrooms, sleeps four. Open May to October, from £160-£180 a week.

Cnoc Mhairi: Viewfield Road, Portree, IV51 9EU (tel 01478-613513). Three-star, overlooking Portree bay, 15 minutes' walk from town centre.

Duntulm Coastguard Cottages: Duntulm Castle Hotel, Duntulm, IV51 9UF (tel 01470-552213; fax 01470-552292; e-mail info@duntulmcastle.co.uk; www.duntulmcastle.co.uk). Three-star, quiet and secluded with sea views. Three coastguard cottages, two with three bedrooms sleeping 6-7 people, the other has four bedrooms, sleeps 8-10, and luxury bungalow, five rooms, sleeps 10-12. Open fires, everything provided. Facilities at adjacent hotel for food and drinks. Open all year, from £160-£550 a week.

Mrs MA Grant: 2 Fisherfield, Portree, IV51 9EU (tel 01478-612269; fax 01478-613553; e-mail mgrant@ultramail.co.uk). Three-star, listed 1830s Georgian house, one house, one apartment, 1-4 bedrooms, sleeps 2-8. Open all year, from £120-£500 a week.

Kiltaraglen House: Portree, IV51 9HR (tel 01478-612435). Two-star, one house, one cottage, 1-2 bedrooms, sleeps 2-4. Open all year, from £160-£300 a week.

Minch View: 1 Totescore, Kilmuir, IV51 9YW (tel 01470-542297; fax 01478-612036). Two-star, one house, three bedrooms, sleeps 5-7. Open all year, from £160-£280 a week.

Mrs D Ross: 6 Ellishadder, Culnacnock, Staffin, IV51 9JE (tel 01470-562321). Two-star, two bedrooms, sleeps 4. Open all year, from £180-£310 a week.

Staffin Bay Holiday Homes: Keepers Cottage, Staffin, IV51 9JS (tel/fax 01470-562217). Three-star, 2-4 bedrooms, sleeps 4-8. Open all year, from £150-£250 a week.

Hostels

Dun Flodigarry Hostel: Flodigarry, by Staffin, IV51 9HZ (tel/fax 01470-552212). Independent, family-run, 54 beds, twin and family rooms available. Open all year, from £8 a night.

Glen Hinnisdal Bunkhouse: Glenhinnisdal, Snizort, IV51 9UZ (tel/fax 01470-542293; e-mail rlyddon@aol.com). Six beds, open all year, from £8 a night.

Portree Backpackers Hostel: 6 Woodpark, Dunvegan Road, Portree, IV51

9HQ (tel 01478-613641; fax 01478-613643). Independent hostel with 24 beds, open all year, from £7 a night.

Portree Harbour Backpacker: The Pier, Portree, IV51 9DD (tel 01478-613332).

Portree Independent Hostel: Old Post Office, The Green, Portree, IV51 9BT (tel 01478-613737). 60 beds, open all year, from £8 a night.

Uig Youth Hostel: Uig, IV51 9YD (tel 01470-542211). Two-star. Hostel reception opens at 5pm. Access until 11.45pm. Views over Uig Bay. Open March to October. 62 beds, two rooms with 4 beds, five rooms with 5-8 beds, one room with 9+ beds, family rooms (aged 5+). Hostel store, shop a mile away, bus nearby, ferry 2 miles.

Camping

Staffin Caravan and Camping Site: Staffin, IV51 9JX (tel 01470-562213). Two acre park accommodating 50. Open mid-April to September, from £7.50 a night.

Torvaig Caravan and Camping Site: Torvaig, Portree, IV51 9HS (tel 01478-612209). Open April to October, 90 touring pitches, from £7 a night.

EATING

Ben Tianavaig Vegetarian Bistro: 5 Bosville Terrace, Portree (tel 01478-612152). Caters for vegetarians and vegans with a seafood kebab for any non-vegetarians. No-smoking. Open end-February to end-October from 6pm to 11pm.

The Chandlery Seafood Restaurant: 9 Bosville Terrace, Portree (tel 01478-612846; fax 01478-613434). Local produce. Open all year. (See *Accommodation*).

Cuillin Hills Hotel: Portree (tel 01478-612003). Award-winning restaurant offer a selection of local seafood. Highland game and traditional Scottish dishes. Open daily from 6.30pm to 9pm. Sunday lunch carvery buffet for £9 for adults; bar meals served at lunchtime and evening from £4.

The Granary Restaurant & Coffee Shop: Somerled Square, Portree (tel 01478-612873). Coffee shop and licensed restaurant offering home cooking and baking. Open all year.

Harbour View Seafood Restaurant: 7 Bosville Terrace, Portree (tel/fax 01478-612069). Open all year.

Portree House: Home Farm Road, Portree (tel/fax 01478-613713; e-mail nigel@portreehouse.demon.co.uk). Lunch, dinner and carry-out menus. Choice of vegetarian foods. Licensed bar-restaurant in an 1810 listed building. Open all year, in summer Monday to Saturday from 11am to 11.30pm, Sunday midday to 11pm; winter Monday to Friday from 11am to 2.30pm, 5pm to 11.30pm, Saturday 11am to 11.30pm, Sunday 12.30pm to 11pm. B&B and self-catering accommodation available.

Pub at the Pier: Uig (tel 01470-542212). Bar restaurant at Uig ferry terminal. Open all year.

Uig Hotel: Uig (tel 01470-542205; fax 01470-542308). Views across Uig Bay. Locally sourced produce.

White Wave Activities and Café: 19 Linicro, Kilmuir (tel 01470-542414). A cross-between an outdoor centre, an inn, a *ceilidh* place and family home. Noted for its soups and home cooking. Opening times depend on season. High season open 8am to 8pm.

SHOPPING

The Brewery Shop (Buth An Leanna): The Pier, Uig (tel 01470-542477). Specialises in Skye Brewery souvenirs and the full range of Skye ales, local whiskies, preserves and confectionery. Open from May to October, Monday to Saturday fromm10am to 6pm, Sunday 12.30pm to 4.30pm.

Castle Keep: Unit 7B1, Portree Industrial Estate (tel 01478-612114; e-mail robmiller86@hotmail.com). Hand-forged swords, knives, daggers and dirks, showroom and display. Open all year.

The Crafts Shop: Hungladder, Kilmuir (tel 01470-552279). Stocks sheepskin products and knitwear, tweeds, tartans, rugs, pottery, wood and horncraft, as well as silverwork, and paintings. Open May to October.

Dun Studio: No 30 Borve, Skeabost Bridge, by Portree (tel 01470-532402). Paintings and prints, watercolours, acrylics and collage. Open all year 10am to 7pm daily.

Skye Woollen Mill: Dunvegan Road, Portree (tel 01478-612889). Range of knitwear, Skye and other tartans, gifts and souvenirs. Open April to October, seven days a week; November to March, six days a week.

Tippecanoe: 1 Wentworth Street, Portree (tel/fax 01478-612970). For gifts and souvenirs. Open all year, Monday to Saturday from 9am to 5.30pm. Extended opening in season.

Trotternish Art Gallery: Kilmaluag, by Duntulm (tel 01470-552302). Specialises in original Skye scenes. Open daily all year.

Uig Pottery: The Pier, Uig (tel/fax 01470-542421; e-mail greatpots@ uigpottery.co.uk; www.uigpottery.co.uk). Functional and original pieces of high-fired reduced stoneware inspired by the colours, landscape and animal life of the island. Open throughout the year, May to October, every day from 9am to 6pm, November to April, Monday to Saturday from 9am to 5pm.

Raasay

Raasay used to be called the 'Isle of the Big Men' because it was believed to be the last stronghold of giants who once inhabited all the western islands. It became the property of the Macleods of Lewis around 1493 and they built Brochel castle as their fortress on the north-east shore. Malcolm, 9th Chief of the Macleods of Lewis, gave Raasay and South Rona to his younger son in 1510. During the 15th and 16th centuries South Rona became such a robbers' haunt that its vicar, Dean Monro, described it as 'a haven good for fostering thieves, riggers and reivers' and one cove in the bay of Acairseid Mhór is still known as *Port nan Robaireann*, or the 'Port of Robbers.' The Macleod of Raasay was known to have Jacobite sympathies and after the defeat of the clans at Culloden the authorities sent troops to lay waste the island and torch Raasay House. Even so, the fugitive Prince was hidden on Raasay for two days before returning to Skye on his way back to the mainland en route for France.

The house where Dr Samuel Johnson and James Boswell were guests in 1773 was built in 1746 after this attack and the old rooms where they ate with their host and danced with his 10 daughters are now at the back of the house. It gained a new sandstone Georgian-style frontage in the 19th century. Many of the original 3 ft (1 m) thick walls and some of the original deep-set narrow windows still remain. You can still see the first-floor room where Dr Johnson slept and if you stay at Raasay House you have a choice of 11 rooms, four of them haunted. A ghostly dog is also occasionally spotted in the kitchen. The impoverished Macleod family was finally bankrupted by the artistic tastes of the Chief, who sent an artist to Italy to find two life-sized stone mermaids for the terrace of his rebuilt house. The artist spent years touring Europe at the Chief's expense. He eventually returned with two huge mermaid statues – and an even more enormous bill. The Chief refused to pay, saying he had ordered life-size mermaids and these were larger than life. The dispute went to the courts, which dithered over the question, 'What is life-size for a mermaid?' Litigation dragged on until the family was financially ruined and obliged to sell Raasay to George Rainy of Edinburgh, a businessman who ruthlessly evicted families from his land to make way for sheep. In 1854, 129 families were shipped to Australia to join their Chief who had emigrated there in 1846. The costly mermaids can be seen near the battery of two cannon on a knoll overlooking the Sound in front of the house.

Edward Herbert Wood, a Warwickshire landowner, owned Raasay from 1876 to 1912. He used the land cleared of tenants by Rainy for private sport. Pheasants and deer were raised for shooting and rabbits were allowed to proliferate. Islanders were forbidden to shoot either vermin or game. In Victorian times Raasay was 'a sporting Hebridean paradise' according to a *Times* correspondent. In one season 1,250 brace of grouse were killed on the 19,000-acre (7,689 ha) estate, along with 700 woodcock. Woods sold Raasay in 1912 and it was bought for its iron ore deposits by Baird & Co, which began to mine it in 1913. The mine was worked intensively between 1916 and 1919 with the help of 250 German prisoners-of-war. After 1922, when the government bought it, Raasay had a succession of landowners until the most recent, Highlands and Islands Enterprise, took over the holdings of its predecessor, the Highlands and Islands Development Board.

EXPLORING

Raasay is a long sliver about 14 miles long and a maximum of 4 miles wide (23 km x 6 km) guarding Portree's harbour and stretching down Skye's east coast from the Storr mountains to the mouth of Loch Sligachan. The distinctive flat-topped summit of **Dun Caan**, Raasay's highest point, rises to 1,453 ft (443 m) over a landscape of southern woodland areas and wilder terrain running up to the northern tip of the island. During his 1773 tour of the Hebrides with Dr Samuel Johnson, James Boswell ended his climb of Dun Caan by singing a Highland song and dancing a reel on the summit. Whether the intoxicating view was responsible or the brandy punch he'd drunk with breakfast is unclear. Raasay is a microcosm of the geology of the region and Dun Caan's lava cap is a reminder of the huge volcano that created Skye and its islands in ancient times. **Inverarish** is the island's main village and has a post office, a shop and two telephone kiosks. You can't buy petrol on the island. The village is a cluster of terraced cottages less than a mile from the jetty at Suisnish and was built to house German prisoners-of-war mining the nearby iron ore deposits during World War I. The cottages now house about two-thirds of the island's 170 population. At Clachan, north of Inverarish, is a recently discovered **souterrain**, or underground dwelling and passage, thought to be more than 2,000 years old. Not far away are the remains of the Iron Age broch of **Dun Borodale**.

The imposing building housing the **Raasay Outdoor Centre** is **Raasay House**, built by the Chief of the MacLeods of Raasay in 1746. Long years of neglect have left their mark on Raasay House but it is still a commanding presence. As well as accommodation, the Centre (tel 01478-660266; fax 01478-660200; e-mail info@raasayoutdoorcentre.co.uk) offers sailing and windsurfing, kayaking, rock climbing and abseiling, walking, orienteering, and archery. It has a licensed café and day visitors are welcome. Bike hire available. The gift and craft shop has information on island walks and places to visit. In the west wing is **Raasay Heritage Museum** (tel 01478-660207) displaying memorabilia of Raasay through the ages. The clock above Raasay House stables stopped the day 36 men left there in 1914 as volunteers in World War I. The 13th century **Chapel of St Moluag** stands beside Raasay House, overlooking the shore where an ancient stone carving of a Celtic cross and a Pictish symbol commemorate the saint's 11th century landing place. Behind Raasay House is **Temptation Hill**, so named, it's said, because it was from its summit that EK Wood, the Victorian English laird, looked down and, tempted by the magnificent view, decided in 1876 to buy Raasay House and the island.

The island's single-track road winds up the western side of the island before crossing to the east coast at Brochel, where the ruins of a 15th century MacLeod castle dominate a rocky spur over the sea. The next two-mile (3 km) stretch of road from Brochel to Arnish is a local legend. It was built single-handedly by postman Calum MacLeod. He started work on it in 1966 and it took him eight years of back-breaking work with a pick and wheelbarrow to finish the road. By the time he had finished all the other residents who had agitated for a road in the first place had left. A cairn marks his achievement, for which he was awarded a BEM. From where the road ends beyond the castle, there's a further seven miles (11 km) or so to the northernmost tip of the island. You can cross a slippery rock ledge here at low tide to *Eilean Tigh*, an island which consists entirely of a hill rising to 365 ft (111 m). This offers arresting views of north Raasay and the adjacent uninhabited island of Rona. From Arnish, you can also walk across a causeway at low water to the tidal island of **Fladday**. Keep an eye on the tide on both these jaunts.

There is no road along the precipitous east coast of the island but a path runs from Screapadal in the north to Hallaig in the south, a fine walk where you might see golden eagles swooping from the cliffs and deer roaming the slopes. The southern part of the island offers a circuit of moorland and lochs as well as some dramatic coastal scenery. You can see the remains of iron mine workings near Fearns and Suisnish. There are other pleasant walks around the island and six of them are detailed in the useful free leaflet *Isle of Raasay – A Guide to Island Walks & Forest Trails*, published by Forest Enterprise and Raasay Social Services Association.

FLORA AND FAUNA

The grassy fields of the south-west, the heather moorland of the north, and the mixed Forestry Commission woodland at Inverarish and Brochel, provide a wide range of habitats for flora and fauna. Most exclusive inhabitant is the **Raasay vole**, a tiny creature that bears a close resemblance to its Alpine cousin. **Red deer** graze in the forests. Some 60 species of bird frequent Raasay's shores woodlands, and open moors. **Golden eagles**, **kestrels** and **buzzards** hunt the uplands, **herons** fish the waters of the lochs, and **snipe** are common on the moors. The Inner Sound provide a good hunting ground for **otters**, **porpoises**, and occasionally **whales**. In early to mid-spring, **bluebells** blossom and in late spring, the island is ablaze with pink **rhododendrons**. **Orchids** include the lesser butterfly, the early purple, the green winged, and the spotted orchid.

GETTING THERE

From Portree you look out across the Sound to the island of Raasay, but to get there you have to drive for 20 minutes down the A850 coast road towards Broadford to board the ferry at Sconser. It's a short trip, but check the timetable and arrive at least 30 minutes before scheduled departure to be sure you get on. CalMac operates the *MV Loch Striven* car-passenger ferry from Sconser to Suisnish pier about nine times daily, Monday to Saturday, from 8.30am to 6.45pm or 9.30pm during summer. The journey takes 15 minutes and the single fare costs £2.30 for driver and each passenger, £9.35 for a car, £9.35 for a caravan, boat/baggage trailer and motorhome, £4.70 for motorcycles, and £1 for bicycles. The passenger day return fare is £4.05 and car day return fare is £16.75. A 'Day Saver' ticket is available which costs £20.80 for a car and up to four occupants, available daily from mid-April to mid-October. There's a hot-drink vending machine on board.

ACCOMMODATION

The *Churchton Guest House:* tel 01478-660260. Has a good reputation, three-star, with fine views of Skye and the Cuillin mountains, ideal for walkers and cyclists. Three double/twin en-suite rooms, £19 B&B. Dinner costs £12. Open all year.

Isle of Raasay Hotel: tel/fax 01478-660222. Two-star, 12 en-suite rooms. Open all year, B&B from £25 and £40 with dinner.

Mrs RS Mackay: 6 Osgaig Park (tel 01478-660207). Has three-star B&B accommodation. Open all year, from £20 night.

Raasay Outdoor Centre: Raasay House, Raasay, IV40 8PB (tel 01478-660266; fax 01478-660200; e-mail info@raasayoutdoorcentre.co.uk). Offers B&B accommodation at £17.50 a night, full board £35 a night, half board £30 a night. There is also bunkroom accommodation for backpackers at £9 a night, and camping facilities with hot showers, toilets, drying room and laundry facilities at £4 a night. The *Dolphin Café*, at Raasay House, serves meals and snacks throughout the day. During the evenings it is transformed into a candlelit restaurant/bar renowned for its food and live music. Late night diners can book transport back to Skye on the Outdoor Centre's boat. There is a late ferry (9pm) on Friday nights in summer, but other days the last ferry from the island leaves at 6pm. A community 'ceilidh place' adjacent to the centre provides entertainment, live music sessions, dances and performances by visiting theatre companies. It also houses a small museum.

Self-Catering

Mrs Anne Gillies: 5 Mill Park, Raasay, IV40 8PA (tel 01478-660284). Two bedrooms, sleeps five. Open all year, from £150-£400 a week.

Mrs MA McDonald: Westcroft, Achnagairn, Kirkhill, Inverness, IV5 7PD (tel 01463-831333). Two-star, two bedrooms, sleeps 4-6. Open all year, from £200-£300 a week.

Hostel

Raasay Youth Hostel: Creachan Cottage, Raasay, Kyle, IV40 8NT (tel 01478-660240). One-star. Reception opens at 5pm, access until 11pm. Open May to October. 30 beds, one room with 4 beds, one with 5-8 beds, and two with six beds, shower. Shop 2 miles (3 km) away, ferry (except Sundays) three miles (5 km) away.

HELP AND INFORMATION

Fire, Police, Ambulance: tel 999.

Raasay doctor: tel 01478-613200.

For information about walks contact *Raasay Social Services Association* (at Raasay House) or Forestry Enterprise (Fort Augustus Forest District Office, Strathoich, Fort Augustus, Inverness-shire PH32 4BT; tel 01320-366322; fax 01320-366581).

RONA

This small uninhabited island north of Raasay lies between Skye and the mainland of Torridon. An automatic lighthouse rises to 42 ft (13 m) and can be seen for 21 miles (34 km). Rona occasionally appears in Scottish history as South Rona. Dean Monro despaired of it as the home of lawless men who made a living despoiling 'pure pepill'. On the east coast, across the island from Acairseid Mhór ('Big Harbour') is the **Church Cave**. Cut into the rock it extends for 50 yards (46 m) into the cliff wall. The cave is arched like a Gothic cathedral, huge stone slabs forming its ceiling. Rows of seats were hewn out of the rock for the congregation. In front, a large boulder served as the altar. Water trickles down one wall into a hollow stone used as the font. In 1921 seven families left Rona to look for better homes. They chose Fearns and Eyre, on the east coast of Raasay because of their fertile land. The 'Rona Raiders' didn't ask for permission to settle from the island's owners, the mining company of Baird. When Baird told them to move they refused, so the company prosecuted them. The head of each family was jailed in Inverness to await trial. The public outcry resulted in the Department of Agriculture taking over Raasay from Baird in 1922 and crofters were then allowed holdings there. On their return a piper played the jailbirds off the boat and led them round Raasay House before piping them all the way home to Fearns. There are non-landing ferry cruises to the island in summer, run by *Brigadoon Boat Trips* (tel 01478-612641).

SCALPAY

South-east of Raasay and separated from Skye by the shallow and narrow strait of Caolas Scalpay is the privately owned island of Scalpay. There's no regular access and you need permission from Scalpay House to visit (manager's cottage tel 01471-822539). Hilly, rough and heather-clad, Scalpay's highest point is Mullach na Càrn ('Hill of the Cairn'), 1,286 ft (392 m) above the central plateau of the 6,128-acre (2,480 ha) island and overlooking Loch an Lèoid, Loch Dubh and a sprinkling of surrounding lochans, all bearing fine brown trout. Scalpay was first developed in the 19th century by Sir Donald Currie, the shipping magnate who established the Castle Line. He laid out the island's roads and began its plantations. A large area of the north-east is fenced to keep in the island's large herd of red deer. Offshore is the barren islet of Longay. Scalpay House is in the well-cultivated south-east corner of the island, where it is served by a small tidal harbour looking out to the rocky bird islet of Guillamon.

The Small Isles

In 1991, Rum reverted to its correct spelling after being mistakenly known for a century or so as Rhum. It's said Victorian laird John Bullough decided to make his island's name respectable by spelling it Rhum, even though no words in Gaelic begin with 'Rh'. Each of the Small Isles used to be known in Gaelic by its 'sea-kenning', a name used at sea to avert bad luck. Rum was known as 'The Kingdom of Wild Forests' because it was once the deer-hunting preserve of the Lord of the Isles, Eigg was the 'Island of the Big Women', Canna was 'The Island Cross' because of its location between the Uists and Skye, and Muck was the 'Island of the Pigs', perhaps meaning whales, whose Gaelic name translates literally as 'sea-pigs'. The four islands were shepherded together in 1740 to become the Parish of the Small Isles. The parish was abolished in the 1950s because of the fall in populations and the islands now fall under the *Small Isles Community Council*. The council meets to discuss matters of benefit or concern to the islands and this gives the four neighbours close bonds, both socially and politically. There are regular events such as **The Small Isles Gathering**, when people from the islands come together for *ceilidhs*, barbecues, and sports days.

GEOGRAPHY

The Small Isles lie to the south of Skye, 10-25 miles (16-40 km) from the mainland. In descending order of size they are Rum, Eigg, Canna and Muck. **Rum** is the largest of the four islands, nearly nine miles (15 km) from north to south and almost the same from east to west, covering a roughly diamond-shaped area of 25,850 acres (10,461 ha). The mountains of the **Rum Cuillin** cover almost all of the southern half of the island and contain Rum's five highest peaks, Askival, the loftiest at 2,664 ft (812 m), Ainshval (2,562 ft/781 m), Sgùrr nan Gillean (2,507 ft/764 m), Hallival (2,372 ft/723 m), and Trollaval (2,303 ft/702 m). The rivers of Kilmory, Kinloch, and the Abhainn Sgathaig radiate from Long Loch in the centre of the island. The low-lying reef of **Oigh-sgeir** is nine miles (15 km) to the west of Rum and is a breeding ground for kittiwakes, eider duck, terns and seals.

On **Eigg** (pronounced 'egg'), the distinctive bulk of An Sgurr seems to tower much higher than its 1,289 ft (393 m), but that's probably because the island is barely 7,540 acres (3,051 ha) in size. Entrance to Eigg's shallow harbour is narrow and stoppered by the rocky island of Eilean Chathastail ('Castle Island'). Although only about one-third the size of Rum, Eigg's population of 68 is more than double that of its neighbour.

Kidney-shaped **Canna** is the furthest out of the Small Isles, some 25 miles (40 km) from the mainland. It lies about three miles (5 km) north-west of Rum. It is five miles long and 1½ miles wide (8 km x 2.4 km) and with the satellite islet Sanday has an area of 3,250 acres (1,315 ha). Tidal Sanday is about 2½ miles long by ¾ of a mile wide (4 km x 1 km) and is linked to Canna by a footbridge. An upland spine runs across Canna and much of the island is barren wilderness, rising to 689 ft (210 m) at its highest point on Carn a'Ghaill. The northern coastline of Canna is bounded by high cliffs. At the western end the remains of various ancient cliff-top forts are a reminder of the days when visitors didn't come as tourists.

Unfortunately named **Muck**, the most southerly of the Small Isles, lies nearly four miles (6 km) south-west of Eigg and 10 miles (16 km) north of Ardnamurchan, the most westerly point on the British mainland. Muck is the smallest of the islands. It has an area of 1,380 acres (558 ha) and is less than two miles wide and a mile long (3 km x 1.6 km). It rises to only 450 ft (137 m) at its highest point on Beinn Airein.

Geology

The 19th century geologist John MacCulloch referred to the island quartet as 'The Cocktail Isles', presumably because of their intricate mix of geological ingredients. **Rum** is built on the remains of an ancient volcano which was active 50-60 million years ago and which was subsequently subjected to intensive glacial erosion. The island's complex of igneous rocks provides an unrivalled outdoor laboratory for the study of basaltic volcanoes and the cataclysmic processes which forge them, and this draws geologists here from all over the world. In 1998, platinum deposits were found in Rum, although not in viable mining quantities. Most of **Eigg** is composed of volcanic rocks, basalt lavas with hexagonal columns. The columnar pitchstone bastion of An Sgurr, the largest such residual mass in Britain, gives the island its distinctive crouching lion outline from the sea. On the north-west coast Jurassic sandstone cliffs have weathered into impressive caves and arches and helped to create Eigg's quartzite 'Singing Sands' beach. In the north, shales and limestones have yielded fossils rare in Scotland, including plesiosaur bones. From the sea, dramatic volcanic landforms dominate the skyline of **Canna**. At the east end of the island and to the north of the harbour is **Compass Hill**, whose basaltic rock is so rich in iron that it can cause compass deviations on passing ships up to three miles (5 km) away. **Muck** is mainly sheet basalt, striated by dolerite dykes, and is reckoned the most fertile of all the islands.

GETTING THERE

The Small Isles are easily accessible by ferry from the mainland. The port of Mallaig – famed for its kippers – is the main gateway, and you can also get there from Arisaig, which is now a yachting centre, with piers, slipway, a Land, Sea and Island Information Centre and other useful facilities. The Hebridean Cruises to the Small Isles leave daily in the summer and charters are available.

From Mallaig

Caledonian MacBrayne (The Ferry Terminal, Gourock, PA19 1QP; tel 08705-650000; fax 01475-635235, reservations; tel 01475-650100; fax 01475-637607, general enquiries; e-mail reservations@calmac.co.uk; www.calmac.co.uk) operates a ferry service to Eigg-Muck-Rum-Canna. November 2000 saw the inaugural voyage of the first vehicle-carrying ferry, *MV Loch Nevis*, on the Small Isles and Skye run, but as yet there are no vehicle slipways ready on Canna, Eigg, and Muck, although they are planned. Canna already has a pier where passengers can land and Rum has a new ro-ro slip, although private vehicles are not allowed on the island. Passengers for Eigg and Muck still have to transfer to small flit-boats to get ashore. Eigg's flit boat lands goods and passengers on the pier in the lee of Eilean a'Chathastail; Muck's flit boat ties up at the jetty if the tide is up. If it's not, you make the final landfall by rowing boat.

The ferry leaves Mallaig once a day Monday to Thursday, and twice a day on Friday and Saturday. The adult single fare is £4.75 to Eigg, £7.25 to Muck, £7.10 to Rum, and £8.10 to Canna; bicycles are £2 between any two places. CalMac also have 'Day Sails' from Mallaig, either with time ashore or as a non-landing trip, during summer only. The cruise to Eigg leaves Mallaig at 10.30am on Monday and Thursday and takes 1 hour 20 minutes (4½ hours ashore). It arrives back at 5.20pm on Monday and Thursday at 3.45pm and costs £8.30. The trip to Rum leaves Mallaig at 12.50pm on Monday, 10.30am on Wednesday and Friday (3 hours 20 minutes ashore). It takes 2 hours 15 minutes and returns at 5.30pm on Monday, 5.20pm on Wednesday, and 4.50 on Friday. The cruise fare is £12.35. From Mallaig to Muck leaves at 10.30am on Tuesday and returns at 3.45pm (2½ hours ashore). It takes 1½ hours and costs £12.85. Passengers on these cruises are transferred to and from the island by small boat. The cruise to Canna leaves Mallaig at 10.30am on Wednesday (1 hour 35 minutes ashore), arriving back at 4.50pm. It takes 2 hours 15 minutes and costs £13.80. The non-landing cruises leave Mallaig at 10.30am Monday to Thursday; at 9am and 12.50pm on Friday; and 6.30am and 1.40pm on Saturday. The cruise fare is £12.65 and operates during summer only. Check the island combinations with CalMac at the Ferry Terminal in Mallaig; tel 01687-462403.

From Arisaig

Arisaig Marine (Murdo Grant, Arisaig Harbour, Inverness-shire, PH39 4NH; tel 01687-450224; fax 01687-450678; e-mail info@arisaig.co.uk; www.arisaig.co.uk) operates services to Rum, Eigg, and Muck with *MV Shearwater*, a 130-passenger vessel.

To Eigg and Muck on Monday, Wednesday and Friday, departing at 11am, arriving Eigg at midday. Leaves Eigg at 12.30pm and arrives at Muck at 1pm. The return trip leaves Muck at 3.15pm, arrives at Eigg at 4pm; and then leaves Eigg at 4.30pm arriving in Arisaig at 5.30pm.

To Eigg and Rum on Tuesday (Sunday June to August), departing at 11am, arriving Eigg at midday; depart Eigg at 12.30pm, arrive Rum 1.30pm. Return journey leaves Rum at 3.30pm, arrives Eigg at 4.30pm; and then leaves Eigg at 5pm and arrives in Arisaig at 5pm.

To Rum on Thursday, departing at 11am, arriving Rum 12.30pm. It leaves Rum at 3.45pm, returning to Arisaig at 5.30pm.

There is also a trip to Eigg and Rum on Saturday during the main May-August season. This departs Arisaig at 11am and returns via Eigg and Rum at 5pm. You can spend five hours ashore on Eigg or two hours on Rum. Alternatively, you can go to Eigg on Sunday during Easter, May and September, leaving Arisaig at 11am and returning at 5pm. This gives you four hours in Eigg.

The return fares to Eigg are £13, Muck £13, and Rum £17. Children under three years are free, 3-12 years £3, and 13-16 £6.

Naturetrek (tel 01962-733051) offers a seven-day walking tour, with four days and nights on Eigg, and the rest of the time on Muck.

Rum

At Kinloch archaeologists have discovered traces of human settlement stretching back 8,500 years, the earliest known in Scotland. Rum is notably lacking in workable fertile land, so it must have been the island's bloodstone that attracted the Mesolithic settlers. This dark green, red-spotted volcanic rock was used as a substitute for flint and fashioned into tools and weapons. A number of bloodstone arrowheads have been found on Rum and Eigg and Rum bloodstone has also been found at prehistoric sites on the west coast of Scotland, indicating that these Middle Stone Age people were sea voyagers. The Vikings arrived about a thousand years ago, but apart from place-names and the names of the main mountain peaks the Norsemen left little to signal their presence.

In 1156, Somerled, an Argyll chieftain of mixed Norse and Celtic blood, became ruler of the southern islands. His descendants were granted territory stretching from the Butt of Lewis to Islay in the 14th century for their support of Robert the Bruce, leading to John of Islay declaring himself Lord of the Isles. After a period of the feuding and fighting characteristic of the times King James VI subdued the Hebridean clans and with the ending of the internecine warfare and the introduction of a new convenience food – the potato – Rum's small population suddenly began to increase, peaking in 1795 at nearly 450. This put such a strain on Rum's resources that landlord Maclean of Coll received next to no rent from his tenants. In July 1826, he evicted 300 people to make way for sheep and transported the displaced tenants to Nova Scotia. Two years later all but one of Rum's remaining families followed them. Areas occupied before these Clearances are visible at Kilmory and Harris where you can see the remains of ruined blackhouses. Sheep gave way to deer after the price of mutton plummeted and in the mid-19th century Rum became the sporting estate of the Marquis of Salisbury, father of the Victorian Prime Minister. In 1886, the estate was bought by wealthy Lancastrian textile manufacturer John Bullough. His son, George, built the pretentious red sandstone 'castle' at Kinloch, whose weird and wonderful fitments and furnishings have made it an eye-popping tourist attraction. Sir George died in 1939 and was buried in the bizarre, Grecian-style stone-pillared mausoleum he'd built on the shore at Harris as his father's tomb. His wife died in 1967 and her body is also interred there. The mausoleum was not included in the 1957 sale which turned the island into one of Scotland's first National Nature Reserves, and the Bullough family has perpetual access to it. Rum has been owned and managed by Scottish Natural Heritage since 1992. Rum's importance as a natural heritage site since then has brought it a host of protective designations, among them Biosphere Reserve (1976), part of The Small Isles' National Scenic Area (1978), Special Protection Area for Birds (1982), Site of Special Scientific Interest, seven Geological Conservation Review Sites (1987), and Proposed Special Area of Conservation (1995). In 1996, 17 sites were scheduled as nationally important ancient monuments.

EXPLORING

There are nearly 200 sites in Rum tracing human activity from the time of Stone Age hunter-gatherers, through the Middle Ages, to the Edwardian era which produced pseudo-baronial **Kinloch Castle** standing at the head of Loch Scresort. This turreted sandstone edifice was completed in 1901 in time to celebrate playboy laird George Bullough's knighthood. Hundreds of stonemasons from Lancashire had laboured on it for nearly three years, being paid an extra shilling a week to wear kilts and two pence a day for smoking tobacco to keep Rum's bloodthirsty midges away from their knees. The castle was designed to be the last word in Edwardian luxury. Its crenellated walls, arched loggia, Italian gardens, lawns, orchard, greenhouses, and turtle ponds were rivalled only by the splendour of its interior. Topsoil was imported from Ayrshire for the lavish landscaping, bowling green, and nine-hole golf course. Glasgow was the first place in Scotland to get electricity, Rum was the second. The castle was lit with electricity generated by its own power-house. It was also the first private residence in Scotland to install an internal telephone system. Its furnishings are intact and include a mechanical orchestra called the Orchestrion, the Edwardian equivalent of a juke-box, which uses large perforated rolls of paper to create the effect of a 40-piece orchestra. Equally impressive is the array of gadgets at the end of each 7 ft (2 m) bath, which includes one for making waves, as well as showers and high-pressure hoses. If a guest pressed the wrong knob the bath turned into a violent whirlpool. When Sir George Bullough invited guests during the two or three months a year he spent on Rum a piper in full regalia would parade along the glass-roofed colonnaded veranda every morning to play until all were roused for breakfast. No one is ever surprised to hear that Kinloch Castle's architect had only ever designed factories before creating this monument to bad taste. Scottish Natural Heritage encourages visitors to experience this flamboyant building and its contents and there are hour-long guided tours conducted four or five times a week by the castle manager at £3 a head (tel 01687-462037). The island's little flit-boat is the *Rhouma*, named after the Bullough family steam-yacht, which was so big that the South African government borrowed it to use as a hospital ship during the Anglo-Boer War.

Apart from jolly Kinloch Castle, Rum's fascination lies in its wild, desolate hill country, its trails and its flora and fauna. It is world-renowned as an open-air laboratory for the ongoing study of red deer, wild goats, Highland cattle and Rum's wild ponies. In the north at Kilmory is a fine beach and the ruins of an old settlement and chapel, St Mary's, with a fine early Christian cross. Kinloch Castle's original laundry was sited here and the family washing used to be spread out on the green turf to dry. Day visitors are welcome and anyone spending only a few hours on Rum between ferries should have enough time to at least tour the castle and/or walk one of the island's three short Heritage Trails. For visitors with permission from the Reserve Office for longer stays the burns and mountains call (see *Sport and Recreation*).

FLORA AND FAUNA

Flora

Rum has been a National Nature Reserve since 1957. A staggering 630 flowering plants, ferns and stoneworts have been recorded, with three plants which are national rarities – the **Norwegian (or arctic) sandwort**, the **Lapland marsh orchid**, unrecognised in Scotland until 1988, and an **eyebright** micro-species that grows at only one known place, on the shores of Loch Scresort. Mountain flowers are among the most distinctive flora locally. The uplands of the south-west are the best place to look for them. **Scottish asphodel**, **stone bramble** and **mountain everlasting** flourish high in the hills, with **purple saxifrage**, and **northern rock-**

cress abundant right up to summit level. **Sundew, butterwort, tormentil, milkwort,** and **bog asphodel** brighten the moorland. **Bitter-vetch** and **pyramidal bugle** occur on the low-lying sandstone soils, while **gentians, trefoils, pansies** and a variety of orchids, including **marsh, spotted,** and **frog orchid,** grow around the sandy bays of the north coast.

Fauna

As Rum has been an isolated island since the last Ice Age there are few indigenous species, with the **otter** and the **pipistrelle bat** the most common. The Loch Scresort Heritage Trail goes through an area popular with otters and their young, and pipistrelle bats are resident in Kinloch. **Pygmy shrews** are also common and widespread, as are the **field mouse** and the **brown rat.** Rum has always been noted for its **ponies,** small dun-coloured animals which are reputed to be descendants of either horses brought by the Vikings, or of those which swam ashore from wrecked Spanish Armada galleons. Native Rum ponies stand between 13.1 and 13.3 hands and were regarded as embodying everything a good horse should be: '*Heded of an ox, tailed as a fox, comely as a kyng, nekkyd as a dukyng, mouthyd as a kliket (fox), witted as a woodkok, mylled (easily guided) as a wedercoke*'. All native **red deer** on the island were exterminated by the late 18th century. They were subsequently reintroduced and now number about 1,400 animals. There are also about 200 **wild goats** on the island. One creature that is definitely a world first for Rum is the pale **flea** *Ceratophyllus fionnus*, which was discovered in a Manx shearwater nest on Hallival. Rum residents say the **midges** that plague man and beast between May and September are the most ferocious in Scotland. Midge nets and repellents are best-sellers in the village store. Biting **clegs,** horse-flies, are also plentiful. More attractive are the 19 species of butterfly.

    Harbour porpoises and **minke whales** are fairly common around Eigg and Rum. The whales usually pass close late in summer and autumn. Schools of up to 100 **common dolphins, white-beaked dolphins, Risso's dolphins** and occasionally **bottlenose dolphins** are sometimes spotted around Rum and Canna. **Killer whales** are infrequent visitors, but have been seen in six-strong pods. **Common seals** can regularly be seen in Loch Scresort and a few **Atlantic grey seals** come ashore between Harris and Papadil in September and October to pup.

Bird-Watching

Rum's commonest bird is one that is hardly ever seen on land. **Manx shearwaters** are seabirds par excellence; they never go ashore except to breed. They spend most of their lives at sea and winter in the waters off Brazil, but migrate north in March to breed in burrows above 1,476 ft (450 m) on the slopes of Rum's highest mountains. The island population of more than 60,000 pairs is one of the largest breeding colonies in the world. The Vikings probably named Trollaval ('Hill of the Trolls') because the weird calls of the shearwaters in their underground burrows there reminded them of these hobgoblins of Scandinavian folklore and this dates the colony back to at least the 11th century. The shearwaters are preyed on by **gulls, peregrine falcon, buzzard** and **golden eagle.** A more surprising predator has also been identified. Red deer regularly chew on dead shearwaters and live chicks for the calcium in their bones. Rum's other breeding seabirds include 4,000 **guillemots,** 700 **razorbills,** 500 pairs of **fulmars,** and 1,500 pairs of **kittiwakes.** The trees around Kinloch Castle originally provided the only habitat for woodland birds such as **robin, blackbird, song thrush** and **dunnock.** Plantings of an additional million trees and shrubs now attract these four species, along with **chaffinch, willow warbler, wren** and **goldcrest.** Other breeding birds on Rum include **merlin, raven, red-throated diver** and **corncrake,** and there are modest seabird colonies along the southern cliffs. The last native **white-tailed sea**

eagle was shot on Rum between 1908 and 1912. In 1975, a reintroduction programme began and by 1985 a total of 82 young sea eagles from Norway had been released here. By 1996, 55 wild sea eagles had fledged in Scotland, and this is one of conservation's most heartening stories. The sea eagle's striking yellow eyes gives the bird its poetic Gaelic name *Iolaire-sùil-na-grèin* ('The Eagle with the Sunlit Eye'). The **best time** for twitchers is between April and October. For more information contact the *Sea Eagle Project Team* (c/o International and Biodiversity Branch, Scottish Natural Heritage, 2 Anderson Place, Edinburgh EH6 5NP; tel 0131-554 9797).

ACCOMMODATION

Accommodation on Rum is limited to 125 a night so visitors are expected to book in advance of their arrival.

Kinloch Castle. Four rooms with oak four-poster beds available at £25 a person a night. Contact Clive Hollingworth (tel 01687-462037).

The Hostel. The hostel in the castle grounds has 48 beds, £11 a person a night, room only. Open all year round. Bring your own sleeping bag as the hostel does not provide sheets. The *Bistro Restaurant* is open from the beginning of April to the end of September, otherwise kitchen facilities are available for self-catering. Non-resident visitors can also use the Bistro, but should book meals in advance.

Village Bothies. Converted farm buildings providing clean, warm, but simple self-catering accommodation for 34 for £5.50 per person a night. Gas stove, electricity, toilet, shower, kitchen and eating utensils. Bring your own sleeping bags and pillows. Blankets are available for an extra charge to cover laundry. Four bothies normally open from March to October.

Mountain Bothies. Two mountain bothies are also available at Guirdil and at Dibidil. Maximum stay of three nights. These cannot be pre-booked.

Camping

The campsite holds 50 and costs £1 a night. The site has a cold water supply and two toilets, with designated areas for camp fires. Open March to September. Booking essential. For camping and bothies contact the Reserve Office (tel 01687-462026).

EATING AND DRINKING

The ancient inhabitants seemed to have lived on seabirds and heather ale. In summer there was a plentiful supply of fat young Manx shearwaters (*fachachs*) which Timothy Pont described in 1596 as the 'the most delicate birds to be eaten...except that they doe taste oyld'. At an archaeological site the remains of 4,000-year-old pots revealed signs of what appeared to be heather ale, brewed from a fermented potion of oats and barley flavoured with heather honey, meadowsweet, bog myrtle, and royal fern. Nowadays you can try the *Castle Bistro* for breakfasts, packed lunches and evening meals, and self-caterers can raid the well-stocked general store/Post Office. This little store has an off-licence, and serves as an informal gathering place in the evenings.

SPORT AND RECREATION

Cycling. There's only one road – Kinloch to Harris (6 miles/10 km) – and this calls for a mountain-bike. A few old pony tracks lead into the remote western parts of the island. Take your own bike but be warned, the road and tracks are equally rough. You are not allowed to bike off-road.

Fishing. The rights in the burns and lochs are owned and managed by Scottish National Heritage. Permits to fish are required, and SNH can restrict fishing in certain areas in the interests of birdlife conservation, particularly red-throated divers.

Heritage Trails

There are three of these trails all starting from the Information Point beside the Reserve Office, where trail leaflets are available. Walks are the circular Kinloch Township trail (1.5 km, 45 minutes), the Loch Scresort trail (5 km out and back, 2 hours), and the circular Kinloch Glen trail (8 km, about 2 hours). One of the most strenuous hikes on Rum is the Cuillin Ridge walk, which involves traversing the principal mountains on the island. This traverse of the main ridges and summits is rated one of the finest island mountain treks outside of Skye. Allow 8-11 hours from Kinloch, but plan with care and first get advice from the Reserve Office. Serious hill walkers usually prefer May, but whenever you arrive in summer you'll have to deal with Rum's two main hazards – steady rain and ferocious midges. So if you are heading for the heights dress well, and take plenty of anti-midge lotion.

HELP AND INFORMATION

Maps, details of walking routes (and route cards for safety), fishing and climbing permits and wildlife information are available at the information centre in the middle of Kinloch village. Contact the Reserve Manager (The Reserve Office, The White House, Rum PH43 4RR; tel 01687-462026; fax 01687-462805).
Rum Post Office: tel 01687-462026.

CANNA

Nearly all the islands of the west coast lie on a north-south axis; Canna is oriented east to west. This means that spring comes earlier here than anywhere else in the Hebrides as the island is protected from the early cold north and north-east winds. This yields early crops, good vegetables and fruit and has given Canna its reputation as the 'Garden of the Hebrides'. It also has the only deep-water harbour in The Small Isles, tucked in between the sheltering tidal island of Sanday and the promontory of Rubha Carr-innis. Canna has been occupied since the Stone Age and during the Middle Ages belonged to the Benedictine monks of Iona, then falling under the successive rule of the Vikings, the Lords of the Isles, and a variety of good, bad, and indifferent owners. Canna had its share of the hardships and turmoil such historical changes brought to all The Small Isles. Canna and Sanday were owned from 1938 until 1981 by Dr John Lorne Campbell, a distinguished Gaelic scholar and lepidopterist of note who collected in **Canna House** a prestigious Celtic library, which he gave to the National Trust for Scotland (NTS) when he handed over the twin islands into its care. His widow, Dr Margaret Fay Shaw, welcomes visitors to Canna House. About 260 varieties of butterflies and moths have been recorded on Canna, among them at least one species of moth identified by Dr Campbell as unique to the island. Canna and Sanday are home to fewer than 20 people, most of them living on the smaller island around the harbour basin. The NTS runs the larger island as a sustainable farm. There are no shops or other facilities apart from a telephone box and a Post Office in a small wooden shed.

The first thing you see as the ferry enters the snug little harbour is a large rock face covered in garish graffiti, mainly names and dates of yachts and fishing boats that have visited over the past century. In the fields above the harbour are the sites of 7th century **St Columba's Chapel** and **A' Chill**, until its population of 238 was cleared in the mid-19th century, the island's original village. In the vicinity are a **Celtic cross** and a **standing stone** pierced by a semi-circular hole said to have been where wrongdoers had their thumbs jammed as punishment. Overlooking the harbour is **Canna House (1865)**, which was the home of Dr Campbell. This is approached through a magnificent arch of *Escallonia*. In and around the house are prehistoric and religious artefacts collected by Dr Campbell. There's one short unmade road on Canna, but you can walk round the island along a number of cliff-top tracks. The cliffs which encircle Canna rise dramatically at the eastern end to some 600 ft (183 m) and include the steep rocky knoll of **An Coroghon** where, washed by sea on three sides, you can see the ruined fortified keep which legend says was used by a jealous Clanranald chief in the 17th century to sequester his wife from the attentions of an amorous MacLeod.

Compass Hill (458 ft/140 m) is in the eastern corner of the island, an overgrown volcanic crater giving fine views north to Skye. To the west is **Carn a' Ghaill**, at 690 ft (210 m) high, the highest point on Canna. Offshore are the inaccessible stacks of **An t-Each** and **Iorcail**. In the south of the island a rough road follows the coast from the pier to the deserted steading of **Tarbert**, on a hillside in the waist of the island. This was cleared of tenants in the mid-19th century but not finally abandoned until the 1950s. The path from Tarbert Bay follows the cliffs to Sròn Ruail at the western end of the island. Along the way you'll see a typical **promontory fort** below the cliffs at Rubha Nic Eamoin and further on a steep track leads down to a grassy terrace on a flat black lava shore where you'll find the **ruined nunnery** of Rubha Sgòrr nam Bàn-naomha ('Headland of the Holy Women'). The path down calls for extreme caution. On a clear day you can see most of the islands of the Outer Hebrides from the point of Sròn Ruail and below on a rock stack are the remains of the Iron Age fort of **Dun Channa**. There's another ruined fort a short walk to the north.

Canna has been a sanctuary for birds since Dr Campbell bought it in 1938 and on the rough walk back to the harbour along the high coastal cliffs of the north you should see many of the 150 species that have since been recorded. The cliffs are home to **shag, fulmar, kittiwake, guillemot, razorbill, Manx shearwater,** and **puffin,** and provide habitats for spray-tolerant grassland and ledge flora. Birds of prey include **golden eagle** and **white-tailed sea eagle** visiting from Rum. One of the clearest signs of Norse occupation has been found at Rubha Langanes, where a **Viking boat burial** has been uncovered.

Sanday

Sanday is linked to Canna by a small footbridge which can be a test of nerves in windy weather. Maybe that's why there's a small white shrine to the Virgin Mary at the Sanday end of the bridge. The island's most prominent feature is the Catholic church of St Edward, which has been restored and converted to a Gaelic study centre, complete with computers. The centre was opened by HRH The Princess Royal, Princess Anne, in June 2001. From the centre there's a pleasant walk to the east end of the island where there's a small automatic light. **Seals** are common along the way. In the south-east are several large caves and the sea stacks of **Dun Mor** and **Dun Beag**, which are favourite puffin hang-outs. A short distance to the south-west of the footbridge is the lovely sandy beach of **Traigh Bhan**.

Pony trekking for riders with some experience is available from Easter to end-September with *Hebridean Trekking Holidays* (tel 01687-462829).

ACCOMMODATION

Wendy MacKinnon: tel 01687-462465. Has one double and one twin room. B&B, evening meal and packed lunch.

Self-Catering

Tighard: National Trust for Scotland (tel 0131-243 9331; fax 0131-243 9594; www.nts.org.uk). Is a large comfortable house, a short walk from Canna Pier. Sleeps 10, £335-£550 a week, includes electricity, gas and solid fuel.

Bothy

Winnie MacKinnon: tel 01687-462466. Has a bunk room and living-room with outside toilet and shower. Sleeps eight. £15 a day (including fuel).

Camping. Permission to camp must be obtained from the NTS, which maintains a small campsite.

Sanday

The converted church of St Edwards has dormitory-type accommodation for up to 12 people. There's a sitting-room, dining-room and a study centre with computers, helped by recent infrastructural improvements including 24-hour electricity powered by diesel generators.

Eigg

The *Isle of Eigg Heritage Trust* bought the island in 1997 after a period of troubled relationships between residents and successive owners which saw much of the infrastructure in tatters and the future of both community and environment extremely precarious. The Trust is a partnership between the local community, the Eigg Residents Association, the Scottish Wildlife Trust and The Highland Council, which gives the island the largest and most structured community in the Small Isles.

Unsurprisingly for this part of the world the island has had turbulent history, starting in the Celtic annals with the murder in the early 7th century of St Donnan and 52 other monks by the women warriors of a pagan queen who lived on a *crannog*, an artificial islet, in Loch nam Ban Móra ('Loch of the Big Women'). Eigg was gifted by Robert the Bruce to MacDonald of Clanranald in 1309, a windfall that helped to fuel centuries of feuding between the MacDonalds and the MacLeods. Massacre was a common occurrence for the islanders, who suffered this at the hands of the Vikings as well as other clans, most notoriously the MacLeods, who in 1577 wiped out the entire population of MacDonalds on Eigg by burning brushwood at the entrance to a cave in which they were hiding. About 395 people were suffocated to death by the smoke and the cave, not far to the south-west of the pier at Galmisdale, is still known as the **'Massacre Cave'**. The MacDonalds eventually took revenge for this on the MacLeods at Trumpan, on Skye, in 1580 but even there it was a pyrrhic victory as they were massacred before they could escape in their galleys to Eigg. Further west is the **'Cathedral Cave'**, where persecuted Catholics once secretly attended services. In 1588, there was yet another massacre when Sir Lachlan Maclean of Duart, Mull, aided by 100 mercenary soldiers from a Spanish Armada galleon which had limped into Tobermory Bay, raided and pillaged Eigg, Rum, and the other Small Isles *'in maist barbarous, shameful and cruell manner...not sparing the pupils and infants'*.

The island is rich in archaeological sites, prehistoric hut circles, cairns, Viking burial mounds, early Christian stones, a pre-Clearance village, and 19th century field systems. At **Kildonnan** you can see the ruins of a 14th century church, which stood where St Donnan established his early monastery. Eigg has many superb walks and it takes only a couple of hours from the harbour to climb the **Sgurr of Eigg**. The soaring sugarloaf looks unassailable, but an easy scramble gets you to its grassy summit for unsurpassed panoramic views of Coll, Tiree, the Outer Hebrides, and the Cuillin of Skye. The remains of an Iron Age fort can be seen near the summit. The rocky tower of the **Scuir of Eigg** rears a further 300 ft (91 m) above the summit plateau at the eastern end of the one-mile (2 km) ridge. On the north-west side of the island is the **Bay of Laig**, with the settlement of Cleadale. To the north of the bay below the eroded cliffs at Camas Sgiotaig, are Eigg's famous **'Singing Sands'**. The sands sing only when they're dry. When you walk or slide your feet over the sand the quartzite grains emit a long musical note. Stroking the sand has the same effect. Another odd sound in the bay area is caused by waves rattling hundreds of limestone fragments trapped in rocky hollows. Above the main village of Galmisdale is **The Lodge**, the empty but still attractive 1920s country house that has been home to a succession of the island's lairds. At the harbour is a community centre, **An Laimhrig** ('The Anchorage'), with a Visitor Information Centre, Post Office, craft shop, tearoom, toilets, and showers. Residential summer courses on art, geology and landscape history are held at the Field Study Centre and talks can be arranged with the island's resident historian. The centre is the hub of the *Feis Eige*, or Eigg Festival, held every July. For more information on the island contact the *Eigg Project Officer* (tel 01687-482476; e-mail andrewbinnie@iselofeigg.org).

There is a taxi/minibus service and bike hire on the island.

FLORA AND FAUNA

Eigg is managed as a wildlife reserve by the Scottish Wildlife Trust and for its size has a wide range of habitats and wildlife within its 7,500 acres (3,000 ha). There are nearly 190 species of bird, 130 of which are recorded each year and the 68 bird species known to breed on the island include **red-throated diver, long-eared** and **short-eared owl**, and **golden eagle**. Other regular species include **puffin, Manx shearwater, snipe, raven**, and **buzzard**, as well as a wide variety of smaller woodland species. More than 480 species of flowering plants grow on the island, including more than a dozen kinds of **orchid**, a fair mix of alpine/arctic flora and a rich and varied woodland community. There are 15 species of **butterfly** and two species of **bat**. Wildlife around the island includes **minke whales, dolphins, otters**, and **seals**. Several basking sharks have recently been seen around Eigg pier.

ACCOMMODATION

Kildonan Farm Guest House: Mrs Marie Carr, Kildonan House, PH42 4RL (tel 01687-482446). One family and two twin rooms. Shared bathroom, lounge and dining room. B&B, evening meal and packed lunch, £30 a night. Under 14, £15 a night.

Mrs Sue Kirk: Lageorna, PH42 4RL (tel 01687-482405). Has a refurbished croft house, five minutes from the beach. One double, one twin and one single room. Comfortable sitting/dining room. B&B, evening meal and packed lunch, from £27 a person a night. B&B £14 a night. Also two more self-catering cottages, each sleeping six. £200-£350 per cottage a week. Open all year.

Self-Catering

The Glebe Barn: Simon and Karen Helliwell, Cleadale, PH42 4RL (tel 01687-482417; e-mail simoneigg@cs.com). Accommodation in converted barn for up to 24 people. The place for any group interested in bird-watching, botany, geology, archaeology or photography. Individual backpackers also welcome. Open April to October, but all year for groups. £9.50 a person a night, £22 a night in a twin room.

Bothy

Smithy Bothy: Kenneth and Sheena Kean (tel 01687-482438). £90 to £130 a week, including linen, towels, kitchen equipment. Outside toilet and shower.

Camping

Facilities for camping are sparse and no charge is levied. Donations, however, are welcome. Contact Mrs Maggie Fyffe (Secretary, Isle of Eigg Heritage Trust; tel 01687-482486).

For details of other accommodation, or general information, call Mairi Kirk (tel 01687-482416).

EATING AND DRINKING

Two minutes from the pier is the *New Pier Tea Room and Craftshop* (An Laimhrig PH42 4RL; tel/fax 01687-482476; e-mail jmcdonell1@compuserve.com) where there's a waiting room, café and tea-room with freshly baked cakes and cooked meals daily, as well as a craft shop with locally produced items. Open 11am to 5pm, May to September.

MUCK

Muck is an island that radiates peace and quiet. It was bought by the MacEwen family in 1896 and more than a century of considerate ownership and management has provided the island with real stability ever since. Small-scale farming, fishing and tourism provide a living for a population of around 30 people. Most of Muck's residents are clustered around the small harbour of Port Mór in the south-east, where there's a tearoom, a craft shop, and a telephone box, and where there will soon be a new slipway. A few people live around the laird's farm at Gallanach in the north, where you might see **otters** and **porpoises** in the bay. **Minke whales** are becoming common around the island and visitors have even been close enough to complain of their smell. More than 80 species of birds nest on and around the island, which has an embarrassment of **greylag geese**. A single car and a couple of tractors are the only vehicles on the island, and with only one short stretch of road between Port Mór and Gallanach this would seem to be plenty. Farming, crofting and fishing keep the local economy going, supplemented by tourist income in the summer months. There are a few good sandy beaches if you feel like beachcombing or chilling out, and you can visit the island's fine **puffin** and **seal** colony. For good views, 450 ft (137 m) Beinn Airein, the highest point on Muck, is an easy climb.

ACCOMMODATION

Godag House: Helen Martin (tel 01687-462371). Half a mile (0.8 km) north of the harbour, two double rooms, one twin, and one single room. B&B, evening meal and packed lunch, £20 a person a night.

Port Mor House: Ewen MacEwen, Port Mor, PH42 4RP (tel 01687-462365). Near the pier, four double, two family, and one single room. B&B, evening meal, and packed lunch, £23 a person a night.

Self-Catering

Gallanach Farmhouse: Lawrence MacEwen (tel 01687-462362). Two houses each sleeping nine, from £200-£400 a week.

Rosie Soutter: tel 01687-462042. Bunkhouse with three bedrooms, one family and two twins. Sitting/dining-room. Bathroom. Open all year. £8.50 per person a night with bed linen provided. £7.50 a person a night with own bed linen.

Camping

This must be the only place in the isles where campers have the option of renting a tipi or a Mongolian yurt. For information about these, campsites, and anything else contact the laird, Lawrence MacEwen (tel 01687-462362).

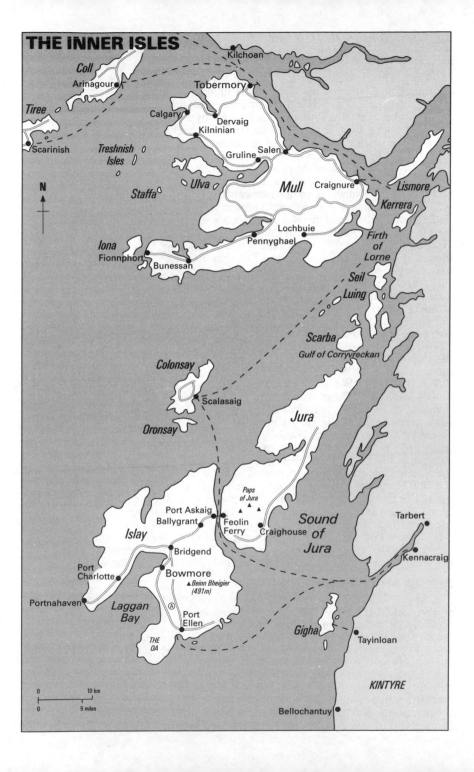

THE INNER ISLES

Coll
Arinagour
Tiree
Scarinish

Kilchoan
Tobermory
Calgary
Dervaig
Kilninian
Treshnish Isles
Staffa
Ulva
Gruline Salen
Mull
Craignure
Lismore
Kerrera

Iona
Fionnphort
Bunessan
Lochbuie
Pennyghael

Firth of Lorne

Seil
Luing

Scarba
Gulf of Corryvreckan

Colonsay
Scalasaig

Oronsay

Jura

Sound of Jura

Port Askaig
Ballygrant
Islay
Feolin Ferry
Paps of Jura
▲ ▲ ▲
Craighouse

Tarbert

Kennacraig

Bridgend
Port Charlotte
Bowmore
▲ Beinn Bheigier (491m)
Portnahaven
Ⓐ
Laggan Bay
Port Ellen
THE OA

Gigha

Tayinloan

KINTYRE

Bellochantuy

N

0   10 km
0   5 miles

the castle, near the RSPB's **Totronald Reserve**, is an airstrip which can be used by private aircraft. Beyond the airstrip is Coll's highest hill, Ben Hogh at 341 ft (104 m). This is well worth climbing for panoramic views and to see the enormous boulder balanced clear of the ground on three smaller rocks. This is what geologists call a 'perched erratic', left behind by the last Ice Age; Collachs say it was brought from Rum and placed there by a giant.

Overlooking Loch Breachacha are the **Breachacha Steadings**, once the home farm of the castles and the site of the creamery where Coll's famous cheese – prized at Westminster – was made until the industry collapsed at the start of World War I. On the other side of the beach is **Hangman's Hill**, site of the last executions on Coll around 1593. At Arnabost, a roofless building that was once a school can be found at the T-junction. In the 19th century, bones, shells and pottery shards, as well as a large bronze pin and a gold brooch were found beneath the building in an underground gallery and circular chamber, known as a souterrain. Visible from the B8071 road from Arnabost near the Old Parish Church at Clabbach is **Grishipoll House**, built around 1750 as a laird's house. It's now a roofless ruin, but when visited by Johnson and Boswell in 1773, they found an 'excellent slated house of two storeys'. More than 70 lochs and lochans dot the length of the island, most of them home to lively brown trout, and six still bear traces of the early fortified artificial island dwellings known as *crannogs*. Throughout the island there are standing stones, and the remains of a chambered cairn, duns, or Iron Age forts, a hut circle, and Neolithic, Bronze, and Iron Age sites. The best preserved of Coll's five duns is **Dun an Achaidh**, which can be found on a ridge to the south of the B8070 road, near Acha Mill. Pottery fragments can be seen among the debris on the slopes near the dun. Of the prehistoric standing stones, the most obvious are those at Totronald, where two granite monoliths known as *Na Sgeulachan* ('The Tellers of Tales') stand on a rocky ridge. In this area in 1593 the Macleans fought a bloody battle with Duart clansmen from Mull. This ended with the defeat of the invading force and the burn that flows into Loch Breachacha was so choked with the severed heads of the Duarts that ever since it's been known as *Sruthan nan Ceann* – 'The Stream of the Heads'.

As you head east, the landscape becomes noticeably more rock-strewn and rugged in contrast with the West End. From Arnabost the road heads east, up over the Windy Gap, the steepest section of road on the island. To the seaward side of the B8072 coastal road the ruined church of **Cille Ionnaig** in the walled burial ground is thought to have been Coll's parish church in the Middle Ages. The burial ground contains several post-Reformation gravestones of Maclean family members, including that of Johnson and Boswell's host in 1773, 'Young Coll', who drowned off Mull the year following their visit. At the road end is Sorisdale, where in 1976, a burial pit and a beaker vessel dating to about 1800 BC were discovered in a sand dune, along with skeletal remains of a young woman.

FLORA AND FAUNA

The Royal Society for the Protection of Birds (RSPB) has a 3,017-acre (1,221 ha) reserve (tel 01879-230301) 6 miles (9½ km) west of Arinagour with a variety of typically Hebridean habitats. Plantlife includes several rare water plants, such as the **slender naiad**, and, on the flower-rich expanses of machair, several hundred species of flowering plants have been identified, including **lady's bedstraw**, **wild thyme**, **cranesbill** and various **orchids**. Other rare plants recorded include the little **bog orchid** and **Irish lady's tresses**. The reserve is a refuge for one of the densest gatherings of **corncrake** in Scotland, which fly all the way from southeast Africa in May to breed here. With Tiree, Coll is of international importance for corncrakes and the two islands attract more than 20% of Britain's total. The rasping call of this elusive bird is **best heard** between 11pm and 2am, and the

best areas are north of Breachacha Castle, at Arinagour, around Arnabost, and along the Arnabost-Sorisdale road. There are also high densities of waders in the reserve, including **lapwing, snipe, redshank** and **dunlins**, and a wide range of seabirds – **puffin** and other **auks, shearwater, red-throated diver, tern** and **gannet**. Coll has one of the largest **heronries** on the west coast of Scotland. You might also spot **otters, seals, dolphins, killer** and **minke whales**, and even giant **basking shark**. In winter, large numbers of **barnacle** and **Greenland white-fronted geese** visit. Reserve facilities include a car park and an information bothy at Totronald. There are guided walks in summer.

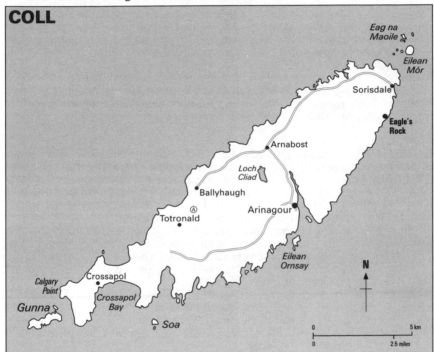

GETTING THERE

By Sea

Caledonian MacBrayne (The Ferry Terminal, Gourock PA19 1QP; tel 08705-650000; fax 01475-635235, reservations; tel 01475-650100; fax 01475-637607, general enquiries; e-mail reservations@calmac.co.uk; www.calmac.co.uk) operates a car-passenger ferry from Oban to Coll and Tiree. The ferry leaves at Oban at 6.30am on Monday, Wednesday, Friday and Saturday and at 2.50pm on Tuesday. The trip to Coll takes 2 hours 40 minutes. The ferry then leaves Coll and goes on to Tiree, which takes 55 minutes. The single adult fare to either island is £11.40, cars £65, motorcycles £32.50, and bicycles £2. The 'Five-Day Return' and 'Six-Journey' ticket is available on both routes. If you go on from Coll to Tiree the single adult fare is £2.90, cars £16.65, motorcycles £8.35, and bicycles £2. The ferry berths at the New Pier (1969), on Loch Eatharna, where there's an office and a waiting room. Outside is a water tap for campers and caravanners. For more information contact the CalMac office in Oban; tel 01631-566688. There are moorings across the loch from the Middle Pier for visiting yachts.

CalMac also has a non-landing cruise to Coll and Tiree on Tuesday from April to October. The ferry leaves Oban at 2.50pm and returns at 10pm. The cruise costs £12.50 and there are fully licensed bars, cafeteria meals, teas and snacks available on board. There is also an Evening Dinner Cruise for £30 (including wine) on this ferry.

GETTING AROUND

Virtually all 20 miles (32 km) of road are narrow, single track. Moped riders and cyclists should watch out for loose gravel on corners, as well as sheep, cattle, farm vehicles, pedestrians, rabbits, hedgehogs, and other cyclists. There is no public transport or taxi service on the island. Bicycles are available for hire from Achamore (tel 01879-230430), Coll Pottery, New Pier, (tel 01879-230382), and Taigh Solas (tel 01879-230333), which also does boat trips.

ACCOMMODATION

Hotel

Coll Hotel: Arinagour, PA78 6SZ (tel 01879-230334; fax 01879-230317; e-mail joliphotel@aol.com). Three-star, at the head of Arinagour Bay with views of Treshnish Isles and Mull. Open all year, from £25 B&B.

B&B

Achamore: Esther and Jim Houchen (tel 01879-230430). Three-star, in the centre of the island, two miles (3 km) from the pier. Good cooking. Open all year, from £18. Self-catering caravan sleeping six also available.

Arileod Farmhouse: Moira MacIntyre (tel 01879-230412). At the West End, about five miles (8 km) from the pier, bordering on RSPB reserve. Three rooms, evening meal optional. Collection from pier can be arranged.

Taigh Solas: Roy and Elaine Barrie, Arinagour, PA78 6SY (tel/fax 01879-230333), three-star, overlooking village bay on the south shore, 1/2 mile from ferry terminal. One twin and one family room. Open all year, from £19. Lunch and dinner also available.

Talla Lan: Julianna Nicholls (tel 01879-230440). Two en-suite twin bedrooms. Packed lunches provided but no evening meals.

Tigh Na Mara: Ruth Sturgeon (tel 01879-230354; e-mail ruthsturgeon@ freenet.co.uk). Overlooks Arinagour Bay with views of Mull and the Treshnish Isles. Courtesy car meets you at the pier. Eight bedrooms with private facilities, and mini-bar, from £17.50. There's also a self-catering chalet, sleeps two adults and two children, from £175 a week.

Self-Catering

Benmeanach: Pamela Garnett (tel 01879-230342). On the north side, close to sandy beach. Sleeps five in double twin-bedded and single rooms. Open all year.

Bousd: tel 01879-230346. At the East End, temporary moorings available and purpose-built slipway to facilitate the launching of boats. One double room, one twin. Linen provided.

Gallanach: Val and Neil Smith (tel 01879-230348). Farmhouse and annexe, sleeps seven.

Greenbank: Fiona Kennedy (tel 01879-230395). At the East End, luxury caravan. One double, one twin. Linen available.

Rosebloom: Cathie MacLean (tel 01879-230408). Traditional village cottage. Double bedroom, open all year.

Round House: Kip Poulson (tel 01879-230479). Traditional whitewashed cottage, sleeps four.

Uig Caravan: Steve and Karlijn Dickison (tel 01879-230491). Four miles (6 km) west of Arinagour, adjacent to 1,000 acres (405 ha) of RSPB nature reserve. Two bedrooms.

Camping

Garden House Camping and Caravan Site: Pat Graham (tel 01879-230374). On the west end of the island, five miles (8 km) from the pier, 24-acre (10 ha) small farm with an old walled garden built in 1750. Open May to September, 20 pitches for tents, three caravan sites. Toilet and cold water available.

Wild camping is allowed behind the *Coll Hotel* (tel 01879-230334) and at *Tigh-an-Lochan* (tel 01879230395/400). The ground near the Church of Scotland is regularly used by campers.

EATING AND DRINKING

The *Coll Hotel* (Arinagour; tel 01879-230334) has good food, a regular bar menu and a la carte using the best of local seafood, beef and lamb. You can enjoy afternoon teas at *Caolas* (tel 01879-230438), at the end of Crossapol Beach, and *The Lochside* (Arinagour; tel 01879-230484).

SPORT AND RECREATION

Diving

The clear waters around Coll abound with life, kelp forests and reefs, where coral once grew in abundance. There are a number of **seal colonies**, which attract such powerful predators as **killer whales**. Coll is visited by **pilot whales, minke whales**, and **dolphins**. The sea around the island has become warmer over the past decade (53-59°F/12-15°C) and **basking sharks** and **rays** are no longer uncommon.

Coll Diving: Achamore (tel 01879-230430). Compressed air for divers. Limited diving equipment for hire. Try-dives and instruction available with BSAC advanced instructor.
Uig Cottage: tel 01879-230491. Small boat services, compressed air.

Fishing
Frank Anderson: tel 01879-230376.
Randy Anderson: tel 01879-230473.
Innes Henderson: tel 01879-230377.
Jimmy Houchen: tel 01879-230430.
Roy Barrie of *Isle of Coll Sea Charters* can take you out boating, fishing, whale and dolphin watching in *MV Perseverance*. He holds a DoT Boatmaster's licence.

Golf. There is a golf course at Cliad. Contact the *Coll Hotel* (tel 01879-230334) for more information.

SHOPPING

Shops are usually open on ferry day mornings, although opening hours are extended in summer. The Post Office sells a small directory which lists local information. There are usually queues for fresh milk and bread in summer so if you are doing your own catering you should place an order. You can buy freshly baked bread from Mull at the *Island Stores* (Arinagour; tel 01879-230335).
An Acarsaid: tel 01879-230395/400. Near the Post Office, gift shop, traditional Scottish crafts.
Coll Pottery: tel 01879-230382. On the ferry pier. Ceramics for sale, classes and community workshops.
Kilbride Wood Workshop: tel 01879-230359.
Lighthouse Gallery: tel 01879-230398. Behind the hotel, paintings, pottery and crafts.
The Corner Shop: Arinagour (tel 01879-230484).

HELP AND INFORMATION

Coll Medical Centre: tel 01879-230326.
Coastguard: tel 01879-230376.
Caledonian MacBrayne: tel 01879-230347.
Post Office: tel 01879-230329.
RSPB Reserve: tel 01879-230301.

There are no banking facilities on the island. Petrol, diesel, and bottled gas are available in the village at limited opening times. There are no garage services, although islanders are usually able to help with car problems. There is no police officer on the island, Tiree (tel 01879-220366) is the nearest police station. The village hall hosts *ceilidhs*, dances, and other social events.

BREACHACHA CASTLE, COLL.

Tiree

Climate in the islands is much of a muchness but Tiree's does deserve a special mention as it holds the record for the maximum amount of sunshine in a month. It had 329 hours in May 1975, an average of 10.6 hours per day. The complete absence of trees on Tiree causes it to record the lowest rainfall in the British Isles as well as some of the highest hours of sunshine. Tiree has a mean temperature in winter of 41°F (5°C) in the coldest months and 57°F (13.9°C) in summer.

EXPLORING

Of all Tiree's poetic names its Gaelic nickname *Tir-fo-Thuinn* ('Land Beneath the Waves') is the most descriptive. Not only is the island a mere pencil line on the horizon until you are virtually in the harbour at Scarinish but the centre of the island, sometimes called 'The Plain of the Reef', is reputedly below sea level and protected from inundation only by a slightly higher shoreline. In severe storms waves have swept right over the island from both sides to meet in the middle. When Tiree was two islands this plain, less than two miles (3 km) wide, was once the bottom of the sea. Few places on Tiree rise more than 49 ft (15 m) above sea level, especially in the central and eastern parts and from a few miles to seaward only houses show against the skyline. The absence of high hills also accounts for the island's low rainfall. The west of Tiree is a plain of fertile sandy soil with two hills, **Ben Hough** (390 ft/119 m) in the north and **Ben Hynish** (463 ft/141 m) with its communications radome 'golf ball' in the south. In between them the land rises to Ceann a' Mhara headland, an overhanging cliff full of ancient remains. Its ledges are beds of **bluebells**, **geraniums**, **sea-thrift**, **vetch**, and **ferns** in summer, and shelter **wild geese**, **swans**, **falcons**, **goosanders**, and **great northern divers**. The lower ledges are white with the guano of **cormorants**, overlooking a colony of **seals**. At sea level are two caves.

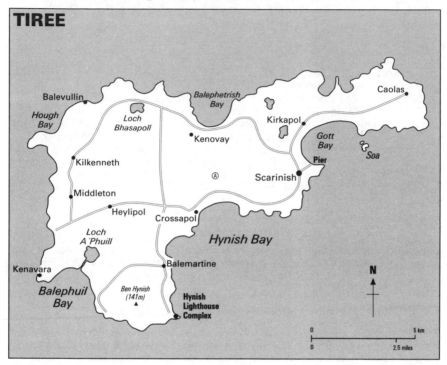

Twelve miles (19 km) to the south-west of this headland is the **Skerryvore Lighthouse**, built by Alan Stevenson, uncle of Robert Louis Stevenson, on a reef uncovered only at low tide. This lonely lighthouse is one of the most exposed in the world, where the force of the waves has been measured at up to three tons a square foot. The tower was completed in 1844, and is 138 ft (42 m) high. Pink granite from Mull – 4,308 tons of it – was used in its construction and when finished RL Stevenson called it 'the noblest of all extant deep-sea lights'. The Skerryvore lighthouse was gutted by fire in March 1954. After renovation diesel-powered electricity was installed and the light automated. Before the lighthouse was built rents on the Hynish side of Tiree were higher than on the eastern coastline because of the rich pickings swept ashore from ships wrecked on the Skerryvore rocks. *The Hebridean Trust* (Lower Square, Hynish, or write to 75a Banbury Road, Oxford OX2 6PE; tel 0865-311468; fax 0865-311593) has restored the old Signal Tower at Hynish as the **Skerryvore Lighthouse Museum**. Before the days of radio this was used to communicate with the keepers at the lighthouse. The associated harbour has also been restored and can be used by visiting boats. Also at Hynish is the **Alan Stevenson House**, created by the Trust out of old store-rooms to accommodate up to 28 people. It is used as an activity centre by a wide range of groups, including disadvantaged children and those with special needs. To the north-west of Hynish, at Sandaig, the Trust has renovated three traditional thatched buildings and these now house the **Sandaig Island Life Museum**, which exhibits a collection of local artefacts, and furniture which replicates a late 19th century interior. Admission is free to both museums, which are open only in summer.

Tiree is swept by boisterous winds, which make the island ideal for the windsurfers who compete in the annual Wave Classic, usually held in October. During summer, sailboarders take part in the **Lug Sailing Regatta**. Each July, Tiree hosts a rollicking Gaelic *feis* (festival). All Tiree's villages are referred to as townships, with Scarinish and its pier, on the east side of the island between Gott and Hynish bays, being regarded as the island's capital. In St Columba's time there were seven monastic settlements on Tiree. To the north of Gott Bay are the ancient chapels of **Kirkapol** (North Church Town) and **Oran's Graveyard**. Close by is the **Little Graveyard** with the ruins of an 11th or 12th century chapel. One of St Columba's contemporaries, St Findchan, founded the monastery of Artchain in Tiree.

Like neighbouring Coll, Tiree is rich in prehistoric duns and brochs. The best example is **Dun Mór Vaul**, just west of Vaul Bay. It measures 35 ft (11 m) in diameter. Within its 13 ft (4 m) thick walls, galleries and cells can be seen. Further west along the coast is the *Clach a' Choire*, the **Ringing Stone**. This is a huge rock of about 10 tons, balanced on one edge. When struck with another stone the rock emits a high ringing note. This is best heard with your ear to the rock, although the pitch can be painful. The note is the result of vibrations in the crystals of the stone and in pitch is 20,000 vibrations a second, just below the upper threshold of human hearing. The rock gong has cup marks on it which probably date it to the late Neolithic period. Local legend says there's a crock of gold inside the hollow rock, but if ever it's broken open, Tiree will sink back beneath the waves. You can hear the sound of the Tiree ringing rock on *The Kilmartin Sessions* CD (Kilmartin House Trust, Kilmartin, Argyll PA31 8RQ; tel 01546-510278; fax 01546-510330; e-mail museum@kilmartin.org; www. kilmartin.org.uk).

GETTING THERE

By Air

British Airways (tel 08457-733377; www.britishairways.com), through *Loganair*, flies to Tiree from Glasgow at 11.10am Monday to Friday, and at 9.10am on Saturday. You can connect with these flights from Aberdeen, Birmingham, London and Manchester. The 15-seater Twin Otter flight take 50 minutes, while the larger 36-seater Shorts 360 aircraft take 35 minutes.

Tiree Airport (tel 01879-220309) is at The Reef on the south-east coast. The airport is open Monday to Friday 11am to 3pm, Saturday 10am to midday (and by arrangement subject to tide variations at Barra). Closed on Sunday. There are ramp facilities at the terminal entrance for the disabled and staff are always ready to help. The Postbus which collects mail from arriving flights will take passengers to Scarinish.

By Sea. The CalMac ferry from Oban to Gott Bay takes about 3 hours 40 minutes, calling in at Coll on the way (see *Coll: Getting There*).

GETTING AROUND

Transport services are sketchy. A **Postbus** operates daily, except Sunday, and there's a shared mini-bus taxi service. Private hire taxis are available and vehicles can be hired from either of the two petrol stations on the island. Hire bikes are popular as Tiree is more of less flat. All the roads are of good standard tarmac single carriageway with passing places.

Buses

John Kennedy: 10 Crossapol (tel 01879-220311). Operates a shared taxi service on the island, Monday to Saturday. It is a request service linking Scarinish, Baugh Surgery, the ferry terminal, Crossapol, and Tiree High School Library. For all other points on the island contact the operator in advance.

DA & AJ MacLean: Rhinns, Scarinish (tel 01879-220342). Operate the bus services. There are two routes from Kenovay-Crossapol-Balemartine-Moss-High School-Scarinish; and Caoles-Scarinish-Crossapol-Kenovay-High School. The service runs Monday to Saturday.

Royal Mail: tel 01246-546329; www.royalmail.co.uk. Operates a four-seater Postbus service from Scarinish post office around the island (with at least 13 stops) to the ferry, and the airport, from Monday to Saturday. Times are subject to flight arrivals, so confirm times and route at Scarinish Post Office (tel 01879-230329).

Taxis

J Gorman: tel 01879-220344. Private taxi.
A MacKechnie: tel 01879-220469.
Vehicle Rental
MacLennan Motors: tel 01879-220555.
Tiree Motors: tel 01879-220469.
Cycle Hire: *MacLean Cycle Hire* (tel 01879-220428).

ACCOMMODATION

Many of the houses on Tiree are available for self-catering rental. Details from Tiree Business Centre (tel 01879-220520).

Hotel

Tiree Scarinish Hotel: Scarinish, PA77 6UH (tel 01879-220308; fax 01879-220410). One-star, at the old harbour. Open all year, from £25.

Guest House

The Glassary: Mrs M MacArthur, Sandaig, PA77 6XQ (tel/fax 01879-220684). Three-star, close to beach, extensive a la carte menu in restaurant. Open all year, from £28.

Kirkapol Guest House: Gott Bay, PA77 6TW (tel/fax 01879-220729). Three-star, converted Victorian church overlooking Gott Bay, en-suite rooms, non-smoking. Open all year, from £25 a night.

Mrs Margaret MacDonald: tel 01651-872216. Self-Catering, one-star, centrally situated traditional croft house, sleeps 6-8. Open all year, from £100-£180 a week.

There's a **hostel** at the Alan Stevenson Centre in Hynish (tel 01879-220726; fax 01879-220730) for groups of up to 28 and individuals can get a bunkbed and full board for less than £25.

HELP AND INFORMATION

Police Station: Scarinish (tel 01879-220366).
Tiree has a resident *doctor* (tel 01879-220323).
Caledonian MacBrayne Pier (tel 01879-220347) is at Gott Bay.
Post Office: Scarinish (tel 01879-220301).
Royal Bank of Scotland: Scarinish (tel 01879-220307).

Daily newspapers are brought by air to the newsagent's shop in Crossapol township, which is also where you'll find the *Argyll & Bute Council Offices* (tel 01879-220349), and the *Tiree Business Centre* (tel 01879-220520).

There's a nine-hole golf course at Vaul, two miles (3 km) from Scarinish. Contact the secretary for more details (tel 01879-220334).

Mull

Mull is the second largest island in the Inner Hebrides and although it's half the size of Skye its 216,299 acres (87,535 ha) offer a dramatic landscape that's very similar, with many wild, remote places accessible only on foot. The island lies in the seaward approaches to Loch Linnhe and is separated from the mainland coast of Morven by the narrow but deep Sound of Mull, and from Oban and the mainland coast by the Firth of Lorn. Islands ranging from semi-submerged rocks and skerries to such larger inhabited islands as Iona and Ulva lie scattered off the west coast. Mull is roughly 24 miles (39 km) from top to bottom and 26 miles (42 km) across at its widest, with an indented mainly rocky coastline nearly 300 miles (483 km) long. Loch na Keal almost cuts Mull in two at its centre from the west and the shape of the island has been fancifully likened to a crouching dog with its neck the central three-mile (5 km) strip of land between Salen and this sea loch. North of this the landscape is mainly gentle, terraced moorlands. The south-west leg is the 20-mile (32 km) long, low-lying moorland peninsula of the Ross of Mull extending out towards Iona and into the Atlantic.

Loch Ba and Loch Frisa are the only substantial inland stretches of water but in the west are the three major sea lochs of Loch Tuath, Loch na Keal, and Loch Scridain, with Loch Buie in the south. Nearly three-quarters of the terrain is above the 500 ft (152 m) contour line and Mull has in 3,169 ft (966 m) Ben More the only Munro peak outside Skye. Mull means 'mass of hill' and as well as improving the skyline the hills bring a notoriously high rainfall, ranging from 50 inches (1,270 mm) a year in the Ross of Mull to 125 inches (3,175 mm) in the mountainous central areas. **Tobermory** is the capital town with a quarter of Mull's total population of around 3,000. About 30 per cent of the islanders, the *Muileachs*, speak Gaelic.

Geology

Mull is unique in Scotland in having its own geological tartan, which gives you the island's underlying structure in a nutshell. The pattern represents a cross-section of the rocks from Fionnphort in the west to central Glen More. Pink is for Ross of Mull granite, grey for the Moine schists at Bunessan and the Jurassic shales at Carsaig, black for the basalt lava flows, yellow represents Mull's ring dyke, and dark green the dolerites and gabbros of the mountains. The green and white represents Iona's famous serpentine marble and the blue is for the sea. Visiting geologists are fascinated by Mull as it has some rocks and structures found nowhere else in the world, such as the Loch Ba ring dyke igneous intrusion which is unique in being comprised of both basic and acid igneous rock. There are also xenoliths, or 'strange rocks', whose appearance is a rare phenomenon. Examples can be seen in the Ross of Mull, where greyish chunks of billion-year-old Moine schist are found in pink and red granite less than half its age.

CRAIGNURE AND THE SOUTH

Mull has a long and colourful history, dating back to 3000 BC when the first Neolithic farmers settled on the island. In spite of the fact that the Vikings were in Mull for 400 years they haven't left much evidence of their occupation, and the sites you see around the island are more likely to be prehistoric or mediaeval.

Soon after leaving Oban the ferry for Craignure passes **Lady's Rock**, at the entrance to the Sound of Mull. This was the scene of a famous attempted murder in 1523 by a MacLean chief who chained his wife and left her on the rock to be drowned by the rising tide. She was rescued by fishermen and taken to her father, the Earl of Argyll. When MacLean went to tell his father-in-law the sad news, she was presented to him alive and well. Shortly afterwards MacLean was murdered by her brother.

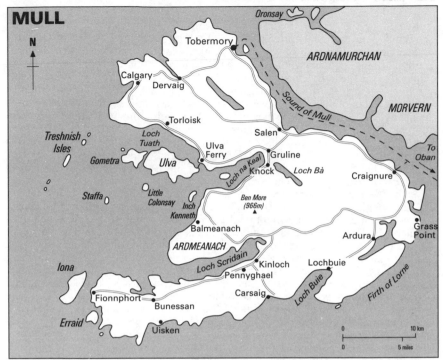

As the island's main ferry port, Craignure is a busy little village at the entrance to the Sound of Mull. From Craignure you can drive, walk or ride the miniature railway the 1½ miles (2.4 km) to Torosay Castle, unique as the only stately home served by a private railway. The narrow gauge **Mull Railway** (tel 01680-812494; fax 01680-300595) operates along a picturesque coastal and woodland route from the Old Pier Station at Craignure to the castle, using steam and diesel locomotives. Scheduled departures from Craignure and from Torosay are hourly early and late in the Easter-October season, and half-hourly in the high season. Fares are reasonable and a variety of tickets and discounts are available. Train buffs enjoy the gift shop selling railway memorabilia.

Torosay Castle (tel 01680-812421; fax 01680-812470; e-mail torosay@aol.com), is an imposing family residence built in 1858 and set in 12 acres (5 ha) of beautiful grounds. The gardens have been designed on a grand scale with Italianate terraces and niche statuary and woodlands giving way to superb seascapes, much enjoyed by Winston Churchill when, in his early days, he was a frequent guest. The interior is decorated in fine Victorian style, with paintings by Landseer and stag heads adorning the walls. Both the castle and its gardens are open to visitors. The gardens are open all year round, daylight hours in winter, and 9am to 7pm in summer. The castle is open daily from Easter to mid-October, 10.30am to 5.30pm. There's a tearoom and a craft/gift shop. Free parking. Admission for adults £4.50, concessions £3.50, children £1.50. In the grounds of the castle is the **Isle of Mull Weavers** (see *Shopping*), where only 66 yards (60 m) of any pattern is ever made. The weaving machine is based on the design of a dobby loom from the mid-1800s. For a demonstration you'll have to don a pair of heavy earphones to protect your ears from the clatter.

Within sight on the stark headland across the bay is 13th century **Duart Castle** (tel 01680-812309), the ancient seat of Clan MacLean chiefs from 1390 until they forfeited the castle in the 18th century for their support of the Jacobite cause. It was recovered by the family in 1911, when work began to restore it to its present condition. You can visit 'prisoners' coughing in the dungeons, learn about the sunken Cromwellian man-of-war lying nearby, and tour the ancient keep with its family portraits, regimental flags, and handsome collection of Highland silver. An exhibition tells the turbulent story of the Clan MacLean chiefs from 1174 until 1990, and there's a display of the decorations given to the 27th Chief Maclean when he was Chief Scout of the Commonwealth. The castle has a gift shop and its tearoom in the old byre is renowned for its homebakes. Open daily from 10.30am to 6pm, May until mid-October. Admission for adults £3.50, concessions £3, children £1.75. Near Duart Point is a castellated beacon built as a **memorial** to the Scottish novelist William Black (1841-98), whose *Macleod of Dare* ends in this setting.

From Duart the road strikes west, passing the head of Loch Don, to almost land-locked Loch Spelve, where a minor road to the left follows the loch shore through fine mountain scenery, dominated by Creach Bheinn, 2,290 ft (698 m). This is a magical road passing dark, landlocked Loch Uisg and ending at Lochbuie. At Loch Uisg is a roadside **memorial plaque** commemorating Queen Victoria's Diamond Jubilee in 1897 and at the road end is an enormous cairn celebrating the 1902 coronation of Edward VII and Alexandra. Westwards along the coastal track is a cliff that presents a remarkable natural rocky profile of Queen Victoria. Bronze and Iron Age sites abound in Mull. Standing stones can be found all over the island, but there's only one **stone circle** and that's at Lochbuie, a 35 ft (11 m) diameter ring of nine stones, with a number of standing monoliths in the vicinity. Also here is ruined **Moy Castle** (*Caisteal Magh*), once the seat of Maclean of Lochbuie. It has been uninhabited since 1750. This gaunt 15th century stronghold is everyone's idea of what an ancient castle should be and was used in the movie *I Know Where I'm Going*. It's not open to the public so you can't see the dungeon where prisoners used to perch on a stone when it was flooded twice a day by the tide. Off the headland at the mouth of the loch is an island that seems an oddity among all the Gaelic names – **Frank Lockwood's Island**. It was named after the 19th century Solicitor General who was related to the then Maclean of Lochbuie. A six-mile (10 km) walk along the coastal path below Ben Buie (2,343 ft/714 m) to the west of Lochbuie brings you to the village of Carsaig and beyond Carsaig Bay to the **Nun's Caves**, whose early Christian carvings are said to be original designs for crosses on Iona. It's a further two-hour hike to Malcolm's Point and the spectacular **Carsaig Arches**, basaltic tunnels among the sea caves and columns of towering cliffs exceeded in height in Scotland only by the sea cliffs of St Kilda, Foula, and Hoy. Massively horned **wild white goats** often browse along the cliffs here.

The main A849 into the **Ross of Mull** runs through Glen More and along the southern shore of Loch Scridain. At Pennyghael you can branch off and drive through Glen Leidle to Carsaig to avoid the coastal hike from Lochbuie. A cairn and a cross dated 1582 stand on the loch shore near Pennyghael commemorating the Beatons, the hereditary physicians of the Lords of the Isles and later of the Macleans of Duart. Close to Bunessan is an attraction that's especially popular with children, the **Angora Rabbit Farm** (Janna and David Greenhalgh, Rehmor Croft, Bunessan; tel 01681-700507). It's open Monday to Friday between Easter and the end of October from 11am until 5pm. Daily demonstrations include clipping at midday, and Angora wool spinning at 3pm. You can buy Angora knitwear and other yarns at the gift shop. Bunessan, at the head of Loch na Làthaich, is the largest village in the Ross of Mull. The **Ross of Mull Historical Centre** on Pier Road near Bunessan Hall (tel 01681-700659; fax 01681-700669; e-mail tania.noddings@ukonline.co.uk) contains a wealth of information about local people and places. It's open April to October, Monday to Friday from 10am to 4.30pm. Admission £1. There are pleasant short walks around the low-lying eastern headland of Ardtun, taking in the **fossilised**

leaf beds sandwiched between sheets of basalt and a favourite spot with fossickers and geologists. A minor road south from Bunessan will take you to the lovely crescent sandy beaches at Uisken and nearby Ardalanish Bay.

The road ends at **Fionnphort** (pronounced *finnafort*), the ferry port for Iona, on the tip of the red granite peninsula. Every year this tiny village is inundated by a tide of around half a million people heading for Iona. To mark the 1,400th anniversary of the death of St Columba in 1997 Fionnphort's **Columba Centre** (tel 01681-700660) was opened, five minutes' walk from ferry. This interpretation centre focuses on the life and work of St Columba and the religious community he founded on Iona in 563. Open Easter to October, Monday to Saturday, 10am to 6pm, Sunday 11am to 6pm.

Just north of the village is the Torr More quarry which provided the superb pink granite used to build Iona Cathedral, the Skerryvore lighthouse and, in London, the Holborn Viaduct, Blackfriars Bridge, and the Albert Memorial. South of the village, facing Fidden, is the tidal island of **Erraid**, forever on the literary map as the place where David Balfour and Alan Breck were stranded after their ship the *Covenant* was wrecked on the Torran Reef in Robert Louis Stevenson's *Kidnapped*. The author knew the island well as he helped his father, Thomas, here during the building of the Torran Reef lighthouse, Dubh Artach, between 1867 and 1872. Stone for the lighthouse was quarried and dressed on Erraid and towed by barge 15 miles (24 km) out in the Atlantic to the reef that had virtually been claiming a ship a year since 1800. Erraid is farmed and managed by members of the **Findhorn Foundation**, who welcome visitors and guests.

For the next leg return to the head of Loch Scridain and turn left along the B8035 road into the **Ardmeanach peninsula**. Apart from its geological interest the peninsula shelters abundant wildlife and the remains of cairns and forts along the coast are evidence of human activity as early as Neolithic times. At Kilfinichen the branch road to the left leads to **Burg**, the Scottish National Trust's 2,000-acre (809 ha) farm property at the western end of the beautiful peninsula, in an area known as the **Wilderness**. There's a small NTS car park at Tiroran. It's then a 3½-mile (6 km) walk to Burg. Almost the same distance again along a tricky cliff-top goat track brings you to **MacCulloch's Tree**, a 40 ft (12 m) high conifer that became a stone fossil about 50-million years ago when it was engulfed by molten lava which preserved the upright 5 ft (1½ m) diameter trunk. The tree is on the shore in a recess in the cliff above high-water mark to the north of the waterfalls near Rubha na h-Uamha. Time your visit to arrive at low tide. The remains of a smaller tree can be seen embedded in lava at the entrance to a cave further along the coast.

Most of the peninsula is trackless and tough going so to get to **Mackinnon's Cave**, famed as the largest in the Hebrides, return to the B8035 at Kilfinichen Bay and follow it across the peninsula through Glen Seilisdeir to the turn-off for Balmeanach farm. From here it's a walk of about a mile (1.6 km) to the cave, which can be entered only at low water. Take a torch. Dr Johnson said the cave was 'the greatest natural curiosity' he had ever seen. It's 600 ft (183 m) deep – although some say it has a subterranean tunnel going right through the peninsula, probably because of the legend that the Mackinnon piper who entered to test the acoustics of the 100 ft (30 m) high cavern was never seen again. His dog, shivering with terror, reappeared miles away with all its hair burnt off. At the back of the cave is **Fingal's Table**, an enormous stone thought to be the altar used by early Christian hermits. The peninsula road linking Mull's south-east corner with Gruline and Salen on the island's narrowest neck of land skirts the feet of the sheer lofty cliffs of Gribun. Beware of falling rocks. One huge boulder which fell here completely flattened a cottage and crushed to death a young honeymooning couple.

Offshore in the mouth of Loch na Keal is the little (136 acres/55 ha) island of

Inch Kenneth, in the 1930s and 1940s home of the Mitford family of Lord Redesdale. They lived in the 19th century mansion near the ruins of the ancient chapel whose graveyard contains the elaborate tombstone of the Maclean chief who entertained Dr Johnson and James Boswell when they spent the night here in 1773. At Gruline, near the head of Loch Ba, is a little bit of Australia, the **Macquarie Mausoleum**, which is managed on behalf of the *National Trust of Australia* (NSW) by the National Trust for Scotland. Major-General Lachlan Macquarie (1701-1824), born on nearby Ulva, replaced the unpopular Captain William Bligh of the *Bounty* as Governor of New South Wales and served from 1809 to 1820. He was known as the 'Father of Australia' and left his name on the map 'Down Under' with the Lachlan and Macquarie rivers and Macquarie Island. Around the tomb on the estate he once owned are prehistoric cairns, standing stones, and a crannog in the loch facing Gruline House.

Three miles (5 km) along the road across the waist of the island is **Salen**, a convenient centre for exploring Mull and an alternative to Craignure as the route to Iona and at 39 miles (63 km) only three miles (5 km) longer. The A849 to Craignure, passes Mull's airstrip, built by army engineers in 1966. At Pennygown, near the foot of Glen Forsa, is a ruined mediaeval chapel, but the area is better known as the abode of the 'Wee Folk' who used to perform tasks for locals until some Smart Alec left a scrap of wood for them to turn into a mast for his boat. They haven't done any jobs since then. Six miles (10 km) from Craignure is the Fishnish ferry terminal and the surrounding campsite of Balmeanach Park.

TOBERMORY   M.S

TOBERMORY AND THE NORTH

From Salen it's a pleasant 10 miles (16 km) on the A848 road along the Sound of Mull to Tobermory. On a promontory at Salen Bay is ruined 14th century **Aros Castle**, once the main stronghold on Mull of the Lords of the Isles. Until Tobermory was established this was the most important place on the island. Rebellious clan chiefs were invited to Aros Castle in 1608 and dined on the *Moon*, the flagship of the Lord Lieutenant of the Isles moored nearby. As they downed an end-of-meal dram they were seized and taken to Edinburgh, where they were imprisoned for more than a year until they had sworn loyalty to James VI of Scotland. A minor road runs north from Aros through Glen Aros and past Loch Frisa to Dervaig. In the 18th century this was the main route used by drovers of black cattle moving stock from the little north coast port of Croig where they were landed from the outer isles. On the way is the site of an ancient market with the longest place-name in Mull, *Druimtigh-macgillechattan* ('the ridge of the house of the Cattenach chap'). Running along the east shore of Loch Frisa through the Salen Forest is a cycle trail which effectively links Aros with Ardmore Point.

Until 1788, **Tobermory** ('St Mary's Well') was a small fishing village on one of the most picturesque anchorages in the Hebrides. In that year the *Society for the Encouragement of the British Fisheries* adopted it as a fishing station and built the handsome row of houses whose multi-hued fronts are such a colourful sight coming into the bay around sheltering **Calve Island**. One of the many film makers who have used Mull for location shoots was responsible for the brightly painted frontages which have given this little island capital such a continental air and

---

The Spanish Armada Treasure Ship

Somewhere at the bottom of Tobermory Bay lies the answer to two questions that have long intrigued marine archaeologists and exasperated wreck divers. What caused the galleon *Santa Maria de Gracia y San Juan Bautista*, generally known as the *San Juan de Sicilia*, to sink on 5 November 1588, and was the 800-ton carrack of the ill-fated Spanish Armada carrying a fabulous treasure in gold ducats? Trying to return to Spain the long way round the north of Scotland, the *San Juan* sought refuge in the bay in September to patch up her hull and rigging and take on food and water after taking a battering fleeing the disastrous engagement with the British fleet in May. Chief MacLean of Duart allowed them to refit and provision in Tobermory on condition the Spaniards provided a hundred of their mercenary soldiers to help him attack Coll, the Small Isles, and Mingary Castle on the mainland. This they did, and the story then becomes hazy. Either an agent of Sir Francis Walsingham, Queen Elizabeth I's Secretary of State and spymaster, smuggled himself on board the ship, or the MacLean of Duart took action when he thought the Spanish were about to sail away without paying for their stores – or there was simply an accident. Whatever the reason, there was an almighty explosion in the *San Juan's* powder magazine which sent the carrack and 350 of her men to the bottom in 60 ft (18 m) of water. Early in the 17th century the Earl of Argyll, then Admiral of the Western Isles, was the first of the unsuccessful treasure seekers and ever since there has been a steady stream in his wake, including divers from the Royal Navy. Finds over the years have been tantalising: pieces of timber, lead sheeting, cannon and shot, silver medallions, a skull, various artefacts – and one Spanish gold coin, a 'Piece of Eight', brought up on the anchor of a Norwegian barque in 1873 and now in the British Museum.

made it so well known. The possibility that a fortune in sunken treasure lies within sight of these 18th century houses has been another great attraction over the years.

The **Mull Museum** (tel 01688-302208) in Tobermory's Main Street has a fine display of small artefacts recovered from the wreck, as well as from other notable shipwrecks around the island. The museum is itself a treasure trove, small but packed with interesting exhibits reflecting every aspect of Mull's history and culture, including an imaginative display on Johnson and Boswell's visit in 1773. It also has reference and photo libraries and an extensive archive. The museum was originally a bakery and contains a Scotch oven built around 1875. Yule Bros ships' biscuits were famous among seamen and fishermen and the artificial ones displayed by the museum continually have to be replaced. They look good enough to eat and vanish regularly whenever children visit. Open Easter to mid-October, Monday to Friday 10am to 4pm, Saturday 10am to 1pm. Admission £1, children 20p.

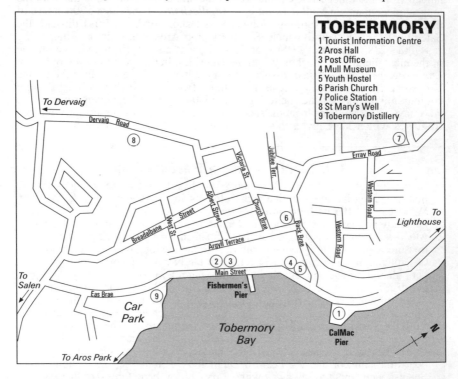

At the **Hebridean Whale and Dolphin Trust** on Main Street (tel 01688-302620; fax 01688-302728; e-mail hwdt@sol.co.uk) you can watch films of whales and dolphins in the Hebrides and listen to their haunting songs. The Trust works to conserve all cetacean species found in the west of Scotland and studies many of the 24 species – nearly a third of all cetacean species – known to roam Hebridean waters, from minke to killer and pilot whales, bottlenose and common dolphins, to the diminutive harbour porpoise. The centre and its shop are open in summer Monday to Friday, from 10am to 5pm, Saturday and Sunday from 11am to 5pm; winter Monday to Friday, from 11am to 5pm.

A small stream tumbles over a pretty double cascade behind the town and next to a ruined mediaeval chapel towards the north-west is **St Mary's Well**, once believed to have healing powers. The lighthouse at Rubha nan Gall ('Strangers' Point'), on the cliffs north of the town was built by the famous Stevensons and is a pleasant walk of about a mile (1.6 km), past the Tobermory golf course. The lighthouse was automated in the 1960s, a century after it was built. About two miles (3 km) from town in the other direction are the **Aros Waterfalls**, in the beautiful grounds of Aros Park, where Forest Enterprise has waymarked a number of walks. Before you head out of town on the B8073 you can set your watch by the **Town Clock**, built by Mrs Isabella Bishop as a memorial to her sister Henrietta, a typhoid victim. Mrs Bishop was better known as Isabella Bird (1831-1904), one of the 19th century's most remarkable women travellers and the first female Fellow of the *Royal Geographical Society*.

The whole northern area of Mull is ideal walking and cycling territory and there are plenty of waymarked hikes and nature trails. Here, five miles (8 km) from Tobermory, is **Glengorm Castle**, whose Gaelic name means 'Castle of the Blue Glen'. Although it sounds poetic it is a grim reference to the smoky blue haze created when tenants here were evicted and their cottages set on fire during the 19th century 'Clearances'. The castle is not open to visitors, but you can enjoy its walled gardens (tel 01688-302368) and buy shrubs, plants, and farm produce. Below Ardmore Point on the tip of the island facing Ardnamurchan, the most westerly point on Britain's mainland, is **Bloody Bay**. In the 15th century this was the scene of a sea battle between John, last Lord of the Isles, and his son Angus. On the opposite shore across the Sound you can see Kilchoan, with ruined Mingary Castle nearby.

The narrow B8073 skirts the three freshwater **Mishnish Lochs** (good for trout) and produces some hairpin bends over stepped lava terraces on the way to **Dervaig** ('The Little Grove'), held to be the most beautiful village on Mull. It is notable for a church with a pencil-shaped steeple and for what is said to be the smallest professional repertory theatre in the UK, the **Mull Theatre** (tel 01688-302828, box office, or 01688-400377, theatre administration; e-mail mulltheatre@tesco.net). Performances are staged in a 43-seat converted coach house in the grounds of Druimard Country House (tel 01688-400345) from May until the end of September. A mile (1.6 km) south of Dervaig is the **Old Byre Heritage Centre** (Glen Bellart; tel 01688-400229), where an exhibition recreates Mull's history with the help of miniature models and a video film show. A 'Taste of Scotland' recommended tearoom serves cakes, teas, coffee and light lunches and a gift shop sells souvenirs and craftwork. The centre is open April to October, daily 10.30am to 6.30pm. Entrance fee is £3 for adults, OAPs and students £2, children £1.50. On the nearby headland near Croig are some ancient cairns and a noted viewpoint which looks out to Skye and the Small Isles. On the way to Caliach Point, the north-west extremity of the island, is **Sunipol House**, where the poet Thomas Campbell (1777-1884) once lived as a tutor, and composed some of the epic works which earned him a tomb in Westminster Abbey's Poet's Corner. As the road swings down the west coast it passes Mull's most famous beach on **Calgary Bay**, with its matchless stretch of white sand. The sea is cold but the bathing is safe. Calgary gets its name from the Gaelic *Calagharaidh*, the 'Haven by the Wall'. The Canadian city of Calgary, Alberta, got its name after Colonel JF Macleod, a Skye man in the Royal North-West Mounted Police, spent a holiday in the Mull village.

The western coast is sparsely populated, with only the occasional croft or farmhouse, the result in the main of the potato famine and the Clearances of the 19th century which reduced the island's population of 10,000 by more than two-thirds. The abandoned crofting township of **Crackaig**, on a peninsula looking out to the Treshnish Isles, was one of the more extensive clearances. Rather than leave, one man hanged himself from an ash tree still growing here. Close by is another substantial deserted village, **Clach Gugairaidh**. The entire western seaboard from Calgary Bay along the shore of Loch Tuath to Ulva Ferry is dotted with cairns and ancient forts.

Although an 18th century building, **Kilninian Church** probably stands on the site of a mediaeval chapel and is worth visiting to see the carved mediaeval Celtic grave slabs in its vestry. Facing the island of Ulva is the spectacular cascade of **Eas Fors**, a repetitive name in Gaelic and Old Norse meaning 'waterfall waterfall'. It's best viewed from the shoreline. Just before the coastal B8073 road joins the B8035 at the head of Loch na Keal there's a pleasant walk from one side of Mull to the other. This is a 2¹/2-mile (4 km) trail from Killiechronan to Salen, most of it through forest plantation. Allow 1¹/2-2 hours.

FLORA AND FAUNA

Flora

Mull's main habitat is its extensive moorland, as its natural and semi-natural woodland exists only in pockets and patches, mainly in the south-east of the island. Most forest cover consists of the sitka, spruce, larch and other coniferous plantations of Forest Enterprise. **Bog myrtle, cotton grass, ling, cross-leaved heath, bilberry, bell heather, bog asphodel, sundew, butterwort, bogbean, heath-spotted orchid, lousewort, milkwort,** and **tormentil** flourish on the moorland. At higher altitudes you'll find **alpine lady's mantle, northern bedstraw, fir clubmoss, woolly hair moss, sea pinks, mossy** and **starry saxifrage, mountain everlasting,** and **roseroot.** The Ardmeanach peninsula is notable for its rich and varied plant life, and for the butterflies attracted by the wealth of summer flowers.

Fauna

You are more likely to see **red deer** than anything else in Mull's hill country. **Wild goats** roam the unstable precipices of Mull's southern coastline and Mull's **hares** are all a mountain sub-species, turning white in winter. The **polecat** is common, although a more likely sighting is **mink,** escapees become resident. Eight cetacean species visit the waters around Mull, with four regularly sighted, the **common porpoise, common dolphin, killer whale,** and the plankton-eating **minke whale,** which returns to local waters every summer.

Sea Life Surveys: Torrbreac, Dervaig PA75 6QL (tel/fax 01688-400223; e-mail sophie@sealifesurveys.co.uk; www.sealifesurveys.co.uk). Offers whale-watching and wildlife cruises, maximum of 12 people in *Alpha Beta,* a 40 ft (12 m) all-weather launch which promises close encounters with minke whale, dolphin, porpoise, seal, basking shark, orca, and seabirds. Operates daily from Tobermory Easter to October. An all-day whale-watch trip will cost you £48 in peak season.

Bird-Watching

Mull is becoming a haven for the **white-tailed sea eagle,** reintroduced in 1975 nearly 60 years after the last two native to Scotland were shot in Skye. One of only 18 breeding pairs in Britain first made an eyrie on Mull in 2000 and reared two eaglets, watched by an estimated 1,200 twitchers who crept into the hide built in a forest exclusion zone by rangers working with the RSPB and Scottish Natural Heritage. If the eagles continue to use the nest site the hide will be open for viewing between May and August, by prior arrangement with Forest Enterprise (Lorne Forest District, Millpark Road, Oban; tel 01631-566155; fax 01631-566185).

Among other birds of prey the **buzzard, kestrel,** and **sparrowhawk** are common and the **golden eagle, peregrine falcon,** and **hen harrier** are seen fairly frequently. Just over 200 species of bird have been recorded, and *Birds of Mull* by Mike Madders and Philip Snow (Saker Press, Islay 1987) is useful to track them down. April, May, and August until October are the **best months** for migrants and from late May until early August for seabirds. Wintering species such as the **great northern diver** begin to arrive from October and most stay at least five months. Generally, the most rewarding month for twitchers is May.

Island Encounters: Richard Atkinson, Arla Beag, Áros (tel 01680-300441). Offers wildlife and bird-watching outings guided by a local expert. Comfortable eight-seat vehicle, lunch snack and drinks. Pick-up can be arranged at all ferry terminals. Adults £23, children £19, including lunch.

Isle of Mull Expeditions: David Woodhouse, Ulva House Hotel, Tobermory (tel/fax 01688-302044). Has day-long 4x4 excursions for sightings of golden eagle and other birds of prey, otters, seals, red deer, porpoise, and dolphins and basking sharks at certain times of the year. Leaves Tobermory at 10am and can collect you from any of the three ferry points. Costs £25.50 for adults, £18.50 children under 12.

GETTING THERE
The ferry services from Oban make it the gateway to the islands of the Outer and Inner Hebrides. The port is just over 90 miles (145 km) north of Glasgow and just under 50 miles (80 km) south of Fort William. It is well served by both road and rail services from all parts of Britain.

By Air
There are no commercial scheduled flights to Mull, although there is a grass over gravel airstrip at Glen Forsa used by private planes and the air ambulance. The runway is 864 yards (790 m) long and is situated $1^1/2$ miles (2.4 km) east of Salen village. The airport is funded by Argyll and Bute Council. From October to the end of April sheep have grazing rights on the airstrip, so 24 hours' notice is required for the runway to be cleared. For flight information contact David Howitt (Airport Bungalow, Glen Forsa; tel 01680-300402).

By Sea
Caledonian MacBrayne (The Ferry Terminal, Gourock PA19 1QP; tel 08705-650000; fax 01475-635235 for reservations; tel 01475-650100; fax 01575-637607 for general enquiries; e-mail reservations@calmac.co.uk; www.calmac.co.uk) operate three ferry routes to Mull. There is a passenger and car ferry from Oban to main entry port Craignure with about six sailings a day, seven days a week throughout the year. The single adult fare is £3.55, cars £24.55, motor cycles £12.30 and bicycles £1. The 'Day Saver' ticket for a car and up to four passengers costs £55. 'Five-Day Return' and 'Six-Journey' tickets are available. The journey takes 45 minutes.

There is also a passenger and car ferry service from Lochaline on the Morvern Peninsula to Fishnish, about six miles (10 km) north of Craignure, which operates from June to August only, seven days a week with as many as 15 departures a day (about nine on Sunday). The journey takes 15 minutes. The single adult fare is £2.15, cars £9.65, motorcycles £4.85, and bicycles £1. 'Five-Day Return' and 'Six-Journey' tickets are available.

The third route is from Kilchoan, on the Ardnamurchan peninsula, to Tobermory. It operates Monday to Saturday, about seven departures a day, and on Sunday, during June to August only, with about five departures a day. The crossing takes 30 minutes and the single adult fare is £3.40, cars £18.05, motorcycles £9.05, and bicycles £1. 'Five-Day Return' and 'Six-Journey' tickets are available. There is also a Kilchoan-Tobermory 'Day Tripper' ticket, valid for a car and two occupants, for travel out and back on any sailing the same day. It costs £36.

CalMac also has 'Day Sails' from Oban to Craignure, 10am, midday, 2pm and 4pm, Monday to Sunday. There are additional sailings on Monday and Friday but check with the office in Oban. The passenger return fare is £6.10, cars £42, and bicycles £2. A 'Day Saver' ticket for a car and up to four passengers is £55, but this is not available on a Saturday. You can also sail from Oban to Craignure, then drive either to Fishnish or Tobermory and cross to Lochaline or Kilchoan. The cost for this Hopscotch Oban-Craignure-Fishnish-Lochaline ticket is £5.15 for a driver and each passenger, car £32; Oban-Craignure-Tobermory-Kilchoan is £6.30 for driver and each passenger, car £38.50. For more information contact CalMac's local offices in Oban; tel 01631-566688, Craignure; tel 01680-812343, or Tobermory; tel 01688-302017.

Tours

The *Mull Experience* (tel 01680-812309/421) coach tour visits Duart Castle, Torosay Castle and Gardens, and includes a ride on the Mull Railway. It operates from May to September, three times a day on Sunday to Thursday, and twice on Friday. The ticket, which costs £17 for adults and £8.50 for children, includes all three attractions, the return ferry from Oban to Craignure, and coach travel on Mull. Tickets from *Caledonian MacBrayne* office at the ferry terminal in Oban.

GETTING AROUND

Maps and Guides

You realise how big Mull is when you find that you need three Ordnance Survey maps to cover it – 1:50,000 Landranger sheets 47, 48, and 49. *About Mull* is a useful little booklet and is a community production whose profits are donated to the *Progressive Care Centre Trust Fund*. It has interesting snippets on all aspects of Mull, as well as Iona, Ulva, and the Treshnish Isles. It also contains discount vouchers which should quickly recoup your £3 outlay. *Mull in the Making*, by Rosalind Jones, will help you to get to grips with the complex geology of the island.

By Road

Almost without exception all roads are winding single-track with passing places marked by black and white poles.

Buses

Bowmans Coaches (Scallastle, Craignure; tel 01680-812313) and *RN Carmichael* (9 Erray Road, Tobermory; tel 01688-302220) operate bus services around the island on behalf of the Argyll & Bute Council (tel 01546-604695). Buses run from the pierhead at Craignure to Tobermory, via Salen; from Craignure to Fionnphort and the ferry to Iona, via Pennyghael and Bunessan; and from Tobermory to Calgary, via Dervaig. These services operate Monday to Saturday only.

Postbuses travel less used or more remote routes. *Royal Mail* (tel 01246-546329; www.royalmail.co.uk) operates a Postbus service from Salen Post Office to Gruline, Ulva Ferry, Lagganulva, Burg, and Achleck. This operates Monday to Saturday. Check times and route at the post office as departures are subject to Oban-Craignure ferry arrivals.

Taxis

MacDougall's Garage: Fionnphort (tel 01681-700294).
Minibus Taxi Service: Jimmy Poulson, Tobermory (tel 01688-302204).

Vehicle Hire

Bayview Garage: Craignure (tel/fax 01680-812444).
MacDougall's Garage: Fionnphort (tel 01681-700294).
MacKays Garage: Ledaig, Tobermory (tel/fax 01688-302103).

Mull Car Hire: The Pierhead, Craignure (tel 01680-812487, evenings tel 01680-300402).

Cycle Hire

Tom A'Mhuillin: Tobermory (tel 01688-302164).
The Ferry Shop: Fionnphort (tel 01681-700470).
On Yer Bike: Inverinate, Salen, Aros (tel 01680-300501).
Pedal Power: Tobermory.
Travel & Crafts: Craignure (tel 01680-812487).

ACCOMMODATION

Hotels

Argyll Arms Hotel: Bunessan, PA67 6DP (tel 01681-700240; fax 01681-700717; www.argyllarms.demon.co.uk). One-star, en-suite accommodation. Open all year, from £25. Friendly bar.

Assapol House Hotel: Bunessan, PA67 6DW (tel 01681-700258; fax 01681-700445; e-mail alex@assapol.com; www.assapol.com). Four-star small hotel. Open April to October, DB&B from £68, no smoking throughout. Vegetarians welcome by prior arrangement. Taste of Scotland.

Bellachroy Hotel: Dervaig, PA75 6QW (tel 01688-400314; e-mail bookings@bellachroy.8m.com). One-star, traditional 16th century droving inn in picturesque surroundings. Open all year, from £18. Good home-cooked food, fully licensed.

Calgary Farmhouse Hotel: near Dervaig, PA75 6QW (tel 01688-400256; fax 01688-400465; e-mail calgary.farmhouse@virgin.net; www.calgary.co.uk). Three-star, nine en suite rooms, from £32 B&B. Open April to October. *Dovecote Restaurant* has an a la carte menu which changes four times a week according to seasonal produce. Smoking discouraged while others are eating. Vegetarians welcome. Taste of Scotland. The *Carthouse Gallery* tea-room is open all day for light lunches and home-bakes.

Craignure Inn: Craignure, PA65 6AY (tel 01680-812305; fax 01680-812306; www.craignure-inn.co.uk). Three-star, 17th century hostelry, centrally located, rooms en-suite. Open all year, from £28. Lively bar.

Druimard Country House: Dervaig, PA75 6QW (tel/fax 01688-400345; e-mail druimard@hotels.activebooking.com; www.druimard.co.uk). Four-star, restored Victorian country house, seven en suite rooms, from £63 DB&B. Open end March to end October. Taste of Scotland. Vegetarians welcome. No smoking restaurant.

Druimnacroish Hotel: Dervaig, PA75 6QW (tel/fax 01688-400274; e-mail taste@druimnacroish.co.uk; www.druimnacroish.co.uk). Three-star, six en suite rooms, 1¹/₂ miles (2.4 km) from village. Open all year, from £35 B&B. No smoking in dining-room. Vegetarians welcome. Taste of Scotland.

Glenforsa Hotel: Salen, by Aros, PA72 6JW (tel 01680-300377; fax 01680-300535). Two-star, panoramic and sea and mountain views, Scandinavian style. Good food and cosy bar. Open all year, from £30.

Highland Cottage: Breadalbane Street, Tobermory, PA75 6PD (tel 01688-302407; fax 01688-302727; e-mail davidandjo@highlandcottage.co.uk; www.highlandcottage.co.uk). Four-star, six en suite rooms, from £33 B&B. Open all year, facilities for disabled visitors. Imaginative cuisine. Member of the Scotch Beef Club and Taste of Scotland. No smoking in dining-room.

Killiechronan House: Killiechronan, PA72 6JU (tel 01680-300403; fax 01680-300463, e-mail me@managed-estates.co.uk; www.highlandholidays.net). Four-star, six rooms, former lodge at head of Loch na Keal. Open from March to October. £130 B&B per night for a double. No smoking in dining-room and bedrooms. Gourmet cooking. Vegetarians welcome. Taste of Scotland.

Pennyghael Hotel: Pennyghael, PA70 6HB (tel 01681-704288; fax 01681-704205). Three-star, lochside, home cooking, en-suite rooms. Open Easter to October, from £31.

Salen Hotel: Salen, PA72 6JE (tel 01680-300324; fax 01680-300599). Two-star, centrally situated overlooking the Sound of Mull. Open all year, from £25.

Tiroran House: Tiroran, PA69 6ES (tel 01681-705232; fax 01681-705240; e-mail colin@tiroran.freeserve.co.uk; www.tiroran.com). On Craignure-Iona ferry road. Six en suite rooms, from £39 B&B. Open 1 April to 28 October, no smoking. Vegetarians welcome. Taste of Scotland.

The Tobermory Hotel: 53 Main Street, Tobermory, PA75 6NT (tel 01688-302091; fax 01688-302254). Three-star, on waterfront overlooking the bay, 16 rooms with private facilities. Open all year, from £35 a night. Restaurant with fresh local seafood.

Ulva House Hotel: Strongarbh, Tobermory, PA75 6PR (tel/fax 01688-302044). Four-star, Victorian house, overlooks bay. Open March to November, from £48 DB&B.

Western Isles Hotel: Tobermory, PA75 6PR (tel 01688-302012; fax 01688-302297; e-mail wihotel@aol.com; www.wihotel.com). Four-star, set above the village of Tobermory. Open all year except 17 to 28 December, from £90 B&B for a double. *The Conservatory* serves bar lunches and *The Dining Room* offers four-course dinners. Vegetarians welcome. Taste of Scotland.

Guest Houses

Achaban House: Fionnphort, PA66 6BL (tel 01681-700205; fax 01681-700649). Three-star, former manse, close to ferry. Open all year, from £18 a night.

Baliscate Guest House: Tobermory, PA75 6QA (tel 01688-302048; fax 01688-302666). Three-star, set in garden overlooking Sound of Mull. All rooms en suite. Open all year, from £23 a night.

Copeland House: Emily King, Jubilee Terrace, Tobermory, PA75 6PZ (tel 01688-302049; e-mail EK@copeland2049.freeserve.co.uk). Three-star, at the top of the town with views over the Sound of Mull and Tobermory Bay, three bedrooms, guest lounge, from £23 a night.

Fairways Lodge: Golf Course, Tobermory, PA75 6PS (tel/fax 01688-302238; e-mail derek_mcadam@msn.com). Four-star, on the golf course, five rooms, all en-suite. Open all year, from £29.

Gruline Home Farm: Gruline, near Salen, PA71 6HR (tel 01680-300581; fax 01680-300573; e-mail gruline@ukonline.co.uk). Five-star, recently converted farmhouse dating from early 19th century set in five acres of grounds, en suite bedrooms. Centrally situated on the island and ideal for touring. Open all year.

B&B

Ardtun House: Bunessan, PA67 6DG (tel 01681-700264). Two-star, traditional stone-built house with sea views, 10 minutes' drive to Iona ferry. Open all year, from £15.

Brockville: Raeric Road, Tobermory, PA75 6AS (tel 01688-302741). En-suite rooms, non-smoking. Open all year, from £18.

Dee-Emm: Janet and Peter Hall, Druim Mhor, Craignure, PA65 6AY (tel 01680-812440, mobile 07780 601177; e-mail jayteehall@supanet.com). About ¹/2 mile (800 m) from the ferry terminal, one double room with private bathroom. Open all year, from £20 a night.

Staffa House: Fionnphort, PA66 6BL (tel/fax 01681-700677). Three-star, highland house, en-suite rooms. Open March to October, from £20.

Self-Catering

Achnadrish House: by Tobermory, PA 75 6QF (tel 01688-400388; e-mail achnadrish@hotmail.com). Three-star, former shooting lodge in eight acres (3 ha) with waterfall, sleeps 2-6. Open all year, from £200-£500 a week.

Ardfenaig Farmhouses: Tiraghoil, Bunessan, PA67 6DU (tel/fax 01681-700260). Three-star, two detached stone farmhouses. Open all year, from £180-£400 a week.

Arle Farm Lodge: Aros, PA72 6JS (tel/fax 01680-300343). Two-star, on working farm, eight twin rooms and two family rooms. Disabled access on ground floor.

Callachally Farm: Mrs MacPhail, Glenforsa, by Salen, PA72 6JN (tel/fax 01680-300424). Three-star, overlooking sea, near beach, one cottage, sleeps eight. Open all year, from £160.

Caol-Ithe: Mrs M Dickson, Fionnphort (tel/fax 01681-700375; e-mail mary@caol-ithe.demon.co.uk). Spacious bungalow, well located for boat trips to Iona and Staffa. Private parking available.

Druimghigha Bothy Cottage: June Winfield, Dervaig, PA75 6QR (tel 01688-400228). Four-star, well-equipped stone house, sleeps six. Open all year, from £375-£425 a week.

Dungrianach: Ms A Rimell, Fionnphort, PA66 6BL (tel 01681-700417). Two-star, one bungalow, sleeps six, views of Iona, situated above the beach. Open all year, from £198-£380 a week.

Glengorm Castle: near Tobermory, PA75 6QE (tel 01688-302321; fax 01688-302738). Baronial castle offering B&B (four-star) and self-catering (two-star) accommodation. Three double rooms, or two flats. Open March to November. B&B from £35, self-catering £244-£468 a week.

Treshnish Farm: Carolyne Charrington, Calgary, PA75 6QX (tel/fax 01688-400249). Two-star, traditional crofters' cottages on working farm, six cottages, sleep 2-6. Open all year, from £100-£240.

Hostels

Arle Bunkhouse: Aros (tel 01680-300343). On the bus route from Tobermory to Aros. Self-catering accommodation for 24 people in eight twin and two family rooms of four. Large communal kitchen and living area, showers, laundry and drying facilities. Ground floor is wheelchair friendly. Ample car parking space.

Dervaig Hall: Dr Richard Foster (tel 01688-400338). Has two bunk rooms, use of kitchen and showers, and can accommodate 10. Additional camping outside the hall can be arranged.

Tobermory Youth Hostel: Main Street, Tobermory, PA75 6NY (tel 01688-302481). Three-star. Hostel reception opens at 5pm. Access until 11.45pm. Overlooking harbour. Open March to October. 40 beds, seven rooms with 5-8 beds. Shop, bus, and ferry nearby.

Camping

Balmeanach Park: Fishnish, Salen, Argyll, PA65 6BA (tel/fax 01680-300342). Three-star caravan and camping site, halfway between Craignure and Salen. A 20-minute walk to Sound of Mull and Fishnish ferry terminal. Open April to October, hot showers, laundry facilities, licensed tearoom on site open for breakfast, lunch and dinner.

Shieling Holidays: David and Moira Gracie, Craignure, PA65 6AY (tel/fax 01680-812496; e-mail graciemull@aol.com). Five-star camping park run by family owners, 12 carpeted cottage tents. Open April to October, hot showers, hook ups, laundry, dishwashing, pay-phone. Stroll to ferry, pub, café, steam railway and buses for Iona, Staffa, and Tobermory. From £10 a night.

The southern end of the beach at **Calgary Bay** is a popular place for camping. Toilets but no other facilities.

EATING AND DRINKING

The best food on the island is in the hotels or in the dishes you whip up yourself with local produce. If you like cheese head for *Sgriob Ruadh* ('Red Furrow') Farm (Glengorm Road, Tobermory; tel 01688-302235; fax 01688-302546; e-mail mull.cheese@btinternet.com) which makes internationally renowned Mull cheese from milk produced by their Friesian herd. It's the only dairy farm in the Highlands and Islands still making traditional farmhouse cheddar. You can try it in the leafy surroundings of their *Garden Barn*. Open Easter to mid-October, Monday to Sunday. Garden Barn is closed on Saturday. Farm shop open daily from 10am to 4pm.

The Anchorage Restaurant: 28 Main Street, Tobermory (tel 01688-302313). Imaginative seafood dishes using local produce, fresh fish and shellfish. Three-course meal £20, excluding wine.

Assapol House: Bunessan (tel 01681-700258; fax 01681-700445). Is an old manse, with views over Loch Assapol. Open at 6.30pm, dinner only. No smoking.

The Black Brae: tel 01688-302422; fax 01688-302666. Tobermory's oldest restaurant, specialises in fresh local seafood. Licensed. Open each evening from Easter to end October from 6pm until late. Weekends only during winter.

At Tobermory ferry terminal is the *Posh-Nosh Café and Takeaway*. Open 11am to 11pm.

Craignure Inn (tel 01680-812305) and *MacGregor's Roadhouse* (tel 01680-812471) are open all year, in summer from 8am to 11pm, and in winter from 11am to 5pm. Opposite ferry in Craignure.

For some of Mull's finest oysters *Croggan Oyster Farm* (An Clachan, Croggan; tel 01680-814224) supplies retail and wholesale all year round.

The Dive, MacGochan's café-bistro-bar overlooking Tobermory harbour (tel 01688-302821; fax 01688-302046; e-mail macgochans@aol.com; www. macgochans.co.uk), is open 11am to 1am daily. Food from midday to 10pm, Monday to Sunday. Weekend brunch (every Saturday and Sunday) £2.95 for full breakfast. Live music. Disabled facilities.

Druimard Hotel: Dervaig (tel/fax 01688-400345). Victorian country house in a quiet north-west hamlet. Open for dinner only from 6.30pm to 8.30pm, closed November to March. No smoking.

Highland Cottage: Breadalbane Street, Tobermory (tel 01688-302030; fax 01688-302727). Open for dinner only from 7pm to 9pm, closed 14 October to 6 November. No smoking.

The Island Bakery: 26 Main Street, Tobermory (tel 01688-302225; fax 01688-302478; e-mail islandbakery@msn.com). Is the place for freshly baked bread and confectionery.

The Keel Row: tel 01681-700458. Fionnphort's favourite pub, home cooking, local seafood, live music. Open all year, summer from 11am to 11.30pm Monday to Sunday.

Killiechronan House: tel 01680-300403; fax 01680-300463. Country house hotel close to the shore of Loch na Keal. Five-course dinners. Open for dinner only from 7pm to 8.30pm, Sunday lunch from noon to 1.45pm, closed November to February. No smoking. Jacket and tie preferred.

Lochinver Restaurant: Main Street, Tobermory (tel/fax 01688-302253). Local fish, Highland venison and Aberdeen Angus steak. Open late March to early November from 11.30am to 3pm, and 6pm to 9.30pm.

The Old Byre Heritage Centre: Dervaig (tel 01688-400229). Licensed tea-room has a range of light meals, homebakes and daily specials such as crofter's soup, Tobermory trout, and clootie dumpling with cream. Vegetarians welcome. Open 8 April to 30 October. Taste of Scotland.

Drinking
Tobermory single malt and Ledaig single malt are both produced by *Mull Whisky Distillers* of Tobermory (tel 01688-302645; fax 01688-302643). The distillery is on Main Street at the bottom of the hill near the waterfront. The complex was built between 1798 and 1823 and is one of the oldest distilleries in Scotland. Tobermory single malt is light amber in colour and produced using water from a private loch and unpeated malted barley. It's regarded as an ideal introduction to island malt whiskies. Open Easter to end-September, Monday to Friday 10 am to 4pm; and October to Easter by appointment. Admission charge for guided tour and tasting, with redemption in shop. Children free.

Brown's Wine Merchants & Ironmongers (21 Main Street, Tobermory; tel 01688-302020; fax 01688-302454). The drink section of this general store sells a wide range of single malts and such curiosities as the 'Smallest Bottle of Whisky in the World' (in the *Guinness Book of Records*) and the 'Original Oldbury Sheep Dip'. Also miniatures of Tobermory 10-year-old single malt and 'Bilgewater' gin. Open Monday to Saturday 8.45am to 1pm and 2.15pm to 5.30pm. Columba Cream and Scottish Highland (sloe whisky) are unusual liqueurs produced and exported by John Murray & Co (Mull) Ltd. As well as at *Brown's*, you'll find them at the *Ferry Shop*, Fionnphort (tel 01681-700470). Open daily.

Regulars say the *Mishnish Bar* in Main Street, Tobermory, is the liveliest place to share a drink with locals. Live music.

SPORT AND RECREATION
Walking and Climbing
Mull and Iona Ranger Service (Forest Enterprise, Salen, Aros; tel 01680-300640) runs an information service on all countryside matters, such as walking, fishing, wildlife, cycling, access, and camping. It also offers guided walks, talks and outdoor activities.

Ben More at 3,169 ft (966 m) is Mull's only Munro, or mountain over 3,000 ft (914 m). Its name translates from the Gaelic as 'Big Hill', and while it's certainly this it can be climbed by anyone in moderate trim. Allow 4-7 hours up and down for either of the two main routes from Loch na Keal and remember that compass readings on Ben More can't be trusted. Not only do readings vary within a short radius, Ben More has a geological surprise: its magnetic polarity is reversed because when its volcanic lava was disgorged the magnetic pole was in the southern hemisphere, not the north. You can climb Ben More and explore other less well-known mountains in Mull with *North-West Frontiers* (18A Braes, Ullapool, Ross-shire IV26 2SZ; tel/fax 01854-612628; e-mail NWF@compuserve.com).

Cycling
Forest Enterprise's cycle route network covers roads and tracks established to access timber in the plantations. All routes are open for biking but it's best to follow those that are waymarked. Remember that you are cycling through working forests. For more information about trails on Mull contact *Lorne Forest District*, Aros (tel 01680-300346).

Diving
The seabed around Mull is dotted with dozens of wrecks dating from the 16th century to modern times. Undoubtedly the most famous is at the bottom of Tobermory Bay, the wreck of a Spanish Armada galleon that sank here in 1588. Its timbers were last visible in 60 ft (18 m) of water in 1740 before it vanished under silt. Despite centuries of endeavour only a cannon and a collection of nondescript artefacts have been recovered. The presence of rumoured treasure has yet to be

proved. Another old wreck lies in 50 ft (15 m) of water off Duart Castle. This is thought to be *The Swan*, a Cromwellian vessel which sank in a storm in 1653. The wreck is a protected site but you can follow an underwater trail guided by a marine archaeologist. Contact the *Lochaline Dive Centre* (Morvern, Argyll, PA6G 5XT; e-mail lochaline.divecentre@virgin.net). Another protected British naval wreck is that of the sailing frigate *HMS Dartmouth*, which went aground in 1690 on Eilean Rubha an Ridire, opposite Scallastle Bay. Most of the wreck sites are in the 20-mile (32 km) Sound of Mull and among the more accessible and popular are the *SS Thesis*, which sank in 1889, *SS Shuna* (1913), *SS Rondo* (1930), virtually on end with her bows in 164 ft (50 m) and her stern in 20 ft (6 m), and *SS Hispania* (1954), which went down in 85 ft (26 m) with the captain standing on the bridge saluting. MacBrayne's 188-ton paddle steamer *Mountaineer* tried to live up to her name in September 1889 by running high up on Lady's Rock between Oban and Mull, staying perched high and dry for 10 days until she broke in two and slipped off the rock. Wreckage lies to the south-west of Lady's Rock, which still has the groove gouged out of it by the keel of the *Mountaineer*. Be guided by Mull, Morvern, or Oban dive centres if you want to dive around the island. The tide races and currents can be treacherous and the coastline is turbulent.

Seafare Chandlery & Seamore Diving: Jane Griffiths, PADI, Main Street, Tobermory, PA75 6NU (tel/fax 01688-302277, and Fionnphort; tel 01688-302686; e-mail janeo@dialstart.net). Diving, sailing all-weather gear. Courses and guided dives, all equipment provided. Open all year, Monday to Saturday from 9am to 5.30pm.

Silver Swift Charters: Raraig, Tobermory, PA75 6PS (tel 01688-302390). Diving charters, fishing trips, and pleasure cruises.

Fishing

There are no coarse fish on Mull, apart from eel and the odd perch, but there are lots of opportunities to catch **brown trout**, **sea trout**, and **salmon**. The **brown trout season** is 15 March to 6 October. There are a dozen hill lochs throughout the island, some with impressive brown trout. Although the **salmon** and **sea trout season** is 11 February to 31 October, the fish don't usually enter the rivers until the first big spate in early July. The *Tobermory Angling Association* (Carna, 7 West Street, Tobermory, PA75 6QJ; tel 01688-302062/056; fax 01688-302093; e-mail olivebrown@msn.com) issues permits for bank fishing only. Other places for information about boats and permits include:

Brown's (21 Main Street, Tobermory; tel 01688-302020; fax 01688-302454).

C Campbell: Fidden Farm, Fionnphort (tel 01681-700214).

Killiechronan Estates: Aros (tel 01680-300403).

Forest Enterprise: Aros (tel 01680-300346) office hours Monday to Friday, 9am to 5pm.

James McKeand: Scoor House, Bunessan (tel 01681-700298).

I Moody: Pennyghael (tel 01681-704232).

Tackle & Books: Main Street, Tobermory (tel 01688-302336).

Hotels are also good sources of information and often have fishing rights.

Golf

Mull has two golf courses. Both welcome visitors. *Tobermory Golf Club* (Honorary Secretary; tel 01688-302338; fax 01688-302170), cliff-top nine-hole course. Green fees £13 per day and £50 a week for adults, juniors £6.50 a day and £25 a week. Green fees payable in advance at *Western Isles Hotel* (tel 01688-302012), *Brown's* (tel 01688-302020; fax 01688-302454), or *Fairways Lodge* (tel/fax 01688-302238, 8am-1pm only). *Brown's* also hires out clubs for £5. *Craignure Golf Club* (tel 01680-812487/300402), nine holes, 18 tees, links course at Scallastle. Limited clubhouse. Tickets available in Craignure, also clubhouse honesty box, £11 per day, under 15 half-price.

Sea Fishing

Sea fishing is rewarding around the island, particularly in the Sound of Mull where catch and release has allowed the common skate (*Raja batis*) to come back from near extinction. Skate of 100 lb-plus (45 kg) are common and gigantic 200-pounders (90 kg) are caught and released every year during the prime March to September season. The British rod and line record for common skate is a 227 lb (103 kg) fish caught off Tobermory in 1986, although even bigger fish have been caught and returned. Conger eel, cod, tope, spurdog, mackerel, coalfish, ling, pollack, and a variety of rays are all common in this area.

Boat Trips

The *MV Amidas*, based in Tobermory (Charlie Laverty, Baloscate House; tel 01688-302048; fax 01688-302666; e-mail bb@baliscate.freeserve.co.uk), runs 3-hour family fishing trips which cost £15 for adults and £12 for children under 12. Rods and tackle are provided. Full-day trips are also available for more serious anglers at £30 an adult, and £24 for children under 12. *Craignure Charters* (Gorsten, Loch Don, PA64 6AP; tel 01680-812332) has skate and general fishing outings aboard a 33 ft (10 m) motor cruiser. Operates May to October, 6am to 9pm. For charter cruising and sea angling aboard *Laurenca II* from Tobermory, contact *Andrew Jackson* (tel 01972-500208).

Other Activities

Squash. There is club at Glengorm Castle which is open all year round. Visitors are welcome. Booking and key available during shop hours from *Togs* (10 Main Street, Tobermory; tel 01688-302379).

Horse-Riding. During the summer months rallies are held every second Sunday by the *Mull Pony Club* (J Hall; tel 01688-302521, or J Kennedy; tel 01680-300583). Shows and rallies take place at Killiechronan.

SHOPPING

Airgiod Gu Leor: Angus J Milne, Willow Cottage, Salen (tel 01680-300494). Large selection of silver and 9ct gold Celtic crosses.

An Tobar Arts Centre, Gallery and Café: Argyll Terrace, Tobermory (tel 01688-302211; fax 01688-302218). Is based in a renovated Victorian primary school. The gallery has local art and craft exhibitions, music, workshops and talks and is a focus for art activities on the island. Open all year, Monday to Saturday from 10am to 6pm. Admission free. Wheelchair access.

Barbara Bisset: Log House, Knockan (tel 01681-700430). Mull and Iona landscapes in pastels.

Brown's: 21 Main Street, Tobermory (tel 01688-302020; fax 01688-302454). Sells just about everything, from screws, nuts and washers to torches, cycle parts, fishing tackle, pocket knives and Wellingtons. Wide range of wines, spirits, malt whiskies and beers as well.

The Carthouse Gallery: Calgary Farmhouse Hotel, Dervaig (tel 01688-400256). Stone-arch gallery near Calgary beach with pictures, pottery, woodwork, etchings, and furniture. Teas, homebakes, light lunches. Open April to September, daily from 11am to 4pm; weekends only in October.

Celtic Originals: Craigmore, Aros (tel/fax 01681-300366; e-mail celtic@originals.freeserve.co.uk). Mail order cottage industry retailing St Columba, Isle of Mull, and Jones tartans, marble soaps, guidebooks, cards and badges.

The Ferry Shop: Fionnphort (tel 01681-700470; fax 01681-700366). The nearest thing to a one-stop shop on Mull. As well as groceries and fresh bread, fish and meat, you'll find hardware, books, videos, a fax and photocopy service, tourist leaflets, and a variety of other useful items. Open seven days.

Island Images: Unit 4, Baliscate, Tobermory (tel/fax 01688-302758). Locally crafted goods and gifts. Handmade basketry, ceramics, stained glass. Incorporates art gallery of local artists. Open April to September and December from 10am to 5pm.

Isle of Mull Silver Company: Main Street, Tobermory (tel/fax 01688-302345; e-mail mullsilver@btinternet.com). Has a large selection of silver and gold jewellery as well as interesting gifts. Open all year, Monday to Saturday from 9.30am to 5pm.

Isle of Mull Weavers: The Steading, Torosay Castle, Craignure (tel 01680-812381). Where you can buy tweed, travel and floor rugs, and other items traditionally woven on old dobby looms. Open all year, 9am to 5pm. Closed on Sunday January-March and November-December.

Kells Gold and Silversmiths: The Hall, Farm Square, Torosay Castle, Craignure (tel 01680-812526; fax 01680-812599; e-mail kells@mull.com). Hand-crafted traditional Celtic, Pictish, and contemporary silver and gold jewellery, set with Iona marble and Hebridean semi-precious stones. Open all year, daily from 9am to 6pm.

Mull Furniture: Ian Slade, Shore House, Fionnphort (tel 01681-700631). Furniture-making, restoration and woodturning.

Mull Pottery: 45 Main Street, Tobermory (tel 01688-302057). Has hand-thrown pottery with contemporary designs at their gift shop in Tobermory and the studio/ gallery (Baliscate Estate, Salen Road, Tobermory; tel/fax 01688-302347; www.mullpottery.co.uk). Open all year.

Seafare, Chandlery and Marine Services: Portmore Place, Main Street, Tobermory (tel/fax 01688-302277). Sells maritime goods, chandlery, diving gear, chart agent, wet-weather gear.

Tobermory Antiques & Collectables: 11A Main Street, Tobermory (tel/fax 01688-302132; e-mail tobantiques@talk21.com). Specialises in whisky-related antiques and collectables. Open all year.

The Tobermory Chocolate Factory: Main Street, Tobermory (tel 01688-302526; fax 01688-302595; e-mail info@tobchoc.co.uk; www.tobermorychocolate. co.uk). Turns out irresistible handmade chocolates. Open Monday to Saturday, 9.30am to 5pm (Sunday 11am to 4pm summer only).

Tobermory Fish Co: Main Street, Tobermory (tel 01688-302120; fax 01688-302622). Does hampers and baskets of fish, chocolate, cheese, Mull shortbread, and other goodies. Also mail-order smoked trout, haddock, and smoked and whisky cured salmon.

Tobermory Treasure Shop: Columba Buildings, Main Street, Tobermory (tel/fax 01688-302278). Has a range of traditional and modern giftware and is Mull's only kilt outfitter.

Angus Stewart's Studio (Breadalbane Street, Tobermory; tel 01688-302781), watercolour landscapes. Open Tuesday and Thursday 10am to 10pm.

HELP AND INFORMATION

Craignure Tourist Information Centre: The Pierhead, Craignure, PA65 6AY (tel 01680-812377; fax 01680-812497; e-mail info@mull.visitscotland.com; www.scottish.heartlands.org). Open April to June from 8.30am-5.15pm, Monday to Friday, Saturday 9am-6.30pm, Sunday 10.30am-5.30pm; June to August from 8.30am-7pm, Monday to Thursday, Friday 8.30am-5.15pm, Saturday 9am-6.30pm, Sunday 10am-7pm; September to mid-October from 8.30am to 5.15pm, Monday to Friday, Saturday 9am-6.30pm, Sunday 10.30am-5.30pm. During winter (mid-October to April), Monday to Saturday 9am-5pm, Sunday 10.30am-midday and 3.30pm-5pm.

Tobermory Tourist Information Centre: Main Street, Tobermory (tel 01688-302182; fax 01688-302145; e-mail info@tobermory.visitscotland.com). Open April to June from 10am-5pm Monday to Friday, Saturday and Sunday midday-5pm, July to August from 9.30am-6pm, Monday to Saturday, Sunday 11am-6pm; September to mid-October, Monday to Friday from 10am-5pm, Saturday and Sunday midday-5pm. Both centres offer local booking, Book-a-Bed Ahead, and advance accommodation booking services. There is a 'What's On' board on which locals advertise forthcoming events.

Police: Tobermory (tel 01688-302016); Salen (tel 01680-300322); Craignure (tel 01680-812322); and Bunessan (tel 01681-700222).

Doctor: Tobermory (tel 01688-302013); Salen (tel 01680-300327); and Bunessan (tel 01681-700261).

Hospital: Salen (tel 01680-300392).

Dentist: Tobermory (tel 01688-302105).

Coastguard: Tobermory (tel 01688-302200/419).

Lifeboat Station: tel 01688-302143.

Post Offices are at Tobermory, Salen, Dervaig, Craignure, Lochdon, Loch Buie, Kinloch, Bunessan and Fionnphort.

Caledonian MacBrayne: Tobermory (tel 01688-302017); Craignure (tel 01680-812343.

Clydesdale Bank: Tobermory (tel 0345 826818; fax 01688-302505). Cashpoint outside for accepted cards and Link cards.

Council Office: Tobermory (tel 01688-302051).

Ranger Service: Aros (tel 01680-300640).

Mull and Iona Community Trust: tel 01688-302770.

Petrol is available in Craignure, Salen, Tobermory, and Fionnphort.

Round & About (Mull Print, Acharonich Cottages, Ulva Ferry, Mull, PA73 6LY; tel 01688-500111; fax 01688-500262; e-mail roundandabout@ukonline.co.uk) is a free monthly newsletter for Mull and Iona which tells you where to go and what to see.

Am Muileach (Salen; tel 01680-300386; fax 01688-300308; e-mail millerlow@clara.co.uk) is a monthly community newspaper for Mull and Iona, run by unpaid volunteers.

The *Information Service*, an information and advice project for Mull and Iona, is open Tuesday and Thursday from 9.30am to 5.30pm, and Saturday from 9.30am to 2pm. For internet access pay at the *An Tobar Arts Centre* (Argyll Terrace, Tobermory; tel 01688-302211; fax 01688-302218; e-mail arts@antobar.co.uk) at the top of the Post Office Brae.

CALENDAR OF EVENTS

April	Traditional Music Festival.
June	Mull and Iona Provincial Mod, festival of Gaelic music, song, and poetry.
	Gathering of Clan MacLean.
	Tobermory Yacht Race, organised by the Clyde Cruising Club, a three-day race, from Bute to Tobermory, via the Crinan Canal.
July	Mendelssohn on Mull Festival.
	Mull Highland Games.
	Western Isles Yacht Club Regatta
August	The Bunessan Show and the Salen Show both have agricultural and craft exhibits.

Mull Half-marathon

October   The Tour of Mull Rally is a popular car rally which attracts
motorsport enthusiasts from all over the UK.

A detailed Iona, Mull and Tobermory Diary can be accessed at
www.tobermory.mull.com. For the latest information and dates contact the Tourist
Information Centre.

Iona

Only a mile (1.6 km) of choppy water separates Iona from Mull. It is a low-lying
island, only 3 miles long by 1½ miles wide (5 km x 2 km) with low craggy hills
overlooking pale sandy beaches and small coves on the east coast and beaches of
more dazzling shell-sand in the north and west. The coastline is more rugged in
the south, which is where St Columba is said to have landed in AD 563. The
island is treeless and its 2,000 acres (809 ha) might look barren and rocky, but the
soil is fertile. Iona has been in the care of the National Trust for Scotland since
1979, except for the Abbey, other sacred buildings and historic sites which, in
1889, were made over to the *Iona Cathedral Trust* by the then owner, the Duke of
Argyll, and are now run by *Historic Scotland*.

Geology

Iona is markedly different from Mull and other surrounding islands. It is so old that
no fossils are found in its hills. It lies across one of the great geological dividing
lines of Scotland where rocks to the west are some of the oldest in the world. Iona's
bedrock may have been created as much as 600-million years ago. Various Lewisian
gneisses, Torridonian sandstone, flags, dark shales and conglomerate can be seen
around the coast and in one or two places limestones have been metamorphosed to
produce the prized white 'Iona marble,' shot through with green serpentine.

EXPLORING

Iona occupies a unique place in the cultural and spiritual history of Scotland and every
year half a million people are drawn to this magical isle, described by Dr Johnson as
'that illustrious island, which was once the luminary of the Caledonian regions.' It was
a sacred island and a centre of worship in the time of the ancient Druids and became
the cradle of Scotland's Christianity with the arrival here from Ireland in AD 563 of St
Columba and his 12 missionary monks. After Columba and his companions
established their monastic settlement the island ceased to be called *Innis nan Druinich*
('Isle of the Druidic Hermits') and became known as Icolmkill, from the Gaelic *I
Chaluim Cille*, or 'The Island of Columba's Church.' Although all the buildings of St
Columba's original monastery are long gone their sites are full of the ruins of a later
ecclesiastical era, spread out around the magnificently restored mediaeval **Abbey** (tel
01681-700404; fax 01681-700460; e-mail ionacomm@iona.org.uk).

Everything on the island is within walking distance of the ferry jetty at **Baile
Mór** ('Big Town'). Heading towards the Abbey from there the first monastic
building you come to is the ruined but still graceful Augustinian **Nunnery of St
Mary**, built in rosy granite in 1203 by Reginald Macdonald of Islay, Lord of the
Isles, who made his sister Beatrice first Abbess. In Columba's time no women were
allowed to stay on Iona. He was fond of saying, *'Where there is a cow there will be
a woman. And where there is a woman there will be mischief'*. so he banished all
the island's females to Eilean nan Ban, the 'Island of the Women' in the Sound of

Iona. Next to the nunnery is **St Ronan's Chapel**, now used as a museum. The road to the Abbey parallels the ancient processional **Road of the Dead** leading to the royal burial ground in **St Oran's Churchyard** (*Reilig Odhran*), which contains the graves of some 60 Scottish, French, Irish, and Norwegian kings, princes and chiefs, testifying to their belief that to be laid to rest on Iona was to be buried in the closest earthly place to heaven. The last Scottish monarch to be buried here was Macbeth (1005-1057), who followed Duncan I, the king he murdered to gain the throne.

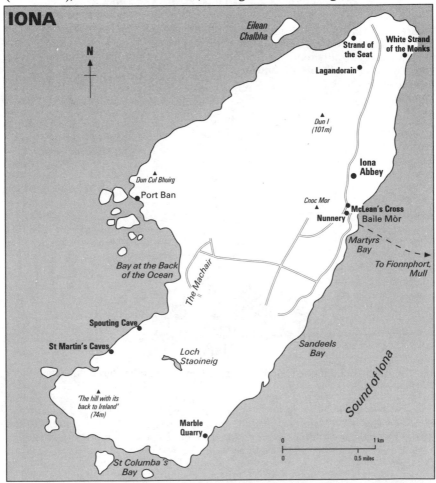

Richly carved in the Celtic tradition, free-standing 15th century **MacLean's Cross** stands 11 ft (3 m) high at a bend in the road near the **Parish Church** and its manse, both built by Thomas Telford in 1830. The manse is now home to the **Iona Heritage Centre** (tel 01681-700576; fax 01681-700328) and has a wealth of information about the history of the island, covering its geology, crofting, fishing, shipwrecks, lighthouses, art and artists, and a Children's Corner. There's a small shop and tearoom which also caters for vegetarians and vegans. Exhibition admission £1.50. Discounts for OAPs, students, groups and children 12-18. Open April to October, Monday to Saturday from 10.30am to 4.30pm.

The restored Romanesque **St Oran's Chapel**, in the royal burial ground to the south-west of the Abbey, is the oldest building on Iona and is believed to have been built in AD 1080 on the site of St Columba's original church by Queen Margaret, wife of Scottish king Malcolm Canmore. From the 8th century on the monastery was destroyed time and again by raiding Vikings and the monks slaughtered. A typical entry of the time in the *Irish Annals* notes, 'Devastation of all the island by the heathen'. Each time the monastery was rebuilt until, in AD 806, after a massacre of 68 monks at **Martyr's Bay** (near the present jetty), the Abbot and most of the community retreated to the monastery of Kells, in Ireland, where they finished working on the fabulous illuminated manuscript of the Gospels now known as *The Book of Kells*. The monks they left behind bore the brunt of further raids until the last one in AD 986 when the Norsemen herded them down to the **White Strand of the Monks** (Tràigh Bhàn) in the north-east and killed all 16.

ST MARTIN'S CROSS,
IONA.

The Abbey buildings seen today are based on those of the Benedictine monastery established in the early 13th century, although the surviving structure of the Abbey dates mainly from the late 15th and 16th century, when it became the Cathedral Church of St Mary. After the Reformation the Abbey fell into ruin and remained in this state until the Church of Scotland meticulously restored it between 1902 and 1910. The secular buildings were restored by the **Iona Community** (Community House, Pearce Institute, 840 Gowan Road, Glasgow, G51 3UU; tel 0141-445 4561; fax 0141-445 4295; e-mail ionacomm@ gla.iona.org.uk; www.iona.org.uk) and date from 1938, when the ecumenical Christian community was founded by the late George MacLeod, later the Very Rev Lord MacLeod of Fuinary. The present cruciform structure has a 70 ft (21 m) square tower, and is 160 ft long by 24 ft wide (49 m x 7 m). Its architecture is mainly Norman and Early Pointed, but peacemeal additions and changes are evident from the mixture of styles. Inside the Abbey are pier capitals carved with a variety of birds, animals and flowers. Such mediaeval remnants as the Romanesque carvings on the capitals of the south aisle arches, and the trefoil arch of the sacristy doorway are particularly striking.

The Abbey and its museum, once the infirmary, are repositories of one of the most comprehensive collections of Christian carved stones in Scotland, more than

180 of them dating from AD 600 to 1600. You can also see what is regarded as St Columba's stone pillow. The richly carved 10th century Great Cross of Iona, or **St Martin's Cross**, nearly 14 ft (4.3 m) high dominates the approach to the Abbey. The earlier Celtic **St John's Cross** was blown down by a gale in 1957 and damaged and the cross now close to the west door is a replica. The remains of the original are in the Abbey museum. Near the west entrance is a small stone cell called **St Columba's Shrine**. For further information on sites contact Historic Scotland (Longmore House, Salisbury Place, Edinburgh, EH9 1SH; tel 0131-668 8600; e-mail graeme.munro@scotland.gov.uk; www.historic-scotland.gov.uk). Once you've explored the Abbey complex a short walk and climb of 10 minutes takes you to the 332 ft (101 m) summit of Dùn I (pronounced *doon-ee*), the highest point on Iona. St Columba must once have enjoyed the views from the top of this modest hill, although his favourite spot was on the **Hill of the Seat** further north, between the beaches of White Strand of the Monks and Strand of the Seat. The walk to the southern end of Iona is a fairly strenuous round trip from Baile Mór of at least four hours. At the southern tip is **St Columba's Bay** (*Port na Curaich*, or 'Port of the Coracle'), the inlet traditionally regarded as the place where Columba first stepped ashore on Iona from his skin-covered boat in October AD 563. From the nearest high point, the 242 ft (74 m) hill now known as **Carn cul ri Eirinn**, the 'Cairn with its Back to Ireland', Columba looked west to see if he could still see his homeland. He couldn't. Multi-coloured pebbles shine like jewels on the beaches of Port na Curaich and adjoining Port an Fhir-bhréige, the most sought after being sea-smoothed fragments of green-streaked Iona marble. Round the south-east headland of Rubha na Carraig-géite are the disused workings where for centuries the prized Iona marble was quarried. It finally closed in 1914. On the west coast is the **Spouting Cave** which sends up sensational fountains of water in stormy weather. Further up the coast are the dazzling white sands of the 'Bay at the Back of the Ocean' (*Camas Cuilan t-Saimh*) below the grassy stretch of the Iona golf course. Near a headland to the north is the small Iron Age fort of *Dun Cul Bhuirg*. Like Skye and Tiree, Iona has some interesting **ringing rocks**. One is not far from the Abbey, an unusual saddle-shaped rock on the foreshore at Port na Fraing to the north, and there's another at Lag Odhar, close to the track leading to St Columba's Bay, but as they have no distinguishing marks you'll need local guidance to find them. If you can't, you can always buy *The Kilmartin Sessions* CD (Kilmartin House Trust, Kilmartin, Argyll, PA31 8RQ; tel 01546-510278; fax 01546-510330; e-mail museum@kilmartin.org; www.kilmartin.org.uk) which features the sounds of these natural rock gongs.

GETTING THERE

Caledonian MacBrayne (The Ferry Terminal, Gourock PA19 1QP; tel 08705-650000; fax 01485-635235, reservations; tel 01475-650100; fax 01475-637607, general enquiries; e-mail reservations@calmac.co.uk; www.calmac.co.uk) operates a passenger-only ferry from Fionnphort, Mull, to Iona throughout the year. There are frequent daily departures from 8.45 am to 6pm. The trip takes five minutes and costs £3.30 return, bicycles are free. The 'Five-Day Journey' ticket costs £9.65.

Bowman's Coaches (tel 01680-812313) provide a link between the Mull ferry terminal at Craignure and Fionnphort. There are four services Monday to Saturday and one on Sunday. The journey takes about 1 hour 15 minutes.

Highlands and Islands Coaches (tel 01631-566999) promise a relaxed tour of Iona, avoiding busy peak times. Leaves Oban at 10am and returns on the 7pm ferry.

GETTING AROUND

The only way to get around is by foot or bike as there are no roads for vehicles. Ordnance Survey's 1:50,000 Landranger Sheet No 48 covering Iona, Ulva and West Mull puts everything into perspective and the Iona Community produces an excellent 6¹/2 inches to the mile (16¹/2 cm to 1.6 km) map of the island, which is useful for walkers.

Bicycles can be hired at *Finlay Ross* (Martyr's Bay; tel 01681-700357; fax 01681-700562), open all year.

ACCOMMODATION

There are only two hotels on the island, no hostels, and no campsites.

Argyll Hotel: tel 01681-700334; fax 01681-700510. Two-star, 19th century hotel, has six single and nine double-twin rooms. Home-cooking, vegetarians welcome. Open April to October, from £43.

St Columba Hotel: tel 01681-700304; fax 01681-700688; e-mail columba@btconnect.com; www.stcolumba-hotel.co.uk. Two-star, opposite the Abbey, nine single rooms, 14 double, and four family. Home-cooked meals. Open April to October, from £36 a night.

The Iona Community (tel 01681-700404; fax 01681-700460; e-mail ionacomm@gla.iona.org.uk) also offers accommodation. *The Abbey* living quarters have been restored and have space for up to 45 guests, mainly staying six nights (£205 per adult). Accommodation is mostly in bunk-bed rooms for two. Disabled access is severely limited, as meals are taken in the first floor Refectory and there's no lift. Share daily prayer and washing up.

The MacLeod Centre – better known as the 'Mac' – has accommodation for about 50, mostly in bunk-bedded rooms for four, five, six and 10 people, £193 a week per adult. Limited disabled access. Religious services, chores, concerts, and *ceilidhs* are shared with the guests and staff from the Abbey. Children of all ages welcome.

B&B

Finlay Ross: Martyr's Bay, PA76 6SP (tel 01681-700357; fax 01681-700562). Two-star, well-appointed bedrooms, some en-suite. Continental breakfast, from £24. Open all year.

Iona Cottage: J&L Mcintyre (tel 01681-700579). Convenient for ferry.

Camping

The nearest camp and caravan site is across the Sound at Fidden Farm (Mrs C Campbell; tel 01681-700427), one mile (1.6 km) from Fionnphort near ferry, £3 a night. Open land with showers and toilets

The Iona Community's *Camas Adventure Centre* on Mull (tel 01681-700367), about three miles (5 km) from Fionnphort, has accommodation for up to 16 guests. It offers outdoor experience for young people particularly those from urban backgrounds. Spartan, no electricity.

EATING AND DRINKING

The two licensed hotels provide meals for non-residents from April to October. *Martyr's Restaurant* is to the left at top of pier, and there's a restaurant at the Abbey, good for vegetarians.

SHOPPING

Finlay Ross: Martyr's Bay, PA76 6SP (tel 01681-700357; fax 01681-700562). Celtic jewellery, designer knitwear, books, and maps. Open all year, April to October from 9.30am to 6pm; November to March from 11am to 1pm and 2pm to 4pm. Closed Sundays November to March.

Iona Community Shop: tel 01681-700404; fax 01681-700772. Opposite the Abbey, stocks a selection of pewter, silver, and gold locally crafted jewellery in traditional Celtic designs, as well as a wide range of gifts and souvenirs, maps and the Community's Wild Goose publications, CDs and cassettes.

Iona Gallery and Pottery: Gordon Menzies, Burnside Cottage, PA76 6SW (tel 01681-700439; fax 01681-700580; e-mail sales@ionagallery.com). Workshop and gallery just beyond the Iona Abbey Coffee House, for decorative stoneware, local landscape paintings and etchings. Open April to September, Tuesday to Saturday from 9am to 5pm, Monday 10.30am to 5pm.

Iona Scottish Crafts: tel/fax 01852-300434. Sells a large assortment of cards, books, jewellery, knitwear, ceramics, woollens and other items.

ULVA

Known to the Vikings as 'Wolf Island', Ulva is by far the largest of the islands around Mull. It lies across a narrow channel off the west coast, its 5,000 acres (2,023 ha) joined by bridge to the smaller island of Gometra. In the centre of Ulva is **Beinn Chreagach** ('Rocky Mountain'), its highest point at 1,027 ft (313 m), with nearby **Beinn Eolasary** only 23 ft (7 m) lower.

Ulva was for years a very private island with owners dedicated to striking a balance between community needs and the preservation of an enchanted little island. Happily they now welcome visitors. If you go to Ulva and Gometra to enjoy peace and some pleasant walks you'll be far from the madding crowd, as the islands draw a mere 6,000 visitors a year and, if they are all at home, there are only 26 residents. You are free to go anywhere around Ulva's 8 sq miles (21 sq km), or you can follow waymarked circular trails which take you through woods, moorland, and along the shore. A longer out and back ramble of five hours follows the rough farm track to the far end of the island. You'll find the Ulva Sheet NM33 1:25 000 map useful. It's available at **The Boathouse Visitor's Centre and Tearoom** (tel 01688-500241/264; e-mail ulva@mull.com) near the ferry landing. A visit to the display here in the **Heritage Centre** will tell you all you need to know about Ulva's history, its walks and where to view natural attractions and ancient sites. It's open Easter to October, Monday to Friday from 9am to 5pm; Sunday June to August only. Closed Saturday. The tearoom is licensed and has homebakes and such specialities as local marinated salmon, oysters, and other shellfish. You can have a cup of tea or a three-course meal any time between 9am and 4.30pm. Nearby is **Sheila's Cottage**, a restored traditional thatched croft house, which supplements the Boathouse display with depictions of Ulva from the Stone Age to the present day. Among the exhibits is evidence that people lived on Ulva nearly 9,000 years ago – flint artefacts and fragments of animal and human bones found in a huge raised sea cavern known as **Livingstone's Cave**.

Ulva was owned for 800 years by the MacQuarries and has had its share of fame. The chief entertained Dr Johnson and Boswell here in 1773. Major General Lachlan Macquarie, first Governor of New South Wales and known as 'The Father of Australia', was born on Ulva, and the grandfather and father of famous African explorer and missionary David Livingstone also lived on the island. Ulva inspired 19th century poet-laureate Thomas Campbell's epic poem *Lord Ullin's Daughter*, which laments the drowning of a chief of Ulva and his bride, who are said to be buried on the opposite shore. Beatrix Potter was a frequent visitor and found inspiration for several of her books here, and the Himalayan climber Hugh Ruttledge lived on Gometra. In the heyday of the kelp industry the island supported more than 600 people. All around the island you can see the ruined cottages of the people who were evicted after the industry collapsed. Off the north-west shore on the tiny islet of Dun Ban are the ruins of a castle, **Glackindaline**. The **Standing Stones** to the south of Beinn Chreagach are a legacy of pre-Celtic settlers who lived here around 3,500 years ago.

The island has been designated an Environmentally Sensitive Area, as well as a National Scenic Area and on your walks you might see **otters**, **red deer**,

mountain hares, **common** and **Atlantic grey seals** and many of the 123 bird species recorded on Ulva, including **white-tailed sea eagles**, **golden eagles**, **herons**, **arctic terns**, **woodpeckers**, **peregrine falcons**, and **corncrakes**. There are around 500 species of trees, wild flowers, and ferns.

From the bridge which links it to Ulva a track crosses **Gometra** to a popular anchorage in a little secret bay almost blocked by Eilean Dioghlum. The highest point on Gometra is 509 ft (155 m). Walkers should be aware that from spring onwards bracken on both islands can grow head-high, making it difficult to find or see off-route sites.

GETTING THERE

Getting to Ulva takes a couple of minutes by ferry, which carries foot passengers and bicycles only and can be called over by following the instructions on the side of the pier shed. Ferry crossings Easter to end-September Monday to Friday on demand between 9am and 5pm. Also Sundays from June to end-August. No Saturday service. Ferry charges of £4.50 return, children £2, include entry to all visitor facilities. If doubtful of weather conditions contact Donald Munro (tel 01688-500226), the ferryman whose brown and white collie Bertie is celebrated for performing cartwheels.

Buses run to Salen from the ferry terminals at Tobermory, Craignure, and Fishnish and from there you can get to the Ulva ferry by **Postbus**. Contact *Aros Post Office* (tel 01680-300321) for times.

Driving time to Ulva ferry from Tobermory, via Salen, 1 hour; Salen, 30 minutes; Dervaig, 30 minutes; Craignure, 45 minutes; Bunessan via Craignure, 90 minutes.

ACCOMMODATION

There's no accommodation and camping is strictly by permission. Organised camping groups should contact estate manager Jamie Howard (Farm Manager's House, Ardulum, Ulva Ferry; tel 01688-500264; e-mail ulva@mull.com) for advice well beforehand. Camping guidelines are on display at The Boathouse.

Staffa and the Treshnish Isles

GETTING THERE

There are regular boat trips to Staffa and the Treshnish Isles from Oban, Mull, and Iona in summer, which is the **best time** to expect the kind of conditions you need to land on Staffa to admire its spectacular caves and fantastic geology and to see breeding birds on the Treshnish group.

Bowman's Tours: 3 Stafford Street, Oban (tel 01631-563221; e-mail bowmanstours@supanet.com; www.bowmanscoaches.sagenet.co.uk). Depart from the CalMac terminal at Oban. The **Mull, Staffa and Iona** tour costs £32 for adults and £17 for children. Check the details with Bowman's.

Gordon Grant Marine: Achavaich, Iona (tel 01681-700338). Has a cruise to **Staffa** and excursions to the **Treshnish Isles**. The cruise leave Fionnphort daily, except Saturday, at 9.45am and 12.15pm and on Saturday at 10.15am and 12.45pm, June to August only. Adult fare £12.50, children £6. The excursion to Treshnish leaves Fionnphort at 10am and returns at 4pm. It operates on Sunday, Tuesday, Wednesday and Thursday, May to July. The adult fare is £25, children

£12.50. It sails to Lunga and lands for two hours.

Inter-Island Cruises: Ardrioch Farm, Dervaig, PA75 6QR (tel/fax 01688-400264; e-mail jenny@mull.com; www.jenny.mull.com). Has full-day inter-island cruises and wildlife trips with landings on **Staffa** and the **Treshnish Isles**. Minimum four passengers, £35 per person, £30 a child under 10. All trips leave from Croig, on Mull, about three miles west of Dervaig, and depart at 10am.

Staffa Boat Trips: Carol Kirkpatrick, Tigh na Traigh, Iona, PA76 6SJ (tel 01681-700358; e-mail dk@staffatrips.f9.co.uk). Has daily trips to **Staffa** from Iona and Mull with at least an hour ashore. It leaves Iona at 9.45am and 1.45pm and from Fionnphort at 10am and 2pm. The adult fare is £12.50, children £5.

Turus Mara: No 1, The Waterfront, Railway Pier, Oban (tel 01631-566999 or 08000 85 87 86; e-mail turus.mara@dial.pipex.com; www.turusmara.com). Has day cruises to **Staffa** from Oban from May to September, leaving at 10am on Monday, Wednesday, Friday, and Sunday. It lands for one hour on Staffa and also visits Ulva. It returns to Oban at 7.40pm, 5.40pm on Friday. The adult fare is £24, children £12.50, and family (2+2) £65. The circular day cruise to **Treshnish** leaves Oban at 10am on Monday, Thursday, and Sunday from June to August, and 10.30am on Staruday. It lands at Staffa for one hour, and Lunga for two hours (from August one hour on Staffa and one hour on Treshnish). It arrives back in Oban at 7.40pm and 7pm respectively. The adult far is £33.50, children £17, and a family (2+2) £90. You can also join a cruise to Staffa and the Treshnish Isles from the Ulva Ferry. The Turus Mara office in Mull is at Penmore Mill, Dervaig (tel 01688-400242/297).

STAFFA

Staffa and its celebrated Fingal's Cave is about seven miles (11 km) to the west of Mull and six miles (10 km) from Iona. The towering formations of mainly hexagonal columns for which the island is famous are composed of dark greyish fine-grained basalt, of such symmetry that early visitors thought they were man-made. The legend

FINGAL'S CAVE.   M.S.

that they were created by a race of giants was given credence until fairly recent times because the natural white calcite deposits between the joints of the columns look just like cement. These volcanic landforms dominate the island and led the Vikings to name it 'Stave' or 'Pillar Island'. Uninhabited Staffa is about 1½ miles (2.4 km) in circumference and has an area of 82 acres (33 ha) and was produced by the same vast, ancient volcanic eruptions that created the Giant's Causeway, 80 miles (129 km) away, in Ireland. Staffa's columns are a good example of the structure that results when a lava mass cools on contact with colder bedrock. For the most part the pillars are hexagonal, a few are pentagonal, while others have seven, eight, and even nine sides. There is said to be only one square stone on the island.

Staffa is honeycombed with caves. The main attractions are **Fingal's Cave**, the **Boat Cave**, the **Clam Shell** or **Scallop Cave**, and **MacKinnon's Cave**. All the caves except Clam Shell face south-east and are best seen by morning light, so plan your visit accordingly. Fingals' Cave is 227 ft (69 m) long and 42 ft (13 m) wide at the entrance, narrowing to about 20 ft (6 m) at its far end. The roof is 66 ft (20 m) above high-water mark, when the water is about 25 ft (8 m) deep. Landings are made near the Clam Shell Cave and the path to Fingal's Cave lies along The Causeway, with cliffs on one side and a brisk, narrow tide-race on the other which separates Staffa from the pyramidal pile of columns called the **The Herdsman**. In moderately calm weather the cave may be entered by boat or by a narrow pathway, which has a protective handrail. The large cave to the west of Fingal's Cave, accessible only by boat, is the **Boat Cave**. Between them is the **Colonnade** or **Great Face** with impressive columns rising to a height of 60 ft (18 m). Beyond is **MacKinnon's Cave**.

Fingal's Cave was unknown to the outside world until visited by famous English naturalist Sir Joseph Banks in 1772. From then on it was acclaimed as a natural wonder of the world and visited by such 19th century notables as Queen Victoria and Prince Albert, the landscape painter JMW Turner, the poets William Wordsworth, John Keats, and Alfred, Lord Tennyson, the writers Jules Verne, Robert Louis Stevenson, and Sir Walter Scott, and the composers Wagner and Mendelssohn – a cavalcade which sent the price of a boat trip soaring to 15 shillings and two bottles of whisky. Mendelssohn was inspired to write his evocative Hebridean overture, *Die Fingalshöhle* ('Fingal's Cave') after hearing the waves crashing in the stupendous basaltic grotto, appropriately known in Gaelic as the 'Musical Cave' (*An Uamh Bhinn*). When he returned to the mainland Mendelssohn was so keen to start composing he immediately sat at the piano, only to be stopped in mid-note by his Scottish host who piously reminded him that it was the Sabbath.

Staffa is a natural sanctuary for the hundreds of **puffins** and **razorbills** which nest here in June and July above the colonies of **seals**. **Whales** and **dolphins** are also frequent visitors. The island is owned by the National Trust for Scotland. Enquiries to NTS Regional Office in Oban (tel 01631-570000).

THE TRESHNISH ISLES

Lying off the west coast of Mull are the uninhabited Treshnish Isles, an eye-catching 6-mile (10 km) chain of skerries, reefs and rocks, with five main islands notable for their varied and curious shapes. At the southern end of the group is conspicuous **Bac Mór**, whose 282 ft (86 m) hump surrounded by a brim of lava has made it better known as the **'Dutchman's Cap'**. Central **Lunga** is the largest in the group, **Fladda** is the flattest, and at the northern tip of the chain are the almost inaccessible twin rocky islets of **Cairn na Burgh More** and **Cairn na Burgh Beg**, separated by a narrow chasm. The ruins of a fort dating back to the time of the Lords of the Isles can be seen on Cairn na Burgh More, which tradition says also still conceals books and records from Iona, buried there by monks to save them from the Vikings. There's also a smaller ruined fortress on Cairn Burgh Beag, used during the Jacobite Rising of 1715.

Lunga is the island you are most likely to visit if you go to the Treshnish Isles. Although it's the biggest island in the group it's only 1¼ miles (2 km) long and 600 yards (549 m) across at its widest. The northern part rises in a hump to 338 ft (103 m) at the summit of **Cruachan**, from which you can see the whole Treshnish group. Below are the ruins of some blackhouses last occupied by visiting summer graziers in 1857. Off the west coast below Cruachan is the 98 ft (30 m) high pinnacle of **Harp Rock** (Dun Cruit), separated from Lunga by a sea channel barely 7 yards (6 m) wide and a popular tenement with puffins.

Lunga is a **puffin** island and there are excursions to Lunga from mid-June until mid-August when they stage a mass departure from their breeding burrows. More than 50 other bird species have been recorded, among them **fulmars, shags, herring gulls, greater black-backed gulls, kittiwakes, arctic terns, razorbills, guillemots**, and **black guillemots. Barnacle geese** winter here. As a sanctuary for birds and a breeding place for Atlantic grey seals the island group has been designated a Site of Special Scientific Interest.

Lismore

Surrounded as much by land as water and lying in the lower reaches of Loch Linnhe, Lismore only just qualifies as an Inner Hebridean island, but is nonetheless an interesting one. The name of this little green and fertile island is popularly supposed to derive from the Gaelic *Lios Mòr* ('The Big Garden'), but it's equally possible that it means 'The Great Enclosure', referring to the holding around the 6th century religious community established by St Moluag. Another possibility is that as the older meaning of the Gaelic *lis* is fort, or stronghold, the name was suggested by St Moluag's fortified monastery. Lismore was long an ecclesiastical centre and gained added fame from *The Book of the Dean of Lismore*, an anthology of Gaelic poetry compiled here in the 16th century.

EXPLORING

The island has a resident population of 160. Its size, 10 miles long and about a mile wide (16 km x 1.6 km), and its gently undulating terrain make it ideal for pleasant walks along and off the main single-track road which runs almost the entire length of the island. A wide range of antiquities, 129 species of birds, and 293 recorded wild plants add to the interest en route, and there are also numerous, if shy, otters. The highest hill on the island is 417-ft (127 m) **Ben Mór**, in the south between lochs Kilcheran and Fiart. You can get good views of the flat summit of Ben Nevis and the sharp twin peaks of Ben Cruachan to the north-east, and the mountains of Morven to the west. The Paps of Jura are sometimes just visible in the south.

Look to the north as the Oban ferry nears Achnacroish and you'll see ruined **Tirfuir Castle**, one of Lismore's most prominent landmarks. This tall Pictish broch overlooks the narrow Lynn of Lorn separating Lismore from the mainland. The Iron Age drystone broch, one of the largest known, is a 2¹/₂-mile (4 km) walk from the pier and is well worth a visit. About half a mile (0.8 km) further along the coast is Port Moluag, where the Pictish monk St Moluag is said to have landed from his skin-covered curragh in AD 562. A local tradition says he raced St Columba to be the first missionary ashore and to make sure he won he severed a finger and threw it ahead on to the beach, greatly displeasing his Celtic Irish rival. St Moluag founded his now-vanished monastery at Clachan. The mediaeval Cathedral of St Moluag was built on the site between 1250 and 1350 and the present **Lismore Parish Church** was in turn built on the ruins of the cathedral in 1750, incorporating some of its fabric and features. A number of carved stones inside and outside of the church date back to when the cathedral was in daily use. Other links with the Pictish saint are a natural rock seat further north along the roadside known as **St Moluag's Chair**, and his blackthorn pastoral staff or crozier, the *Bhachaill Mor*, which can be seen by appointment at Bachuil House, home of the hereditary keepers, the Livingstones. The missionary and explorer David Livingstone was a descendant of this family.

Probably the oldest man-made structure on the island is the large Bronze Age cairn of **Cnoc Aingeil** ('Hill of Fire') to the west of the road near Lismore Parish Church. At 141 ft (43 m) in diameter and 24 ft (7.3 m) high this is the largest in Lorn and, uniquely, from the top six castles can be seen – Dunollie, Duart, Glensanda, Stalker, Shuna, and Barcaldine. At the top of the church glebe is the smaller cairn of **Carn Mor**, near the remains of **Castle Coeffin** on the west coast. This castle was probably built in the 13th century by the MacDougalls, Lords of Lorn, on the site of a Viking fortress. Legend says it once belonged to the Norse warrior Lochlann, who 'neither allowed his galleys to rest nor his arms to rust'. Close by are barely visible signs of a prehistoric promontory fort and on the shore below is a man-made tidal fish trap. In the south-west are the ruins of another 13th century stronghold, square-tower **Achinduin Castle**, which was built as the pre-Reformation seat of the Bishop of Argyll and abandoned around 1510. Not far from the castle is **Bernera Island** which can be reached at low tide. Tradition says St Columba preached here under a yew tree whose branches could shelter a thousand people. It was chopped down in the 19th century to make a staircase for Lochnell Castle on the mainland. You can see St Columba blessing this great yew in a stained glass window in the east gable of the Parish Church. On the southern tip of Lismore is **Eilean Musdile** with its now automated lighthouse, built in 1833 by Alan Stevenson. The lighthouse guards some treacherous waters and islets, one of which is **Lady's Rock**, totally submerged at high tide. In 1523, a Maclean of Duart marooned his wife on this rock at low tide because she failed to produce a male heir. She was rescued by passing fishermen and the callous husband was subsequently killed by his brother-in-law.

Signs of Lismore's more recent history can be seen at **Port Ramsay**, about 1¼ miles (2 km) round the coast from the ferry jetty at the Point. To the north of the hamlet is the kiln which used to prepare the lime quarried on the west coast for shipment to the mainland. The hamlet's houses, now mainly holiday homes, were originally built for the families of men who worked in the kiln and lime quarry at An Sailean. Another lime kiln was operating near a Catholic seminary just south of Kilcheran Loch when Sir Walter Scott visited early in the 19th century. He noted in his diary: 'Reports speak well of the lime, but indifferently of the progress of the students'.

If you'd like to find out more about the island a visit to the **Lismore Historical Society** (*Comman Eachdraidh Lios Mòr*) is recommended. It's near the jetty at Achnacroish and it's open every day from 10am to 5pm, May to October. £1.50 entrance. Contact Donald Black (Achnacroish, PA34 5UG; tel 01631-760257) or Margaret MacDonald (3 Newfield Terrace, Achnacroish, PA34 5UJ; tel 01631-760285).

GETTING THERE

From Oban

Caledonian MacBrayne (The Ferry Terminal, Gourock PA19 1QP; tel 08705-650000; fax 01475-635235, reservations; tel 01475-650100; fax 01475-637607, general enquiries; e-mail reservations@calmac.co.uk; www.calmac.co.uk) operates a small car-passenger ferry to Lismore at 8.45am and 2.25pm Monday to Saturday, with an extra sailing at 10.45 on Tuesday, Thursday and Saturday, and at 4.45pm on Tuesday and Friday. The eight-mile (13 km) crossing takes 50 minutes. The single adult fare for driver/passenger is £2.45 each, car £21, caravan, boat/baggage trailer £21, motorcycles £10.50, bicycles free. 'Five-Day Return' and 'Six-Journey' tickets are available. There is also a 'Day Sail' from Oban which leaves at 8.45am Monday to Saturday and 10.45am on Tuesday, Thursday and Saturday. The passenger day return fare is £4.10, bicycles free. For more information contact the CalMac office in Oban (tel 01631-566688).

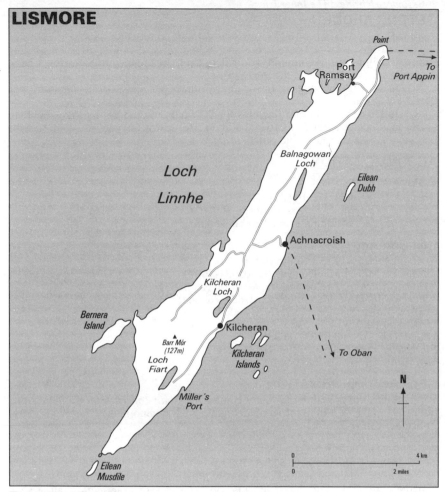

LISMORE

(map labels)

Point
To Port Appin
Port Ramsay
Balnagowan Loch
Loch Linnhe
Eilean Dubh
Achnacroish
To Oban
Kilcheran Loch
Bernera Island
Barr Mór (127m)
Kilcheran
Kilcheran Islands
Loch Fiart
Miller's Port
Eilean Musdile
N
0   4 km
0   2 miles

From Port Appin

There's a small foot passenger ferry to Point, at the northern end of Lismore. This can carry 12. Scheduled departures every two hours throughout the day 8am to 6pm inclusive (12 hours' notice for a 7.25 am crossing and 24 hours' notice for a 9.30pm crossing on Friday and Saturday). The ferry returns from Lismore every two hours from 8.15am to 6.15pm inclusive (12 hours' notice for 7.40am crossing and 24 hours' notice on Friday and Saturday for 9.45pm crossing). There are no 7.25am and 8am services on Sunday from Port Appin, and no 7.40am and 8.15am services from Lismore. Reduced sailings on public holidays. The crossing takes six minutes. Adult return fare is £2, children £1. Contact the ferryman's answering service and leave a message on mobile number 01893 053274, or tel 01631-730311. There's a small prefab waiting room at the Lismore pier with a toilet and washbasin.

If you miss the last ferry from Port Appin the *Pierhouse Hotel and Seafood Restaurant* (tel 01631-730302; fax 01631-730400) at the jetty is noted for oysters, scallops, prawns, salmon, langoustine, and mussels. Double-twin bedded room (per person sharing) with breakfast, October-March £60-70, April-September £70-80.

GETTING AROUND
Royal Mail (tel 01246-546329; www.royalmail.co.uk) operates a four-seater **Postbus** from Lismore Post Office and Achnacroish Pier to Clachan and Port Ramsay, Baligrundle, Achinduin, and Kilcheran from Monday to Saturday. Check departure times and route at the Post Office.

There's a **taxi service** on the island. Contact Mr and Mrs Livingstone (tel 01631-760220).

Cycle Hire. You can hire bicycles for £10, full day, and £6, half day, helmets available. Contact Peter (tel 01631-760213). He'll wait for you on Lismore with bikes and advise on routes and points of interest.

ACCOMMODATION
B&B
Brynalan: C Lutyens (tel 01631-760298).
The Old Schoolhouse: Mrs Crossan (tel 01631-760262). Also teas, coffees, lunches and evening meals when booked in advance.

Self-Catering
No 3 Achnacroish: Mr R Smith (tel 01631-760246).
An-Airidh: Mrs M MacDougall (tel 01631-760213).
Ballimackillichan: Archie and Ina MacColl (tel 01631-760247).
Calgary: Mrs DA Livingstone (tel 01631-760284).
Ceol-na-Mara: K Carter (tel 01631-760241).
Mrs Drew: tel 0141-339 5433.
Mrs MacGregor: tel 01631-760304.
Pierhouse: Miss A Stewart (tel 01631-760221).
Mrs Willis: tel 01631-760204.

HELP AND INFORMATION
For more information about Lismore contact the *Oban Tourist Information Centre* (tel 01631-563122; e-mail info@oban.org.uk; www.oban.org.uk).
Police: tel 01631-730222.
Doctor: tel 01631-730271.
Post Office: tel 01631-760272.
Argyll & Bute Council: tel 01631-567900.

Souvenirs available at the Post Office/village shop (tel 01631-760272) include Lismore glass, dram and glass, and Lismore whisky – 12 year single malt, 8 year blend, and standard blend. You can buy a video of Lismore's history, legends, music, and songs at the Lismore Historical Society centre.

The island has a well-stocked shop which includes the Post Office (tel/fax 01631-760272), about a mile south of the church, where you can order your bread, milk and papers in advance. It is open throughout the summer, Monday to Friday (except Wednesday) from 9am to 1pm and 2pm to 5pm; Wednesday and Saturday from 9am to 1pm. During the height of summer Lismore Light Lunches provide snacks and teas at the Public Hall, open every day from 12.30pm to 3.30pm.

KERRERA

The low-lying island of Kerrera, only four miles long by two miles wide (6 km x 3 km), acts as a natural breakwater for Oban Bay and shelters the town and its harbour from the worst of the south-west winds. The island is only 3,000 acres (1,214 ha) in area, but it's geologically rich and complex and scenically an attractive mix of small rocky and sandy coastal bays, cliffs, caves, and raised beaches, with boglands in the interior, and hill pasture rising to the island's highest point, 620 ft (189 m) **Carn Breugach**. A short climb to the summit will give you views of Ben Cruachan, the Paps of Jura, the mountains of Morvern and Mull, and the little islands of Seil, Easdale, and Luing to the south.

EXPLORING

A rough road almost circles the centre of the island and this and a number of well-beaten tracks makes it easy to explore on foot. The prominent obelisk at the north end of the island is a **memorial** to David Hutcheson, founder of the steamship company which passed to his assistant and son-in-law, David MacBrayne, in whose name the ferry service is known throughout the islands. Nearby **Ardantrive Bay** has a jetty and slipway and is a sheltered anchorage normally crowded with visiting yachties in summer. The **finest beach** on Kerrera is on the west coast at Slatrach Bay, which can be reached by track from Ardantrive and directly across the middle of the island from the ferry jetty. South of the bay are the **caves** of Uamh nan Calman ('Cave of Doves') and Uamh Fhliuch ('Wet Cave').

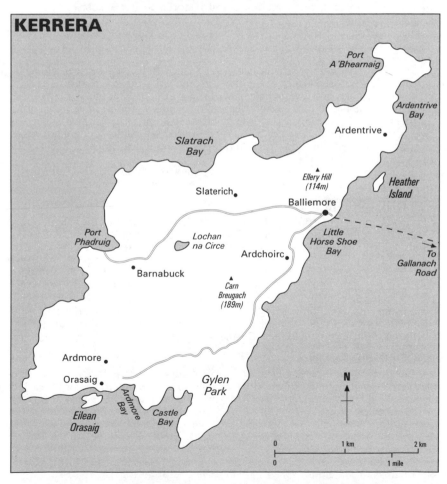

KERRERA

A pleasant walk leads south from the ferry jetty past the bay known as the **Little Horse Shoe**, where the galleys of King Alexander II of Scotland were moored when he died of fever, or was poisoned, in July 1249 at the start of an expedition to bring to heel the MacDonald who had proclaimed himself 'King of the Isles'. A hut was prepared for the King in a field on the bay still known as **Dalrigh**, or 'The King's Field', and his body was taken from there to Melrose Abbey for burial. In the field is a spring called 'The King's Well' where tradition says Alexander drank. It was also in this bay that King Haakon of Norway anchored his Viking fleet before sailing south to the Battle of Largs in 1263 and a defeat that finally ended nearly five centuries of Norse rule in the west coast islands. Perched on a sheer rocky point in the south-west below Carn Breugach stands **Gylen Castle**, ruined but still imposing with its turrets and high walls. It was once a stronghold of the MacDougalls of Lorn, who built it in 1587, but was torched in 1647 during the Convenanting Wars by Cromwell's troops under General Leslie. When the castle was sacked the MacDougalls' famous Brooch of Lorn, a massive bejewelled silver disc said to have once pinned the plaid of Robert the Bruce, was part of the booty. It then disappeared for nearly 200 years, to be produced and restored to its owners in 1825 by a descendant of the Campbell officer who had originally snaffled it. There are a number of caves in the headland of Rubha Seanach, south of Gylen Park, which overlooks Ardmore Bay and the tiny tidal islet of Eilean Orasaig. The island visible to the extreme west is Bach Island.

There's a **seal colony** off the west coast and **otters** may be seen along the shoreline. It's not unusual to see **porpoises** and occasionally **dolphins** feeding quite close inshore, and even **whales** have been sighted further out. A herd of **wild goats** roams the island in the south-east and their kids can be seen in early spring. **Gannets** may be seen diving off the south-west point, and all three species of divers overwinter in the western bays. **White-tailed sea eagles** and **golden eagles** visit the island, and **hen harriers**, **buzzards**, **peregrines**, **falcons**, and **kestrel hawks** are not uncommon.

For more information about Kerrera contact the Oban Tourist Information Centre (tel 01631-563122; e-mail info@oban.org.uk; www.oban.org.uk).

GETTING THERE

Kerrera Ferry (tel 01631-563665). This is the only ferry to the island and is situated two miles (3.2 km) south of Oban on the Gallanach Road. In summer bus service number 431 connects with the 10.30am and 4pm ferries. The crossing takes about five minutes. Free parking is available. The ferry goes across every two hours from 8.30am in the morning until 12.30pm, and then from 2pm to 6pm. Times change in winter and can also change because of weather and tides. When you get to the ferry sign turn the board over to black so that the ferryman opposite knows someone is waiting. Turn the board back once the ferry approaches. Adult return £3, children £1.50, bicycles 50p. Other ferries and boat trips by arrangement. **Getting Around:** Pony trekking (tel 01631-563668).

ACCOMMODATION

Kerrera Bunkhouse: Lower Gylen, PA34 4SX (tel/fax 01631-570223 or 567412; e-mail kerrerabunkhouse@talk21.com). Two miles (3 km) from ferry. A converted 18th century stable, fully equipped with bunks, bedding, sink, cooker, microwave, fridge and cooking utensils. Luggage can be transported from the ferry by arrangement (24 hours' notice). Open all year. Booking is advisable, preferably by daytime telephone or letter. Booking essential in winter (October to March). You can eat at the *Kerrera Tea Garden* at Lower Gylen, which is adjacent to the Bunkhouse. Organic home-grown vegetables, soups, salads and jams available, as well as sandwiches, cakes, scones, hot and cold drinks. Open April to September from 10am to 5pm.

COLONSAY

Colonsay and its semi-detached neighbour Oronsay lie 20 miles (32 km) from the mainland, nine miles (14 km) to the west of Jura, and 15 miles (24 km) south of Mull. Just visible to the south-west from a high point on a clear day is the coast of Donegal, in Ireland, and the only thing between here and Canada is the lighthouse of Dubh Artach, on an isolated reef 16 miles (25 km) away. Colonsay and Oronsay are separated by a mile-wide (1.6 km) shallow strait known as The Strand, which dries out between tides, giving you about two to four hours to walk or drive across.

EXPLORING

Scalasaig is the ferry port and main village in Colonsay, an island of 108 inhabitants with an area of 20 sq miles (52 sq km), which means that no point is more than five miles (8 km) from the harbour. This makes it ideal for exploring on foot or by bike. The island's economy is based on fishing, farming and crofting and Gaelic is the everyday language.

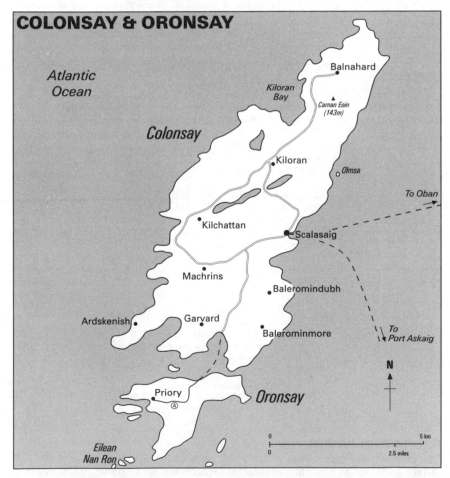

The **obelisk** visible on the hill opposite the hotel commemorates Duncan McNeill, Lord Colonsay, laird of the island in the late 19th century. It's a 20-minute walk up the track behind the church to the monument, for fine views of the harbour and Jura to the south-east. Colonsay has 14 miles (23 km) of road, an eight-mile (13 km) circular route round the centre of the island, with branches off to the north and south. From Scalasaig, the circular loop takes you past a number of standing stones and Iron Age duns to Kilchattan, where there's a ruined **mediaeval chapel** close to the two standing stones known as '**Fingal's Limpet Hammers'**.

At Kiloran, the road skirts the gardens of **Colonsay House** to end two miles (3 km) on at the track leading to **Kiloran Bay** and its famous beach. Its half-mile stretch of white sand has been described as the finest beach in the Hebrides. At the far end of the beach is **Lady's Cave** where many Neolithic remains have come to light, along with flint tools and weapons, and Bronze Age brooches and earthenware pottery. A Viking boatgrave has been unearthed in the dunes behind the beach complete with the remains of a Viking warrior interred around AD 855 with his weapons, horse and harness, and a portable scale with decorated weights, now displayed at the National Museum of Scotland, in Edinburgh. Five other such dune burials have been found on Colonsay and five on Oronsay.

The island has been owned by the family of Lord Strathcona since 1904. Colonsay House (1722) their old residence, a mile or so away from Kiloran Bay, is surrounded by **sub-tropical gardens** famed for their rare and exotic plants. In the grounds is *Tobar Odhrain* ('The Well of Oran'), with a carved stone from the nearby burial ground at Riasg Buidhe. Parts of the gardens are open to the public (tel 01951-200221/369). The 18th century house has largely been converted into holiday apartments. Above the dunes overlooking the beach another well-defined trackway leads to Balnahard, known for its wild goats, passing Colonsay's highest hill, 470 ft (143 m) *Carnan Eoin* ('Cairn of the Birds'), where you might spot an eagle drifting on the thermals, and *Tobar Challuim Chille* ('St Columba's Well'). Beyond Balnahard is a ruined **mediaeval chapel** and cemetery with a **stone cross** and if you don't mind walking over rough, hilly ground this northern finger of land is full of interest.

About a mile (1.6 km) up from the hotel and left on a single track for two miles brings you to the tidal flats separating Colonsay from Oronsay. On the way you'll pass a small ruined chapel to the right of the road. This is the **Temple of the Glen**, known as the 'Monks' Waiting Room' because they used to wait here for the tide to fall so they could cross the sands. If you walk across The Strand be sure to check the tide table before you set off and avoid using your car. Corrosion from seawater is a risk and if your vehicle should stall it will quickly vanish under 7 ft (2 m) of water. The **Postbus** crosses three times a week. This costs £2 per adult return from Post Office, or 50p from shore to shore. If you are walking, be sure to leave Oronsay in good time for the lengthy walk back. Spring tides (new and full moon) give three to four hours access.

Halfway across the sands is the **Cross of Refuge**. It's made of rocks and covered with seaweed, so it's difficult to see. In the past, fugitives reaching it were safe from arrest so long as they stayed a year and a day on Oronsay. Overlooking the crossing place on the Colonsay shore is **Hangman's Rock** on the crags below Beinn Eibhe where cattle thieves used to be executed, most of them from Islay. The hole piercing the flat-topped rock makes it unmistakeable. The rope was passed through this hole and held by a large knot. Victims died within sight of the sanctuary of Oronsay.

FLORA AND FAUNA

The **curlews** and **corncrakes** which circle over Colonsay are just two of the 150 different species of resident and migrant birds, from the common to the rare and protected, found on Colonsay. The botanist can wander among a variety of habitats supporting more than 500 species of plants. More than 40 per cent of Britain's plant species be found in an area of 12 sq miles (30 sq km), the greatest variety in the Hebrides. The most unforgettable floral display is in May when the machair bursts into bloom. **Atlantic grey** and **common seals** can be spotted all round the coast. **Otters** are present, but they're more elusive. Look for them around the southern coastline. **Wild goats** frequent the rugged northern end of the island.

GETTING THERE

Caledonian MacBrayne (The Ferry Terminal, Gourock PA19 1QP; tel 08705-650000; fax 01475-635235, reservations; tel 01475-650100; fax 01475-637607, general enquiries; e-mail reservations@calmac.co.uk; www.calmac.co.uk) operates a car-passenger ferry service from Oban, Kennacraig, and Port Askaig. It leaves Oban on a Sunday at 3.30pm, 3.15pm on Wednesday, and 6pm on Friday. The ferry leaves Kennacraig at 8.15am on a Wednesday. Both journeys take about two hours and the adult single fare is £10.10, cars £48.50, motorcycles £24.25, and bicycles £2. 'Five-Day Return' and 'Six-Journey' tickets are available on this route. The ferry from Port Askaig leaves on a Wednesday at 10.40am and takes 1 hour 10 minutes. The adult single fare is £3.55, cars £18.75, motorcycles £9.40, bicycles £2. A 'Day Saver' ticket is available on this route which costs £44 for a car and up to four occupants. There is also a day return ticket which costs £6 for adults, car £32, motorcycles £16, and bicycles £2. For more information contact the CalMac office in Oban (tel 01631-566688). CalMac operates a large car ferry Islay-Colonsay-Islay service on Wednesdays.

CalMac also has a 'Day Sail' to Colonsay departing Kennacraig every Wednesday at 8.15am and returning at 9.45pm. This gives you six hours ashore and the day return ticket costs £17.20 which you pay at Kennacraig at time of travel; no advance bookings. There are also non-landing cruises and 'Evening Dinner Cruises' from Oban leaving at 3.30pm on Sunday, returning at 8pm; and departing 6pm on Friday, returning at 10.45pm. These cruises operate between April and October only and the fare is £11.40 and £30, including wine, respectively.

Firth of Lorn Ferry Services (tel 01951-200320; e-mail boat@ colonsay.org.uk) is a new passenger and bicycle only service which began operating between Colonsay, Mull, Islay and Jura at the end of March 2002. Landfall and uplift at Jura and Mull is by dinghy and unsuitable for anyone with impaired mobility. All trips are weather dependent. The service operates 30 March to 19 October. Booking is essential. The ferry leaves Colonsay for Uisken, Ross of Mull, at 12.15pm and 4.15pm on Tuesday and Sunday, returning at 3.30pm and 7.30pm. The trip takes 1½ hours. The Colonsay to Jura ferry leaves at 10.30am on Tuesday and Friday, returning at 12.15pm. It takes 1 hour 45 minutes. The Colonsay to Islay ferry leaves at 10am on Thursday, returning at 1.15pm. It takes 45 minutes. All these routes cost £15 for adults; under 16 half-price.

There is an **airstrip** on Colonsay at the Machrins golf course, primarily for the use of the emergency air ambulance service, and an overgrown, disused landing strip on Oronsay.

GETTING AROUND

Buses

Royal Mail (tel 01246-546329; www.royalmail.co.uk) operates a 4-seater **Postbus** service from the Colonsay Post Office (tel 01951-200323) around the island, with about eight stops, and across to Oronsay. It operates Monday, Wednesday, Thursday and Saturday. The timetable is subject to ferry arrival and trips to Oronsay depend on the tide. Departure times should be confirmed at the Post Office.

From Monday to Saturday *C&M McKinnon* (Kilchattan; tel 01951-200341) operates a circular bus service Kilchattan-Kiloran-Uragaig-Glas Aird-Post Office-Pierhead-Scalasaig-Blackgate-The Strand-Machrins-Golf Course. McKinnon also runs a **taxi service.**

Boats Trips: For boat trips contact *Frank Nicholson* (tel 01951-200354).

Cruises: The 12-passenger Lochin 33 *Lady Jane* (K&C Byrne Partnership; tel 01951-200320/242, on-board mobile 07833-902318; e-mail boat@ colonsay.org.uk) offers trips around Colonsay and the Firth of Lorn islands. Special trips on request. Available for diving, fishing, whale-watching, and other charter at £45 an hour (underway) and £10-£15 an hour (waiting time).

Cycle Hire: For bike hire contact *A McConnel* (tel 01951-200355).

Tours

Three to five-hour topography, archaeology, and natural history tours are available. Contact Kevin or Christa Byrne (tel 01951-200320).

ACCOMMODATION

The hotel and *Colonsay Estate Cottages* (Mrs McNeil, Machrins Farm PA61 7YR; tel/fax 01951- 200312; e-mail eleanor@colonsaycottages.swinternet.co.uk; www.colonsay.org.uk) are the largest providers of accommodation. Much of the accommodation is booked well in advance, particularly in the summer months.

Hotel

Isle of Colonsay Hotel: tel 01951-200316; fax 01951-200353; e-mail colonsay.hotel@pipemedia.co.uk. Is the sole hotel, three-star, built in 1750, a listed historic building, lively bar where light meals are served, close to ferry. Open all year, from £69 a double. Fun quiz night every Wednesday evening at 9.30pm.

Self-Catering

Colnatarun Crofthouse: Archie and Susan MacConnell (tel 01951-200355). Sleeps eight.

   Druim Buidhe: Angus and Jenni MacFadyen (tel 01951-200229).

   Drumclach Crofthouse: Mr DM MacNeill (tel 01951-200238). Sleeps six.

   Island Lodges: Kevin and Christa Byrne, Scalasaig, PA61 7YR (tel 01951-200320; fax 01951-200242; e-mail byrne@colonsay.org.uk). A-frame, four self-catering chalets, sleeps two or three and five or six, open all year, long and short lets. Open all year, from £150 to £495 a week, daily from £45.

   Seaview: Annie Lawson (tel 01951-200315). Two-star, one cottage and one studio flat near the standing stones of Kilchattan. Open all year, from £120-£495 a week. Also three-star B&B in croft house, three double rooms, can also make evening meals. Open April to October, from £23.

   Sgreadan Crofthouse: Duncan and Margaret McDougall (tel 01951-200304/300). Sleeps seven.

   Uragaig Crofthouse: Mrs EB MacArthur (tel 0141-580 0619).

B&B

Corncrake Cottage: Rhona and Nigel Grant (tel 01951-200315). Sleeps seven.

   Kiloran Bay: Kirsty MacAllister (tel 01951-200307, or Jenni McFadyen; tel 01951-200229).

   Smiddy Cottage: Helen and Angus MacPhee (tel 01951-200275).

Hostel

Keepers Backpackers' Lodge: Mrs McNeill, Colonsay Holiday Cottages, Machrins Farms (tel 01951-200312; e-mail eleanor@colonsaycottages.

swinternet.co.uk). Former Victorian gamekeeper's house and two adjacent stone bothies, in the centre of the island. Three twin rooms and a four-bedded dormitory. Bed linen provided. £10 a person in twin rooms, £8.50 in dorms. Minimum booking two nights. A mini-bus collects backpackers, or luggage, from the ferry.

Camping

This is not normally allowed although organised educational and research groups may camp provided they get permission well in advance from Colonsay Estate (Colonsay House, Argyll, PA61 7YT; tel 01951-200312). As the island is so small, caravans, trailers and motor-homes are not permitted. There are a number of sheltered anchorages for private boats.

EATING AND DRINKING

Andrew Abrahams: Poll Gorm (tel 01951-200365; e-mail andrew@ aabrahams.junglelinks.co.uk; www.colonsay.org.uk/honey). Can supply fresh Colonsay oysters at £5 per dozen. They'll keep fresh for up to four days. He also sells wildflower honey from his own bees.

Colonsay Hotel: Scalasaig (tel 01951-200316; fax 01951-200353). Open noon to 2pm and 7.30pm for 8pm. Bar food available.

Colonsay House Gardens: tel 01951-200221/369. Open every Wednesday for al fresco meals, organic produce.

The Pantry: May McKinnon (tel 01951-200325). Tearoom, near pier, behind Heritage Centre. Baking, ice-cream, crafts, teas, coffee, toasted snacks, lunches, high tea, for take-aways, order in the morning. Open in winter on Monday, Wednesday and Friday from 10am to 2pm, Saturday 10.30am to 3pm. Local honey for sale. Phone to book for evening meals. In summer open Monday to Saturday 9am to 6pm, Sunday 3pm to 5.30pm.

SPORT AND RECREATION

Clay Pigeon Shooting

The local gun club (tel 01951-200312) has regular shoots, advertised in the local shop and hotel. No need to bring a gun, but a licence must be produced. All firearms must be declared before boarding any ferry.

Fishing

Colonsay Fly Fishing Association controls most of the loch fishing on the island, including **brown trout** fishing on Lochs West Fada, Mid-Fada, East Fada, an Sgoltaire and Turamin. **Best months**, May, June and September; fish average 10-16 oz (283-453 g); fly only. Boats for hire at £2 a half-day. Permits covering all water £10 from Isle of Colonsay Hotel (tel 01951-200316) and shop at Scalasaig (tel 01951-200323). Season is from 17 March to 30 September. Catch is restricted to four good-sized (over 8-inch/20 cm) fish per person a day. All the rest must be returned.

Sea fishing is also available and while saithe is the most common catch, mackerel and other varieties are regularly caught from the pier.

Golf

There's an 18-hole golf course (4,775 yards/4,366 m) swept by Atlantic winds and kept trimmed by rabbits and sheep. Golfers will have to adapt their normal putting style to the Colonsay greens, but 18 holes on Colonsay's links should be an experience to remember. It's a members-only course, but membership is open to all at £10 a year. There are no green fees (tel 01951-200316). The course is also a landing strip for light aircraft.

McPhie-Bagging
Any hill on the island of 300 ft (91.46 m) or more is Colonsay's answer to the mountaineering fraternity's Munros, or peaks over 3,000 ft (914 m). The aim is to climb all the McPhies on Colonsay and Oronsay during the course of one walk. There are 22 of these over a distance of 20 miles (32 km) and the record stands at 6 hours 44 minutes.

Sailing. Sailing dinghies and other small craft can be launched from a slipway within the inner harbour. Contact the Port Supervisor (tel 01951-200320). Boardsailing is popular.

SHOPPING
You'll find plenty of local produce available, whether crafts or foodstuffs. Colonsay lamb and mutton are noted for their flavour and quality. Contact Rhona or Nigel Grant (tel 01951-200303; e-mail rhonag@colonsay.swinternet.co.uk). Exhibitions of local craft work are often displayed in the local *Heritage Centre*, near the pier. *Colonsay Bookshop* (tel/fax 01951-200232; e-mail bookshop@colonsay.org.uk; www.colonsay.org.uk) in the middle of the island is a tiny shop, but it's one of the best island book stockists we've come across. New and antiquarian books, special orders and book search, OS maps and local guides. If the shop is closed call Kevin and Christa Byrne (tel 01951-200230; e-mail byrne@colonsay.org.uk) or Georgina (tel 01951-200375) to make an appointment or ask for access to shop. Jenni is likely to be in the shop on Tuesdays, Thursdays and Saturdays for at least some of the afternoon. Linked to the bookshop is the island's own publishing company, *House of Lochar* (tel/fax 01951-200232; e-mail lochar@colonsay.org.uk; www.colonsay.org.uk), specialising in Scottish books.

HELP AND INFORMATION
Police: tel 01951-200303/350.
Coastguard: tel 01951-200344.
Coastguard Hut: tel 01951-200243.
Pier: tel 01951-200308.
Port Supervisor: tel 01951-200320.
Colonsay Post Office (Office a' Phuist), Shop, and Tourist Information is open Monday to Wednesday 9am to 1pm and 2pm to 5.30pm, Thursday 9am to 1pm, Friday 9am to 1pm and 2pm to 5.30pm, Saturday 9am to 1pm. It sells everything from buckets, plastic footballs, beans and sardines, to postcards and water chestnuts. There's a single petrol pump opposite the shop. Regular *ceilidhs* are held throughout the summer in the Village Hall at Kiloran. At the Heritage Centre, Scalasaig, exhibitions of local crafts are regularly on display.

Colonsay has good telecommunications links with the mainland. There is a well-equipped **medical surgery** (tel 01951-200328) and an air ambulance service on call.

Services at both Church of Scotland (Scalasaig) and the Baptist Church (Kilchattan) are held regularly, although there is no resident minister.

Colonsay has an on-line magazine, *The Corncrake* (e-mail byrne@colonsay. org.uk; www.colonsay.org.uk/corncrake), which lists forthcoming events.

ORONSAY

Oronsay's name is Norse in origin and means 'tidal island'. It is renowned for its ancient priory, regarded in importance as second only to Iona, and for the bird reserve established on its 1,421 acres (575 ha) by the Royal Society for the Protection of Birds (RSPB). The reasonably well-preserved ruins of the 14th century Augustinian priory, with its superbly sculptured Celtic cross, lie about 1¹/2 miles (2.4 km) along the track from The Strand. A magical place of great beauty, the site is believed to have been a centre of worship and healing even before Christian missionaries arrived from Ireland in the 6th century. Legend says that Oronsay was St Columba's first landfall after he left Ireland. From the summit of Ben Oronsay (305 ft/93 m) he could still see the hills of his native Ireland, so to strengthen his resolve he sailed on to Iona, where he established the religious community that became the fountainhead of Christianity in northern Britain. A monastery was also founded on Oronsay in AD 563. The Lords of the Isles established the magnificent priory on the same site between 1330 and 1350. In the 15th and 16th centuries the priory was celebrated for its stone-carvers, regarded as the most highly skilled craftsmen of their time. The famous 12 ft (3.7 m) high **Oronsay Great Cross** on a grassy mound at the south-west corner of the priory church and 27 superbly carved tombstones on display in the Prior's House (Oronsay Priory; tel/fax 01951-200300) are testament to the artistry of these mediaeval masons. All around the island are traces of earlier occupation, shell middens, standing stones, hut circles, 13 duns, and eight forts spanning a time frame from the Mesolithic and Neolithic to the Bronze and Iron Ages.

FLORA AND FAUNA

Only seven people live on Oronsay, which is a microcosm of Hebridean habitats and still a working farm managed as part of the RSPB conservation programme to encourage such endangered and declining species as **corncrakes, choughs, lapwings** and **skylarks**. Areas of tall grass are left to provide cover for the corncrakes that arrive in May. Nesting can continue into August, so the hay is cut late, and slowly from the centre of the field outwards, to give the birds time to escape to safety. Now extremely rare in England, the chough is found here all year round. There are also **gannets, guillemots, cormorants** and **shags**, three species of **diver, mergansers** and **shelducks**. During winter **barnacle** and **white-fronted geese** from Greenland shelter on Oronsay, and spring sees the passage of such waders as **dunlins, turnstones** and **greenshanks**. Oronsay is also a haven for **redshanks** and **snipe. Rock** and **meadow pipits, wheatears**, and shore birds such as **ringed plovers, oystercatchers, gulls, terns** and the beautiful **eider** also nest on the island. In summer the flowers come into bloom – marsh marigolds, followed by irises and many species of orchid, including the **frog orchid** and the **lesser butterfly orchid**. Wildlife all year round includes **Atlantic grey seals, otters** and **dolphins** along the coast. Off the southern tip of Oronsay is *Eilean nan Ron* ('Seal Island'), home to a colony of Atlantic greys. For more information contact the RSPB (Oronsay Farm, Oronsay; tel 01951-200367).

Islay

Islay (pronounced *eye-la*) is the most southerly of the islands of the Inner Hebrides, lying off the west coast of Kintyre and separated in the east by the narrow Sound of Islay from its smaller but much wilder and hillier neighbour, the island of Jura. The Antrim coast of Ireland is as close as the mainland of Scotland. Islay is 25 miles long and some 20 miles wide (40 km x 32 km) and enjoys such a mild climate that the island is greener throughout the winter months than most other parts of Britain. On the west side of the island is the fine coastal district known as the Rinns of Islay, saved from total detachment only by a narrow neck of land between the deep inland thrusts of sea lochs Gruinart and Indaal. South beyond Laggan Bay are the lofty cliffs of the Mull of Oa peninsula and inland a series of hills rising to no more than 1,500 ft (457 m). Off Port Ellen is Texa, at 120 acres (48 ha) the largest of the four islets of note around Islay. The others are Orsay, off Portnahaven, and Nave and Eilean Beag off Ardnave Point in the north. The highly indented coastline runs for more than 130 miles (209 km), a succession of sandy beaches, extensive intertidal flats, cliffs and rocky shoreline.

Geology. A highly complex mix changing from one locality to another, but principally containing Lewisian gneiss and schist in the south and sandstone, limestone and quartzite in the northern areas.

EXPLORING

Islay occupies a special place in the history of the islands of the west. It's known in Gaelic as 'Queen of the Hebrides' (*Bannrigh Innse Gall*) and for nearly four centuries was the heart of the kingdom of the Lords of the Isles, the MacDonalds who ruled all the western islands and a large part of the mainland coast from their loch-bound capital of Finlaggan. Islay has the longest recorded history of any of the western isles, for Celts arrived from Northern Ireland in the first half of the 3rd century and then went on in the 6th century to colonise mainland Argyll, where they were known as *Scotti*. As well as its historical associations, Islay's other attractions include unrivalled birdlife, notable golf links, miles of unspoilt beaches and, of course, what many see at its greatest contribution to civilisation, the distinctive malt whisky produced by seven different distilleries.

Port Ellen

Islay has a wonderful timeless air about it. As the island's largest settlement and main ferry terminal **Port Ellen** is Islay's front door and a good place to begin a tour. This attractive village was established in 1821 by Walter Frederick Campbell, Laird of Islay, and named after his first wife, Eleanor (Port Charlotte,

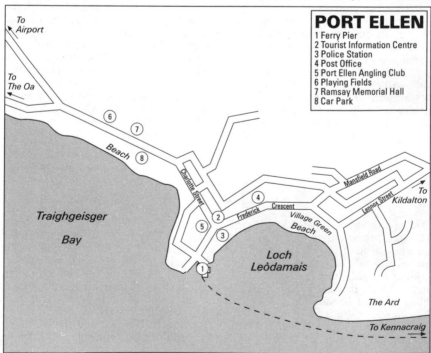

PORT ELLEN

1 Ferry Pier
2 Tourist Information Centre
3 Police Station
4 Post Office
5 Port Ellen Angling Club
6 Playing Fields
7 Ramsay Memorial Hall
8 Car Park

founded in 1828, was named after his mother). The parish encompasses the seaside **whisky distilleries** of Laphroaig – with its visiting otters – Lagavulin, and Ardbeg. Beyond the twin pagoda roofs of Lagavulin distillery the coastal road east passes the ruins of 16th century **Dunyvaig Castle**, built on the promontory site of an earlier stronghold of the MacDonald Lords of the Isles. The crumbling castle keep dates from the 17th century, when the defences were severely damaged during a siege by royalist forces. The ruins are now unstable.

Three miles (5 km) further on is the churchyard of Kildalton, where there are two finely carved Celtic crosses. One, the 9th century **High Cross of Kildalton**, is as famous as St Martin's Cross on Iona. This outstanding cross is intricately sculpted from one piece of local grey-green epidiorite and is widely regarded as a masterpiece of early Christian carving. The smaller, apparently unfinished, 14th century cross stands close by in a railed enclosure. Only the walls and gable ends of the 12th-13th century church still stand. Inside among the mediaeval grave slabs is one with a fine effigy in relief of a knight in armour. The road peters out above Claggain Bay on the east coast, but a cliff-top path continues to **McArthur's Head lighthouse** at the entrance to the Sound of Islay. Inland are rugged uplands dominated by Islay's highest hill, **Beinn Bheigier** (1,611 ft/491 m). All along the route from Port Ellen to the road's end are examples of standing stones, chambered cairns, hut and stone circles, and duns in varying states of preservation; for beach lovers there are good sandy stretches at Ardilistry Bay, Aros Bay, and Ardtalla. Look out for Islay's **red, roe**, and **fallow deer**, especially around Ardtalla and Kildalton.

The Oa. a short wooded walk round the bay to the west of Port Ellen is the sheltered beach of Kilnaughton Bay, popular but never crowded. On the headland is the oddly shaped lighthouse of **Carraig Fhada**, one of five around Islay. The lighthouse is solar-powered. Nearby is the beach of **Traigh Bhán**, with sands that 'sing' when disturbed. A road runs west through the middle of the **Mull of Oa** (pronounced without the 'a'), the peninsula at the south-west end of the island. Scattered around the Oa are the ruins of deserted houses and villages from a time when the peninsula had a population of 4,000, now the total for the whole island. Notable are the abandoned settlements of Lurabus to the south of the road, Grasdal and Tokamal to the north, near Kintra. The Oa is a wild, bleak, place that's ideal for walking and bird-watching, which is why the new **RSPB Upper Killeyan Farm Nature Reserve** has been established here to entice the rare chough (see *Flora and Fauna*). The road traverses the reserve to end at a car park about a mile (1.6 km) from the highest point on the cliffs where the tall stone broch-like **American Monument** stands. This was erected by the American Red Cross in memory of the 697 US servicemen who were drowned in 1918 when the troopship *Tuscania* was torpedoed by a German U-boat and went down south of Oa and the *HMS Otranto* sank further north eight months later after colliding with another convoy ship during a storm. On a headland to the south-east is the Iron Age hill fort of **Dun Athad**, on an impregnable 354 ft (108 m) high stack connected to the mainland by a narrow grassy neck. The easiest way to get to the northern part of the Oa peninsula is to return to Kilnaughton Bay and take the fork to Kintra, with its nearby large forested area and the beginning of the magnificent seven-mile (12 km) beach known as the **Big Strand**, the longest stretch of sand on Islay.

Bridgend. Two roads head north from Port Ellen, the main A846 known as the 'low' road, and inland across the peat moor the B8016 secondary road known as the 'high' road. They meet near Bridgend – the centre of the island road system. At Machrie, on Laggan Bay, golfers will find lots to interest them in the Machrie Hotel, the premier golfing hotel (see *Accommodation*) with its splendid bayside links. A little further on is Glenegedale Airport. **Bowmore** is the administrative 'capital' and shopping centre of Islay, a lovely spacious village on the shore of Loch Indaal. It is the home of the Bowmore whisky distillery and is noted for the curious circular **Parish Church of Kilarrow** which was built in 1767 by Islay laird Daniel Campbell, who also planned Bowmore. Open daily, it is one of only two round churches in Scotland and was designed like this so there were no corners in which the devil could lurk. The body of the kirk has a diameter of 60 ft (18.2 m). The whitewashed buildings of the **Bowmore Distillery** are just off The Square and to the south of the complex is Islay High School, whose pagoda roof mirrors the distinctive shape of that at the distillery.

THE ROUND CHURCH, BOWMORE

On a hill overlooking the tidal flats of Loch Indaal near Bridgend is a railed white obelisk, a **monument** to John Francis Campbell (1821-1885), folklorist and Gaelic scholar. Behind the obelisk to the south-east of Bridgend are the overgrown ramparts and ditches of the Iron Age fort of **Dun Nosebridge**, on a long raised crag offering a wide view of the Laggan Valley. If you are not up to the walk 4x4 vehicle trips can be arranged (tel 01496-810274). In a wooded setting at the head of the loch is **Bridgend**, where a road junction gives you the choice of turning west to the Rinns of Islay or east to Port Askaig. Islay House stands in wooded grounds on the outskirts of Bridgend. A village stood on the shore here in the 18th century, but was uprooted by the Campbell laird of the time because he thought it spoilt the view from Islay House.

Roughly five miles (8 km) from Bridgend along the A846 to Port Askaig is the straggling village of Ballygrant which, unremarkable in itself, sits in the centre of an area full of remarkable ancient sites. A short distance down a narrow road signposted Mulindry will take you between two small lochs to Lossit Farm, on whose land is Islay's only Iron Age broch, **Dun Bhoraraig**. The ruins of the galleried stone tower are on the summit of a hillock, offering glorious views of the whole Sound of Islay and across to the Paps of Jura. A mile past Ballygrant is the turn-off to **Finlaggan**, once the centre of the powerful mediaeval fief of the MacDonald Lords of the Isles. The MacDonalds were virtually independent princes from the end of Norse rule in the 13th century until their land and titles were annexed by King James IV. The Lords of the Isles ruled, appropriately from two islands in Loch Finlaggan. The larger, Eilean Mòr ('Large Island'), is accessible by walkway or by boat, provided by the *Finlaggan Trust* (tel 01496-810629; e-mail lynmags@aol.com), which runs the site and its information centre. On the highest point are the ruins of a roofless 14th century chapel and a burial ground containing elaborately carved grave slabs dating from 1350 to 1500. The path across the island goes over the remains of its 13th century defences. The foundations of the mediaeval great hall once used for lavish feasting and entertaining can still be seen. Eilean Mòr was covered with the houses, kilns and barns of a farming township in the 16th century, their drystone walls now reduced to low mounds. Off the southern tip is smaller Eilean na Comhairle ('Council Island') where the Lords of the Isles debated and passed judgment according to the laws made by Reginald, son of Somerled, the ancestor of all MacDonalds. The foundations of the Council Chamber are on those of a 13th century castle, which in turn stood on the site of an Iron Age fort. The two islands are connected by a stone causeway. The **Finlaggan Visitor Centre** (tel 01496-840644) is open in April on Tuesday, Thursday and Sunday from 2.30pm to 5pm; from May to September daily, except Saturday, from 2.30pm to 5pm, and during October on Sunday, Tuesday and Thursday from 2pm to 4pm.

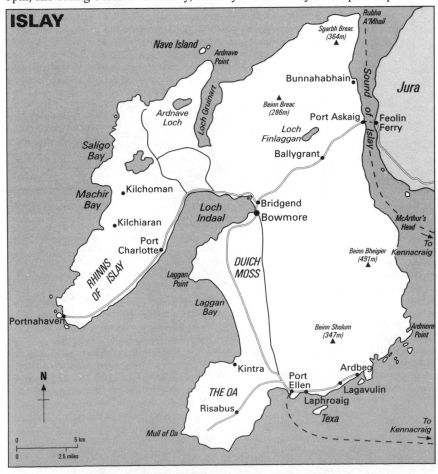

The A846 road ends at **Port Askaig**, the alternative CalMac ferry terminal to Port Ellen and the departure point for the local ferry to Feolin, on Jura. It is also the base for the Islay lifeboat, a station with a long and proud record of saving life at sea. The **Islay Lifeboat Station** (tel 01496-840245) is open daily. Visitors are always welcome and given a guided tour. On Thursday afternoons from May to September, Ladies Guild members sell souvenirs and present visitor certificates. Just south of Port Askaig is **Dunlossit House**, whose gardens provide views over the Sound of Islay. On the outskirts of the port is the **Caol Ila Distillery** (see *Eating and Drinking*). There is no road to the northern tip of the island, it ends three miles (5 km) beyond one of Scotland's most remote whisky distilleries, **Bunnahabhainn** (pronounced 'bu-na-ha-venn'). The going is tough, but you can walk from here across open moorland to the lighthouse at Rubh' a' Mhàil and the caves, cliffs and beaches of the northern coast. High and dry on the rocks of the Sound is the wreck of the 338-ton trawler *Wyre Majestic*, which ran aground in October 1974. For superb views along the way climb **Sgarbh Breac** (1,192 ft/364 m). Two miles (3 km) west of Bridgend, on the coast at **Blackrock**, is a safe and sheltered sandy bathing beach. The B8017 road goes north from here to **Loch Gruinart**, whose tidal mud flats and salt marsh are a magnet in winter for vast flocks of migratory swans and a variety of geese. Land to the south and along the west side of the loch is an RSPB farm and nature reserve (see *Flora and Fauna*). From the RSPB centre at Aoradh Farm the road heads along the western shore of Loch Gruinart to **Kilnave**, with its ruined 12th century chapel of **Cill Naoimh**. Set in lawns of springy turf are carved grave slabs around an 8¹/2 ft (2.63 m) high Celtic cross, somewhat battered and broken but still imposing. It's thought to date from around AD 750. Inside this beautiful little chapel 30 Maclean clansmen from Mull were burnt to death in 1598 by Islay MacDonalds. The Macleans had sought sanctuary in the chapel after a battle with their enemies on the shores of the loch. The track ends near Ardnave Loch, with its crannog, and from the parking place here you can take an easy circular 4-mile (6 km) walk around the headland to **Ardnave Point**, which gives you good views of nearby **Nave Island**, almost cut in two by a narrow defile called Sloc na Maoile. A ruined chapel stands near the edge of this abyss. The remains of Bronze Age dwellings have been uncovered in the sand dunes near Ardnave.

It's worth a detour from the RSPB centre to the west along the B8017 to the area around the largest freshwater loch on Islay, Loch Gorm, where a little island holds an ancient MacDonald castle. All around are cairns, standing stones, ancient forts and some splendid coastal cliff walks. At Ballinaby Farm, on the north shore of Loch Gorm is the tallest **standing stone** on Islay, a monster Bronze Age monolith standing more than 16 ft (5 m) high. The walk along the cave-riddled cliffs south from Saligo Bay brings you to Machir Bay, with its huge white dunes and its two-mile (3 km) stretch of golden sandy beach – **neither safe places to swim**. Half-way along the route is Coul Point, where the 322-ton brig *Exmouth Castle* foundered in April 1847 while carrying 240 emigrants to Canada. Only three survived. Above the bay is **Kilchoman**, noted for the free-standing carved Celtic cross in the graveyard of a rather dilapidated church. The elaborately sculpted cross stands 8¹/2 ft (2.7 m) tall and was erected in the late 14th century. It is regarded as one of the most beautiful of Islay's 17 such crosses. The cross is also remarkable for surviving intact the Reformation period when many other religious works of art were smashed or defaced by zealots. There's also a modern walled cemetery to the south where the bodies washed ashore from *HMS Otranto*, lost in 1918 in Machir Bay, lie under rows of identical gravestones. After exploring this north-west corner return via the B8018 to Loch Indaal. Before reaching the coastal road again you'll pass **Foreland Walled Garden and Nursery** (tel/fax 01496-850483; e-mail foreland@isle-of-islay.com), surrounded by woodlands. The garden has a large range of perennial plants, trees, roses, shrubs, hedging, bedding plants, and herbs for sale and a wild flower garden with benches where you can sit to enjoy the view. Open all year, March to September, Tuesday to Saturday from 11am to 5pm, Sunday 3pm to 5pm; October to February, open Thursday only midday to 3pm. After a halt on the way to sample the wares at lochside **Bruichladdich Distillery** you come to the picturesque village of **Port Charlotte**, also known as 'Queen of the Rinns' and the main settlement on the western peninsula. All the street names are in Gaelic and all the houses are white with windows and doors painted in a pleasing contrasting colour. Port Charlotte has a typically ingenious island solution to the problem of keeping pedestrians and traffic apart. In Sraid Ard ('High Street') one pavement is walled and raised above the road, while the one on the other side runs below road level.

This picture-postcard conservation village has converted an old Free Church kirk into the award-winning **Museum of Islay Life** (tel 01496-850358/310). The museum covers life in all its aspects from the earliest to recent times. There are finds from archaeological excavations, displays of tools used by wheelwrights, coopers, leather, and distillery workers, as well as an illicit still. Living conditions in the 19th century are portrayed in room settings, including a croft room with all the features of a home of that period. Divers should find the exhibits relating to island shipwrecks fascinating. The **Museum of Childhood** section has a delightful model farmhouse, toys, and children's clothing. The **Gordon Booth Library** contains an important collection of reference books, papers and documents relating to Islay. A shelter in the old graveyard has a collection of carved stones dating from the 6th to the 16th centuries. Open daily from Easter to end-October from 10am to 5pm, Sunday 2pm to 5pm. Suitable for wheelchairs. Admission for adults £2, concession £1.20, children £1. In a former distillery warehouse in the village is the **Islay Wildlife Information Centre** (tel 01496-850288), which shares the building with a fine 42-bed hostel on its upper floor. The centre is managed by the Islay Natural History Trust and it has displays and exhibitions of Islay's wildlife, plus a reference library with identification books and files of the island's natural history records. The centre is open from 9 April to 28 October every day except Wednesday and Saturday from 10am to 3pm (5pm in July and August). Admission £2 for adults, concession £1.20, children £1, and family £5. All tickets are valid for multiple visits for a week. The Trust publishes free checklists of birds, mammals, butterflies and dragonflies and wild flowers.

Nearly three miles (5 km) further along the road is **Nerabus**, where in three adjoining burial grounds you can see some of Scotland's finest carved graveslabs, a few of them recently unearthed in a turnip patch. Another four miles (6 km) on are the twin villages of **Port Wemyss** and **Portnahaven**, where the road ends above an attractive little bay sheltered by two islands, **Orsay** and **Mhic Coinnich**. Orsay is crowned by the white Rinns of Islay lighthouse (1825), designed by Robert Stevenson, which towers over a ruined 14th century chapel. The two fishing and crofting communities use the same church at the head of the bay, but enter through different doors. A revolutionary wave-powered generator has been built near Portnahaven but it's largely underground so there's not much to see. A rough and narrow road leads to the north along the rocky west coast to Kilchiaran Bay. On the way, to the west of the road, is the **Cultoon Stone Circle**. Only three of the 12 stone monoliths are standing, the others lie on the ground near the holes dug for them as the circle was never completed. There's a burial ground and a partly restored but still roofless 14th century church at **Kilchiaran** dedicated to St Ciaran on the site where legend says St Columba stayed on his way from Ireland to Iona. A roughly hewn mediaeval font stands in the chapel and several ancient weathered grave slabs have also been moved inside. Sightings of the rare chough are virtually guaranteed around Kilchiaran, which can also be reached by a shorter road inland from Port Charlotte.

FLORA AND FAUNA
Woodland, moor, hill, sea cliff, machair, sand dune, agricultural land, river, marsh, freshwater and the two great sea lochs of Indaal and Gruinart give Islay as diverse a variety of habitat as can be found anywhere in the islands. Islay is one of the world's major wintering resorts for **barnacle geese**. **Greylag** and **Greenland white-fronted geese** are also regular visitors. Throughout winter from the end of October the fields and tidal flats are turned black and white by up to 50,000 of these visitors. Wild **orchids** and a variety of spring and summer flowers are also a lure and sightings of **minke whales, bottlenosed dolphins, porpoises,** and **seals** enliven coastal walks. There are two nature reserves on Islay run by the Royal Society for the Protection of Birds (RSPB). At **Loch Gruinart Nature Reserve** (tel 01496-850505; fax 01496-850575; e-mail loch.gruinart@interramp.co.uk) you can join guided walks over its 4,087 acres (1,654 ha) every Tuesday at 10am, use the bird-watching hides, and spend time looking at displays in the informative Visitor Centre where a live video camera gives you even closer views of the birdlife. Open April to October from 10am to 5pm; November to March from 10am to 4pm. Wheelchair accessible hide and toilets. Admission free, although donations are welcome. There's an incredible variety of wildlife here. Breeding waders share the reserve with **hen harriers, golden eagles, peregrines, buzzards, merlin, kestrels, corncrakes,** and the rare **chough,** and in winter there's the spectacle of the migrant geese. There are 110 different kinds of birds breeding here and more than 270 species have been recorded. **Curlews** and **oystercatchers** are the most numerous, but **ringed plover, dunlin, sanderling, turnstone** and **bar-tailed godwits** can be seen virtually throughout the year. The spring migration is a good time to spot unusual birds such as **great white egret, marsh harrier, wood sandpiper** and **blue-winged teal.** Tiny **roe deer** fawns are reared among the rushes around Loch Gruinart and **red deer** stags feed close by. **Otters** often hunt in the shallows.

The RSPB's newest nature reserve is at **Upper Killeyan Farm** on the Mull of Oa, in southern Islay, 351-acres (142 ha) of cliffs and coastal grassland. It is administered by the RSPB office at Gruinart (tel 01496-850505). The main aim is to make the habitat here attractive to **choughs,** the rarest and perhaps most beautiful member of the crow family. Islay is home to 49 breeding pairs of choughs out of a Scottish total of 66. The dramatic headland, with cliffs rising to 656 ft (200 m), is also home to a variety of seabirds and plantlife. Admission to the reserve is free.

GETTING THERE
By Air
British Airways (tel 08457-733377; www.britishairways.com), through *Loganair* (tel 01496-302300), operates a 40-minute flight to Islay from Glasgow at 9.10am Monday to Saturday, and at 5.10pm Monday to Friday. There are also connections from London, Manchester, Birmingham, and Aberdeen, Monday to Friday. Contact the airline to check fares and flight times.

Islay Airport (tel 01496-302361; fax 01496-302096) is owned and operated by Highlands and Islands Airports. It lies in the south-west, a short drive from the two main villages of Port Ellen and Bowmore. Public transport and a taxi service are available. A bus meets scheduled arrivals and departures, but will not wait if arrivals are more than 20 minutes late. In the summer months the airport is busy with private and charter aircraft from as far afield as the US. The airport is open Monday to Friday 9.45am to 6.30pm, Saturday 10.45am to 11.30am (and by arrangement). Closed on Sunday. There are ramp facilities at the terminal entrance for the disabled and staff are always available to assist. There's an Open Day during the summer when you can see various aspects of the airport, aircraft displays, and overhead aerobatics.

Aircraft charter

Edinburgh Air Charter: tel 0131-339 8008.
Executive Air: tel 0141-887 83480.
Highland Airways: tel 01667-462664.
Paul Keegan: tel 01631-720215.
Woodgate Executive Air Charter: tel 01849-422478.

By Sea

Caledonian MacBrayne (The Ferry Terminal, Gourock PA19 1QP; tel 08705-650000; fax 01475-635235, reservations; tel 01475-650100; fax 01475-637607, general enquiries; e-mail reservations@calmac.co.uk; www.calmac.co.uk) operates a car-passenger ferry to Islay from Kennacraig, Kintyre, to Port Ellen and Port Askaig. It can be diverted en route from one port to the other if the weather is bad. The ferry leaves Kennacraig for Port Ellen at 7.15am on Monday, Tuesday, at 7.15am and 6pm on Thursday to Saturday, and at 12.50pm on Sunday. It sails to Port Askaig at 12.50pm and 6pm on Monday and Tuesday, 8.15am on Wednesday, and 12.50pm Thursday to Saturday. The single passenger fare is £7.05 to Port Ellen or Port Askaig, cars £37.50, motorcycles £18.75, and bicycles £2. From April to October an 'Early Bird Saver' is available for £72 for a car with up to four passengers. It's valid on the first sailing of the day, returning on the last sailing of the same day. 'Five-Day Return' and 'Six-Journey' tickets are also available. For more information contact the CalMac office at Kennacraig (tel 01880-730253) or Port Ellen (tel 01496-302209).

CalMac also has an **Afternoon Cruise** from Kennacraig to Islay on the *MV Hebridean Isles*. The cruise leaves at 12.50pm every day except Wednesday and returns to Kennacraig at 5.30pm, 5.45pm on Sunday. There is also an **Evening Cruise** every Monday and Thursday, leaving Kennacraig at 6pm and returning at 10.15pm on Monday and 10.40 on Thursday. Both cruise fares are £9.50, payable at Kennacraig at time of travel.

CalMac has a 'Grand Tour of Islay' cruise leaving Kennacraig for Port Ellen at 7.15am on Tuesday from June to August only. Passengers then board a coach for an island tour. The coach returns to Port Askaig for the ferry back to Kennacraig at 5.30pm. The tour costs £18. For a family (two adults and two children) it costs £45. There is also a 'Cross Islay Excursion' which leaves Kennacraig at 7.15am every Monday, Tuesday, Thursday and Friday. A bus then takes you across the island to Port Askaig in time for the return sailing to Kennacraig at 5.30pm. The inclusive fare (ferry and bus ticket) is £15.50, family (two adults and two children) ticket costs £38.75.

GETTING AROUND

By Sea

Caledonian MacBrayne (tel 01496-302209) sails from Port Askaig to Colonsay every Wednesday throughout the summer months and *Islay Marine Charters* (tel/fax 01496-850436; e-mail info@islaymarine.co.uk) operate day-long wildlife cruises from Port Askaig to Oronsay, as well as half and full-day fishing trips.

Serco Denholm (Port Askaig; tel 01496-840681) runs a small car-passenger ferry regularly every day from Port Askaig, Islay, to Feolin, Jura.

Wildlife Study Weeks (Richard Gulliver, Carraig Mhor, Imeravale, Port Ellen, PA42 7AL; tel 01496-302432), week-long residential courses on natural history, ecology and wildflower identification on Islay and Colonsay.

By Road

No road circles Islay, but there are well-surfaced, classified roads linking the coastal villages, and other smaller, narrow roads and tracks branching off in all directions.

Buses

Islay Coaches: Auchnaglach, Keills, Port Askaig, PA4 6RB (tel 01496-840273). Operates two daily tours of Islay during the summer.

Mundell Bus Company: Auchinghach, Port Askaig, PA46 7RB (tel 01496-840273; fax 01496-840655). Meets every ferry apart from evening crossing.

Royal Mail (tel 01246-546329; www.royalmail.co.uk) operates a 10-seater **Postbus** service on two routes Monday to Saturday. One is from Port Askaig to Ardbeg with stops at Keills, Ballygrant, Bridgend, Bowmore, Airport, and Port Ellen. The other is from Portnahaven to Ardbeg, with stops at Port Wemyss, Port Charlotte, Bruichladdich, Bridgend, Bowmore, Airport, and Port Ellen. Check departure times and route at a Post Office.

Taxis

Carol's Cabs & Mini Bus Hire: tel 01496-302155.
L Campbell: tel 01496-801534.
L&H Campbell Car & Mini Bus Hire: tel 01496-840651.
Fiona's Taxis: tel 01496-302622. 24-hour service.
Carole MacDonald: tel 01496-302155.
John Woodrow: tel 01496-810313.

Vehicle Hire

McKenzie: Jamieson Street, Bowmore (tel 01496-810206).
D&N MacKenzie: Glenegedale, PA42 7AS, by Port Ellen (tel 01496-302300; fax 01496-302324). Car and van hire, delivery to ferry and airport.

Cycle Hire

Bowmore Post Office: Main Street (tel 01496-810366). Reasonable rates. Monday to Friday 9am to 5pm, Saturday 9am to 1pm.
Mrs MacAulay: Frederick Crescent, Port Ellen (tel 01496-302053).

ACCOMMODATION

Hotels

Ballygrant Inn: Ballygrant, PA45 7QR (tel/fax 01496-840277). Two-star, three-bedroomed family-run inn. Open all year, from £23 a night.

Bridgend Hotel: Bridgend, PA44 7PQ (tel 01496-810212; fax 01496-810960). Three-star, 10 well-appointed rooms. Bar and restaurant make use of local produce. Open all year, from £41 a night.

Glenegedale House Hotel: Glenegedale, Port Ellen, PA42 7AS (tel 01496-302147; fax 01496-302210; e-mail dunstan.gallery@virgin.net). Three-star, six bedrooms in 17th century farmhouse. Open all year.

Harbour Inn: The Square, Bowmore, PA43 7JR (tel 01496-810330; fax 01496-810990; e-mail harbour@harbour-inn.com). Three-star, overlooking Loch Indaal, adjacent to Bowmore Harbour. Family-run, en-suite rooms. Award-winning restaurant. Open all year, from £38. Special events for autumn/winter include cooking weekends to enjoy the informal tuition and tasting of local produce including shellfish and game, matched with Islay malt whisky.

Lochside Hotel: Shore Street, Bowmore, PA43 7LB (tel 01496-810244; fax 01496-810390; e-mail ask@lochsidehotel.co.uk; www.lochsidehotel.co.uk). Two-star, eight en-suite rooms. Centrally located with views over Loch Indaal. Claims world's largest selection (400) of single malt whiskies. Open all year, from £20. Also has speciality malt whisky weekends, from £135 a person.

Machrie Hotel and Golf Links: Port Ellen, PA42 7AN (tel 01496-302310; fax 01496-302404; e-mail machrie@machrie.com; www.machrie.com). Three-star, built more than 250 years ago as a farmhouse but with 21st century facilities. Accommodation for up to 90 – 32 in hotel, rest in annexe cottages. Busiest time is May, June and September. Airport five minutes, Port Ellen 3¹/2 miles (6 km), Bowmore 8 miles (13 km). Close to beach and golf links. Restaurant serving local produce. Sit at a magnificent 30-seater dining table once used by Palmerston, Disraeli, Dickens, Yeats, and Irving at the Garrick Club, London. Open all year, from £35 B&B. Hotel's own 8-seater Islander aircraft is based at Cumbernauld, Strathclyde. Can pick you up anywhere, costs on application.

Marine Hotel: Bowmore, PA43 7LB (tel 01496-810324; fax 01496-810764). Three-star, five en-suite bedrooms overlooking Loch Indaal. Open all year, from £33.

Port Charlotte Hotel: Port Charlotte, PA48 7TU (tel 01496-850360; fax 01496-850361; e-mail carl@portcharlottehot.demon.co.uk). Four-star, Victorian hotel on shore of Loch Indaal. Ten en-suite rooms with sea views. Restaurant featuring local seafood, beef and lamb. Open all year, from £28.

Port Askaig Hotel: Port Askaig, PA46 7RD (tel 01496-840245; fax 01496-840295; www.portaskaig.co.uk). Two-star, 400-year-old inn overlooking the Sound of Islay and ferry pier. Eight bedrooms. Home-cooked food, bars open all day. Open all year, from £36.

White Hart Hotel: 2 Charlotte Street, Port Ellen, PA42 7DF (tel/fax 01496-300120).

Guest Houses

Abbotsford Guest House: Bruichladdich, PA49 7UN (tel/fax 01496-850587). Four bedrooms, family-run, overlooking Loch Indaal. Open all year, from £25.

The Bothy: 91 Lennox Street, Port Ellen, PA42 7BW (tel 01496-302391). Two-star, two bedrooms. Open all year, from £17.

Glenmachrie: Port Ellen, PA42 7AW (tel/fax 01496-302560; e-mail glenmachrie@lineone.net; www.glenmachrie.com). Four-star, five en suite rooms, no smoking throughout, facilities for disabled. Beside golf course and beach. Open all year, from £30. Family-run working farmhouse. Home cooking. Taste of Scotland member. Unlicensed. Open all year, from £30.

Kilmeny Country Guest House: Ballygrant, PA45 7QW (tel/fax 01496-840668; e-mail info@kilmeny.co.uk; www.kilmeny.co.uk). Five-star, three bedrooms. No smoking throughout. Open all year, from £36 B&B. Taste of Scotland member. Unlicensed.

Trout-Fly Guest House: Port Ellen, PA42 7DF (tel 01496-302204; fax 01496-300076). Two-star, three bedrooms. In the village adjacent to ferry terminal, residents lounge. Open all year, from £19.

B&B

Caladh Sona: Ian and Rhona Scott, 53 Frederick Crescent, Port Ellen, PA42 7BD (tel/fax 01496-302694; e-mail hamish.scott@lineone.net). Three-star, en-suite on Port Ellen Bay, near ferry terminal. Open all year, from £20 a night.

Ceol-na-Mara: Mr and Mrs McDonald, Bruichladdich, PA49 7UN (tel 01496-850371). Three-star, three bedrooms. On shore of Loch Indaal. Open March to November, from £20.

Loch Gruinart House: Gruinart, Bridgend, PA44 7PW (tel/fax 01496-850212). Two-star, four bedrooms, family-run. Home cooking. Open all year, from £29.

Mrs Margaret MacFarlane: 2 Mulindry Cottages, Bridgend, PA44 6PZ (tel/fax 01496-810397). Three-star, two miles from Bridgend.

Joy Prentice: tel 01496-302536. One family room and one double/twin room, private facilities. £20 a night.

Sheiling: Flora Street, Bowmore, PA43 7JX (tel/fax 01496-810634). Three-star, four bedrooms, centrally situated. Open all year, from £18.

Self-Catering

Ardtalla Cottages: tel/fax 01496-302441; e-mail info@ardtallacottages.co.uk. Three-detached, self-contained cottages, comfortable and well-equipped, on 15,000-acre (6,070 ha) Ardtalla Estate. Eight miles (13 km) from Port Ellen and Bowmore. More than 1,000 red and fallow deer on the doorstep, eight miles (13 km) of deserted coastline with seals and seabirds.

Foreland Estate: Mrs DH Doyle, Bruichladdich, PA49 7UU (tel 01496-850211; fax 01496-850337). Two-star, cottages on private estate. Open all year, from £220-£300.

Kilchoman House Cottages: Ian and Margaret Brooke, Bruichladdich, PA49 7UY (tel 01496-850382; fax 01496-850277; e-mail kilchoman@aol.com). Three-star, close to sandy beach. Five cottages, sleeping 4-6. Open all year, from £200-£475 a week.

Knocklearach Farm: Mrs C Bell, Ballygrant, PA45 7QL (tel/fax 01496-840209). Two-star, self-contained apartments, sleep 3-8. Open all year, from £140-£260 a week.

Catriona Leask: Bayview, 83 Frederick Crescent, Port Ellen, PA42 7BG (tel 01496-302356). Three houses in peaceful location. Open all year, from £200-£400.

Farmhouse flat: Mull of Oa (tel 01496-302140). Sleeps five, from £180 a week,

Lorgba House: Mrs S Roy, Port Charlotte, PA48 7UD (tel/fax 01496-850208). Three-star, five traditional cottages on safe sandy beach. Open all year, from £105-£365 a week.

Mrs JD Macauley: 102 Frederick Crescent, Port Ellen, PA42 7BQ (tel 01496-302053). House in own woodland, four bedrooms. Open all year.

Mrs A MacDonald: High Street, Bowmore, PA43 7JE (tel 01496-810524). Two-star, modern cottage with garden. Three bedrooms, sleeps six. Open all year, from £80-£250 a week.

Fiona McFarlane: tel 01496-302243. Cottage overlooking the sea, two bedrooms.

Mrs M McKerrell: Island Farm, Bowmore, PA43 7JF (tel 01496-810229). Three-star, centrally situated. Open all year, from £180-£250.

Neriby Farm: Mrs EC Cunninghame, Bridgend, PA44 7PZ (tel 01496-810274). Four-star, luxury three-bedroomed cottage, sleeps six. Open all year, from £250-£410 a week.

Newton Cottage: Mr and Mrs J Adamson, Bridgend, PA44 7PN (tel 01496-850546). Three-star, spacious cottage in rural setting. Open all year, from £230-£320.

Mrs H Roxburgh: tel/fax 01496-302251; e-mail ballivicar@tinyworld.co.uk. Two apartments in renovated barn on farm, pony trekking, golf and beaches nearby.

Mrs M Shaw: 10 An Creagan Place, Port Charlotte, PA48 7TW (tel 01496-850355). Three-star, on working croft. Open all year, from £250-£350.

Tighcargaman: P&J Kent, Port Ellen, PA42 7BX (tel/fax 01496-302345). Two-star, overlooking bay, ferry 1/2 mile (0.8 km), airport four miles (6 km). Open all year, from £100-£300.

Hostels

Islay Dive Centre: 10 Charlotte Street, Port Ellen, PA42 7DF (tel 01496-302441; e-mail ann@islaydivecentre.co.uk). Also has two flats, sleep 10, in secluded garden. Showers, toilets, sitting rooms and central heating. Bottom flat equipped for self-catering. Other facilities include full board, all linen and towels, drying room, airing area, laundry and wash down area. Dining-room for 16 dedicated to all aspects of underwater Islay, which doubles as a meeting room featuring maritime exhibits and photos. Open all year, from £26.

Islay Youth Hostel: Port Charlotte, PA48 7TX (tel 01496-850385). Two-star, 42 beds in what was once a distillery. Hostel reception opens at 5pm. Access until 11.45pm. Open March to October, from £8. Hot showers, laundry, hostel store, shop and bus nearby, ferry from Port Askaig 13 miles (21 km) away, ferry from Port Ellen 20 miles (32 km) away. Self-catering facilities.

Kintra Bunk Barns Hostel: Kintra Farm, Port Ellen, Islay, PA42 7AT (tel 01496-302051). Independent hostel. Open April to September, from £8.50 a night. On the long beach nearby the farm has a good camping and caravan site, serving food and drink evenings only from May to August.

If you take the ferry from Kennacraig to Islay and need to overnight somewhere close try the *Victoria Hotel:* Barmore Road, Tarbert, Loch Fyne (tel 01880-820236; fax 01880-820638), three-star inn. Open all year, from £30.

EATING AND DRINKING

There's no chip shop on the island (strange, considering its prized potatoes), but the *Colina & Ann Fish & Chip Van,* known as the 'Nippy Chippy,' is in Bowmore on Thursday evening, and Port Ellen on Friday and Saturday evening from 7.30pm to 10.30pm.

An Sabhal: Portnahaven (tel 01496-860308). Bar meals available all day. Open March to October from 10am to 8pm.

Cottage Restaurant: 45 Main Street, Bowmore, PA43 7JJ (tel 01496-810422), licensed family restaurant and coffee-shop with take-away. Open all year from 10am to 7pm.

The Croft Kitchen: Port Charlotte (tel/fax 01496-850230; e-mail douglas@croftkitchen.demon.co.uk). Bistro-style, licensed restaurant. Homebakes and soups, snacks and a good range of daily specials. Try raspberry and Bowmore malt whisky cranachan. Taste of Scotland. Open mid-March to mid-October, from 10am to 8.30pm; closed the second Thursday in August (Islay Show Day), no smoking.

Heather Hen Restaurant: Glenegedale, PA42 7AS (tel 01496-302147). Bistro restaurant opposite the Airport. Open February to December from 9am to 4pm and 7pm to 11pm.

Spirit of Islay

As the wind and sea lashes the island, the spirit inhales the atmosphere, and a shot of Hebridean wildness is locked into the matured whisky...People who don't understand probably don't like oysters or caviar, either – Michael Jackson (the writer, not the pop singer).

Single malt whisky is like chateau-bottled wine, there's nothing else quite like it. Islay is famed as an island with seven different distilleries each producing its own distinctive nectar. In the south are Laphroaig, Lagavulin, and Ardbeg. These are heavily peated malts: you either love them or you hate them. Connoisseurs of classic malts love them. On the west coast are Bowmore and Bruichladdich, and in the north-east are Bunnahabhain and Caol Ila.

Laphroaig (tel 01496-302418; www.laphroaig.com). In Gaelic its name means 'The beautiful hollow by the broad bay'. Malted barley is dried over a peat fire to give Laphroaig its particularly rich and distinctive flavour. Laphroaig has its own loch and peatlands. Malts available at 10, 15, and 30 years. The only Islay whisky supplied 'By Appointment' to HRH Prince Charles. Open all year. Tours by appointment, Monday to Friday 10.15am and 2.15pm. Disabled facilities. Whisky and souvenirs for sale. Register as a 'Friend of Laphroaig' and the distillery gives you a lifetime lease on one square foot of Islay and pays you annual ground rent of a dram of Laphroaig, to be collected in person.

Lagavulin (tel 01496-302400; fax 01496-302733; www.scotch.com), built beside the picturesque ruins of Dunyvaig Castle, three miles (5 km) east of Port Ellen. It's the spiritual home of White Horse Scotch Whisky. Open all year. Distillery tours (£2), Monday to Friday only, 10.30am, 11.30am and 2.30pm. Admission charge with redemption in shop.

Ardbeg (tel 01496-302244; fax 01496-302040; www.ardbeg.com), established in 1815 in an isolated area of great beauty. Ardbeg is a monster of a dram, available at 17 and 30 years, also 1978, 1975 and 1974 vintages. Gift shop and café in The Old Kiln. Sample the famous Clootie Dumpling. Open all year, Monday to Friday from 10am to 5pm; June to September open seven days a week from 10am to 5pm. Regular tours from 10.30am, last tour at 3.30pm. Admission charge with redemption in shop. Limited wheelchair access.

Bowmore (tel 01496-810441; fax 01496-810757). **Visitor Centre** (tel/fax 01496-810671; www.bowmorescotch.com). Islay's oldest distillery has stood on the shores of Loch Indaal since 1779. Open all year, Monday to Friday, tours 10.30am and 2pm; tours in summer at 10.30am, 11.30am, 2pm, and 3pm; Saturday at 10.30am. Admission charge with redemption in shop £2 for adults, £1 for OAPs, disabled facilities. Shop has branded merchandise and a full range of malt whisky available at 10, 12, 21, 25 and 30 years.

Bruichladdich (tel 01444-412337; fax 01444-440732; e-mail isabel@ bruichladdich.com; www.bruichladdich.com), Islay's only independent distillery, celebrated its re-opening and inaugural distillation on 29 May 2001 after being closed for six years. When it was built in 1881, it was a state-of-the-art plant, and structurally has remained very much the same, with some of the original equipment still in use. Available are 10, 15, and 20-year-old single malts. Bruichladdich Vintage (46%) is an occasional bottling from a single vintage.

Bunnahabhain (tel 01496-840646; fax 01496-840248) lies on a secluded bay at the end of one of the island's most scenic roads. Small informal visitor centre and shop. Guided tours and tasting. Available at 12 years. Bunnahabhain is the lightest of all the Islay malts and is also the spiritual home of Black Bottle Scotch whisky. Open all year, Monday to Friday from 10am to 4pm; March to October at 10.30am, 1.30pm and 2.45pm. By appointment rest of the year. Four luxury five-star self-catering cottages lie alongside the distillery and are available for weekly bookings all year round.

Caol Ila – pronounced *cull-eela* (tel 01496-302760; fax 01496-302763). Founded in 1846 close to Port Askaig. Distillery tour followed by a dram of 15-year-old single malt, which is available from the shop. Open all year Monday to Friday. All visits by appointment. The distillery suspends production at various times of the year, though visitors are welcome and tours still available. There is an adult admission charge which includes a discount voucher, redeemable at the distillery shop.

SPORT AND RECREATION
Diving
There are more than 200 wrecks recorded around Islay and range in depth from a few fathoms to more than 100 ft (30 m), from a U-boat to a passenger liner. In the bar of the Port Charlotte Hotel is a fascinating display of items recovered from some of the offshore wrecks and there's also a wreck display at the Museum of Islay Life in Port Charlotte. Contact Ann or Gus Newman at *Islay Dive Centre* (10 Charlotte Street, Port Ellen; tel 01496-302441; e-mail ann@islaydivecentre.co.uk) for diving from their heavy weather catamaran. 12-litre dumpy cylinders and air provided. Experienced skipper-divers with knowledge of local waters. Rockface, drift, and wreck dives on 15,000 ton American troop carrier (46 ft/14 m), and submarine (39 ft/12 m), among others. Tim Epps of Port Charlotte (tel 01496-850379) is a local wreck diving expert with ownership rights to a number of wrecks.

Fishing
Fly-fishing for **brown trout** and **salmon** is available by permit only on rivers and well-stocked inland lochs on island estates. The season is 15 March to 30 September. Boats are available for hire on a number of lochs at reasonable rates, although bank fishing can be equally productive. Some lochs are exposed, so it's a good idea to wear buoyancy aids/lifejackets when boat fishing. For boat and bank fishing permits on a number of lochs, contact *Islay Estates* (Head Game Keeper; tel 01496-810293/221). *Dunlossit Estates* has boat and bank fishing on its lochs. Contact the Estate Office (tel 01496-840232). *Foreland Estates* (tel 01496-850211); *Laggan Estate* (tel 01496-810388); and *The Oa* (tel 01496-302264).

Port Ellen Angling Club (Iain Laurie, 19 Charlotte Street, Port Ellen; tel 01496-302264), can help with permits and wild brown trout fishing on five lochs. *Bridgend* permits and self-catering accommodation from B Wiles, Headkeeper (tel 01496-681293). *Port Askaig Hotel* (tel 01496-840245) has loch trout and river salmon fishing, and *Machrie Hotel* (tel 01496-302310) has salmon and sea-trout fishing.

There's good **sea fishing** throughout the summer season on reefs and wrecks for coalfish, pollack, wrasse, conger, ling, cod, pouting, and many other species, including plentiful mackerel. *Islay Marine Charters* (Roger and Isobel Eaton, Erasaid, Gruinart, Bridgend, PA44 7PL; tel 01496-850436; e-mail islaymarine@ileach.co.uk) operate sea angling trips, cruises and private charter on the *Angie*, a 37 ft (11 m) boat licensed to carry 12. Rod hire available, hooks and weights sold on board. A 4-hour sea angling trips cost £13 a person, £22 for an 8-hour outing. Rod hire £2 and £3 respectively. Open all year from 9am to 10pm.

Golf
Islay Golf Club: Machrie Hotel, c/o Western Cottage, Port Ellen (tel 01496-302409; fax 01496-302392; e-mail islaygolf@btinternet.com). 18-hole championship golf course which is listed 56th in Britain's top 100 golf courses. Designed in 1891 by Willie Campbell on natural terrain along Laggan Bay, few courses match Machrie for first-class golf in an out-of-the-way place. A defiantly old-fashioned links, with half the shots blind. The Machrie's main claim to fame is its own Open Championship of 1901 which included the great triumvirate of Harry Vardon, John Henry Taylor and James Braid. £30 a game, £40 for a day ticket. Hire clubs cost £10-£15. For a caddy, contact Creig (tel 01496-302023) or John (tel 01496-300009).

Horse-Riding
Ballivicar Pony Trekking Centre: Port Ellen (tel 01496-302251). Small family-run

pony trekking centre for all standards. Rides tailored to suitability. Beach riding. Open all year.

Rockside Farm Trekking Centre: Rockside Farm, Bruichladdich (tel 01496-850231; fax 01496-850209; e-mail enquiries@rocksidefarm.u-net.com). Rides along sandy beaches and hillside tracks, with a choice of horses to suit your experience. Open April to October, 9am to 7pm.

Shooting

There are three main private shooting estates: Ardtulla, Dunlosset, and Islay. They offer red and roe deer, and bird shooting. *Cultoon Shooting Ground* (Jim and Lynn Wilson, Cultoon Farm, Porthahaven; tel/fax 01496-860323) offers clay pigeon shooting from beginner to experienced levels. Guns and cartridges available. Open all year in the afternoon. *Cultoon Live Shoot* has access to 1,800 acres (728 ha) of sport shooting over farmland and woodland. Family-run operation offers accommodation, food and shooting with keepers. Packages available from mid-October to January for three days including two-three guns, B&B, and evening meal.

Other Activities

Bridgend Bowling Club welcomes visitors. The bowling green is opposite the hotel in Bridgend. Visitor's fees may be paid at the Hut (daytime Monday to Saturday) and at the green on Sunday and in the evenings (£2 per adult). Bowls are available from the shed at no extra charge. The green is usually open from May to October, 2pm until dusk.

Mactaggart Leisure Centre: School Street, Bowmore (tel 01496-810767; fax 01496-810924). Open all year, closed on Monday. This small leisure complex with its 27-yard (25 m) swimming pool, fitness studio, sauna, solarium, sunbed, and sports shop is owned by the islanders of Islay and Jura through their own company, Islay and Jura Community Enterprises Ltd.

Port Ellen Playing Fields Association: 16 Cnoc-na-Faire, Port Ellen (tel 01496-302349). Open daily 10am to 9pm, midday to 9pm, May to September for putting, tennis, pitch and putt, bowls, and bicycle hire.

SHOPPING

As well as the island's famed malt whisky there are several other local products you can take home as souvenirs. The local cheese is a popular buy, as well as woollens and fabrics which have even established a reputation in Hollywood.

Carraig Fhada: tel 01496-302114. Near Port Ellen lighthouse. Original paintings, prints of Islay, hand-spun knitting wool, knitted garments, and many locally made items. Open seven days a week, 10am to 6pm.

Celtic House: Shore Street, Bowmore (tel/fax 01496-810304; e-mail colinroy@ukgateway.net). A wide range of gifts, jewellery, Celtic crafts, whisky mementoes, Scottish books, OS maps and knitwear. Open all year from 9.30am to 5pm. Closed Sunday.

Country Crafts: Neriby Farm, Bridgend (tel 01496-810274). Craft and floristry supplies, silk and dried flowers, découpage, baskets, ribbons. Open all year on Tuesday and Thursday from 2pm to 5pm.

Islay Arts and Crafts Guild: Secretary, Liz Sykes (tel 01496-850357) or Ted Turner (tel 01496-302140). Organises craft fairs throughout the summer and at Christmas, Easter and *Feis Ile* time in Bowmore Hall.

Islay Craft Shop and Gallery: Main Street, Bowmore. Next to the Post Office, has a selection of local hand-crafted goods, original paintings, designer mugs and T-shirts, jewellery, pottery, gifts and souvenirs. Open Monday to Saturday.

Islay Heathers Craft Shop: Glenegedale (tel 01496-302147). Workshop and shop producing crafts, flowers, heather baskets, quilts, cushions, scented goods, custom made items. Open all year, Monday to Saturday from 9am to 5pm, Sunday 10am to 3pm.

The *Islay Whisky Shop:* Shore Street, Bowmore (tel 01496-810684; fax 01496-810353; e-mail dram@islaywhiskyshop.com; www.islaywhiskyshop.com). Specialises in Islay whiskies. They'll deliver to anywhere in the UK.

Islay Woollen Mill: Bridgend (tel 01496-810563; fax 01496-810677; www.islay.woollenmills.co.uk). Fabrics from here were used in the Mel Gibson movie *Braveheart* and in Tom Hanks' *Forest Gump.* The mill has a unique example of antique machinery, a rare 'Slubbing Billy,' which is the only one of its kind in existence. Open all year, Monday to Friday 10am to 5pm, and Saturday 10am to 4pm.

Persabus Pottery: tel 01496-840243; e-mail pottery@persabus.co.uk; www.persabus.co.uk. A few miles from Port Askaig on the Bunnahabhain road, hand-crafted pottery, including lamps, clocks, whisky decanters jugs, and planters. You can also order on-line.

Port Ellen Pottery: Tighcargaman, Port Ellen, Islay (tel 01496-302345). Watch pottery being handmade on the premises. Open all year, except November.

Elizabeth Sykes Batiks: Port Charlotte (tel 01496-850357). Batik pictures, scarves and garments, hand-dyed. Showroom open seven days a week. Also one-day introductory batik courses.

Tighcargaman Pottery: tel 01496-302345. All pottery handmade on the premises on the outskirts of Port Ellen.

Tormisdale Croft Crafts: Port Charlotte (tel 01496-860239; e-mail ann@tormisdale.fsnet.co.uk). Handmade crafts include designer knitwear, sticks, staghorn work, patchwork, hand-spinning, paintings, rare breeds' wool, and black Hebridean sheep wool. Open all year, 9am to 6pm, later by appointment.

HELP AND INFORMATION

Bowmore Tourist Information Centre: The Square, Bowmore (tel 01496-810254; fax 01496-810363). Open February to October.

Fire, Coastguard, Emergency 999.

Police: Bowmore (tel 01496-810222). Port Ellen (tel 01496-302002).

Doctors: Bruichladdich (tel 01496-850210); Port Ellen (tel 01496-302103); Bowmore (tel 01496-810273).

Islay Hospital: Bowmore (tel 01496-810219).

Airport: Port Ellen (tel 01496-302202).

Caledonian MacBrayne: The Pier, Port Ellen (tel 01496-302209).

Serco Denholm: Port Askaig (tel 01496-840681). Jura ferry.

Post Offices: Ballygrant (tel 01496-840656); Bowmore, Main Street (tel 01496-810366); Bridgend (tel 01496-810335); Bruichladdich (tel 01496-850319); Port Askaig (tel 01496-840245); Port Charlotte (tel 01496-850232); Port Ellen, Frederick Crescent (tel 01496-302382); Portnahaven (tel 01496-860200).

Scottish Natural Heritage: Main Street, Bowmore, PA43 7JJ (tel 01496-810711; fax 01496-810665).

Bank of Scotland: Shove Street, Bowmore (tel 01496-810437).

Royal Bank of Scotland: The Square, Bowmore (tel 01496-810555). Pierhead, Port Ellen (tel 01496-302314).

Mactaggart Community Cybercafé: Mansfield Place, Port Ellen (tel 01496-302693; e-mail café@cyber.fq.co.uk). Serves food and will handle your e-mail. Open Monday to Saturday 11am to 10pm, Sunday midday to 9pm. Meals till 7pm. Eight computers online, surf the net; e-mail, play games, word processing. Full disabled access,

Ileach: Bowmore (tel 01496-810335; www.ileach.co.uk). Community newspaper for Islay and Jura, published fortnightly, costs 60p.

The Black Bottle Islay Jazz Festival (www.islayjazzfestival.org.uk) is held every year in September. It's organised by *Assembly Direct* and *Islay Art Association* (Fiona Alexander, 89 Giles Street, Edinburgh EH6 6BZ; tel 0131-553 4000; e-mail Fiona@assemblydirect.ednet.co.uk; www.jazzmusic.co.uk).

The *Islay Pipe Band* appears at the Islay Show in early August and at various other events and festivities throughout the summer.

Jura

Jura is about 16 miles (26 km) across the Sound of Jura from the Argyll mainland and separated from the island of Islay by the 14-mile (23 km) long, half-mile-wide (800 m) Sound of Islay. The island is nearly 30 miles (48 km) long and eight miles (13 km) across. The huge sea loch of Tarbert nips in the island's waist and almost divides Jura into two equal parts. The mountains known as the Paps of Jura, all around 2,500 ft (762 m) in height, dominate the rugged landscape in the south. A group of islands forms a natural breakwater across the Small Isles Bay in front of Craighouse. Off the north coast is the Gulf of Corryvreckan, famed for its enormous whirlpool, which makes a noise that can sometimes be heard on the mainland. Only one 25-mile (40 km) road exists, following the southern and eastern shoreline. The western half of the island is virtually trackless, making Jura one of the wildest and emptiest of Britain's inhabited islands. The west coast is notable for its caves and famed for its unsurpassed raised beaches, great stretches of boulders stranded 30-100 ft (9-30 m) above present sea level, and created by the land being relieved of the weight of the last Ice Age's glacial deposits. The raised beaches are best seen on the west coast, especially between Ruantallain and Shian Bay, although the most easily accessible are a two-mile (3 km) walk north of Inver.

Geology

The metamorphosed sediments which make up Jura quartzite cover 90 per cent of the island. These tilted beds of hard white, pink and grey quartzite, especially evident in the landscape around the Paps, form the largest area of quartzite in Scotland. This ancient rock was originally laid down as horizontal sedimentary beds, contorted about 350-million years ago in the great geological mountain-building era when the Caledonian mountains rivalled the Himalayas. Cracks later filled with molten magma to form basalt igneous dykes, all pointing like arrows towards Arran as the volcanic centre which created them about 50-million years ago. Along the south and east coast a narrow band of schist has weathered to provide the only soil suitable for agriculture and the reason why since prehistoric times settlement has been concentrated along these shores.

EXPLORING

Jura's name is believed to come from the Old Norse meaning 'Deer Island,' a description that's still apt as red and roe deer outnumber the 200 population by at least 25 to one. Although there's little evidence of them the Vikings must have been on Jura until driven out in the 12th century by Somerled, whose descendants became the MacDonalds and Lords of the Isles. In the early 17th century they fell out of favour with the Scottish Crown and most of their land on Jura was granted to the Campbells of Argyll, who stayed for 300 years. The last Campbell left in 1938 and the island's 90,000 acres (36,422 ha) are now divided between seven private estates.

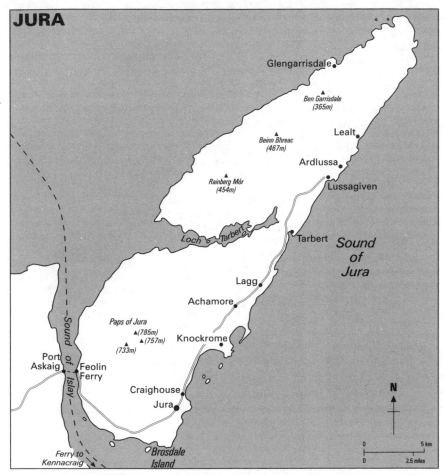

The single road links many of the island's attractions. About three miles (5 km) along the road from the ferry is **Camus an Stacca**, at 12 ft (4 m) high and 4 ft (1 m) broad the largest of Jura's eight standing stones. Offshore is the islet of Am Fraoch Eilean ('Heather Island'), with the ruins of **Claig Castle**, the fortress built in 1154 by the great Somerled. A mile (1.6 km) on is **Jura House** (tel 01496-820315), built by the Campbells in 1812 and known for its **Walled Garden**. The garden was designed as a Victorian kitchen garden, with boxwood hedges, a rose garden, vegetables and fruit trees and now also has an extensive range of Australian and New Zealand plants which flourish in the frost-free climate. Access to the garden is opposite the roadside car park where a booklet is available from the Information Point. Admission to garden and walks (including booklet) is £2 for adults, £1 for students, children under 16 free. Open all year 9am to 5pm. There is an attractive circular walk through the grounds of the estate as well as a scenic walk along the cliffs. The longer of the two walks along the cliff-top to Poll a' Cheò ('The Misty Pool') will take you to Jura's only example of a Neolithic **chambered cairn**, dating from around 2000 BC. There is also a Bronze Age **burial cairn** nearby. Scuff your feet on the beach at the southern tip of the island and you'll hear the sand 'sing'.

The main village of **Craighouse** has a hotel, shop, Post Office, tearoom, village hall, and the island's sole whisky distillery, birthplace of *Isle of Jura Malt*. Whisky has been distilled here since 1810, although the present distillery was built and enlarged between the late 1950s and 1970s. *Isle of Jura Malt* is ranked No 10 in the world market, not bad for a small island distillery employing only a dozen people. Arrange a tour by contacting the office (tel 01496-820240; www.isleofjura.com/). Try a dram in the **Jura Hotel**. In the passage to the bar are some interesting old work tokens, and communion tokens issued and used at Jura Parish Church and at the Free Church of Scotland, Leargybreak. There's an excellent exhibition of old photographs in a room at the rear of 200-year-old **Jura Parish Church**. At the main door of the church is a stone bench where Gaelic parishioners used to sit until the service in English was over. The old crofting settlement of **Keils** is a beautiful conservation village where you can compare traditional crofthouses with their modern equivalent. A fold in the land makes it unnoticeable from the road.

Beyond Keils is the cemetery of **Killearnadil** ('Church of Earnan') which contains a Campbell mausoleum that commemorates the family which dominated the island for three centuries. It is also where Gillour MacCraine is buried. He is said to have kept '180 Christmases in his own home and died in the reign of Charles the 1st'. When the Earl of Argyll asked Gillour what he thought about whisky the old man replied, *'I have never at any time turned aside from my path to partake of it, nor have I ever avoided it when it met me in the way'*. One of MacCraine's descendants, Mary, is buried at Killchianaig cemetery, Inverlussa. She died in 1856 aged 128. At the end of the bay from Craighouse is the only beach on the east side of the island, a lovely stretch of white sand a mile (1.6 km) long and safe for bathing. **Corran Bridge**, or Three Arched Bridge, was built in 1804 by Thomas Telford, who also built one of Craighouse's two piers 10 years later. There are a number of Iron Age forts on Jura, but the most spectacular is that at **An Dunan**, on Lowlandman's Bay. The remains of what is believed to be a Viking drydock are close by. The bay used to be a fishing boat anchorage. It's now a favourite haunt for basking seals.

Corryvreckan Whirlpool

The road follows a coastline north giving wonderful views to seaward, and inland to the bold hills which draw stalkers and walkers alike. The A846 road ends above little Lussa Bay and becomes and even narrower track until a mile (1.6 km) beyond Lealt a chain prevents vehicles going further. You can park here and slog the remaining seven miles (11 km) to the northern tip overlooking the Gulf of Corryvreckan and its notorious **whirlpool**. On the way you'll pass the stone farmhouse at Barnhill, which is where Eric Blair – better known as George Orwell – wrote his famous novel *1984*. He originally planned to call his opus *The Last Man in Europe* but settled on its title by reversing the last two numbers of 1948, the year he finished writing it. Orwell nearly lost his life here when his boat overturned in the Corryvreckan whirlpool. The renowned whirlpool boils when currents of up to 10 knots rush through the strait between Jura and Scarba from opposite directions and meet over an underwater pinnacle. The whirlpool is best seen on a rising tide when there is a strong wind from the west. At its peak, its roar can be heard up to 12 miles (19 km) away. Writing in 1695 Martin Martin said that *where the white waves meet and spout up: they call it the Kaillach, ie 'an old hag,' and they say that when she puts on her kerchief, ie the whitest wave, it is then reckoned fatal to approach her*. The Gulf of Corryvreckan is officially classed as unnavigable by the Royal Navy although, as one old account puts it, 'when they [currents] are asleep the smallest bark may pass with impunity'. According to legend, the Danish prince Breacan fell in love with the daughter of an island chief who would permit their marriage only if Breacan anchored in the whirlpool for three days and nights to prove his courage. To hold his anchor, Breacan had three cables made, one of hemp, one of wool, and one woven from virgins' hair. The hemp rope failed on the first night and the wool on the second. The rope of virgins' hair bore the strain until the final hour, when it also parted, apparently because the hair of one of the maidens did not meet the strict specification. Breacan was drowned and his body was washed ashore in Bagh Gleann nam Muc. He was buried in a deep cave which is still called Uamh Bhreacain ('Breacan's Cave'). This legend is disputed by modern scholars, but when the cave was excavated some years ago a stone coffin was found. Scholars have also toyed with the theory that the ancient Greek hero Odysseus visited Jura. Based on Homer's *Odyssey* it's said to be conceivable that the classical whirlpool of Charybdis is that of Corryvreckan and the island Thrinacia, meaning 'three-pronged,' is Jura with its three Paps. The theory draws further support from the northern stellar constellations Odysseus recorded on his voyage. Mike and Joan Richardson (tel 07899-912116) run a four-wheel-drive service to the Gulf of Corryvrechan and Barnhill from Kinuachdrachd Farm. A single journey of up to three people costs £15, with £5 for each additional adult. Return costs double. They also do guided walks from the farm. In the north-west is the site of **Glengarrisdale Castle**, scene of notable battles between the Campbells of Jura and the Macleans who owned the northern part of the island, and **Maclean's Skull Cave**. The reason for this grisly name, a human skull mounted on a stone cairn after a major clash between the two clans in 1647, weathered for nearly 350 years before it was removed.

FLORA AND FAUNA

Most habitats can be found on Jura and the mild climate has favoured the development of a remarkably rich flora and fauna, with several rare and very rare plant species. There are alpine varieties on the mountain slopes, wild fuschia abounds, and palm trees grow in the hotel grounds at Craighouse. The last census recorded more than 5,000 **red deer**. When you leave the ferry at Feolin you might see some grazing on seaweed along the shoreline, and it's said there is a pair of **otters** for every three miles (5 km) of coastline. There are upwards of 100 species of birds, with everything from **blackcock, grouse** and **snipe** to the **golden eagle** inland, and practically every known variety of seabird on the shore, making Jura a haven for twitchers. Small **wild goats**, supposedly descendants of those from Spanish Armada ships wrecked here in 1588, abound on the uninhabited west coast, which they share with **Atlantic grey seals**. The **rabbit** is the commonest mammal, but the **hare** and the **stoat** may also be spotted.

    Deer Cull. Between 1 July and 15 February, the legal season, deer culling takes place to control their population. This is a major contributor to the island's economy, both financially and in the number of locals employed in the industry. No shooting takes place on Sundays. If you are walking or otherwise moving about off-road on the island during this period you should be aware of when and where stalking is taking place. Check with the following estates:

> *Ardfin:* tel 01496-830396.   *Inver:* tel 01496-820223.
> *Ardlussa:* tel 01496-820323.   *Ruantallain:* tel 01496-820292.
> *Forest:* tel 01496-820332.   *Tarbert:* tel 01496-820207.

GETTING THERE

By Sea

Serco Denholm (tel 01496-840681) operates the small ferry between Port Askaig, Islay, and Feolin, Jura, on behalf of Argyll & Bute District Council. The ferry does the 10-minute crossing every 30-45 minutes, Monday to Saturday, with three sailings on Sunday. Car and driver single costs £6.20, day return costs £10, and adult single is 90p. Pay on ferry.

The Small Isles Bay at Craighouse offers good, safe anchorage for visiting yachts and other vessels.

Farsain Cruises: Craobh Haven Marine, Watersports Centre, Craobh Haven (tel 01852-500664). Cruises and trips daily from Craobh Haven to Jura and other neighbouring islands.

Gemini Cruises and Water Taxi Service: based at Crinan Harbour (tel/fax 01546-830238; e-mail murrcrinan@aol.com; www.gemini-crinan.co.uk). Offer seal-spotting, bird-watching, cruises to the Gulf of Corryvreckan, Loch Craignish and the Sound of Jura. You can take a two or four-hour boat trip.

GETTING AROUND

There is only one single-track road on Jura which goes up the east coast from Feolin ferry for about 25 miles (40 km). Seven miles (11 km) from the ferry is the main village of Craighouse. The road continues to Ardlussa and on to a mile (1.6 km) beyond Lealt. From here it's a private road which deteriorates into little more than a track, closed to vehicles. You can leave your vehicle at the road-end and walk a further seven miles (11 km) to the northern tip of the island.

Buses

Jura Bus Service has three mini-buses and covers the island from Feolin ferry in the south to Ardlussa in the north via Craighouse, Knockrome, and Lagg. The service operates from Monday to Saturday, timetables are available from tourist information centres, ferry terminals, on the ferry, or from the operator, Alex Dunnachie (tel 01496-820314/221; e-mail alex@jurabus.co.uk). Also available for private hire and tours for groups of up to 16.

Tours

Exploration Jura: Mike and Joan Richardson, Kinuachdrachd Farm (tel 07899-912116; fax 01496-820301). Guided walking and wildlife holidays; half and full-day or weekly packages. Open primrose time (March) to red deer run (October).

ACCOMMODATION

Jura is not over-endowed with accommodation. There's only one hotel and the road is too narrow for caravans. The two-star *Jura Hotel* (tel 01496-820243; fax 01496-820249; e-mail jurahotel@aol.com) is a warm and friendly place. It has 18 bedrooms, often heavily booked. Open all year.

B&B

Gwen Boardman: 7 Woodside, Craighouse, PA60 7YA (tel 01496-820379). One twin, one family room. Open April to September, from £20.

Dwin Capstick: tel 01496-820384.

Davie Gilmour: tel 01496-820319.

Liz Mark: tel 01496-820332. B&B and bunkhouse/bothy for six. Close to beach. Meals available on request.

Self-Catering: *Cottage,* Mrs Fletcher (tel 01496-820323). With four double rooms, remote location on sandy bay.

Camping

Camping is allowed in the field in front of the Jura Hotel. There's no charge but check with reception before pitching your tent and don't forget the donation box at reception for local charity. No vehicles allowed in field. Showers (£1 in the slot) and toilets at the back of the hotel.

EATING AND DRINKING

The *Isle of Jura Distillery* (tel 01496-820240) is opposite the Jura Hotel in Craighouse, on the shore overlooking the Small Isles Bay. This is the island's only distillery. The original part dates from the early 19th century. It was rebuilt in 1963 and produces an elegant 10-year-old malt. All visits by appointment. Open all year, Monday to Thursday 9am to 4pm, Friday 9am to 1pm.

In summer, you can get a cuppa while touring the gardens at Jura House, or at the Post Office in Craighouse, or you can get something more substantial at the Jura Hotel, where a venison burger costs £5.95. There's a vegetarian menu for around £6.

SPORT AND RECREATION

Walking and Climbing

You can enjoy many miles of hill, moor and coastal walking, though small areas may necessarily be restricted during the deer-stalking season and you should check this with the Jura Hotel or one of the estates (see *Flora and Fauna*). There are few well-defined paths, but plenty of deer trails you can follow. Expect rough going. For the climber, the three conical quartzite mountains known as the **Paps of Jura** offer several challenging climbs. There are also fairly easy routes for walkers up all three of these mountains, **Beinn a'Chaolais** ('The Mountain of the Sound'), **Beinn an Oir** ('The Mountain of Gold'), and **Beinn Shiantaidh** ('The Sacred Mountain'). A traverse of the three peaks can conveniently be undertaken from Craighouse. Another route starts at Inver, to the north of the Feolin landing. Strong boots are advisable as the upper slopes are mainly scree and large lumps of quartzite. On a clear day there are breathtaking views of many Hebridean islands and if it's exceptionally clear you might from the summit of Beinn an Oir make out the Isle of Man, well over 50 miles (80 km) away, as well as the distant coast of Ireland. The peaks of the Paps, together with four other lesser peaks form part of the route for the **Bens of Jura Fell Race**, held each year at the end of May. This is considered to be one of the toughest fell races in Britain, involving a distance of more than 16 miles (26 km) and a total climb of more than 7,000 ft (2,134 m). It starts and ends at the distillery in Craighouse and the first home is likely to have completed the gruelling course in under 3¹/₂ hours. A popular outing is known as the '**Evans' Walk**', which follows an out-and-back path from the main A846 road above Lowlandman's Bay across the island to Glenbatrick, just over 5 miles (8 km) away. The west coast is not otherwise easy to reach on foot. It's a wild coastline of caves, sandy coves, arches, stacks, and miles of raised beaches.

Cycling: The Jura Hotel keeps a small number of bicycles for free loan to guests. They can be hired for longer periods by arrangement.

Fishing

Mackerel, saithe and pollack are just a few of the fish you can catch from the rocks or off the coast. On the Ardfin Estate you can fly-fish in mountain burns and lochs for trout. If you are staying at the Jura Hotel you have use of the hotel's equipment. Trout and shore fishing are free of charge to guests, but sea fishing other than from the shore or one of the hotel's dinghies involves a boat hire charge. Ardlussa Estate also offers trout and salmon fishing (tel 01496-820323).

Deer Stalking: There is a great demand for this seasonal activity and it is usually necessary to make arrangements through the Jura Hotel well in advance.

HELP AND INFORMATION
Dr Mike Acres: Craighouse (tel 01496-820218).

Mountain Rescue: David Ewen Darroch, Inver (tel 01496-820223); Duncan Bure, Craighouse (tel 01496-820237); and William MacDonald, Ardfin (tel 01496-820396).

The *Post Office* in Craighouse also has a gift shop and tearoom.

Jura Stores in Craighouse is a general store and has a petrol pump.

Serco Denholm: Jura ferry (tel 01496-840681).

Jura Bus: Alec Dunnachie; tel 01496-820314/221. A mini-bus runs from the Feolin landing to Craighouse, and on to Inverlussa.

Royal Bank of Scotland's Mobile Bank calls at Craighouse, Jura, on Thursday 1pm to 2.30pm.

The Village Hall at Craighouse is the venue for frequent *ceilidhs* and other island gatherings.The **Jura Music Festival** is held towards the end of September every year.

GIGHA

Gigha (pronounced *gee-ah*) lies across the Sound of Gigha, 2¹/₂ miles (4 km) from the Tayinloan ferry pier on the west coast of Kintyre. It is only about 6 miles long and 1¹/₂ mile (10 km x 2.4 km) wide, with 30 miles (48 km) of indented shoreline made up of black rocky inlets, little bays and some lovely white sandy beaches. A single track road runs its length from north to south. Gigha's name is said to come from the Old Norse for either 'Isle of God' or 'Good Island'. It's certainly a fertile and well cultivated little island. Softened by warm Gulf Stream currents, its kindly climate has produced a renowned garden and given Gigha a name for its dairy herd and some excellent cheese. It has a population of 110, who bought the island from owner Derek Holt in 2001. About ¹/₂ mile (1 km) off the southern tip is its calf, the islet of Cara, which remains the property of the MacDonalds of Largie, the last link with the Lord of the Isles.

EXPLORING
The main village of Ardminish begins as you leave the pier and from here, at the road junction, you come to the island stores and Post Office, stocked to overflowing. To the scenic northern point of the island from the village is 4 miles (6 km), to the old pier in the south it's about two miles (3 km). The **Parish Church** (1923) has the original stone font from nearby Kilchattan Church and some interesting memorial windows, one dedicated to Kenneth MacLeod, the Gaelic scholar once of Gigha parish, who composed *Road to the Isles*, and another to former laird Sir James Horlick. Past the hotel are the remains of the **Church of Kilchattan**, dedicated to 6th century St Catan. The 18th century church is an elegant ruin and stands on 13th century foundations. The church is floored with about 30 mediaeval grave slabs, with more in the churchyard. Some retain their beautiful designs of foliage, animals and the great Highland sword, the claymore (*claideamh-mòr*). One showing the figure of an armed and kilted warrior is that of Malcolm, first MacNeill Laird of Gigha, who died in 1493. Close by is a standing stone bearing a carved inscription in the curious Celtic shorthand known as Ogam, or Ogham. This has been identified as a burial stone, probably dating from AD 500-700.

Sir James Horlick left his name on the night-time malted drink that enabled him to buy Gigha in 1944 and on the flowering shrub *Rhododendron horlickianum*, which grows with other ornamental species in the famed gardens he created in the 50 acres (20 ha) around **Achamore House**, near Kilchattan Church. When Sir James bought the estate the woodlands around the house were a wilderness. By the time he died in 1972 he had created the celebrated gardens which draw gardeners and plant lovers from around the world. He gifted his plant collection to the National Trust for Scotland in 1962, along with a small endowment for its future maintenance and to ensure that rare species are propagated and shared with other great gardens. **Achamore Gardens** (tel 01583-505254; fax 01583-505244) are noted for their rhododendrons, azaleas, camellias, hydrangeas, and rare exotic trees and plants. The gardens are open all year, 10am until dusk. Admission £2 adult, £1 child, family ticket £5. May is the **best month** to visit.

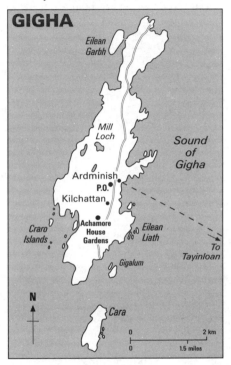

At the southern tip of Gigha the scant remains of a fortification are crowned by two curious stones representing an old man and a hag once believed to have mysterious powers. Further on is a landmark known as **The Druid Stone** (*Clach a' Thairbeirt*) and **The Hanging Stone**, from a tradition that people found guilty at Court Hill nearby were executed here. From the top to bottom of Gigha and the adjacent island of Cara there are traces of around a hundred ancient dwellings, burials, and other archaeological sites, most of them difficult to find and even harder to interpret. Helpful is RSG Anderson's book *The Antiquities of Gigha*, which you'll find on the island.

Gigha is a mini-paradise for twitchers and nature lovers. More than 120 different species of breeding birds have been recorded, including the **buzzard, barn owl, hen harrier, peregrine falcon, sparrow hawk**, and **raven**. Seabirds include **shelduck, eider, red-breasted merganser, guillemot** and **gannet**. Seals are common, although not so much off the western coastline, and appear to be musical. Locals say if you sing the same line of a song over and over the curious seals swim closer. **Otters** can be seen with patience, **rabbits** are everywhere. A wealth of wild flowers includes **bluebells, yellow iris, marsh marigolds,** gentians, **foxgloves, dogroses, red campion, tormentil, sea thrift**, and **Grass of Parnassus**. Orchids – marsh, fragrant, and spotted – grow all over the island and are so common it's almost impossible to walk without crushing them.

GETTING THERE

Caledonian MacBrayne (The Ferry Terminal, Gourock, PA19 1QP; tel 08705-650000; fax 01475-635235, reservations; tel 01475-650100; fax 01475-637607, general enquiries; e-mail reservations@calmac.co.uk; www.calmac.co.uk) operates a car-passenger ferry from Tayinloan every hour from 8am to 6pm Monday to Saturday, and from 11am to 5pm on Sunday. The crossing takes 20 minutes. The return fare for driver/passenger is £4.75 each, cars £17.90, boat/baggage trailer £17.90, motorcycles £8.95, and bicycles £2. A 'Day Saver' ticket is available at £20.85 for a car and up to four occupants from April to October. A 'Five-Journey' ticket is also available. For more details contact CalMac, Kennacraig (tel 01880-730253). For schedule of sailings on Gigha (tel 01583-505217).

Yacht Station. A favourite haunt for cruising yachtsmen with anchorages off South Pier (water and fuel) and at Ardminish, where the nearby *Boathouse* provides hot showers, drying and washing facilities.

Gigha airstrip, south of the island, is suitable for private light aircraft. Landing fees are £15 for single-engine planes, £25 for twin, and £10 for a microlight. There's a £5 discount if you stay overnight in the hotel. Contact the hotel (tel 01583-505254) for prior permission to land.

GETTING AROUND

There is no **bus** service, and the **taxi** is part of the school car run. Petrol is available next to the Post Office only. You can hire **bikes** from the Post Office for £3 an hour or £9 a day. Mountain-bikes from Gigha Hotel, £10 a day, £5 for half-day, adults £40 and children £35 a week.

ACCOMMODATION

Gigha Hotel: Gigha, PA41 7AD (tel 01583-505254; fax 01583-505244; e-mail william@isle-of-gigha.co.uk; www.isle-of-gigha.co.uk). Three-star, 13 en-suite bedrooms, bar, restaurant. Short stroll from the ferry slip. Open March to October, from £40 a night. The hotel also owns six holiday cottages around the island. *South Lodge*, built in 1895, is two miles from Ardminish village; *Ferryman's House* is close to a beach a short walk from the village, two bedrooms, sleeps five; *Ferry Crofts 1 and 2* are above Ardminish Bay, as is *South Ardminish* which sleeps six in two twin-bedded rooms and one double room; and remote *Ardailly House*, sleeps six, north on the island's main road.

Post Office Guest House: Gigha, PA41 7AA (tel 01583-505251; e-mail postoffice@gigha.net), also self-catering cottage. Phone or write for details.

No **camping** without permission from Gigha Hotel. No **caravans** allowed.

EATING AND DRINKING

'There is only one inn on the isle' said a visitor in 1700. This is still the case, although the *Gigha Hotel* (tel 01583-505254) has been modernised and enlarged and is noted for its cuisine and its friendly atmosphere. The bar – open all day – serves pub grub and is the local gathering place.

The *Post Office shop* has a wide range of Gigha's famous cheeses, including some shaped like apples (chives and garlic flavour) and some like oranges (orange liqueur flavour). Round cheeses (200 g) are Captain's Claret, Highland Chief, Poacher's Choice, Lazy Ploughman, Mature Cheddar and Herbs, Laird's Mustard, Ben Gunn, and Old Smokey. Mild cheeses £5/kg and mature £5.60/kg.

SPORT AND RECREATION

Nowhere in Gigha is much more than three miles (5 km) from the ferry, so undemanding **walks** and **bike rides** are pleasant options. The best walking can be found on the springy machair, the sea-turf of the coastal strip between the rocky shore and farmland, or on the hill ridge that forms the centre of the island and culminates in **Creag Bhan**, the highest point at 330 ft (101 m).

The Gigha Hotel has three **trout lochs** and **salmon fishing** rights around the island. **Sea fishing** off rocky outcrops is great fun for both novice and expert anglers.

Gigha Golf Club (John Bannatyne, Secretary; tel 01583-505242) has a nine-hole par 65 course, half a mile (0.8 km) from the Post Office shop. £10 a day for a round, £5 under 16. Weekly ticket £40, country membership £55. Pay at the shed on the course.

HELP AND INFORMATION

Dr NJ Gourlay: Greenhill, Muasdale (tel 01583-421206).
Post Office and shop: tel 01583-50525. Can sell or tell you anything you need to know.
Caledonian MacBrayne: tel 01583-505217.

The Slate Islands

Huddled together close to the Argyll mainland are the small islands of **Seil**, **Easdale**, and **Luing**, collectively known as the **Slate Islands**. Seil, just 14 miles (23 km) from Oban, is the gateway to these islands in the Firth of Lorn and is connected to the mainland by bridge. Even so it is comparatively isolated and has remained, like its neighbours, a definite island community. Seil is about five miles long by 2½ miles wide (8 km x 4 km) and has a population of around 450. To the west, across a narrow stretch of water, is tiny Easdale, with a population of 45, and nowhere more than a mile (1.6 km) wide. Confusingly, the main village on Seil facing Easdale island is also known as Easdale, although it's officially Ellenabeich. Across the narrow but fast-flowing strait in the south is Luing, the largest and most fertile of the Slate Islands, with a population of 130. In the north-west is Luing's main settlement, the little village of Cullipool which, like Toberonochy in the south-east, grew up around the old slate quarries. Blue slate from here was used to re-roof the Abbey on Iona. Around the three islands is a scattering of smaller and largely uninhabited islands.

Geology

The whole area interests geologists. Everywhere is evidence of the ancient volcanic activity that created today's landscape. The Dalradian bedrock of the district comprises some of the oldest sedimentary rock exposed in Britain, laid down 650-million years ago. Subsequent deposits were heated and compressed about 440-million years ago until they were transformed into slate.

SEIL

You can cross the Atlantic Ocean without leaving Scotland if you visit Seil. To get there take the **'Bridge Across the Atlantic'**, the humpbacked Clachan Bridge designed by Thomas Telford in 1792 to link the first of the Slate Islands to the mainland. He achieved this by spanning the sound with a simple but elegant stone bridge where the Atlantic is as narrow as a Scottish burn. Its 70 ft (21 m) long single arch is high enough for ships to sail under and the sound here is deep enough to take a 40-ton vessel at high tide, which has caused problems for whales in the past. In the early 19th century a 78 ft (24 m) whale with a 21 ft (6 m) lower jaw failed to make the passage, as did 129 pilot whales in 1837. In summer the bridge is a purple haze of tiny rare fairy foxgloves festooning the masonry. The old inn nearby is *Tigh an Truish*, which is Gaelic for **'House of the Trousers'**. This takes its name from the turbulent time following the suppression of the clans after their defeat at Culloden in 1746. The kilt was officially banned so islanders used to change into trousers at the inn before venturing on to the mainland. A path from the bridge offers a pleasant walk over to **Puilladobhrain** at the north end of Seil. The north-west corner of Seil is wild and lovely where you might see **otters**, **deer**, **duck**, and other wildlife. Millions of film fans and TV viewers have seen Seil without even realising it, as the island has been used as a location for a number of films, including *Ring of Bright Water*, and *Kidnapped*, and the popular BBC *Para Handy* series. Mrs Frances Shand Kydd, mother of the late Princess of Wales, lives on the island.

A single road runs the length of the island from the bridge to the Luing ferry slip at Cuan, branching west at Balvicar in mid-island to Ellenabeich and Easdale island. **Balvicar** is one of several villages built during the 19th century to house workers in the slate quarries. It has a fine nine-hole golf course and near the junction of the B844 and the B8003 is Balvicar Stores and Post Office, open seven days a week and stocking just about everything. The old churchyard encloses the remains of the medieval church dedicated to St Brendan, one of seven churches Seil has had over the centuries. The earliest was the chapel at Ballachuan Loch where St Brendan is believed to have had his cell when he was preaching here around AD 540. There was also a Covenanters church at Ballachuan, now a ruin, the 'Tin Church' at Kilbride, a corrugated iron building no longer used, and the Free Church at Balvicar, now a private residence. **Kilbrandon Parish Church**, further south, was built in 1864 to replace the smaller church at Cuan. It has some striking **stained glass windows** by Douglas Strachan, unusual in a Presbyterian kirk.

If you are energetic you can follow the shore from Cuan Sound to **Ellenabeich**. Prehistoric **Dun Mucaig** ('Fort of the Boar') is perched on a dramatic crag along the way and nearby, but difficult to find, is the **Fairy Cave**. The trim little conservation village of **Ellenabeich** is also known as Easdale. Most of the village was once an island called **Eilean-a-Beithich** ('Isle of Birches'). Over the years the quarry waste was tipped into the channel between the two and by the early 19th century the island was joined to Seil and known as Easdale. Like Easdale island the village grew up around the slate quarries and in its heyday some 600 families lived on Seil and Easdale. A policy of strict conservation has since protected the village from modern development with the result that it has a pleasing forgotten air about it. Single-storey whitewashed cottages stand in neat rows around a square alongside the small harbour. Around the square are little shops, all in original slate-roofed buildings. Next to the Post Office on the square is **The Slate Islands Heritage Centre** which provides a fascinating window into the history, natural heritage and economy of the Slate Islands through the 20th century. This is a varied display of photographs and artefacts, with some realistic models. Admission adults £1.50, concessions £1.25, children 25p. A combined ticket for the Heritage Centre and the Easdale Island Museum is available with a special fare on the ferry. In the Village Shop you can book a boat ride with *Sea.fari Adventures* (tel 01852-300003) through the Gulf of Corryvreckan and around Scarba. Climb the cliffs above the village for one of the most breath-taking views of the Inner Hebrides. On a clear day you can see 30 islands. Tucked in below the cliffs is **An Cala** (tel 01852-300237; fax 01852-300237), reputedly one of Scotland's finest small gardens. Open 1 April to 31 October 10am to 6pm. Designed by Thomas Mawson in the early 1930s, much of the original planting of its five acres (2 ha) survives in the beds of Poulsen roses, banks of Ghent azaleas, and *escallonia* hedges. An Cala is also known for its groves of ornamental Japanese cherries, including the lovely late-flowering Prunus *Oku Miyako*. May and June are the **best months** for visiting.

ACCOMMODATION

Inshaig Park Hotel: Easdale, Seil, PA34 4RF (tel/fax 01852-300256). Three-star, family-run hotel next door to An Cala gardens. Stands high above the road in attractive grounds. En suite bedrooms and a fine dining-room, as well as good bar meals. Open all year, from £27 a night.

    Tigh an Truish Inn: Clachan, PA34 4QZ (tel 01852-300242). Stands near the 'Bridge Across the Atlantic' which joins Seil to the mainland. £45 a room.

    Willowburn Hotel: Jan Wolfe and Chris Mitchell, Clachan Seil, PA34 4TJ (tel 01852-300276; fax 01852-300597; e-mail willowburn.hotel@virgin.net; www.willowburn.co.uk). Four-star, between the road and Seil Sound, with delightful gardens stretching down to the water's edge and an excellent licensed restaurant. Open March to December, from £53.

B&B

Clachandubh Farmhouse: John and Sue Brownlea, Balvicar (tel 01852-300317).

    Dunfillan: Mr and Mrs T Goodwin, Cuan Ferry (tel 01852-300258).

    Mutiara: Mrs E Nee, Clachan Seil (tel 01852-300241). Three-star, large modern house with bay views. Open May to November, from £15.

Self-Catering

Balvicar Holiday Chalets: Alan and Liz Macaskill (tel/fax 01852-300221; e-mail info@balvicarchalets.uk.com). Two-star, seven chalets on a small farm. Fully furnished for four with two bedrooms, bathroom, living-room and kitchen area. Open March to November, from £150-£310 a week.

    Caolas: Mrs B Nathan, Ellenabeich (tel 01852-300209).

    Innishmore: Mrs H Simcox, Ellenabeich (tel 01852-300222).

    Kilbride Croft Cottages: Mary and Brian Phillips, Balvicar (tel 01852-300475; e-mail kilbridecroft@aol.com). Two renovated old stone cottages, sleep 4/5. Each cottage is equipped with fridge, cooker, wood-burning stove, dishwasher, microwave, showers, and washing machine. Open all year, from £160-£350 a week.

    Oban Seil Steadings and Cottages: Oban Seil Farm, Clachan Seil, Nic and Bette Hunter (tel/fax 01852-300245; e-mail obanseilfarm@ukonline.co.uk). Four-star, luxurious houses in converted steading. Open all year, from £120-£500 a week.

    Old Clachan Farmhouse: Dr and Mrs A Henderson (tel 01852-300493).

    Seil Island Cottages: J Kidd (tel 01852-300440).

    Tramway Cottages: Donald and Lynn MacPherson, 34 Ellenabeich, Easdale (tel/fax 01852-300477). Four-star, fully-equipped cottages. Open all year, from £190-£375 a week.

EATING AND DRINKING

Non-residents can eat at all three hotels. On the square in Ellenabeich *The Seafood and Oyster Bar* (tel 01852-300121/269) licensed restaurant has an extensive seafood menu, and the tearoom has snacks and meals throughout the day. Take-aways available. Locals say their fish and chips are the finest in

Scotland. Their ice-cream is also tops. *Kilbrandon Oysters* (Portmor Limited, Kilbrandon House; tel 01852-300586; fax 01852-300584) in Easdale sells succulent oysters to visitors and to hotels and restaurants throughout the UK. Open all year 9am to 5pm.

SPORT AND RECREATION

Isle of Seil Golf Club (tel 01852-300373) has a challenging nine-hole course which uses natural water hazards, with play around Balvicar Bay and old slate quarries. Tickets available from Balvicar Stores or caravan at car park. Adults £5 a day, week £20; junior £2.50 a day and £10 for a week.

SHOPPING

You can't miss the *Highland Arts Studio* in Ellenabeich (tel 01852-300273; fax 01852-300271; e-mail highland.arts@ukonline.co.uk; www.highlandarts.co.uk), an Aladdin's Cave of gifts and an amazing exhibition of the works of the late C John Taylor, artist, poet and composer. You can listen to his compositions and read his poetry. Open all year, summer from 9am to 9pm, winter 10am to 4pm.

HELP AND INFORMATION

Oban Tourist Information Centre: tel 01631-563122; e-mail info@oban.org.uk; www.oban.org.uk. Informal tourist information from Easdale village shop.

Doctors and **district nurses** at surgery between Clachan and Balvicar.

Groceries and *Post Offices* at Balvicar (tel 01852-300373) and Easdale (113 Ellenabeich; tel 01852-300341).

EASDALE

Although at 650 by 500 yards (594 x 457 m) by far the smallest of the three neighbouring islands, Easdale gave its name to the blue-back slate they all produced and to a geological band stretching through the Scottish Highlands. First recorded in 1554, the slate of Easdale was used to roof Armaddy Castle, Lorn, Castle Stalker, at Appin, Cawdor Castle, near Inverness, and Glasgow Cathedral. On the islands locals used it as durable flooring and to make their tombstones. Slate boats returning from Ireland carried soil as ballast which was used by the islanders to create plots to grow vegetables. Grain came from more fertile Seil and Luing. The Slate Islands were among the earliest in the Sound of Lorn to become the property of the Breadalbane family, a branch of the Clan Campbell, which over 400 years became one of Europe's greatest landowning families. In the year that Bonnie Prince Charlie was raising the clans in rebellion the Breadalbanes were establishing the Marble and Slate Company of Netherlorn. By the late 19th century 11-million slates a year were being produced, each hand-cut in sheets as thin as 6-12 mm and exported as far afield as Canada, America, Australia, New Zealand, and the West Indies. The workmen were paid once a year, and then only for slates sold. It all came to an end on 22 November 1881 when the sea flooded the workings during a violent storm. From then on the industry went into terminal decline. The Easdale slate quarries finally closed down in 1911, although groups of men worked to meet local demand until the 1960s. Time has healed many of the old scars on the landscape and former quarry workings now look like pleasant lagoons, and one is a popular summer swimming spot. Some are nearly 200 ft (61 m) deep. There are no cars on Easdale, and the pretty little cottages, once rented by quarry families for 25p a year, are laid out around a grass square and connected by gravel paths. It's possible to walk around the island in half an hour. Near the ruined Smithy is a path to the top of the hill which is worth the climb for the glorious view. To learn more about the quarries, the men who worked in them, and social life in the 19th century visit the **Easdale Island Folk Museum:** tel/fax 01852-300370) off the square near the harbour. Open April to October, weekday from 10.30am to 5.30pm, Sunday from 10.30am to 4.30pm. Adults £2, concessions £1.50, children 50p.

GETTING THERE
Easdale ferry (tel 01852-300472) is run by the Argyll & Bute Council and carries passengers only for the three-minute crossing from Ellenabeich, on Seil. Press the button in the little wooden shed at the terminal to call the ferry from Easdale island. It runs partly on demand and partly to schedule. Monday to Saturday, April to October, there are frequent sailings from 7.15am to 8.50pm. Sunday from 9.30am to 12.50pm, 2pm to 3.50pm, and 4.20pm to 5.50pm. Monday to Saturday, November to March, 7.15am to 7pm, 11pm on Friday and Saturday, and Sunday 9.30am to 12.50 and 2pm to 4.50pm. Adult return £1, children 50p, bikes free.

ACCOMMODATION
Mr and Mrs M Baldock: 22 Easdale Island (tel 01852-300438). Run a B&B.

EATING AND DRINKING
The Puffer (tel/fax 01852-300579; e-mail info@pufferbar.com; www.pufferbar.com), bar and restaurant is housed in a restored quarryman's cottage. The bar is open all year round. Beer buffs will find some unusual Scottish bottled beers to try, as well as draught 'Caledonian 80/-'. The restaurant is open from spring to autumn. All-day menu. This is the centre of island activity. Various entertainments, including the occasional *ceilidh*.

LUING

Luing (pronounced 'ling') is the largest of the three Slate Islands. It has excellent facilities for yachtsmen, some good fishing and pleasant walks, ancient sites, and wildlife which should include a sighting of the Luing hare. The island is effectively one large farm and owned in the main by a family which has developed the famous chocolate-brown Luing cattle, a breed prized throughout the world for its ability to cope with extreme conditions. A narrow road runs for about four of Luing's six-mile (10 km) length, from the ferry slip to Toberonochy, with branches off to the old slate villages of **Cullipool** and **Black Mill Bay** on the west coast. Cullipool is a pleasant holiday village with a small Post Office and shop. It's the site of the UK's first seawater lobster storage pond built to hold up to 100,000 crustaceans. A mile (2 km) to the west of Cullipool is the small island of **Belnahua** and closer in is **Fladda**, whose lighthouse beam can be seen for 11 miles (18 km).

A short walk to the east is **Cnoc Dhomhnuill**, at 308 ft (94 m) Luing's highest point. The island of **Torsa** ('Thor's Island') and its linked islet of **Tora Beag** lie in the north-east off Ardinamir, where to the south are a number of prehistoric remains. Near the north end of Luing at Port Mary is a ruined village dating back to before the Clearances that displaced so many of the island families. Above the village of Toberonochy on the east coast is **Kilchattan Church**, the ruins of an earlier chapel last used for worship in 1685, and the island's only graveyard, where there's a memorial to crew members lost when the 1,951 ton *SS Helena Faulbaums* foundered off Belnahua in October 1936. Alex Campbell is also buried here, a Covenanter who, according to the inscription on his slate tombstone, 'digged my grave before I died'. Offshore is the wooded island of **Shuna**, left to the Glasgow Corporation in 1829 by owner James Yates for the benefit of the city's poor. The city's response to this charitable gesture was to sell the island.

About thee miles (5 km) west of Luing, at the entrance to the Firth of Lorn, are the **Garvellachs**, an archipelago of small islands nearly three miles (5 km) long and also known as the 'Isles of the Sea'. On **Eileach-an-Naoimh** ('Holy Isle'), the most southerly island, are a considerable number of Celtic monastic remains, including beehive cells, a chapel, and a burial ground, associated in local tradition with St Brendan and his nephew, St Columba. The northern island of the group is **Dun Chonnuill** which has the ruins of 13th century castle said to have been raised on the site of a 1st century fort built by Conal Cearnach, an Ulster king. Between Luing and Jura to the south is the strange island of **Scarba**, barely three miles (5 km) long, yet rising to a height of 1,470 ft (448 m), with great cliffs overlooking the Gulf of Corryvreckan and its awesome whirlpool (see *Jura*). Sea and weather conditions dictate whether you can land on these and any of the other small islands surrounding Luing. Check with *Dunaverty* (Easdale, PA34 4RF; tel 01852-300203, boat 0771 2202133) for large, fast boat charters.

GETTING THERE

A small Argyll & Bute Council vehicle-passenger ferry operates all year from Cuan, Seil, to Luing every half hour from 7.30am to 6pm, Monday to Saturday. On Sunday there is a passenger-only ferry from 11am and half hourly until 6pm. In June to August there's an extra car ferry on Friday and Saturday at 10.30pm, and an extra passenger ferry Monday to Saturday until 11.30pm. Return £5.40 car and driver and £1 for each passenger. It takes a couple of minutes to cross the narrow Cuan Sound.

GETTING AROUND

Royal Mail (tel 01246-546329; www.royalmail.co.uk) operates a 15-seater **Postbus** from Blackmill Bay-Toberonochy-Cullipool-Cuan Ferry, Monday to Saturday. Check departure times at the Post Office.

Isle of Luing Bike Hire, Cullipool (tel 01852-314256), will deliver bikes to the ferry. Apart from 'ferry hill' most of the island's roads are easy pedalling and provide a good half-day's exploration. Cost for half-day hire (four hours) is £6, full day (eight hours) £10. Book in advance by phone (evenings).

ACCOMMODATION

Sunnybrae Caravan Park (tel 01852-314274) at South Cuan has six modern, clean and well-equipped mobile homes, with fitted kitchen, bathroom with shower, bedrooms with pillows, blankets and duvets, gas heater. Open March to October, from £100-£300 a week.

Firth of
Clyde Islands

Corrie, Arran

The Firth of Clyde is one of the most attractive estuaries in Britain and an historic seaway from the heart of industrial Glasgow to the Atlantic. It is dotted with islands ranging in size from the isolated sentinel rock of Ailsa Craig in the Firth's wide mouth to the islands of Arran, Bute and the two Cumbraes. All are a hop, skip and a jump from the mainland and for many island-hoppers their accessibility makes them an easy introduction to the wider world of the Western Isles.

Arran

Arran is nearly 20 miles long and 10 miles wide (32 km x 16 km) and the largest and most picturesque of the Firth of Clyde islands. It lies some 14 miles (23 km) from Ardrossan on the mainland coast, its western shore separated from the Mull of Kintyre by the Kilbrannan Sound, which at its narrowest point is less than 4 miles (6 km) wide. A good road, 56 miles (90 km) long, encircles the island. Two others cross it from east to west, the best known being the road called 'The String' which runs for 10¹/₂ miles (17 km) from Brodick to Blackwaterfoot, the other 'The Ross'. running from Lamlash Bay to near Sliddery. Brodick and Lamlash are the main settlements on the east coast, both with lovely bays. Other settlements and farms straggle around the thin coastal strip. Arran has a population of around 4,500, nearly a third resident in and around Brodick. With Skye and Bute, Arran attracts the most tourists of any island and at the height of the season its normal population swells tenfold.

Goatfell and its attendant granite peaks and ridges climbing to nearly 3,000 ft (900 m) give the northern half of Arran an impressive wildness in sharp contrast to the rolling heather moorlands of the south. The gently undulating southern plateau seldom exceeds 1,300 ft (400 m) in height. Sandy bays edged by cliffs, often riddled by sea caves, punctuate the coast.

Holy Island is the larger and more accessible of Arran's two satellite islands, its two-mile (3 km) 1,030 ft (314 m) spine almost blocking the entrance to Lamlash Bay to create a natural sheltered harbour. **Pladda** island lies in the south just a mile (1.6 km) off Kildonan. Although separated by often turbulent seas it's a popular picnic spot. With a height of 66 ft (20 m), it is the haunt of **seals** and seabirds, including **common** and **arctic terns, eider, shelduck, mallard, red-breasted merganser**, and some rarer migrant commuters. Out in the mouth of the Clyde further south is **Ailsa Craig**, a 1,109 ft (338 m) high cone of rock that's better known as 'Paddy's Milestone' and famous as the source of the fine red granite once used to make the smooth, heavy stones used in the old Scottish game of curling.

Geology

Mention 'Hutton's Unconformity' to geologists and their eyes light up. Arran is one of the world's classic geological locations whose remarkable variety of rocks and structures was discovered in 1787 by eminent Edinburgh scientist Dr James Hutton, known today as the 'Father of Geology'. His most important discovery on Arran was the unconformity near Lochranza, an unusual geological formation with rocks of different periods meeting at a discordant angle which provided the first definite proof of the earth's great age. The Highland Boundary Fault slicing Scotland into the Highlands and Lowlands continues through Arran, effectively dividing it in two to replicate Scotland in miniature. A raised beach of nearly 26 ft (8 m) circles the island, the result of ground levels rising at the end of the last Ice Age. The effects of glaciation can be seen in the spectacular corries, hanging valleys and knife-edge granite ridges of the northern mountains. In the uplands, crystals of smoky quartz, cornelian, jasper, agate, as well as cairngorms are fairly common. The discovery in 1975 of the fossil trail of a giant centipede preserved in the rock of one of the island's quarries added to Arran's geological interest. The standard work for rock buffs is Dr James Bryce's *Geology of Arran*, and Scottish Natural Heritage produces a geological booklet, *Arran and the Clyde Islands*.

EXPLORING

Arran shares many of the natural beauties and attractions of the more far-flung islands of the Hebrides, but its closeness to mainland Scotland has for more

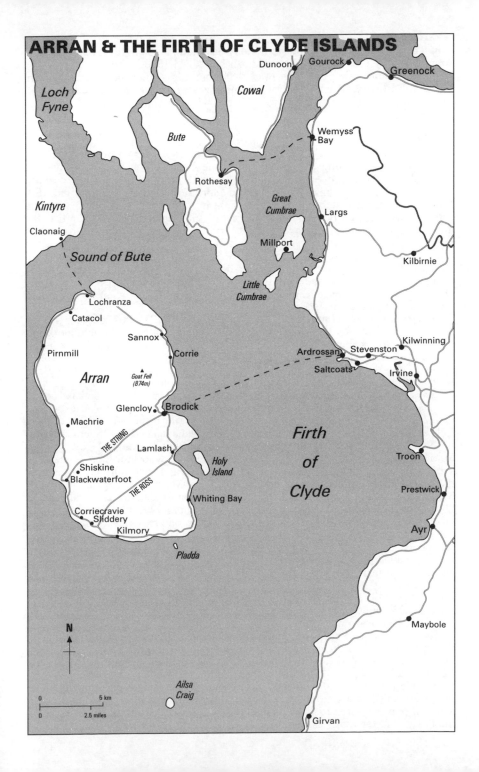

ARRAN & THE FIRTH OF CLYDE ISLANDS

Loch Fyne

Cowal

Dunoon

Gourock

Greenock

Bute

Wemyss Bay

Rothesay

Kintyre

Great Cumbrae

Largs

Claonaig

Millport

Kilbirnie

Sound of Bute

Little Cumbrae

Lochranza

Catacol

Sannox

Corrie

Kilwinning

Pirnmill

Ardrossan

Stevenston

Arran

Goat Fell (874m)

Saltcoats

Irvine

Glencloy

Brodick

Machrie

Firth

THE STRING

Lamlash

of

Shiskine

Holy Island

Clyde

Troon

Blackwaterfoot

THE ROSS

Prestwick

Corriecravie

Sliddery

Whiting Bay

Kilmory

Ayr

Pladda

N

Maybole

0   5 km

0   2.5 miles

Ailsa Craig

Girvan

than a century made it a favourite holiday destination. 'Delightful at all times is Arran' is how one old Irish bard described the island, whose name means 'high' or 'kidney-shaped'. The road that rings the kidney bean island offers access to virtually all its attractions in the space of a day. The two cross-island roads launch you into uplands to visit the wilder natural features and many ancient sites.

NORTH

From **Brodick** ('Broad Bay'), the island capital, most attractions and villages are conveniently strung like beads along the circular A841 road. About 1¹/2 miles (2¹/2 km) north of Brodick is the **Arran Heritage Museum** at Rosaburn (tel 01770-302636; e-mail arranmuseum@brinternet.com), a converted 18th century croft farm which provides an insight into the Arran way of life over the centuries. A cottage gives an authentic feel of Victorian and Edwardian life, the museum's geological display exhibits Arran rocks formed in environments ranging from tropical seas and deserts through successive Ice Ages, and the outstanding archaeological section deals with Arran's Neolithic and early Bronze Age. There are also regular demonstrations of such traditional occupations as weaving and spinning, as well as horse-shoeing in 'The Smiddy'. Open April to October, every day 10.30am to 4.30pm. Gift shop, tearoom and picnic area. Wheelchair access. Car park.

  Brodick Castle, Garden & Country Park (tel 01770-302202; fax 01770-302312; e-mail brodickcastle@nts.org.uk; www.nts.org.uk). The landmark red sandstone castle is administered by the National Trust for Scotland and is a beautiful setting for a treasury of porcelain and silverware. Its walls are hung with priceless paintings and the rooms are full of furniture from all over the world. Italian glass, Dutch marquetry tables, Japanese carvings and 18th century Chinese serving dishes are just some of the exquisite items on display. Brodick is one of Scotland's most battle-scarred castles and has been rebuilt many times. The site of the ancestral seat of the ducal Hamiltons was a fortress even in Viking times. The 13th century fortified tower was developed in the 16th century and extended by Oliver Cromwell in the 17th century. The main Victorian extension was laid in 1844 by Princess Marie of Baden, wife of the 11th Duke of Hamilton, who built her a pine-cone summer house in the grounds to remind her of Bavaria. She introduced the now rampant rhododendrons. Her granddaughter, Lady Mary Louise, 6th Duchess of Montrose, lived in the castle until 1957. As you might expect, the castle has several ghosts, the most benign a figure usually seen in the library wearing breeches, a long green jacket, and a powdered wig. During a plague outbreak three female visitors believed to be carrying the disease were reputedly walled up to prevent its spread and the wandering ghostly Gray Lady is said to be a reminder of this cruel act.

  The walled garden dating from 1710 has been restored as a Victorian garden and in the **Country Park** you can accompany a ranger naturalist on one of a series of guided walks from the nature centre or wander along some 11 miles (18 km) of waymarked trails among waterfalls, gorges, and wildlife ponds. The castle is open 1 April to 30 June and 1 September to 31 October, daily from 11am to 4.30pm (last admission 4pm); 1 July to 31 August, daily from 11am to 5pm (last admission 4.30pm). Reception Centre and shop open 10am to 5pm. Walled garden open all year, daily 9.30am to 5pm. Country Park open all year, daily from 9.30am until sunset. Disabled facilities, picnic site, and licensed restaurant. Admission £2.50 gardens and park, £5 for the castle.

  Corrie is a delightful hamlet of picturesque white cottages on the coast at the foot of Arran's loftiest mountain, Goatfell. Its closeness to beautiful Glen Sannox makes it popular with artists as well as climbers and fell walkers. White posts on the hillside as far north as Sannox Bay indicate the 'Measured Mile' set up for

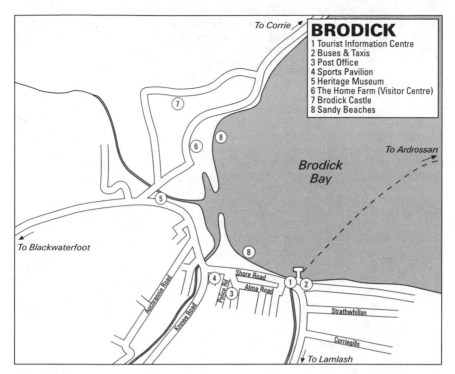

BRODICK

1 Tourist Information Centre
2 Buses & Taxis
3 Post Office
4 Sports Pavilion
5 Heritage Museum
6 The Home Farm (Visitor Centre)
7 Brodick Castle
8 Sandy Beaches

To Corrie

To Ardrossan

Brodick Bay

To Blackwaterfoot

Shore Road

Alma Road

Auchrannie Road

Police Rd

Knowe Road

Strathwhillan

Corriegills

To Lamlash

vessels on speed trials. The coastal path leaving the road at North Sannox leads to the **Fallen Rocks**, landslips of huge Old Red Sandstone blocks piled up to 600 ft (183 m) above the sea shore. The road north-west from Sannox runs through North Glen Sannox and Glen Chalmadale, crossing the Witch's Bridge over Ballarie Burn to **Lochranza** ('Loch of the Rowan Trees') at the head of a deep sea inlet at the northern end of the island. It's picturesque, even by Arran standards. The hills sweep down to the attractive lochside village, dominated by the half-ruined square double towers of 16th century **Lochranza Castle** on a grassy promontory where you might see sheep and deer sharing the grazing. The castle was made famous by Sir Walter Scott in *Lord of the Isles*. Robert the Bruce is said to have landed at Lochranza from Ireland in 1306 at the start of his long struggle to liberate Scotland. From **South Newton** on the opposite side of the loch there are some fine walks around the **Cock of Arran**, the northernmost headland, where **basking sharks** are often seen in August and September. This wild area produced the family which gave Britain a Prime Minister, Harold Macmillan, Lord Stockton, and a leading publishing company. The road south hugs the west coast, which is one long stretch of rock, pebbles and shingle.

The delightful bay at **Catacol**, on Kilbrannan Sound, penetrates into the hills towards Arran's biggest stretch of inland water, mile-long (1.6 km) Loch Tanna, which lies at an altitude of 1,051 ft (320 m). Catacol has an intriguing row of a dozen identical cottages called the **'Twelve Apostles'**. They are also known as 'Hungry Row' because they were built to house locals evicted from their hill village to make way for deer. The little settlement of **Pirnmill** lies on the coast below Beinn Bhreac and Beinn Bharrain, both more than 2,300 ft (701 m) high. The mill here once produced the *pirns*, or pine bobbins, for the worldwide textile thread industry supplied from Paisley. Further south are **Whitefarland**, with its interesting old shoreline burial ground, the spectacular **palm trees** of **Imachar**, and beyond **Dougarie** some interesting caves near the seaward end of long and desolate Glen Iorsa, which stretches into the heart of the northern mountains.

There are as many as ten **stone circles** on Arran and most of them are on the west coast around **Machrie**. At **Auchagallon**, not far from the Machrie Golf Course, is a single circle of graded stones around a Bronze Age burial cairn regarded by experts as a perfect example of its type, and worth visiting for the panoramic views across Kilbrannan Sound. Nearby **Machrie Moor** is the site of Arran's most outstanding collection of prehistoric remains, with at least six enigmatic stone circles surrounded by Neolithic and Bronze Age burial cairns and hut foundations. The most spectacular site on the moor has three sandstone monoliths standing up to 18 ft (5.5 m) high, each weighing 8-10 tons.

Through a coastal plantation a signposted footpath descends to follow the raised beach to the **King's Cave**. Allow about 45 minutes for the walk. This large sandstone cave is one of several here and was reputedly once used by Robert the Bruce. Legend says that in 1306 he was encouraged to continue his resistance to domination of Scotland by Edward I, the 'Hammer of the Scots', after watching a spider in the cave struggle to fix its web until eventually it succeeded. Smaller caves here are known as his **Kitchen**, **Cellar**, and **Stable**. There are carvings of Pictish and early Christian origin in King's Cave, which is protected by a locked iron gate. Ranger-led walks visit during May. Contact the local Forest Enterprise office (tel 01770-302218). South along the beach to the village of **Blackwaterfoot** there's a standing stone and the ruined ramparts of a great Iron Age fortress near Drumadoon. The 'String Road', built by Thomas Telford in 1817, offers a short cut back to Brodick from Blackwaterfoot. Two miles along (3 km) is **Shiskine Church**, where a crudely carved tombstone is believed to mark the burial place of St Mo Las.

SOUTH

On the shore near Kilpatrick is the **Church Cave**, also known as **Preaching Cave**, which was used for six years early in the 19th century by parishioners at odds with the minister foisted on them by the duke. There are traces of a hill fort near here and another south of Corriecravie. At **Sliddery**, the transverse road 'The Ross' snakes between the hills and plantations to Lamlash. On the shore at Sliddery is a green mound, the shape of a Viking burial. Torrylin Creamery, at **Kilmory**, is the home of Arran cheese. **Lagg** is a little oasis of tropical plants which also boasts the oldest hotel on the island, an 18th century inn. A signposted track to the north leads through woodlands to a stone circle and to **Carn Ban**, the great stone cairn at the head of Kilmory Water. Its remote location – a round trek of about 7 miles (12 km) – has made this the best preserved cairn in Arran.

The most southerly point on Arran is **Bennan Head**, where seals often congregate among the boulders in front of the **Black Cave**, which runs into the cliffs for about 50 yards (46 m) and is 80 ft (24 m) high. On the main road is **South Bank Farm Park** (East Bennan; tel 01770-820221), where you can watch sheepdog demonstrations on Sunday, Tuesday and Thursday at 2.30pm. Open April to October from 10am to 5pm. Facing offshore Pladda is Kildonan, which is the location of Arran's third and least known stronghold, ruined **Kildonan Castle**, which moulders on an elevated site overlooking the sea. It was once the hunting seat of Scottish kings. Past Dippin Head the broken shore and cliffs of the south give way again to farmland and long sandy stretches all the way back to Brodick. The sedate resort of **Whiting Bay**, the southernmost of the three main east coast villages, straggles for more than a mile around the shallow bay. It has good sea fishing, sea bathing, and some attractive walks through Glenashdale Forest, taking in **Glenashdale Falls**, which leap 200 ft (61 m) in two cascades. The second fall at the head of the glen is **Eas a Chranaig**, the highest waterfall in Arran. Not far from the falls on the northern side of the glen is an Iron Age fort and in the forest nearby are the remains of ancient iron ore furnaces known as bloomeries. Turn sharp left up a staircase of 315 steps in the early stages of the Glenashdale Falls walk and the forest trail takes you to the **Giants' Graves**, chambered cairns known as 'horned gallery graves' because of their semi-circular forecourts. These held the remains of Neolithic people interred in crouching positions.

On the headland between Whiting Bay and Lamlash Bay, looking out to Holy Island, is **Kingscross Point** where Robert the Bruce embarked for the mainland in 1307. On the point is an Iron Age fort and a substantial Viking burial mound, which a recovered 9th century coin dates to the time when Norse warrior 'Ivarr the Boneless' was sacking York. **Lamlash** stands on a wide but sheltered sand and cliff-fringed bay south of Brodick and is where King Haakon of Norway rested his Viking armada before attacking Scotland in 1263. It is also where Arran's gentler southern contours merge into the mountainous scenery of the north. At one time Lamlash was a base for the vessels of the North Sea Fleet, now it is a popular haven for yachts and pleasure boats of all kinds. It's also the place where shopkeeper Donald McElvie (1866-1947) developed Arran's prized varieties of potato. Inland from Lamlash, 'The Ross' road climbs through Monamore Glen to nearly 1,000 ft (305 m), descending through Glen Scorrodale to the south-west coast near Lagg. About a mile (1.6 km) along the road is a parking place and a path leading through the forest to the chambered cairn called **Meallach's Grave**, where excavations in 1961 revealed signs of fire and feasting a thousand years ago. From here it's about 4 miles (6 km) back to Brodick.

FLORA AND FAUNA

Flora

Nothing indicates Arran's mild climate more than the **palm trees** thriving outdoors all around the island. The warm Gulf Stream gives the island a rich and unusual plantlife, including varieties of **primula** usually found only in Britain's southern islands. One of the more unusual plants is the **Tonbridge filmy-fern** which likes the damp deep ravines around Brodick Castle. The more inaccessible slopes and crags of the steep-sided gorge in the 24-acre (10 km) **Glen Diomhan National Nature Reserve**, about two miles (3 km) south-east of Catacol, shelter two rare species of **whitebeam** which are found nowhere else in Britain. Moorland plants such as **tormentil, lousewort, bog asphodel, milkwort** and **heath spotted orchid** grow on the lower ground and in the glens, where dwarf juniper also occurs. High on the peaks **starry saxifrage, mountain sorrel, goldenrod** and **alpine buckler-fern** grow on the granite pavement. The Forestry Commission has been on Arran since 1950 and since then has reafforested most of the southern half of the island. These woodlands are managed so that visitors can walk, cycle, or pony-trek through the plantations.

Fauna

There are around 2,000 **red deer** running wild and you might catch a glimpse of a rare albino, the source of the legend of the White Stag, which in earlier times was said to herald the death of someone in the island's ducal Hamilton family. Red deer are easily seen north of the 'String Road' at most times of the year. There is a strong population of **red squirrels** and a scattering of **badgers**. Sightings of **basking sharks** and **porpoises** are not infrequent and around the coast you'll spot lots of **common seals**.

Bird-Watching

Birds of prey are a fairly common sight. On moorland and in forest clearings **hen harriers** hunt for **red grouse**, and there are breeding **peregrines**. Dusk may reveal a **barn owl**, many of which nest in barrels put up by local wildlife rangers. **Crossbill** first bred in the forestry plantations in 1980, **goldcrest** and **siskin** are well established, and **sparrowhawk** and **buzzard** are on the increase. Both **red-throated** and **black-throated diver** occur. **Fulmar** nest along the west coast and a few pairs of **black guillemot** breed at Dippin Head.

Golden eagles are often seen over the glens of the National Trust for Scotland's 6,605-acre (2,673 ha) **Goatfell Nature Reserve** and **ravens** patrol the high corries. On the moorland slopes of Beinn a Chliabhain a few **golden plover** breed, and **redpoll** nest in the woodlands of lower Glen Rosa. **Brodick Country Park's** 178 acres (72 ha) provide habitat for **chiffchaff**, **garden warbler** and **blackcap**; **nightjar** breed in the more open woodland, and nearby **Merkland Wood** attracts many other woodland birds.

GETTING THERE

There are two car-passenger ferry services to Arran, one from Ardrossan, Ayrshire, to Brodick and the other from Claonaig, Kintyre, to Lochranza. Both are operated by *Caledonian MacBrayne* (The Ferry Terminal, Gourock, PA19 1QP; tel 08705-650000; fax 01475-635235, reservations; tel 01475-650100; fax 01475-637607, general enquiries; e-mail reservations@calmac.co.uk; www.calmac.co.uk). The Ardrossan to Brodick ferry leaves daily from 7am to 6pm, Monday to Saturday, and 9.45am to 6pm on Sunday. The crossing takes 55 minutes. The single adult fare is £4.40, car £25.50, caravan, boat/baggage trailer £25.50, motorcycles £12.75, and bicycles £1. 'Day Saver' ticket costs £60 for car and up to four occupants. The 'Five-Day Return' and 'Six-Journey' tickets are also available. This ferry has a wheelchair lift, cafeteria, and bar.

The ferry from Claonaig operates in summer only. It leaves daily from 8.50am to 7pm and takes 30 minutes for the trip. The single adult fare is £4, car £18.05, caravan, boat/baggage trailer £18.05, motorcycles £9.05, bicycles £1. There is a 'Day Saver' ticket which costs £36 for a car and up to four occupants available from April to October, except Saturday during July and August. 'Five-Day Return' and 'Six-Journey' tickets are also available.

CalMac also has 'Evening Dinner Cruises' from Ardrossan, Monday to Friday, April to October. These are non-landing cruises during which a three-course dinner, with wine, is served. It leaves at 6pm (8.30pm on Friday) and returns at 8.15pm (10.35pm). The cruise, including meal, costs £20. There is also a 'Day Out' ticket which leaves Ardrossan at 7am and returns at 7.20pm from Brodick. The return fare of £48 includes the ferry crossing for car and two adults, full Scottish breakfast, and 10% discount on meals on the return trip. Tickets are available Monday to Friday, April to October. Booking is advised. The Sunday 'Lunch Cruise' leaves Ardrossan at 12.30pm and returns at 2.45pm from April to October. This is a non-landing cruise, includes a three-course meal and costs £12.50. The other option is a day sail from Claonaig to Lochranza. There are about six sailings a day from 8.50am to 3.05pm. A day return tickets costs £6.80, car day return £31. For more information contact CalMac at Ardrossan Harbour (tel 01294-463470; fax 01294-601063) or Brodick Pier (tel 01770-302166; fax 01770-302618).

Waverley Excursions (Waverley Terminal, 36 Anderston Quay, Glasgow,G3 8HA; tel 0141-221 8152; fax 0141-248 2150) has cruises down the Clyde on the *Waverley*, one of the world's last sea-going paddle steamers. Operates Easter to October but check the specific dates and times of the cruises with the operator. There are cruises from Greenock and Glasgow to Brodick, which cost £25.95. From Rothesay £17.95, and from Millport £15.95. The 'Five Islands' cruise from Greenock costs £27.95, with views of Arran, Bute and Cumbrae, steaming to Pladda and round Holy Isle. From Glasgow the same route costs £28.95, from Rothesay £21.95, and from Millport £18.95.

Buses

A bus service operates between Claonaig, Kennacraig and Tarbert (contact Argyll & Bute Council; tel 01546-604695); for bus service between Lochranza and Brodick contact *Strathclyde Transport* (tel 0141-332 7133).

GETTING AROUND

Maps and Guides

When you buy maps check prices around town. The ones in the Tourist Information Centre in Brodick cost more than those in, for instance, the Post Office. The 1:50 000 Ordnance Survey Sheet 69 covers all of Arran, but Harvey's Isle of Arran 1:40 000 waterproof map not only has more detail, its reverse side has an enlarged 1:25 000 sheet of the northern mountainous half of Arran with 49ft (15 m) contour intervals. Ideal for walkers and climbers.

There's an interesting £7.95 Banton Press pocket reprint of *All About Arran*, by R Angus Downe, which shows that little has changed since it was originally published by Blackie & Son in 1933.

Buses

The bus station is in Brodick, alongside the ferry terminal building. Buses leave from here for Corriegills, The String, Blackwaterfoot, Lamlash, Whiting Bay, and Lochranza, Monday to Sunday. An 'Arran Day Ticket' is available for £3 and you can buy it on the bus. This entitles you to unlimited travel all day, or a 'Ride-around-Arran' which, by combining journeys on the services offered, gives you a 55-mile (89 km) circular tour of the island starting and ending in Brodick. Contact *Stagecoach: Western Scottish* (tel 01770-302000).

Royal Mail (tel 01246-546329; www.royalmail.co.uk) operates a four-and-eight-seater **Postbus** from Brodick on a circular route around the island, with at least eight stops, Monday to Saturday. Check the route, departure times, and fares with any of the island post offices.

Vehicle Rental

Arran Transport: The Pier, Brodick (tel 01770-302121; fax 01770-302123).
Blackwaterfoot Garage: tel 01770-860277; fax 01770-860258.
Glencoy Garage Auchrannie Road, Brodick (tel 01770-302224; fax 01770-302012).
Whiting Bay Garage: Shore Road, Whiting Bay (tel 01770-700345; fax 01770-820286).

Cycle Hire

Balmichael Visitor Centre: tel/fax 01770-860430. Near Shiskine, on 'The String' road, has guided cycle tours and quad bikes.
Brodick Boat and Cycle Hire: tel/fax 01770-302868. On Brodick beach, cycles delivered and collected.
Brodick Cycles: tel/fax 01770-302460. Opposite village hall.
Mini Golf Cycle Hire: Brodick (tel 01770-302272; fax 01770-302903; e-mail admin@biIslands.co.uk). Close to the pier. Cycles delivered and collected.

Tours

AC Hendry: tel 01770-302274, Private hire, half-day, full day and evening tours. Golfers and climbers catered for. Transport to and from ferries.

ACCOMMODATION

Hotels

Auchrannie Country House Hotel: tel 01770-302234; fax 01770- 302812; e-mail info@auchrannie.co.uk; www.auchrannie.co.uk. Sumptuous four-star hotel, one mile (1.6 km) north of the Brodick ferry terminal. Extensive leisure club has pool, sauna/steam, gym, aromatherapy and reflexology. Open all year, B&B from £61. Assisted wheelchair access. Award-winning garden restaurant (no smoking) offers formal dining with a table d'hôte menu offering a good range of local Scottish meat and fish dishes, and daily vegetarian special. *Brambles Café Bar* (smoking area) is an informal venue for snacks and meals. Taste of Scotland.

Glenartney Hotel: tel 01770-302220; fax 01770-302452; e-mail glenart@ dalriada.co.uk. Two-star, all rooms en suite. Open March to December, from £28.

Kilmichael Country House Hotel: Glen Coy, near Brodick (tel 01770-302219; fax 01770-302068; e-mail enquiries@kilmichael.com; www.kilmichael.com). Five-star, one single, seven double rooms. Open from April to October, facilities for disabled, no smoking in dining-room and bedrooms, B&B from £60. Menus with French and Italian influences. Taste of Scotland.

Guest Houses

Blackrock Guest House: Corrie (tel 01770-810282). Two-star, en suite accommodation. Open February to November, from £18.

Carrick Lodge: Mrs Thompson (tel/fax 01770-302550). Three-star, Victorian sandstone manse in own grounds, panoramic views. Ample parking. Open February to November, from £21.

Dunvegan House: Shore Road (tel/fax 01770-302811). Four-star, on the shore of Brodick Bay, en suite accommodation. Open all year, from £29.

The Invercloy: tel 01770-302225; fax 01770-302495; e-mail invercloyhotel@ sol.co.uk. Four-star, open March to October, from £29.

Tigh-na-Mara: The Seafront (tel 01770-302538; fax 01770-302546; e-mail arran.tighnamara@btinternet.com). Two-star, built in 1897, five minutes' from the ferry terminal. Open all year, from £18.

B&B

Alma House: Alma Road (tel 01770-302628). Two-star, within walking distance of ferry terminal. Open April to October, from £17.

Belvedere Guest House: Alma Road (tel 01770-302397; fax 01770-302088; e-mail belvedere@vision-unlimited.co.uk). Three-star, open all year, from £18.

Connemara: Knowe Road (tel 01770-302488). Two-star, overlooks golf course. Open all year, from £16.

Crovie: Corriegills (tel 01770-302193). One mile (1.6 km) from town. Open April to October, from £16.

Self-Catering

Cir Mhor Cottage: Glen Rosa (tel 01770-302274). Three-star, sleeps two. Open all year, from £145 a week.

Gran's Cottage: Glen Rosa Farm (tel/fax 01770-302380). Five-star, period 17th century cottage, sleeps four. Two miles (3 km) from the ferry terminal. Open all year, from £200-£450 a week.

Middle Cottage: Chelan, Whitefarland (tel 01770-302564; fax 01770-850258). Three-star, sleeps 4-6. Open all year, from £200 to £260 a week.

Camping: *Glen Rosa Farm* (tel/fax 01770-302380; e-mail campbellseaton@ hotmail.com). Open all year, from £5 a night.

North: Hotels

Butt Lodge Country House Hotel: Lochranza (tel 01770-830240; fax 01770-830211; e-mail butt.lodge@virgin.net; www.buttlodge.co.uk). Four-star, overlooking golf course. Open all year, from £28.

Lochranza Hotel: tel/fax 01770-830223; e-mail hotel@lochranza.co.uk. Three-star, overlooks Lochranza Bay harbour. Open all year, from £20.

North: Guest Houses

Apple Lodge: Lochranza (tel/fax 01770-830229; e-mail applelodge@easicom.com). Four-star, Edwardian country house. Open all year except Christmas week, B&B from £30, no smoking in dining-room and bedrooms. High quality home cooking, vegetarians welcome. Taste of Scotland.

North: Self-Catering

Ornsay: Lochranza (tel 01770-830304). Three-star, sleeps two. Open April to October, from £160 to £180 a week.

Primrose Cottage: Lochranza (tel 01770-830636). Three-star, sleeps seven. Open March to January, from £375 a week.

North: Hostel

Lochranza Youth Hostel: tel 01770-830631. Two-star. Hostel reception opens at 5pm. Access until 11.45pm. Open March to October. 68 beds, two rooms with four beds, eight rooms with 5-8 beds, one room with 9+ beds, family rooms (aged 5+), laundry, hostel store, shop nearby, bus nearby, close to ferry to Claonaig, Brodick ferry 14 miles (23 km). Well placed for walkers and climbers.

North: Camping

Lochranza Golf Caravan and Camping Site: tel 01770-830273; fax 01770-830600; e-mail sitc@lochgolf.demon.co.uk. Four-star, own golf course. Open April to October, from £6.

South: Hotels

Argentine House Hotel: Whiting Bay, KA27 8PZ (tel 01770-700662; fax 01770-700693; e-mail info@argentinearran.co.uk; www.argentinearran.co.uk). Three-star, 8 miles (13 km) south of ferry terminal, on the seafront. Open March to mid-January, B&B from £23, no smoking in dining-room. Scottish produce with continental touch, vegetarians welcome. Taste of Scotland.

Blackwaterfoot Hotel: Blackwaterfoot, KA27 8EU (tel 01770-860202). Two-star, Victorian building, 10 bedrooms. Open March to December, from £30.

Breadalbane Hotel: Kildonan (tel/fax 01770-820284). Rooms en suite, dining-room and south-facing sun lounge with panoramic views. Reputation for good home cooking. Open all year, from £20.

Burlington Hotel: Shore Road, Whiting Bay, KA27 8PZ (tel 01770-700255; fax 01770-700232; e-mail burlhotel@aol.com). Three-star, family-owned, views to Holy Isle. Open Easter to October, from £26.

Kinloch Hotel: Blackwaterfoot, KA27 8ET (tel 01770-860444; fax 01770-860447; e-mail kinloch@cqm.co.uk). Three-star, 44 rooms. Heated indoor swimming pool, sauna, fitness room, and snooker room. Open all year, from £35.

The Lagg Inn: tel 01770-870255. 14 en-suite bedrooms, lounge and public bar. Bar meals served midday to 2.30pm and 6pm to 8.30pm. *Burnside Restaurant*, reservations only. Sunday lunch carvery.

South: Guest Houses

The Lilybank: Lamlash, KA27 8LS (tel 01770-600230; e-mail carol.berry@virgin.net). Four-star, on the shores of Lamlash Bay overlooking Holy Isle, en suite bedrooms. Open March to October, from £25.

Marine House: Lamlash, KA27 8JZ (tel/fax 01770-600298). Three-star, views over Lamlash Bay, en suite rooms. Open March to October, from £25.

South: B&B
The Greannan: Blackwaterfoot (tel/fax 01770-860200). Three-star, views over Shiskine valley. Open March to December, from £20.

Morven House: Blackwaterfoot (tel 01770-860254). One-star. Open all year, from £17.

The Shore: Millhill, Lamlash (tel/fax 01770-600764). Four-star, Swedish designed home on the beachfront. Open all year, from £21.

Westfield: Lamlash (tel 01770-600428). Two-star, sandstone house near the beach. Open all year, from £15.

South: Self-Catering
Alba: Lamlash (tel/fax 01770-600307). Three-star, sleeps four. Open all year, from £200 to £360.

Braeside: Swallowbrae, Torbeg, Blackwaterfoot (tel 01770-860219). Three-star, sleeps four. Open all year, from £150 to £225 a week.

Carraigh Dhubh: Whiting Bay (tel/fax 01770-700563). Three-star, sleeps 4-7. Open all year, from £220 to £320 a week.

The Smiddy: Norwood, Smiddy Brae, Whiting Bay (tel 01770-700536). Four-star, sleeps four. Open all year, from £280 to £400 a week.

South: Hostels
Burncliffe: Shiskine, KA27 8HD (tel 01770-860245). Independent hostel.

Kildonan School Houses, situated in the village of Kildonan at the southern end of Arran, are three-star properties open all year round for weekly and weekend breaks (tel 01436-820956; fax 01436-821770). Egmond Estates, Egmond, Torwoodhill Road, Rhu, Helensburgh, G84 8LE, or Arran Holiday Properties, Invercloy House, Brodick, KA27 8AJ (tel 01770-302303/2310; fax 01770-302713; e-mail arran.estateagents@virgin.net; www.arransites.co.uk/ahp). Views of Pladda, Ailsa Craig, Mull of Kintyre, and Ireland.

Whiting Bay Youth Hostel: Shore Road, Whiting Bay, KA27 8QW (tel 01770-700339). Two-star. Hostel reception opens 5pm. Access until 11.45pm. Open March to October. 48 beds, five rooms with 4 beds, four rooms with 5-8 beds, family rooms (aged 5+). Shop and bus nearby, Brodick ferry 8 miles (13 km).

South: Camping
Breadalbane Caravan and Camping Site: Breadalbane Lodge Park, Kildonan (tel 01770-820210). Views over Clyde Estuary, from £3.50 a person a night.

Middleton Caravan and Camping Park: Lamlash, PA27 8NQ (tel 01770-600251/255). Three-star, on seven acres (3 ha). Open April to October, £8 a night.

Seal Shore Camping and Touring Site: Kildonan (tel/fax 01770-820320). Take-away food, shop within two miles (3 km). Some disabled facilities. Open all year, from £8.50 a night.

EATING AND DRINKING
Arran is a bountiful island and most places emphasize their use of fresh seasonal produce. In particular, a lowly staple takes pride of place here – the potato. Arran's 30 varieties are known worldwide, particularly the descendent Maris Piper, but look for the renowned Arran Victory spuds for a real taste treat.

Brodick
Brodick Bar: Alma Road (tel 01770-302169). Has good fresh fish, especially scallops, roast monkfish and sea bass. Mouth-watering daily blackboard menu. Expect to pay £8-£14 for a meal. Open all year, Monday to Saturday lunch from midday to 2.30pm. At night Monday to Thursday 5.30pm to 9.30pm, Friday and

Saturday 5.30pm to10pm.

Brodick Castle Restaurant: tel 01770-302202; fax 01770-302312; e-mail Brodickcastle@nts.org.uk. Large self-service restaurant in the old servants' hall, home cooking and baking. Taste of Scotland. Open 1 April to 31 October, from 11am to 5pm, and winter weekends until 31 December. Licensed, vegetarians welcome, facilities for disabled, no smoking throughout.

Café Rosaburn, enter through Arran Heritage Museum in Rosaburn (tel 01770-302636). There are tables on a lawn stretching down to the river and a range dishes prepared fresh daily. Try the delectable carrot cake.

Creelers of Arran: Home Farm (tel/fax 01770-302810). Seafood restaurant, smokery and fish shop. Seafood dominates the blackboard, daily changing menu in informal bistro-style restaurant. Expect to pay £11-15 for a main course. Open Easter to September for lunch from midday to 2.30pm, dinner 6pm to 9pm. Closed Monday, except Bank Holidays.

The Wineport: Cladach (tel 01770-302977). Has fresh, seasonal produce. Blackboard menu changes daily. Expect to pay £5-7 for main courses. Open Wednesday to Sunday from midday to 3pm and 6pm to 9pm. Closed Tuesday.

North

Harold's Restaurant, Lochranza Distillery (tel 01770-830264; fax 01770-830364; e-mail visitorcentre@arranwhisky.com; www.arranwhisky.com). This is one of the island's leading dining establishments. Cuisine has gained Taste of Scotland accolades. Open daily April to October (with reduced winter hours), closed Monday evening. Vegetarians welcome, facilities for disabled, smoking area in restaurant. Open 10am with a daytime tea and coffee snack menu which runs throughout the day until 5pm. Lunchtime bistro menu midday to 2.30pm. Booking is advised for dinner.

Lochranza Pier Tearoom and Restaurant: tel/fax 01770-830217. This is a self-service restaurant and also the island's only internet café. Daytime blackboard menu with a range of bistro-type dishes. The menu changes for dinner. Open Easter to mid-October.

South

Carraig Mhor Restaurant: Lamlash (tel 01770-600453). £23 fixed price for three courses, £18.50 for two courses. Reputation for fine cuisine with an Austrian richness. Booking is advised. Open all year, except from the first Sunday after New Year to mid-February. Dinner from 7pm to 9.30pm. Closed Sunday and Monday but open Sunday on Bank Holidays.

The Lagg Inn: tel 01770-870255. At Lagg, near Kilmory, serves pub grub during the week, grill night on Friday at 7pm, and a full menu restaurant at the weekend.

Machrie Bay Golf Course Tearoom: tel 01770-840213. Homebakes which see pilgrimages from the other end of the island for their meringues with lemon curd and fresh cream. A useful pit-stop for refreshments on the quieter side of the island, frequented by golfers and cyclists. Snack blackboard menu. Open April to mid-October.

The Pantry: Shore Road, Whiting Bay (tel 01770-700349). The first island venue offering a wide variety of coffee styles, from cappuccino to espresso. Freshly roasted coffee from the company's South American arabica and other blends. There's a carvery on Friday and Saturday 6pm to 9pm and on Sunday midday to 4pm. Open all year, Monday to Saturday 10.30am to 9pm, Sunday midday to 4pm.

The *Isle of Arran Taste Trail* booklet, available from the Tourist Information Centre for £1, will point you in the direction of other eateries.

DRINKING
Arran Brewery Co Ltd: Cladach Visitor Centre, Brodick (tel 01770-302353; fax 01770-302653; e-mail info@arranbrewery.co.uk; www.arranbrewery.co.uk). Produces three ales at its hi-tech micro brewery, *Arran Light,* a delicate, aromatic brew; *Arran Dark,* a stronger and more bitter brew; and *Arran Blond,* a pale golden, zesty brew. Methods are traditional and no artificial additives are used. Visitor Centre open Monday to Saturday from 9.30am to 5pm, Sunday from midday to 5pm. Admission £2.

Isle of Arran Distillers: at Lochranza (tel 01770-830264; fax 01770-830364; e-mail arran.distillers@btinternet.com; www.arranwhisky.com). Traditional distilling in beaten copper stills and Oregon spruce fermenting mash tubs. It started production of a single malt whisky in 1995 and its first bottling began in late 1999. Range includes Arran Single Malt, Lochranza Premium Blend Whisky, and Holy Isle Cream Liqueur. Visitor Centre with a restaurant, tours, exhibition, and gift shop. Open April to October daily, and November to December restricted hours. Admission charge. Restaurant 11am to 5pm, evenings 7pm to 9pm (except Monday).

SPORT AND RECREATION
Walking and Climbing
A variety of peaks and ridges concentrated in a relatively small area make Arran an exciting place for all mountain lovers – the ramblers, scramblers, and rock climbers often lumped together as 'wenders, ascenders, and suspenders'. The area of the **eastern peaks** provides ridge-walking circuits of various lengths, with the great glens of Ross and Sannox effectively splitting them in two. The **hills of the west** provide a ridge traverse that's ideal for a short day out. Although widely separated, the ascent of all the main hills in the two groups can be done in a single day by the keen and fit. Coastal walks in the south of Arran can make a relaxing change from the tops.

Goatfell. Arran's highest peak rises steeply between Brodick Bay and Corrie to a height of 2,866 ft (874 m), not quite a Munro. Goatfell (from the Old Norse *Gast Bheinn*, meaning 'Windy Hill') is every visiting walker's goal summit. Allow a fairly strenuous 3 hours up and 2 hours down. The mountain is in the National Trust for Scotland's Goatfell Nature Reserve and is open all year, with a year-round ranger service (NTS Ranger Centre, Brodick Country Park; tel 01770-302462. Open from 9am to 5pm). Main access points for Goatfell are from Brodick Country Park and from Cladach, on the A841 Brodick-Lochranza road. A slightly less popular alternative route leaves the A841 road near the most southerly houses of Corrie. Most people begin the Goatfell walk from the car park at Cladach, which runs through the woodlands around Brodick Castle. The distance from Cladach to the summit is about 3¹/2 miles (5¹/2 km). The final 650 ft (200 m) is steep and rocky and calls for caution. On a clear day the view from the top is magnificent, stretching from Ireland to Mull. According to the summit indicator, Skiddaw, 105 miles (169 km) away in the English Lake District, can be seen in ideal conditions.

For more information on walks contact Forest Enterprise in Brodick (tel 01770-302218). The Forestry Commission has produced a leaflet *A Guide to the Forest Walks of the Isle of Arran* which lists seven graded walks with a small route map for each. These are available at the Tourist Information Centre for £1.

Climbing
Arran is a close second to Skye, offering some really severe ascents and abseiling. The southern half of the island, barely topping 1,640 ft (500 m) at Ard Bheinn, is of little interest to climbers, but Cìr Mhor (2,621 ft/799 m) and the Rosa Pinnacle offer some testing pitches, as do Caisteal Abhail (2,818 ft/859 m), Beinn Tarsuinn

(2,710 ft/826 m), and Beinn Nuis (2,598 ft/792 m). The A'Chir ridge traverse is recognised as 'for mountaineers only' and regarded as Arran's most delightful climb; Cìr Mhor ('The Great Comb') ranks as one of Scotland's most magnificent peaks. For more detail consult WMM Wallace's *Climbers Guide to Arran* (Scottish Mountaineering Trust).

Stalking Season. Anyone heading for the hills in the northern half of the island – above the B880 road – between August and October should be aware that this is the main deer stalking season. Recorded messages on **Hillphones** will tell you where stalking is taking place and which routes are unlikely to affect stalking, as well as giving a forecast of stalking activity over the next few days. Recorded messages are updated by 8am each day and calls are charged at normal rates. While the stag stalking season ends in October, the hind cull continues until 15 February. There is no stalking on Sunday.

Cycling

The only waymarked cycle route on the island is a 10-mile (16 km) forest track climbing through woodland in the south-east above Lamlash Bay to eventually join the coastal road in the south and returning by way of the quiet narrow road known as 'The Ross'. This makes it a 20-mile (32 km) circuit of 4-5 hours. The route is graded strenuous, with two major climbs: one to the high point of 850 ft (260 m) in the forest then a second to 985 ft (300 m) on the minor road on the way back. For a longer spin, cycle the 55-mile (88 km) coastal circuit of the island. You can split this into two rides using the B880 to form a northern 35-mile (56 km) loop and a southern 33-mile (53 km) circuit. The flattest and quietest section of the coastal road in the north-west is between Machrie and Lochranza. The east coast road north from Brodick to Sannox is also much flatter than the road south to Lamlash and Whiting Bay.

Diving

Johnston's Marine Stores: Old Pier, Lamlash (tel 01770-600333). Has diving
    equipment for sale, air to 3,000 psi (207 bar). Information on wrecks, drop-
    offs, shore dives, and underwater photography.

Fishing

Between them, the island's six freshwater lochs and its rivers contain **brown**, **rainbow**, **golden**, **brook**, and **sea trout**. Rivers are short spate, with good runs of sea trout and occasional **salmon** from mid-July onwards. The salmon, sea trout and brown trout season is generally from 1 May to 31 October, although this varies around the island. There is no Sunday river fishing. The Tourist Information Centre at Brodick pier provides a free information sheet detailing all the main freshwater fishing areas on Arran, with charges. It also issues day and six-day permits for the various waters of the *Arran Angling Association* (Celia Sillars, secretary; tel 01770-302327). Association membership for the season is open to all for £30. Permits are also available from Kilmory Post Office and General Stores; Bay News, Whiting Bay; Jimmy the Barbers, Lamlash; Corrie Golf Club, Sannox; and the Kildonan Hotel. Average fees are between £7.50 a day (£37.50 a week), and £10 a day (£50 a week). Juniors under 16 half price.

Other contacts:
A & C Cameron: Blackwaterfoot Post Office (tel 01770-860220).
Estate Office: Dougarie (tel 01770-840259; fax 01770-840266).
John Knox: Head Bailiff, Riverside Cottage, Machrie (tel 01770-840241).
Machrie Fishing: Secretary, 10 Leys Mill, by Arbroath, Angus (tel 01307-
    466699).
Port-na-Lochan Fishery: Kilpatrick, Blackwaterfoot (tel 01770-860276).

Sea Angling
Big specimen fish include **skate, ray, tope, dogfish, conger, whiting,** and **wrasse.** The Scottish rod and line record **garfish** was caught in Brodick Bay and Lamlash's **Spring Festival** attracts competitive anglers from all over the UK.
Contacts include:

Blackrock Boat Hire: Wee Port, Corrie (Blackrock Guest House, Corrie; tel 01770-810282). Has boat trips, sea angling, sightseeing, 2-4 hours from £10 a person. Rod hire.

Brodick Boat and Cycle Hire: The Beach, Brodick (tel 01770-302868/840255), has fishing dinghies with engine (4 people) available for hire. Fishing rods for hire with boats, tackle for sale, bait available.

Lamlash Boat Hire: Old Pier, Lamlash (tel 01700-600998/349). For mackerel fishing trips, June to September, Monday to Saturday. £10 a person, two-hour trip. Rods provided if required. Booking essential. Also has self-drive 16 ft (5 m) motor boats for sea angling. Daily from 10.30am to 5pm, two-hour minimum hire. Four people maximum per boat. Rods for hire and bait available. Booking is advisable.

Golf
Arran is a golfer's paradise, offering a choice of seven lush courses with varying degrees of difficulty but all with magnificent views.

Brodick Golf Club (tel/fax 01770-302349), parkland and links 18-hole course, par 65, with views of Goatfell. Daily green fee is £25 (£30 for Saturday and Sunday), or £18 (£22 for Saturday and Sunday) for a round at any time. You can use the clubhouse, including the changing rooms and showers. Bar snacks available. Caddy cars, buggies for hire.

Four miles (6 km) to the south is *Lamlash Golf Club* (tel/fax 01770-600296), heathland, par 64, 18-hole course. The views from the 1st green to Holy Island are inspiring.

Continuing south is *Whiting Bay Golf Club* (Golf Course Road; tel 01770-700487), five miles (8 km) north of Kildonan. An average 18-hole parkland, par 63, course with views across the Clyde and to the Ayrshire Hills. Daily green fee for adults is £17.50, or £13.50 for a round at any time. Buggie hire £10 a round. Use of clubhouse, changing rooms and showers. Bar snacks available.

The course at Blackwaterfoot, *Shiskine Golf Club* (Shore Road; tel 01770-860226; fax 01770-860205), an unspoiled 19th century links, is highly rated even though it has only 12 holes. It is a short, tight links course, par 42, with miniscule greens and views over to the Mull of Kintyre. Daily green fee for adults is £18 (£22 Saturday and Sunday), or £13 (£16 Saturday and Sunday) for a round of golf. Use of changing rooms and showers. There is a tearoom but no bar. Booking preferred. Caddy cars, electric buggies for hire.

The tiny nine-hole *Machrie Bay Golf Club* (tel 01770-850232; fax 01770-850247) is on the west side of the island. This simple holiday links, par 66, course is ideal for beginners and juniors, running along the shore and straddling the road with views over Kilbrannen Sound to Kintyre.

Lochranza Golf Course (tel 01770-830273; fax 01770-830600; e-mail golf@lochgolf.demon.co.uk; www.arran.net/lochranza), is known as the 'Augusta of Arran'. It's a friendly nine-hole seaside course with two sets of teeing positions making an effective 18, par 70. Wild red deer stags enjoy the sweet, pesticide-free grass so much they graze on the fairways.

A few miles further on and heading back to Brodick, the road brings you to the *Corrie Golf Club* at Sannox (tel 01770-810223) on hilly heathland. The challenging 9-hole par 65 course is flat for the first and final few yards but in between it climbs towards its magnificent mountain backdrop.

Horse-Riding
Brodick Riding Centre: Gavin Bell, Corriegills (tel/fax 01770-302800). Offers trekking and hacking on quiet cobs, off-road riding. Transport available to and from centre.

Cairnhouse Riding Centre: Dawn Murchie, The Stables, Blackwaterfoot (tel/fax 01770-860466; e-mail cairnhouse@stables70.freeserve.co.uk). Caters for novices to experienced riders on horse or pony over farm land, tracks and beaches. Open all year.

North Sannox Pony Trekking Centre: James McKinnon, Sannox (tel 01770-810222). Has one and two-hour treks through the countryside.

Sailing
There's excellent sailing out of Brodick, Lamlash and Lochranza, where public moorings are available. Visiting boats can touch base with the *Arran Yacht Club* (committee member-secretary: tel 01770-600242; or treasurer: tel 01770-600705).

Other Activities
Auchrannie Leisure Club: Brodick (tel 01770-302234, ext 308). Swimming pool, sauna, steam room and solarium. Open daily to non-members, Monday to Sunday 9am to 4.45pm, Monday to Saturday 7.30pm to 9.30pm, Sunday 7.30pm to 8.30pm.

Kinloch Sports Club: Blackwaterfoot (tel 01770-860444). Swimming pool, sauna, solarium and squash. Open to non-members, daily from 10am to 5pm.

You can go paragliding with *Flying Fever* (No 2 Coastguard House, Kildonan; tel 01770-820292), a registered school offering international standards of training. Good flying sites for beginners and experts. A Funday which allows you to try the sport and get your feet off the ground costs £55. A tandem flight with a qualified instructor is £35.

SHOPPING
There's a multitude of interesting shops, galleries, speciality stores, and craft centres, but in particular Arran produces excellent cheese, malt whisky, chocolates, and smoked seafood.

Brodick
On the outskirts of the town is Home Farm Shopping Centre, where you'll find the *Island Cheese Co* (tel/fax 01770-302788) whose board features its own Arran Blue and soft cheeses, such as plain crowdie, crowdie with garlic, fromage frais, créme fraiche, sour cream and goat's milk crotins. Also a range of flavoured cheddars. Most of the milk produced by Arran's 10 diary farms is processed here. Sample the cheese and watch the cheesemaker at work. There's also a range of wines, Scottish ales, pottery, and other gifts. Alongside is the *Arran Aromatics Visitor Centre* (tel 01770-302595; fax 01770-302599; e-mail info@arran-aromatics.co.uk; www.arran-aromatics.co.uk). Watch toiletries and candles being made and shop in the factory outlet. Open all year, November to Easter, Monday to Saturday from 9.30am to 5.30pm, Sunday 10am to 5pm. Winter hours vary.

James's Chocolates at Invercloy, Brodick (tel/fax 01770-302873) is home to the *Arran Chocolate Factory*, where you can see chocolates and fresh cream truffles being made. Open all year, seven days a week from 9.30am to 5pm.

North
Arran Pottery: Thunderguy, Prinmill (tel 01770-850238). Hand-thrown and decorated stoneware.

Castlekirk: Lochranza (tel 01770-830202). Has workshops run by 'Project

Orchil' in traditional crafts, such as spinning, weaving and dyeing.

Corrie Craft and Antiques: Hotel Square, Corrie (tel 01770-810661; fax 01770-810248). Has an ever-changing stock of interesting antiques, collectables and small items of furniture. Open Easter to end October, seven days a week, from 10am to 12.45pm and 2pm to 5.30pm.

Lochranza Studio Gallery: tel 01770-830651. Sells original works of art in a variety of media. Open April to October from midday to 6pm daily, except Tuesday; November to March on Wednesday, Thursday, Friday and Saturday from 11am, or by appointment.

Old Byre Showroom: Auchencar Farm, Machrie (tel/fax 01770-840227). Has a range of hand-knitted Arran sweaters and cardigans, sheepskin and travel rugs, leather and small gifts. Open seven days from 10am to 5pm.

The Whins Craftshop: Lochranza (tel 01770-830650). Home of the Arran stonemen, hand-painted stone characters and animals, decorative candles, and stag-horn products, all handmade. Open all year, seven days a week from 10am to 6pm.

South

Arran Fine Foods: The Old Mill, Lamlash (tel 01770-600606; fax 01770-600225; e-mail enquiries@paterson-arran.com; www.paterson-arran.com). Has a tasty range of island mustards, preserves, marmalades, dips, chutneys and savoury sauces. Open May to September, Monday to Friday from 9am to 5pm, Saturday and Sunday from 10am to 4pm; October to April, Wednesday and Saturday from 10am to 4pm.

Arran Woodwork and Candlemakers: Tigh-an-Air, Lamlash (tel 01770-600917; fax 01770-600474). Craft shop and gallery stocking woodwork, candles, pots, wallhangings, baskets, and stained glass. Candlemakers' workshop open Tuesday, Wednesday and Thursday from 10am to 5pm at Spion Kop, between Lamlash and Whiting Bay (tel/fax 01770-600474).

Crafts of Arran: Village Centre, Whiting Bay (tel/fax 01770-700251). Local Arran crafts and Scottish gifts. Open all year, from November to Easter. Access to craft shop on request.

Balmichael Visitor Centre, near Shiskine (tel/fax 01770-860430). Has craft shops, a working pottery and showroom, selection of handmade crafts, gifts, antiques and tapestry in converted farm buildings and courtyard. Heritage area with working mill wheel. Coffee shop. Facilities for the disabled, free parking. Open April to October, Monday to Saturday 10am to 5pm, Sunday midday to 5pm.

Kilmory Workshop: tel 01770-870310. Handmade woodwork and pottery, turned work, furniture and stoneware pottery. Open all year, Tuesday to Friday 10am to 5.30pm.

Island Porcelain: Kilmory, KA27 8PQ (tel/fax 01770-870360). Specialises in hand-painted birds, seals and dolphins. Gift shop has factory seconds at reduced prices. Open Monday to Friday 9am and 5pm.

Roslyn Gibson: Glenside, Kilmory (tel 01770-870224). Artist and hand-knitter. Paintings and drawings in most media. Knitwear to individual designs, based on traditional knitting-in-the-round. Open by appointment.

Silk and Stained Glass Studio: The Wishing Well, Lagg (tel 01770-870344; e-mail alison.f.bell@btinternet.com). Open studio, gallery. Gift range includes scarves, ties, shirts, waistcoats, cushions, throws, paintings, jewellery, and wall hangings. Silk painting classes held daily from 2pm to 4pm, £20, booking advisable. Open all year, daily from 11am to 4.30pm, except Monday.

Torrylin Creamery: Kilmory (tel 01770-870240). Watch prize-winning cheese being made from the viewing gallery, then taste it at the shop, which has a selection of cheese, ice-cream, honey, and other products. All cheese suitable for vegetarians as no animal rennet is used. Open April to October, Sunday to Friday,

10am to 4pm (closed Saturday); November to March, Monday to Friday, from 10am to 4.30pm.

HELP AND INFORMATION

Tourist Information Centre: The Pier, Brodick (tel 01770-302140; fax 01770-302395; e-mail arran@ayrshire-arran.com). At the ferry pier. Open Monday to Thursday from 9am to 5pm, Friday 9am to 7.30pm, Saturday 10am to 5pm. There are toilets for the disabled at the Tourist Information Centre, and at the *North Ayrshire Council* offices in Lamlash (tel 01770-600338).

Police: tel 01770-302574/573; fax 01770-302673.

Coastguard and Inshore Rescue: In an emergency tel 999.

Mountain Rescue: tel 01770-302625. Or in an emergency tel 999.

There are **doctors** at the Medical Centre in Lamlash (tel 01770-600516); Brodick Health Centre (tel 01770-302175); and Inglewood, Shiskine (tel 01770-860247).

Arran War Memorial Hospital: tel 01770-600777.

Brodick Post Office: tel 01770-302245. Open May to mid-September, Monday to Friday 9am to 5.30pm, Saturday 9am to 12.45pm; mid-September to April, Monday to Friday 9am to 12.45pm and 1.45pm to 5pm, Saturday 9am to 12.45pm.

Blackwaterfoot Post Office: tel 01770-860220.

Forest Enterprise: tel 01770-302218.

Bank of Scotland: Brodick (tel 01770-892000). Open June to September on Monday, Tuesday, Thursday and Friday from 9am to 5pm, Wednesday 10am to 5pm; October to May, Monday, Tuesday and Thursday 9am to 12.40pm and 1.30pm to 5pm, Wednesday 10am to 12.30pm and 1.30pm to 5pm, Friday 9am to 5pm.

Royal Bank of Scotland: Shore Road, Brodick (tel 01770-302222). Open June to September on Monday, Tuesday, Thursday, Friday from 9.15am to 4.45pm, Wednesday 10am to 4.45pm; October to May on Monday, Tuesday, Thursday from 9.15am to 12.30pm and 1.30pm to 4.45pm, Wednesday 10am to 12.30pm and 1.30pm to 4.45pm, Friday 9.15am to 4.45pm. Autoteller available.

Arran Library: Brodick Hall (tel 01770-302835), open Tuesday 10am to 5pm, Thursday 10am to 1pm and 2pm to 7.30pm, Friday 10am to 7.30pm, Saturday 10am to 1pm.

The local newspaper is *The Arran Banner*, published in Brodick every Saturday at 40p. Good for what's on.

Calendar of Events

Arran Folk Festival, week-long festival throughout the island. Concerts, workshops. Contact Nici McLellan in High Corrie (tel 01770-302311/810289; www.netreal.co.uk/arranfolkfest), or Iain or Maggie Frame (tel 01770-302623; e-mail info@arranfolkfestival.org; www.musicscotland.com/arranfolkfest).

Goatfell Race, starts from Ormidale Park, Brodick. Contact Mr C Turbett, Rannoch, Shiskine (tel 01770-860427).

Brodick Castle Victorian Day – beginning of August.

Farmers' Society – first week in August.

Brodick Highland Games – second Saturday in August.

Harvest Home Sunday – end of September.

HOLY ISLAND

The 625-acre (253 ha) island, once an early Christian monastic settlement, has been owned since 1992 by the Buddhist group **Kagya Samye Ling Monastery** (Eskdalemuir, Langholm, Dumfriesshire DG13 0QL; tel 01387-373232; fax 01387-373223; e-mail office@holyisland.org; www.holyisland.org) which is implementing a 'Holy Island Project' designed to make the island a sanctuary by returning it to its early spirituality and restoring its degraded environment. The island has been recognised as a UK Sacred Site by the Alliance for Religions and Conservation.

As well as planting 30,000 indigenous trees, the Buddhist community has renovated lighthouse cottages to provide accommodation for visitors on retreat. Volunteers have also renovated a farmhouse and this is now a guest house. The community welcomes visitors and if you'd like to stay on the island telephone 0793-208 6481 between midday and 1pm or 6pm to 7pm. You will be met at the north jetty and told about the island's geography, history, wildlife and plans for the future. The best time to visit is during the late spring and summer months. Wildlife includes **Eriskay ponies**, **Soay sheep**, **feral goats**, and other small animals. There are also many species of birds, including nesting **peregrine falcons**, **buzzards**, **ravens**, **gulls**, **stonechats**, **whinchat**, and **wheatear**. Like Arran, the island is home to a few **adders**, or vipers.

In the 6th century the Irish monk St Mo Las, a disciple of St Columba, lived in a cave on Holy Island until he died at the age of 129. The **Saint's Cave** is a deep water-worn recess in the sandstone rock, about 80 ft (24 m) above sea level on the west coast. There are some early Christian and runic Norse inscriptions carved in the cave wall, the latter probably dating from 1263 when King Haakon's Viking fleet anchored in the bay at the time of the Battle of Largs. Below the cave is **St Mo Las's Well**, whose water was once reputed to cure disease. The well is also known as the **Saint's Bath**. The **Saint's Chair**, or **Judgment Stone**, is a large almost circular chunk of sandstone with a number of seats cut into its sides. From high point Mullach Mór (1,030 ft/314 m) there's a fine view of Arran's northern peaks.

HOLY ISLE, LAMLASH BAY, ARRAN.

Getting There

Holy Isle Ferry (Lamlash Boat Hire, Old Pier, Tom Sheldon; tel 01770-600998, or Harold Kyte; tel 01770-600349) runs to the island from Lamlash Bay pier, May to September, on the hour from 10am, with the last trip at 4.45pm. It leaves the Holy Island jetty at a quarter past the hour from 10.15am, with the last departure at 5pm. There is a reduced service from Easter to end-April and September to October. The return fare is £7 for adults and £4 for children under 12. Departure times for the 10-minute crossing are subject to wind and tide.

Bute

Bute is 15 miles long and five miles across at its widest point (24 km x 8 km) and lies to the south of the Cowal Peninsula, separated from it by the long narrow Kyles of Bute and from the mainland ferry port of Wemyss Bay seven miles (11 km) away by the broad Firth of Clyde. Across the Sound of Bute six miles (10 km) to the south is the larger island of Arran; less than a mile off the west coast is the islet of Inchmarnock. The two Cumbraes lie off to the east.

Topographically, Bute falls neatly on either side of the Highland Boundary Fault, which gives it craggy hills divided by deep Glen More in its northern half and gentler farmlands in the south edged in places by precipitous cliffs. Windy Hill at 912 ft (278 m) is the island's highest point. In the south, conical St Blane's Hill rises to less than half this height. The main lochs also lie in the south – Fad, Ascog, Quien, Dhu, and Greenan. Most of Bute's 30,000 acres (12,200 ha) are owned by the Marquess of Bute, who is heir to one of the wealthiest land estates in Britain. Rothesay is the island's capital – and only – town, where most of Bute's 7,000 people live. During the May to September season the population can swell to around 100,000.

Geology. The rich agricultural land of the south is the result of its underlying Old Red Sandstone, with marked intrusions of basalt. The uplands of the north are largely igneous rock. Much of Bute's shoreline is rocky with ridges and pinnacles chiselled by the sea.

EXPLORING

In Bute's heyday steamers sailed 'doon the watter' from Glasgow with holidaymakers and day trippers. The ships are long gone but in the summer months you might still see the old *Waverley*, the last sea-going paddle-steamer in the world, reliving the past among Caledonian MacBrayne's ferries and Clyde Marine's vessels.

ROTHESAY

The historic town of Rothesay has been a royal burgh since 1400, with the eldest son of each Scottish king dubbed Duke of Rothesay, today the premier Scottish title held by Charles, Prince of Wales. The town overlooks a small but busy harbour and marina on a lovely bay and still has a whiff of the Victorian and Edwardian eras that brought it fame as the unchallenged holiday resort of the Clyde. The imposing granite and sandstone villas along the shore were once the homes of wealthy 19th century Glasgow merchants and these examples of late Victorian architecture, embellished with ornate ironwork, are now protected by the largest Scottish conservation area designation outside of Glasgow, along with Rothesay's recently restored glass and cast iron Art Nouveau-style **Winter Garden**, which dominates the shoreline among the gardens of the esplanade. The wrought iron arch next to the Winter Garden marks the **Highland Boundary Fault.** Walk through and you move from Highlands to Lowlands in a step.

You'll find locals are more likely to point out the town's truly **palatial toilets,** opened on the pier in 1899, than Rothesay's historically important mediaeval castle – but then the toilets and their splendid Victorian ceramic tiling, marble and enamel alcoves, and glass-sided cisterns have featured in a TV series about the nation's architectural gems.

Although it's in the middle of town, it's easy to miss **Rothesay Castle** (tel 01700-502691) as the stately ruin is hidden in a maze of small streets. It was originally built around 1098 in the days when Vikings still ruled the Western Isles. Although substantial restoration work has been carried out you can still see where

Vikings breached the east wall during their 1230 siege. It is now an outstanding example of a 13th century castle, with massive sandstone curtain walls fortified by protecting drum towers. The walls enclose a circular courtyard, a plan unique in Scotland. Inside is the ruined 14th century **Chapel of St Michael** and around the castle is a deep moat. You can explore the dungeons, thick outer walls and the restored grand hall. Open all year, April to September from 9.30am to 6.30pm; March to October 9.30am to 4.30pm. Closed Thursday afternoon, Friday and Sunday in winter. Admission for adults is £2, senior citizens £1.50, children 75p. Behind the castle is **Bute Museum** (Stuart Street; tel 01700-505067) which affords a glimpse of bygone island life, and highlights the Clyde's famous steamers. Bute has been inhabited for 6,000 years and is rich in antiquities and exhibits from several excavations can be seen in the museum. One archaeological treasure is a Bronze Age jet necklace found in 1953 on Inchmarnock. There's also a fine display of Bute's Christian sculpture. The **Bute Natural History Society** is part of the museum. Open April to September, Monday to Saturday 10.30am to 4.30pm, Sunday 2.30pm to 4.30pm; October to March, Tuesday to Saturday 2.30pm to 4.30pm. Adults £1.20, senior citizens 70p, children 40p.

The ruined chancel of ancient **St Mary's Chapel** stands in the churchyard of the **High Kirk**, at the top of High Street near **Kirk Dam**, the portion of Loch Fad which is Rothesay's reservoir. Once the mediaeval parish church of Rothesay, it served as Cathedral of the Isles in the 17th century. Among the tombs is one bearing a carving of a 14th century knight and another containing the remains of Napoleon's niece, Stephanie Hortense Bonaparte, wife of a Sheriff of Lancaster. The mausoleum of the Marquesses of Bute also stands in the churchyard. On the western shore of **Loch Fad** ('Big Lake') is **Kean's Cottage**, occupied in 1824 by Edmund Kean (1789-1833), the famous English actor. The road along the loch's eastern shore passes smaller **Loch Quien** and is an alternative route to Kilchattan Bay. The reedy islets off the west and south banks of Loch Quien conceal two ancient fortified sites.

North

The resort of **Port Bannatyne**, on Kames Bay, is almost part of Rothesay. At the head of the bay is 14th century battlemented **Kames Castle**, and in the grounds is the tower house of Wester Kames, built in the 17th century, and rebuilt in 1900. These are not open to the public. At the turn of the century the village was a busy port of call for Clyde puffers and passenger ships. In 1943 midget submarines exercised in the bay before setting off to attack the German battleship *Tirpitz* in Norway. Today the port is popular with yachts, golfers, and watersports enthusiasts. You'll get a good view of Arran from the top of **Kames Hill** (883 ft/269 m), which is an outlier of Bute's highest point, **Windy Hill**.

The road westwards across the narrow waist of Bute leads to the broad sandy expanse of **Ettrick Bay**, Bute's most accessible beach and relatively safe for confident swimmers. The road narrows and continues along the west coast as far as Kilmichael, site of the ancient ruins of the **Chapel of St Michael**. There are several chambered cairns in the vicinity. The east coast road from Kames Bay along the Kyles of Bute ends at the little ferry point of Rhubodach. Cliffs along the bare northern tip of the island mean that the two stone slabs of the **Maids of Bute** and intriguingly named **Buttock Point** can be appreciated only from the sea.

South

The mild climate encourages fine gardens and plant displays. **Ardencraig Garden** (High Craigmore, Rothesay; tel 01700-504644) has been developed as a walled propagation, education and show garden, with new plant cultivars introduced annually. The extensive fuchsia and bedding displays contain many of

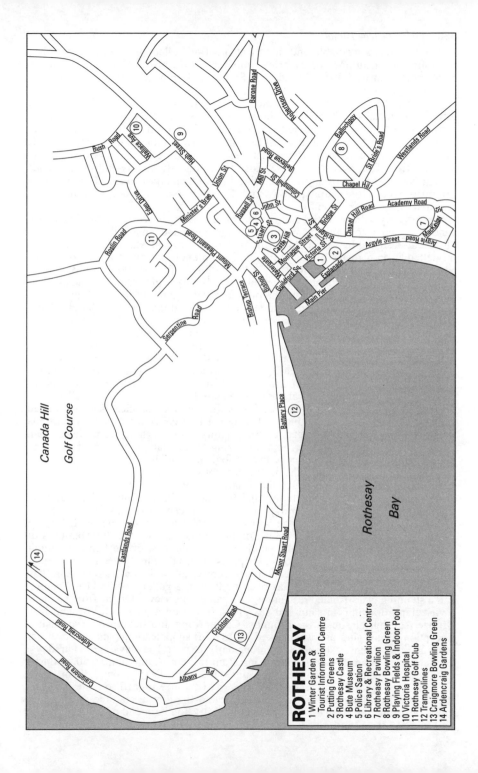

ROTHESAY

1 Winter Garden &
  Tourist Information Centre
2 Putting Greens
3 Rothesay Castle
4 Bute Museum
5 Police Station
6 Library & Recreational Centre
7 Rotheasy Pavilion
8 Rothesay Bowling Green
9 Playing Fields & Indoor Pool
10 Victoria Hospital
11 Rothesay Golf Club
12 Trampolines
13 Craigmore Bowling Green
14 Ardencraig Gardens

Canada Hill

Golf Course

Rothesay
Bay

Barone Road
Robertson Drive
Ballochgoy
Bush Road
Wallace Ave
Hall Street
Ballyvane Road
Westlands Road
St Bride's Road
Chapel Hill
Chapel Hill Road
Academy Road
Union St.
Mill St.
Columshill St.
Eden Drive
Minister's Brae
Russell St.
John St.
Bridge St.
Bridgend St.
Argyle Street
Mackinlay St.
Argyle Road
Roslin Road
Mount Pleasant Road
Stuart St.
Castle Hill
Montague Street
Victoria St.
Esplanade
Serpentine Road
Bishop Terrace
Bishop St.
Wyngate
Guildford Sq.
Main Pier
Battery Place
Eastlands Road
Mount Stuart Road
Craigmore Road
Ardbeg Road
Crichton Road
Albany Rd

the best cultivars available and there's also a fine collection of cacti. There is a tearoom and a number of aviaries housing exotic birds. Open 1 May to 30 September 9am to 4.30pm Monday to Friday and 1pm to 4.30pm Saturday and Sunday. Admission is free.

Three miles (5 km) south of Rothesay ferry terminal is **Ascog Hall Fernery and Garden** (tel 01700-504555), built around 1870 and restored in 1997. It's a remarkable Victorian fernery, the only one of its kind in Scotland, with an impressive collection of sub-tropical fern species from all over the world. In pride of place is a huge *Todea barbara* that's estimated to be around 1,000 years old. The bus from Rothesay to Mount Stuart runs frequently all day and stops outside Ascog Hall. No cars are allowed up the drive. Open April to mid-October from 10am to 5pm, closed on Monday and Tuesday. No dogs. Admission £2.50, children under supervision free.

Kerrycroy village at the end of the shore road south of Rothesay has a fine sandy bay and a stone pier, as well as a village green and a maypole. It was built in 1802 and designed by Maria North, the wife of the second Marquess of Bute, who modelled it on a rustic English village. The splendid avenue leading to **Mount Stuart House and Gardens** (tel 01700-503877; fax 01700-505313; e-mail contactus@mountstuart.com; www.mountstuart.com) begins here. The house was built in 1877 after fire destroyed the original family home of the 3rd Marquess of Bute, who created the wonderful gardens and parkland that surround Mount Stuart today. The 300-plus acres (121 ha) contain a wide variety of horticultural gems. To the south of the house lies the secluded eight acre (3 ha) 'Wee Garden', created in 1823 and containing mainly southern hemisphere plants and a rock garden with water feature designed by Thomas Mawson in 1893. The new Kitchen Garden, the plant collection in the octagonal Glass Pavilion, and the young conifers in the extended Victorian Pinetum are new additions, part of an ongoing plant conservation programme for rare and endangered species. The house reflects the diverse interests of the 3rd Marquess. The profusion of astrological designs, stained glass and marble is breathtaking, and there's a fine collection of family portraits illustrating several hundred years of Bute family history. There are no fewer than three libraries and a horoscope room for gazing at real stars, with painted panels of planets below a ceiling decorated with astrological symbols.

The 3rd Marquess created the most sumptuous Victorian interiors in Britain and even the outside drainpipes carry the Stuart coat of arms and are decorated with castles and lions. Mount Stuart was the first house in Scotland to have electric lighting (1883), a telephone (1887), and a modern central heating system. It was also the first private home in the world with a heated swimming pool. Former Formula One racing car driver John Colum Crichton-Stuart, the 7th Marquess of Bute, opened Mount Stuart to the public in 1995, the first of the family to admit paying visitors to his ancestral home. He plans to turn the family seat into a money-spinning corporate leisure and conference centre, as well as attracting more day visitors. A new visitors' centre has been built with a gallery, audio-visual centre, and a stunning glass-fronted restaurant with panoramic views. On the front lawns is a vast 'land drawing' in sand and sea grass, based on a jet necklace found in a Bronze Age burial site in the grounds. Car parking and ticket office at Visitor Reception. Picnic sites and waymarked walks. Gift shop, tearoom, and audio-visual presentation. Open Easter to September daily except Tuesdays and Thursdays. Gardens from 10am to 6pm, house from 11am to 5pm. Admission £6.50, children £2.50, students and senior citizens £5. Guided tours cost £2 (last tour 3.30pm).

Just over a mile (1.6 km) down the road from Kingarth on the A844 is sheltered **Kilchattan Bay** where you can spend the day in solitude on the pink sands or follow the Kingarth trail around the hilly southern end of the island. The trail takes in the **Standing Stones of Lubay**, the **Iron Age fort** at Dunagoil Bay, and the ruined **Chapel of St Blane**, not far from Garroch Head and **St Blane's Hill**, which rises steeply to 404 ft (123 m) above the southern tip of the island. The 12th century Romanesque chapel is set among the trees in a quiet valley near Plan Farm. The names of three 8th century abbots and two 17th century bishops are recorded among the tombs, which lie in a graveyard that is an early example of sex discrimination, a men-only burial ground. Women were interred in a separate lower graveyard. The ring of boulders in the enclosure is known as the **Devil's Cauldron**. No one knows why. The west coast road skirts the sands of Scalpsie Bay, where there's a **seal viewing point**, and secluded St Ninian's Bay, with its ruined chapel dedicated to the 6th century Irish saint. Twin monoliths stand on the moor, looking out to the island of Inchmarnock.

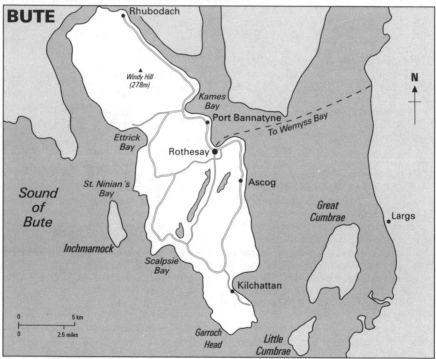

FLORA AND FAUNA

Colonies of **seals** sport around Scalpsie Bay, there are large populations of **moles** and **hedgehogs**, and a **long-tailed field-mouse** is unique to the island, but Bute is more rewarding for twitchers with around 150 recorded species of birds. Summer sees such migrants as **wheatear, wood-warbler, redstart** and **blackcap**. Six species of **hawk** rest on the island regularly and the coastline is home to **oystercatchers, ringed plovers, curlews, redshank, turnstones, dunlin**, and **red-breasted merganser**, plus large numbers of **eider**. The biggest gatherings can be seen in the sandy bays of Kilchattan, Scalpsie, St Ninian's and Ettrick.

Two areas have been designated Sites of Special Scientific Interest: the north, with its woodland and open moorland holding steady populations of small birds, as well as raptors such as **sparrowhawk** and **buzzard**, and the cluster of freshwater lochs of the south which attract substantial winter populations of **greylag, barnacle**, and **Greenland geese**, as well as great numbers of **teal** and **goldeneye**

duck. Greenan Loch has an attractive summer show of **water lilies**, and **yellow poppies, sea pink, purple cranesbill**, and **wild geranium** thrive around the island.

GETTING THERE

Caledonian MacBrayne (The Ferry Terminal, Gourock, PA19 1QP, te; 08705-650000; fax 01475-635235, reservations; tel 01475-650100; fax 01475-637607, general enquiries; e-mail reservations@calmac.co.uk; www.calmac.co.uk) operates a car-passenger ferry from Wemyss Bay to Rothesay, and from Colintraive to Rhubodach. The Wemyss Bay ferry leaves every day, every 45 minutes from 7.15am to 6.50pm Monday to Saturday, and from 10.15am to 20.40pm on Sunday, with one early morning sailing at 8.45am. The trip takes 35 minutes. The single adult fare is £3.25, car £13.15, caravan, boat/baggage trailer £13.15, motorcycles £6.60, bicycles £1. The 'Day Saver' ticket costs £34 for a car with up to four occupants available daily from April to October. 'Five-Day Return' and '10-Journey' tickets are available. Contact CalMac at Rothesay (tel 01700-502707) or Wemyss Bay (tel 01475-520521).

A regular 50-minute rail service from Glasgow to Wemyss Bay connects with Rothesay ferry. Contact *National Rail Enquiries* (tel 08457-484950; www.nationalrail.co.uk), or CalMac.

The car-passenger ferry from Colintraive leaves for Rhubodach (9 miles/15 km from Rothesay) every half hour from 5.30am to 7.55pm, Monday to Saturday, and Sunday from 9am to 7.55pm. The trip takes a couple of minutes. The single adult fare is £1, car £6.60, caravan, boat/baggage trailer £6.60, motorcycles £3.30, bicycles free. A 'Day Saver' ticket for a car and up to four occupants costs £14.60 and is available from April to October. Contact CalMac at Colintraive (tel 01700-841235).

CalMac also has cruises to Rothesay, May to September, from Gourock, every Tuesday, £12; Largs, every Monday, Wednesday, Friday and Sunday, £10; and Dunoon, every Tuesday, £10.

Bute Berthing Company: 15 Watergate, Rothesay, PA20 9AB (tel 01700-500630; fax 01700-503389) fixes up visiting boats with pontoons, water, and electricity. Contact Rothesay Harbour on VHF Channel 12, 16, or 1. Open 24 hours all year round.

Clyde Marine Charters: Princess Pier, Greenock, PA16 8AW (tel 01475-721281) offers a variety of cruises from June to August.

Waverley Excursions: Waverley Terminal, 36 Anderston Quay, Glasgow G3 8HA (tel 0141-221 8152; fax 0141-248 2150) operates cruises to Rothesay on one of the world's last paddle steamers, the *Waverley*. These sail from Anderston Quay, Glasgow, and Custom House Quay, Greenock, from June to September. Check timetables and fares with the operator.

GETTING AROUND

Maps and Guides

Free maps from Tourist Information Centre, but best is still the one you pay for, Ordnance Survey 1:50 000 Sheet 63. TIC also has a free but flimsy *Bute, the Unexplored Isle* visitor guide, but it's short on info, heavy on advertisements. Interesting for history buffs is Christine Wiener's *Arran & Bute* (S Forsyth, London 1996, 164 pages, £10.50).

By Road

One of the best ways to enjoy the scenery of Bute is from one of the open-toppers operated by *Stagecoach Western Buses* (17 High Road, Port Bannatyne; tel 01700-502076). There's a regular daily service from Guildford Square from late May until late September, including a 'Grand Island Tour', with a commentary pointing out local features. SWB runs a bus service throughout the island on behalf of Argyll & Bute Council (tel 01546-604695). Council bus stop signs are blue and white. An area transport guide is available from the Council offices and the Tourist Information Centre. There's also a *Dial-a-Bus* (tel 01546-602869) service. This door-to-door service operates anywhere on Bute on Tuesday from 10.30am to 2.30pm, and Saturday from 10am to 4pm. For more information phone between 10am and 4pm, Monday to Friday.

If you have a vehicle, **parking** everywhere costs 20p for 20 minutes, 60p for up to two hours until 6pm.

Taxis
A&A: tel 01770-502275.
David Gaston: tel 01700-505050.
Radio Taxis: tel 01700-505511.
Sandy Ross Taxis: tel 01700-504224.
Stewart Sweet: tel 01700-504000.
David Zan-Kreyser: tel 01700-504499.

Cycling
Bute Cycle Centre: 24 East Princes Street, Rothesay (tel 01700-502333; e-mail robbcycles@hotmail.com). Has bikes for hire, including pump, repair kit and helmet. Adult bikes from £6 for half-day and £10 full-day. Open April to September, daily from 8am to 8pm.

ACCOMMODATION
Hotels
Ardmory House Hotel: Ardmory Road, Ardbeg, PA20 0PG (tel 01700-502346; fax 01700-505596; e-mail ardmory.house.hotel@dial.pipex.com). Four-star, in grounds overlooking the Clyde. Open all year, from £38. Restaurant bar serves dinners, Sunday lunch and snacks. Open to non-residents.

The Ardyne-St Ebba Hotel: 37-38 Monstuart Road, Rothesay, PA20 9EB (tel 01700-502052; fax 01700-505129; e-mail ardyne.hotel@virgin.net). Three-star, elegant Victorian hotel on the seafront, views across Rothesay Bay, ³/4 mile (1 km) stroll from the main ferry. Open all year, from £25 B&B. Good Scottish fare in the restaurant, which is open to non-residents. Three-course dinner for residents £13.95, non-residents £15.95.

Bayview Hotel: 21-22 Mountstuart Road, Rothesay, PA20 9EB (tel 01700-505411). Three-star, Victorian house hotel with views over Rothesay Bay. Open all year, from £21.

Cannon House Hotel: Battery Place, Rothesay, PA20 9DP (tel 01700-502819; fax 01700-505725). Four-star, Georgian townhouse close to harbour. Licensed restaurant open to non-residents. Sailing available on hotel's private 40 ft (12 m) yacht. Open all year, from £35.

Craigmore Hotel and Leisure Centre: Crichton Road, Rothesay, PA20 9JT (tel/fax 01700-503533). Two-star, family-run, views of Firth of Clyde. Open all year, from £20.

Kingarth Hotel: Kingarth, PA20 9LU (tel/fax 01700-831662), two-star, overlooking the bay, on bus route. Open all year, £20 a person B&B. Cream teas available. Lunch and dinner in garden restaurant.

St Blane's Hotel: Shore Road, Kilchattan Bay, PA20 9NW (tel/fax 01700-831224). Two-star, family-run on water's edge. Meals served in bar or garden. Open all year, from £22.

Guest Houses
Ardbeg Lodge: 23 Marine Place, Ardbeg, PA20 0LF (tel 01700-505448). Two-star,

close to golf course. Open all year, from £23.

The Commodore: 12 Battery Place, Rothesay, PA20 9DP (tel/fax 01700-502178). Three-star, seafront house. Open all year, from £18.

Glendale Guest House: 20 Battery Place, Rothesay, PA20 9DU (tel 01700-502329). Three-star, Victorian house on seafront. Minute's walk from pier and town centre. Home cooking. Open all year, from £16.

Lyndhurst Guest House: 29 Battery Place, Rothesay, PA20 9DU (tel 01700-504799). One-star, overlooking Rothesay Bay, five minutes' walk from the pier. Open all year, from £17.

B&B

Abergwaun: Mrs D Smith, 15 Argyle Place, Rothesay, PA20 0BA (tel 01700-502088). On the sea front, close to the pavilion, overlooking Rothesay Bay. Open all year, from £16.

Avion: Mrs A Smith, 16 Argyle Place, Rothesay, PA20 0BA (tel 01700-505897; e-mail avion@compuserve.com). Two-star, short stroll along the promenade. Open all year, from £17.

Glecknabae Farmhouse: Mr Gimblett, North Bute, PA20 0QX (tel/fax 01700-505655). Four-star, renovated farmhouse. Open all year, from £20. Self-catering cottage available at £150-£325 a week.

New Farm B&B and Restaurant: New Farm, Mount Stuart, PA20 9NA (tel/fax 01700-831646). Seven rooms, five en suite, from £25. Facilities for disabled. Creative cooking and baking. Vegetarians welcome, and you can pick your own dinner veggies.

Waverley: Karen Thompson, 37 Argyle Street, Rothesay, PA20 0AX (tel 01700-502390). One-star, on seafront. Open all year, from £16.

Self-Catering

An interesting option is a Victorian cottage in the 22-acre (9 ha) grounds of *Kames Castle* (Peter and Jennifer Hardy, Port Bannatyne, PA20 0QP; tel 01700-504500; fax 01700-504554; e-mail kames-castle@easynet.co.uk). Three-star, six cottages, 2¹/2 (4 km) miles from Rothesay. Sleep 2-4 and 4-9. Open all year, from £230-£595 a week. A cottage comprising a double bedroom and a room with two singles costs £315-£345 for a week.

Balmory Hall: Tony and Beryle Harrison, Ascog, PA20 9LL (tel/fax 01700-500669; e-mail mail@balmory-hall.com). Country home, three apartments, one cottage. Open all year, from £235-£650 a week. B&B from £50.

East Colmac Farm: Mr Robertson, North Bute, PA20 0QT (tel 01700-502144). Three-star, two apartments in farmhouse on working farm. Open all year, from £180-£250 a week.

Guildford Court: 3 Watergate, Rothesay, PA20 9AB (tel/fax 01700-503770). Two-star, harbourside apartments, opposite ferry. Open all year, from £155 to £345 a week.

Prospect House: Mrs P Shaw, 21 Battery Place, Rothesay, PA20 9DU (tel/fax 01700-503526; e-mail islebute@aol.com). Three-star, luxury apartments, cottage and conservatory, seafront. Open all year, from £189-£376 a week.

Shalunt Farm: Mr and Mrs, PA Mason, North Bute, PA20 0QL (tel 01700-841283). One-star, flat in secluded farmhouse, sleeps 4-6. Open May to October, from £150-£250 a week.

Hostel: *Bute Back Packers* (Esplanade, Rothesay tel 01700-504446). Open all year, from £7 a night.

Camping

Lanerly Garth Park: Serpentine Road, Rothesay, PA20 9EH (tel/fax 01700-

502048). Six self-catering holiday caravans. Open March to October, from £105-£240 a week.

Roseland Caravan Park: Canada Hill, Rothesay, PA20 9GH (tel 01700-504529/505819). Pitches for caravans, tourers, and tents, from £6. Caravans to let, from £140 to £160 a week. Open March to October.

EATING AND DRINKING

The Black Bull: 3 West Princess Street, Rothesay (tel 01700-502366; fax 01700-504466). Bute's oldest pub, opposite Rothesay harbour. Good food. Open all year.

Craigmore Pier Licensed Tearoom and Restaurant: Mount Stuart Road, Rothesay (tel/fax 01700-502867). Fresh home-made snacks and meals. Open all year, daily from 10am to 5pm, 7.30pm to 11.30pm Friday and Saturday.

Fowler's: The Winter Garden, Rothesay (tel/fax 01700-500505). Waterfront restaurant serving freshly prepared food. Open from Easter until October, daily (except Monday evening and Tuesday); winter for lunches daily, except Tuesday, dinners Thursday, Friday and Saturday. Closed in January.

The Kettledrum: 32 East Princes Street, Rothesay (tel 01700-505324). Bistro café, overlooking harbour and pontoons, serving everything from freshly ground coffee to a three-course meal, all day, all home-made. Open all year, from 10.30am to 6.30pm.

La Dolce Vita: 72 Victoria Street, Rothesay (tel 01700-502938). Lounge bar, open all day. Bar snacks served midday to 2.30pm, seven days a week. Open all year, 11am to 1am, seven days a week.

New Farm: Carole Howard, Mount Stuart (tel 01700-831646). Home-baked breads, herbs and vegetables gathered from the kitchen garden. Reservations essential. Open all year for lunches, afternoon teas, and dinners.

For fish and chips try *The New Ferry Fry*, at Brodick Pier (tel 01700-302656), open Monday to Saturday 8.30am to 10pm, Sunday 10am to 10pm.

Drinking

The *Glue Pot Bar* in the 17th century Argyll Arms (Watergate Street, Rothesay; tel 01700-502643), is up from the square, opposite the pier. Music on Friday and Saturday. Open Monday to Saturday 11am to 1am and Sunday 12.30 to 1am. No food, but there's a beer garden.

Golfers Bar: 3 East Princes Street, Rothesay (tel 01700-502095). Friendly town centre pub with live music every Friday and Saturday. Open daily all year, 11am until late.

The Grapes Bar: 70 Montague Street, Rothesay (tel 01700-503803). Open all year, seven days a week from 11am to 1am.

Mac's Bar: 14/18 Castlehill Street, Rothesay (tel 01700-502417). Public house opposite Rothesay Castle. Open all year, Monday to Saturday from 11am to 1am, Sunday 12.30pm to midnight.

The Scottish Mead Company: Mount Stuart Visitor Centre (tel fax 01294-823222; e-mail scotmead@aol.com). Small craft-based operation producing an historic Scottish drink. Three kinds of mead – Bute (apples), Cumbrae (cinnamon), and Oransay (honey), each 10% alcohol by volume. Open late summer, from 11am to 5pm.

SPORT AND RECREATION

Walking

Bute was the first Scottish island to establish its own long distance trail, the West Island Way covering 26 miles (42 km). It begins in the south and winds to the northern end before swinging round again to finish at Port Bannatyne. On the way it traverses some of Bute's more remote areas and guarantees spectacular views across to Ayrshire in the east, and the hills of Arran and Argyll in the west. The trail covers a variety of terrain, suitable for both beginners and more experienced walkers. Coastal walks, particularly in the west, are pleasant excursions. A ranger service, operating from Mount Stuart but covering the whole of the island, is available for advice on this and other walks in and around Rothesay, or contact the Tourist Information Centre (tel 01700-502151).

Cycling

Good surfaced roads run north and south from Rothesay, joined by minor branch roads adding several central and southern loops. Flat coastal roads and light traffic make for enjoyable cycling. If you haven't brought a bike it's easy to hire one (see *Getting Around*). There are pleasurable short runs from Rothesay to Kerrycroy (4 miles/6 km), Ardberg (1¹/2 miles/2.4 km), Ettrick Bay (5 miles/8 km), Kilmichael (7 miles/11 km), and Rhubodach (9 miles/15 km).

Fishing

Bute's brown trout boat or bank fishing season runs from 15 March to 6 October, however *Loch Fad Fishery* (tel 01700-504871) offers fly fishing (boat and bank) for brown and rainbow trout on Bute's largest loch from 1 March to 22 December. There are 30 boats available. The **best rainbow** record catch so far is 19 lb 2 oz (9 kg), and the **best brown** is 7 lb 8 oz (3 kg). Rods for hire, tuition by arrangement. Open during the season from 8am daily. Admission for adults £15, senior citizen £10, children £6.

No matter the time of year you can haul **pike** and **perch** at Loch Ascog, and Greenan Loch is well stocked with **tench, roach** and **carp**. Permits from the *Isle of Bute Angling Club* (Alister McFarlane, secretary/treasurer; tel 01700-504871, daytime; tel 01700-505420, after hours), the *Tourist Information Centre*, or *Bute Angling & Outdoor Centre* (Alan McDougal, Albert Place, Rothesay; tel 01700-503670).

Sea fishing from the rocky shore is popular and productive or by boat from Rothesay pier.

Golf

Rothesay Golf Club (Canada Hill; tel 01700-503554) has a scenic 18-hole course with panoramic views. Full catering and bar service during the season. Open all year, seven days a week. Various green fee options for visitors.

Port Bannatyne Golf Club (Main Road; tel 01700-504544; fax 01700-505267) is a well-maintained hillside, 13-hole course overlooking Kames Bay, Loch Striven and the Cowal Peninsula. This is a par 67, based on 13 plus five holes. Clubhouse facilities. Visitors welcome. Open all year. Green fees from £8.

There's a challenging 9-hole course at **Bute Golf Club** (Kingarth; tel 01700-504369), set by the shore, looking out to Arran.

Sailing

The waters around Bute are said to offer some of the safest and most fascinating sailing in the west of Scotland. There's pontoon berthing at Rothesay pier, right in the middle of town, as well as moorings in three sheltered bays (tel 01700-500630; fax 01700-503389, mobile 077 8736 5104). Charter a yacht or bring your own. Five-day RYA sailing courses for all proficiency levels are available. *Bute Sailing School* (Ray Dalton, Cannon House, Battery Place, Rothesay; tel 01700-502819; fax 01700-505725; e-mail butesail@claranet.co.uk; www.butesail.clara.net) offers shore-based tuition and trips as far as St Kilda. An RYA recognised teaching establishment, offering all RYA courses, adventure cruises and day sails aboard a luxury yacht.

You can use local slipways for **windsurfing, dinghy sailing, water** and **jet-**

skiing.

Horse-Riding
Kingarth Trekking Centre (Linda McMIllan, Old School, Kilchattan Bay, Kingarth; tel 01700-831673), close to sandy beach, moors, hills and tracks. Mini-breaks, full weeks or casual rides. Small camp and caravan site. Open all year from 10am to 4pm.

Other Activities
Ardberg Bowling Club: The Terrace, Ardberg Road, Rothesay (tel 01700-502164). Bus service from town centre. Visitors welcome. £1 a game. Open May to September from 10am to midday, 2pm to 4pm, and 7pm to 9.30pm.
Rothesay Bowling Club: Ballochgoy Road (tel 01700-502315). Close to the ferry terminal. Afternoon and evening sessions, visitors welcome. Open all year, daily from 2.30pm to 4.30pm and 6.30pm to 9pm.
For rainy days there's *Rothesay Leisure Pool* (High Street; tel 01700-504300 ext 217), a 27-yard (25 m) main pool with beach area, sauna, solarium, fitness facilities, and private showers. Open every day May to September until 5pm at weekends and 9pm weekdays.
You can enjoy a lively game of **tennis** during summer (May to September) at the *Meadows* in High Street, Rothesay, and **badminton, table tennis** and **snooker** are played at the *Moat Centre* in Stuart Street.

SHOPPING
Bute Island Foods: tel 01700-505117; fax 01700-500131. Vegan factory above town in Columshill Street. Non-dairy foods, including alternative hard cheese ('Scheese') and vegetarian ice-cream.
The Grapevine: 49 Victoria Street, Rothesay (tel/fax 01700-504414). The only retail health food shop on the island. Also sells Touchwood Celtic wood crafts, local pottery, and handmade soaps. Open daily except Sunday, from 9.30am to 5.15pm.
James McIntyre: 74 Montague Street, Rothesay (tel 01700-503672). Haggis, island cheeses, Bute honey, and game. Open Tuesday to Saturday 8.15am to 5pm.
Ritchies of Rothesay: Montague Street (tel 01700-505414). Mail order smokies. Open Monday and Wednesday 8am-1pm, Tuesday, Thursday, Friday and Saturday 8am to 5pm.
The Tartan Shop: 7 Albert Place, Rothesay (tel 01700-503399). Wide range of souvenirs, including scarves, travel rugs, commemorative spoons, and tea towels. Open April to October, 10am to 5pm.

HELP AND INFORMATION
Tourist Information Centre: The Winter Garden, Victoria Street, Rothesay (tel 01700-502151; fax 01700-505156; e-mail rothesaytic@aillst.net).
Police: High Street, Rothesay (tel 01700-502121).
Victoria Hospital: High Street, Rothesay (tel 01700-503938).
Rothesay Health Centre: tel 01700-5022990.
Dentist: West Princes Street, Rothesay (tel 01700-502041).
Bannermans Pharmacy: Victoria Street (tel 01700-502836).
Moss Pharmacy: 26 Montague Street (tel 01700-502362).
Post Offices: Guildford Square, Rothesay (tel 01700-503514); Ardbeg (tel 01700-502504); Gallowgate (tel 01700-503722); Kilchattan Bay (tel 01700-831628), and Port Bannatyne (tel 01700-502911).
Bank of Scotland: 36/42 Montague Street, Rothesay (tel 01700-503253/3531).
Royal Bank of Scotland: 37 Victoria Street, Rothesay (tel 01700-502539; fax 01700-502358). 24-hour Cashline, Visa, Mastercard and Eurocard accepted.

Open all year, Monday, Tuesday, Thursday, Friday from 9.15am to 4.45pm, Wednesday 10am to 4.45pm.

Caledonian MacBrayne: Rothesay (tel 01700-502707); Colintraive (tel 01700-841235); Wemyss Bay (tel 01475-520521).

Library: Stuart Street (tel 01700-503266).

Laundry in Rothesay at Sud-U-Like, 4 Argyle Street (tel 01700-502074). Open Monday to Saturday.

The local weekly newspaper is *The Buteman,* 10 Castle Street, Rothesay (tel 01700-502503; fax 01700-505159), published on Friday at 35p. Good for it's Infoline, what's on, coming events, and tide table.

CALENDAR OF EVENTS

Bute's *Country Music Festival* and its *Cycling Weekend* both take place in September.

Bute Highland Games: Public Stadium, Rothesay. Every year around August. Pipe bands, athletics, Highland dancing. Contact Gordon Sutherland, Honorary Secretary (tel 01700-831610 – evenings).

International Folk Festival and World Ceilidh Band Championships, Scotland's biggest festival, four days of non-stop music, song and dance in July. Check dates and times with Gillie Banks (tel 01700-831614; e-mail gillie@butefolk.freeserve.co.uk).

Isle of Bute Jazz Festival: 4 Ettrickdale Road, Port Bannatyne, PA20 0QZ (tel 01700-502800; fax 01700-502860). Usually held over the May Day Bank Holiday weekend. Booking up to a year in advance.

Royal Rothesay Regatta is usually held in June.

Great Cumbrae

Great Cumbrae island lies between Bute and Ayrshire, just off Largs, and with its neighbour to the south, Little Cumbrae, is a popular outing from many Clydeside resorts. Cumbrae is thought to derive from a Gaelic word meaning a shelter or a refuge. Great Cumbrae is about 4 miles long and 2 miles wide (6 km x 3 km), and covers an area of nearly five sq miles (13 sq km). Little Cumbrae, separated by about half a mile (800 m) of water – The Tan – is less than two miles long and a mile across (3 km x 1.6 km). With around 1,500 inhabitants Great Cumbrae is the most densely populated of all the islands of comparable size.

Geology. Oddly, the two islands don't share the same structure. Great Cumbrae is composed principally of Old Red Sandstone and notable for the intrusions and variety of its igneous dykes. Little Cumbrae is composed predominantly of a 600 ft (183 m) thick tiered pile of carboniferous basalt rock of volcanic origin, and is a geological outpost of the vast Clyde Lava Plateau.

EXPLORING

The Cumbraes have been recording visitors since AD 500, when they were known as 'The Isles of the Virgins' and formed part of the Kingdom of Strathclyde. One notable visitor was Norse King Haakon, who rested his fleet here in 1263 before the disastrous Battle of Largs. The resort town of Millport didn't exist until 1700 and most of the islanders lived in *clachans,* small farming or fishing hamlets. The earliest village was at Kirkton, about ½ mile away from Millport Pier. Organised catering for tourists began in the late 18th century, when the harbour was built and a ferry linked it to Largs. This commercial turn seems to have had a profound affect on the idyllic rural island. The Statistical Account for 1793 describes residents as 'sober, regular and industrious in a remarkable degree', but by 1840 was noting reprovingly, 'there are nine ale or public houses in the parish, the effect of which upon the morals of the people is most pernicious'.

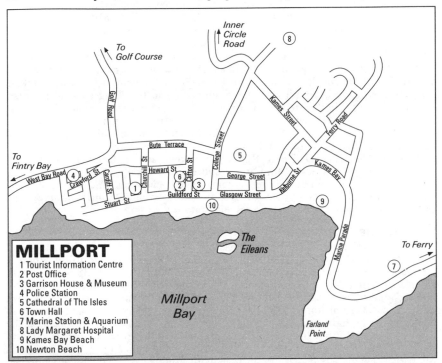

MILLPORT

1 Tourist Information Centre
2 Post Office
3 Garrison House & Museum
4 Police Station
5 Cathedral of The Isles
6 Town Hall
7 Marine Station & Aquarium
8 Lady Margaret Hospital
9 Kames Bay Beach
10 Newton Beach

Millport

Great Cumbrae is often known simply as **Millport,** after the chief town situated in the south on a spacious bay with good bathing, boating, and other watersports. The small rocky islets in the bay are called **The Eileans**. Close to town the sloping sandy stretches of Kames and Newton beaches are regarded as the best areas for swimming, with deep water but no strong currents or sandbanks. Interestingly, Victorian bye-laws specifying different bathing areas for men and women have never been repealed and a fine of £2 is still on the cards for offenders. Impressive **Garrison House** standing in the middle of the bay area was built about 1745 in the same style as Sir Walter Scott's home 'Abbotsford', and houses the **Museum of the Cumbraes**. The house was built by Captain James Crawford, who leased the land from the Marquess of Bute, paying a single rose for rent every 11 July. Crawford commanded the revenue vessel *Cumbrae Cutter* stationed here to prevent the smuggling that was a traditional pastime in Cumbrae. On occasion the minister had to postpone Communion because the wine had not been smuggled ashore in time. Along the northern and western coast there are still inlets known as Wine Bay and Brandy Bay.

Island Circuit

A popular outing is the 10½ mile (17 km) trip around the island along the flat coastal B896 road, best done by bike, trike, or tandem. Along the west coast is **Fintry Bay**, a shingle crescent that's a favourite place with picnickers and bathers. At one time it was a Bronze Age burial ground and nearby are the remains of a prehistoric stronghold. Half-way around the bay a refreshing well springs from the rock with water noted for its purity. At the island's northern tip is **Tomont End** with its monument to the two midshipmen of *HMS Shearwater* who drowned here on 17 May 1844. Tradition says that Vikings killed at the Battle of Largs were buried at this point. At the Cumbrae Slip ferry terminal, three miles (5 km) from Millport, the statue of two sandstone figures symbolically watching over travellers has become the target of mindless vandalism. Heading south along the coast the road passes the **National Water Sports Training Centre** and the rocky outcrop of **Douncraig**, the site of a vitrified fort. Towards the south-east corner of the island is **Lion Rock**, a projecting rocky mass with a vague resemblance to the King of Beasts. Other natural likenesses in the area popular with visitors are garishly painted **Crocodile Rock** and the rocky profile of **Queen Victoria** on the headland of Farland Hills. Near private Keppel Pier is the **Marine Biological Station** and its aquarium and museum, the ideal place to spend a wet day. This complex owes its existence to a remarkable Victorian, Dr David Robertson, known as the 'Cumbrae Naturalist'. Marine biology classes for university and other students are a feature of the station, which has its own diving decompression chamber. The station is open Monday to Friday from 9.30am to 12.15pm and 2pm to 4.45pm, Saturday (June to September) from 10am to 12.15pm and 2pm to 4.45pm.

Inner Circle Road

This loops round the island's hilly backbone, giving access to the highest point, the **'Glaidstone'** at 417 ft (127 m), a roadside well, and the **Standing Stone** at Craigielea Woods. On the way down into Millport is the 123 ft (38 m) landmark steeple of Britain's smallest cathedral, the **Cathedral of the Isles**, built in 1851 and recognised as an early masterpiece of architect William Butterfield. It is open daily. The cathedral library contains some priceless old volumes and the superb acoustics of its nave make it a popular venue for Sunday concerts. Among the tombs of other local worthies in the churchyard is the grave of the Rev James Adam (1748-1831), remembered for his unshakeable belief in the importance of his parish. He always ended his sermons with a prayer for 'The Great Cumbrae, the Little Cumbrae, and the adjacent islands of Great Britain and Ireland'.

FLORA AND FAUNA

There are few mammals, but the island is rich in bird species. The coast road provides easy viewing of waders and sea birds, with small terrestrial birds in the shrub vegetation of the raised beaches. Sea cliffs have breeding **fulmars** and **ravens**. Inland, the inner circle road gives access to moorland and woodland species, including **buzzards**, **sparrowhawks** and **kestrels**, while the Cathedral and Garrison grounds are home to **tawny owls** and **collar doves**. Eider ducks nest on the islets in the bay, which have a claim to fame as the site of the discovery in 1812 of the **roseate tern**. Visiting rarities have included a **white-billed diver** in 1972, the first ever recorded in the west of Scotland.

In winter a **seal** colony moves into Millport Bay. Summer sightings are common but less frequent. Animals in evidence include **rabbits** (some black), **ferret/polecats**, **hedgehogs**, **voles**, **slow-worms**, **lizards** and **newts**. Wild flowers and ferns abound, but the island is a particular haven for marsh and moorland species. At least nine species of **orchids** can be found and, to quote one authority, 'the island is awash with them'. In summer the road verges are colourful with **yellow rattle**, **marsh lousewort**, and clumps of yellow **bird's-foot-trefoil**, pink **thrift**, and pinky-white **English stonecrop** brighten the shoreline. Harmless plankton-eating **basking sharks** are often seen cruising around the island in July and August.

GETTING THERE

At one time you had to summon the ferry from Largs by lighting a fire. Now *Caledonian MacBrayne* (The Ferry Terminal, Gourock, PA19 1QP; tel 08705-650000; fax 01475-635235, reservations; tel 01475-650100; fax 01475-637607, enquiries; e-mail reservations@calmac.co.uk; www.calmac.co.uk) operates a car-passenger ferry from Largs to Great Cumbrae every half-hour, Monday to Saturday from 6.45am to 8.15pm, Sunday from 9.15am to 8.15pm. The trip takes 10 minutes. The return adult fare is £3.15, car £13.35, caravan, boat/baggage trailer £13.35, motorcycle £6.70, bicycles £2. A 'Five-Journey' ticket is available.

Waverley Excursions (Waverley Terminal, 36 Anderston Quay, Glasgow G3 8HA; tel 0141-221 8152; fax 0141-248 2150) has cruises to Millport Easter to October on its sea-going paddle steamer, the *Waverley*. Fare from Greenock £19.95, from Glasgow £22.95, and from Rothesay £13.95. There is also a cruise around Great and Little Cumbrae from Millport for £11.95. Check dates and times with the operator.

GETTING AROUND

Buses

A connecting bus meets every ferry to take foot passengers to Millport. For more information on other routes and fares contact Strathclyde Transport (tel 0141-332 7133).

Taxis: *Caldwell's Newsagent* (tel 01475-530344).

Cycle Hire

Rental costs are the same at all three cycle hire shops in Millport: £1.50 an hour, £2.80 for two hours, £3.20 for three hours, £3.80 for six hours, £14 a week, and £20 for two weeks.

Bremner's Stores: 17 Cardiff Street (tel 01475-530707/309). Hire by hour, day, week, or longer.

Mapes of Millport: 3/5 Guildford Street (tel/fax 01475-530444; e-mail mapes@mapesk.freeserve.co.uk). Tandems and helmets also available. Bike deposit £5.

AT Morton: 4 Mount Stuart (tel 01475-530478).

ACCOMMODATION

Royal George Hotel: Millport (tel 01475-530301). On the Quayhead overlooking the bay. B&B, bar meals, and a la carte restaurant.

Cathedral of the Isles and College of the Holy Spirit: Millport (tel 01475-530353; fax 01475-530204). B&B, half-board and full board available.

Guest Houses

Ambler Guest House: 1-3 Craig Street, Millport (tel 01475-530532).

Denmark Cottage: 8 Ferry Road, Millport (tel 01475-530958). Small family-run guest house close to beach and local amenities.

Eastneuk Guest House: Kames Bay, Millport, KA28 0EA (tel 01475-530799).

Millerston Guest House: 29 West Bay Road, Millport (tel 01475-530480). Rooms en-suite. Also self-catering caravans available.

Self-Catering

Mrs B McLuckie: Muirhall Farm, Larbert FK5 4EW (tel 01324-551570). Has four flats with sea views, sleep 2 to 10; and one house which sleeps eight. Open all year, from £110 to £490 a week.

Cumbrae Holiday Apartments: tel 01475-530094. Centrally situated. Open all year.

Camping

Millport Holiday Park: Golf Road, Millport, KA28 0HB (tel 01475-530370). Also hire and sells caravans.

EATING AND DRINKING

Crocodile Chippy: tel 01475-531111. For delicious fish teas. Take-away and sit-down restaurant.

Deep Sea: tel 01475-530443. Licensed take-away at the pier.

Fintry Bay Tearoom: Millport (tel 01475-530426). Lunches, homebakes. Open from 10.30am daily.

Grannie Jean's Coffee Shop: 24 Glasgow Street, Millport (tel 01475-530852). Fresh meals and homebakes. Home-made soup every day. Open from 10.30am to 5pm daily.

Kelburne Bar: tel 01475-530080. Local pub. Disabled toilet facilities.

Munchie's: 52 Stuart Street, Millport (tel 01475-530873). Freshly cooked meals and snacks. Sit in or take-away.

Newton Bar and Hiccup's Lounge: tel 01475-530920. Licensed restaurant and public bar. Entertainment all year round.

Ritz Café: tel 01475-530459. Tea, coffee, filled rolls, toasties, home-made ice-cream. Open 10am till late.

The Sweet Shop: 7 Guildford Street, Millport. The home of the renowned Millport tablet.

SPORT AND RECREATION

Walking

There are lots of walks on the island, ranging from easy rambles of an hour to a two-hour cross-country walk for the fit to Farland Hill. Some are detailed in *Favourite Walks on Cumbrae*, a leaflet available from the Tourist Information Centre.

Cycling

The size of the island makes it ideal for cycling. There are virtually no traffic lights, few hills and the 10¹/2 mile (17 km) round-island road provides great views. The inner route is more hilly but has stunning panoramas over the Firth.

Fishing

Two redundant reservoirs known as **Top Dam** and **Bottom Dam** are stocked by the Cumbrae Angling Club (The Firs, Westbay Road, Millport) and provide excellent catches of rainbow and brown trout. The season is from Easter to end-October. Fly only. Open sunrise to sunset. Tickets £10 a day, available at *MacFarlane's Newsagent* (Glasgow Street, Millport; tel 01475-530324), *Ritz Café* (Stewart Street, Millport;tel 01475-530459), and from the secretary of the angling club.

Sea fishing is excellent from shore and boat, with catches of mackerel, pollack, wrasse, whiting, and rock cod the most common. Deep-sea angling excursions can be arranged with pick-up at Millport pier. There's good rod fishing around the islets in the bay and at Farland Point.

Golf

Millport Golf Club: Golf Road, Millport (tel/fax 01475-530306). Heathland 18-hole course has existed since 1888. The course is slightly hilly over the first five holes and the mountains of Arran form a striking backdrop. Visitors welcome.

Horse-Riding: *Millport Riding School*, Upper Kirkton Stables, Golf Road, Millport (tel 01475-530689).

Watersports

Scotland's National Water Sports Centre (Anne Dipple; tel 01475-530757) is close to the ferry pier. Cruising, dinghy, catamaran, canoeing, power-boating, windsurfing, VHF courses, and diesel maintenance. All instructors are RYA qualified.

Help and Information

Tourist Information Centre: 28a Stuart Street, Millport (tel 01475-530753). Open Easter to October only.
Strathclyde Police: Millport (tel 01475-530316).
Millport Lady Margaret Hospital: tel 01475-530307.
Caledonian MacBrayne: Largs (tel 01475-674134).
Post Office: Millport (tel 01475-530319).
Cumbrae Local Office: Millport (tel 01475-530741).

LITTLE CUMBRAE

Little Cumbrae is privately owned by Mr and Mrs Peter Kaye and maintained as a nature reserve. While visitors are not encouraged you can land if you first get permission (Little Cumbrae Estate, PO Box 1, Millport, KA28 0AA) and excursion boats are available from Largs. Robert II, heir of The Bruce, was a frequent visitor to **Little Cumbrae Castle**, and two of his charters dated 1375 and 1384 were signed here. The walls of the now ruined castle are more than 6 ft (2 m) thick and surrounded by a rampart and a fosse. It was razed in 1653 by Cromwell's troops. The island is rich in archaeological remains, including **St Vey's Chapel** (she was one of the Virgins mentioned in the ecclesiastical *Annals of Ulster*). One of the cairns excavated in 1813 at Sheanawally Point, on the northern tip of the island, produced the remains of a large sword, a helmet, and some chain-mail. Robert Stevenson (1772-1850), the grandfather of Robert Louis, built the lighthouse in the centre of the island in 1793. It has been rebuilt and altered several times since then and became fully automatic in 1974. Cliffs above the raised beach in the rugged south are good muscle-stretchers for climbers and cavers. No one should leave without admiring the view from the 'Hill of Hills'.

GLOSSARY

Broch – An Iron Age defensive stone tower with inner wall, named from the Old Norse *borg*, or castle.

Chambered cairn – A Neolithic burial tomb.

Cist – A grave or box made from stone slabs.

Crannog (lake dwelling) – A small islet, usually man-made, on which a dwelling was built, linked to the shore by causeway. Some probably date from the late Bronze Age.

Dun – Gaelic for a hill fort, a small drystone fortification usually dating from the Iron Age or later.

Henge – Usually a circular or elliptical area enclosed by a ditch and an external bank and often enclosing a stone circle. Usually regarded as a meeting place for ceremony and ritual.

Iron Age – Final period of prehistory in Scotland, beginning around 500 BC and lasting into the early centuries of the first millennium AD, when iron superseded bronze as the preferred metal for tools and weapons.

Mesolithic (Middle Stone Age) – The period between the Palaeolithic and Neolithic ages, from around 7000 BC to 4000 BC. The Mesolithic groups were hunter-gatherers like their predecessors.

Midden – An accumulation of domestic rubbish, usually built up over a long period.

Neolithic (New Stone Age) – Period between the Mesolithic and the Bronze Age in Scotland, dating from around 4000 BC to 2000 BC and characterised by the introduction of settled farming communities.

Ogam, or **Ogham** – A script in which letters are represented by groups of parallel lines meeting or crossing a straight base line. Thought to have originated in Wales or Ireland around AD 300. Used by the Picts until the 9th century.

Palaeolithic (Old Stone Age) – In Britain, beginning with the earliest occupation by man around 450,000 years ago, and ending with the Mesolithic around 7000 BC.

Runes – A stick-like angular script developed for carving on wood and stone around AD300. First recorded use was in Scandinavia.

Souterrain – An earth-house with a long, underground passage, often having drystone walling and a flagged roof, and sometimes a chamber. Usually attached to a settlement and used for storage. They date from around 800 BC to about AD 200.

Stone Circle – Circles or ellipses of standing stones, mostly dating from the Bronze Age and believed to be connected with ritual ceremonies and possibly astronomical observations.

Wheelhouse – Round drystone house usually dating from the late Iron Age, in which partition walling, possibly roof supports, radiate in from the wall like the spokes of a wheel.

INDEX

Vacation Work publish:

	Paperback	Hardback
Summer Jobs Abroad	£9.99	£15.95
Summer Jobs in Britain	£9.99	£15.95
Supplement to Summer Jobs in Britain and Abroad *published in May*	£6.00	–
Work Your Way Around the World	£12.95	–
Taking a Gap Year	£11.95	–
Taking a Career Break	£11.95	–
Working in Tourism – The UK, Europe & Beyond	£11.95	–
Kibbutz Volunteer	£10.99	–
Working on Cruise Ships	£10.99	–
Teaching English Abroad	£12.95	–
The Au Pair & Nanny's Guide to Working Abroad	£11.95	–
The Good Cook's Guide to Working Worldwide	£11.95	–
Working in Ski Resorts – Europe & North America	£10.99	–
Working with Animals – The UK, Europe & Worldwide	£11.95	–
Live & Work Abroad - a Guide for Modern Nomads	£11.95	–
Working with the Environment	£11.95	–
Health Professionals Abroad	£11.95	–
Accounting Jobs Worldwide	£11.95	–
The Directory of Jobs & Careers Abroad	£12.95	–
The International Directory of Voluntary Work	£11.95	–
Live & Work in Australia & New Zealand	£11.95	–
Live & Work in Belgium, The Netherlands & Luxembourg	£11.95	–
Live & Work in France	£11.95	–
Live & Work in Germany	£10.99	–
Live & Work in Italy	£10.99	–
Live & Work in Japan	£10.99	–
Live & Work in Russia & Eastern Europe	£10.99	–
Live & Work in Saudi & the Gulf	£10.99	–
Live & Work in Scandinavia	£11.95	–
Live & Work in Scotland	£10.99	–
Live & Work in Spain & Portugal	£11.95	–
Live & Work in the USA & Canada	£11.95	–
Drive USA	£10.99	–
Hand Made in Britain - The Visitors Guide	£10.99	–
Scottish Islands - The Western Isles	£12.95	–
Scottish Islands - Orkney & Shetland	£11.95	–
The Panamericana: On the Road through Mexico and Central America	£12.95	–
Travellers Survival Kit: Australia & New Zealand	£11.95	–
Travellers Survival Kit: Cuba	£10.99	–
Travellers Survival Kit: India	£10.99	–
Travellers Survival Kit: Lebanon	£10.99	–
Travellers Survival Kit: Madagascar, Mayotte & Comoros	£10.99	–
Travellers Survival Kit: Mauritius, Seychelles & Réunion	£10.99	–
Travellers Survival Kit: Mozambique	£10.99	–
Travellers Survival Kit: Oman & the Arabian Gulf	£11.95	–
Travellers Survival Kit: South Africa	£10.99	–
Travellers Survival Kit: South America	£15.95	–
Travellers Survival Kit: Sri Lanka	£10.99	–
Travellers Survival Kit: USA & Canada	£10.99	–

Distributors of:

	Paperback	Hardback
Summer Jobs USA	£12.95	–
Internships (On-the-Job Training Opportunities in the USA)	£18.95	–
How to Become a US Citizen	£11.95	–
World Volunteers	£10.99	–
Green Volunteers	£10.99	–

Plus 27 titles from Peterson's, the leading American academic publisher, on college education and careers in the USA. Separate catalogue available on request.

Vacation Work Publications, 9 Park End Street, Oxford OX1 1HJ
Tel 01865–241978   Fax 01865–790885

Visit us online for more information on our unrivalled range of titles for work, travel and gap years, readers' feedback and regular updates:

www.vacationwork.co.uk